An Astonishing Infantryman

The Life and Letters of
Jack Hill, Royal Welch Fusiliers
1778-1838

Steve McCarthy

Grosvenor House
Publishing Limited

This book is published by
Grosvenor House Publishing Ltd
Link House
140 The Broadway, Tolworth, Surrey, KT6 7HT.
www.grosvenorhousepublishing.co.uk

A CIP record for this book
is available from the British Library

Hardback ISBN 978-1-83615-299-6

To my late mother and father
who first inspired my interest in history,
and to Dawn who inspires me in every way today.

Contents

Credits

The illustrations on pages 188 – 191 and 390 to 393 are reproduced by kind permission of the following:

Page 188: Portrait courtesy of Ed Hill
Page 189: Portrait of Rev. John Hill courtesy of Philip Hill
'Old' Blundell's courtesy of Blundell's School
Page 190: letters courtesy of Ed Hill
Page 191: Valk memorial courtesy of Ed Hill
Martinique eagle courtesy of RWF Museum
Page 390: Prayer book and case shot courtesy of Philip Hill
Page 392: Ellis & Pearson portraits and medals courtesy of RWF Museum
Page 393: Portrait courtesy of Philip Hill

All other illustrations: the Author.

Foreword

The words 'remarkable' and 'extraordinary' are frequently used about books and probably overused in most cases. This, however, is a book by Steve McCarthy that fully deserves those adjectives. The military life of Jack Hill of the 23rd or Royal Welch Fusiliers surpassed in experience, danger and success all but a few others. He was present at pretty much every major engagement of the Revolutionary and Napoleonic Wars in which British troops were involved, including campaigns in the Low Countries, the Americas and Iberia. He was there at the end of the great war, at Waterloo, where he was wounded, joining that band of men marked forever by their presence at that great, decisive, battle; a battle that remained in folk memory for a generation or more. 'If you were at Waterloo, it matters not what else you do, if you were at Waterloo'. Jack also served with the Portuguese army, adding further experience to his curriculum vitae.

While reading this book, we gain a clear idea of what motivated Jack Hill and others like him during those years and we also catch glimpses of what the Regiment, and the Army, were like at that time. Jack had some remarkable contemporaries, especially Henry Walton Ellis, who commanded the regiment's 1st Battalion for five years, only to be killed on the last day of the war at Waterloo. There was also Thomas Pearson, a fearless soldier but a ferocious disciplinarian – no friend to Jack – whose biography was written some years ago by Donald Graves. There is more written about the Royal Welch Fusiliers, and written by its members, than any other regiment, in any army list, anywhere in the world. As well as Ellis and Pearson, there are numerous personal accounts from the period that Steve has rightly used to illuminate events. These include accounts by ordinary soldiers like Drummer Bentinck; the diaries and letters of officers like Thomas Henry Browne; and asides from family members: Browne's sister was Felicia Heamans, the celebrated Victorian poetess who outsold Jane Austen in her day. This book joins that great canon of military literature and is a most welcome addition.

Jack Hill ended his service with a pension – not all it should have been – a raft of medals including the Order of the Bath, the Army gold medal and gold cross and the Waterloo medal. But the last chapters make hard and sad reading, for his treatment at the end of his service can only be described as shabby. He was not the first to have been so treated and I doubt he will be the last. The gratitude of nations for their salvation is always short.

It has been a pleasure and a privilege to write the Foreword for this book. I wish it every success and commend it to the Regiment and to all those who share the fascination for things military and times Napoleonic.

Jonathon Riley CB DSO, Lieutenant General, Late Colonel, the 23rd Royal Welch Fusiliers

Introduction

The village of Hennock sits at the eastern edge of Dartmoor. It remains a relatively rural place, with houses surrounded by farms, and amenities limited to a village pub, hall and school and St. Mary's church. Near the church door stands a plain box tomb, its iron railings long gone; this is the Hill family vault. John Hill was rector of St. Mary's from 1775 until his death in 1828; his remains now lie alongside those of his wife Margaret and other members of their family, including Lieutenant-Colonel John Humphrey Edward Hill, CB, Royal Welch Fusiliers.

The eroded inscription on the vault is now hard to read unless you catch it in the right sunlight. On the wall inside St. Mary's, however, is a prominent white marble plaque commemorating John Humphrey Edward Hill. The 23rd Regiment of Foot, the Royal Welch Fusiliers (RWF), were as active as any British regiment during the Revolutionary and Napoleonic Wars. Global transportation in those days meant long, slow and perilous voyages under sail, yet at the height of the wars the 23rd fought on 3 continents in a single decade - in Holland in 1799, Egypt in 1801, and the Caribbean in 1809 - and then across the Iberian Peninsula from Lisbon to southern France between 1810 and 1814. In 1811 they faced perhaps their biggest test on a day that saw more casualties than any other of the Peninsular War and a few years later helped end the Napoleonic Wars at Waterloo.

Through these journeys, battles and marches, including sometimes in the Portuguese army, John Humphrey Edward Hill, known to his army colleagues as Jack, fought, was wounded several times and yet survived, despite being shipwrecked and nearly drowned almost before his career had begun.[1] Jack Hill was born and buried in Hennock, but between those events, he rose to become one of the most senior and longest serving members of his regiment, be appointed to one of the nation's most senior chivalric Orders and participate in some of the most memorable military events of the early 19th century.

---

1 He signed all his letters 'J. Hill'; in other letters his brother William calls him John. To avoid confusion, I call him Jack throughout.

This book is based significantly on Jack's letters, mostly written to his mother and father. Some eighty of his letters and other documents have survived in the possession of the Hill family, though transcripts of many of them are held by the archives of both Blundell's school and the RWF museum. The letters offer a contemporary record of one man's experiences and enable a glimpse of both his personality and life in the British army at an important time in its evolution. Jack's descriptions of the events he participated in align well with current knowledge, though they also challenge generally accepted versions of some aspects, such as the performance of Sir Thomas Graham's column at Vitoria, the efforts of the Portuguese army at the battle of St. Pierre in 1813 and on the Adour the following winter. History is often a matter of interpretation; as the 1st Duke of Wellington commented 'every man who can write, and who has a friend that can read, sits down to write his account of what he does not know'.[2] Still, looking back over 200 years later, Jack seems to have done a reasonable job; if his letters change some longstanding narratives, that is good.

My text is intended to give the letters context, starting with Jack's boyhood, through his career, and eventual retirement from the army. The battles he was in of course play a vital part in the story. Something about each is included, but not a blow-by-blow description of everything that took place; my focus is what Jack and those he led did. Some may find my coverage of certain battles scant, but anyone wanting to know more will find a vast array of original and secondary sources to select from. The bibliography includes contemporary sources I have used to bridge a couple of gaps in the chronology of Jack's letters. Unfortunately, there are none between 1805–1807, or from 1812 or 1814, though much of what he was up to at those times can be discerned from other records.

As I thought it important that Jack's own voice came through as strongly as possible, I have re-transcribed his letters from the original manuscripts wherever possible and limited my editing to minor punctuation and other tweaks intended to help today's reader. For example, because writing paper was sometimes a scarce commodity on campaign, common practice was to avoid paragraph breaks; I have inserted a few to break up an otherwise lengthy text. I have made suggestions for occasional missing words and tried to explain some obscure contemporary references. The Appendices include biographical notes on Jack's RWF officer colleagues. These were the people he spent many hours with, sharing entertainment, boredom, gossip or violence; as they pop up in Jack's letters, it seems fair to include something about

---

2 Quoted in *The Armies of Wellington* Philip J. Haythornethwaite 1994

them. Unfortunately, it has proven impossible to find anything about some neighbours and family contacts he mentions who are now sadly erased from history. I have not changed the spellings Jack used for locations which have either changed over time or which were known to English speakers by Anglicised versions; I have only included current spellings where the place referred to is not obvious - for example some Basque towns in Spain, which Jack marched through in 1813. Peninsular War historian Sir Charles Oman said: 'certain names of Basque villages are never written with the same letters by any two persons who have occasion to mention them'.[3] Spanish language names of the time, and some tortured spellings used by British soldiers, often bear no relationship to the current Basque names.

Short extracts from fewer than half Jack's letters appeared in a 1988 booklet entitled *Letters to a Vicarage 1796–1815*, selected by Enid Case and edited by Jenny Currie. Extracts have also appeared in some military history books. The full text of all his letters is, however, published here for the first time. Even in wartime, a soldier's life is mostly not about fighting; from schoolboy concerns before he joined up, ambitions for promotion, gossip on colleagues, the scenery he passed through and events he witnessed, financial concerns, or the homesickness he suffered, Jack offers insights on army life at home and abroad during the Revolutionary and Napoleonic Wars. His family did not have the connections of aristocratic or other 'interested' families, but Jack's letters show how the Hills sought to use their Devonian contacts to further Jack's career. They also underline the difficulty of maintaining regular communications in the early 19th Century. Jack's complaints about the lack of mail from home (no letters sent to him survive), sometimes attributed unfairly to laziness on his family's part, were more often caused by mail not getting through due to enemy action, bad weather or simply the difficulty of a letter sent from perhaps thousands of miles away reaching the person it was addressed to - the reason that official letters were often sent in triplicate, by different routes, and carefully timed and dated in case they arrived out of sequence. That said, Jack more than once commented that he had nothing worth the postage to write about.

The letters tell a tale of endurance, adventure, frustration and reward at a time when life was very different from today in many ways and yet similar in others. Personal communications over any distance being handwritten and hand-carried meant the only means of transporting mail were foot, horse, carriage or boat, all of which Jack employed to stay in touch with his family. But roads were often reduced

---

3 A History of the Peninsular War Volume VII Sir Charles Oman 1914

to mud and sea voyages were perilous; even when things worked well, the time for any letter to go from writer to reader, and for a reply to return (if it did) could be filled with concern about a loved one's wellbeing. When Jack served, life expectancy was much shorter than today and for military personnel it was shorter still, as much from accident and disease as from the risks of warfare. Jack experienced those and many other challenges but survived. Through it all he looked for news from home, for confirmation that his family were well and always asked to be 'remembered' to them. He deserves his story to be told, and this book, based around his own words or those of people who were in the same place he was, is an attempt at that.

All authors rely on an army of supporters, contributors and reviewers to bring their work to fruition. I am greatly indebted to Ed Hill, Jack's great-great-great grandson and himself a Welch Fusilier, for first sharing with me copies of the transcripts and the manuscripts of the letters, granting permission to publish them in this book and for his enthusiasm for the idea. I am also most grateful to Phillip Hill and Susan Hill for other information about the Hill family and access to photographs of memorabilia. I also owe a great debt to my former colleague Colonel Nick Lock at the RWF Museum for launching the project in my head, his enthusiasm and 'above and beyond' help since then, a personal guided tour of the outstanding RWF Museum in Caernarfon and the opportunity to share my research about Jack's life at the excellent 'RWF Fest' in September 2025. I am pleased to donate the royalties from this book to the Museum in small return for these kindnesses. Nick also introduced me to various people without whose input this book would have suffered significantly. These include Jane Ap Thomas, Collections Officer, Wrexham Museum & Archives and Al Poole of the Wrexham Museum & Archives team. My thanks to them both and especially for Al's heroic efforts on my behalf, including scanning all the Archives' copies of the Hill manuscript letters, which enabled me to check the earlier transcripts and correct some errors. Other people Nick introduced me to include Donald E. Graves, who helped me with several aspects concerning the 23rd Foot during the period that arose from my reading his excellent book *Dragon Rampant*; Lieutenant-General Jonathon Riley, who boldly undertook to read the whole draft, providing numerous invaluable edits and other comments, and who most generously wrote the Foreword; Mick Crumplin, who provided more help than I could have hoped for, including a mock X-ray, on the injuries Jack suffered at Waterloo, his treatment and the consequences of his wound, including putting me on the trail of John Hennen's record of that treatment; and Ben Collins who tipped me off to the mention of Jack Hill in von Wacholtz's memoires and has been encouraging throughout.

This book would have been far less complete or interesting without the input of Moisés Gaudêncio whose invaluable contribution to knowledge about the Portuguese army during the Peninsular War, through his book with Robert Burnham, *Wellington's Fighting Cocks*, was amplified by his finding and sending me material relevant to Jack Hill held by the Portuguese National and Military Archives. I am deeply grateful to Moisés for his efforts and for helping me understand many aspects of Portuguese service at that time, including the complex command arrangements of the 4th Infantry when Jack took them over. Moisés provided so much detail on Jack's Portuguese service that what I initially thought likely to be one thin chapter became three substantial ones, which Moisés also patiently read at least twice and improved massively in doing so. At Blundell's School, Catherine Flavelle, History Teacher and Archivist, was outstandingly helpful in showing me Blundell's archive material on Jack and his contemporaries at the school, providing illustrations, answering numerous subsequent questions, and providing a copy of an unpublished piece on the value of the letters. Cathy also put me in touch with Rupert Casey, to whom I am grateful for the background to the donation of a bound copy of the letter transcripts to the school. I must also thank Jill Drysdale at Totnes Archives for uncovering material on Jack Hill's life (and death) at Dartington, and Peter Michael Nielsen for reading the section on the Copenhagen expedition of 1807 and for taking me on a highly enjoyable trip to key locations of that campaign. It is always good to visit battlefields; it is better to do so with a good friend.

On the subject of good friends and battlefield visits, most of all I thank my wife, Dawn, for her love, constant support, encouragement, genealogical and other online research, for ploughing through many weighty tomes at the National Archives in Kew, proof-reading the entire text, enduring innumerable battlefield and other out-of-the-way trips 'because Jack went there' and for allowing into our family a man from a tiny village nestled on the edge of Dartmoor who became one of Wellington's 'astonishing infantry'.

Steve McCarthy
Hennock, Devon
2025

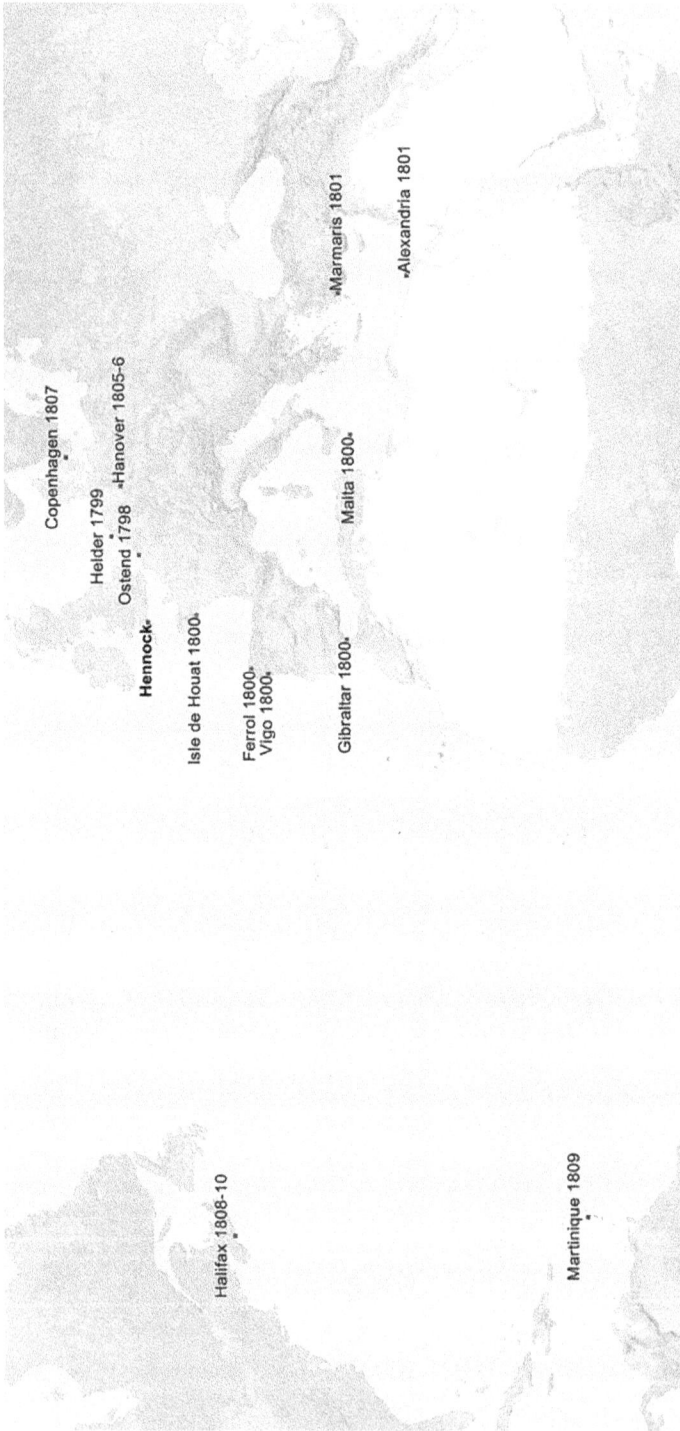

Map 1: The Voyages of Jack Hill 1798 – 1810

Copenhagen 1807

Helder 1799
Ostend 1798   •Hanover 1805-6

Hennock•

Isle de Houat 1800•

Ferrol 1800•
Vigo 1800•

Gibraltar 1800•

Malta 1800•

•Marmaris 1801

•Alexandria 1801

Halifax 1808-10

Martinique 1809

CHAPTER 1

A TIME OF REVOLUTION

'I had the honour of being appointed to a 2nd Lieutenancy in the 23rd
or R.W.F. Regt...Promoted to a First Lieutenancy...
and appointed to the Lieut. Colonels Company'.

Statement of Services, 1816

What used to be the vicarage in Hennock sits at one corner of a
triangle with St. Mary's church and the Palk Arms pub. To quote from
the estate agent's literature when what is now called the Old Vicarage
was sold in the 21st Century, the house 'occupies a truly unique
position...with lovely views across the Teign Valley to the Haldon
Hills'. The house has changed over the years but remains at the centre
of the village today, just as it was at the end of the 18th Century, when
the vicarage was home to the Hill family.

Hennock today comprises a string of houses on the eastern edge
of Dartmoor overlooking the Teign Valley; it claims some of the best
views in Devon. Few people know of it, though the village has a little
history.[1] A hilltop position and abundant water sources running off
Dartmoor may have made it attractive to early settlers. The Domesday
Book notes a holding called Hanoch, comprising nine villagers, six
smallholders and five slaves whose Lord in 1066 had been Alnoth but
by 1086 was Roger, son of Payne; there were more sheep (sixty) than
people and in summer there may still be. At 400–600 feet above sea
level, Hennock was later the site of a warning beacon connecting the
south coast to the capital, used for example during the approach of the
Spanish Armada in 1588 and at various times of national celebration
since. Local legend has it that Thomas Fairfax, Oliver Cromwell and
the Parliamentary army marched through in January 1646, with
Cromwell staying overnight in the most impressive house in the village
centre, Longlands. The Parliamentarians reputedly captured a Royalist
officer, a handful of his troops and a Colour near the village then, on 8
January 1846 surprised a Royalist detachment in the valley below,

---

1 *Hennock: A Village History*. Ian Fraser 2004

capturing over twenty officers, 140 men and 150 head of cattle in a small skirmish known as the battle of Bovey Heath.[2] By the late 18th century, Hennock was home to almost 500 people.[3] This was primarily agricultural land. Mining, for minerals, lead, copper and even silver, and quarrying would come in later years (and go: Great Rock mine, just outside the village, was the last metal mine in Devon). Much of the surrounding area, once part of the Torre Abbey estate, was in the late 1700s owned by the Templer and Palk families, both of which made their fortunes through the East India Company. Robert Palk rose to become a Council member of the Company and a Baronet. The Palk Arms, now Hennock's only pub, is named for the family.

The spiritual home for residents of Hennock was, and is, St. Mary's church. In 1651 control of the rectory and parsonage of Hennock, together with associated tithes, barns, houses and glebe lands, passed to the aldermen of Exeter. Just over one hundred years later, one of those aldermen, and a former Mayor of the city, was Humphrey Hill. Humphrey fathered six children - three boys, three girls - with his wife Margaret. One of the boys, John, went to Balliol College, Oxford aged 18 in March 1770 to study for holy orders, eventually graduating with a Batchelor of Arts degree.[4] Ordained as a deacon by Frederick Keppel, Bishop of Exeter, in September 1773, John was appointed curate of Exeter Holy Trinty Church.[5] He held that role until July 1775, a big month for John Hill. On the 3rd he married Margaret Scott and at the end of the month was ordained as a priest. With perfect timing for the newlyweds, the benefice of Hennock fell vacant when the Bishop of Exeter offered the incumbent, Malachy Hitchins, a vicarage in his native Cornwall.[6] So it was that on 4 October 1775 John Hill, son of Exeter alderman Humphrey Hill, and friend of Bishop Keppel, was appointed rector of St. Mary's. The appointment was not an entirely free gift, though it was a lucrative one. The newly appointed rector was required to pay an annual lease to the mayor of Exeter of £42, plus a further £7 annually to the Lord of the Manor of Bovey Tracey. In return, according to evidence he gave to a Parliamentary enquiry in 1834, John received an income from tithes

---

2 Information board, Bovey Heath Battlefield and Fraser, *Hennock*
3 John Hill's Episcopal Visitation Return, 1779. FODA.org.uk
4 *Alumni Oxoniensis (1715–1886) Vol. 2* Joseph Foster (ed.) 1888 – 1891
5 Clergy of the Church of England Database. https://theclergydatabase.org.uk/jsp/persons/index.jsp. John Hill is person ID 145041
6 Hitchens was also a mathematician and astronomer who played a significant role in the development of The Nautical Almanac. *An 18th-century astronomical hub in west Cornwall* Caroline Kennett, in *The Antiquarian Astronomer, Issue 11, June 2017*

and other payments totalling £260 per year. Thus, at a cost equivalent to perhaps £5,000 today, he received an income worth now about £30,000.[7]

John and Margaret Hill, together with one of John's younger sisters, another Margaret (known as Peggy, helpfully avoiding confusion with her mother and her sister-in-law), moved from Exeter and into the vicarage at Hennock, just across a narrow lane from both St. Mary's and the village poorhouse. They would stay there for over fifty years. Between 1777 and 1794 John and Margaret produced six children. Their first born, Caroline Margaret, lived only three years. But four sons and another daughter survived childhood:

- John Humphrey Edward (Jack), born on 17 December 1778;
- Caroline Rebecca (1780);
- William (1783);
- Charles Abraham (1785); and
- Frederick Carne (1794).

John's clerical duties were busy, if not untypical for the time. In a survey return to the Bishop of Exeter in 1779, he noted that he performed services twice every Sunday, performing them also at Lustleigh, about three miles away, catechising children on 'Saturdays, in the Afternoon'. He ministered to eighty-seven families, some '491 souls', though it seems not all of them were regular churchgoers; John noted that when the 'Sacrament of the Lord's Supper is administered four Times a Year, Easter, Whitsunday, Xstmas [sic] & the Sunday nearest to the twenty ninth Day of September…The Number of Communicants are from 30 to 40'.[8] As an Anglican at a time when Catholicism was considered by some to be close to treachery, with some sense of relief John also noted: 'We have no reputed Papists nor any meeting Houses for dissenting Congregations & amidst our 491 Souls but one Dissenter who professes himself to be a Presbyterian'.

As well as his spiritual role, managing charitable finances was also a key responsibility; John's return noted receipts from the rent of a plot of land 'of two Pounds twelve shillings…is to be expended in Bread, to be distributed to the Poor, inhabiting the Poor-House'. There was also a bequest of £5 paid annually for the vicar of Hennock to distribute 'to such poor of the parish not receiving monthly pay, as he should think fit'. Like many clergymen then, John was an amateur student of natural

---

7 *Parliamentary Papers: Accounts and Papers relating to Corporate Offices and Charitable Funds* 1834. Comparative values using the Bank of England inflation calculator

8 Devon Episcopal Visitation Returns, 1779. FODA.org.uk

history. When in later years his sons travelled the world, they regularly sent back descriptions of the geology and flora and samples of seeds and rocks for their father's collection. John Hill was also well connected. The letters Jack later sent home name many of the great and good of the area with whom he was familiar through his father. The Reverend and his wife were well enough acquainted with members of the local gentry to share with Jack news of events that happened to them and even sometimes ask them to intervene with relevant authorities in support of their sons' military careers. The notable families include the Palks and Templers, the Cliffords of Ugbrooke House, the Bastards of Kitely and Ashprington and the Mallocks of Cockington. Connections with the City of Exeter also continued through John's older sister Elizabeth who was married to John Pinhey, Sheriff of Exeter in 1790 and Mayor in 1792. John of course also tapped into the clerical network across Devon and beyond, many of whom had family in the military too.

The Act of Parliament commissioning a national census in 1801 gave John Hill another job: local vicars were to gather the numbers of inhabited houses and resident families in their parish, calculate the total residential population and record how many were employed in agriculture, trade, manufacturing or handicrafts. John's return for 1801 shows nearly half the population of Hennock were agricultural workers: a harsh life with the incomes of even those fit for regular employment being subject to the vagaries of the weather, the success of the harvest, and the market value of produce. Many men, women and children who worked the land were employed on a daily or piece rate basis, not knowing if they would have an income, or how much it would be, from week to week. Unsurprisingly, therefore, Hennock was not wealthy. In 1790 a labourer might earn as little as one shilling a week, perhaps £6 today. Those unemployed, ill or injured relied on alms from the church to survive. A contemporary guide to Devon noted of Hennock 'the parish has been regularly inhabited by peasantry. The houses mud built, thatched, not neat. Orchards to all the farms; except those on the downs. The farms very small, the property divided, in good state of cultivation. 56 farms. These farms are occupied by 6 freeholders and 44 rackrenters. Total of cot[tage]s and farm-houses, 76....Roads bad, tho' amidst the best of materials.[9]

The Hill family of course enjoyed a relatively affluent middle-class lifestyle compared to most in the area and no doubt held a central place in village life. As they grew older the children would help their parents minister to the community; the clergy would have been considered as a suitable future career for the boys. Perhaps with this in mind, when he

---

9 *The History of Devonshire*, Rev. Richard Polwhele 1793

became a teenager Jack was sent to Blundell's School in Tiverton, around 30 miles from Hennock. The school Register for 1792 shows 'John Humphry Edward, son of John Hill, Clerk, of Hennock, Devon; aged 13, admitted August 7, left June 29, 1796'.[10] Blundell's had around 100 pupils at the time and was named for Peter Blundell, a businessman who had accumulated his fortune from cloth, financial dealings and property holdings. Blundell never married; when he died in 1601 his will left £20,000 - some £5 million today - to establish a school at Tiverton for up to 150 boys. A staunch Protestant, Blundell's motivation included ensuring future generations were brought up in that faith. The school opened in 1604, teaching boys aged between 6 and 18, provided they were literate to a standard of 'grammar scholar' – i.e. that they should be proficient in Latin and Greek. The school was for boys from Tiverton and the immediate area, but pupils from further afield would be allowed to fill the places if there were insufficient locals. When Jack joined, new pupils came from across Devon, Somerset, Cornwall, Wales and even London: non-Tiverton boys being collectively called 'forreyners' in Blundell's will.[11] The Master, the Reverend Richard Keats, had been in the job for 17 years. Keats was a man of 'peculiar' methods mixing sternness with humour which 'could scarcely be recommended as a pattern for other masters'.[12] He apparently had a nickname for nearly every boy in the school, but carried with him always his 'discipline', a piece of knotted whip cord tied to a stick whose use can readily be imagined. He reputedly improved the weapon's effectiveness by 'feinting at a boy sitting nearer [to him] so as to throw off his guard the real victim'.[13] More positively, Keats introduced the school's first formal prize, the Keats medal, awarded for literary and oratorical abilities. Overall, a later assessment claimed he 'certainly ran a happy ship'.[14] A day at Blundell's began at 6.30am, with lessons between 7am and 9am followed by breakfast, two hours further class before lunch (also of two hours duration), then another two hours of lessons from 2pm, with supper served at 6pm.[15] Physical activity – fishing, swimming, hunting, walking and ball games – was encouraged but as well as English, numeracy, Roman and Greek history and classic poetry, the school focused its curriculum significantly on Latin and

10 *Register of The Scholars Educated in Blundell's School 1770 – 1809.* Benjamin Inceldon
11 *The Book of Blundell's* Charles Noon 2002
12 *'Blundell's Worthies'* in *The Blundellian* 1902
13 *'Blundell's Worthies'*
14 Noon, *Blundell's*
15 *A History of Blundell's School*, M. Sampson 2001

Greek.[16] The objective was to prepare pupils for university entry, often with the aim of qualifying them as clergymen, clerks or lawyers. Blundell's was therefore ideal for a clergyman's first son who might in time join his father's profession; two surviving letters from Blundell's suggest Jack enjoyed himself and thrived (later letters show signs of an education in the classics, his enjoyment of field sports, and that numeracy was probably not his favourite subject).

It was, however, a time of war and revolution. When Jack was born the American Colonies were in revolt, supported by France, Britain's longstanding enemy. Peace would not come until Britain recognised American independence with the Treaty of Paris in 1783. In the year after Jack was born revolution swept France, an event that may have altered the Hill's views on their sons' future careers. For the British, events in France were divisive. Some saw the merits of popular rule replacing government by hereditary rulers; others feared the consequences of revolution as extremism followed the initial uprisings in France. This was no academic matter; unrest grew across Britain, even as violence increased across the Channel. French military successes saw the revolutionary cause begin to spread across northern Europe; the country 'seemed closer than it had ever been to revolution'.[17] The British government sought to repress agitation, prosecuting those producing what it considered seditious material and suspending the writ of *habeas corpus*, allowing imprisonment without trial. The militia was mobilised on 1 December 1793 to help contain domestic disorder and in preparation for renewed hostilities with France.

The Hills, like much of the middle class, avidly read the newspapers, with which Devon was well served; 'the news was part of daily life'.[18] Moreover the turbulence reached even the Hills' little corner of the world. A Baptist minister, William Winterbotham, was arrested in Plymouth in 1792 charged with seditious preaching against the King; tried in Exeter in 1793 he received a fine and four years imprisonment. Then, on 21 January 1793, came the shock of Louis XVI's execution and on 1 February France's ruling Convention declared war on Britain. The official cause was French demands for freedom of navigation on the River Scheldt, closed since the Treaty of Westpahlia in 1648 to limit (Bourbon) French expansionism. This latest phase of war between Britain and France would, with varying casts of allies and only two brief interruptions, be fought across the globe for more than the next two decades.

16 Noon, *Blundell's*
17 *A History of Britain, Vol. 3.* Simon Schama 2002
18 *In These Times: Living In Britain Through Napoleon's Wars 1793 – 1815.*
   Jenny Uglow 2014

Renewed war with France did not quell discontent at home; indeed, the need to supply the fleet and the army increased food prices. A combination of a severe winter in 1794/5, failure of the following year's harvest and premiums paid by military procurement agents put the price of wheat up by 75%. Mass protests led to riots, including on the Hill's doorstep. In April 1795 a mob armed with clubs and axes from Bovey Tracy and Ilsington, Hennock's neighbours, attacked Bellamarsh Mill near Chudleigh, accusing the owners of 'engrossing' the price of flour. The militia deployed and ringleaders were arrested; one, Thomas Campion, was tried at Exeter and found guilty of rioting. On 6 August he was transported to Bovey Heathfield, at the foot of the hill on which Hennock stands, and hung. The Exeter and Devon Volunteers and part of the 25th Light Dragoons attended to prevent any rescue attempt. Similar incidents flared across the country until October when as George III drove to the opening of Parliament his coach was mobbed, pelted with mud and had its windows broken. On returning he was stopped again, and had to be rescued by his Household troops. The government made gatherings of more than fifty people illegal and clamped down further on seditious publications. This authoritarian response was criticised, but the Government was simultaneously buoyed by patriotic indignation at the King's close call. Suffering and depravation continued, but domestic strife temporarily eased in the face of an enemy massing troops over the Channel.

The turmoil, tension and trepidation of discontent, revolution and war was the background against which young Jack Hill was studying at Blundell's and his parents were considering his future. As solid members of the establishment, John and Margaret may have felt a mixture of concern and patriotism in response to apparent threats to the fabric of their society. As one historian recently put it 'the ends of Revolution were ends of principle and ideology: the fight against it was a fight for the survival of Britain's constitutional monarchy (and to many, therefore, for the survival of Britishness)'.[19] The French Revolution even attacked religion: the French church was stripped of rights; had property confiscated; thousands of priests were killed or exiled; and the Christian calendar was replaced. Liberty and reason became the basis for holidays, not saints or religious events. The Hills also witnessed the military implications of the threat as Devon prepared for war: Plymouth, the county's second largest town, was a major Royal Navy base just thirty-five miles away; the road to it from London ran past Hennock. Dartmouth built naval ships; warning stations appeared along both coastlines, with local corps of 'Sea Fencibles' recruited to man them; militia and regular

19 Schama, *History*

army recruitment stepped up; barracks and coastal batteries were built, together with fortifications at Berry Head, begun in 1794, to protect the important anchorage of Tor Bay. The whole county was put on a war footing because French threats had caused numerous scares and raids over the years. Teignmouth, at just over 10 miles away the nearest port to Hennock, was briefly captured and burned by the French navy in 1690.[20] In August 1779, when the Hills' firstborn son was barely six months old, a combined French and Spanish fleet appeared off Plymouth and people living near the coast made ready to flee: 'every person is packing and removing such valuables as they can' reported *Trewin's Flying Post*, the Exeter newspaper.[21] There was no invasion, but it was nevertheless a genuine threat and the risk of raids and attacks on coastal shipping remained. In July 1793 a sloop from Dartmouth was chased into Salcombe by a French privateer, and a year later customs officials boarded a brig that had been taken by another French privateer shortly before. Such incidents were regular occurrences throughout early years of the Revolutionary war and in June 1793 the first naval action in home waters of that war took place off Devon's southern coastline between the frigates HMS *Nymphe*, commanded by Captain Edward Pellew, and the French *Cleopatre*. It became known as the Battle of Prawle Point.

At national level the Secretary for War, Henry Dundas, noted 'When an enemy lands...the great object must be constantly to harass, alarm and fire on an enemy, and to impede his progress till a sufficient force assembles to attack him...every inch of ground, every field may to a degree be disputed, even by inferior numbers...The country must be driven, and every thing useful within his reach destroyed without mercy.'[22] Not for the last time, Britons were being told to be ready to fight on the beaches, in the fields and in the streets. Devon clergymen were instructed to prepare their flocks for evacuation should the enemy choose one of the county's coastlines as a landing point. The instructions issued in the village of Molland, about 40 miles due north across Dartmoor from Hennock illustrate the type of preparation that John Hill was expected to make:

> On receiving orders or in case of an enemy landing in your
> immediate neighbourhood, without waiting for such orders you
> are to repair to [the assembly point in the centre of the village]

---

20 Teignmouth was the last foreign capture of English soil. The French ransacked the town, destroyed around a dozen fishing vessels, burned houses, plundered churches, and killed livestock.

21 *Trewin's Flying Post* 20 August 1779

22 Quoted in *How the Army Made Britain a Global Power 1688 – 1815* Jeremy Black 2021.

there to take under your charge the wagons and carts appointed for the removal of the sick and infirm, and to conduct them by such route and to such place as you shall receive orders to do, taking care in all cases, to avoid travelling upon the public roads, which are to be left open for the King's use, namely for the conveyance of Ammunition and Provisions for troops, and for their march and to order to this if necessary, you will have proper tools with you for the purpose of making breaches in hedges etc. You are to be very careful of all those placed under your charge, and provide for them in the best manner you shall be able.[23]

The plan was that the route for evacuation from each village would be published in *Trewin's Flying Post*, with a copy to be delivered by horse to each parish.

While world events influenced John and Margaret's thinking, there were other considerations too. John's income was comfortable, but any family of their size faced financial challenges. Putting four boys through school and perhaps further education was costly, even for a relatively affluent country rector. Whether driven by patriotism or practicality, rather than have them follow their father's footsteps or take other paths in civilian life, the Hills determined that their boys would enlist for military service. Clergymen's sons often became military officers; the most famous being Nelson, whose father was a vicar. Their decision meant the Hills would make a significant personal contribution to Britain's fight. All four of their sons would eventually face the perils of war. There seems to have been no military tradition in the Hill family before John and Margaret's decision. Their ostensible patriotism may therefore have been underpinned by financial reality: the Royal Navy was a cheap option as a career for middle-class boys. There would be some expense for kitting out, but a sailor had to be a competent seaman to be commissioned as an officer; naval lieutenant's commissions were not bought, but awarded after an examination had been passed. That examination could not be taken before six years had been spent at sea, at least two of which had to be in the position of midshipman or master's mate. Another advantage was that young men with aspirations to be officers would be educated aboard ship, while simultaneously learning their profession. The upshot was that while Jack was still away at Blundell's, in January 1795 his younger brother William joined the navy as a 1st Class Volunteer, the precursor to becoming a midshipman. As the name implies, this was an unofficial position, but it was a common entry route for anyone seeking a career. William was all of 11

---

23 https://www.devonheritage.org

years old. His brother Charles, some two years younger, joined with the same status shortly afterwards. Going to sea at such ages was normal, but William was thrown in at the deep end: he saw his first fleet action within six months, aboard HMS *Colossus*, a 74-gun ship of the line, part of a fleet that engaged twelve French ships of the line off L'Orient in north-western France on 23 June. Three French ships were taken; *Colossus* had five men killed and thirty wounded. It is easy to imagine William being terrified and thrilled at the same time by this literal baptism of fire. It easy to imagine Jack, the Hill's eldest son, feeling jealous sitting at Blundell's contemplating his own future.

Unlike his brothers, Jack was to be a soldier. This was not without its drawbacks. The navy, Britain's 'wooden walls', was a highly respected service with recent victories to boast of, while the army's recent track record was mixed. Soldiers were less respected than sailors because they were used as an internal security force and because, unlike sailors who were either at sea or based in a few anchorages around the coast, soldiers were billeted in towns across the country. Throughout history, a combination of soldiers, drink and locals has often ended badly. Then there were financial matters: in the army a commission might have to be purchased. Further purchases might be necessary to gain promotion too, perhaps accompanied by a dose of patronage, or 'interest', as senior officers ensured their own or their friend's relatives had the best opportunity to gain advancement. The selling of army commissions dated at least to the 17th Century and in principle helped ensure officers came from families with means and a nominal stake in the well-being of the country. For the Government, money raised from commissions paid the bounties used to recruit men for the ranks and provided the officer with a saleable commodity on resignation or retirement ('selling out'), avoiding the need for a pension. The purchase system is caricatured today as reserving senior ranks for those who could afford it, leading to the over-promotion of incompetents. By the beginning of the 19th century, however, purchase represented only a minority of advancements, with seniority in rank being the usual means for officers to gain a step.[24] Time served did not guarantee the best officers reached the top; there were certainly cases of the opposite. But the largely successful record of the British army through the Napoleonic Wars suggests that combining purchase, which allowed some to make early advancement, with seniority, which in a time of war was arguably

---

24 During the period of the Peninsular War only 20% of first commissions and promotions were purchased. *The Purchase of Commissions: A Reappraisal* Michael Glover Journal of the Society for Army Historical Research Vol 58, No. 236 (Winter 1980)

more likely to equate to useful experience, broadly worked. The regular generation of vacancies through death, invalidity and resignation also kept the system flowing. As has been often noted, the early career of the man who became the Duke of Wellington resulted from a combination of purchase and interest, so the system cannot be considered entirely flawed. To quote one historian 'had Arthur Wellesley been compelled to languish in the lower echelons of the army list by a system which would be today considered more acceptable, it is not inconceivable that the whole course of European history might have been different'.[25]

The reality of the system, however, meant not being overly wealthy or having noble connections could impair one's prospects. Nevertheless, John Hill approached the office of the army's Commander-in-Chief, the Duke of York, to ask whether a commission for his son might be available. At the end of April 1796 the Duke's Military Secretary, Colonel Robert Brownrigg replied that His Royal Highness had 'shewn a disposition to serve him'.[26] Before a commission could be arranged, however, Jack needed to be interviewed by a General Officer to ensure his suitability. It seems the Hills were initially tempted for Jack to join the cavalry. His first surviving letter, written from Blundell's, reports that he had been probing suitably connected schoolmates about the prospects; but joining the cavalry seemed problematic, as commissions were apparently in great demand.

Tiverton
April 11, 1796

Dear Father,

I have further enquired if there was a cornecy vacant in the 27 L. Dragoons now going to India, and there is not a single vacancy. All of them have been filled up about six weeks ago when they had ten subalterns join them. I had this intelligence from one that went to school here about a year and a half ago in which he is Lieutenant.[27]

There are three other Regiments of Horse going with them besides the 25 and 27; the 23 and 24 are two of them the other I do not know - they all go out dismounted and expect to sail in about a

25 Haythornthwaite *Armies*. The purchase system is also discussed in depth in *Wellington's Military Machine* Philip J Haythornthwaite 1989 and *Soldiers* Richard Holmes 2011.

26 TNA WO31/49: *Memoranda of appointments, promotions and resignations: July 1796*. Captain Bradford to General Grenville

27 William Whitter, from Holcombe in Devon, left Blundell's on 21 December 1794. Whitter's father was also a churchman; Holcombe is only some ten miles from Hennock. *Register* Inceldon

month. I have enquired of Shawe his father is L[ieutenant] Colonel in India and there purchased an Ensigncy for his son.[28] I have desired Carrington to write home to his Father at Ide who, I believe, has or will have a commission in the Horse for his son, for which of the sons it is, the one that is here tells me, is not determined on - however, if it be so, I shall be able to get from him a very particular account and will; as soon as I have it you shall have it the day after.[29] Mr. Garrett, I think, will be able to give you a very good account by applying to the Regiments agents in London that are now going or already gone there.[30] The 74th, in which Col. Shaw is, is coming home immediately.[31] It seems all the regiments will be crowded from Lieutenant Witter's account.

If you will give me leave, I can have a p[ai]r. of foils here at a week's notice. It will be more for amusement than trouble for one of the boys here who fences very well to teach me. Give my love to Charles when you write him and also to William. Let me know when the former joins his ship – & to Caroline. Duty to Mother and Aunt Peggy. Mr K gave me a knife for keeping the boys so well in house during Easter. I saw Uncle Pinhey here and Mr. Barter of Bath last week.[32]

I remain,
Your Dutiful Son,
J H E HILL

Monday, 12 o'clock

---

28 Two Shaw brothers attended Blundell's. Musgrave and Robert Shaw were admitted aged 11 and 10 respectively on 1 October 1794; both left on the same day as Jack, 29 June 1796. They were the sons of Robert Shaw of the 74th Regiment. Inceldon, *Register*

29 Robert Palk Carrington, son of William Henry Carrington of Ide, Devon, was admitted to Blundell's aged 7 on 3 February 1789 and left on 29th June 1798. Inceldon, *Register*

30 The Reverend John Garrett was Master at Pynsent's Free School in Chudleigh. John Pynsent (a Chudleigh native) died in 1668 and left money for a school for the education of 20 boys from the area. Garrett became master in 1771 and remained there until his death in July 1811. Garrett and John Hill undoubtedly knew each other; it is possible that Jack attended Pynsent's school before Blundell's, but there is no surviving evidence. The school closed in 1912.

31 The 74th in fact remained in India until 1803. Colonel Shawe (or Shaw) was mentioned in despatches for his 'gallant manner' during the battle of Seringapatam on 4 May 1799.

32 John Pinhey was married to John Hill's sister; their son (also John) enrolled at Blundell's the year after Jack.

The celebrated 'Mr K' in this letter was the Master, Richard Keats. The knife was almost certainly a reward for overseeing other boys; Jack was a senior pupil by then, so might well have held a position with some responsibility as one of the school 'monitors'. It has been suggested that the boys had mutinied and Jack helped restore control.[33] This cannot be ruled out. There is a record concerning a 'rebellion' at the school in 1787, sparked by allegations of harsh treatment by Thomas Wood, the under-master, but that was 5 years before Jack's time at Blundell's. There were also 'rebellions' by boys at other schools in this period: at Eton in 1783, Winchester 1793, Rugby 1794 and Harrow in 1805. If there was an incident at Blundell's in 1796, however, there is no record of it (though that is unsurprising, as the school would not have made such things widely known).

Jack may have thought of fencing as preparation for military life. By 1796 the wearing of swords by civilians was declining as fashions changed, but military officers of course still carried them. The unavailability of cavalry commissions may have been a relief to Jack's father who was going to have to foot the bills. Joining any regiment was expensive; aside from purchasing a commission, an officer had to buy his own equipment and pay for accommodation and rations; 4 shillings and 8 pence daily pay was far from sufficient for this.[34] The relatively recent innovation of officer's messes made money go further, but the joining fee was between £3 and £4 for a new junior officer.[35] Pay deductions were taken for the upkeep of the Royal Hospitals at Chelsea and Kilmainham, the widows and orphans fund and regimental agent's fees.[36] This was for the infantry; the cavalry was significantly more expensive with a commission costing around double and an officer having to provide his own horses, saddlery and other tack.

Whether because of cost or availability, the view formed that Jack should not join the cavalry but should become an infantryman. Even this was not straightforward; some regiments were decidedly more attractive than others and if the war ended there could be reductions or disbandments. Jack's next letter, also from Blundell's, suggests his father had been investigating such issues, but had not reached a conclusion. He was, though now being advised by two people with a particular interest.

---

33 *Letters to a Vicarage 1796 – 1815* by Enid Case and Jenny Currie (1988)
34 An Ensign's daily pay rate after the Government agreed to a rise for all ranks of the Army and Navy in 1797. On active service all officers also had to contribute 6d per day for rations.
35 Nearly £300 at today's prices.
36 *Officers and NCOs in the late 18th Century Army* Lieutenant-General Jonathon Riley 2013

Dear Mother,

I received yours yesterday (Friday), but I had it not in my power until now to answer it. I am sorry to hear that the advantages of a Soldier are so few with respect to what we imagined. I think that the commissions mentioned by Mr. Garrett are not the best for this one reason - the Scotch Brigade it is uncertain if they will be kept in pay during so long a peace as may ensue after this war. It is now in your pow'r for once to chose where to go: once entered into a Regiment necessity forces the officers to go where it is ordered. A commission may be bought in another Regiment besides those in the West Indies I should think at equally as cheap a rate; however, I do not think myself that I am able to determine which is the best.

C[aptain] Bradford can inform Father in every thing he wants to know; what an Ensign pay and what other perquisites are? If he can maintain himself upon what Government allows him? If it would be better abroad at first or at home where he would best be able to maintain himself and get promotion? There are, I should think, some other regiments at Gibraltar besides S[cotch] Brigade; if it were certain they would not be disbanded at the end of the war, I should think it a very good Corps and good station, though the People in general do not like it.

I should like to know if it would be necessary to join the 13th immediately on the purchase of the commission, and how many years they have been there; they would, I suppose come home about a twelve months' time. Captains Bradford and MacKenzie can inform and advise better than most people.

Remember me to Charles. William, I see, is sailed. Do let me know what C[aptain] B[radford] says as soon as you know. Please give my duty to Father. Love to Aunt P[eggy] and Caroline.

I remain yours,
J HILL

PS My Nankeen Breeches are almost torn to pieces. Do send me some others.

Jack's hesitancy to join a regiment in the West Indies was wise; in the late 18th Century it was a graveyard for many soldiers. An estimated 40,000 British military personnel died, with as many again invalided, in the West Indies between 1794 and 1796, mostly from disease:

in 1796 over 40% of troops stationed in the Windward and Leeward Islands died - over 6,500 from fewer than 16,000 personnel. In October 1796 alone 1,273 men died of disease there. Unsurprisingly, commissions in regiments stationed in the West Indies were affordable; the official price for an 'entry-level' commission at the time was around £400, but prices for more fashionable regiments could be higher. Establishing 'what an Ensign pay [is] and what other perquisites are; and if he can maintain himself upon what Government allows him' was also a wholly valid question. Bradford's answer may have been that initially pay alone would not be adequate. Contemporary commentators thought it essential for an officer to have private means. In 1804 one of Britain's leading soldiers, Sir John Moore, estimated that a private income of £50 to £100 was necessary; others thought twice that. Start-up costs were also significant, like the cost of acquiring uniforms and other clothing, including boots, and perhaps a pistol. A sword might cost four guineas, more than two weeks' pay for a new officer.

The 'Scotch Brigade' was newly revived, returning to active establishment only in 1794. Perhaps this was why it was thought an option. In Gibraltar when Jack wrote, it moved to South Africa later in 1796 and India in 1798. Renamed the 94th Foot in 1802, the regiment was not disbanded until 1818. Speculation on their demise was ill-founded, but Jack could not know that. The reference to 'the 13th' is puzzling; the 13th had been in the West Indies but after very significant losses from disease were effectively broken up in August 1795 with survivors drafted to other regiments and officers and NCOs returned to England. When Jack wrote, therefore, they were effectively in suspension. The references to Captains Bradford and Mackenzie and Jack's speculation about when the regiment mentioned would return from the West Indies strongly suggest he meant the 23rd Foot, the Royal Welch Fusiliers. The 23rd had been in the West Indies since 1794 but returned in April. Bradford and Mackenzie were officers of that regiment, so Jack wrote 13th, not 23rd, in error. George Bradford and James MacKenzie had local connections. The Bradfords lived in Ideford, just 6 miles from Hennock, where George's father was the vicar. The clerical connection meant the Bradfords and Hills knew each other. MacKenzie's father, himself a former officer of the 23rd, was an important man in Exeter, with which John Hill retained close connections. The 23rd had 'suffered so severely from the climate [of the West Indies] that the regiment returned to England a perfect skeleton'.[37]

---

37 *Historical Record of the Royal Welch Fusiliers* Major Rowland Broughton-Mainwaring, 1889

375 members of the regiment had died in 1794, another 152 the next year, and eleven more in the few months of 1796 before they left; in June 1796 the regiment was just 103 strong - around 90% below official strength. They needed new officers and their Colonel, Lieutenant-General Richard Grenville, wanted the junior vacancies filled quickly. The captains knew this; having learned the Hills foresaw military careers for their sons they lobbied for Jack to join their regiment, possibly suggesting that Grenville would support his acquiring a commission without purchase.

As the Duke of York's office had already been approached, Bradford and Mackenzie now moved fast to ensure Jack would join the 23rd. Finding a General Officer to vouch for their protégé was easy; Major-General Richard Donkin, also a former Welch Fusilier and colleague of Mackenzie's father Frederick, would meet Jack in the sure knowledge that he would give a favourable opinion. In short order Donkin duly confirmed this:

Colonel Brownrigg
Secry. To H.R.H Field Marshal
The Duke of York
Saville Row
London

Exeter 7 May 1796

Sir

In consequence of your letter of the 29th April addressed by command of H.R.H. Field Marshal the Duke of York to the Rev'd. John Hill, Hennock near Chudleigh, I have seen & conversed with his Son, John Humphrey Edward Hill, between 17 & 18 years of age, full 5 feet 8 inches high; and can with great safety certify him fit for a commission in His Majesty's Army from Education, Address and Figure.

I am, Sir your most obedient
Humble Servant
R. Donkin
Major General[38]

---

38 TNA WO 31/49

Soon after, Bradford wrote to Grenville:

Lt. General Grenville
Royal Welch Fusiliers
Burlington Street
London

Ideford May 20th

Sir

Having been informed by Capt Mackenzie of your wish to fill up the vacancies amongst the Junior Officers of the Corps, with respectable young men, who may be disposed to accept the same, I take the liberty of mentioning the name of Mr John Humphry [sic] Edward Hill, who is greatly desirous of embarking as a Soldier in the 23rd Regt.

His Father is a most respectable Clergyman of this Country with a large family, to whom a Commission is a very great object. The young man has had a very good classical education, & is reputed a good scholar, he is between seventeen & eighteen years of age, & is on the point of leaving School, is a very personable, well grown young man, about 5 foot 9 Inches high, has a very decent knowledge of the French language, & is in every respect calculated for a Military Life.

The Duke of York has, by letter from his Secretary to his father, shewn a disposition to serve him & only waits a recommendation from a General Officer.

If the above particulars meet your approbation, & you will have the goodness, to mention his name for a Commission in the 23rd Regt. you will confer a very great favor upon a very deserving family & [through] this the obligations of

Sir
Your very faithful & very obedient servant
Geo. Bradford
Capt. 23rd Regt.[39]

Grenville passed both Donkin's and Bradford's letters to Brownrigg. His covering note, however, noted an awkwardness: he had also recently recommended another candidate. But as he finished writing, unfortunate yet timely news provided a way ahead.

39 TNA WO 31/49

Lt Col Brownrigg

My Dear Brownrigg

I must by leave trouble you with the enclosed, to which I have given the answer, that having recommended Mr James Dawson West to His Highness for a commission, I could not in justice to Him recommend Mr Hill, but that I w'd lay his name before you to be put upon the list.

Yours most sincerely
R Grenville

Thursday May 26th 1796

PS I have just rec'd a letter from Lt. Col. Ellis to acquaint me that 2nd Lieut. Morse of the 23rd Regt. who was upon the recruiting service, has shot himself.[40]

Morse's untimely demise cleared the way; on the reverse of Grenville's letter is the comment

to be noted for a 2nd Lt^{cy} in the W Fuziliers.

A month after he left Blundell's, on 29 July 1796, Jack was commissioned into the Royal Welch Fusiliers. His commission was published in the *London Gazette*: 'John H.E. Hill, Gent. To be 2nd Lieutenant'.[41]

At 17 Jack was young, but about 10% of officer recruits to the army at the time were between 15 and 17 years old; some were even younger.[42] Even today no two British army regiments do everything the same way, as was true in 1796. The most junior officer rank in most of the infantry then was Ensign, but in Fusilier regiments this rank was called 2nd Lieutenant. Jack's joining the Royal Welch Fusiliers has no Welsh angle; affiliations of British regiments at the time implied little about where they recruited from.[43] An aspiring officer would obtain a commission in the most attractive regiment he could afford (or which

---

40 TNA WO 31/49
41 *London Gazette* Issue No. 13919 dated 6 August 1796
42 *A Gentleman Volunteer: The Letters of George Hennell from the Peninsular War, 1812–13* Michael Glover [ed.] 1979
43 Haythornthwaite notes 'that most Welsh of regiments, the 23rd (Royal Welch) Fuzileers at Waterloo contained (of those men whose origin is recorded) 405 English, 62 Irish, 7 Scots, 1 Dutchman, 1 Canadian, 1 Italian and only 191

was offering him one for free). The 23rd had officers born in all four home nations and America, where it had served with distinction through the War of Independence. Just as 'Welch' did not make the regiment exclusively Welsh, so 'Fusiliers' no longer implied different equipment to other regiments. In the 17th Century they had been one of the first regiments armed with 'fusils', a type of gun fired by a spark from a flint striking a piece of steel (better known as a 'flintlock'), rather than by a burning piece of cord (a 'matchlock'). By 1796 Flintlocks were standard army equipment, but the original 'Fusiliers', the 7th, 21st and 23rd Foot, kept their name as a title of honour - one of the many distinctions by which the regiment sustained their identity.[44] Jack now received the formal Commission document granted to every officer in the army on appointment. Despite the free entry, his father would have had to pay the fee which nominally covered the cost of producing this. In the 23rd, as a more fashionable Fusilier regiment, the fee was £6 11s 10d.[45] The document was, however, magnificent and signed by the King himself:

> George the Third, by the Grace of God, King of Great Britain, France and Ireland, Defender of the Faith, &c., To Our Trusty and Well-beloved John Humphrey Edward Hill. gent.,
> Greetings: we repose especial Trust and Confidence in Your Loyalty, Courage and good Conduct, do, by these presents, constitute and appoint you to be 2nd Lieutenant in a company of the 23rd Regiment of Foot...[46]

In the weeks after leaving school Jack visited tailors and suppliers to buy his various uniforms (to be worn as appropriate on formal 'dress' and less formal 'undress' occasions), a 12-inch tall fusilier bearskin cap for ceremonial events and a two-pointed cocked hat for regular wear, a sword, perhaps of the new 1796 pattern, a sword belt to hang it from,

---

Welshmen' and by 1815 the regiment had recruited in Wales for some years. As a Devonian, Jack was certainly not unique.

44 Sometime spelled fuzileer, fusileer, or fuzilier. 'Welch', the original spelling is the regiment's preference, although when Jack served the official spelling was 'Welsh'.

45 One drawback of fusiliers having 2nd lieutenant as their lowest officer rank: the cost of an Ensign's commission in other line regiments was £2 less. Glover, *Commissions*

46 The Act of Union of 1801, which established the United Kingdom of Great Britain and Ireland, dropped the phrase 'King of France', used since Edward III, from the formal list of the sovereign's titles. Britain's formal claim to France remained until March 1802, when the Treaty of Amiens recognised the Republic.

shirts, waistcoats, breeches, stockings, footwear, gorget, officer's sash and greatcoat. Other 'necessaries', included a 'canteen' or mess kit and sundry other baggage. Preparations completed, and farewells made to relatives and friends, in October he travelled to join his battalion, based at that point in Chatham. On route, he may have called in to the regimental agents, Messrs. Greenwood & Cox, at their offices in Craig's Court, off Whitehall. The agents, though private companies, were a critical part of regimental machinery, managing pay and other financial affairs and arranging many aspects of a soldier's personal administration such as forwarding baggage and mail when the regiment moved. The road from Exeter to London was good, but was probably two or three days travel, depending on how much his father spent on the fare. Recruitment had by now increased the regimental strength but Jack was joining a small band: in November 1796 they had just 229 officers and men, against a full establishment of 1,010. In 1796 officers and soldiers were required to have long hair tied in a short pigtail, or queue. In the 23rd the officers wore this tied with ribbons and fixed up against their heads by a small comb; the men wore theirs greased and rolled up into a ball, or 'club', at the top of the neck. On arriving, Jack had his hair styled into a Fusilier officer's plait with short, frizzy side locks and donned for the first time the red jacket with royal blue facings that he would remove for the last time nearly three decades later.[47]

The army Jack joined was not an impressive force; 'In 1795...the army's stock stood as low as the life expectancy of its troops' commented one recent author.[48] It was, though, starting a significant regeneration championed by the Duke of York. The army's administration, size, processes, promotion arrangements, service periods, pay, accommodation, uniforms, equipment, tactics and drill were all changing. Together with the development of a core of experienced officers and men, these reforms would help deliver consistency across the service. Previously the Colonel of a regiment, then effectively its 'owner', determined what manoeuvres his men would be trained in; the reforms now being introduced would in due course 'turn a collection of regiments into an Army'.[49] Education and housing would also be critical. When a young British army officer joins a regiment today, they are probably newly-graduated from the

---

47 The Guards and all regiments designated 'Royal' had dark blue facings and Colours.

48 *The Making of the British Army.* Allan Mallinson 2011

49 Black, *Global Power.* As Black notes, the whole country was undergoing major change at the time, with the introduction of income tax (1799), parliamentary union with Ireland (1800–1) and the first national census (1801) all part of a period of wider reform.

Royal Military College (Sandhurst) and accommodated in officially provided quarters in or near their barracks. In 1796 there was no prior training, it being widely considered that 'fine education was inappropriate in a soldier; it was enough that he took some tuition by rule of thumb when he joined his regiment'.[50] A Military Academy had been founded at Woolwich in 1741, but that was for the technical roles of artillery or engineer officer. What became the Royal Military College, training infantry officers, was not founded until 1801. Before then, a new officer received on the job training. Jack's introduction to the 23rd may have been similar to that outlined by a lieutenant in the 43rd Regiment, who was required 'to drill with a squad composed of peasants from the plough and other raw recruits, first learning the facings, marchings and the companies' evolutions. That being completed, the officer put on cross-belts and pouches and learnt the firelock exercises; then again he marched with the same; and when it was considered that the whole was perfect, with and without arms, they began to skirmish in extended file, and last of all learned the duties of a sentry, and to fire ball cartridge at a target.'[51] At least this approach meant an officer started at the bottom, and should have a good understanding of what he was ordering his men to do.

Accommodation was similarly informal. Military barracks were rare; many were not built until the 19th Century. Officers and men instead were billeted in 'inns, livery stables, alehouses, victualling houses, and all houses selling brandy, strong waters, cyder or metheglin [mead] by retail to be drunk on the premises.'[52] Officers pooled resources to buy more and better food and drink from the innkeeper, so inventing the officer's mess, an unofficial establishment run by the officers themselves - but no less regimented for that. By 1795, the mess of the 23rd had 46 rules, covering the costs of membership, the appointment of a treasurer and management committee, the pay due to those providing food, strict rules on not removing utensils and the nature of the drink to be consumed (Rule 14: 'none but port be the wine in general use of the Mess except where the whole body then present chuse to drink any other, or where it cannot be got so good and cheap as other wines'). Perhaps most important was Rule 35: 'no person whatever can become a member of the Mess unless he either is, or has been an Officer of the regiment'.[53] Jack's early letters show him a thoughtful and responsible young man, but any 17-year-old just out of

---

50 *Scientific Soldier: A life of General Le Marchant.* R. H. Thoumine 1968
51 Quoted in Holmes, *Redcoat*
52 Quoted in Holmes, *Redcoat*
53 The full 'Rules of the Mess' of the 23rd, first codified in 1787 are in Appendix II of *Regimental Records of the Royal Welch Fusiliers (Formerly 23rd Foot) Vol. I 1689–1815* A D L Cary, OBE and Stouppe McCance 1921, reprinted 1995

school must have experienced significant culture shock as he plunged in at the deep end with new people, a new job and a new home. Boarding at Blundell's may have prepared him a little, but the regiment was an entirely new way of life, governed by new rules.

No letters survive from his initial days in uniform, though circumstantial evidence suggests Jack settled in well. Having family friends like Bradford and Mackenzie to guide him must have helped, while Mackenzie's younger brother George, another new officer in the regiment, would become a close friend and confidant. Within a year of joining Jack was promoted, without purchase, to Lieutenant.[54] This first promotion offers an example of how advancement through a combination of purchase, seniority and interest could benefit several officers within a regiment. In April 1797, Captain Peter Buchanan died; the vacancy was filled by the promotion of Lieutenant Henry Ellis, son of the regiment's former Commanding Officer, and still formally one of its Lieutenant-Colonels, John Joyner Ellis. The younger Ellis had been the regiment's senior lieutenant, a position then known as captain-lieutenant, not least due to a very early start to his military career: his father had bought Henry an Ensigncy in the 89th regiment before he was a year old. To quote the 23rd's official records 'on [the 89th] being disbanded a few months later, the baby was placed upon half-pay, but brought on full pay again as ensign, at the age of six, on 21st September 1789, in the 41st Foot.' Henry Ellis was promoted lieutenant in 1792, aged 10, transferring to the 23rd when his father assumed command the following year. Ellis's promotions were all bought; his making captain in 1797 aged just 14 shows how purchase enabled rapid progress for those with connections and wealth. Ellis' stepping up to captain enabled another lieutenant, Holland Lecky, to become the captain-lieutenant and, in turn, for Jack Hill to be promoted to the lieutenancy vacated by Lecky. None of this would have happened if the captaincy had not been obtained by Henry Ellis; Ellis would become a close friend to Jack and his abilities would live up to his rapid rise, though that could not have been foreseen in his early teens. Jack himself made a good impression on his senior officers; in his *Statement of Services*, written many years later, he proudly noted that he was appointed to the Lieutenant-Colonel's Company by Ellis senior himself, though according to the 23rd's records, this did not formally happen until May 1799.[55]

When Jack joined the 23rd it had a single battalion of ten companies, each nominally of seventy-five men, one or more sergeants,

---

54 His promotion, vice Lecky, was in the *London Gazette* Issue No. 13999 dated 4th April 1797.

55 TNA WO 12/3963 *Regimental General Muster books and Pay Lists, 23rd Foot,* 1799

three to six corporals and two drummers. Each company was commanded by a captain, usually supported by two lieutenants and two 2nd lieutenants.[56] Historically, one company was nominally commanded by the regimental colonel and another by the lieutenant-colonel. These were accordingly designated as the 'Colonel's' and 'Lieutenant-Colonel's' companies. By 1796, the practice of such senior officers commanding a company of men in person was outdated, though it was not formally abolished until 1803. The Colonel's company was instead usually commanded by the captain-lieutenant and the Lieutenant-Colonel's by a lieutenant. Jack did well to be talent spotted while still an inexperienced 2nd Lieutenant, whose status in the regiment was formally listed as *'en second'*, in effect a supernumerary position somewhat akin to probation. Perhaps his connection to Bradford and James Mackenzie, the latter shortly to become one of the regiment's majors, helped. That said, Jack's promotion and appointment also underlined the 23rd's continuing shortage of manpower. Their monthly pay list for December 1797 (which incidentally lists Jack as being 'absent by leave', having presumably been allowed to go home for Christmas) shows his company to have two other officers, six sergeants, five corporals, three drummers and just fifty-two 'Private Men' (one of whom, Thomas Williams, had deserted on 27 December).[57] One of these men would have acted as Jack's personal 'soldier-servant', a position that provided extra pay, another expense for the officer's pocket, and sometimes excused the man from other duty.[58]

The sergeants and corporals, or non-commissioned officers (NCOs), provided essential support to their company officers, especially in ensuring discipline. When not commanding on parade, on the march or leading in action, officers generally had little to do with their men while in barracks, though an officer was expected to ensure his men were provided for before he looked after himself; in practice the NCOs ran the company.[59] Unlike commissioned officers, however, they remained at risk of flogging and being returned to the ranks if they failed to live up to their responsibilities. The relationship between a company officer and his NCOs and men was nonetheless critical for

---

56 Company establishments increased to 100 in 1805. A typical company establishment from then had five corporals and ninety-five men. *British Army Establishments During the Napoleonic War* Roderick MacArthur *Journal of the Society for Army Historical Research* 2009

57 Sergeants: John Bowman, John Callaghan, William Gregory, William Johnston, Richard Love, Theophilus Sutton. Corporals: Robert Crew, William Chappell, John Dobbins, Joseph Scott, William Watson.

58 Haythornthwaite, *Armies*

59 Riley, *Officers and NCOs*

military effectiveness: 'the rules of discipline, subordination, and good order teach the Officers their duties towards the soldiers; and how to render them efficient, and to preserve them in a state of efficiency to serve the State. They teach the soldiers to respect their superiors, the non-commissioned Officers and the Officers; and to consider them as their best friends and protectors. The enforcement of these rules will enable the officers to conduct with kindness towards the soldiers those duties with which he is charged.'[60]

The NCOs and men filling the thin ranks of the 23rd came almost inevitably from society's lower reaches. Straightened personal circumstances attracted most individuals to join when a recruiting party comprising an officer, sergeant and party of smartly-uniformed men and a drummer, arrived in their village 'spinning wild tales of the adventures of their countrymen [and] of the glories of war.'[61] The offer of the quasi-mystical 'King's shilling', actually a signing-on bounty of perhaps around ten guineas, was too tempting for many to resist, though most of it was quickly taken back in payment for 'necessaries', including a uniform and other equipment, and what remained was often soon drunken away.[62] For those who faced poverty, hunger and few prospects at home, the incentive was regular food, drink, shelter and pay. Joining for patriotic reasons was not unknown, and the chance to travel, serve and fight the King's enemies was also not an uncommon motive for enlistment. Some who joined may have served in their local militia, giving them a modicum of experience. Others joined the army rather than face jail; pardons for those enlisting were common practice. Once joined, the men faced regular drilling, iron discipline enforced if necessary via corporal punishment and the risk of a violent death or disfigurement from enemy action or disease: in 1796, enlistment in the ranks was for life; time-limited service was not introduced until 1806. If a soldier suffered serious wounds or grew too old or infirm to serve in the line he might be transferred to garrison duty or a veteran's battalion (which tended to guard fixed fortifications) or discharged - for the lucky few as an in or out Pensioner in the Royal Hospitals. An alternative route out was the one Thomas Williams took, desertion, but there were very serious consequences if an absconder was caught.

Since the middle of the 18th Century, the standard British infantry weapon, carried by fusiliers and every other infantryman, was a flintlock

---

60 The Duke of Wellington, 1834. Quoted in Haythornthwaite, *Armies*

61 *Wellington's Regiments* Ian Fletcher 1994

62 The amount varied by regiment, the number of recruits needed and competition from the navy, who paid more than most army regiments. *Recruiting the Ranks of the Regular British Army During the French Wars* T H McGuffle Journal for the Society of Army Historical Research 1956

musket affectionately known as the Brown Bess. Nearly 5 feet long, with a smooth-bore unrifled barrel, the weapon weighed around 10 pounds. It fired a lead ball weighing about 1oz that was rammed down the muzzle after powder had been poured into the barrel. The weapon was not aimed but 'presented': pointed from shoulder height towards the enemy. It was unquestionably an inaccurate weapon; but fired in volley by a company standing shoulder to shoulder in two or more ranks, it would hurl sufficient lead through the air to be devastating at ranges of up to 100 yards and possibly beyond. The best infantry could fire at a rate of up to three shots per minute, though doing so in the chaos of a battle took serious discipline. Firing generated a cloud of smoke which, coupled with that from artillery and exploding shells rapidly obscured vision; in battle it was often the case that nobody from the commander of the army to the individual soldier could see much at all. For close-in work, and often used to unsettle the opponent, the Brown Bess could be fitted with a triangular bayonet with a 17-inch blade; a fearsome weapon that was hard to stand against when used offensively and difficult to overcome when grouped into a defensive hedge.

Some of the men Jack oversaw could have been boys of 15 or less, but most were older than him. A minimum recruiting height was set at 5 feet 4 inches, though some exceptions found their way in. As civilians they might have been labourers, miners, weavers, clerks, cobblers, metalworkers, tailors, barbers, carpenters, or a host of other trades, some of which skills would be useful in their military life. At least one in ten, possibly one in three, were illiterate. Ostensibly medical tests had to be passed before anyone joined, though in the 23rd's situation these may have been loosely interpreted to fill the ranks. Significantly, and unlike the conscripted troops they would often face, all were in one form or another volunteers who had sworn an oath, in front of a magistrate or Justice of the Peace, attesting to their name, age, occupation and health and that they would 'be true to our Sovereign Lord King George, and serve Him honestly and faithfully in defence of his Person, Crown, and Dignity, against all His Enemies or Opposers whatsoever: And to observe and obey His Majesty's Orders, and the orders of the generals and Officers set over me by His Majesty'. Once sworn in, the regiment provided men with comradeship and a strong sense of belonging. In regiments with proud histories like the RWF, these were virtues based on strong traditions, but it was drill, discipline and, over the next twenty years, experience that would turn those who survived into part of one of the most successful military forces that Britain ever produced. But first, Jack and his new colleagues would experience a few missteps along the way.

CHAPTER 2

HIGH ADVENTURES IN
THE LOW COUNTRIES

'Ostend, having charge of a detachment to cover the Artillery...
taken prisoner and confined in Lille; Holland, had the command
of the above Company in every action...on returning embark'd
on board the "Valk" Dutch Frigate...wrecked'

Memorandum to the Duke of York, 1823

As the 23rd, with Lieutenant Hill now proudly in their ranks, recovered their strength and trained their recruits, the political and military situation in continental Europe worsened. There was also continuing trouble at home. In April 1797 the 23rd moved to Chelmsford as part of a force assembled to suppress a naval mutiny about pay and conditions at the Nore. Pay rises and other concessions already made following mutiny at Spithead in April and a refusal to go further by the Government was coupled with firm punishment of the ringleaders; the Nore mutiny ended within a month. Meanwhile in Europe a promising young general named Napoleon Bonaparte had just led the French *Armée d'Italie* in a lightning campaign across the northern Italian provinces, culminating with victory at Rivoli. The Treaty of Campo Formio that ended the campaign brought temporary peace between Austria and France and made Britain the latter's only major enemy. In 1796 a French fleet of over forty ships with 15,000 troops aboard sailed towards Ireland to support an uprising; as with the Spanish Armada centuries before, Britain was saved by its bad weather. A planned landing near Cork proved impossible due to storms in Bantry Bay.[1] On 22 February a small affair which became known as 'Britain's last invasion' took place at Fishguard in Wales.[2] Though both abject failures, these raids showed the French threat was real: en route to Fishguard the fleet was spotted off the north coast of Devon (some frigates stopped at Ilfracombe), where the local militia turned out. One historian has

---

1 Schama, *History*
2 *Britain's Last Invasion: Fishguard 1797*, J. E. Thomas 2007

suggested that by 'the end of the eighteenth century the threat of French invasion was a way of life'.[3] In November 1797 Bonaparte was appointed to command the French *Armée d'Angleterre* (French armies were routinely named after the place they were looking to conquer). An invasion force began to assemble. This was a potential game-changer: Bonaparte had championed the notion of France landing a blow against Britain: 'Our Government must destroy the English monarchy...Let us concert all our activity on the navy and destroy England. That done, Europe is at our feet.'[4] It was good propaganda, but Bonaparte recognised that the Royal Navy's dominance of the Channel was the reality. After visiting the Channel ports, he recommending keeping the threat of an invasion only as a deception: a strong French army poised across the Channel could not be ignored by the British government and would help keep their army pinned down at home.

It was as well that the Royal Navy was so powerful, because Britain was unprepared for invasion. Jack's first surviving letter from his service life is only partially dated; he missed off the year.[5] But it was written shortly after the regiment moved from Chatham to Chelmsford in April 1797 and underlines how unready his men were, needing more training, better quality uniforms and fewer desertions. They were typical of the poor state of an army which might have to fight for their country's existence.

Thursday, August 10 [1797]

My Dear Mother,
I shall await your next with some impatience as I wish to know every particular respecting William. Charles you mention is gone to Denmark, but he is but halfway there. I saw by Tuesday's paper that he is with Admiral Duncan.[6] I much wish he may be in the India service as that will employ him during peace, he will be sent to the[re] right about as soon as the war is over.[7] The servant I now

---

3 *Napoleon's Obsession – The Invasion of England* Nick Lipscombe *British Journal for Military History, Volume 1, Issue 3, June 2015*
4 Quoted in *The Campaigns of Napoleon* David Chandler 1966
5 In Case and Currie, *Letters*, this letter is dated to 1800, but it is from 1797
6 Duncan was Commander-in-Chief, North Sea. Which ship Charles Hill was on is not clear, but Jack's calling him 'halfway' to Denmark is consistent with his being in Duncan's fleet, Sheerness being almost exactly halfway to Denmark from Devon!
7 This comment reflects a continuing doubt about the war's duration and of the probability of military reductions in the event of peace. That Charles might be better off in 'the India service' is a suggestion he might join a ship of the Honourable East India Company, whose fleet did depend on the war.

have was one to an old mate on board the Canton. From the report he makes of it, it seems to be an enviable situation. His promotion will go on in the Navy another way all the same. I recollect Mr. Grey's having the Dart, Charles having been fitted out for the East Indies is another great point, consider he is provided for during his life by entering into that service. Your idea of our coming into Devon I think is not likely to happen, we imagine we shall go to Guernsey, Gibraltar, or some such place. Our men are deserting so fast the Col[onel]'s Company to which I belong alone has lost six men by it since we came from South End; of the 10 other Companies, some more few less, we are now near an 100 men weaker since we left Chatham. Some stop or other will be put to so infamous a practice; we all imagine from that, that our stay in England will be short. I wish we may go abroad for some time. I should get high up among the Lieut[enant]s - some are about to retire, some to purchase, it will hasten them off, and make many steps for me.[8]

I should be very glad to come into Devon, if we do I shall be more expensive still to you, it would cost £10 which I assure you is more than I can manage yet to get over without your assistance but many things would be cheaper there, or rather that I could get done for nothing which cost me a great deal and badly done after all. Some of my linen I have laid aside that is rent in hopes to get you to mend them, you will hear for a greater certainty where we are to go when Cap^n. B[radford] joins[you].[9] You may then send what I desired you: after we have been reviewed we shall know if we move.

The Garrison of Plymouth has its complement of troops: the Dutch fleet will keep all the military in this Kingdom that are in it now, two Troops of the 1st Fencible Cavalry are here the same as were at Exeter some time ago. The Lancasters, who marched from this when we came here, do not like their Quarters at Plymouth. I suppose they have something to do there. I often envy them the advantages they are discontented with. I shall say everything that Capn. B[radford] should wish me with respect to his health. It was thought here that he would get into a decline, I shall say his friends fear it now, he well deserves his leave, there is a Boy in the Reg^t an old 1st Lieut. who has lately got six months' leave by the interest

8 Postings abroad were unpopular; officers routinely transferred to another regiment to avoid it. Those who remained rose up the seniority list.
9 Another indicator of the closeness of the Hills and Bradfords; Jack clearly expected him to call at Hennock while at Ideford.

his friends have: he would soon quit were we to go abroad, if he can get it is hard the Capⁿ. could get so short a time. [10]

I rubbed out that part of your letter wherein you mentioned that, because no one shall see it. Charles in a letter to me 29 June last says: "H. Rogers has been home these 2 months past, I suppose you know there is a nephew of Mr. J. Templer's with us, he expects that his Father will live at Stover shortly". I did not at first understand who he meant would live at Stover, Sr. F. R. or Mr. J. Templer.[11] I see now that it is the latter, say if this has taken place. He also adds: "Every time I think about the Navy I lose my patience, I am most heartily tired of it. I wish I was in the Merchant service and capable of taking charge of a vessel which I hope I shall very soon do - to do my duty and to carry it on properly is a very great punishment it is very difficult". I mentioned this some time ago and that I thought Evans would teaze Charles more than ever after the hint Capⁿ. Hunt said he would give him, of his ill-treatment to Charles. He now from the stile my Brother writes in, is his most inveterate enemy, he has not more duty to do now than formerly. If he should come up the River I will go and see him, I could do it for a Guinea it is worth that to know how he is situated with Evans and Capⁿ. H[unt]. Admiral Duncan's fleet always repair at Sheerness. I am sorry Capⁿ. Hunt should ever have left the Concorde or the squadrons stationed at Falmouth. [12]

We have every officer except eight who are either recruiting or on the staff with us here, so that our mess-room will not hold us all. We now have two or three times a week a field-day; we have a curious General here he knows but little of the manoeuvres in the Field: we have two Field Pieces attached to the Regt. lately. The whole Reg^t. will learn the great gun exercise: we had the Reg^t. fire ball, some time ago, about 4 in an hundred hit the target: we

---

10 The 'Boy' was Lieutenant Francis Offley (who was about 16 at the time), who was granted six months leave from March 1796; Bradford got two months in July. TNA WO 17/125 *23rd Foot Monthly Returns to the Adjutant General 1764 – 1805.*

11 Sir F[rederick] R[ogers], 5th Baronet Blachford, had been mayor of and MP for Plymouth. He died on 21st June 1797; news that had clearly not yet reached Jack. That the Hills knew the Rogers (and the Palks) shows how well connected they were. 'J. Templer', whose nephew was apparently at sea with Charles, is James Templer, by now head of the Templer family who owned much land near Hennock, including Stover House.

12 Captain Anthony Hunt commanded HMS *Concorde*, a former French frigate, from August 1794 to November 1796. 'Evans' may therefore be Robert Evans, *Concorde's* 3rd Lieutenant, suggesting Charles was aboard her and, at only 12 years old in August 1797, was being bullied.

should make a poor Reg^t. of Yagers or Riflemen: it is no wonder, some of them do not know how to load their piece. The badness of the musket, the ball not fitting, the powder some of the best I ever saw, come from the King's stores, such as you would give 2s.6d. per 1b; all together made a fine business. It seems strange soldiers are not taught to shoot with more precision. Col. Ellis has been for some days in London, he returned last night. I shall often trouble you with letters under cover to Mr. Palk, say if he would be displeased by my frequently taking that liberty.

Please to send the Bullet mold and shot pouch if you send the Gun. The Gun powder I suppose Charles showed you where it is; in case he has not I will tell you that it is in the little cellar up over the ceiling of the staircase leading to the room I last used when at home. I wrote this day in hopes it might reach Ashburton by Saturday as I know I have recd. your letter sometimes in that time. I should much like to come and see you. I should be not a little pleased to march into Devon it is what I much wish: our march down there would cost Government in extras expences about £900. That would not trouble me if we were ordered down there. I think it would be of great service to the Reg^t. if we could go there with our General. The men would not desert so fast there, here the people entice them away. I do not imagine I should be reduced if peace comes & I should be where I now am. I should do duty & receive full pay altho' a supernumerary.

What account does William give of the state of the West Indies? I hear that the yellow Fever is not so prevailing as it was some time ago. The men who are ran away from my company are the best belonging to it, at least the tallest. Our band some time ago had their Master and Trumpeter dangerously ill. The first with a white swelling in his arm, he is now perfectly recovered, the other in a deep decline who is now going home to his friends; if he dies the band will suffer much they now are improving very fast. But peace alone will, after most of what we now have been discharged, bring us a fine Reg^t. The Duke of York's new-fashioned Austrian cloathing is much scorned.[13] It takes up as much cloath as the old, and by wearing the facings in front, they got dirtied and rubbed in pieces in a very short time. Our Reg^t. never had such bad cloath[s] before as they now have.

Please remember me to Father who I suppose is very well. I imagine he is a letter in arrears with me. I wish I could stay some time with him if it was only to study Botany with him. Tell him

---

13 Uniforms were modified in January 1796; long lapels were abolished ('bringing the facings in front') and a new cap introduced.

here would be a fine country for him. Two plants I see here would be great ornaments to any Garden, the one the white water-lilly or Lotos; its leaves are sometimes a foot and half broad with as beautiful a flower as can be imagined floting from a great depth of water by its side. The other a varigated thistle; its mottled leaves are its greatest ornament. The flower is much the same, but larger, as the common ones.

You did not say a word about Caroline. I want to see Fred. Aunt Peggy visited Exeter in an unfortunate time, you will give me a long description of Mrs. Siddons in your next. I was at a play last night for the first and last time, the Windsor set are here. A great deficiency appears after being at Drury. I am almost tired of a good thing, but I did not like to put this letter off to another time.

Yours,
J. HILL

Jack's might have felt it 'strange soldiers are not taught to shoot with more precision' but regular British infantrymen were not required to aim at targets. He does not say what the range was, but 'about 4 in an hundred hit the target' is not a bad return for the Brown Bess, which in some tests failed to register a single hit beyond 150 yards.

Jack did not get his wish to go to Devon; the regiment moved to Norwich in January 1798 and Canterbury in April. Meanwhile, the government learned that invasion vessels were being built at Antwerp and Flushing. These could be moved to Ostend by canal, thus avoiding the Royal Navy in the Channel. Captain Home Popham RN suggested disruption of this inland waterway system by destroying locks at Slykens near Ostend. In an early and for the time unusual example of combined arms planning, Popham persuaded Lieutenant-General Sir Charles Grey, commander of the army's Southern District, and together they convinced the government to support the scheme. Major-General Eyre Coote was appointed to command the landing force, with Popham commanding the transport vessels and supporting warships. Preparations were underway by April 1798. The 23rd were one of the regiments designated for the expedition, together with 1st Guards, 11th and 49th Foot, some Royal Military Artificers and Labourers (forebears of the Royal Engineers) and a group of civilian miners employed with the promise of bounties. The plan was ambitious: after the canal, it was hoped the force could go on to attack Ostend and Flushing and capture the island of Ameland, believed to have Royalist sympathies. Weather delayed departure until 16 May, when the ships set sail from Margate.

Strong winds prevented their arrival off Ostend until early on 19 May. The ship carrying the Guards lost contact with the fleet; they should have been first to land and that combined with the continued bad weather might have meant a delay, but Popham and Coote determined to continue. The troops were ordered to pack a day's rations, water and all the ammunition they could carry and were put ashore as quickly as possible.

Only the Grenadier and Light Companies of the 23rd landed, the rest remained afloat as a diversion: they 'took up a position so close to the enemy's batteries...that in a very short time no less than 11 seamen were killed and wounded, and of the 23rd one private was killed and 5 wounded.'[14] While his company remained aboard, Jack did not. Perhaps the officer contingent of the two flank companies needed to be brought up to strength before landing; perhaps George Bradford, the Grenadier's captain, wanted Jack to taste his first action. Jack recalled what happened in the *Statement of Services* he wrote at the end of his career:

> Was employ'd in the expedition to Ostend under General Sir E. Coote and was embark'd in H.M. S. "Harpy", Capn. Basely with a detachment of the 23rd Regt. on board which there was a party of Artillery with a 6-pounder. As this ship led in, the troops on board her were the first landed - Lieut. Coles of the Navy having charge of the sailors, but in getting on shore the boats were swamp'd on the beach and the ammunition spoiled.[15]

Despite the soggy landing and loss of their ammunition, by 5am Jack and the initial landing party were marching under command of Major-General Harry Burrard to cover the military artificers as they successfully destroyed the locks. Jack noted:

> I advanc'd and surprised a signal station suppos'd to have been a battery, and remain'd in front of it till daylight when other troops disembark'd.

Unfortunately, having carried out their mission, continuing bad weather made it too rough to re-embark. Coote's entire landing party of some 1,200 men found themselves stuck on the beach and highly vulnerable: an after-action report noted 'the risk we ran, in staying in an enemy's country naturally exasperated against us for the damage we had

---

14 Cary and McCance *Regimental Records;* Broughton-Mainwaring *Historical Record*

15 *Statement of the Services of Brevet Lieut. Col. J.H.E. Hill of the 23rd or Royal Welch Fusilier Regiment* January 1816

recently done them'.[16] All attempts to get away failed, so they dug in for a night amongst the sand dunes.

Early the next morning French troops and artillery were seen advancing. After skirmishing for a couple of hours, the British 'found that our front was broken and our flanks completely turned - the enemy pouring in upon us on all sides'.[17] The British spiked their guns and surrendered. As Jack put it years later:

> 'On the succeeding day after some resistance, the whole were taken prisoners, conducted to Lille and confined in the Citadelle's.'[18]

Possibly as few as 500 French troops had attacked; if so, this was not the best day for the British army. A clue to such poor performance may be Jack's comment that their ammunition was spoiled on landing. If this was true of even half the landing force, once trapped ashore their ability to resist was seriously compromised: little ammunition, food or water and with an untenable sea at their back. Eyre-Coote was wounded and eight other officers and some 150 men were killed, wounded or missing. Four of those killed and eleven of the wounded were from the 23rd. Over 1,000 men surrendered unharmed, including Jack and 182 of his regimental colleagues, not least their commanding officer Lieutenant-Colonel Richard Talbot. Interestingly, Jack is not listed in Eyre-Coote's subsequent despatch to London as one of the 23rd's officers captured, probably because of his last-minute attachment to the landing party but also because Eyre-Coote did not accompany the captives because of his injury. Jack is listed on a return by Burrard, who took command when Eyre-Coote was wounded and accompanied his men into captivity.[19]

Jack's first taste of war came to an ignominious end; he and the others were marched nearly 50 miles south to Lille and imprisoned in the Citadelle, a 17th Century fortress built in marshland to the north of the city. To reduce sickness and maintain proper appearances, military discipline was firmly maintained, as General Orders issued by Burrard on 31 May made clear:

> Cleanliness at all times but particularly in this present confined situation being absolutely necessary for the welfare of the men... the Orderly Officer attended by a Serjeant will visit the several

16 Burrard, quoted in *The Raid on Ostend 1798: Combined Operations Against Revolutionary France* Andy Phillipson 2003
17 Burrard, quoted in Phillipson, *Ostend*
18 Hill 1816 *Statement of Services*.
19 TNA WO 28/11: *Entry book of orders and other records relative to British prisoners of war at Lille, with returns of prisoners, etc.*

quarters of his Regiment at Half after Twelve o'clock and minutely examine them seeing that the Beds & Blankets are rolled up, the rooms well swept and the court yards and cooking places quite clean and all windows and doors wide open...the men are to get up at 6 o'clock in the morning and go to bed at eight...An officer of a Company will parade their Company near their Quarters every morning at half past eight o'clock and see that they are clean and well washed...at all times when the men are fell in profound silence is to be observed for nothing can give the Troops who surround us so contemptible an opinion of our national discipline as noise and confusion on the Parade and the Commanding Officer is convinced the men have too much proper pride to wish to become a reproach to their own country. [20]

As prisoners of war, they of course also had to follow rules imposed by the French. The prisoners were paraded in the square twice a day, at 9am and 7pm and a roll was called in the presence of a French officer who checked the numbers. The prisoners could walk in the square between these times, but after the evening parade men had to return to their quarters on threat of confinement if found 'straggling about the square or beyond the district of their quarters'. Officers were to be in their barracks by 10pm. Anyone confirmed sick by the surgeon was immediately removed to the town hospital.

Prisoners of War were sustained by their own Government, so Colonel Cotes, a British commissary liaison officer in Paris, contracted with one Citoyen Gregoire to provide provisions: 'Beef shall be delivered in whole quarters in the prison...it ought to be the best, if not it is to be rejected. Hind and Fore quarters are to be served by turns and without the least deviation'. Bread, cheese and butter (to be 'sweet and well flavoured') was also procured, as was wood for cooking and heating and candles for lighting. Two ounces of soap were 'to be delivered to each Prisoner on Mondays'. Small financial allowances were made too; each officer received a 'gratification of 12 Sols per day, or in lieu of rations 36 Sols'; private soldiers received 3 Sols per day. Cotes established means for prisoners to receive and send mail, though asked Burrard to make clear this privilege was allowed by the French on condition that 'they are not to write anything but of their family concerns'. The men were asked 'to write their letters on small sheets of paper', to reduce bulk. The arrangements made prison relatively comfortable: on 6 June Burrard wrote to Cotes 'I cannot say we are unhealthy' and later confirmed to William Windham, the Secretary at

---

20 TNA WO 28/11

War, 'our situation here has been made as comfortable as it is capable of being and it is but justice to this [French] Government to say that we are treated with Humanity'. But even with good treatment, Jack and his colleagues were still incarcerated in the enemy's country. Long period of boredom mixed with desire for release. There was inevitably some trouble among the men and although Burrard reported to England that 'the disorders most frequent among the men are such as are easily caught and do not endanger them', on 11 June he had to issue a General Order noting that he was 'very sorry to observe that many men by frequent drunkenness and riot bring dishonour upon themselves and... disgrace upon their country'. He ordered that gratification payments would no longer go direct to the men, but to their officers who would disperse it in a way that would 'check the drunken and encourage the good'. [21]

Cotes wrote at the end of May 'it is probable your stay in Lille will not be long'. In June he told Burrard 'a new proposition is come over for an Exchange of Prisoners and presented to the Commission of Exchange'. Still, the weeks and months ticked on. The prisoners knew that following the French Revolution negotiations for exchanging prisoners of war, previously normal practice, had broken down. Few exchanges were being agreed by the Revolutionary government.[22] A few men in Lille decided to try to take things into their own hands, resulting in Burrard ordering on 29 August that a directive from the French Government be read to the troops, reminding them that anyone 'who shall quit the place of his residence or confinement without permission [is] to be kept in irons for six years, but if found in the Department of Paris shall suffer death'.

As things turned out, Jack and the other British captives from the Ostend raid were lucky. On 13 September a 'Cartel for the Exchange of Prisoners between Great Britain and France' was signed. Five officers to every one hundred men would be sent from France and, on their arrival, an equal number of French Prisoners ('man for man and Rank for Rank') would go the other way. The reciprocal exchanges would continue until all were home. Despite the continuing state of war, the British would be transported in French vessels and the French in British ones. En route, the British prisoners would daily receive a pound each of bread and beef, plus two quarts of beer and one of wine; the French were to receive the same except the wine, presumably because it was

---

21 All quotations in this section are taken from documents in TNA WO 28/11.
22 Once Bonaparte assumed power he refused to release British captives, arguing that any able-bodied man could fight against France. Many British prisoners from the early years of the Napoleonic war were not released until 1814; many French prisoners ended their lives in Britain.

less readily available in Britain. The agreement took time to implement though and meantime the French authorities toughened up their regime. On 25 October the Commandant of the Citadelle wrote to Burrard apologetically that he was now 'obliged to adopt a measure most disagreeable to me', having received orders that all prisoners were to be closely confined. While the Commandant soon lifted these tighter restrictions, conditions in the prison were deteriorating. In early November the senior British officer remaining, Colonel Cunninghame of the Guards (Burrard had been among the first to go home) wrote to Cotes asking for supplies of additional woollen jackets and trousers for the men, adding 'from the late rain and now from the hard frost our men were getting very sickly for want of firing to warm the rooms and dry their linen'. Their ordeal would shortly be over. Having been held for nearly half a year, that same month Jack, most of the other officers and their soldier servants were released on parole. This meant they could return to Britain but were not allowed to rejoin their units until formally exchanged under the terms of the Cartel. Jack was listed in a return of officers and soldiers 'on Parole in England' dated 8 November.[23] A handful of officers from each regiment remained in Lille 'to see justice done to the Men, [and] to take charge of them on their March when the exchange which is soon expected takes place'. For the 23rd, this fell to Major Phillip Skinner, Captain Alexander Halkett, and Lieutenants Jacob Van Courtlandt and Henry Hanson. Those who returned to Britain were still listed in regimental records as Prisoners of War with the NCOs and men based at Eling Barracks, near Southampton, until February 1799 when Jack, the other paroled officers and all the men were formally exchanged and rejoined the regiment.[24]

Despite the wholesale capture of his force, Eyre-Coote called the Ostend expedition a 'complete and brilliant success' and the Government hailed the destruction of the sluice gates, and therefore the mission, as a triumph. But this was a combination of self-promotion and politics; in practice the raid had little effect and was strategically otiose as by the time it took place the French Directory had agreed Napoleon's proposal to invade Egypt, not Britain. Bonaparte wasted

---

23 TNA WO 28/11

24 Broughton-Mainwaring, *Historical Record* suggests the men rejoined in November, but Jack and his colleagues, including Lieutenant-Colonel Richard Talbot, are still listed as 'prisoner with the enemy' in January 1799 in TNA WO 12/3963 and as 'Prisoners of War' in TNA WO 17/125. The discrepancy is because while the parolees physically returned in November, the formal exchanges were not completed until February. Despite being in England, those on parole were still formally Prisoners of War.

little time in quitting the Channel coast, crossing the Mediterranean and landing in Africa. Jack would eventually follow him, but before that he and his colleagues would again land on a hostile European shore. At the end of his first military adventure, Jack had been confined as a prisoner of war; at the end of his next one he would survive the narrowest escape of his early life. Many of his regiment would not be so lucky.

Napoleon's departure for Africa, plus French expansionism in Switzerland and on the Italian peninsula meant Britain sustained its naval blockade and continued to seek allies to oppose the spread of revolutionary ideology. In 1799 a new understanding, the 2nd Coalition, saw Turkey, Austria, Portugal and Russia agree to join Britain in trying to reverse French territorial gains. In part because France's best general was on a different continent, the Coalition had early success. Austrian forces pushed the French back across the Rhine and in combination with Russia recovered most of Italy. Britain's primary role was to provide funding and naval support, but the Government also sought an opportunity for direct military involvement. The low countries across the Channel were again to be the target. In 1795 the Dutch people, with French support, had rebelled against the Stadtholder, William V, Prince of Orange-Nassau, and established the Batavian Republic. Batavia was effectively a French puppet state; British intelligence suggested popular support for revolutionary ideals was not universal. Britain and Russia therefore planned jointly to invade the new Republic, capture or destroy the Dutch fleet to prevent its use by France and generate a popular uprising in favour of restoring William to power. The Duke of York was to command the operation; he had led previous British military endeavours, though none blessed with success and history has adjudged York a brilliant administrator, but not a great field commander. An Anglo-Russian convention of June 1799 promised Russia would provide some 17,500 troops in return for British subsidies. Prussia having declined to join the Coalition or to allow the troops to march through her territory, the Russians would have to be transported by sea and would take several weeks to arrive. Another challenge was that the British army was significantly understrength, through a combination of losses and sluggish recruitment, both driven in part by service in the West Indies.[25] The Government's answer was to draft members of the militia, with the Militia Act amended in July to facilitate it. On the clear

---

25 Henry Dundas, the Secretary for War, considered the army 30,000 below the level needed to defend Britain, never mind any amount needed to mount offensive operations. *'Fairly Out-Generalled and Disgracefully Beaten': The British Army in the Low Countries 1793–1814*. Andrew Robert Limm 2014

proviso that anyone transferring to the regulars would serve only in Europe, some 10,000 militiamen were quickly enlisted, leaving little time for them to train. With hindsight the entire operation seemed a rushed and dubious proposition.

To commence operations before the season was too late, Lieutenant-General Sir Ralph Abercrombie took command of an initial force of around 3,000 men to land and establish an initial foothold. York would follow with a second wave, of British and Russian troops, for the main operations. Abercrombie was an experienced and capable soldier, arguably the best general Britain had at this period: 'he was a soldier who delivered the goods. His war record was astonishing.'[26] The 23rd, in the first wave, moved to Barham Downs near Canterbury where the invasion force was being assembled and exercised. On 9 August they and the rest of Abercrombie's force moved to Ramsgate and embarked. Putting to sea on 13 August, they immediately experienced similar weather to that faced on the way to Ostend the previous year; it was to be 'a tedious and tempestuous voyage'.[27] At sea for over a week, the fleet finally began to appear off Texel island from the 20th. Preparations for landing began on the 22nd, but the weather failed to co-operate, and the fleet put to sea again. It finally returned only on the 26th, when conditions had eased sufficiently to get the men ashore. Spending almost two weeks aboard crowded ships in heavy seas with food and water running low cannot have been pleasant. The expedition was supposed to have been secret, but much had been reported in newspapers and the fleet's arrival, departure and return confirmed to the defenders not only that that they were coming, but 'it became evident to their general that the British would commence to land next morning'.[28] Some 6,000 Batavian soldiers awaited in the sand dunes behind the beaches of the narrow Helder peninsula. About 7,500 more, including French troops, were a few miles further back.

At around 3am on 27 August, the British climbed into shallow boats and were rowed towards the beaches, under covering fire from the ships. Some boats overturned in the strong surf, but Jack and his men landed safely north of Callandsoog near Groot Keeten. Like at Ostend the units became mixed up; Major-General John Moore, commanding a brigade, said afterwards 'we landed with great confusion and irregularity'.[29] The 23rd, brigaded with the 55th Foot in the

---

26 *Britain's Victory in Egypt: The End of Napoleon's Conquest* Piers Macksey 1995
27 Broughton-Mainwaring, *Historical Record*
28 *The Campaign in Holland 1799* 'A Subaltern' 1861
29 *The Diary of Sir John Moore Vol. I* Major-General Sir. J F Maurice, KCB (Ed.) 1904

Reserve commanded by Colonel McDonald of the 55th, were among the first to reach the shore.[30] 'Reserve' was a misnomer; MacDonald's formation was routinely amongst the first ordered to attack. Advancing into the dunes, the 23rd quickly found themselves engaged with the defenders. Both sides fought doggedly, and the contest continued until around 3pm when the Batavians began to retire. The Reserve had borne the brunt of the fighting; the 23rd lost eighteen men killed, with three officers, Captains Thomas Bury, Henry Ellis and Godfrey MacDonald and more than seventy men wounded.[31] But the beaches were secured, and this initial success was amplified when an abandoned arsenal at Den Helder, on the northern point of the peninsula, was captured. This gave the British command of the Marsdiep, the channel between the mainland and Texel island, enabling the Royal Navy to sail in and force the Dutch fleet to surrender without resistance.

The scene was set for further advances, but a flaw in the plan now became apparent. Abercrombie's instructions were to establish a foothold for the main British and Russian force, but that force was not yet available. Abercrombie felt unable to advance further without them. Following the stiffness of the initial resistance, he worried about the strength of the enemy in front of him. He also was rightly concerned that the terrain ahead of him was difficult, with few roads and crossed with canals and drainage ditches. Against that, his position amongst the sandhills was far from comfortable, 'the whole of the troops are without tents, and the weather is uncommonly bad'.[32] The men were 'suffering severely from the weather, having no other shelter than trenches, which they dug for themselves in the sand'.[33] Abercrombie decided on a limited further advance to improve his defensive line. On 1 September he moved south and established a position on the Zijpe polder, behind two dykes in a line running north-west broadly from Petten on the coast to the Zuider Zee. The dykes were a ready-made defensive position, fronted by a wide canal and with good fields of fire.

This new line established, Abercrombie told London he could go no further: 'the Dutch troops are on the right...and the French in Alkmaar, Bergen and Egmont. The French may be estimated at six thousand men and the Dutch at nine or ten thousand...they have since drawn [together]...everything they could collect. The country between us and the enemy is entirely intersected with ditches and canals, except

---

30 *A Narrative of the Expedition to Holland, in the autumn of the year 1799* E Walsh 1800
31 Broughton-Mainwaring *Historical Record*. Full casualty details are listed in 'A Subaltern' *Campaign*
32 Moore *Diary*
33 Broughton-Mainwaring, *Historical Record*

on the right opposite Petten, where the sand hills of the Camperdown begin. In this situation I have judged it better not to risk an action, until the arrival of reinforcements'.[34] But problematic weather continued, and those reinforcements did not land until 3 September; the main body and the Duke of York did not arrive for over another week. All the while Abercrombie had little choice but to remain on the defensive. The Batavians/French though were not so immobile, and at dawn on 10 September launched a surprise attack against the British line, which fortunately held. The Reserve were briefly engaged late in the action, pursuing some of the enemy as they retreated.

By 15 September, Jack and those from the initial landing had been on shore in hostile territory for over a fortnight, but the full allied force of around 30,000 men was finally assembled with the Duke of York in command; an advance inland could finally begin. On the 19th the allied army formed into four columns. The largest was some 10,000 strong under Abercrombie and included the Reserve. Their objective was not the enemy's line, but the village of Hoorn, across the Helder peninsular to the south-east on the shoreline of the Zuider Zee. York's plan was that taking Hoorn would enable Abercrombie to move around the enemy right and threaten the town of Purmerend, due south of Hoorn, in the enemy rear and on the road to Amsterdam. This looked a reasonable strategy on paper, but in practice meant a third of York's army moving away from where the main fighting was to take place. The distances involved and the difficulty of the terrain meant that they would be out of easy contact. That was risky enough, but York's orders for the British and Russian advance attack stated, 'If the attack on the right proves successful, Sir Ralph Abercrombie risques nothing in pushing every advantage'.[35] The further advance to Pumerend by Abercrombie's detachment therefore depended on the Allies' success in the main attack. This placed a heavy emphasis on communication across bad roads being sufficient for Abercrombie to know what was happening twenty miles away and with an opposing army between him and his commander.

Abercrombie's detachment moved off on the evening of the 18th. It was a difficult march. The waterlogged terrain and broken bridges caused delays and detours. This was no swift flanking movement, but a drawn-out muddy flog that left the troops exhausted on arrival at Hoorn. The town was, though, captured with little opposition. Information operations played a part. Henry Bunbury, an aide to the Duke of York, recorded many years later that a show was made of the bringing up of cannon to threaten to blow the town doors open, with

34 TNA WO1/179: *Dispatches Helder expedition* Abercrombie to Dundas 4 September 1799

35 TNA WO1/180 *General Dispositions for the attack upon the enemy's position*

much shouting of 'make way for the guns', to alarm the occupants of Hoorn. Bunbury claimed that not only the townsfolk were alarmed but 'our jaded infantry were roused from their unconscious slumbers by the sudden clatter of the horses on the pavement, the rattling of the cannon wheels, and this unhappy cry of 'back, back'. In an instant the 23rd and 55th broke like a flock of sheep, plunging into the deep mud at the sides of the causeway, and dreaming for some minutes that they had been surprised by a sortie of cavalry'.[36] Bunbury was writing well over fifty years after the event, so his colourful account should be viewed with caution. Even if it is true that the men were startled by the commotion, that is hardly surprising when they had fallen exhausted into sleep. Abercrombie could hear gunfire from the rest of the army near the coast but knew his men needed to recover before they could attempt the further ten miles to Purmerend. He sensibly decided to halt. 'Our men were much jaded'..[they]...were directed to lie on their arms upon the road' Moore wrote.[37]

Things were going less well with the main attack. The Russian column moved off earlier than intended and in darkness. It was hard to determine their direction. In the confusion, they began firing on their own men. The two British columns started later then encountered stiff resistance which slowed them down and left the Russians unsupported. As a result, when the Russians reached the village of Bergen they were quickly outflanked and forced to retreat. This in turn meant the entire allied line had to fall back to their starting positions. British officers quickly assigned the failure to Russian incompetence; Russians to lack of British support. Moore concluded the Russian 'retreat was precipitous and as unsoldierlike as their advance...the first check caused confusion, and there was nobody to remedy it'.[38] It was a bad start for the Duke of York, who also blamed the Russians, but the whole attack was badly coordinated. York's dispersal of his columns across a wide front did not help. Abercrombie's column saw no action in what was to be called the battle of Bergen, simply exhausting itself by fruitlessly marching to Hoorn. It was also fortunate that they did not press on to Purmerend; if they had they would have found enemy troops posted there and would have been isolated when the main attack was defeated, with their backs to the Zuider Zee and exposed to the entire enemy force. After the failure of the main attack, Abercrombie was ordered to return; as one history of the 23rd notes 'there was no opposition in [their] quarter, but the column...resumed its former position'.[39]

---

36 *Narrative of Some Passages in the Great War with France* Henry Bunbury 1854
37 Moore, *Diary*
38 Moore, *Diary*
39 Broughton-Mainwaring, *Historical Record*

The Helder campaign saw the first ever British Field Post Office established for private mail to and from the army. NCOs and private soldiers could send and receive mail at a concessionary rate of one penny per letter.[40] Officers had to pay the full rate, but this seems not to have deterred Jack from writing home. Two letters from this operation survive, the first written from the village of Basinginhorass (Barsingerhorn), where the 23rd were deployed as an advanced outpost of the allied line. He composed the letter over a period of over a week, starting shortly after the battle of Bergen. This letter has an intriguing comment written on the outside of the envelope: 'Sir, Is Mr. Hill wounded? Taylor.' He was not, and it is not clear who Taylor was or why he thought he might be.

Tuesday, 23 Sep[r]. 1799.
Basinginhorass

Dear Father,

I had the pleasure of receiving yours of the 12th Sept. [on] the 21st of the same month, last Sunday. I am sorry I had not the pleasure of seeing you at Deal. We were but a little while there, I intended but found it impossible to ask leave to go and see Charles. I am very glad to hear that Charles is at home, and likely to do well; by an old English newspaper I saw that the Woolwich is going again to the E. Indies. I suppose if that is the case, Charles will not return to that climate again.[41]

Capn. Bury is, I heard yesterday, is [sic] getting better. He is able now to sit up a little while in the day. I have heard since two shot hit him and not one as I mentioned in my former. The wound in his face is, I believe, well. It is the shot that went in just below his collar-bone that now punishes him.

You mention having had very bad weather for your harvest. I think I never saw such at this time of the year, the corn looks nearly as green as it did in June. I am sorry to hear Aunt Pinhey has been so ill - recollect and say how your farm gets on. I intend to write you every week almost, unless by the distance of our Quarters should prevent me from sending to the head Q[uarters]. I am very much obliged to you for your kind offer of money. I have just compleated my debt to Capn. B[radford] to 5 Guineas as I mentioned in my last. I told him I would request you to pay his friends. I will not draw for

40 See *The Postal Service of Wellington's Army*, Peter B Boyden in *The Road to Waterloo* Alan J Guy (ed.) 1990
41 This suggests John Hill had collected Charles from Deal. As a Volunteer, Charles had the right to leave at any time.

the sum you mentioned unless I am forced, at present I am not. I am living as frugally as circumstances admit of.

In my last I informed you the division of the army to which we belonged was going to move forward. I think it was the 18 of this month, we marched about 3 in the afternoon towards Hoorn, we marched all night and arrived there between 3 and 4 o'clock of the morning of the 19, we summoned the town and they would not surrender till they saw the muzzle of our six-pounder close to the gate and the Port fire burning, ready to blow them open, we marched in and took between 2 and 3 hundred prisoners.[42] Our Light Company and part of the 55th remained in the town, the other part of the Corps remained outside Hoorn till about six o'clock we began to march back to this place. The Lt. Compy. arrived here after a march of all night during which it was raining the greatest part, about 5 o'clock in the morning our Lt. Comp. and the 55th came up the next day. We retired in consequence of things not turning out as we could wish on the right. The Russians & ourselves suffered very severely, the loss one way & another was pretty equal in both sides; we have taken 3,500 Prisoners, their number of killed I know not, ours I suppose the Gazzette will inform you of. The 17th & 35th lost the most men. The Russians drove the enemy from all his entrenchments, 3 times he marched up at the beat of the Drum in ordinary lines and turned the French out, units afterwards advancing so far that ammunition could not be brought up to him, they were dispersed when the enemy came down on them with nearly all his Force.

Their Commander in Chief is taken and another of their Generals.[43] Since we have evacuated Hoorn, the enemy appeared before it and wanted to come in, the Inhabitants shut the gates on them and now do duty for themselves under the Prince of Orange's Colours. Sunday and Monday last we heard a very heavy cannonade. We are not acquainted what it was, it appeared to be the Shipping up the Zuyder Zee.

Report says Admiral Mitchel has taken a town near Amsterdam with a number of shipping.[44] A[msterdam] is very well affected

---

42 Other sources suggest the march began at around 8pm, but Jack presumably knew whether it was mid-afternoon or evening. If his timing is correct the march took some 12 hours to complete.

43 Lieutenant-General Ivan Herman von Fersen, Commander in Chief of the Russian Troops, was captured at Bergen.

44 This was probably Enkhuizen and Medemblik, which hastily surrendered following the arrival of Mitchel's squadron; a handful of vessels were taken. *The Secret Expedition* Geert Van Uythoven 2018.

towards us. Alkmaar as an obstacle is the greatest we have, the greatest part are Patriots. The Hills in its neighbourhood present a strong position among which they have entrenched themselves.

We are continually receiving reinforcements, 8,000 Russians have arrived since the last action. Report mentions some Swedish ships are also at Helder. It is supposed the King of Prussia is moving, he will turn the ballance [sic] I suppose either side. I have not purchased a horse yet, we have no baggage to carry scarcely, and they are scarce, being all wanted for the guns. George Mackenzie was slightly wounded the other day in the outside of his arm just below the shoulder.

Remember me to the Miss Mallocks if they are staying in your neighbourhood. I will place this aside for a little while and go a-gossipping for news.

We are again ordered to march. I know not when we shall make a second attack on them in a few days. The letters are ordered in every Wednesday. I shall continue my correspondence weekly. I shall fold this up and continue when I have time and opportunity. Remember me to all our neighbours.

25 Sept.

We are at present at Oude Sluys quite in the rear of all, it is supposed we shall act as the corps de Reserve to the Russians in their next attack. Cap^ns. Bradford and the Mackenzies are well. I have heard a circumstance this moment. The French placed a great quantity of Gin in the way of the Russians as they advanced after having driven them from their Batteries which unfortunately many of them could not resist.

Remember me to all at home and give my love to them. I much fear this will not arrive so soon as I could wish and that it will miss the week's packet

We had a march last night from night-fall till between 1 and 2 o'clock this morning through the most infamous roads. This place is situated on the Zuyder zee. I am sorry you should have lost your maps of Holland as they were on a larger scale than any I have seen and, tho' old, would have shown you every inch of the country.

I am yours
J. HILL.

30 of Sep all well. We marched up to the sandhills, intending to attack them, but could not pass for the surf - letters go twice a week.

The bad weather, which had barely let up since the start of the operation, continued. New offensives were impossible throughout much of the rest of September. Meantime, ill feeling simmered between the British and Russians. The rumour Jack heard during his 'a-gossipping' of the Russians being distracted by French gin indicates the disdain many British officers developed for their allies. There is evidence that some troops took opportunities for plunder during the Russian advance and that some Russian soldiers had drunk all their double rum ration before setting off; contemporary soldiers from most countries would have done both. There is no evidence to suggest the French laid a deliberate trap with alcohol.

As a third Russian division of around 6,000 and further British reinforcements arrived, food supplies were becoming problematic. Buying supplies ashore was difficult, the weather impeded resupply from the sea, and transporting anything to the front was hard. Some 40,000 men were now concentrated in a relatively small, low-lying and wet area; everywhere was churned up. On 24 September the Reserve was relieved from its advanced position on the army's left. Its move to the centre of the line was the early morning march on 'infamous roads' Jack recorded on the 25th. York tried to attack again on the 29th, but 'it was found impossible to proceed, as the roads, from having no hard bottom, were in such a state that the infantry march almost knee-deep in mud, while the wide sandy beach, on the right, was rendered equally impassable by a high tide, with heavy surf, breaking upon it',[45] just as described by Jack in his 30 September postscript. It was another wasted effort by the troops, who had assembled at 3am, marched south and then turned back. 'The troops were disappointed at this counter-order' said Moore understatedly, 'they got back to their cantonments just as day broke.'[46]

When October arrived the rain finally eased. The howling wind became a temporary friend, helping to dry the roads a little. York's next attempt was on 2nd October. Abercrombie's formation had been reinforced and now comprised about 8,000 infantry and some 900 cavalry. The Reserve was now on the right, near the village of Petten. Their task was again to outflank the enemy, this time by their left, marching down the coast to Egmont-op-Zee, and then attacking the French rear at Bergen. Abercrombie made good initial progress, with the Reserve setting off at 6.30am along the sea-dyke and rapidly capturing a French redoubt near Campe. Turning into the sand hills, they pressed on. Unfortunately, things were not progressing as well across the rest of the line, where well-entrenched French forces proved

45 'A Subaltern' *Campaign*
46 Moore, *Diary*

difficult to dislodge. After 'several hours with the greatest obstinacy on both sides'[47] exhaustion set in, and the main attack stalled. Abercrombie had advanced 6 miles down the beach before turning inland, but his ability to support and be supported by the rest of the army was compromised by inability to capture the sand hills, some of which were over 20 metres high. The terrain significantly favoured the defenders, not least as the soft sand was difficult to traverse. 'It is impossible to give you an adequate idea of the ground,' said one officer 'which I can only compare to the sea in a storm'.[48] There was later criticism of Macdonald for taking his force into the sand hills and closer to the Russians, rather than staying right to support Abercrombie, but making any progress on this ground was tough going. The advance of the Reserve consequently slowed, as fighting down the length of the sand hills was much more difficult than moving along the beach. One officer serving with Macdonald's force recorded:

> the line of hills as it sloped towards the level country was partly covered with long slips of scrubby wood or coppice; affording shelter for such troops as the enemy might please to keep in concealment. Through all this region it was impractical to bring up Artillery, even the Hussar horses of the French that were opposed to us were frequently up to their shoulders in the loose sand, and the difficulty of even moving infantry in any shape was very great.[49]

The French reinforced their left, and Abercrombie now found himself in a tough fight in front of Egmont-op-Zee. After hours of effort, and finally rejoined by Macdonald's Reserve, he managed to take the sand hills. With his troops now exhausted and at risk of being cut off from the rest of the army if he advanced further, Abercrombie paused for the night as bad weather again set in: 'You cannot conceive of our wretched state, as it blew and rained nearly the whole time. Our men bore all this without grumbling, although they had nothing to eat but the biscuits they carried with them, which by this time were completely wet'.[50] The next day their opponents, concerned that the British and Russians now held much of the high ground and could still outflank them along the beach, withdrew. Abercrombie occupied Egmont-op-Zee.

---

47 'A Subaltern' *Campaign*
48 Isaac Brock, quoted in *A Matter of Honour: The Life, Campaigns and Generalship of Isaac Brock* Jonathan Riley 2011
49 *A Waste of Blood and Treasure: The 1799 Anglo-Russian Invasion of the Netherlands* Philip Ball 2017
50 Isaac Brock, quoted in Riley, *Honour*

The second of Jack's letters from this campaign is incomplete but was written from Egmont-op-Zee. Oddly, it is dated 5 September. While the whole letter has not survived, the part which has includes a reference to Abercrombie having two horses shot from under him. This must refer to the fight on 2 October, which became known as the Battle of Alkmaar (sometimes alternatively the second battle of Bergen). The date is confusing, but Jack may have inadvertently written the wrong month, an easy mistake to make by someone who had been living in horrendous conditions for months and had just taken part in the most significant engagement of his life so far. What remains from this letter confirms the difficulty of the terrain, with Jack's company being deployed into open formation (or as he puts it 'to act as Light Infantry') and records his escape from a couple of near misses.

Egmont Op Zee,
Sep. 5 99

... Russian [at] Alkmaar we marched from Oude Sluys within two days after I wrote you from thence.[51] Tuesday, ten o'clock at night, we rec'd orders to march; at twelve we proceeded from thence, which is situated on the Zuyder Zee, to Petten which is on the North Sea, and arrived just after day-break; at Petten the chain of sandhills is broken and for about 2 miles the shore is flat with only the Dyke towards it. Both the hills were posts of the opposite armys. We had advanced on Petten, where the division of the army for attack on the right was assembled, consisting of about 15,000 men; at five we began to move forward along the beach against a breastwork of the enemy's on the flat and a gun on the top of the hills; the Reserve is reinforced by 12 flank companies from the Regts. who have been filled up from the Militia, and very fine men they are.[52]

They led the way, the rest of the Reserve followed supported by all the remainder of the troops. We did not lose more than 4 or 5 men altogether in getting possession of the first hill. We remained at the foot of the hills near an hour while two Brigades marched past, one to the right along the North Sea, the other on the left of the

---

51 The partial letter starts halfway through a sentence. These opening words probably refer to the regiment's role in supporting the Russians in the previous action.

52 It was common practice to combine the Grenadier and Light companies, together known as the 'Flank' companies, into a single 'composite battalion'. Flank companies were considered elite; putting a composite battalion of them in the Reserve strengthened it, but weakened the battalions they came from.

sandhills. We followed soon after the last-mentioned Corps for near a mile, when we inclined to the right and began to make our way down the centre of the sandhills, which are in some places 3 miles broad. They were engaged when we came up. We marched against a large body of the enemy posted along the top of the hills, with a gentle ascent without a hollow near them within musket shot.

We drew up in line just out of musket shot; when I was ordered with the Col[onel's] company forward - to act as Light Infantry and give notice to the enemy's yagers, to quit their lurking places, the first rifle shot fired from them hit the hairs of my bearskin of the helmet, the third wounded one of the company, we then began firing, when some more companies on the right coming up and, advancing on them, we soon turned them out of a wood, but before this their line had moved off. We went on skirmishing a considerable way, till we came to a large hollow with small wood. Between them on each side the hostile troops were, and the sharpshooters in the cover between. We were firing near two hours in this situation, when small parties of ours began to get into the wood against the enemy's rifle men. At this time our right was also gaining ground, and the enemy was passing off along the hills just before mentioned. Some troops on our left began to charge. We passed through the wood up the hills cheering as we passed through the copse. We had two of our Officers wounded in this business - young Keith and Maclean. The enemy, who were French, did not like this movement, and began to go off in quick time. The troops on the right, where General Abercrombie commanded in person, were very much engaged for near an hour. General A. had two horses killed, Halkett of ours, who is his Aide de-Camp, had his horse also shot in the head, but it is yet alive. The troops there have suffered very severely. The Regts. were the 25, 49, 69, 79, 92. There were many others which I do not know, the last-mentioned Regt. charged and carried their point but in it they lost 200 men. We have lost in killed, wounded and missing upwards of 70. A spent ball afterwards hit the brass of my helmet as I was considerably in the rear of the Regt. when they had faced to the right and were going across the sandhills to N. Sea. In the latter part of the day I had laid down to rest myself for near half an hour and was coming up. I was sent for orders to know if we might retire to...' [text ends]

As Jack noted, the day had been costly, with over 2,000 British and Russians killed and wounded and perhaps 3,000 of their opponents. The 23rd got off lightly, with just 7 men killed and Lieutenants Alexander McLean and William Keith plus around 60 others wounded or missing.[53] Jack narrowly avoided joining his colleagues as a casualty - a few inches further down and either of the bullets that hit his Fusilier cap - one in the bearskin part and one in the metal front plate - could have been fatal. That he wore this headgear is interesting as the distinctive (and expensive) Fusilier fur-cap was often not worn in battle during the later years of the Revolutionary wars but was kept for ceremonial occasions. Instead, officers usually wore a bicorne hat, or (after 1801) a shako. The timing of when the 23rd implemented this change is not known, and there was often significant discretion on officers' headdress; it seems unlikely Jack was the only officer who wore the cap that day.

York's army now controlled the line of sand hills as far south as Egmont, but he had wanted a more decisive outcome that would enable him to go on and attack Amsterdam. The French and Batavians had fallen back to a shorter and more defensible line and been reinforced, bringing the numbers almost to parity on both sides. A further allied attack, in bad weather, on 6 October, the battle of Castricum, had little success. Jack and the Reserve were again on the right of the line, advancing along the beach west of Bakkum. As they moved forward the French counter-attacked and some of the militia failed to stand, breaking and running back along the beach in disorder. Fortunately, they found their salvation in the form of the 23rd. One of those involved later wrote: 'we perceived some regiments advancing to our succour; among them was the 23rd, which advanced in line, and showed so good and steady a front as quite delighted us'.[54] The fleeing men rallied behind the 23rd and the French were repulsed. The afternoon saw a series of attacks and counterattacks by both sides, but the two lines ended the day more or less where they had started. The British and Russians lost more than 1,400 killed, wounded and missing, of which the 23rd accounted for around forty.

York now faced a series of problems. After the successful landings and the capture of the Dutch fleet in mid-August (both before he arrived), the combined Anglo-Russian force had fought four battles, lost some 11,000 men and gained just a few miles of sodden ground and sand hills. Their opponents had retreated from their original positions but were now reinforced in a better one. Meanwhile, the weather continued to hamper supply efforts and the uprising in support of Orange rule had been a damp squib. Perhaps 5,000 locals had declared themselves for the Stadtholder, but they were too ill-equipped and ill-fed to be of immediate military use. Lastly, if the weather had not been bad enough already, winter was coming, and northern Holland was no place for an army to

---

53 'A Subaltern' *Campaign*
54 *Twenty-Five Years in the Rifle Brigade* W Surtees 1833

be exposed in that season. On 7 October York decided his entire army should fall back to its former position along the Zijpe dykes. The 23rd were in the centre of this line, at Kolhorn. After further skirmishing between the two sides, on the 14th York proposed an armistice. Under its terms, the Anglo-Russian army would withdraw entirely, after releasing 8,000 Prisoners of War.[55] On returning home, Abercrombie and his men were voted the thanks of Parliament, but there was serious criticism of the government: one MP called the enterprise 'a waste of blood, and expense of treasure'.[56] The government emphasised the capture of the Dutch fleet, but there was no escaping the conclusion that otherwise the expedition was an expensive failure. The Dutch fleet was captured within hours of the initial landing; nothing was achieved in the months after that except a breakdown of relations between the British and Russian armies. The French and Batavians rightly considered themselves victorious; York never again commanded troops in the field.

The 23rd marched from Kolhorn to Den Helder and prepared to sail home. Jack was looking forward to getting back to England, but he had no idea of what he was about to endure to get there. On 28 October, with his company and eventually all or part of nine others, he boarded a fifty-year old captured Dutch frigate named '*De Valk*', ready to sail back across the North Sea. While waiting to collect troops they missed the morning tide.[57] This, which Jack understatedly described as 'in all human probability an unfortunate delay' sealed their fate. Jack wrote to his father after he finally made it home almost a month later outlining what happened next:

Portsmouth
20th November 1799

Dear Father,

I am happy to inform you of my arrival here, which took place this morning.

I have had a charming passage, very different to our first essay to get to Old England.

We sailed in company, the 28th of last month, with another Dutch Frigate. In the 'Valk' there were the Grenadier, Capt[n]. Bradford's and the Lieut. Col's with parties of near every other Company except the Light.

---

55 Limm *Out-Generalled*
56 Richard Sheridan MP in the House of Commons, 10 February 1800
57 The 23rd Foot had briefly formed an 11th company, commanded by Captain George Mackenzie.

During all the time we were beating about the N. Sea we had very terrible weather when, imagining ourselves within seventy miles of Yarmouth about three o'clock in the morning of the 10th Nov^r., the ship struck on the Island of Ameland. All of our Regt. except nineteen and myself perished. Of the Dutch seamen – five [survived].

Twenty-four saved out of near five hundred men, women and children on board. I hope no intimations reached you of the loss in consequence of our not being heard of for so long a time.

I stuck by the forecastle till it was tumbling over on me. At this time every other part of the vessel was broken in pieces which either sank or drifted away.

I got on another piece of the wreck which I found to be entangled in the rigging, and was washed from that and several other pieces; at last I got on a good one and lashed myself on with my gallins [braces] and pocket handkerchief, and was floated on shore just at daylight. I was the only person saved out of the cabin. Lieut^s. Hanson, Vischer, Maclean, and Hoggard perished. My left hand is not yet well, having the flesh and nails carried away from the first joints of the two first fingers, but the bones are not hurt - my left knee was much bruised. My left eye is still very weak and blood-shot from the difficulties I experienced in escaping with my life.

I had a passage given me in the Rosylite Frigate - thirty-two guns - and accordingly put the few survivors on board of her, but afterwards went to pay the hire of a vessel from Ameland by which means I lost my passage, and my party is gone to Yarmouth.[58] Excuse a tavern pen.

J. HILL
Direct London

The story Jack tells here is dramatic enough, even allowing for his heavy irony in describing his eventual safe arrival via 'a charming passage' compared to what he had just gone through. But he told his family a sanitised version. As the only officer who survived the disaster, Jack had made notes about what transpired while still on Ameland. Granted three months leave to recover, he was asked to produce an official report which he completed while at home and submitted to the Duke of York on 1 February 1800. Jack's report forms the basis of the summary description of this event in the official history of the 23rd and

---

58 There is no record of a ship called *Roslyte*. It was probably HMS *Proselyte*, another former Dutch frigate that in 1799 was commanded by Captain George Fowke.

numerous histories of the regiment and the Helder campaign.[59] Its full text, incorporating supplementary notes he added by way of further explanatory detail, is at Appendix 1. It is a tale of bravery and terror, with perhaps an undertone of poor seamanship by the Dutch captain and his inexperienced crew.[60] The Duke of York's Secretary, Colonel Robert Brownrigg, acknowledged receipt of Jack's report, noting that he had 'lost no time in communicating it to H.R.H. the Commander in Chief who directed me to convey to you many thanks for the very interesting narrative which your letter contains of the melancholy loss of the Valk Dutch Frigate, & of the officers & men of the 23rd Regt. who were on board that ship'.[61]

Jack's report also acknowledges the generosity of the Amelanders, who cared for him and the other survivors for a week while they recovered from their traumatic experience and injuries. One history of the 23rd records that the locals 'received the survivors in the kindest manner, and performed the last offices to those who were washed ashore, with as much decency as their poverty would permit'.[62] They did so despite having suffered from the British blockade of the European coast; the island economy depended on the sea. One islander, Cornelis Pieter Sorgdrager, recorded the events in his diary, noting that four days after the disaster, Amelanders removed wet tobacco and flour from the wreck. They were pleased to be able to benefit a little in this way as Ameland was poor and supplies were short. The generosity of the islanders in feeding and clothing the survivors is underlined by Sorgdrager's blunt comment that 'if all these people had arrived here alive, our country would have been in embarrassment, because there was so little to eat'. As it was, there was insufficient wood on the island to make coffins for all the bodies washed ashore, though Jack asked that these be made for the two officers whose remains were recovered and for one of the women who perished, Mrs. Darcie. Some 150 other bodies which came ashore were initially buried in the dunes but were subsequently moved to the cemetery in Ballum, one of the island villages. When Jack and the survivors finally left Ameland, via a fishing boat he had hired to take them to Den Helder, many of the men still

---

59 For example, Broughton-Mainwaring *Historical Record,* and Cary and McCance *Regimental Records.*
60 *Lieutenant ter Zee* Dithmar Martinius, who captained *De Valk,* sailed with Abercrombie in the first wave of the invasion; he had helped to recruit some 272 captured Dutch sailors being held on British prison hulks to join the British fleet as volunteer crew before the expedition sailed. Van Uythoven, *Expedition*
61 Letter from Brownrigg to Hill dated February 5th 1800. See Appendix 1.
62 *Historical Record of the Twenty-Third Regiment or Royal Welsh Fusiliers,* Richard Cannon 1850

needed medical assistance and a local surgeon accompanied them. The fishing boat apparently cost Jack 130 Guilders (which he equated to over £210 pounds), with the doctor's assistance another 80 Guilders.[63] During the Helder campaign his father had written offering to provide funds; Jack had assured him that he was living frugally, but he must now have had to draw on his father to be able to afford these bills.

The generosity of the Amelanders is even more notable as they had a reason to want their guests to leave quickly. When the campaign was underway, the population of Ameland had declared for the Prince of Orange; the island had been the personal property of the House of Orange until as recently as 1795. But the fortunes of war went against them and now the arrival on their shore of 20 British soldiers gave Ameland's municipal leaders a presentational problem. After the armistice was signed the Batavian government sought confirmation from local authorities in the surrounding area that the invaders had fully withdrawn. Inconveniently, at the precise moment the question was asked, the presence of the *Valk* survivors meant Ameland, whose loyalty to Batavia was questionable to say the least, was hosting twenty members of the invading force, albeit that they were in no condition to fight. The Ameland authorities decided to take their time in responding and to be economical with the truth when they did. They held their reply until 17 November, as the survivors of the 23rd were either departing or only just gone, and they were very precise with their choice of words. Their response said:

> there are no English people here on the island, nor have there been during the war...we have sent the rescued men of the shattered transport ship *De Valk* that was wrecked here on the 10th November with a ship hired for this purpose on the 15th November to Den Helder...most of them were sick and injured. Among them was an English officer who gave us a certificate of good treatment. We trust that you will approve...Nothing of importance has been recovered from the wrecked ship *De Valk*...Forty or 42 bodies have been found here on the beach, so that a large number are still missing.[64]

This is a masterpiece of careful wording. The surviving Fusiliers may even have still been on Ameland on the 17th (Jack says they were on the

---

63 There are, however, some problems with Jack's conversion (maths was not his strong point). See the footnotes in Appendix 1

64 *The municipal council of Ameland lied!* Roel Cazemier 2002. Historical Association Northeast Friesland https://www.hvnf.nl/2012/02/het-gemeente bestuur-van-ameland-loog.

island for a week; they were shipwrecked on the 10th), but the Amelanders knew that the British soldiers would be well on the way home by the time their letter reached the Batavian authorities.

Jack was apparently not reimbursed for the cost of the boat he hired to take the survivors from Ameland to Den Helder. After his death one of his sons, Charles Frederick Hill, wrote a summary of his services which differs in a few details from the two such summaries Jack himself wrote towards the end of his military career. One difference is a pointed comment in relation to the *Valk* incident 'He brought the Survivors to England on his own expense & was never repaid'.[65] Jack was not only out of pocket, but he had also lost all his possessions other than the clothes on his back. According to the letter to his father, he even missed joining the frigate which brought the other survivors home, following instead on another ship. This is confirmed by the *Naval Chronicle*, which records that on 20 November, in Portsmouth:

> The Pelter gun brig, Lieutenant John Walsh (second) Commander, from the Texel, having been ashore on the Dutch coast, was sent on Wednesday into this harbour for refitting, having lost her anchors, cables, and false keel.
>
> She has brought Lieutenant Hill, of the Welch Fusileers. He was one of the twenty-five persons, and only officer saved out of 529 that were on board the Voolk, a Dutch frigate wrecked in the night of the 10th instant, on the island of Ameland. Among the above passengers were three companies of the said regiment. Lieutenant Hogart, who had got safe on a piece of the wreck, died instantly in a state of delirium, caused by excess of joy, after exclaiming "Thank God, my Lads, we are once again safe on shore".[66]

The *Pelter* sounds barely seaworthy herself, but she got Jack home alive after a stern test of his determination, initiative, ingenuity and luck. Most of his colleagues and shipmates were less fortunate. The 23rd lost more than six times as many men in the disaster than it had through fighting and sickness in the entire Helder campaign; this would turn out to be the biggest single loss the Royal Welch Fusiliers suffered through the Revolutionary and Napoleonic Wars.[67] The 23rd's monthly pay

---

65 Manuscript document *Colonel Hill (CB) Services*, written by Charles Frederick Hill, in the possession of the Hill family.

66 The Naval Chronicle Vol II 1799

67 At Albuera the regiment lost 76 killed and 257 wounded; while some of the latter died of their wounds, many rejoined the regiment after recovering. See Chapter 10.

records for November 1799 show a succession of entries with the annotation '(dead)' in the Remarks column for each man. Just twenty-five people survived the *Valk*, twenty of them RWF. Only Captain Alexander Halkett's Light Company lost nobody in the disaster (it lost 5 men during the campaign). The complete list of NCOs and privates who died, together with a note of any money they were owed by the regiment or that they owed to it, is included in the regimental pay record for June 1800.[68] The list covers six foolscap pages; it shows that four officers, eleven sergeants, twelve corporals, six drummers and 203 private men, a total of 236, were lost in the wreck, not the 265 recorded in the tally at the end of Jack's report (and in most subsequent histories of the regiment). The total of RWF dead for the entire Helder campaign, including those lost in battle, to sickness and the *Valk* disaster was 268; this suggests Jack was inadvertently given that higher figure (possibly by the Regimental Paymaster, William Keith) for use in compiling his report to the Duke of York. More speculatively, if the last digit were mis-transcribed or mis-read by Jack as a '5', the numbers would tally exactly.[69] In some cases, the money the dead were owed was used to pay off their debts to the 23rd or other regiments with whom they had presumably previously served. Against a few, there is a note that the money owed to them was paid to their fathers, mothers, brothers, sisters and most poignantly 'paid to widow'.

The wreck of the *Valk* is one of the greatest maritime disasters in Dutch history. A high dune north of Hollum, Ameland's main town, where the bodies washed ashore and were initially buried subsequently became known as 'Engelsmanduin' - the Englishmen's dune. In

---

68 TNA WO 12/3964 *Regimental General Muster books and Pay Lists*, 23rd Foot, 1800.

69 The list in the June 1800 pay records is entitled 'State of the Effects and Credits of the Noncommissioned Officers and Privates of the 23 Regt of Foot (or Royal Welch) who have died from 25 June to 24 December 1799, according to what has been paid by the Paymaster to the friends & co of the Deceased, and also the Balances which remains Due'. 264 names are listed, of which 232 are recorded as 'dead 10 November', the date of the Valk disaster. The others are recorded as having been killed on, or died shortly after, the dates of battles during the campaign (especially the initial landing on 27 August), with one recorded as 'died in General Hospital date unknown'. Adding 264 NCOs and privates to the 4 officers killed during the period (all in the *Valk*), brings the total regimental loss resulting from the Helder campaign to 268. The list is handwritten, as would be any note sent to Jack while on leave at home in Devon about what the number lost was. A mis-transcription or mis-reading of '268' for '265' seems a reasonable possible explanation of what would otherwise be an odd overstatement of the *Valk* losses in Jack's official report.

November 1999, 200 years after the *Valk* was lost, a memorial was unveiled near Engelsmanduin to commemorate the disaster. The memorial is made from granite recovered from another ship that foundered off the island. Illustrated with a sketch of the *Valk* and the badge of the RWF, the memorial bears an inscription in Dutch which reads: 'On November 10, 1799, the frigate "De Valk" stranded north of Hollum. Only 25 of the 444 people on board survived the disaster. Among the 419 casualties were 265 men of the English 23rd regiment "Royal Welch Fusiliers". R.I.P.' Taking part in the unveiling ceremony for the memorial was a party from the RWF, one of whom, holding the same rank as Jack at the time of the wreck, was Lieutenant Edward Hill, his great-great-great-grandson.[70]

The combined casualties from the campaign and the shipwreck meant the strength of the regiment was reduced to about 400 men. As well as the loss of life, much of the regiment's weapons and other stores had also gone down on the *Valk*. The manpower numbers were made up via drafts from the Irish militia, with a few recruits raised in England, but 'the supplies were far from placing the regiment on its former establishment.'[71] The manpower and equipment shortages were still not rectified three months after the disaster. The 23rd were inspected by Major-General Lord Charles Somerset on 28 February, who reported 'there are 283 firelocks and bayonets wanting to complete to the present strength of the 23rd. I am happy to have it in my power to state that the 23rd Regiment is extremely correct and expert in the field, and in every respect except the want of arms, it is in high order'.[72] The cold rules of the army promotion system offered a silver lining for Jack. Three of the officers who died were above him on the regimental lieutenants' seniority list. Henry Hanson had held that rank since October 1794, Harman Vischer since November 1794, Alexander Maclean since February 1796. Only John Hoggard, promoted lieutenant in May 1799, was less senior than Jack; the deaths meant Jack, promoted lieutenant in April 1797, advanced in seniority within the regiment, bringing promotion closer. Despite their manpower shortages, in March the 23rd, along with a number of other regiments, were asked to send one officer and thirty-six men to Horsham to train as riflemen, potentially to become part of a newly formed Experimental Rifle

---

70 'The 'Valk' Memorial Dedication, 10th November 1999 in *Y Ddraig Goch, The Journal of the Royal Welch Fusiliers* March 2000, which also contains the article 'A Real Life Richard Sharpe: Lieutenant Colonel John Hill of the 23rd Foot' Major Nick Lock RWF.
71 Broughton-Mainwaring, *Historical Record*
72 Cary and McCance *Regimental Records*

Corps.[73] The original intention was for these men to form the basis of a rifle detachment within each regiment, but that was not pursued (though some years later the men of Jack's company would be temporarily issued with rifles, which they used with great effect during the expedition to Martinique - Chapter 8). Instead, the Experimental Rifle Corps became a line regiment and subsequently found fame as the 95th Rifles. One can imagine the 23rd not being overly impressed at the time to have to lose another chunk of manpower; they selected men from across their companies, rather than further denude one. Private Berry was one of those to go from Jack's company. The detachment did not return to their parent regiment until December.[74]

---

73 Lieutenant Thomas West led this detachment, taking two sergeants and a bugler as well as the private soldiers. TNA WO 17/125
74 TNA WO 12/3964

CHAPTER 3

FIGHTING AROUND THE MEDITERRANEAN

'Employed on the coasts of France, Ferrol and Cadiz. Commanded a
Company in the Egyptian Campaign. At Gibraltar'

Memorandum to the Duke of York, 1823

In May 1800 the 23rd moved again, this time to the Devon/
Somerset border, stationed in Honiton, Chard and Crewkerne. At the
end of June, they marched to Plymouth; on the way Jack stopped off to
see his family, rejoining the regiment before what would become their
longest and most dangerous overseas deployment since he joined. The
Valk disaster might reasonably have put Jack off ships, but on 1 July he
found himself at sea again, as the 23rd sailed on the frigates HMS
Naiad and HMS *Alcmene*.

They were part of a force commanded by Lieutenant-General Sir
James Pulteney whose task was to support another reported royalist
uprising, this time in the west of France. In mid-July they disembarked
on the Isle d'Houat in Quiberon Bay. The intention was to use the
island as a base to capture nearby Belle Île, but 'the orders had changed
with every contradictory report of the enemy's strength'.[1] It became
apparent that the defences of Belle Île were too strong for an attack to
succeed and nor was there much sign of the expected uprising. Captain
Richard Wyvill of the 79th called Isle d'Houat 'a rocky, barren place,
occupied by a few fishermen'.[2] Yet the British stayed there for nearly a
month until embarking again on 19 August. Wyvill said the 'regiments...
have been very sickly' while stuck there. Reinforced by troops who had
left Britain a month later, the fleet set sail the next day for a new target:
the major naval base and shipyard at Ferrol in north-western Spain.
There, Jack's fourth amphibious landing generated no better results
than the first three, though took less time to fail. The expedition arrived
outside Ferrol on 25 August. A fort near the port was bombarded and
some 8,000 troops and sixteen guns were landed near Cape Prior. They

1 *British Victory in Egypt: The End of Napoleon's Conquest* Piers Mackesy 1995
2 *Sketch of the Military Life* Richard Augustus Wyvill 1820

were 'ordered to climb up a very steep and difficult ascent...the road was so extremely narrow, hilly, and bad that the troops were obliged to ascend by Indian [single] files, and it was one o'clock in the morning before we reached the summit'.[3] An initial attempt to drive the British back into the sea failed and early on 26 August a larger body of Spanish attacked on the heights of Brión and Balon, overlooking the town and harbour. They too were repulsed with British casualties of sixteen killed and sixty-eight wounded; one and three of whom respectively were from the 23rd. While the defenders failed to drive the invaders away, after observing the strength of the town's fortifications, Pulteney decided he had insufficient force to carry them. That evening the landing party re-embarked and the fleet sailed away the next day to try elsewhere, arriving in Vigo Bay on the evening of the 29th. Some of the soldier's wives accompanying the troops were landed on Isla de Baiona to wash linen, while the ships underwent a thorough cleaning and fumigation, took on water and supplies and rode out storms. A couple of ships were lost when driven onshore by the wind, while others collided. After two weeks, Pulteney concluded 'that nothing was to be gained by landing troops'[4] and on 10 September they sailed away. Thwarted again, the fleet headed for Gibraltar where they joined a larger force under Sir Ralph Abercrombie, now the British army's Commander in the Mediterranean. Jack was on the transport ship HMS *Heroine*, a converted frigate, from which he landed with a small detachment of men on 25 September in Tetuan Bay (in modern Morocco) to stand guard while a naval party obtained water supplies. Touching dry land was a rare pleasure; the 23rd had spent all of September (and would spend most of October) afloat. Wyvill described the landing site: 'there is a large pool of water, into which a rivulet flows, and the sailors have only to run their casks into the water, and they fill themselves...Our sailors bought some very fine grapes on shore, as many as eleven of us in the cabin could eat, for half-a-crown. The natives will take our soldiers' buttons as money, and a cartridge is of great value.'[5]

Abercrombie had left Britain in Spring carrying numerous orders, including attacking Cadiz, another important Spanish naval base. Now with Abercrombie's larger force, Jack and the 23rd therefore sailed back the way they had come, arriving off Cadiz on 7 October. Another farce ensued: the troops began to board the ships' boats to land, but the arrangements were botched: 'it is not to be described', said John Moore, 'the bad management and confusion which attended the assembling of

---

3 Wyvill, *Sketch*
4 Cary and McCance, *Regimental Records*
5 Wyvill, *Sketch*

the boats'.[6] First there weren't enough boats available and then Lord Keith, the naval commander, told Abercrombie that if the troops landed, the Navy might be unable to get them off again, just as had happened in Ostend. Added to incompetence afloat were rumours of plague on land. It was enough for the attack on Cadiz also to be abandoned. As the ships turned away, gales blew up and pushed the entire fleet out into the Atlantic. The futile expeditions and increasingly difficult conditions aboard caused some wry comments: 'we are entirely ignorant of our destination. Our colonels call it a political cruise. I wish our politicians who planned it were in our place, living as we have done for upwards of a month on salt provisions, and cooped up together for 73 days'.[7] Even Moore, one of the most senior officers present commented 'the figure we have cut is truly ridiculous, but the shortest follies are the best, and it is lucky we did not land'.[8] The fleet were trying to get back to Gibraltar, but contrary winds meant the 23rd did not arrive at the Rock until 24 October; others took almost another month. Jack's description of these attempts to strike a blow against the enemy gives a rather superficial gloss:

> I was employ'd in the demonstrations at Bell Isle, Ferrol and Cadiz under Sir James Pultney and Sir Ralph Abercrombie.[9]

These were not supposed to be 'demonstrations', though, they were meant to be attacks that would cause harm to the enemy. The failure to achieve anything, said contemporaries, made the army 'the laughing stock of Europe'.[10] Certainly those efforts Jack had experienced so far - Ostend, the Helder, Belle Île, Ferrol, Vigo and Cadiz - had all ended badly, and most didn't even really start. The troops had begun to call themselves 'the floating army'.[11] A turning point was, however, coming. Abercrombie took his force eastwards towards a far more challenging target. They entered Valetta harbour on 22 November; after two further days aboard ship, the weary soldiers stepped ashore in Malta.

A few weeks later Jack wrote home, in a bad mood due to a lack of incoming mail.

---

6 Quoted in Mackesy, *Victory*
7 Wyvill, *Sketch*
8 Moore, *Diary*
9 Hill 1816 *Statement of Services*
10 Black, *Global Power*
11 Dragon Rampant: The Royal Welch Fusiliers at War, 1793 – 1815 Donald E. Graves, *Dragon Rampant* 2010.

Dear Mother,

It is Sunday. I am going to practise one of the greatest virtues of a Christian - namely: forgiveness. I have written you by every opportunity that offer'd. I have heard from you but once. It was directed for me at the Isle de Houat in August, four months after Col. Hall gave it a lift on to Malta, the Mackenzies and Bradford have rec'd a great many, particularly the former. B[radford] got a letter yesterday dated not a month ago, certainly if you had looked about you or his Family written you, I should have heard, if all other resources fail one certain one remains which is by sending them to the Agents. Keith and the Col[onel] have joined us with a part of the Regt. left behind at Plymouth. There was not only an opportunity of sending letters but any little thing you wish'd.

As it happened I had not an opportunity of going on board the Port Mahon.[12] It was well for me that I desired G[eorge] M[ackenzie] to do it in case he was able, he was sent up to Gibraltar to purchase things for the men, who were completely in rags, the Brig was there at the time and he saw a young man who informed him that Charles had gone home in the Lion. I saw the Lion sail from Tetuan, and I believe the same ship will carry home my Brother and Letter. He has been rather inattentive to me, every officer knew almost of what Regts. the army was composed and Charles might have left a letter for me behind him - it appears he has again left quarters that were beginning to bear a very promising aspect, for what reason G[eorge] M[ackenzie] could not find out, his late ship is now on the coast of Egypt and has carried up an officer in the Q[uate]r M[aste]r Gen[era]l Department; the army will soon follow, supported by a Turkish one. Alexandria in all human probability will fall. Capⁿ. Louis in the Minotaur is in the Harbour with the Minotaur [sic]. [13] The shipping in Alexandria will furnish for the navy one of the finest opportunities for promotion this war has afforded. Here is a chance lost, I hope he is

---

12 HMS *Port Mahon*, which Charles Hill should have been on, was an 18-gun brig-sloop captured in 1798.

13 Capt. Thomas Louis was born in Exeter in 1758. Appointed captain of HMS *Minotaur* in 1794, he had been with her in the Mediterranean squadron for some years, participating in the battle of the Nile. She would be part of the fleet which sailed to Marmaris Bay and supported the landing in Egypt. Louis became a Rear Admiral in 1805, but died of disease in Egypt in 1807, aged 49.

gone home with a view which will in the end turn out equally advantageous. If I had seen him I certainly should have advised his acting with the army, there is nothing that I lament so much as Charles being now not with me.

Your letter dated 5 months since particularly mentioned Linquo,[14] I hope the Gentleman is perfectly recovered from his fits. I am happy to hear you go on as usual quiet and with not many things to annoy you. After passage of 12 days with a Gale of wind driving us from abaft, we arrived here, the 22[nd]of last month, disembarked the 24th and have continued on shore ever since, and our ships sent off to Sicily for fresh provisions; we have been taken up so much with our duty that I have had scarcely time to look about me.

The Gazetteer will inform you of all the fine things I saw yesterday. The Grand Master's Garden, the Churches at Civita Vecchia, Catacombs, the one where he was confined and the bay where St. Paul was shipwrec'd. The English Churches are mere Barns when compared with the magnificent edifices dedicated to the supreme Being here. We are quartered in Valetta in the palace belonging to the Grand Captain for Italy; the rooms are immensely large and high but no furniture whatever.

The whole of the army is now embarked except the left wing of our Reg. waiting for a little more wind to sail for Egypt, our left wing is still on shore, to which I belong. The Astrea[15] was sent to Sicily or Italy for provision and money I believe.

This is the 17th and I am now finishing my letter as I see by the Genl. Orders there is an opportunity of writing, this is my birthday,[16] it is some consolation when away to consider that in the same day and hour we are thinking the one on the other, we have had no news here at all scarcely, there is a report of Hostilities having recommenced between Austria and France, that Russia was again coming forward with her troops, that this Island was to be given up in consequence. I should be very sorry if it is given up, it is one of the finest Islands I ever saw, the port is wonderfully fine. Ships may ride there almost without an anchor and cable, while we have such a fleet scarcely anything could possibly take it from us except a negociation.

---

14 One of the family dogs.
15 The transport ship *Astraea*.
16 The letter is dated 14th, yet Jack was again writing over several days, apparently still adding to it on 17th December.

You mentioned William was well at which I was much rejoiced, this winter I hope will see him made L[ieutenan]t.[17] Charles I think might have stood as good a chance had he been with Cap[n]. Lewis in the Minotaur, why he went home I can't imagine, it will never do to be shifting ships or R[egimen]gts; the world does not always know the reason. A short time, I should suppose, will decide the fate of Egypt, before a twelvemonth we meet again. Bradford told me Caroline was to be married to J. Ley.[18] This is a quiz I suppose of Betsy Mallocks which I suppose some of the Girls at Ideford have heard and pass'd on as a thing determined on.[19] Our Devonshire Friends here get on very well; the Macs. are on board. Cooke is quite as ridiculous as ever, he has left our ship. Hall and Jones are our Commanders. On board the Astrea, Bradford, Ellis and Pearson our Cap[ns]. Keith and Humphrey these you all know, I believe, we have been very healthy considering.[20] Write Short at Plymouth and if our Baggage should be ordered out send me scarlet cloath and English boots, Rifle, Buttons, and pack half my heavy baggage up and Send some flannel. Perhaps it's too much trouble for you to go to Plymouth and see it done. I wrote a long letter on business some time ago. Did you get it?

J. HILL

Jack's mail problems reflect the unreliability of communications with overseas military units at the start of the 19th Century. Regimental

---

17 William would not be commissioned lieutenant until April 1803. The letter to which he is responding seems to have been sent in August, so Jack was unaware that HMS *Diligence*, William's ship during 1800, had been wrecked near Cuba on 8 October. Fortunately, the entire crew of *Diligence* survived.

18 Caroline married Jacob Ley, Rector of St. David's, Ashprington, Devon on 24 April 1801.

19 The Mallocks were another important Devon family. Roger Mallock purchased Cockington, near Torquay, in 1654. The family produced Members of Parliament, Justices of the Peace, clergymen and attorneys.

20 Of the regimental officers mentioned: Lieutenant-Colonel John Hall commanded; he had only recently caught up with his battalion, having not been with them in Portsmouth. Evan Jones was one of the relatively few Welshmen in the regiment; 'Humphrey' is Richard Humfrey, the regimental surgeon; 'the Macs' are James and George Mackenzie; Pearson, another vicar's son, joined the regiment around the same time as Jack in 1796, but his father must have been better off, as Pearson was now a Captain. Cooke was commissioned 2nd lieutenant on 1 March 1800. Perhaps his newness explains why Jack found him 'ridiculous'.

Agents knew where a unit had been sent, and forwarded mail accordingly, but that did not mean they would still be there when it arrived. Mail might therefore shuttle from one location to another, risking loss on the way, in the hope eventually of reaching an intended recipient, but possibly never doing so. One of the safest alternatives was for a member of the Regiment joining later to bring mail with him, as Colonel John Hall did.

Jack was not the only unhappy person in Valetta. Abercrombie was less than impressed with the condition the 23rd presented upon inspection, as Jack would report in his next letter. Jack admits that his own appearance was less than ideal, but after months at sea and little opportunity to drill since they left Isle d'Houat in mid-August, it would be surprising if the 23rd's overall military bearing was not all it might be. The regiment were censured and placed under special oversight,[21] while Jack set about renewing his wardrobe in the relatively cheap markets of Malta. In assessing his displeasure with the condition of the 23rd, Abercrombie may also have been reflecting on the challenge he was about to face, for he had been ordered to do no less than recapture Egypt. He was ordered to pursue this in co-operation with the Ottoman Empire. British troops were about to undertake yet another amphibious landing, working with a foreign partner about which they knew little. It must have felt familiar to Abercrombie as he reflected on the lessons of the Helder expedition and the more recent abortive efforts around the coasts of France and Spain. Abercrombie determined to do better this time. For that he needed good co-operation with the navy, so his army arrived ashore in good order. Conversely, he felt he needed rather less co-operation with his new allies. Reportedly the quality of the Turkish army was poor. It was therefore agreed that the Turks would approach Egypt overland, separately from the British. Lastly, Abercrombie meant to ensure that his own army was fit, drilled and ready to fight immediately they reached the Egyptian beaches, as they would be landing to face a far more serious opponent. The *Armée de l'Orient* was composed of veterans from Bonaparte's Italian campaign; they had beaten the Marmelukes who controlled Egypt, captured Cairo and subjugated a swathe of the Eastern Mediterranean coastline. Abercrombie set sail for Turkey to meet his new partners and rehearse. Just before Christmas, the 23rd embarked yet again; on New Year's Day 1801, they reached their next temporary home, the bay of Marmaris.

---

21 Graves, *Dragon Rampant*

Marmora Bay, near Rhodes.
11 Jany. 1801.

Dear Mother,
    We sail'd from Malta the 21 of last month, arrived here the 1 of Jany. This place is situated in the continent of Asia just above the Gulph of Marmara. The fleet at present consists of about an hundred sail; we have not yet seen anything of the Turkish forces of any description except two small frigates. Report says we shall not sail from here this month. In my last I think I gave you a fine scolding for not writing to me. I hope you will profit by it. I have now written at least twenty letters and have rec'd one only from you dated 20th August.[22] We are all seated round the table writing, and asking each other for a hint of something to say. The Fleet is anchored in a most beautiful Bay, every way surrounded by immense high rocky mountains between which there are some very fruitful vallies [sic]. I have been several times shooting on shore, we saw a number of wood-cocks, having not proper implements, we did not get much to bring on board, we make a grand party soon, armed at all points, as there are a great number of Bears, wolves, leopards here on the mountains.
    Charles' ship, the Port Mahon, is here. I have not been on board which I intend doing to find out how he got on there, and his reason for leaving her. We are tolerably healthy having lost only a few men by the flux.
    A salute has just been fir'd on account of a two-tail'd Turkish Bashaw having come on board the Admiral, he arrived last evening in their town on shore from Constantinople.[23] You have a very good description of the Turkish town in the French intercepted letters therefore I shall not trouble you with it.[24]
    At Malta I recruited my kit in great stile having bought a new jacket and scarlet waistcoat, 4 shirts and pocket h-k-chiefs, several pr. of thin pantaloons, stockings, etc.; what we most want is good

---

22 Letters being carried by HMS *Swiftsure* were lost when she was captured in June 1801. Had they got through, Jack's family would have no doubt kept them as they did his others.

23 'Bashaw', an alternative spelling of 'pasha', generally refers to a high-ranking official, admiral or general. 'Two-tailed' refers to the number of horse tails tied to the officer's standard, akin to 'one-star' or 'two-star' used today as shorthand for the ranks of modern generals.

24 Intercepted letters written by French officers from Egypt had been published in Britain. Jack doesn't seem to consider that letters sent home by British soldiers could have suffered a similar fate.

boots, remember and keep a good look-out at Plymouth and if our Reg^{tal}. cloathing for the men is sent out you can get in a couple prs. of strong boots. A little shot would not be amiss as we only pay 1/2 a crown a pound for very bad here. I shall write soon to Major Fletcher. The French have thrown a reinforcement into Egypt it is thought we shall have something to do there.

At Rhodes we have about an hundred Gunboats fitting out. Cap^n. Bradford is writing opposite, and he will give the best account of himself. I hope the widow has had plenty of fun this Xmas, the home duty of the Fusiliers is much more pleasant of a winter's evening at Hennock or Ideford than amidst the Turks in Asia. Credit we got nowhere, at least not from Sir R. Abercrombie. He has expressed his astonishment at the state of the Reg^t. after all their advantages which they had at the Isle d'Houat, as for myself I can say I have worn out nearly the whole of the portmanteau of clothes which I brought from Hennock the evening before we embarked. Give my love to Caroline and ask her to inform me in her next how Mr. J. Ley is, also to all our friends at Hennock.

Yours
J. HILL

Jack thought the bay 'most beautiful'; others agreed it was impressive, 'remarkably fine, spacious, and deep, perfectly land-locked...This bay is almost circular; it is fifteen miles in diameter, and capable of containing all the navies of Europe' said Wyvill, though he was less impressed by the town of Marmaris, which he called 'abominably filthy'.[25]

Abercrombie was about to test an army whose recent record was failure, against a French army which knew little but success. He described the operation as 'arduous, and perhaps doubtful'...I am not confident of success'.[26] But he had to try, and he had one major advantage: Bonaparte himself was no longer there. Having persuaded the Directory to threaten British interests in India, in May 1798 Bonaparte crossed the Mediterranean with nearly 40,000 soldiers, plus over 150 'savants'; eminent scientists and experts whose role was to unlock the secrets of ancient Egypt. Avoiding Nelson and capturing Malta en route (recaptured by Britain the following October), Bonaparte and his army landed near Alexandria on 1 July and captured Cairo within a month. But at the beginning of August Nelson found the French fleet anchored in Aboukir Bay and eliminated it in the battle of

25 Wyvill, *Sketch*
26 Quoted in Mackesy, *Victory*

the Nile. Stranded, but not cowed, Bonaparte fought his way west and north along the Mediterranean coastline until he was eventually stopped in May 1799 at Acre, which was defended by a Turkish garrison supported by the Royal Navy. Returning to Egypt, Bonaparte departed (or fled, depending on your perspective) for France, claiming that he needed to save his country from the armies of Russia and Austria, which were again advancing across Europe. This he did, ultimately defeating the Austrians at Marengo in June 1800. He also arranged a coup d'etat, was appointed First Consul (in effect ruler of France) and confronted his wife Josephine about the affair she had been having while he was away. Returning to France was unquestionably the right move for Bonaparte's career, but his abandoned army in Egypt could be forgiven for not seeing things that way. Peace negotiations were expected after Marengo and French possession of Egypt meant they would argue to keep it. That would be problematic for British trade with India and the rest of Asia. The pressure was on for Abercrombie to succeed in driving France out.

Bonaparte had left the capable General Jean-Baptiste Kléber in command in Egypt, but Kléber too was not a factor in Abercrombie's calculations; he was assassinated in June 1800. Kléber was succeeded by Jacques-François Menou, a man 'as sedentary as Abercrombie was active, though at 48 he was sixteen years Abercrombie's junior'.[27] Despite changing commanders and campaign losses though, the *Armée de l'Orient* remained a powerful and experienced force of some 10,000 men; Abercrombie's preparations needed to be thorough. His stay in Marmaris provided a unique opportunity: while waiting for supplies, especially horses for his cavalry and artillery, he planned. Abercrombie had the diplomatic skills to work closely with the Royal Navy, ensuring the naval and army components of the mission were fully coordinated. He also recognised the need to keep his men as healthy as possible through regular supplies and arrangements to care for the sick. He gave careful thought to logistics, for example issuing orders to ensure adequate water supplies. Finally, having established that his Turkish allies would not be ready in time, he planned for the initial part of the operation to be British only. That would reduce his manpower but would avoid the problems cooperation brought. Abercrombie was also astute tactically. While still drilling his men for manoeuvre in large formations, he also 'placed considerable emphasis on light infantry work',[28] using some troops in loose formations to skirmish with the enemy and protect his front lines. There was rivalry in the British Army

---

27 Mallinson, *Army*
28 *Abercromby in Egypt: The Regeneration of the Army*, Piers Mackesy in *The Road to Waterloo* Alan J Guy (ed.) 1990

between a so-called 'German' school, following the legacy of Frederick the Great by favouring the power of close formations and disciplined movement in open terrain; and an 'American' school, who had experienced the utility of looser formations and lighter troops in close country during the American Revolution. Abercrombie believed both had their place, depending on circumstances, and that the army needed sufficient flexibility to adopt either.

Perhaps most importantly, Abercrombie inspected, trained and rehearsed his men. His chosen landing site was Aboukir Bay, where Nelson had destroyed the French fleet nearly three years before. The shoreline there was shallow up to seven miles out, so transport ships would have to anchor at distance from the beach. The landing would have to avoid long intervals between waves of troops and exhausting the sailors who rowed the army ashore. Abercrombie's answer was an ingenious piece of reverse thinking. The men of his second wave would be pre-positioned in small boats close in, so sailors returning after landing the first wave did not have to row back to the fleet to collect them and the two waves could be delivered in a shorter timescale. Such complex arrangements needed practice and Abercrombie stimulated a competitive spirit during the rehearsals by timing how long individual units took to land and form up on the beach. Jack took part in one trial on 22nd January. The troops 'got into the flat boats, ships boats, and launches, and were all landed in twenty-three minutes. The Turkish admiral witnessed this transaction, and was quite in raptures at the sight'.[29] All the planning and preparation worked. From the 'floating army', who had spent months sailing around the European coastline launching chaotic and ill-fated pinprick raids, Abercrombie forged 'perhaps the most coherent British striking force to take the field in eight years of war'.[30] The regeneration of the army that had just begun when Jack joined in 1795 was not yet complete, but in Turkey Abercrombie took it a long way forward. Now his work would be tested in battle.

By 18 February the troops were embarked, but it was the 22nd before the fleet sailed from Marmaris bay: around 180 ships of all shapes and sizes were crowded with everything needed for a major expedition. The 23rd were again in the *Astraea* and *Heroine*. Conditions aboard were 'misery…like going to prison' said one of the officers.[31] Yet again the weather delayed them and some of the transports became separated from the fleet. Moore noted 'When we left Marmaras we were about 180 vessels of all descriptions. I cannot now count above

29 Wyvill, *Sketch*
30 Mackesy, *Abercromby.*
31 Lord Dalhousie, quoted in Mackesy, *Victory*

140'.[32] The fleet reached the Egyptian coast on 1 March, entering Aboukir Bay the next day. The conditions were too rough to allow an immediate landing, but at around 2am on the 8th, carrying three days of rations, some 5,000 British soldiers loaded into their landing boats and took up the positions they had practiced. On the shoreline 2,500 French troops lined the sand hills overlooking the beach, supported by artillery and cavalry. Jack and the 23rd were again designated as part of the Reserve, this time under Major-General John Moore, alongside the 28th, 42nd, and 58th regiments, plus the Corsican Rangers and detachments of the 40th and cavalry. Again, despite the name, the Reserve were 'the army's crack brigade'[33] and would be among the first to land. The 23rd were at the extreme right of the long line of boats, with only the 40th outside them. At about 8am a flare was fired from the ships and the first wave were rowed in. As they approached the beach, the Royal Navy fired over their heads at the French positions. The French responded with what Moore called a 'really most severe' artillery barrage; it 'churned up the water like hail'.[34] For those in the boats the only defence against this was to reach the shore as quickly as possible. Three boats were sunk by enemy fire in the hour it took to reach the beach, no doubt with many prayers being said, and occasional cheers from the soldiers as they made their way in:

> The sea was smooth and the weather remarkably fine...Never was a thing conducted with greater regularity...the British troops preserving a regular line, as they advanced in their boats, although the wind was directly in their teeth and finally, landing in regular order of battle, under the heaviest fire perhaps ever experienced. Shells, cannon-balls, grape-shot, coming with the wind, fell like a storm of hail about them; yet not a soldier quitted his seat; nor did a single sailor shrink from the hard labour of his oar.[35]

Each company, battalion and brigade got ashore and rapidly formed up: 'the tide of redcoats was as unstoppable as the waves themselves'.[36] The 23rd were among the first to disembark and attacked immediately as Moore led the Reserve directly up a steep sand-hill some 30 metres high. Perhaps previous experience in Holland helped, as despite the difficulty of running up the loose sand, they reached the top before their

---

32 Moore, *Diary*
33 Mackesy, *Victory*
34 'most severe': Moore, *Diary*; 'churned up the water': Cary and McCance *Regimental Records*
35 Wyvill, *Sketch*
36 Mallinson, *Army*.

opponents fired more than a single volley and scattered them, capturing their artillery in the process: 'the 23rd...rushed up the heights with almost preternatural energy, never firing a shot, but charging with the bayonet the two [French] battalions which crowned them, breaking and pursuing them'.[37] The action helped the regiment regain their good name with Abercrombie, who later shook Lieutenant-Colonel John Hall's hand with the comment 'my friend Hall, I am glad to see you; I shall never abuse you again'.[38] Moore later recorded in his journal 'the enemy had had eight days to assemble and prepare; the ground was extremely favourable for defence. Our attempt was daring, and executed by the troops with the greatest intrepidity and coolness'.[39] Elsewhere on the beach the fighting was hard, but within two hours of touching the sand, the British beachhead was secure and the French were retreating down the narrow Aboukir peninsular towards Alexandria. The 23rd lost 6 killed and about 40 wounded out of the overall British loss of over 700. One young man killed was ensign the Hon. Edward Meade of the 40th Foot who, unbeknownst to him, had just been promoted lieutenant and transferred to the 23rd. If he had made the change, he would have been in a different place on the beach and may have lived, rather than suffer the random fortunes of war. Among the wounded of the 23rd were Captains Charles Lloyd, Henry Ellis and Thomas Pearson.

The next day Abercrombie issued a General Order, noting 'The gallant behavior of the troops in the action yesterday claims, from the Commander-in-Chief, the warmest praise that he can bestow; and it is with particular satisfaction that he observed their conduct, marked equally for ardent bravery and by coolness, regularity, and order'.[40] A later assessment called the landing 'perhaps the most skillful and daring operation of its kind that was ever attempted...the patient endurance of the troops as they sat, powerless for resistance, between the peril of a furious fire above and the peril of drowning below, was beyond all praise...the storming of the sand-hill was the most brilliant as it was the decisive moment of the day'.[41] Abercrombie no doubt remembered though that a successful landing also started the Helder campaign; what mattered was what followed. His main objective was to capture Alexandria, around 12 miles to the west between Lake Aboukir and the sea. As stores were unloaded over the next few days, the Reserve moved forward to occupy a line across the narrow neck of land separating the

37 Broughton-Mainwaring, *Historical Record*
38 Quoted in Graves, *Dragon Rampant*
39 *Moore of Corunna* Roger Parkinson 1976
40 Quoted in Mackesy, *Victory*
41 Fortescue, *History* Vol. IV Pt. II

British from their target. Supplies could now be landed from the calmer waters of lake Aboukir, reducing the risk from bad weather. On 12 March the whole army moved up again, demonstrating the value of their training as they advanced in columns, redeployed perfectly when nearing the French and then advanced in line, continually dressing by the Colours of the 23rd, on the extreme right,[42] despite the challenges of the terrain. It was a piece of manoeuvering so well performed that many observers commented on the discipline shown: 'a more perfect manner than I have seen it at any review' said one.[43] After some skirmishing with French pickets, the real fight resumed the next day. Much of the struggle was on the left, while the Reserve remained in column on the right to protect against cavalry. In that formation they were vulnerable to cannon fire, against which they could not fire back. Undaunted, they calmly moved forward, taking casualties all the way. 'Nothing could overcome their cool intrepidity, discompose their order, or prevent their advancing', said Moore of his soldiers.[44] The fighting, the battle of Mandara, cost the British 1,240 killed and wounded, but by the end of the day the French had been pushed back under the guns of Alexandria and Abercombie's army occupied a strong line about 3 miles long, anchored on Lake Aboukir on the left and some Roman ruins on the Mediterranean shore to the right. Jack and the Reserve were posted near these ruins. The discipline they demonstrated was impressive, causing one historian to argue that Mandara 'might be singled out as the pivotal moment when the regenerated British Army came of age. The precision of its manoeuvres was matched by its steadiness under fire and under attack; and for the first time its light infantry acted as an integral element in a general action'.[45] There were more serious tests to come, but the army had shown it could act coherently and effectively in the face of the enemy.

Despite the success so far, Abercrombie felt an immediate assault on Alexandria would be too costly and spent the following week consolidating the British line, building entrenchments and emplacing artillery. A market was established for local traders to sell food to the soldiers, at set rates to avoid inflated prices. Meanwhile, the French had been reinforced and had aggressive ideas of their own. Just before daybreak on 21 March they launched a diversionary attack against the British left, while the main French force attacked the British right. As the French pressed in, Jack and the Reserve advanced to support their

---

42 Mackesy, *Victory*
43 Major Lowe of the Corsican Rangers, quoted in Mackesy, *Victory*
44 Moore, *Diary*
45 Mackesy, *Abercromby*

colleagues of the 58th Foot, stationed in the ruins. They arrived just in time to meet a French column. Jack takes up the story:

> the 23rd. Regt. moved up to the support of the 58th Regt. and halted about sixty paces from the front face of the ruined Roman buildings, the Light Company being in front, the Lieut. Colonel's company was on the left flank. The head of a French Column was observed entering through the broken wall on the left face; the dawn of day shew'd their hats, on which I wheeled the Company up in silence and gave orders to fire at about thirty-five yards' distance. During the 2nd discharge, Capn. Bradford brought up his Company on the right, and...Henry Ellis his on the left; when the word "charge" was given, the openings gained and about three hundred and fifty prisoners made.[46]

This short summary, in his 1816 *Statement of Services*, contains a wealth of detail. It confirms the 23rd's light company was skirmishing ahead of the main body of the regiment, making Jack's Lieutenant-Colonel's company the leftmost company of the line. It also shows Jack acting on his own initiative by wheeling his men to face the French and fire; at short range this must have had devastating results. The discipline and flexibility with which the 23rd manoeuvered is underlined by Bradford and Ellis' positioning their companies either side of Jack's, thus putting the line 'out of order'. Firing a volley followed by a charge with bayonets was to become a classic British tactic during the many fights that were to follow in succeeding years. Lastly, that Jack wheeled his men against the French when 'the dawn of the day shew'd their hats' presages a comment by the Duke of Wellington some 10 years later when arguing against proposals to change British headgear: 'at distance, or in action, colours are nothing: the profile, and shape of a man's cap, and his general appearance, are what guide us...the narrow top caps of our infantry, as opposed to their broad top caps, are a great advantage to those who look at long lines of posts opposed to each other'.[47]

The fight at the ruins was hand-to-hand and vicious. 'Menou had promised a louis to every French soldier who should be concerned in establishing a position in the ruin; and several attempts were made for that purpose. The 58th had been stationed there in the beginning of the action, with a part of the 23rd, and had already repulsed a column of the enemy...three columns forced in...they were received by the 58th and 23rd...a most desperate conflict ensued. Our men attacked them

---

46 Hill *Statement of Services* 1816
47 Quoted in Haythornthwaite, *Armies*

like wolves, with less order than valour, for having expended all their ammunition, they had to recourse to stones, and the butt ends of their muskets, transfixing the Frenchmen with their bayonets against the walls of the building'.[48] Despite repeated French attacks, the British line held its ground. The Reserve came under serious pressure as the French sought to turn the British right flank. The 'attack on this point was begun by the infantry, sustained by a strong body of cavalry: the contest was unusually obstinate; the enemy was twice repulsed, and their cavalry were repeatedly mixed with the British infantry. They at length retired, leaving a prodigious number of dead and wounded on the field'.[49] Praise for the Reserve was fulsome: 'To Major-General Moore… and the reserve, no acknowledgments are sufficient' and 'The Reserve, against whom the principal attack of the enemy was directed, conducted themselves with unexampled spirit: they resisted the impetuosity of the French infantry, and repulsed several charges of cavalry'.[50] The 23rd suffered 5 men killed; one officer, two sergeants and twelve men wounded in the battle of Alexandria. The officer was Samuel Cooke, who had been in the army just a year and who Jack had labelled 'ridiculous' on the outgoing voyage. Seriously wounded, his leg was amputated; he was far from ridiculous while the operation was taking place. George Mackenzie said 'Poor Sam Cooke received a wound from a splinter of a shell which broke his right leg below his knee, & shattered it in so bad a manner as to render an amputation immediately necessary…The Surgeon tells me that he never in his life saw any one bear an operation with such fortitude: he did not speak a word or utter a groan during the whole time'.[51] Mackenzie gave Cooke money and thought he would make it home, but he was wrong; Cooke died on 2 August. The total price of the British victory was over 240 killed and some 1,100 wounded, most significant by far being Abercrombie. With a bad habit of riding to wherever the battlefield action was hottest, he was lucky at Alkmaar in 1799 when he lost two horses. But his luck ran out: while near the ruins encouraging his men he was shot in the leg. Abercrombie remained on the field fearing the impression on his men should he leave. Nearly passing out from loss of blood, he was finally

---

48 Wyvill, *Sketch*. The 'part of the 23rd' was presumably the Light Company, which Jack describes as being 'in front' before the rest of the regiment came up. In *Dragon Rampant*, Don Graves incorrectly attributes part of this quote to Jack, but it is Wyvill's colourful language.

49 Broughton-Mainwaring, *Historical Record*

50 General Order and official despatch (respectively), Major-General Sir John Hely-Hutchinson, quoted in Broughton-Mainwaring, *Historical Record*

51 RWF Archive Object No. 379. Letter dated 27 March 1801 from 'camp before Alexandria'.

carried off as the battle neared its conclusion. He died a week later. The army had lost 'one of the most worthy and well-liked commanders of the period, experienced, capable and a great humanitarian'.[52]

The authors of the Regimental Records of the Royal Welch Fusiliers clearly felt the Egyptian campaign was now broadly over: 120 years later they wrote 'beyond the taking of Fort Rahmanieh on the 10th May, followed a week later by the surrender to Brigadier-General Doyle of 600 of 'the best troops of France', the evacuation of Cairo by the French and their auxiliary troops on the 27th of June, winding up with the surrender of Alexandria on the 2nd September, which shattered Napoleon's aims in Egypt, nothing of importance remains to be narrated'.[53] This is a highly misleading understatement of the remaining six months of the Egyptian campaign, based on hindsight and the fact that the 23rd did not play the most active part in what was to come. But both their work and that of the rest of the army was far from done, and the outcome of the expedition was still in the balance. The army's new commander, Major-General Sir John Hely-Hutchinson, shared Abercrombie's views about the risk of trying to take Alexandria by assault. But he also faced a dilemma. Despite the victory on 21 March, the French remained a potent enemy. If all their forces in Egypt combined, they would have more than enough troops to attack and possibly defeat him. Menou's subordinate commanders were urging him to do just that. Turkish forces had now crossed the border and were heading for Cairo, where there was a large French garrison, and additional British troops were due to arrive on the Red Sea coast from India any day. But these allied forces were widely dispersed and if the French could unite, they might defeat the parts individually. Hutchinson decided that he had to prevent this. Leaving Alexandria covered by a small force including the 23rd, under the Command of Major-General Eyre Coote, Hutchinson began a remarkable set of moves that remain sadly under-recognised in British military history. What he and 5,000 men did was: march 40 miles to Rosetta, capture it, make a remarkable 150-mile march down the Nile, link up with the Turks, fight at Rahmanieh and ultimately force a French force of over 13,000 men in Cairo to surrender. All in the searing Egyptian early summer heat, and all before the end of June.

The 23rd may have remained at Alexandria because it had been hit badly with sickness. On 28 March they recorded 116 sick out of 591 total present - nearly 20% of total strength. One who suffered was Lieutenant-Colonel John Hall, who returned to the fleet to recover. Hall handed command to Major James Mackenzie, who had himself had

---

52 Haythornethwaite, *Armies*
53 Cary and McCance, *Regimental Records*

been complaining of intestinal problems since returning from the Helder two years previously. Sick again in Malta and after the battle of Alexandria, his brother George tried to convince James also to go back aboard ship, but James procrastinated, not least through a sense of duty. On 22 March his condition worsened. Complaining of severe pains and passing blood, he finally agreed to reboard HMS *Heroine*. Within hours he died. James' passing was a shock; George Mackenzie wrote to his father that 'neither myself, Geo[rge] Bradford, nor the surgeon (Mr. Humphries) had any idea he was so ill'.[54] On 26 March James' body was taken ashore by his brother. The next morning, George reported 'Bradford, Hill and myself saw it decently interred under a Palm tree'. James had been in the 23rd since 1780, but despite his distinguished service on four continents, George's request for military honours was denied. He asked the Admiral's Chaplain to perform a service, but then 'I c[oul]d not find him this morning, and therefore was obliged to request John Hill to read the burial service'. James Mackenzie was a friend since before Jack had joined the army and had been instrumental in his becoming a Fusilier. In his letters from Blundell's Jack called Mackenzie someone able to 'inform and advise better than most people' on army life; he and George were 'the Macs', who Jack cheerfully mentioned in his letter home the previous December. Jack would no doubt have felt honoured to read the appropriate text over his grave, but James's death was a blow. Jack would learn to cope with losing friends over the long career he was to have. George Mackenzie put it well: 'the situation of a soldier's friends is different from that of all others, as they ought at all times to be in some measure prepared for the worst'.[55]

Meanwhile, the north-south line from the Roman ruins near the sea that the 23rd had helped defend was strengthened, so it could be held by Coote's much smaller force while the rest of the army headed for Cairo. The dyke between lake Aboukir and the dry lake Mareotis was breached and the latter flooded, preventing the risk of a French flank attack from the south. All this work was done by the troops, who slept in their clothes at night in case of attack and were required to stand ready and armed every day from 3am - an hour before daylight. This was far from the comfortable non-event the 23rd's official historians implied. The discomfort was added to by swarms of flies and rampant sickness, especially ophthalmia which infected up to a third of Coote's men,[56] but also the plague and other illnesses that killed or

---

54 RWF Archive Object No. 379
55 RWF Archive Object No. 379
56 Mackesy, *Victory*

crippled. The troops were at least well provisioned from local supplies through the market, though the army had not been paid for eight months, and many officers lent money to their men so they could eat better food than salt rations. Those who avoided illness thrived 'As to myself, G. Bradford & Hill, we were never better in our lives' said George Mackenzie 'the army is stationary in camp, & exposed to no fatigues, nor likely to be as we must blockade Alexandria for some time'.[57] 'They were a lean and hardy race of soldiers who had lived in their clothes by day and night for six months, never undressing except to wash or put on a clean shirt, and sleeping in their equipment...very dirty, starved and shabby, without wine, comforts, and even clothing'[58] said one historian of Coote's force. In early August this shambles greeted the British troops sent from India who had marched fully across the Egyptian desert from the south yet still looked a lot better than the colleagues they met outside Alexandria. The troops from the sub-continent had arrived after Cairo had fallen, but Hely-Hutchinson brought them and his own force to Alexandria and rejoined Coote at the siege lines. The fully united and reinforced British-Turkish force spent two weeks tightening their grip on the town, building batteries, bringing in gunboats to blockade and bombard it and sailing across the now-flooded Lake Mareotis to attack from the west as well. The pressure worked. Menou finally surrendered on 2nd September.

Egypt was a stunning success: York's reforms had improved the army's administration; Abercrombie, Moore and others had provided competent command; and the troops had shown they could win in battle. The Egyptian campaign was a turning point for the British army. It had efficiently landed its forces, manoeuvered and fought in a disciplined and modern way, crossed a country in a harsh climate and beaten a veteran opponent. Bonaparte, unsurprisingly, did not agree, later commenting 'no military man, English, Turkish, or French...will deny that the army of Abercromby must have been defeated and destroyed if Kléber had lived'.[59] Perhaps if Bonaparte himself had been there, things may have been different too. But an army can only fight what is in front of it. The campaign cost the British 633 men killed or missing and over 3,000 wounded. 160 men were permanently blinded by ophthalmia and 200 more lost one eye from the disease.[60] The French lost 4,000 dead after the British landed; an astonishing 27,000 in total surrendered. Under the surrender terms, they were shipped to

57 RWF Archive Object No. 379
58 Mackesy, *Victory*
59 Quoted in *Napoleon on Napoleon* Somerset de Chair (ed.) 1992
60 All figures from Mackesy, *Victory*

France by the Royal Navy; the last man from Bonaparte's oriental adventure left Egypt before November.

The British government recognised the significance of what had been achieved: 'the King's ministers could at last see that a well-found and well-generalled British army supported by the Royal Navy could gain decisive results'.[61] The army received the thanks of Parliament and every regiment that fought in the campaign was 'permitted to bear on its colours and appointments the Sphinx, with the word 'Egypt'' - the first time every regiment participating in a campaign was granted such a battle honour, underlining the relief and pride that the army had at last gained a significant victory in a campaign against France.[62] The honour was a small piece of propaganda reminding future members of those regiments what they should live up to and future opponents what they faced. Each officer who fought in Egypt was presented with a gold medal by the Grand Seignior of Turkey. It was Jack's first such decoration but would not be his last.

The death of Abercrombie was especially lamented. His body was placed in a cask of spirits and transported back to Malta, where it was buried with full honours in a bastion of Valetta's Fort St. Elmo. Yet despite his towering achievement in taking a disparate and unready force to another continent, forging it into an army and defeating an experienced and capable opponent, his name is now sadly little remembered. Even his tomb is often missed by visitors to Malta's National War Museum, despite its introductory section telling them that the bastion on which they stand was renamed 'Abercrombie Bastion' after he was buried there. If you walk along the Thames Embankment in London, however, you may find an obelisk popularly known as 'Cleopatra's Needle', which was presented to Britain in 1819 by Muhammad Ali, a member of the Turkish army during the campaign and later ruler of Egypt. The Historic England website says the gift was to commemorate the 'Nelson's victories'.[63] But in fact, it was to commemorate two commanders who fell at their moment of victory. As the plaque at the base reads, the obelisk is 'a worthy memorial of our distinguished countrymen Nelson and Abercromby'.

In October, Jack and the 23rd embarked for Malta, where they spent a few weeks recovering and restocking supplies. On 12 December they sailed for Gibraltar. There the mail finally caught up with them, but there was also very bad news that Jack was at last ready to broach with his family.

---

61 Mallinson, *Army*
62 Broughton-Mainwaring, *Historical Record*
63 https://historicengland.org.uk

25 Dec^{r}., 1801
Gibraltar

Dear Mother,

I had the happiness of receiving yours of the 7th Dec. last evening. It appears very extraordinary so many letters on both sides should have miscarried.

With respect to poor Charles, I wrote Mr. White of it 4 months since, requesting him to mention it to Mr. Pinhey. The letter I rec'd from my Father [which] mentioned Charles being on board the Minotaur immediately suggested a thousand fears for him on account of this ship being for 5 months close to us and his not finding me out - soon after landing in Egypt I wrote to my brother. Cap^{n}. Louis opened it and answered it and enclosed one from you directed to Charles. I immediately became suspicious of some accident. I took my horse and rode to one of the redoubts to whose battery the Minotaur people serving on shore were attached. I could not that day get any satisfactory intelligence and sent Power next day to enquire among the Minotaur's men if any of them knew Mr. Hill.[64] Power very soon returned bringing a seaman who came from Bovey and had served his apprenticeship at Hawkesmore - Harris.[65] Charles had also found him out to be a countryman and had taken notice of him. He very coolly informed me there was no hope whatever.

It appears from him the Minotaur had purchased a poleacre and had put a some of her Guns into her. The Gale, if you recollect, that drove S^{r}. R. Abercrombie['s] army out of the Mediterranean previous to our going up to Malta, was fatal to my poor brother, it is supposed by the seamen that the Guns were too heavy for her. It is now about a year and half since the accident happened - many a melancholy hour have I spent in Egypt when on night duties, the gloomy thoughts that would intrude during the darkness; what was become of my brother - hourly expecting to be engaged when my fate also might be decided - and of the sorrows you might be subjected to, in being deprived of two of us at once.[66] I have

---

64 Power was Jack's soldier servant.
65 Hawkesmoore (or Hawkmoor) was a farm owned by the Harris family on the outskirts of Bovey Tracy, near Hennock.
66 Mounting guns on small boats like poleacres was common practice; HMS Minotaur participated in numerous actions involving such craft, often to bombard land targets. Jack suggests Charles' fatal accident was in the summer of 1800, when HMS Minotaur was at sea off the Italian coast. The storm Jack refers to however was in October 1800.

remained an hour often so absorbed in my reflections respecting you and Charles, till rous'd by a patrol or one of the sentinels challenging, I us'd to rise up and go to the front, walk about there which requires all attention and circumspection and by these means bring my thoughts back from so melancholy a subject and congratulate myself on what I had already escaped and prayed the Almighty out of his infinite goodness to return me safe to you and my Hennock friends once more.

You must perceive from my letter that I entertained some dread for him. I have not mentioned it because as there were no particular accounts when and where it happened, I thought it was better to let Cap^n. Louis himself acquaint you. As soon as I knew of it in Egypt, I wrote Cap^n. Louis saying it was the custom in the army when an officer dies to sell everything, pay his debts, and remit the balance to his nearest relation. I desired that nothing should be sold and that I would pay every debt of his (I had then £35 in dollars) and that if he wish'd to get dollars for bills of exchange, I would among the officers get it at the rate we rec'd it which is 4s.6d. a dollar now; the navy then were paying 6s. 5d, to tenpence each dollar. He said as for debts he knew of none that he would part with nothing of his but wait my father's directions - that he was much obliged to me for the offer of the Dollars, and if he wanted them he would trouble me. His letter was very civil and polite.

I dropt the correspondence there. The other day the Minotaur came in here. Part of the 11th Dragoons came down [on her as] passengers. They belonged to the reserve, in consequence I knew two or three of them. We were walking with [them], and I desired Lutchings in case we met Cap^n. Louis to introduce me.[67] I met him one day riding - Lutchings said I wish'd to know if he'd heard anything of my brother, he said no, and fear'd it was but too true. He said in general invitation, he should be very happy to see me on board the Minotaur - to which I bowed - at that time we had no mess established, and I could not say in return I should be glad to see him on such a day. We wish'd each other a good morning and parted at which I was not sorry. I disliked carrying on a conversation on such a subject with 8 or 9 strangers in the publick street. I know I have not paid Cap^n. Louis perhaps all the attention due him for his kind offers - but after the misfortune I hated the name of the Minotaur, and wanted to avoid every circumstance that might bring to my recollection, my brother, when strangers were by.

---

67 Lt. Benjamin Lutyens, 11th Light Dragoons, which was in the Reserve in Egypt.

I have also written by the M[inotau]r - the letter you got went home in S. J. Warren's ship.[68] You must make an apology if you think proper for my not going on board the M[inotau]r and for not being more communicative in my correspondence with Cap[n]. Louis, as he did not wish to commit me respecting the final selling of his affairs. I was glad of being spar'd a painful task. In my correspondence with Caroline she appear'd to hint something which I returned, as I knew from Louis here that you would get the information from Mr. Kitson.

My letter to Mr. White has miscarried, otherwise you would have heard from Mr. Pinhey as I desir'd him to ride out one Sunday and mention it to my Father, as I thought it was much better to be communicated in that manner. If I had written my Uncle, the girls seeing a letter from me would not rest till they knew its contents. It appears to me that including those lost in the Swiftsure upwards of a dozen of my letters have either miscarried or may perhaps in ½ a year's time turn up when not wanted. I sent you a plan of the army's position before Alexandria and of the French plan and orders for an attack on us of the 21 of March last with an inscription on a piece of marble dug up by a reserve working party. Caroline alluded to letters I never recd. from her. John Pinhey I have not heard from tho' you mention his writing.[69] I recd. no letters for John Orchard, neither do I know to what ship he belongs.

I have just been to see our men get their Xmas dinner. It consists of boil'd beef, plumb-pudding, potatoes, and a bottle of porter each. From the time the Regt. left Plymouth till it came into this garrison, the soldiers never pull'd off their clothes day or night, except to bathe or put on a clean shirt, all the time of the campaign they were force'd to sleep in their accoutrements. It was the case with the officers in the field - but on ship-board private soldiers suffer ten times as much almost, as before an enemy. The poor fellows seemed to enjoy the porter. I left the comp[an]y to themselves as soon as I saw everything right, as an officer looking on would be a check, and consequently make them less comfortable. The Reg[t]. is now reduced to 180 duty-men. We are not fit to stay here unless they complete us with drafts.

I have heard nothing of Mr. Archdale or the Flannel, the 40th know no such man, he is not yet come out perhaps. I have got the scarlet cloath made up and put it on this day for the first time, it is nearly spoil'd in making, but we have no ladies here to please and it

---

68 Sir John Borlase Warren, at that time commanding a Royal Navy squadron of the North Western French coast.
69 This is Jack's cousin, was also an Old Blundellian.

will do as a soldier's coat very well. We shall soon know if we are to stay here [after] the peace [suggested] by the dispatches which brought out your melancholy epistle. I should have liked to have got a few of Charles' things for prime cost, tho' nearly worn out, a common shirt such as I bring from England with me, without cambrick frills costs here [£]1-5-0. For a good shirt such as you afford for visiting will cost a guinea and a half. All my hard earn'd savings in Egypt are here dissipated in purchasing a few necessaries. In shirts I have been extravagant. I first bought three pieces ready made at 25 shillings and after purchased a piece of linning [sic] at an auction, there was a shipload nearly sold at the same time, this I am getting made up. I fear they will cost more than the former. Boots £2-18-6 per pair. Toe shoes 12 and 14 shillings; washing is onerous as we are on an allowance of water and employ women of other Reg^{ts}. The general price for making a shirt in town is 4-6. I have been recommended to a serg^t.'s wife, as they are not very fine, says she, I think I will make them for 3 shillings. At Malta I could have got them made for tenpence each. If we had got to England I could have scraped together nearly £200, which would pay Mr. Ireland, have got me a good new kit and a small corps de reserve, this rascally place has taken five months' pay and upwards of twenty pounds pocket-money almost, away. Our baggage has been within sight of the Rock since last Sunday. Three weeks since we expected them in next morning, they were so close, but in the night the wind shifted, blew hard, they had lost their way again, at present the wind is westerly there is no chance of their getting in.

I delay writing you respecting the agents and Ireland till I get my writing desk which I hourly expect, and am much annoyed at not getting the allowance for my baggage in coming from Holland long ago.[70] Major Fletcher was very well when I saw him last only a few days previous to our embarking. He was much reduced at first when he came out of the Pharos, the horse flesh had not prov'd quite so nutritious as roast beef, but he was mending every day and said he had not been so well for a year and a half before as he then was.[71] Just before we left the country he went to Cairo, we were in daily expectation of going away, otherwise I would have

---

70 This confirms that Jack was not compensated for his uniforms and other baggage lost on the *Valk*.

71 Richard Fletcher, later Wellington's Chief Engineer in Peninsula, was obviously known to the Hills, perhaps because his father was also a clergyman. One of the few engineers assigned to the Egypt expedition, he was captured after being sent ashore to reconnoitre before the landing and held, presumably being fed on horsemeat, until Alexandria fell.

[asked him to] let me make the trip also to the G[rand] Visier's army with him.

Do let me know how J. Pinhey gets on at Crediton, I wrote Caroline about 3 weeks since. I have had this letter of yours for some time. I see now which letter it is you have rec'd. It was a scrawl written just as we were going to turn into bed as the ship sailed at daylight, it was the very day we got in here at nightfall. A new cause of disquiet has wracked me. I wonder you did not mention the Jamaica Hurricane. Report says here 13 men of war are lost, where is William and Cap[n]. Hands? My Father rather forgets the position of Corunna, it is opposite Ferrol and in sight of it. I shall keep about 20 Pounds ready for a start when I get leave, but a man of war is what we look out for. If not that opportunity offers itself, certainly Lisbon is best as being about half-ways - and vessels sailing every wind for London. I have look'd [at] every navy list for W[ilia]m's name among the Lieuts., but have not seen it. I see Cap[n]. Hands has got the Neireide. I was fearfull some accident might have befallen him when I saw the Thunderer home without him. Orchard's death, I fear, will be no great loss, but I am sorry for the very unequal distribution of his property.[72]

Some months hence you will get a batch of letters from me dated Malta. Some of the ships have been five weeks on their passage down. This Garrison before the last mail came in has not been so long without accounts from England during the war. I see the balance is greatly in my favour with respect to letters. I see yours marked 2s-ld. a pretty sum in sending and nearly as much in receiving. It was last April I heard of poor Charles being no more. Remember me to all my friends. I dine in a select party this day, Jones, Bury, Bradford, Keith, Hill. There are a number of strangers at the mess, we get away in peace to drink our dear relatives. You see I have not been forgetful of you on Xmas. Remember me to Caroline and Mr. Ley. I shall one day, I hope, again meet with you. I am sorry the plans did not reach my Father, however, I still have the bits of marble for him. I will send them home in the St. George. Sir J. Saumerez squadron are still in the bay. I shall drink all your healths. I am much rejoiced to hear none of you were ill at home as I fear'd to hear from you almost. Give my love to Aunt Peggy, Frederick and everything to my Father.

---

72 The Orchards were Hennock freeholders. John Orchard seems to have joined the navy. A Lieutenant Joel Orchard took command of HMS *Pike* in 1808; possibly the same person.

Our F[iel]d. Officers have houses to themselves, very snug, it is ½ past four we're going up the hill to Bury's.[73] I hope you will be in better spirits next time I hear. Bradford is ready to go. I will scribble every nonsense rather than let this be vacant. I cannot express how happy I should be to look in on you this very moment - here I am with my coat and waistcoat off, my fire out, while you are enjoying your Xmas fire - however, the evening begins to be cloudy, it has been a delightful day - indeed, except a few days it has always been so since we have been here. Adieu. May ev'ry happiness attend you. Je vous embrasser de tout ma coeur.

I remain yours,
J. HILL

The death of Charles was obviously distressing, yet Georgian formalities apparently precluded Jack from pressing Captain Louis on the circumstances, or for that matter Louis volunteering more information. The circuitous communications Jack sought to use to tell his parents failed when none of his letters from Egypt made it home (none are among the surviving collection). Some were presumably lost when HMS *Swiftsure* was captured on 24 June 1801 by a French squadron.[74] The chances of 'a batch of letters from me dated Malta' appearing now seem slim.

Jack had learned his lesson on mail, however, sending tips to improve the chance of those from home getting through and doubling up on his own messages.

Gibraltar
20th Jany. 1802

Dear Mother,
    I wrote my Father a few days since enclosing a bill of Exchange for £250, desiring him to pay Ireland, and now write this so soon after, because should the first have miscarried you may present this before 'tis paid.[75]
    Mr. Scott with part of our baggage is at last arrived still one half of it is left at Portsmouth, where is my Bedstead, Curtains, etc.

---

73 Thomas Bury had been major in the 23rd Foot since April 1801. The others of Jack's 'select' Christmas Day dining colleagues are Evan Jones, George Bradford, William Keith.

74 *Swiftsure* was taken into the French fleet, eventually giving her the distinction of being in the British fleet at the Nile and the French at Trafalgar.

75 The letter referred to is not in the collection, so apparently miscarried.

In examining my trunks I do not find some scarlet cloth and three pieces of Nankeen, pray do inform me in your next if I sent it home with the other things, or I have lost it as I suppose by my trunks having been opened, while they have been absent. I expected also to have found my coverlet for my bed - I was in such haste when we embark'd from Plymouth that I forgot what I sent home by Charles in the Portmanteau - I have, I believe, now rec'd all your letters, six came with the baggage.

Mr. Archdale has sent down from Malta the Flannel and Boots. Do tell me if you sent out some Green Glass spectacles as I never have rec'd. anything of that kind. If ever I should get home again I will bring you my preceptress a bottle of Otto of Roses which I have by me. Forgiving you the hint with respect to the green silk as it was we foresaw it, Bradford by way of having enough bought - ½-doz. yards of which he is now making lining for sleeves of jackets. I hope her health is by this time re-established, and that you have had as merry a Xmas as usual. I hope I may keep Midsummer Day with you. The Alligator is not come from Egypt. When she does I will give Orchard his letter. I suppose by this time the Minotaur is at home and you have heard from C[aptai]n Louis; you must remember to pay the inland postage of letters, otherwise they will never come out, you must also put them in the post office and not send them to Falmouth, for at Lisbon there is no bag, I believe, made up for this place, or if there is they must miss one packet as at present there is a Frigate waiting there to come off immediately with the Med[iterranea]n Dispatches, etc. Two mails arriv'd here three days since, Bradford got a letter, but it had been once return'd from London to Chudleigh for the postage to be paid, it was mark'd in consequence with double inland postage. I expected to get a letter by the last conveyance from Ashprington. I have recd. at last John Pinhey's letter. Do remember me to him and all our relatives in that Q[uate]r. Remember and not lose a day in acknowledging the Rec[iep]t of this. Pay Hawkes, hatter, Piccadilly and Gardends, Piccadilly, London, accoutrement maker, £4-12-0.[76] I mentioned it in full in my last and do not doubt its arriving in safety.

Remember me to all our circle of friends. G. Mackenzie is not come down as yet - Bradford is very well; there is nothing new here. I will send home by 1 Oct., some things for my Father. I sorry

---

76 Hawkes was the supplier of the British Army uniforms. In 1802 their premises were in Piccadilly; they moved to No. 1, Saville Row in 1912. The company is now Gieves & Hawkes (Gieves supplied the Royal Navy; they combined in 1974).

my present to Aunt Peggy should have been lost in the Swiftsure. I will copy it again one of these days when I feel myself inclin'd. I am sorry it should have been lost as that packet employ'd me several days. I had copied Menou's orders for our attack. Remember me to Fred and Father and Aunt.

J. HILL

Two months after Jack wrote, the Treaty of Amiens ended the Revolutionary War. The British government hoped now to restore trade; prevent France allying with Russia; and quieten Parliamentary opposition to continued war. The Treaty required various territories around the world to be exchanged, including Britain withdrawing from Egypt (which they did) and quitting Malta (which they did not). Peace was marked with fireworks and celebrations across the country and pamphlets, poetry and plays. For the soldiers and sailors though, the downside was possible unemployment; to save money the navy and army were both to be halved, and the volunteer forces disbanded. Despite their Egyptian victory, the future of Jack and his colleagues was thrown into doubt.

CHAPTER 4

HOME

'I am vexed most abominably'

Letter of 21 August, 1803

When the army shrank, officers were not discharged but placed on 'half pay'. This reduced costs, and income for the officer concerned, but left them able to be called back to duty, at any time or location in any regiment, unless the officer resigned his commission. A significant manpower shortfall in the 23rd helped them avoid many reductions: in March 1803 they were 346 men 'wanting to complete', a long way from full strength.[1] Inspection by the Duke of Kent, the Governor of Gibraltar, found the men of the regiment 'low but stout and active and fit for any service'. Jack was not present for the inspection; in September 1802 he obtained a six-month leave of absence, returning to England after more than 2 years away. Reuniting with his family after Charles's death may have been one of the reasons his leave was granted. Before Jack's leave ended, however, peace did: the 'lasting peace' of Amiens lasted only just over a year. On 18 May Britain declared war on France, claiming French violations of the treaty by sending troops into Switzerland and elsewhere across the continent. Britain refused to quit Malta; the planned military reductions were abandoned. The Napoleonic Wars had begun.

The 23rd were still in Gibraltar but were due home soon. Jack and the other officers on leave were ordered to the Isle of Wight to meet them, rather than travel out and back again. On arrival he tried to reunite himself with part of his personal baggage left in Plymouth when he had embarked in July 1800.

---

1 Cary and McCance, *Regimental Records*

Dear Mother,

After leaving you I reached Exeter without any accident befalling me. Whilst there not a single word transpir'd respecting Dinah. In the evening, I was in the Counting house, Campion's son came in with a new flute for Humphrey and Salter to try. Campion enquir'd how Mrs. S. was, I know not how it was but some one enquired if she had not lain in some time, was she not most well?

After supping at my Uncle's where I met E. Walker and J. Wright about ten o'clock, I walk'd up in town to see about my place which I fortunately secured in the Mail and slept that night at the Inn. A Mr. Cartwright, an Attorney, was my only companion till we got to Bridport where we picked up a Bonnie Scotch laddie and went on to Salisbury where Sandy and I were to quit that conveyance.[2] After enquiring at every place for a passage, we found we could not get out by any of the publick conveyances for more than 30 hours. We determined to take a Post Chaise (22 miles) to Southampton. After looking over all Salisbury we arriv'd at South[amp]ton a little after 12 o'clock the same day we quitted Exeter. The morning following (Sunday) 10 o'clock we found a passage boat going down to the Island in which we took our passage and arriv'd at Cowes by one o clock. We then got into a Chaise, I to report myself at Carisbrook to Col. Farquhar who commands in the room of Genl. Hewit - about 5 we return'd to dinner at Cowes and the next day, Monday, went in one of the passage boats to Portsmouth - Sandy to see the yard and your Humble Servant to look after his kit - this job employed me nearly eight hours. I will not tire myself a second time and you also in mentioning the various measures I took to recover it.

However, I did and what is all as good, in a high state of preservation. In the evening as I was walking near the point I remembered John Orchard - when by good luck the very first boat I enquired of to whom she belonged proved the Alligator's. I tore a leaf out of my pocket-book and wrote him a note desiring him to come to me at the Blue Posts which he did the next morning before I was up (Tuesday). I then ordered a private room and gave

2 'Sandy' was a nickname commonly given (by the English) to Scots, alongside Paddy for Irish and Taffy for Welsh. Three characters so named often appeared in cartoons of the day alongside the representation of an Englishman, John Bull.

him a breakfast, he mentioned that he was applying for his discharge from that ship and desir'd me to speak to Cap^n. Richardson in his behalf, which I declin'd as I very well knew how well Capns. of Troopers love applications of that kind from Lobsters. I said his mother wished him to get forward in the line he was in, and that [it] was agreed they should apply to Sir L. Palk to that effect.

After John Orchard had left me I went and found out Cap^n. Raymond who was getting his hair put in order, however, he came out as he was, and I sat with him more than an hour during which time he said the West Country was but everything, after which we went to the Genl. Office when on comparing notes with the Brigade Major I mentioned what I had learnt the day before respecting the Baggage, not fixed on one place where 'twas likely to be found. When after surmounting new difficulties in finding the locks eaten out with rust, I at last recovered my bed in such good order as quite agreeably surprised me. I had quitted Raymond before telling him I should go with the Serg^t. to overhaul the musty packages. All of which had been turned over to the Ordnance as containing arms, when on turning out they found as much Baggage as Arms. They took the arms and put the other things into the first chests that came in the way, on opening the very first I came on what I sought for. Tuesday [I went] back to Cowes. After all I find I am the first of the Regt. here [as] had I come by [chaise]. I now by experience can say that I must have saved 5 Guineas, but we were all zealous to be here in time.

It is now just as cold and uncomfortable as November. I have borrowed some coals and intend keeping in a good fire. Whilst some of you are staying down the country, do go and see about my baggage being sent here. In case the water conveyance does not suit you send them by the Waggon, the direction is Parkhurst B[arrac]ks., Isle of Wight near Newport. I put in what I suppos'd would be sufficient writing paper but I find I am nearly out. One P[ai]r of the Boots Woolscott made me is too small. I know not what to do - one pr. of whole and one of half fit, the other whole are too small in the leg. There is a London P[ai]r of old military Boots at home. Do give him one as a pattern here after. After I have got my Baggage here the King pays all carriage after.

The Reason why our Officers are ordered here is that they have sent from hence all the officers belonging to the E. Indies and in a day or two the Alligator takes out a great number for the West Indies, so that they are very short of officers and are scraping them together from every Q[uate]r. There certainly are Regts. coming home from the Mediterranean, so that as yet no countermands have been sent out for the Welch.

Whenever you send any box advise me of it. I will desire Cap^n. Raymond to look out for it at Portsmouth. I do not know anyone here, which is inconvenient as I want to be introduced at the Mess. At present none of ours are here but they must come in a day or two. They have more rain nearer this place than with you - now I suppose you will have a plenty - I never was colder at this time of year scarcely than I was in my Passage to and from Portsmouth from this Island. There is not the least prospect of Peace, here they talk of nothing but war. Remember to tell me how Aunt. P.['s] family gets on.

Friday 27th: Part of the troops going out in the Alligator to the West Indies went hence this morning. They do not go to Jamaica, some others will in a few days. I got up this morning to write to William but have delayed it in consequence of their going to the Le[e]ward Islands. I shall not feel myself settled till I get the remainder of the Baggage so that you may send it as soon as you like. I shall dine at the Mess this day, they say 'tis a good cheap one. I shall be happy to find it such. I did not enquire for James Garrett at Portsmouth, I had full employ without. Tell me how you like the Fan he sent you; mention should you know where he is. Not one of ours is yet arrived which is awkward however, I begin to know some of them here and I shall very soon find myself comfortable. I did not call on Mrs. Fletcher, I had difficulty to get up to P[orts]mouth at all. Col. Farquhar seemed at first to throw difficulties in the way, and I represented if he wanted me do duty I must get my military baggage as I had then only my plain cloaths. I came back so soon in consequence of returns going to Town that day.

Friday left Hennock, slept at the New London Inn, Exeter.

Saturday left Exeter, slept at Southampton.

Sunday left Southampton, went to Cowes, from thence into the interior of the island, return'd and slept at Cowes.

Monday left Cowes, went to Portsmouth, searched for my baggage.

Tuesday found my baggage, returned to Cowes and slept.

Wednesday left Cowes with my Baggage, slept in B[arrac]ks.

Thursday attended parade and muster

J. HILL

Carisbrooke Castle was in 1803 the base of General Sir George Hewett, Inspector General of Recruiting for the British Army. Parkhurst barracks on the Isle of Wight was one of the centres used for new recruits, including as it happened several Dutchmen who had volunteered to serve with the British Army following the Helder expedition in 1799. Jack's report of his discussion with John Orchard, at the Blue Posts pub in Portsmouth, suggests either that Orchard wished to leave the Royal Navy or perhaps wanted to be assigned to a ship not destined for the West Indies. He was surely correct that he would have more chance of success if Sir Lawrence Palk, head of the influential Palk family, used his connections, rather than Jack intervening as a 'lobster' - a common nickname for British soldiers, arising from their red coats (and the pointed hats of earlier uniforms).

For an ambitious soldier the resumption of war with France was a positive development. The army now needed recruits; the 23rd were far from the only regiment short of men. In June the practice of Field Officers formally commanding companies was ended. The change provided opportunities to recall those on half pay and fostered recruitment by offering promotion to officers who raised a certain number of troops. For officers on full pay like Jack, however, the change brought an odd combination of hope and uncertainty. He had been de facto commander of the Lieutenant-Colonel's company since 1799; the formal commander, Lieutenant-Colonel John Joyner Ellis was permanently listed in the 23rd's records as 'on leave'. The General Order announcing the new arrangements required that all companies should now be commanded by a captain and specified that the former Lieutenant-Colonel's company was to 'be filled by a Captain from the Half Pay Establishment, or in some very peculiar cases by a Lieutenant on Full Pay'.[3] Jack met the latter criterion, but was only second on the lieutenant's seniority list, behind Jacob Van Courtlandt; under the first criterion he might lose his de facto command to a captain from outside the regiment. His uncertainty was reflected in his next letter, written to his father yet opening unusually with a formal greeting:

> June 8th, [1803]
> Army Depot, Isle of Wight

Dear Sir,

From the papers you may see the regulations about to be established respecting the Field Officers Comps. I only heard of it this day

---

3 Cary and McCance, *Regimental Records*

officially, but Shawe of ours came from town a few days since he had seen Genl. Grenville who mentioned that it was in contemplation and that he had recommended Cortlandt and myself in the strongest manner for promotion, but that H.R.H. the D. of York said it was intended to reduce the ½ pay list and that he could not do it. G[eneral] Grenville said he should make another attempt in our favour. In a short time I shall hear more about it - the eldest Lt. is to raise 30 men. This is rather a hard bargain & I doubt if 'tis to be accomplishd. I suppose Cortlandt will immediately commence - the limitation of three months is also hard. Government allow you the regular bounty but something must be added. The season of the year is bad as the Harvests are commencing. Should Cortlandt not accept the offer, there is scarce any doubt but he will, I certainly will attempt it. The scramble is now great for promotion; if it is not now procur'd there will be but very little chance for it for some time; now is the moment in which we may succeed.

I have been enquiring about the best method of getting the Baggage forwarded. From Salisbury it must go to Southampton. Capn. Langer of the Newport Hoy will take it up there and shall get it delivered here among the Government stores - do enquire the charges and pay them for this reason - the less there is to pay the more readily Cap. L. of the Hoy will take them up at the Waggon Office.[4] This by enquiry at Verrels you will soon discover.

I was extremely sorry to hear of Miss Bastard's death in my mother's letter.[5] I have got a letter ready to send out to William by some detachments going to Jamaica. What do you think of all this rain it will do your grass great good I should suppose. I hope after this we shall have some warm weather.

You may expect to hear often from me till it is certain how I shall be affected by these changes. From the debates it seems many of the ½ pay regular officers will be employ'd with the militia.

Remember to let me know when you send the trunk as I will be in readiness to receive it. Should it be necessary I will go to

---

4 A hoy is a small sailing craft, suitable for passenger or freight carriage in coastal waters. That Jack knew Captain Langer's Newport hoy well suggests it was the main ferry service between Newport and the mainland.

5 Edmund Bastard (1758–1816) lived at Sharpham House in Ashprington, Devon. He was Lieutenant-Colonel of the East Devon Militia and MP for Dartmouth from 1787 to 1812. His daughter Jane died in May 1803, aged 12. Jack's parents were staying at Ashprington, probably because Caroline was soon to give birth (hence Jack's later comment 'Let me know soon how Caroline is').

Southampton to receive it. Should I go recruiting I would turn it over to Shawe.[6] Let me know soon how Caroline is.

I am on duty at present and cannot go into town to see the papers. I wrote Col. Mackenzie yesterday to ask his advice on the subject. I shall get an answer in a day or two, I shall be too late for the post. Remember me to all at home [and] at Ashprington.

I remain, yours, etc.
J. HILL
Thursday, Noon.

Colonel Frederick Mackenzie was a good man to seek advice from on promotion prospects. Head of the 23rd's Mackenzie's dynasty, he joined the regiment in August 1756, serving through the American Revolutionary War (leaving a renowned memoir). Later he lived in Exeter and raised and commanded the 1st Exeter Volunteers. The father of James, who died in Egypt, and Jack's good friend George, Frederick Mackenzie would soon become Secretary of the new Royal Military College.

While the British army sought to rebuild its strength, in France Bonaparte had determined to cross the Channel and attack his country's most enduring enemy. In March 1803 he ordered an invasion flotilla built and in June began to assemble an army on the Channel coast from Holland to St. Malo; a planned invasion force of up to 120,000 men. Bonaparte recognised the difficulty of getting past the Royal Navy, but the British government could not risk his succeeding. Recruiting increased for the Volunteers, the militia and, from June, for an entirely new body to support the regular army, an Army of Reserve of 50,000 men. The Reserve was intended to form fifty second battalions for existing line regiments, the men being encouraged through bounties to join the first battalions as they were needed. Recruiting concurrently for three distinct volunteer forces and the regular army meant all levels of the country's military machinery needed to be joined up. Unfortunately, they were not. A confused and sometimes competitive system of recruitment ensued, with differing levels of bounties paid to recruits; differing terms of service between the various types of units; and different levels of training. There were even questions about whether military discipline applied equally to all, the broad assumption being that, unlike regulars, volunteers could change their mind or simply resign if they did not like their orders. Nor were there enough weapons

---

6 Probably Thomas Shaw, at the time a lieutenant in the 23rd.

to go around. The Government could offer only one musket for every four men; the rest were to be armed with pikes (quite how massed pikemen would have stood up to a well-trained and disciplined French army led by the greatest soldier of his age is fortunately only for speculation). This was not all; the Levy en Masse Act, passed in July 1803, required Lords Lieutenant to list all men aged between 17 and 55 in every county (Clergymen, Quakers, school masters, and the infirm excepted). These men were to be trained and armed and would be eligible in case of invasion to be called out and sent anywhere in the British Isles. The measure was never enacted, but it was the closest Britain came to implementing conscription, already commonplace in Europe, until the First World War. Other preparations included earmarking privately-owned wagons for regimental transport and building defensive works including around army camps. The Royal Military Canal was dug between Shorncliffe and Cliff End (near Hastings) to facilitate the transport of men and supplies more rapidly along this key stretch of the south coast and provide a fortified defensive barrier across Romney Marsh. Additionally, a string of cylindrical 'Martello Towers', heavily armed with cannon, was commissioned; over 100 of various sizes were eventually built. As an invasion never came, the efficacy of these works was not tested, but the Royal Military canal was not completed until 1809 and the guns that were to protect it were not in place until 1812, when the chain of Martello towers was also completed; by then the political landscape of Europe looked very different. As Fortescue later noted 'if Napoleon had landed at the end of September or beginning of October, he would have found little to oppose him but a half-armed, undisciplined rabble, composed in many instances of fragments of corps whereof part had marched out to meet him and the remainder, agreeable to their terms of service, had refused to move out of their military districts'.[7] This may be an overstatement, and ignores the presence of veteran regular regiments like the 23rd who were back home by mid-August, but Britain was certainly unready to face an invasion. Fortunately, Bonaparte was also unready to launch one.

The cloud of possible invasion had a silver lining for Jack. While the changes in company commands did not give him immediate promotion, the promotion of Lieutenant Jacob Van Courtlandt put Jack top of the 23rd's lieutenant's seniority list. As future promotion opportunities were usually offered first to those with longest seniority at the rank below, this mattered. The creation of the Army of Reserve would bring more changes, as Jack hinted in his next letter.

---

7 Fortescue, *History* Vol. V

Dear Mother,

A few days since I rec'd at the same time a letter from you &
my Father, the latter announcing the departure of my baggage, the
other yours informing me of the incidence at Ashprington. I am
very happy to hear Caroline is well as can be expected and partake
of the joy the little stranger's arrival has diffused.

I was in hopes of getting something by the abolition of the
Field Officers Companies, but it has only taken in the oldest
sub[altern]n, the Capt[ain] L[ieutenant], the other from the ½ pay.
I am now, I believe, the oldest [i.e. most senior] L[ieutenant]t. of the
Reg[t]. Cortland was expected to have been in the Gazette
last Saturday week. They will be obliged to ransack every place for
the officers of the 50 thousand now raising in case of any farther
augmentation to the Regt. or any of our Cap[tai]ns getting Majorities
in this Army of Reserve, which may if fortune favours present an
opening for your humble servant. It will be hard if there is not
promotion for the old sub[alter]n; 'twill be hard to be commanded
by the Fencible Cap[tain]s who heretofore have not had army rank. I
have not heard any more respecting the Regiment since I left you.
The Agents informed me that they were soon expected home. I have
picked up a man belonging to the Regt. as a servant - tolerably good.

You must not trouble me with many commissions for
Portsmouth. I might as well give you a few for Plymouth. How I
am to deliver these things to Mrs. Fletcher I know not. I had much
rather have paid the carriage for Coach myself. Should I deliver it
in person it would cost me at least a Guinea. I have the whole of the
Island to cross, pay my passage by water to Portsmouth, must sleep
out of Q[uarte]rs,. dine, etc., lay myself under obligations to the
Commanding Officer and loiter about 5 or 6 hours perhaps in the
different Pot-houses waiting for a passage boat.

I volunteered coming to this outpost. Manley, a Capn. in the
63rd, is an old Tiverton schoolfellow - all the others coming out
were very gentlemanly fellows, there was an opening left and I got
out here.[8] My Father may remember the place near the Fort of
Sandown the object is the defence of the Bay. Sunday morning a
vessel with French Colours flying came within musquet shot, we got
under arms and informed the people in the Fort of it who immediately
opened upon her, we sent an officer of the army out to her with some

---

8 Manley is probably Henry Manley, from Craddock, Devon, who started at
Blundell's a week after Jack, leaving a year earlier.

men, when she proved to be a prize in charge of a middy, who not having any other colours on board, thought it finer to wear French than none. They very soon took the hint from the 18 Prs. and downed colours in a short time. We knew not at first what it meant as 16 others were pretty near us, French craft picked up by a Frigate.

Direct my letters as usual. Newport is the only post town. I have not yet heard of my baggage but am rather impatient to have it, as my writing Desk and the etc. are very comfortable companions in a B[arrac]k room. There is very good fishing and bathing here; we intend making ourselves very snug. The moon shines on this coast haunted only by spirits. This watering place is rather out of the way. I know not how to send Mrs. F. her parcel. I know not where they live in or near Portsmouth. Do let me know in your next. Perhaps the Mathematician at Chudleigh is reconnoitering; not a place I should suppose for pleasure or cheapness. I dare say Mrs. __ looks on it in that light. If I go to Portsmouth I will enquire for James Garret - there are six [ships] at the mother bank and a vessel with troops from abroad under quarantine, not known what Regt. I hope Mr. and Mrs. B[astard]. are now recovering from the shock occasioned by so severe a loss. The officer's name of Cavalry at Chudleigh I may suppose.

I have succeeded in getting on my boots - wet weather was a great assistance. I wanted them either for worsted or other stockings for which they are all too small. I was measured when I came from Gib., & got fat at home, but these country fellows will have a way of their own and will not believe that you would wish to have then made large tho' you might swear to it. I should have thought Mr. Bradford might have been safe from Southerton. I have not heard from C[aptain] B[radford] some time. I am daily expecting an answer to my last from him.

Remember me to my Father, Caroline & Mr. Ley with the others of your circle - you must pay the extra postage; I have already thrown away a few shillings.

yours,
J. HILL

How does the hay go on - the apples, etc.?
(Eastern part of the Island Wednesday Morn.)
P.S. I have opened your letter and I shall write Mrs. Fletcher to procure the parcel for the Isle of Wight.

The 'little stranger' was the first son of Jacob Ley and Caroline, also called Jacob, born on 18 Jun 1803. Now the senior lieutenant, Jack's fear of potentially being commanded by 'Fencible Cap[tain]s' shows the level of rumour about the government's new regulations. But there was a prospect of soon being reunited with his colleagues. The return of veteran troops would also boost the security of the nation; the entire south coast of England was now on invasion alert. As the incident with the vessel commanded by a midshipman ('middy') sailing under French colours indicates, everyone was twitchy. It is possible that 'the Mathematician at Chudleigh' was William Mudge of the Royal Artillery who was director of the Ordnance Trigonometrical Survey, forerunner of the Ordnance Survey. In 1803 Mudge established a temporary survey headquarters near Ugbrooke House, Chudleigh, the home of Robert Clifford, an expert cartographer who had been working on the production of maps of Devon. Mudge's grandfather had been vicar of St. Andrew's, Plymouth, so his arrival may well have stirred interest from the Hill family.

Meanwhile, Jack had begun to wonder whether he could swing both a promotion and a billet near home:

Parkhurst Bks,
July 21st, 1803.

Dear Father,

A few days since I wrote Col[one]l MacKenzie requesting his advice with respect of my making an application to H.R.H. the D[uke] of York by a memorial or recommendation sent in through Genl. G[renville]. My situation is this - I now am the eldest Lt.; 'twas reported the other day that the oldest of each Regt. was to have a Comp[an]y in the Reserve; should that take place I shall be provided for without troubling them with superfluous papers, but as I fear that may be too good luck, it is very necessary to keep a good look out on all sides. I wonder what Capn. Bradford is about. We are nearly situated alike. Shall we let this scramble pass and not endeavour to pick up some of the promotion afloat? Advantages - Rank, Pay; Disadvantages - prospect of ½ pay after the war and leaving a high character'd Regt. Capns. pay, I think, would suit me very well, full or ½, but a comp[an]y in the Fusiliers much better. The best thing [that] can happen to me is George MacKenzie getting a Majority. I think its scarcely worth Bradford's while to accept it; he must get the Brevet soon. No such certainty for me. £92 per an[num] should Bonaparte allow me to return to Hennock with a Militia Comp[an]y or any other employ would do tolerably well. Should you think so – set your wits to work and try how in conjunction we can beset H.R.H. I shall, if Mac thinks proper, immediately desire Grenville to forward a memorial from myself with his recommendation. I shall tell his R[oyal] H[ighness] I am an old correspondent and bring Holland to his recollection. I did expect a letter from Col. M. this day - I shall most probably have it tomorrow. The post goes out early from this place which makes it necessary to commence a long letter a day beforehand.

Saty., 23 July

I have recd. no answer from Col. M. Cortlandt is gazzetted for the Comp[an]y. I want much to hear from town. Major Bury has been enquiring for me. I shall go and seek him in hopes of some news or other.

Remember me to Mother, Caroline and Mr. Ley when you see them. Tell Aunt & Fred to eat my [share] of the fruit unless the black birds have done it for me already. No news of the Regt. How goes your Farm & Harvest on Army of Reserve at Hennock, &c.? Tell me in your next. I am in haste to save the post & all short.

J. HILL.

Jack's claim to be an 'old correspondent' of the Duke was a tongue-in-cheek reference to his official report after the *Valk* disaster, but was lobbying the Commander-in-Chief or General Richard Grenville directly for promotion a good idea? It was a delicate matter; some self-promotion was essential; as historian Rory Muir put it 'few British officers of the period rose to prominence by modestly effacing themselves'.[9] But Jack was clearly agitated by the matter and frustrated as he saw others around hlm stepping up. He did not know that George Bradford, now the regiment's senior captain, was considering transferring from the 23rd to gain his majority. Separation from regiment and family, so isolated with his own thoughts, hopes and fears did not help.

Bonaparte too was becoming frustrated. Unquestionably one of history's greatest land commanders, his invasion plans crashed into the reality of naval matters, which he understood rather less. Transports took too long to build, while many that were built, in yards across the French-dominated parts of Europe, were of poor quality, sailed badly and could not be concentrated without risking Royal Navy intervention. The south coast of England has large natural harbours and safe anchorages, but the French coastline had no suitable concentration area for an invasion Fleet between Brest in the extreme west and Texel in the

---

9 *Wellington: The Path To Victory, 1769-1814* Rory Muir 2013

extreme east. Both were too distant from the target. Boulogne was in the right place and protected by a large offshore sandbank, providing an anchorage Royal Naval frigates could not reach; but its harbour was too small without significant improvements that would take many months to complete. Bonaparte therefore abandoned any invasion in 1803, though troop training and transport construction continued, as did Britain's high alert.

One military force that did come up the Channel was Jack's regiment. It sailed from Gibraltar on 21 June, arriving at the Motherbank anchorage off the Isle of Wight at the beginning of August. Their convoy had been spotted off the Isles of Scilly and reported as an enemy force to the British authorities. As the 23rd were sharing transports with the blue-jacketed 26th Light Dragoons and most of their ships were of French or Dutch build the mistake is understandable, but fortunately nobody intercepted them. Reunited with his regiment, Jack would soon be busy preparing to deploy with them, though where to he did not know.

Army Depot,
Newport, Isle of Wight.
6th Aug., 1803.

Dear Mother,

I recd. your last about a fortnight or three weeks since and my Father's of about the same date, forwarded by Mr. Cummings a few days since he left it at the Inn when leaving Newport. As the Regt. is arriv'd you had better not write me till you again hear from me unless you may chance to find out the Hd. Qrs. The convoy in which they came was six weeks on the passage. They will get Pratique about Sunday or Tuesday. Wednesday or so I think we shall be setting off for our destination. I shall wait the arrival of the Post to see if I hear from you. In case I do not I shall have little to say except congratulating you on the fine weather.

The Post is arrived without any intelligence from you. Let me know how the harvest and apples get on. Where are we to be quartered? Do not think of selling the Mare as in case we are ordered into Camp I shall be obliged by the Duke's order to provide one. 'Twill be better if you think proper to let me have it from you than to buy another from a stranger. For a guinea the waggon takes a horse from Exeter to London, the keep will cost me nothing and I will turn over as much as she costs you in case I must have one. I won't positively promise to pay you all. I will if I can.

J. HILL

After 6 weeks travel from Gibraltar, everyone from the regiment had to remain aboard for a few more days before they were formally declared disease-free and disembark, the process known as 'pratique'. Jack of course could not visit them in the meantime, though no doubt messages were passed. The return of the 23rd was welcome but also brought bad news: having toiled to re-acquire the baggage left in Britain when he sailed for the Mediterranean, Jack now learned he had lost the part he had left in Gibraltar.

> Sunday, 21st August, 1803.
> Portsmouth.

Dear Mother,

Capn. Raymond going into Devon will take this part of the way. Our destination is not known. Genl. Whitelock wishes to keep us here - 'tis impossible to say what will be done with us.[10]

I am vexed most abominably. Power has stolen every thing left at Gib. I know not what to do. 'Tis a poor satisfaction to get him a few hundred - All over 5 shirts, 5 Silk H[an]dk[erchief]s, 1 Kerseymere B[lanket]s, 1 Sattinette D[itt]o, one Sattinette Waistcoat, my Japanned Dressing Case, 1 Table-Cloath, one P[ai]r Silk Stockings - indeterminant of Cotton Stockings, Towels and Flannels. This is an Irishmen, depend on it; what I said to you is true. An Irishman one time or another breaks out somehow or other. They will show themselves; a villains nature will break out.

I have called on Major and Mrs. Fletcher - they and the children are well. I rather imagine I shall be obliged to get a horse. We are allowed 10d a day keep - the idea is every officer is to be in readiness to march at a moment's notice. I wish I was nearer you - a Pr. of panniers in case of an invasion would be the best things - but the French have lost the opportunity of making a serious impression; as soon as the harvest is in he will not come with impunity. The villainy and rascallity that I have several times experienced [is such] that now I believe with Bradford every soldier

---

10 Major-Gen John Whitelock, Lieutenant Governor of Portsmouth and General Officer Commanding South West District, would later command the attack on Buenos Aires during the British invasion of the Rio del Plata (1807). The attack failed and Whitelock surrendered. Court martialled and found guilty, he was dismissed from the service and declared 'totally unfit and unworthy to serve His Majesty in any military capacity whatsoever'. If Bonaparte had invaded in 1803 or 1804, Whitelock might have been his opponent; history could have been very different.

is the most infernal scoundrel under the sun - never trust him till you by experience [prove] the contrary. After the box was given into the store he got it out again by some pretence or other, sold box and all: the box is discovered with one of the privates here.

Remember me to Caroline and Mr. Ley. 'Tis now six weeks since I heard from you. I will try not to be angry with you. Mind and tell me how many ships William has taken. I have written him his letter from Parkhurst. I know not if he will get them; the last contained Steel's list. I have forwarded the spoons for Henson's friends. How has your harvest turned out? How does the cider promise? I wish I could get some of the fruit the birds are stealing.

I keep the servant I picked up at the Depot. I am the only officer who has joined the Regt, since their arrival. Bradford is still at Worcester, all the world make of his engagement with Miss N. Remember me to all our friends.

Your
J. HILL

It seems Power, Jack's soldier-servant, had been unable to resist an opportunity for personal gain while separated from his officer. His crime having been discovered, Power faced serious punishment. In a letter written less than a month later, Jack says Power 'got 300' lashes. Jack's opinion of the qualities of enlisted men, while obviously written in anger after discovering Power's crime, is far from an untypical view. Irish troops were widely held to be good fighters, but inveterate rogues. In scolding his mother for not writing, Jack had presumably forgotten that just two weeks before he had told her not to write again until she heard from him! William had been on the Jamaica station since about 1795. Early in 1803, while acting as lieutenant of the sloop HMS *Rattler*, he had been wounded in the right arm and side. His Royal Navy biography says that he was frequently employed in boat service, the sending of a small boat in to capture, or 'cut out', an enemy vessel; hence Jack's wanting to know how many ships his brother had taken. Jack's view that the French 'have lost the opportunity of making a serious impression' once the harvest was in was because the need for volunteers and militiamen to be home to help with the harvest, without which their families might starve, was one of the perceived weaknesses with the government's attempts to recruit such a vast collection of men under arms to defend the country. Once the harvest was complete, the men were more readily available. For the same reason the Levy en Masse Act focussed on those less critical to their families' survival: Lords Lieutenant were required to separate eligible men into four classes: unmarried men under thirty with no living children under ten years old; unmarried men aged between thirty and fifty, with no living children under ten; married men between seventeen and thirty with no more than two living children under ten; and those not included in the previous classifications; call up would happen in this order.[11]

His loss of kit was serious, but Jack's attention now focussed on something far more important; promotion might finally be within reach. George Bradford's appointment as major in the new 2nd Battalion of the 58th Foot was announced in the *London Gazette* on 12 August. This created a vacancy in the 23rd that Jack was desperate to fill. The risk that someone from outside the regiment could purchase the captaincy remained though: Jack did not have the money for purchase and the 23rd was an attractive regiment, with a good reputation. He again wondered how far he should champion his own cause, not least when the goodwill of those above him mattered and he did not want to be considered a nuisance. But presumably Colonel Frederick Mackenzie had endorsed Jack's proposal to set his cause out on paper, for now he wrote a 'memorial' to be forwarded to the Duke of York and submitted it via Thomas Bury, currently commanding the 23rd in the absence of Hall, and Colonel Grenville.

His Royal Highness Field Marshal the Duke of York, Commander in Chief &c &c &c

The memorial of Lieutenant J.H.E Hill 23rd Regiment of Foot or Royal Welch Fusiliers

Humbly sheweth,
    That your Memorialist having seen in the Gazette of the 23rd Instant the Promotion of Captain John George Bradford to a Majority in the 58th Regiment whereby a Company becomes vacant in the 23rd Regiment,
    Your memorialist having served seven years and now being the eldest first Lieutenant in the Regiment, during which period he has been present in every Action the Corps has been engaged in,
    That your Memorialist was taken at Ostend and in consequence confined for a considerable time at Lille; And is the officer who on the return of the Regiment from Holland was saved out of the Valke Dutch Frigate lost on the Island of Ameland, the particulars of which your Memorialist had the honor of stating to your Royal Highness.

---

11 Fortescue, *History* Vol. V

Humbly hoping your Highness will take his case into consideration your Memorialist as in duty bound will ever pray &c &c &c

J H E Hill Lieu[t]. 23rd RWF.
Portsmouth Aug[r]. 24th 1803[12]

Bury's covering note endorsed Jack's suitability for promotion:

Sir

I have the honor herewith to Enclose you the Memorial of Lieut. J. Hill, to H.R.H. The Commander in Chief praying to be appointed in the room of Cap[t.] Bradford, promoted in the 58th Reg[t.] and beg leave to recommend him as an attentive and meritorious officer highly deserving of any promotion which H.R. Highness may be pleased to grant him.

I have the honor to be

Sir
Your most Loyal & Humble Servt.
T Bury
Major R.W.F.[13]

Grenville added his stamp of approval in forwarding both Jack's Memorial and Bury's endorsement to Colonel William Clinton, the Duke of York's Military Secretary:

Butleigh, Somerset
August 27th 1803

My dear Clinton

I have this moment received the enclosed which I must beg the favor of you to lay before His Royal Highness. I think it my duty at the same time to recommend L[t]. Hill most particularly to the Duke's protection as a most deserving officer.

May I beg the favor of you to return my most sincere thanks to His Royal Highness for his very kind attention to my recommendation of Captain Bradford & beg leave to assure you

---

12 TNA WO 31/146 *Memoranda of appointments, promotions and resignations: September 1803*

13 TNA WO 31/146

that I feel most sincerely your readiness to respect my wishes upon all vacancies.

Believe me ever yours most sincerely
R Grenville[14]

It appears that Clinton, himself a veteran of the Helder Expedition which Jack had carefully mentioned, added another positive via a small insert slip:

He is Lieutenant of 1797 but only one Lt. has been promoted in the Regiment

The paperwork was in; all Jack could now do was wait while his paranoia about being superseded by an outsider increased. Charles Sutton, who had been on half pay with 3rd Guards, transferred into the 23rd in May and was formally appointed to command what had been the Lieutenant-Colonel's Company. Sutton had not physically joined the regiment yet (he is listed as 'absent' in the August 1803 muster roll), but the company was listed under his name with Jack as Sutton's subordinate lieutenant.[15] Jack was finding it hard to be patient; one can almost feel the excitement and tension in his words as he wrote home again.

August 27th, 1803
Portsmouth.

My dear Friends,

    I rec'd your letters this morning. I have been with yourself in very anxious expectation of a letter from home, imagine yours and my Father's last, arriv'd about the same time, within two days, yours frank' d dated July 10th, my Father's was forwarded by Cummings. I wrote you a few days ago by Cap^n. Raymond, he is gone into Devon. I mention'd about the horse, he said his servant should bring it up. I at that moment hesitated but now wish I had accepted the offer. I am allowed 10d per day for one. In a few days 'twill be determined if I should not be allowed 3 as there is a very good chance of my getting Bradford's comp[an]y. All the necessary papers are gone into Grenville. How should you like next week to address me by Captain? I hope you may. I think I ought to go to town about it and wait on the Duke in person. This rascally mauvaise

---

14 TNA WO 31/146
15 TNA WO 12/3967 *Regimental General Muster books and Pay Lists, 23rd Foot, 1803*

honte is in my way. I had a mind to go to town at any rate at first, but on recollection General Grenville is not in town nor Hall nor Jones. The Leve [sic] is next Tuesday. If I do not go to the Duke of York, I may dine with Col. Mackenzie; he again can tell me if he thought it proper £5 is worth throwing away in such a lottery. All here think I stand a very good chance - but ours is so good a Regt. a man of interest might get it even in spite of the Duke almost.

Bradford's promotion was in the Gazzette Tuesday, Wednesday morning we heard of it. The same evening my memorial with a very handsome recommendation from Major Bury was forwarded to Somersetshire for Gen. Grenville also to recommend me and transmit it to the Duke of York. Bradford's negligence in not telling me what he was about has annoy'd me, but no time has yet been lost since I knew it. Shall I go to Town? I reason this way - if they are inclin'd to give it me, 'twill be done without, if a man with interest is before me, I cannot dissuade them. A few days will determine. I intended not writing till I knew what turn 'tis likely to take.

First keep yourself cool, I this morning spoke to the Adjutant respecting the horses, we ought to have near 30 among us merely to comply with Duke of York's order - every Regt. has done it except ourselves. I am just come in from a field day, we have just astonished a few of them here. Lord C. Somerset who commands at Gosport all the field officers of Militia said they never saw the manoeuvres in such stile [sic]. When you receive this should you see Raymond ask him to let his servant ride up the horse. The Military want a great number of horses. They are very difficult procur'd in this part. Don't sell her yet awhile if I get a Comp^y, and Francois swares he will come.[16] I shall keep her for nothing. With two for the Comp^y., the more violent exercise I use the better I am, when not carrying my baggage, she shall carry me.

I hope Fred is got well. I shall see Fletcher by and bye. I am just returned, the Duke of York is not in town. Desire Cap^n. Raymond to allow his servant to bring up the horse, he is in the North of Devon, if you hear of any other conveyance embrace the first opportunity. Do persuade Mr. J. Templer to frank you up.[17] How do you like the prospect of your 40,000 new neighbours, troops that are to be sent for your protection.[18] Mention what you think

---

16 'Francois' = the French.

17 From a later letter, it seems James Templer, head of the Templer family of Stover House, wrote to General Grenville lobbying in support of Jack's promotion, presumably at Rev. John Hill's request. This may be what 'frank you up' means in this context - franking being the means of paying for postage.

18 Due to the creation of the Volunteers and, potentially, a Levy en Masse.

the horse worth. I shall write you again very soon. Mention in your answer how Fred is, what is the date of my last letter to you. I wrote on leaving Parkhurst I.W. Nothing has transpir'd respecting our moving. I have delayed in consequence. Wednesday morning - we shall see in the Gazette here if the Comp^y. is fill'd up. One comes out this evening; few regular promotions come out in Sat[urda]ys. Remember me to aunt P. I hope Fred is better.

I remain, etc.,
J. HILL.

Government will give us saddles for the carriage of baggage, I believe, otherwise a pack saddle would be the best thing in the world provided Bonaparte was here. Yourself and baggage must go as you can, I walk. On a march, horse carries its own corn for 3 days or more. My portmanteau blanket and spare provision, tent and pole also must be carried among the officers of the Comp^y. I am the only officer now with the Comp^y. I wish in my next you may dub me Cap^n. I see Sam White Corps is made royal. I congratulate you on the spirited stile Hennock has come forward in. I hope our Regt. may be sent Westward. You never saw a Regt. disciplined in such stile [sic]. A few hundred of the army reserve would soon be made soldiers with our Batt[alio]n. Mr. Fletcher looks very well, the children are very fine. F[letcher's] maiden aunt still with them. This is not one of the most correct letters in the world, but after the bustle of the morning I could not sit as regularly down afterwards. If you send the horse purchase a military saddle, I hope Cap^n. Hill will pay you, I hope I shall find him a decent kind of a fellow.

The King held a levée at St. James's, on 31st August 1803 (in fact a Wednesday) which presumably the Duke of York and the three most senior officers in the regiment, General Richard Grenville; Lieutenant-Colonel John Hall and Lieutenant-Colonel Evan Jones might have been expected to attend. £5 would have been the fare to London if Jack chose literally to 'go to town' in support of his ambition. The Duke of York had made clear that every officer in the army had the right to attend his weekly levée and put his case to the Commander-in-Chief in person if he believed himself to have been unjustly treated.[19] Despite having made his case in writing, following Sutton's arrival Jack was clearly tempted to exercise this right.

---

19 Glover, *Commissions*

CHAPTER 5

LOOKING OUT FOR BONAPARTE

'Promoted and obtained the... late Lt. Col's Company'

Memorandum to the Duke of York, 1823

The waiting was almost intolerable. Everyone in the battalion was saying he would get his captaincy. The vacancy was there; he topped the lieutenant's list; he had support from every senior officer in the regiment; both Bury and Grenville pressed his cause with the Duke of York. They were confident, but it was not their prospects that were at stake. Had Sutton's appointment undermined his chances? What more could he do? Petitioning the Duke of York in person seemed too much. Lieutenant-Colonel Hall was absent when Jack's papers went in so had not visibly given his endorsement. Would his doing so help get Jack over the line? The stressed Lieutenant Hill was indecisive and anxious; he dare not push too much. Meanwhile the regiment was impressing various distinguished visitors. It was something to be proud of, but such displays risked making that vacancy an attractive target for a wealthy militiaman. At this point, every silver lining had a cloud.

Portsmouth, 2nd Sept. 1803

My dear Father,

I this morning recd. yours dated 28th ult. by which you may perceive it has been detained somewhere. I yesterday receiv'd a letter from Caroline dated the 30th [from] Cockington Bury. I rec'd a letter from Genl. Grenville in answer to the memorial and recommendation saying that he had forwarded them to H.R.H. Duke of York with a very strong letter in my favour. We have not heard how it digests with H.R.H. Col. Hall joined us last evening. I do not see how I can get him to be of use to me. Every necessary recommendation required by routine is gone in, in a handsome manner. People here do not doubt of the success. I hope we may not be disappointed.

H.R.H. the Duke of York has said since the review the Regt. was in the highest order possible. H.R.H. the Prince of Wales look'd at the troops here two days since, yesterday came out in a very handsome compliment from him to this Regt. in particular. People who are judges say we move as a body of men in better stile [sic] than they ever saw. General G. said my papers were the first that informed him of the success of his appreciation of Capn. Bradford; he was sorry to lose B. out of the Corps but rejoiced in his promotion. Every[one] admires the Regt. 'Twould be hard were they to supersede me, but 'tis a Regt, every one would be glad to get into. There's the danger.

What I am now anxious to learn is the Duke's answer to G[eneral] G[renville]. They are wonderfully pressed by business in town. I shall go directly and ask Hall what he thinks he can do for me. I will ask him to write to the D[uke] recommending me. He said last night, not to me, he should do it. He is very sanguine about the business. There's no doubt in [him that] he'll get it for me, but [without doubt]ing the man we don't believe it all gospel, but doubt not that he would do everything in his power to serve me. When I know more I will inform you. I want Raymond here. I have been thinking since the Prince has so far committed himself it would be right to say such a thing was vacant in the Regt., and that it would afford general satisfaction if it went in the Corps.

I am glad to hear a good acc[oun]t. of Fred. Aunt's promise of going to Ashprington has certainly occasioned these [doors] to open. We trust they will not be blasted. What sort of a harvest? Remember me to Mother.

Believe me yours
J. HILL

Both the Duke of York and the Prince of Wales inspected the troops at Portsmouth in August 1803. As well as regulars, some 2,000 volunteers, about a third of the adult male population of the area, were turned out. The local paper reported 'The town and neighbourhood have been very unexpectedly honoured with a visit from the Prince of Wales. On Tuesday all the troops in garrison and camp received orders from General Whitelocke to parade the following morning on Southsea Common...About 12 o'clock the Prince arrived on Southsea Common, the cannon saluting as he advanced. His Royal Highness then reviewed the following troops: The Royal Artillery in garrison; The Royal Artificers; the 23rd Foot (Royal Welch Fuzileers,) the North Gloucester, Worcester, Flint, Carmarthen, and Merioneth Militias, and the Portsdown Cavalry. His Royal Highness expressed, thro' General

Whitelocke, his warm approbation both of the appearance and discipline of the respective corps'.[1]

By his next letter, Jack was back on the Isle of Wight, scouting a campsite at the western end of the island. He still had no formal news of his possible promotion, but the absence of any reference to the issue suggests he may have been informally told his claim had succeeded: Grenville's confirming he had made the recommendation was a strong indicator it would. Perhaps also pressing Lieutenant-Colonel Hall had revealed a little slight-of-hand going on: Charles Sutton would not be physically joining the regiment - he was going to a staff appointment. The way was therefore clear for Jack's promotion. The appointment was published in the London Gazette two days before he next wrote; his being now at Freshwater almost certainly means he had not himself seen the formal announcement, but Hall would have known it had been approved.

Camp Freshwater.
8th Sept. 1803.

My dear Father,

The attention of Government is so much engaged respecting the safety of the Capital that I do not imagine any Regt. will be sent West to supply the vacancies occasioned by the embarking of the 9th for Ireland. It is at present suppos'd in case Bonaparte should not attempt an invasion very soon we shall be cantoon'd in this Island for the winter, for which purpose Government are buying all the Barnes, etc., they possibly can. Every week they are looking out for the French, everything is prepared to give them a warm reception, we are busy entrenching ourselves in Freshwater Gate in this part of the Island. I am very sorry to hear of the deaths you mention'd in our neighbourhood, particularly our late pleasant companion Mr Tozer. Respecting the horse you mention'd unless fodder was cheaper in this case you may make yourself perfectly easy as I am allowed the keep of 3 horses provided I have them, but nothing if I have none. 10lb. corn per diem, 14lb. hay for each - no straw. A man per comp^y. to look after it, who at present has only the care of me. A Serg^t. of my Comp^y. has the superintendence of the whole of our Bat horses. I have seen Raymond since his return from Devon.

This has been a complete Spanish Summer, a fine thing 'twill be for them who bought their hay early in the harvest. We find it

---

1 *Hampshire Telegraph and Sussex Chronicle* 5 September 1803

very cold in Camp and have very long patroles [sic] to make along the coast during the night, about 2½ hours work each patrol.

I shall write William in a day or two. Remember me to Mrs. Garrett. I shall write Caroline also in a day or two.

If Bonaparte comes I shall be allowed to carry as much baggage as I chuse [sic] on my own back. Government allowed the Cap^n. £20 and sub[altern]s £12.10. Baggage money, we are now supposed to be enabled to carry our own baggage. Bonaparte, it seems, is collecting his boats in the great canal that runs from behind Dunkirk, Ostend, to Middleburgh near the island of Walcheren. The French troops in that Q[uate]r are very sickly. The F[rench] boats have been taking a cruise you see from Boulogne to Calais and back again. Is Augerou and [his] Bayonne Army to go to Portugal or Ireland[?]What are they about in Italy? Remember in the invasion of France by the Prussians 'twas the national volunteers who defeated them at Jemappes. That was done in spite of P[russian] cavalry. Francois will have none when he comes here, he had better take care how he quits the covering fire of his gunboats that our Navy allow him to keep. We shall be disappointed if he does not come now that we are prepared for his reception.

Remember me to all at home. Col. Hall never rec'd that pointer you sent him. Enquire about it.

Yours ever,
J. HILL

The Tozers were a firm of Devon solicitors (and still are), founded in 1785. The Tozer who died may have been John Tozer, who founded the company in Newton Bushell in 1785. The answer to Jack's question about 'Augerou' was both, or neither. In 1803 Charles Pierre François Augereau, 1st Duke of Castiglione, was dispatched by Bonaparte to Bayonne to organise troops for an invasion of Portugal but before they were ready, Portugal made peace with France. Augereau was then transferred to command at Brest with a view to his forces being part of the invasion of Britain, in their case targeted at a landing in Ireland. Thus, his army was intended to go to Portugal and to Ireland but ultimately did neither. In the Battle of Jemappes on 6 November 1792 the inexperienced French Republican army, as Jack notes largely composed of poorly trained volunteers, defeated a regular but significantly outnumbered Austrian (not Prussian) army.

The Isle of Wight had long been at threat from French invasion, though the last actual incursion there was as long ago as 1545, at the eastern end of the island. Freshwater, not far from the Needles on the southern coast, was considered a vulnerable point. The bay there, known in 1803 as Freshwater Gate, is the only significant break in the line of cliffs extending from the Needles in the west to Shanklin in the east. With a gentle beach at the end of a valley cut by the Western Yar, any invasion force landing there could easily penetrate inland. In 1803 the whole area was largely rural; the urbanisation and gentrification that followed Queen Victoria's adoption of Osborne as her summer home was still forty years in the future, as was the 'Palmerston' fort built in 1856 to defend the area Jack and his men were charged with securing. Freshwater is today a medium sized town, but in 1803 was largely farm cottages clustered round All Saints church. Jack was staying in the village, about a mile from his men. On Sundays he almost certainly worshipped at the church under the rector, Benjamin Holmes.

Manning an entrenched camp on hills overlooking the bay, and the routine patrolling that entailed, was tedious. With few distractions, several of Jack's later letters from Freshwater hint at boredom. But he was certainly excited in early September 1803 when his promotion was finally confirmed and Sutton's taking a staff job cleared the way for Jack to adopt the rank without changing company. His appointment was gazetted as 'Lieutenant J. Humphrey Edward Hill to be Captain of a Company, without Purchase, vice Bradford, promoted to 58th Foot.'[2] There was a double reason for the Hills to celebrate: William was formally commissioned Lieutenant in the Royal Navy on 11 April. His mother, apparently, attributed the joint success to Aunt Peggy's temporary relocation to Caroline's at Ashprington, but Jack knew that he needed to pass proper thanks to the influential men who had supported his cause. His next letter home uniquely has two parts, addressed separately to his mother and his father respectively.

Portsmouth, Sunday.
Sept. 11th, 1803.

My Dear Mother,
    Hereby to gratify you, as you mention'd you had rather correspond with a Cap[tain], than a sub[altern]. I have accepted a Comp^y. in the Royal Welsh Fusiliers. I suppose the same party will be nearly assembled round the fireside to receive the notification as there was when Willy's [promotion] arriv'd. I am much obliged to Aunt certainly. One cannot consent to her leaving Hennock often for fear the charm should loose its effect. Tell Caroline to kiss

---

2 *The London Gazette* Issue no. 15618 dated 6 September 1803.

her little son for me and say to him the Welsh will do their best endeavours to smoothe the road before him. How much I should like to be quartered within a ride of you all.

I rec'd a letter from George Mackenzie; he endeavours to explain the cause of this promotion in the F[usiliers], so gratifying to the West Country folks, another way.[3] It strikes me it was a most fortunate circumstance for Bradford (and [me]) that the D[uke] of Y[ork] was so much pleased with the Regt. as I conceive in a fit of complacency he might have been induced to make some promotion in the corps which unseen might have been forgotten. We are indeed a very favorite Regt. almost everywhere. H.R.H. the Prince of Wales paid the Regt, and Bury the most marked compliments, the Duke of Kent pleas'd as Punch at the Regt. coming off with so much credit. Bury mention'd a circumstance new to me last eve, he was the only Com[manding] officer of the 5 Regts, that did not mutiny that told the Duke of Kent 'I can depend on my men'. The others could not, they could not answer how the men might behave. G[eneral] Grenville is highly gratified with our being in such favour. The P[rince] of W[ales] comes again here on Tuesday. I shall write a letter of thanks to G[eneral]G[renville] to-morrow, you are always first, you see.

I wish I could get Will at Plymouth or this place, we would cram ourselves on the top of a coach and come down to try if we could make you a bit proud on the occasion. Madame Caroline and her heir would come in for a smile in spite of her making you grandmama.

Do let me know where Bradford is, as I have a letter of business and advice of his baggage having been sent to the 3 Crowns, Bristol till call'd for to forward [to] him. I directed one Barnstable which he has not answered. I rec'd my baggage from home safe tho' late, my baggage left at Gib. my servant Power, an Irishman - you know my opinion of them - sold a box full - box and all for which he got the other day 300 [lashes]. I shall purchase a suite of silk Hdks. soon, they save washing, and a few pr. of stockings this week as I intend drawing the whole nearly of my ready money £45 to pay for my promotion to the many Agents' fees, debt of Compy., etc., etc. I shall be able to spare about 3G[uinea]s. and leaving a disposable force of 10 or 12 in my pocket I shall [see] if 9s.5d. a day won't replace it tolerably soon.

I remain ever yours,
J. HILL

---

3 Mackenzie's explanation may have been related to Sutton's move to the staff.

My dear Father,

We are all much obliged to Mr. Templer for putting in a good word to Genl. G[renville], but we are also very fortunate in pleasing the whole nearly of the Royal Family. Our good appearance and conduct has gotten this promotion to go in the Regt, added to Mr. Bonaparte swearing he would come here. He has too much sense to come here, some people think.

The 'circumstance' in Gibraltar arose while Bury was in acting command (Jack was home on leave, as was Lieutenant-Colonel John Hall) and the Duke of Kent was Governor. Kent's obsessive approach to drill and discipline was 'turning life in the Gibraltar garrison into something resembling a penal colony', according to one modern historian.[4] At Christmas 1802 the 1st and 25th Foot mutinied. This was rapidly put down and the ringleaders hanged, with others transported to Australia and/or flogged. The 23rd did not join the uprising and were praised for maintaining discipline. Jack's wish to ride with William to Hennock was not realised; William would be in the West Indies for another two years. But his pride both in the two brothers' achievements and in his regiment's ability to impress their Royal inspectors is obvious. His crediting of 'Mr. Bonaparte' reflects the promotion opportunities from the army's expansion - had the 2nd Battalions not been raised, Jack's path to promotion would not have cleared.

Jack now formally commanded of what a few months before was called the Lieutenant-Colonel's company; it was now called 'Captain Hill's'. He had led these same men as a lieutenant since 1797 but thought he had lost command in June following the new army regulations. He must have been almost as relieved to have secured his position at their head as to have his promotion. Jack had two inexperienced subordinate officers in his company, Lieutenant John Selby Smith, himself just promoted, and 2nd Lieutenant Thomas Fletcher, just joined. But his sergeants were experienced men who Jack knew well: John Beevor, Robert Gregory and William Hargreaves. Beevor had been with the company since October 1802, Gregory since December 1800 and Hargreaves was there when Jack first took de facto command in May 1799. The company was seriously understrength, with four corporals (Michael Howard, Arthur McCormick, Josiah Shelly and Thomas Wickstead), two drummers (John Leeds and John Thorton) and just 33 private men, from John Auriele to Josiah Wilkinson. Each of their names, where they were on the day and the pay they each received for the month are all listed in the *Regimental*

---

4 Graves, *Dragon Rampant*

General Muster books and Pay Lists of the 23rd Foot, 1803, on the page for the period 25 August to 24 September 1803, which is headed 'Captain Hill's formerly Sutton's company'.[5] The muster roll even has an interesting little piece of trivia about one of the men: 'N.B. Peter O'Leary has been mustered by the name of Peter Daily since 25th August last by mistake'. On the following pages Jack signed his name for the first time as 'J Hill, Captain', acknowledging payments totalling £5 13s 2d as 'Extra Allowance paid to Innkeepers for Non-Commissioned Officers, Drummers, & Private Men...billetted upon them' while 'on a March' including the 'Allowance paid to Soldiers lieu of beer'. The life of a Captain of a Company was more routinely filled with administration than glory. The captaincy obtained, Jack returned to fretting about horses.

Little Yarmouth,
17 Sept. [1803]

Dear Mother,

We shall encamp tomorrow in the Western part of the I. of Wight. You must direct to me & Yarmouth via Lymington Hants. Mrs. Fletcher I saw yesterday: she is quite well again. This move is in consequence of their expecting Bonaparte. I know not what to do respecting the Horse. I wish I had her, but I know not how [as] we shall be some distance from town.

In case of an invasion, I shall have no means of conveyance but my own back. I am much obliged to you for the kind congratulations in your last, let me hear from you soon. Humphrey of ours has got the Sargency of the Regt. James White belongs to, they are at Chichester.[6] Is he to join his Regt. again? Get him to bring it [the horse] up.

Yours,
J. HILL
Tell them I will pay all expenses.

He also had an eye on a possible role on the staff of Lieutenant-General John Graves Simcoe, commander of the Western Military District, headquartered in Exeter. Simcoe was a west countryman who, after marrying into wealth, had an estate in Honiton. Staff appointments were

---

5 TNA WO 12/3967

6 Abraham Humphrey was a corporal in Jack's company, now transferring as sergeant-major in another regiment.

highly prized; they were a chance to be 'noticed'. Jack had no staff experience, but such an appointment, based near home depended on influencing Simcoe: it was time to pull some strings again. Meanwhile, the family had decided to send the horse with one of their apprentices, Charles.

Saty. 22 Octr., 1803.
Camp Freshwater

My Dear Father,

I rec'd yours of the 15th a few days since, in your next direct only Yarmouth, Lymington; do not mention Isle of Wight. I shall enclose for your information a copy of the route I think the nearest.

I saw a letter from George Mackenzie a few days since, he mentions Simcoe wanted him to be his A[ide].-de -Camp which he declin'd as he is fishing for something better. If this said Gent. wants one still, can't you contrive it among yourselves to offer your Humble Ser[van]t.? Mackenzie has been so long on the staff that he would be a great acquisition to any Genl. I should not be ready form'd. Get it if you can; never mind if you are qualified. Do enquire of S. White or someone else if G[eneral] Simcoe has got his complement of A.-de-C. before you take any other steps.

I am very sorry of the mortality in your neighbourhood. You certainly are unfortunate in having fevers so often visiting you, you enquire after my health. I am very well, the pain in my back has not annoy'd me for some time, all are saying how fat I am getting. I think I am quite fit to take the field against Bonaparte when he comes. By the bye, they have given us no men yet. The weather has been very fine for us. I know not how you farmers like it. We have now entrenched ourselves up to the wiskers [sic]. If you have bought a new saddle I will repay you. It threatens rain; when it once sets in determined manner we shall retreat to the barns. Col. Hall has brought down his wife, very young and pretty, he keeps his own carriage. We shall be sadly dispersed, I fear. The allowing us so many horses is the only equivalent [i.e. alternative]. I fear we shall be divided into different messes.

I shall write Caroline soon. I do not know exactly the distance from Wareham to Christ Church at the top of Poole Water. On his return, Charles may go to Poole from hence, from Poole to Dorchester in the great road, 17 miles, then 'twill be all plain-sailing. He might go to Torbay. I will meet him at Lymington tho' if I should not be there, never mind. The boatman would take care of the horse. I will be there if possible we [are not] allow'd to sleep out of the Island for fear of [invasion]. Linquo I think might make a soldier if Mother could part with him, the other will protect aunt's turkeys. Raymond promised to send her a tame fox, we have a fine one from Barbary. I will provide Charles accommodation here for two or 3 days and then forward him to you.

Dorchester to Lymington will be the most difficult part of the road. My staying at Lymington one day will assist Charles and the horse for two. Mr. E. Bastard or J. Templer might in case of a vacancy recommend me to Simcoe. You know best about that, the Devonshire District you might object to - for fear of my comp[an]y to kill you some game. Twill be too good luck to succeed but nothing like trying.

I remain yours, etc
J. HILL.

(Note. Charles' route probably):

	Miles
Honiton	17
Axminster	9½
Bridport	13
Dorchester	16
Wareham	17½
Christ Church to Lymington.	11½

Charles was probably the son of a Hennock family. Under rural apprenticeship, children from poverty could be bound to the care of masters till the age of 21 or until marriage, sometimes compulsorily. This provided relief for their parents when food was scarce and cheap labour to farmers and other employers. Compulsory apprenticeship was common practice in Devon until after 1843; it did not require the consent of child, parents or masters. Boys learned a trade, a craft or became skilled labourers. Girls were trained in domestic service. The apprentice was better fed than at home, though not all were happy in their situation. Jack's estimates of how far Charles would have to bring the horse were broadly accurate, to within about a mile, but he missed from his summary the 18 miles leg from Wareham to Christchurch (apparently substituting the distance from Christchurch to Lymington, about 12 miles). The total distance would therefore be just over 100 miles, not 84½, the total of Jack's estimates. Maybe this was a sleight of hand trying to make the journey look shorter. As for Jack's complaint that 'they have given us no men yet', a few months later, on 1 January 1804, the 23rd were still 361 men short, despite recruiting in Wrexham, Yeovil, Worcester and Manchester. In fact so many officers were away on recruiting duty or in staff posts that it became clear to Jack he would not be allowed to pursue a role on Simcoe's staff, as he explained to his mother.

Camp Freshwater
7th Nov. 1803
Monday

My dear Mother,

I rec'd yours of the 31 Oct, & Novr. 3 yesterday. If Genl. Simcoe has two A.D.C. he has his comp[lemen]t. At this moment I do not think I could accept it, as since my last, Capn. Sutton of ours is about to be employ'd in the same manner. Col. Hall would not nor the Capns. allow so many to be away at once as we now have. MacKenzie, Offley, Abercrombie, and Sutton, two recruiting, there's scarcely enough left to do the duty of the Hd. Qrs. At a future period it may be of use; at any rate there's no harm done in letting Genl. Simcoe know there is such a person.

Genl. Ellis is dead, Jones purchases the Lt. Colcy., Capn. Ellis the Majority, Dalmer the Compy. Cap. E. set off a few days since to join his Mother; he has leave till the 24th. With respect to the horse, I think you had best forward it immediately. I must furnish myself with one otherwise here. I will pay you for the saddle &c. if you will let me know by Charles. I am very sorry to hear so bad a report of Mrs. J. Templer. Let me know immediately as you hear from the W. Indies. I wrote Wm. a few days since. I am very sorry for the poor Chudleians. I suppose Miss Mallock's complaint has now come to a crisis, that has been annoying her so long. I very much wish she may live. Master Fred has been a great traveller. What is still more extraordinary first taught to leave his nest by Aunt P. You seem, you say, to have given up the idea of the French, cither you or Ircland will most probably rcccivc a visit within a month as a diversion to their Boulogne fleet. The latest accounts from Brest you see wear a formidable appearance. Provided there was a vacancy with G[eneral] S[imcoe], you see I c'd not accept it, which is my reason for getting the horse.

The Camp will not break up for these some days [and I] wish to enter it in the forage list before we go into winter Qrs. in the farmers' houses, the men in the Barns. The weather is very rough; our rounds are very long, we borrow ponies from one another now. We shall be very much dispersed during the winter, I know not where I shall go, the Regt. will be about 4 miles apart, which is very annoying.

Remember me to all at home & let me hear from you soon. We have received our new arms and are quite ready for Francois.

Believe me ever your
J. HILL

Jack became even more 'ready for Francois' when Charles arrived after his long journey from Hennock with the horse and Linquo the dog. To return, Charles would have to avoid freezing to death in the stormy weather and being press-ganged into the Royal Navy, whose 'recruitment' teams scoured the area from Portsmouth to Plymouth as part of the great mobilization of 1803, when over 10,000 men were forcibly taken into naval service. The gangs were supposed to take only seamen, but landsmen were pressed too, despite having no shipboard experience. The death of General John Joyner Ellis was unexpected, not least as he was in the process of selling his commission to Evan Jones. The succession of officers Jack outlined was consequently disrupted, and caused a dispute between Horse Guards and his son, Henry.

Camp Freshwater,
20th Nov.

Dear Father,
    I rec'd the Horse, safe, for particulars I must refer you to Charles. I shall give the boy £6.10.0. which will pay the sadler's bill [of] £4.0.0. and about £2 to take him home with directions, in case it should not be sufficient, to draw on the 4. I am rather rushed for time in consequence of his being delayed one day longer than I imagined at Lymington in consequence of there being no wind. I do not think there will be any chance of the Hoys getting off to-day. I shall run the risk and not delay him. We have nothing new here, looking out for Bonaparte. Remember me to all at home.

I remain yours
J. HILL

    23rd Nov.: I could not send Charles home the day I wished in consequence of the communication between Lymington and Salisbury being but Mondays and Thursdays. The weather may again be as bad as 'twas yesterday, and he must have lain about on the road in the inside of a Waggon. His great-coat assisted with a little straw will keep him very warm, 'tis slow but sure. In the paper back I put parish apprentice in case the press gang should be inclin'd to make love to him, it will be some kind of protection.
    It was tremendous weather here yesterday. I shall dread to hear the damage that must have been done to our shipping.
    The Mare is much admir'd here. I find [of] her allowance of 10lb. corn and 14lb. hay that the former will be too much at first.

The only expence besides shoeing is not quite a shilling a week for the stable.

I am at present doubled up in Bks. with Capn. Ellis, but in a few days I shall go with my Comp[y]. to a small Bks a mile and ½ to the E. of this place on the coast when I shall have [a] 4-stall'd stable of the Kings.

In case I should sell her, I will remit you the money. Our horses are all for sale in the Regt. provided you give the money ask'd - 30 g[ui]n[ea]s, nothing under.

yours,
J. HILL

The transfer of the horse achieved Jack set about training her and Linquo to military life. Both animals had a better life than the men of his company who, though now out of tents, were instead in unheated barns. Jack's hopes of a post on Simcoe's staff had been dashed by Sutton's appointment, but he was still looking for other opportunities for work closer to home.

Freshwater, 4th Dec[r]., 1803

Dear Mother,

I was rather surpris'd at your not expressing a wish to know when dispatched Charles, and did intend announcing his arrival and departure, but relinquish'd the idea when I remember'd you had not desir'd me to do so. I have delay'd answering your two last, in conscquence of having bccn so busily employ'd in arranging Capn. Bradford's papers and Accts, on leaving this Regt. which I am afraid will not be accomplish'd without his presence. Capn. Sutton, an officer lately join'd about 10 days after I desir'd you to look out for an employment under Simcoe, had the offer of one of the same description. 'Twas a doubt if one could then go, but after he was gone, there was no chance, as Major Mudge says 'tis a good thing to be brought into notice in the Adjutant Genl. Office, and it has cost you nothing.

I am glad to hear Charles got home safe, do report to me how the finances lasted out. I thought when he came here he had been ill and enquir'd of him [if] 'twas the case. I am sorry you lament Linquo so much. He is taken great care of here, which may be one consolation, and has rather to my surprise turned out a very good dog, he is wonderfully attached to me, and half his time sleeps either on the foot of mine or Cap[n]. Ellis' bed. The Mare as well as

Linquo is much admir'd and is getting confidence daily, at a distance of ½ a mile this day she took no notice of the cannon practising with shot. She will improve very fast, I plainly perceive. There will be some difficulty in taking up her carcase in consequence of her sides being so flat. Our men left their canvas habitations last evening. I am doubled up with Cap. Ellis, lately we have had two rooms between us and are tolerably comfortable. Soon I must make another move to a mile distance. I should have had not much objection to have done duty as Brigade Major in Devon for a twelvemonth or so, [if] we have not so many Cap^{ns}. on the staff, more than any Regt. in the service; as soon as one or two come in, I shall make another attempt at it. I understand G[eorge] Mackenzie was playing a higher game than B[rigade]M[ajor]. He wants permanent rank, from accepting what I understood he before refused, I suppos'd he must have been disappointed.

I shall write Caroline soon.

Mon. Morn.: Our men are in Barns. The fireplaces are not fitted up: they must be miserably cold. What think you of the frost? I hope to hear of Fanny Mallock's health improving. Remember me to all at home. These breezes from the North promise to bring on another continental war. I hope Glory and the Foxes may come to action this winter.

Yours,
J. HILL

William Mudge, possibly the 'mathematician' referred to in Jack's letter of the previous June, was soon to be promoted Lieutenant-Colonel and it seems was roped into the Hill's attempts to get Jack a billet closer to home, this time as Brigade Major for the South-West district. A staff appointment at brigade level, Brigade Major was a post, not a rank and was often held by a Captain. The role was largely administrative, for example ensuring proper liaison with higher and lower command levels but it attracted extra pay and gave exposure to more senior officers, which might help advance a career.

While Glory, another of the family dogs, sought action with the foxes of Hennock, there was no sign of the British army coming to action with the French, for all the 'looking out for Bonaparte' that Jack, the 23rd and the entire British regular and volunteer force was doing. Northerly winds would in any case trap the French fleet in port, presumably why Jack predicted the next conflict would be on the continent; he would be proven right, though not everyone was so convinced. George III was contemplating putting himself at the head of his army to face the invader. He wrote to the Bishop of Worcester 'I cannot help thinking [that if] the usurper is encouraged to make the trial that his ill-success may put an end to his wicked purposes. Should his troops effect a landing, I shall certainly put myself at the head of mine and other armed subjects to repel them'.[7] Whether the King's personal leadership would have been a blessing or a trial for his soldiers also fortunately remains speculation. After 6 months of being formally at war, and despite the continuing build-up across the Channel, confidence grew among the troops lining the English coast. A summer invasion would have found Britain's defences in a poor state, but by late1803 the country was far more prepared, even if there were still gaps in the physical defences and shortfalls in the training and equipping of volunteers. Any landing force would certainly be spotted by the British ships cruising the French coast who would signal alerts by semaphore. Repeater posts on hilltops across the south would pass messages on - a message received in Portsmouth could be in London in just 10 minutes. The best British troops were now largely concentrated in the areas most under threat: possible approaches to London from the south-east and the east, plus Plymouth and Portsmouth where the Channel Fleet was based. The 23rd, on the Isle of Wight, were part of the defence of the latter (though Jack would have preferred that they were defending Plymouth, which would have allowed regular trips home). The job of these forward forces was, if possible, to hold any French landing on the shoreline. Once the alert had been issued, via despatch riders and through beacons that had been built across the country during 1803, reinforcements from the Militia and Volunteers move rapidly along pre-planned routes to the landing place. Time was of the essence, as the Duke of York recognised: 'the period of the enemy's greatest weakness would be the moment of his landing and the time he is preparing his artillery and stores to commence his march. There will be no opportunity for manoeuvre...2,000 additional men which could be brought to the beach in the first twenty-four hours [would be] of greater importance than treble that number which might join the army at a later period'.[8]

The soldiers waiting along the south coast were becoming impatient for action. Despite some false alarms, by Christmas, Jack was lamenting that 'Bonaparte is not yet come'; it was all quiet on the Freshwater front.

---

7 Quoted in *The French Are Coming: The Invasion Scare of 1803-5* Peter A Lloyd 1991
8 Lloyd, *The French*

Dear Mother,

I rec'd yours of the 12th some days since and was much gratified to hear from William. I suppose this will arrive just in time to wish you a merry Xmas and happy New Year. George MacKenzie is again plac'd on the staff I suppose in Devon he may perhaps be there during this gay time of the year. He has by this I suppose not succeeded in getting placed on the Q[uarte]r M[aste]r Gen[era]l Staff and thinks being employ'd in the Staff near his dear friends better than doing duty with his Regt.

I am sorry to hear still so melancholy an account from Totnes respecting Miss Mallock. I perceive my Father is employ'd Commissioner in the income tax, is there anything to be got by it except trouble? I wrote Caroline a few days since. I am happy to hear of her and her son's welfare.

Your wheat turn'd out, I understand from Charles, better than it promised when I was home. Our situation in this place is nearly as rusticated as that of Hennock; we live very quietly and get a plenty of exercise. I never, thank God, was better in my life. Major Jones has lent me a single Gun with which I kill half the shots I fire. I wish I was with you. I think now I could venture to promise you a tolerable supply of game. Linquo now is mad after a gun. A hint in making flannel waistcoats, to double over in the seams as much as 'tis probable, will be wanted to let out when half worn. Blacking shoes, 4d. worth of oil sweet, ½-lb. treacle, ld. copperas, 1 quart of vinegar, ivory or lamp black, the oil and black to be first mixed, to be boiled, it must not be made very thick; this will not come off and dirt the clothes, and will shine as well as your Spanish.

The Mare - the other day Lloyd desir'd the servants to take his two and mine to the field where we parade, she had only a halter and cloath on, she tipt him somerset.[9] I sent him home for the bridle, she then took no notice of the drums, when the weather is little better she shall always attend parade by constant practice, she must be quiet. I am allowed 1s. 1d. and 8-lb. oats per diem for her; so that she cannot be much expense. I think in the spring I shall make her cut a very gentlemanly appearance.

Bonaparte is not yet come, what can he be driving at? You spoke of my companion in your last, the Commander in Chief has for the present put a stop to the sale of his father's commission, he is

---

9 Charles Lloyd, at this point a Captain in the 23rd, whose soldier servant suffered being thrown head over heels.

opposite me now drawing up a memorial, should the great man persist and refuse him. I think twill be a most rascally piece of business as his resignation was accepted of before his death, we all feel for him and consider it will be a loss of three thousand five hundred to the family. I hope Fredrick is quite recovered by this time. You have not mention'd what success you have had with the Geese and Turkies. Do you imagine Glory will be as great a favourite at home as Linquo was? I am glad Charles' money lasted him so well. I was afraid he had lived too abstemiously for his hard work and required the butcher in preference to the doctor. I am sorry [you] have not got a company of volunteers again at Bovey as infantry is certainly the best calculated for the defence of Devon. I hope William after the reduction of St. Domingo may come home as I suppose most of the prizes worth taking in the W.I. are now pick'd up.

Friday: I heard from Caroline yesterday, she mentions your having written her of William's welfare, Fanny Mallock is getting better, I understand. There is nothing new in this part of the world. Poor Ellis' affair looks very gloomy. I fear he will not succeed. Remember me to our dear circle at Hennock.

I remain, Ever yours
J. HILL.

Capn. Ellis could not persuade Charles to be a soldier. Have you had many Woodcocks this winter? How does J.O. got on, is he to become a Benedict soon? Or does etiquette prevent it for a few months?

Income tax was first introduced in 1798, to pay for the war. The rate varied between two pence in the pound (for incomes over £60) to a maximum of two shillings in the pound (incomes of over £200). It was abolished after the Treaty of Amiens but reintroduced when war resumed with a lower top rate of 5% but an expanded scope, so more money was raised for the Exchequer. The 10% top rate was later re-imposed, and the broader scope kept. Jack's question 'is there anything to be got by it except trouble?' is an insight into the unpopularity of the measure. The 'companion' referred to was Henry Ellis. His father, former regimental commander John Joyner Ellis, was a Major-General when he died on 30 October 1803, and still held a Lieutenant-Colonel's commission in the 23rd. He had formally resigned, but died before his commission sold. The would be purchaser, as Jack had noted the previous month, was Evan Jones, whose elevation would in turn create a vacancy for Henry Ellis himself. Henry Ellis sought the Duke of York's permission to allow the sale to proceed, which as Jack notes would generate a tidy sum – and no doubt help fund his own promotion. Ellis was fighting an uphill battle, however. Longstanding practice in the army was that commissions were not inheritable; if an officer died before selling out, the value of the commission reverted to the Crown.[10] The argument that Ellis senior had already resigned, so the transaction should be completed, did not carry any weight.

By the end of 1803 the concept of the Army of Reserve had collapsed, plagued by insufficient recruitment, desertion and its members switching to the regulars (where they would receive another bounty for enlisting). The flow of manpower from the militia and volunteers was steadily improving though; by the end of 1803 nearly 400,000 men had answered the call (over 3.5% of the population). Simcoe had offered Jack a staff job, but too many others were already absent: regimental returns show twenty officers were away on staff duties, recruiting, leave or sick, plus three vacant lieutenancies following recent promotions (including Jack's). Only nineteen officers, and only five of ten captains, were present despite the high alert state.[11] Jack was stuck where he was and unable even to visit home. His mother and sister had, however, been keeping him abreast of local gossip.

Freshwater 11 Jany. 1804

Dear Mother,

I rec'd yours of the 29th Decr. some time since, with a great deal of Hennock news. The death of Mr. Abraham I suppose will bring something decisive between J.P. and Phillip P. You did not mention if their brother in India is married - it certainly was a misfortune for Mr. Handcock to have been thrown so early in life among great people, in endeavouring to support his vanity he has probably sacrificed his neck.

I often wish returning home from shooting sometimes I could give you the snipes - woodcocks we have none - the other day we surprised a covey of partridge in a covert they got up one after another. I killed 3 of them. The Mare is improving very fast. I think

---

10 During the Peninsular War exceptions were made allowing post-mortem sales for the benefit of an outstanding officer who had been killed, but it was not until 1856 that a Royal Warrant allowed an officer's widow, children or other relations to sell his commission, though still only if he had been killed in action or died of wounds within 6 months of receiving them (which would not have applied to Ellis). Glover, *Commissions*

11 TNA WO 17/125

if I chance to part with her I may now get £30 for she still does not like the men when under arms – I cannot well train her to it 'til the weather gets a little better. If we should go abroad, or any fair opportunity affect, you shall certainly have Linquo. I will not part with either dog or horse without advice from you.

I have not heard latterly of George MacKenzie's movements. Is he appointed to the Western District? The D. of York will not relax a point in favour of Capn. Ellis, it strikes me that there is a little personal spite in the business. Bonaparte is again on the opposite coast. I suppose he must make an attempt soon. I see no prospect of any of our Cap^{ns}. joining from their staff employments, consequently no hopes of being able soon to take advantage of Gen. Simcoe's offer. We have now a recruiting party at Wells. Pearson got it there, I shall try if I can get it further West should I be employed in that service. Leave of absence there can be no prospect of while things remain in this situation. Bonaparte seems very backward in striking a blow; he has allowed us to organise our volunteers & Bt^{ns}. of Reserve - still very many of the regulars are not compleat. Mr Windham is half in the right perhaps the French imagine the spirit of the country may subside.

[If] John Carne is to be enlisted in the military I would by all means advise them to endeavour to get him into the Engineers. If he attends that branch whilst at the academy there will be but little trouble. Their pay is ½ as much again as the Artillery.

Pray how does the young lady at Stokelake get on? Caroline tells me great things of her. Report says our colonel's lady is in the family way. It is a fortunate circumstance as some people begin to despair - there will be between four & five thousand a year for the youngster. I am sorry the terrier turns out so bad. I was in hopes he would have been a great favourite with Aunt P. from his annoying the foxes when plac'd in - Rabbits Charles says he hunts. I think there will be no occasion to put a covering over Smiler's or Captain's eyes when your troop charge the French, as the Spaniards are oblig'd to do when to their steeds when they attack the wild bulls that they may not see their [horns?].

Many of the Volunteer Corps are in very [good] order, and promise to make as fine troops in the field as any under the sun. We had a false alarm here the other day - we turned out a few hours before daylight & furnished each man with 60 rounds of ammunition. When day light came nothing was to be seen. It had originated at Deal I believe & was communicated to us in a very short time.

You did not say for Fred if he has rec'd my answer to his letter. Remember me to the Mallocks & Donnells when you see them, tell Aunt to take care of the Turkies. I hope not to have a hint from any of my fathers' associates - I understand they have been at Col.

Hall's. We have been disappointed in our expectation of a little dry weather - however it must soon come.

Believe me yours
J Hill

The 'Mr. Abraham' referred to may have been Robert Abraham. The Abrahams were attorneys and bankers at Ashburton; Jack later refers to his cousin John Pinhey ('J.P.') being at Gunnington, which was the Abraham's home. Jack's younger brother Charles had the middle name Abraham, which may suggest a close connection with the Hill family. Stokelake, a property near Hennock, had been purchased by the Rev. W. F. Bayley. That Caroline knew the 'young lady' shows the Devon clerical network in action again. The French camps along the Channel were regularly visited by Bonaparte, sometimes with ill-effect when he vented his frustrations at the slow build-up of transports and poor enthusiasm of French admirals. The newspapers in Britain reported this with a mix of glee and terror, which is how Jack knew that Bonaparte was 'again on the opposite coast'. It is interesting that despite continued manpower shortfalls, Jack encourages someone looking to join the army to join the Engineers on the grounds of better pay; a reflection perhaps on the persistence of his own financial problems, despite his recent promotion - his own regiment could have used men.

The accommodation problems Jack mentioned in his early letters from Freshwater continued to drive minor adjustments in billets. At the end of January Jack and a few of his men moved north to Yarmouth, where he found more comfortable arrangements, the opportunity for plenty of sport and the chance to play a small prank on a colleague's mother, in connivance with the 23rd's Commanding Officer, Lieutenant-Colonel John Hall. All such distractions no doubt helped relieve the boredom.

Yarmouth
Feby. 1 1804

My Dear Mother,

I know not with whom of us the last letter rests, if with me, I have put it aside unanswered. I have search'd my Desk for it but cannot recover it. Another reason, independent of our late silence, induces me to write which is to learn if you have had any accounts from William by the last fleet from the West Indies. He now has a chance of coming home, do give me an early answer, as I am anxious to hear of his welfare. I am at present Quarter'd in

Yarmouth, I know not how long I shall stay here, as there is an idea of their again changing the party in which case 'tis uncertain if I am to stay here with a small party of my men or go to Freshwater again.

I think for few months this will be the most desirable place as I am got into very comfortable lodgings. I am allow'd 8 and pay six shillings per week – Col[one]l and Mrs. Hall live in this place, as there are no accommodations for them near Freshwater. The Col[one]l has been very civil to me. Do send up by the coach directed to me the canister of the Spanish snuff, it is in the drawer of the Study you remember it - it seems they value it at its full price in Nottinghamshire. Hall was laughing at Thornhill's mother the other day for being so stingy over it, this is to be sent there I believe with the idea of making her imagine there is more to be got here and to see how she intends acting on the occasion, it is to be given to Mrs. T['s]. sister to whom Mrs. Thornhill would not give any of the quantity we brought from Cadiz.[12] I hope you have given it house room. I am sure I did not think it worth so much.

I remember in one of your letters of late you enquir'd where the rabbit nets were put - I had but very few, four, I think, they are either in the shooting jacket pocket or at Cornishes. The weather has been so very bad here we have not been able scarcely to move out - the three last times I have been shooting with the Col[one]l. I kill'd a woodcock the only thing brought home between 3 of us - a Mr. Lee whose father has a large estate and manor near this place, making the 3rd.[13] The second time I did not fire once, yesterday I had one shot and miss'd a hare. The gentlemen in this neighbourhood have been civil to us in this respect, we had leave to shoot over their estates on condition of not killing the pheasants and only occasionally to shoot a hare when we wanted it, not to make a practice of killing every one that came our way.

I wrote William a few days since, if he is in the West Indies the letter will be worth having, if he is come home 'twill not find him out. I was thinking one day for more than [once] that in case William should come to [here] if Hennock would be depriv'd of your presence for a week or so. The post here goes out at 9 in the

---

12 Captain William Thornhill joined the 23rd as a 2nd lieutenant in 1799.

13 An area known as Lee Farm at Wellow, near Yarmouth, may have been where Jack and his party enjoyed their sport. Today the area hosts a large solar farm and housing.

morning. Major Jones is here on his way to town. I can write no longer.

I remain yours,
J. HILL.
Remember me to all at home.

The snuff seems unlikely to have been acquired during the abortive raid on Cadiz in 1800, so presumably was brought home by Jack from Gibraltar. A few weeks later rumours of activity by the French fleet sparked a defensive response, but there remained little to do. Even a short deployment to provide electoral security was curtailed, owing to the bespoke nature of democracy in Georgian England.

Yarmouth, Lymington, Hants
25th Feby. 1804

My Dear Mother,
I was much gratified with your last letter in which you gave me an account of William's proceedings. You did not mention how my Father was but I concluded perfectly recover'd. I hope this may not cross yours on the road as our two former epistles have done. With respect to the snuff, I think you had better direct it for me, 23 Reg^t. Freshwater, near Lymington, Hants, via Salisbury & send it by the coach.

Major Fletcher came here yesterday to inspect the works in this part of the Island. He dined with me. His family & Mrs. F. are all well – he mentioned that there has been a bustle between the Carters and the Butlers in consequence of Major C. Marrying Miss B. but all was now settled. Major F[letcher] is gone out this morning to Hurst Castle. I am at present tolerably well, oft having a very good companion in one of the officers of the Reg^t. who is also ordered to remain in this place. I imagined I should have had to have gone over to Freshwater for a few days in consequence of an election here, but instead of 3 days before & after they now compris'd for as many hours – the Detachment will only march out therefore in the morning & return in the evening. I understand it is managed very quietly, the borough being completely in one man's hands – S^{ir} Home Popham is to be the member – I am invited to dine with them.

I see by the Gazzette that you have a Comp^y. of Volunteers in Chudleigh – What is become of Mr. Bayley's brother - does he intend settling after having had enough of the militia. I enquired again when I was at Parkhurst respecting Mrs. B. it was as Cap^n.

Bradford mentioned her father was something in the dock yard. Col[one]l. Hall has an inflammation in his eyes, he is still very much indisposed by it. All idea of Cap^n. Ellis getting any thing from his Fathers' services is at an end. Major J[ones] does not imagine the prize money from St. Domingo will be one half as much as you supposed. I understand the French fleet in the Mediterranean is at sea. In this case I suppose they will not much longer delay making a dash. All the ships have been ordered away from Ports[mou]th in consequence of some intelligence respecting the enemy's movements.

I wrote Caroline a few days since. How does John Pinhey get on at Exeter and Gunnington? Is Lucy Bradford soon to be married? What chance do the other damsels stand of getting husbands? I fear war will take all of the men away from home & send them after Francois.

I hope Glory's grip improves & defends the turkies & geese from the foxes. I hope A[unt] Peggy has been gratified by hearing of a few canards having been worried this winter. I believe you must have had a bad opportunity as there has been so little snow, this weather is very good & seasonable I should suppose for the farmers.

Remember me to all our dear Hennock circle.

I remain ever yours
J Hill

Hurst Castle, across the water from Yarmouth was first built by Henry VIII to protect the western entrance to the Solent. In 1803 a programme significantly to strengthen its defences began; it was completed in around 1807. It was presumably these works that Major Richard Fletcher was inspecting. The election of Home Popham as one of two members for Yarmouth was uncontested and was the first of several seats Popham held during his Parliamentary career.[14] Popham, of course, was the man behind the ill-fated 1798 Ostend raid; discussion over dinner may have been delicate, given that Jack was imprisoned in Lille for six months after that debacle. The edition of the *London Gazette* that Jack had been reading was from January; it recorded the appointment of two officers, William Bond as lieutenant and John Pike as Ensign, to the Chudleigh Volunteer Infantry.[15] Margaret Hill's interest in the French Caribbean colony of St. Domingo (now part of

14 He was MP for Yarmouth until 1806, Shaftesbury from 1806 to 1807 and Ipswich from 1807 to 1812.
15 *The London Gazette Issue Number 15670* January 28 to January 31, 1804.

Haiti) was because William was there aboard HMS *Vanguard*, a 74-gun ship of the line. Following the success of the independence movement led by the former slave Toussaint Louverture, French troops left the island, but their convoy was intercepted, and the Royal Navy captured several ships; William would get his share of the spoils, even if it was less than his mother expected. The melancholy from a long period of inaction can be seen in Jack's comment 'What chance do the other damsels stand of getting husbands? I fear war will take all of the men away from home & send them after Francois'. It was unusual for him to be so reflective in letters to his mother, which were normally far more upbeat.

Jack soon moved back to Freshwater, though the gossip in his previous letters excited his mother, holidaying with relatives in Exeter, to press for details about the young Mrs. Hall. Jack did not feel himself well qualified to respond but provided an approving description anyway.

March 18th 1804
Freshwater

My Dear Mother,

I was much pleas'd at hearing you were gratified in your late excursion. I hope during your residence in Exeter the weather was as fine there as it has been here - we have been rambling through the fields enjoying the return of spring. I moov'd [sic] from Yarmouth about 10 days since and am now at the head[land] in the country at the back of the island. I have now taken up my residence in a house hir'd by the Government, with only one officer besides, his name is Patterson[16] his father the member for Minehead, he lives in Norwich, he is a very fine young recruit. The village in which we are is the church town & about the size of the lower town in Hennock. Its disadvantage is the distance from F[resh]water Gate, which is a mile & is the point we are guarding.

I know not whether I have complied with your wishes in describing Mrs. Hall: her hair is flaxen, her eyes are blue, nearly as good a figure as the elder Miss Packer she is apparently about 18 – from what I have seen of her lately I think her mode of conducting herself particularly correct, much more so than is generally seen among the young fashionable fair of the present

---

16 Robert Dossie Patteson was commissioned 2nd lieutenant RWF on 31 December 1803 and lieutenant on 22 November 1804. In 1804 his father was indeed Tory MP for Minehead.

day. Col. H[all] has been ill lately - a rheumatic affliction in the head - with a sore eye, her behaviour was kind & attentive, without betraying any childish fondness. I lived at Yarmouth within a few doors of them, that detachment now is made a Sub[altern]'s and is kept for the convalescent, very fortunately we cannot find enough description to compose the no. 18 – the whole of our sick does not amount to above 8 that is somewhere about average for the winter, very fair for 380 [the total size of the Regiment]. I forwarded a navy list by an officer going out to join his Regt. in the W.I. to William this is the 3rd or 4th; I hope he may receive some of them. I should imagine if Carnes were to purchase them at Falmouth, enclose & direct them for William, he would stand a good chance of receiving some & the island postage would be good.

With respect to the snuff – I am convinced that the publick conveyances are the best, the smallness of the parcel is no objection. If you remember Mr. Lee sent me a p[ai]r of epaulettes only from London to Chudleigh by coach. You might nearly as well be in Exeter as Portsmouth because there is no regular conveyance through the island. A letter from Newport, distance 12 miles, must go to Cowes (5), Southampton (16), Lymington (18), Yarmouth (7&3) to arrive here – more than 49 miles round to come here. 'Tis for this reason you must not mention in your directions Isle of Wight because it goes to Newport as the capitol, they return it from N[ewport] to us by the above route.

I am glad Bradford has found the Devonshire air better in their attachments than the Irish clovers. I hope it is not one of the Templers that is killed in that unfortunate affair at Teignmouth all apparently were in fault the magistrate meddling in business that could not interest him cuts but an aucquard figure in the story as now told. You did not say how Fanny Mallock was. I hope your silence augurs good. I am in doubts how to direct this letter. Remember me fondly to all our relatives - I have succeeded in making the horse as cool as any after the hounds, I now intend introducing her to the soldiers - I am very glad to hear you are not an absolute fixture at Hennock. I expect to hear from W[illia]m in your next as a pacquet has arrived - Comp[limen]ts to Mr & Mrs A and Aunt & Uncle.

Believe me yours
J Hill

It seems that Jack had been reading *The Kentish Gazette* of 16 March 1804 which carried a letter from Charles Hubbard of the King's Arms at Teignmouth reporting 'a melancholy affair' that occurred there when:

> Captain T. of the T— Cavalry, having given one of his men a severe blow over his eye with a stick, about three days since, while drilling, on account of some insolent language he used towards him; it occasioned a great deal of conversation. Among others, Mr. N—, the Magistrate, observed to a friend of the Captain, that his conduct was ungentlemanly, and that of a b--d; this being told to the Captain, he called on Mr. N. for an explanation, who would give no other answer to his request, than what he had heard was perfectly correct. Captain T. being enraged at the circumstance, sent Mr. N a challenge.[17]

'N' and 'T' met at the King's Arms and the latter was killed in a duel. The Magistrate was arrested. Jack's view that a civilian magistrate ought not to have involved himself in a matter of internal military discipline is unsurprising. His concern that 'Captain T' was one of the Templars seems unfounded; there is no record of anyone of that family being killed in Teignmouth in 1804.

A couple of weeks later, Jack's six-month stint on the Isle of Wight ended. He probably felt relieved to be moving elsewhere, even if he did not go far. He dashed off a quick note home with the news.

Shoreham
8th April 1804

My Dear Mother,

We marched from Freshwater Tuesday last & marched for Newport that Evening. Wednesday we embarked at Cowes & arrived at Portsmouth and marched to Havant & some other small places. Thursday marched from Havant to Chichester, Friday from Chichester to Shoreham & Worthing. We are halted here for some days. Thursday morn we march for Lewes, Friday to Hailsham in Sussex, not far from Battle. The orders were sudden. I rec'd the snuff safe.

Your last letter mentioned in a P.S. that Lucy Bradford was married - I cannot unpack my desk to make any comments on it. I saw Major and Mrs. F[letcher] at Portsmouth. They were all very well. Tell Caroline in your next of our moves. I will write you again when we are settled I am happy at hearing you have been so gay. I

---

17 *The Kentish Gazette* 16 March 1804

think in about a week we shall learn where we are likely to take up our residence for a short time. Remember me to all at Home.

Believe me yours.
J Hill

The move took the 23rd into the Southern Military District, comprising Sussex, Kent and Surrey, the most likely frontline if invasion came. There were some 37,000 troops in the Southern District, well over half of them militiamen.[18] Encamped opposite on the French coast was an army of over 70,000 men, most of them veterans. The distance across the Channel was shortest at this point and the long, shallow beaches offered good potential landing-grounds, if an invading force could make it across. Jack found himself and his men stationed close to the site of the last successful armed invasion of Britain, as the locals were apparently happy to remind him.

Hailsham Bks. Sussex
18th April, 1804

My Dear Mother,
    We arrived here last Friday. The Barracks we occupy are scarcely finished, better calculated for summer than winter. The town near which we are situated is very small and has a market once a fortnight.[19] It is imagined we are not to be encamp'd this summer "provided the French do not come". We are brigaded with the 8th, 48th and 88th under Maitland, the 8th and 23rd are in these Barracks. The others are at East Bourne about 5 miles distant. General Sir James Pulteney commands the district. There is an idea that we are to have a second Battalion - we are among the Regts. intended for one, but Query, where are the men to come from? We have rec'd orders to send in the names of such officers who wish to raise men for rank. To raise the numbers specified is utterly impossible.
    Some extraordinary measures must be taken. The Militia will not part with their men as long as there are so many of its officers in the House of Commons, we are completely in the dark how it is to be effected. A second Battalion is a good thing for the officers to whom it will give promotion but considered regimentally it is a bad

---

18 TNA WO 17/2787 *Quarters of Troops in Great Britain 1 Sep 1803 – 1 Jun 1804*
19 Hailsham recorded a population of 1,029 in the 1801 census. *The History of the Parish of Hailsham* L.F. Salman 1901

thing as you may imagine to collect good recruits for officers, and having formed a good corps, we are equally divided into the 1st and 2nd Battalions, the other ½ comes from whence nobody knows, people of every description. One advantage will accrue to me, which is that the same objection will not then exist to my accepting a Staff employment as now does.

In whatever part of England you go to, the place you are in is the very place, the first to be attacked by the enemy. The reason given in this neighbourhood is because William the Conqueror landed at Pevensey which is very near this place, 6 miles. I have not heard from Caroline lately. She is a letter in my debt. I shall write her soon. Do let me know as soon as possible after you hear from William, lately there have been no despatches from the W. Indies. I see by the papers one of the Miss Bethels is married.

This weather has been so unfavorable since we have been here, that I have scarcely been able to look about me. We are now only 12 miles distant from Battle, this is the old tract of country we have been always used to go through. I should imagine nothing [but] the slippery ground upon which that consummate villain Buonaparte stands only prevents the sailing of the Fleet destin'd for our invasion.

Remember me kindly to our dear friends at home. Some people are come in. I cannot write any more. Pichegreau murdered is the news of the day.

Yours,
J. HILL

The barracks at Hailsham was only begun in 1803, hence its 'scarcely finished' status. The 23rd was one of the first regular battalions stationed there, though clearly Jack felt the newness of the facilities was not an advantage.[20] The reports about raising second battalions for some line regiments were true; this was the latest move in attempting to increase the size of the regular army. Confusion between the various forms of military service available was at the root of the measure. In March the Government was forced to admit the failure of the Army of Reserve concept. The Act - and under it all the recruiting activity for the Volunteers and Militia that was distracting men from joining the Regulars - was to be suspended for a year and the officers of six regiments, including the 23rd, were given permission to recruit men for a second battalion. If they did, they would be promoted; a process

---

20 Salman, *Hailsham*

known as 'raising for rank'. In principle this provided opportunities for advancement without leaving the regiment, but as Jack noted the catch was the numbers of men required. For a captain to obtain a majority required him to raise ninety men. Jean-Charles Pichegru was a French general who had conspired against Bonaparte. Arrested in Paris in February 1804, he was found strangled in his prison cell on 5 April. It was not clear whether he was murdered or committed suicide, though many assumed the former. The many plots against Bonaparte and the allegations that Pichegru was killed on his orders may be the 'slippery ground' to which Jack refers.

This newest recruiting measure failed to pass Parliament. Jack was right that the number of MPs holding military rank, whether regular or reserve, meant such new measures were controversial. The government resigned; their successors reduced the size of the Militia and cut the maximum levels of bounty payable to those who joined the Militia or Volunteers, reducing competition with the regulars. The possibility of enlisting for a shorter service was also introduced, and militiamen and volunteers were encouraged to enlist in the second battalions of the regular army, for a further bounty. These measures made a difference, though the process took time; the second battalion of 23rd was only formally established on Christmas Day 1804. Another change was that line regiments were allocated areas in which to focus recruitment: 2/23rd were to be headquartered in Wrexham, recruiting from Anglesey, Caernarfon, Denbigh, Flint and Merioneth. The Royal Welch Fusiliers would finally nourish their Welsh roots, though recruiting was slow at first both because of the sparce population of rural North Wales and, possibly, because of fear of the punishments regulars could receive. When he later joined the regiment, Private Thomas Jeremiah suggested the risk of flogging meant: 'we could not get any more volunteers from the militia, particularly the Welch militias from whom we their county regiment used to be furnished with [the best] and hardiest men in the army'. [21]

Finding an opportunity to lead a recruiting party was very much on Jack's mind. This would not do anything for his promotion prospects, but it might offer a chance to see his family if he could be arranged to be based in the West Country. In a letter full of the boredom of much of a soldier's life and not a small measure of homesickness, he admitted that this was a dim prospect. There was one small consolation; back on the mainland and nearer to direct mail routes, letters from home were now arriving in record time - a matter of days from Hennock to Hailsham.

---

21 The National Library of Wales MS 22102A. *Autobiography of Private Thomas Jeremiah of the 23rd Regiment of Royal Welch Fusiliers* c.1837

My Dear Mother,

I was extremely gratified at receiving yours of 27th April on the first of May, containing the welcome intelligence of our dear William's welfare. I shall be happy indeed could we all meet at Hennock. I have been making hints lately about volunteering a recruiting party in the West - it is the only chance of seeing Hennock in the present situation of affairs, but an unsuspected obstacle has turned up, we are to have a second battalion, which will take another Capt. from Head Q[uarter]s, leaving only four - none can be spared for the recruiting service. Jones and Ellis are to have promotion provided they raise a given number of men, which is generally thought impossible unless the Legislature, as it is hoped, will open some new source for the Line, by letting some of the Militia volunteer.

The situation here is tolerable, the fine weather has been the principle means of contributing to it, not much amusement going forward during our leisure hours. Your old acquaintances go on very well – Linquo is as fat as ever – the Mare is in high order, not a farthing less than [£]35 for her now. If I can persuade myself that Buonaparte would not come I should turn her for a month into a salt marsh in the neighbourhood with her shoes off to expand her feet. Could I effect this 'tis imagined by all that are judges here she would fetch near £40 at Tattersals.[22] You cannot imagine the high prices horses fetch or how much she is improv'd, she has not conquered her antipathy to a musquet yet she is determined to support her character of a fine Lady. The daily papers are filled with speculations respecting the change of administration, nothing yet is certain, except Mr. Pitt if he does not take the case, will find himself opposed by a very strong party.

I have not Rec'd the letter via Halifax William alludes to. I have mentioned Linquo and the Mare, now you must in answer tell me how Aunt goes on with the Turkies and Geese, [and] my Father with the prospect of the apples and grapes. I hope young Glory improves as she grows older. I told you some time ago that I was become a tolerable shot and Linquo much improved when under good command and fond of the Gun.

---

22 Tattersalls horse sales was founded in 1766 by Richard Tattersall and continues to this day.

How does Fred get on - I hope he is always a good boy and shall be always very happy when you tell me so. You must inform me how Caroline does, as she has not answered [my] two last letters direc't. The 18th is the date of [her] last to me.

In case the 2nd Battalion should be added I shall get several steps, but it will deprive the Rg^t. of several of our best officers. William is higher up among the Lieut[enant]s of the Vanguard than I imagined he would be. Duckworth stands a chance of being recall'd in case L[or]d. Vincent goes out of office.

Remember me to all. I remain yours
J Hill

Jack's pessimism on the difficulty of raising men was misplaced, as Parliament did incentivise recruitment from the Militia. As he predicted, Major Evan Jones was finally promoted to Lieutenant-Colonel and took command of the 2/23rd; Henry Ellis, senior captain since George Bradford left, purchased the Major's vacancy thus created in 1/23rd. Captains Thomas Pearson and George Mackenzie, the next most senior captains, took the two majorities in the 2nd Battalion. Jack therefore got his predicted 'several steps' up the captain's seniority list but five other captains remained ahead of him: Alexander Abercromby, the son of General Sir Ralph, who had joined the 23rd as a captain in May 1801, William Keith, Charles Sutton, Francis Offley and Jacob Van Courtlandt. Admiral of the Fleet John Jervis, 1st Earl St Vincent, became 1st Sea Lord in 1801. His drive against corruption embroiled political allies of William Pitt; when Pitt returned to office, St Vincent had to go; he resigned four days after Jack wrote. Sir John Duckworth, in 1804 Commander-in-Chief of the Jamaica Station (and therefore commanded the fleet including William's ship, HMS *Vanguard*), was not recalled.

The 23rd were in Hailsham barracks for only about a month before they moved into camp near Beachy Head.

Camp near E. Bourne, Sussex
30th June, 1804

My Dear Mother,
I mentioned in my last the probability of our being encamp'd, we pitch'd our tents here last Monday week. The heights are those of which Beachy Head forms a part, on our right about a mile. The line of the camp flanks the Bay of Pevensey render'd remarkable by the landing there of William of Normandy. The old Welch are again at one of the posts of honour.

The Brigade consists of the 8th, 23rd, 48th [and] 88th Reg^{ts}. of the line and the North Hants M[ilitia] with 6 guns, under the command of B[rigadier] Gen[era]l Maitland. We are one of the Reg^{ts}. to have a 2nd Battalion for certain. I imagine it probable we may receive some of Mr. Pitt's men. Come from whence they may we must have men, 220 duty men now compose our strength deducting sick, Bat men and others on paper.

The spoons sent out to Miss Henson I forwarded by an officer of the 85th Reg^t. they live in Spanish town; Kingston is the seaport. William's letters to me are always directed to our Agents in London. It saves the trouble probably of their passing through half a doz[e]n country post offices. I am glad G. Templer has young Glory in preference to anyone else. I may get one in return perhaps from him. I am become a decent shot, I learnt it last Autumn while in camp at Freshwater (I had got a Rifle in Portsmouth) and there us'd to practise with others at a mark. We sometimes by way of amusement go under these very high Chalk Cliffs, I have shot some of the seabirds with a ball from the Rifle. I know not when we may meet again but I shall be very proud to bring my dear Mother home a woodcock. As to recruiting there's no chance from that quarter as all our parties are called in. Our only chance is to get Bonaparte to venture across and bring the business to an issue. I see by the papers an unfortunate fellow by the name of Providence Hansard [is] to be hung in town for forgery, tell me how has the affair terminated in which Handcock was implicated.

I also read this morning an account of an affray at the Exeter Theatre. Lieut. P. excites my curiosity. I flatter myself for the honour of my profession it could not have happened among the regulars. I know not if it be from our very elevated situation that we feel such vicissitudes of the weather, but several evenings we have not cared to leave our canvas habitations. Daily we expect to hear of our chief's being presented with, we flatter ourselves, a son and heir, the period can not be distant.

I think with you with respect to poor William, he has made every sacrifice to his profession in the attainment of his promotion. I sincerely hope he may soon taste the pleasures I have so lately experienced of a hearty welcome at Hennock. I glanc'd my eye over the dispatches from Surinam before I began to read, looking out for the Vanguard's name rather in the same stile as you first look for the sum total of a bill. I rec'd a letter from Caroline a few days previous to yours, she is very moderate in her demands and does not ask for an answer these two months.

The Bat horses are again turn'd over to the Cap^{ns}. of Comp[anie]s so that they may occasionally have the use of two.

Every four years Government allows £18. 18. 0 for the purchase of a new one but in return in case of one being lost the Cap[n]. is to replace it

Young Carew and Jenkins of Sidmouth of the 11[th] D[ragoon]s. with A. Chichester are quartered in this neighbourhood.[23] I shall go and see them soon. Carew has dined several times at our mess. J[enkins] call'd on me one day.

Remember me to all at home, Father, Aunt and Fred.

Believe me ever to be your
J. HILL

Linquo is in my tent with me, he takes notice of no one in the Regt, except myself and servant, he is so fat as scarcely to be able to run about these downs with the least ease to himself.

The 'unfortunate fellow', Providence Hansard, was executed at Newgate on 5 July 1804, having been found guilty of forging an order for payment of £741. A detailed report of the case, trial and execution was published in a printed news sheet at the time, which would have given Jack all the information he needed. The report of the incident at Exeter Theatre that Jack read was probably one the *Morning Herald* printed on 26th June 1804:

Exeter - On Wednesday 18th inst. A meeting took place between Major G. and Lieut. P. in consequence of a quarrel the Friday preceding, at the Theatre, which, we are happy to say, ended without bloodshed. The Major, on his first entrance into the Theatre, glanced his eye on a Mr. M, seated near a Lady of his acquaintance; and having an unfortunate impediment in his speech, found his fist the readiest means of intimating his approach. Upon this, Lieut. P. thought it his duty to interfere, by calling Major G. a 'B-d'; which appellation was returned by that of 'Impertinent P-y', and a blow in the face. The parties soon made their way into the lobby, where blows and hard words passed in pretty quick succession; and not a few of the bystanders were repaid for their

---

23 This is an Old Blundellian reunion. Thomas Jenkins, son of William Jenkins, Clerk, of Sidmouth, Devon, aged 10 and his brother William, aged 8 were admitted to Blundell's on the same day as Jack, 7 August 1792. Thomas left in December 1797, William a year later. Arthur Chichester, whose father Robert was also a vicar, arrived on 8 August 1795, leaving in 1800. 'Young Carew' is Charles Carew, who arrived at Blundell's on 31 March 1796, just before Jack left. Inceldon *Register*

curiosity by bloody noses. The combatants were at length separated, but the subsequent days were consumed in futile attempts at a reconciliation; and on the Wednesday, at three P.M. the parties, attended by their seconds and surgeons, proceeded to Marepole Head, about a mile from the city, where, through the unremitting efforts of their seconds, mutual apologies were exchanged; though all their efforts might have failed of effect had they not hit on the new and excellent idea of making each party begin the apology at the same instant!.[24]

Jack's assertion that 'Lieutenant P.' could not be a regular comes from his professional pride; there is no indication whether he was a volunteer or not. HMS *Vanguard*, with William aboard, was soon to return home after being in the West Indies for nearly 9 years. Bat horses were those designated to carry an officer's baggage. The animal was normally the responsibility of the officer's batman, or servant (both words derive from the French *bât*, meaning pack).

The Duke of York reviewed Maitland's brigade on 26 August: 'They went through their business with great precision and steadiness, particularly the 8th, 23rd and 88th Regiments, and although last, not least, the North Hants Militia. A small corps of Caravan [sic] Artillery surprised the spectators by the rapidity of their motions, always changing their position in full gallop'.[25] By summer 1804 some 70,000 French soldiers under generals Ney and Soult were encamped and training across the water. Just over a week before the Duke of York's inspection a significantly grander equivalent was held in Boulogne, under the eyes of France's own new royal personage: on 18 May the French Senate made Napoleon Bonaparte Emperor of the French. A popular vote approved this by 3.5 million for with 2,500 against, though how genuinely 'free and fair' the vote was is questionable. The now Emperor Napoleon continued to visit, encourage and review his troops on the Channel coast. On 26 August, the whole army was drawn up to see him award the first of the new *Légion d'Honneur* awards to 2,000 selected individuals, to the sound of no less than 1,300 drummers. The Emperor was ready to lead his army, and the army was undoubtedly ready to 'venture across', as Jack and his colleagues hoped it would. But the French navy was not ready to help. Napoleon needed control of the Channel for long enough to enable his army to cross. Yet his fleet was bottled up in ports around France and Spain and was in poor condition

---

24 *Morning Herald* 26 June 1804
25 Cary and McCance *Regimental Records*

both because its ships could not be overhauled and its crews could not train without being at sea. Despite the Emperor's pressing, his navy was unable to provide an invasion window.

No French soldiers yet landed on the south coast, but one English sailor did. Jack's brother William sailed home a prize captured at St. Domingo - *La Virtu*, a 40-gun frigate, arriving in Plymouth on 14 August. William unsurprisingly wasted no time in making the short journey to Hennock. This, and other family good news, further piqued Jack's desire to see home.

Haylsham
20 Sepr. 1804

My Dear Mother,

I rec'd yours of the 12th two days ago announcing the arrival of another little nephew and of our dear Caroline doing as well as could be expected. I have been waiting for this pleasing intelligence which has been the occasion of my silence. I have in the meantime written to my Father, mentioning that I intend having some very weighty affairs to settle about the latter end of October and try my fortune in making an application for leave of absence. In case I should succeed I shall certainly bring Linquo and the Mare with me. I shall be extremely gratified in meeting my brother at Hennock. Whilst the affair of the invasion remains undecided I fear there will be many obstacles in the way of my obtaining leave of absence.

You do not mention what is to become of La Virtu – is she paid off? I must write to W[ilia]m in a day or two – our last letters crossed each other on the road, we have been hesitating who is to write again first. I suspected he might be either at Hennock or Ashprington instead of Plymouth and did not know where to direct. Remember me to Caroline and Mr Ley.

I have not been so successful the two last times I have been out with Linquo. I missed 6 shots. Before I had eleven and killed 5. I have not bought my hand in so well as I did in the Isle of Wight. I hope in Novr. to furnish you with some woodcocks. I hope we may all meet at Hennock this winter. Bonaparte may now expect weather in which his boats will not sail very comfortable. Remember me to Mrs. Caerwithin and the family in Totnes.

Believe me ever yours
J Hill
P.S. Direct Haylsham Barracks, Sussex - we came from camp near a month since.

Jacob and Caroline Ley's second son, John, was born on 12 September 1804. As for *La Virtu*, the Royal Navy did not commission her into British service; she was eventually broken up in December 1810.

Jack's pessimism about being allowed home was justified; no leave of absence was to be had. But intelligence arose of another chance to join General Simcoe's staff in Exeter. If Jack was to stand a chance this time, he needed his father's lobbying quickly geared up again.

Haylsham
30 Sepr. 1804

My dear Father,

There is a fair opportunity now for making an application to Col. Mudge to use his influence with Genl. Simcoe to obtain me a Brigade Majority. George Mackenzie has inform'd me this morning that there is vacancy occasioned by Major Thorley's appointment to the 96th Regt. George M. daily expects a Majority in one of the 2nd Batts, this will give us another Cap^n. at head Q[uarte]rs. I then may stand a chance of getting among you in the District. You must not lose a moment in writing to Col. Mudge nor he to Simcoe that the latter may not fill up the vacancy. The Gen[era]l's application to the Ad[ujan]t-Gen[era]l must be well timed, everything depends on this. You must see George Mackenzie and exert yourself as much as you wish to see me in Devon.

I know not myself whether it is best to make the application as soon as George Mackenzie gets his promotion, or to wait till one of our Lieuts. has got the company. Col. Hall is going away in a few days into Nottinghamshire, Bury will command the Regt. He will give me any recommendations I can wish. Pray is Major Mudge in Wales, I fear he is, do let me know. The Request to be made [to] Simcoe is for his application that Cap^n. H[ill] of the 23rd may succeed to the appointment vacated by Major Thorley and that the objections lately made against Capn. H[ill] do not now exist by the promotion of Capn. Mac[Kenzie]. I have been very explicit on this head, as I know 'tis a subject new to you. From what I understand from MacKenzie it was Col. Mudge's interest, not Col. Clifford, that was of service lately, there is no occasion for your making an application to his lordship when it is of no use. Let me know what measures you adopt. I would advise you immediately to see George M. Call on him with Wm. but he has so much to do I fear you will not meet him unless you send a note to say when you intend calling.

I see by Steele's list the Virtu paid off in which case W[illia]m is with you. Let W[illia]m inform me of his intentions [and] what effect on his movements will a Spanish war have, you did not write me in answer to my letter [on] this subject. One great advantage in [the] Thorley situation, he was not attach'd to any particular Genl. These officers on the staff of the Volunteer Brigades are in waiting in case the French should land and the volunteers turn'd out, those are Staff officers to conduct the Brigade. I shall write George Mac. in a day or two.

Pray, how does Caroline go on?

I have heard nothing of W[ilia]m. Tell Fred I shall write him one day when I can get a moment. I am sorry Aunt has been unsuccessful in her poultry.

I remain yours
J. HILL

Jack's question about a 'Spanish War' was appropriately directed at his naval officer brother, as the ostensible *causus belli* was to be the British seizure of four Spanish treasure ships travelling from Montevideo. But this action took place off the Portuguese coast on 5 October 1804, *after* Jack raised the prospect of war in his letter. It was, however, realised in Britain that Spain would be pressured to ally with Napoleon and that Spain would probably declare war as soon as the treasure ships arrived, which encouraged the British to intercept them.

Hailsham
29th Octr. 1804

My Dear Mother,

On Thursday next we march from this place for Bletchington Barracks, near Seaford which we imagine it is probable will be our winter Quarters.[26] George Mackenzie mentioned he was going to write my Father. I heard lately from him, he has behav'd extremely kind to me in this business. He undertakes directing Genl. Simcoe in making the applications, so that the same answer may not be returned as before. He also has promised to use his Father's influence with Calvert, the A[dujan]t. Gen[era]l. They were formerly brother Fusiliers. Thornley whom it is supposed I am to succeed as B. Major will be detained 2 or 3 weeks longer on a C[ourt] Martial. This again is a fortunate circumstance as about that time Mackenzie will be Gazzetted [sic] and perhaps another of our Cap^{ns}. comes off the staff.

---

26 Blatchington, near Seaford

I am sorry to hear you complain of William's right eye. I should imagine it is occasioned from his so frequently using the spy glass on board. Before he goes, you must desire him to get one of the largest size, as it requires much less exertion than the small ones. I know not what to think of a Spanish war. The Dons harassed by famine, pestilence and insurrection would of themselves not declare wars, but Bonaparte will oblige them to break with this country. I hope at any rate to see William. Was I sick I would come down for a fortnight. Let us hope the best, and imagine I shall succeed in getting a Staff employment. The other Cap^n. I alluded to is Offley, his uncle Genl. Needham has ordered him home from Newfoundland where he is employed as B[rigade] Major in consequence of there being nothing to do there. Should you not mention what is going on for me to Col. Mudge?

I know not exactly how you must direct to us at Bletchington B[arrac]ks, Sussex had better be on your next letter. When we are there I will inform you if it is insufficient to find us. B[letchington] is only 9 miles across the country but to avoid the by lanes of this County we must go 18 miles round. You would never complain of your lanes after being up to the knees in stiff clay here. I have kill'd some Pheasants lately; I wanted to send them to you but Courtlandt having sent some into Wales, about the same distance, and their having not kept good, prevented me. From what I have seen of our new Q[uarte]rs I do not think there will be any shooting except snipes and wild fowl in the winter. The rain has now set in. I do not think we shall have another day here - besides every officer and man had now the pleasing task of being drilled over again, when we are perfect ourselves we have to drill our Comp[any] - this is the consequence of the variance between the Dukes of York & Kent - delirant reges, plectuntur Achivi.

I sincerely hope we may eat our Xmas dinner together in Hennock. Remember me to all. I have not had an opportunity of getting a Frank for Fred. How does Aunt P. get on with the Turkies?

I Remain Your
J Hill

Caroline mentioned to me respecting my standing sponsor to her little John, & added that Mr. Ley did not wish it to be delayed longer than the middle of Novr. I explain'd my situation & said I should be happy to comply with her request, but desir'd that my absence might not interfere with Mr. Ley's arrangements.

This letter both underlines the importance of 'interest' in fostering an officer's career and shows the 23rd's old boy network in action.

Lieutenant-General Sir Harry Calvert had joined the 23rd Foot in 1778 aged 15, serving with them throughout the American War. He became Adjutant General of the army in 1799. A former comrade of George Mackenzie's father Frederick, Calvert might listen to his appeals concerning an officer of his old regiment seeking a staff post. Influence could, however, work two ways as it seems Captain Offley was finding out. Jack's description of his colleague Captain Francis Needham Offley as General Francis Needham's nephew is (probably unknowingly) euphemistic - Offley was in fact illegitimate, his surname being that of the General's grandmother. The records of the RWF Museum coyly note Offley's 'forename implies a connection with his probable father, General Francis Jack Needham'.[27] It is not clear whether Offley called Needham his uncle through discretion or ignorance. Jack shows his familiarity with the classics in employing a quotation from Horace that can be broadly translated 'the rulers err, the people are punished'. The Duke of Kent was a disciplinarian whose methods had provoked the Gibraltar mutiny of 1802 and were criticised by his older brother the Duke of York, Commander-in-Chief of the army, more a progressive thinker. It seems the officers and men of the 23rd, having perfected tighter drill under Kent, now needed to demonstrate the more advanced approaches of York.

George Mackenzie got his promotion to major in the new 2nd Battalion on 24 October, but the lobbying did not get Jack a staff officer post; Jack seems to have accepted this meant he was stuck in Bletchington for the time being. Mackenzie or another senior colleague may have hinted that continued agitation would be unhelpful, and he should keep his head down for a while. The structural changes resulting from creating a second battalion and an unexpected change of 1/23rd's Commanding Officer did not help Jack's chances of getting away.

Bletchington Bks.
23rd Novr. [1804]

Dear Mother,
I was happy at hearing of the safe arrival of my Father and William at home - I had previously learnt about 5 or six days ago from George MacKenzie that Calvert would not give in my name for the situation. I think in consequence it will be useless to annoy them any more, unless Offley may have come home in this Newfoundland fleet that has been dispersed. I arrived safe and in

---

27 *Officer Biographies of the Royal Welch Fusiliers* May 2011 RWF Museum

very good time here from town. I hope that Aunt may feel the comforts of her present. I think Father had better thank L[or]d. Clifford for his kind intentions to me. I have written to Col. Mudge he will make an application in another quarter it is probable through that of the Duke's military secretary - there are no hopes I fear. I know not what to think about applying for a month's leave after what has been going on for me, perhaps 'twould be as well to let them rest for a time.

I know not what to say in respect to the Mare. She is worth the money to any one - I cannot draw the forage unless I actually have a horse. Am I to exchange her, sell her, purchase another or not keep one? There was a very vague report about our going to Canada - no one believes it. This reconciliation of the royal family will perhaps employ the D[uke] of Kent. In this case Dalmer, now a Cap^n., will be employed under him on the Staff. H.R.H has promised it him in consequence of a book on their manoeuvres written by him.

We are at present quartered with a part of the 10 D[ragoon]s, the P[rince] of Wales Regt. You will be a little surprised at hearing that [Lt. Col. John] Hall has quitted the Regt. It was unexpected by us all, even by himself. He had written, enquiring if H.R.H. the D[uke] of Y[ork] had any objection to his quitting his present situation and if H.R.H. would grant him the com[man]d of a recruiting district - on which the Com[mander]-in-Chief gazetted him on the ½ pay of the 20th Regt. - and Hall must now depend on promises when a vacancy offers. I find that the 10 senior Cap^{ns}. will remain with the 1st Batt[alio]n. This is a new arrangement, and is one of the objections to my getting on the Staff. The man appointed to the command of the R.W.F. is nam'd Losack. He is in the A[dujan]t Gen[era]l's Department for the W[estern] District with G[eorge] Mackenzie who has given me a very favourable report of him. G.M. immediately goes to Wrexham to join the Hd Qrs of the 2nd Battn.

I do not understand the letter you copied for me. Calvert not the D. of York objects - this is plain from what I have already heard and for this part "if you see no objections to its delivery request the favour of you to forward the original likewise enclosed etc." - Yet still if you remark he says in the commencement "I have the C. in Chief's objections to enclose" etc. It is signed Calvert – the part underlined cannot belong to the same letter. I imagine [given] Calvert objecting, no good can come from forwarding applications when Calvert has an answer ready cut and dried, we must be content, s[ine] die. There is an idea of giving us 12 shillings a day, £7 extra, in lieu of coals and candles, the expense to government will be scarcely any thing extra, only paying in cash, not in kind.

Friday – I have not heard any thing more by this day's post.

I remain yours
J Hill

The chance of a staff posting near home was unpromising, but Jack had not given up on seeing his brother before William returned to sea. William's next ship was to be the sloop HMS *Inspector*, which was nearby; Jack thought a little pretence might be in order.

Bletchington
Wednesday 12 December 1804

My Dear Mother,

Persuade William to send in a sick certificate that it is necessary for him to go through a course of physic for his eye - A Genl. Leave of absence is come out. I cannot now say if 'twill come to me - I think [if] I can borrow six weeks we may yet meet. You shall hear more in a few days. The Inspector is arriv'd from a cruise at Yar[mou]th. The order is not yet come to us. I am the third, I do not know how many will go.

I remain yours
J Hill

The two brothers did not manage to contrive a rendezvous; regimental records confirm that Jack did not go on Christmas leave of absence. There is no record that William applied for sick leave; he probably preferred to return to sea than start badly with his new captain.

Two weeks later, Jack was still musing to his father about his prospects, speculating about the future of his colleagues, and speculating about a pay rise.

Bletchington Bks,
Dec.ʳ 31 1804

My Dear Father,

I will sell my Mare as you wish the first opportunity. The frost now setting in as it now does prevents any one thinking of a horse, in about a month or so I imagine I shall dispose of her. The Inspector has not yet sail'd. I have not heard from Wm. lately. I heard of Capn. Mitchel lately he is spoken very well of - "a fine young man".

Offley I imagine will very shortly be provided for out of the Regt. – unless the Duke should imagine he has almost promoted enough of our Cap^{ns}. Offley, Abercrombie, Sutton are talked of as being within 3 years to be provided for at the very farthest. The two first I should imagine will [promote] directly.

You might have seen in the papers a Capn. Shawe of our Regt. being very active in taking up some deserters in sum more than 200, he is still going on with his plans for their apprehension and they will not allow him to join us as he wishes. He talks of getting promotion for it - he is below me - I fear he will be on the London Staff and cut me out - when Offley's promotion comes out I intend making another application provided this Shawe has join'd.

I have lately got a few steps among the Capns.- Pearson has a Majority in the Regt. he was Lt. next me. Unless the expedition should require a very large number of men I do not think we shall go - they can muster 20,000 before us, we shall soon have far more than double that number in a short time disposable. We find this a dismal Q[uarte]rs. The Barracks so cold that in my room I have been forced to put up my tent as a screen. No shooting, no riding, from one tile fire which we generally have to ourselves, except every third day when we are tied by the by, having only 3 Cap^{ns} with the Reg^t. We have been this day picking out the Non-Com^d. officers for the 2nd Bat^n. to proceed immediately to Wales. I understand the parishes intend paying the money. This will be issued again for the recruiting of the army by its own officers.

They talk of increasing the pay of the army now the same as in Ld. [Sonne's ?] time. The Pri[mary?] party will vote for it. Pitt pledged himself in 94 to take into consideration of the higher ranks when they increased the Sub[altern]s. Many things in that short time are nearly double. Boots then in Exeter £1-7- 0s now in London are [£]2-12-0. I wrote Caroline a few days since, There is nothing new in this Q[uarte]r. The politicks of Europe appear completely wrapped in mystery.

A large expedition preparing. You remarked the 3 Rgt^s. embarked in Ireland for the W. Indies were suddenly ordered to disembark. Portugal or Swedish Pomerania I think in case of a continental war will be the theatre. Remember to give my love and Comp[limen]ts to all your Xmas parties.

I remain yours most dutifully.
J Hill

Jack's assessment of the promotion chances of his fellow captains, presumably based on talk in the officers' mess, were pretty accurate.

Offley would make major in May 1806; Abercrombie would join the 81st Foot as a major in July 1806; Sutton got his majority in April 1807. All three were ahead of Jack on the regimental captains list. As for 'Shawe', this was Richard Shaw, who did not gain either a promotion nor a staff post and soon returned to 1/23rd. As he speculated to his father, while Jack and thousands of British troops continued to look in anticipation across the Channel, the Pitt Government had resolved no longer to await Napoleon's next move - though at least for now neither Portugal nor Swedish Pomerania would be the target.

CHAPTER 6

BACK TO ACTION

'Hanover during the winter. Copenhagen,
wounded in mistake by our own men.'

Memorandum to the Duke of York, 1823

1805 was a momentous year for Europe, the war and one of the
Hill's sons, but not for Jack. For most of it he remained on invasion
watch on the south coast of England, although in April he finally got
his wish to lead a recruiting party to the west country. Accompanied by
2nd lieutenant Samuel Corfield and Private George Taylor from his
company, Jack was based in Dorchester. A successful recruitment effort
was boosted by several volunteers from the militia who Jack rode to
collect from Berry Head, diverting to Hennock on the way.

Tavistock,
May 5th, [1805] Sunday[1]

Dear Mother,

At going from you on Monday last I found on my arrival at
Berry Head that there was [a] party for us who had volunteered
from the 1st Wilts without any officer to take charge of them, by
which means we lost many; however, we have secured 12 which
now makes our number more than 100. This morning we have
received a route to march into Exeter on Wednesday next, then to
receive farther orders. If you can contrive it, better meet me there. I
have no idea how long we may be detained and better send in my
portmanteau from Hennock provided it is come up from B[erry]
Head; [we can put] the things that are to go into it in yours, and
then we can pack all up.

Having been shut up in this place the greater part of the week,
I know nothing that has been going on at B[erry] H[ead] or at the

---

1 This letter has no year, but 5 May was a Sunday in 1805; the content fits with
that date.

Reg^t. On coming I made application for a route to take the men and put them under Farmers charge. I expect that the parties will meet at Exeter instead of B[erry] H[ead] which will save some days' march. I should imagine we shall be in tolerably early on Wednesday; I shall perhaps get in before the party to report to Simcoe. I have been much annoyed at being detained here, but it could not be prevented - I am the senior officer. I wish they could have given a discretionary route. I should then have marched through Moreton where there would have been plenty of accommodation for 70 men. I am almost afraid I shall not be enabled to steal out to Hennock again.

I remain yours,
J. HILL

The fort and barracks at Berry Head, completed in 1802, protected the important anchorage of Tor Bay (as it was then spelt). Hennock was just a short detour from Jack's route there. Moreton (Moretonhampstead) was in 1805 on the main road from Tavistock to Exeter; if Jack had been able to march his recruits as he wanted, he could readily have called in to Hennock again.

The strategic shape of 1805 was set when Britain persuaded other European nations to resume the fight against Napoleonic France, starting with Russia in April. In part enraged by Napoleon's decision to crown himself King of Italy, the Austrians and Swedes then also committed to renewed war with France; the 3rd Coalition was born. Britain's contribution was again largely financial and naval, though the army would eventually play its role. At the start of the year, however, the question remained whether Napoleon would invade. 1805 was when he arguably came closest. He still needed French control of the Channel for long enough to leap what he considered 'a mere ditch', but the amount of time he wanted shortened as he berated and beseeched his naval commanders to act. By August he was pleading for just 24 hours.

Napoleon had two significant fleets available, of twenty-one ships of the line at Brest and eleven at Toulon, with smaller numbers also in the West Indies, Rochefort and Texel. Combining these fleets with Spain's in Ferrol, Cadiz and Cartagena could potentially generate sixty ships of the line, supported by significant numbers of frigates and smaller vessels. The Royal Navy could at that point probably only generate around fifty-five ships of the line from stations around British and European coastlines. Napoleon envisaged a naval version of his doctrine of concentrating force to overmatch an opponent. To keep the British guessing, misinformation was spread suggesting he might return to Egypt, land in Sicily or elsewhere in the Mediterranean, or attack either the British Caribbean or Ireland. But fleets could not manoeuvre as armies did: winds and tides did not obey anyone's orders.

Natural problems were compounded by the Royal Navy playing a game of naval cat and mouse, directed by the Admiralty. The proximity of Brest to the Channel, with secure anchorages where a large fleet could assemble, meant with westerly winds a fleet from there could quickly render the support that Napoleon needed off Boulogne. Brest was therefore closely blockaded. Off Toulon and Cadiz however, the British maintained an 'open' blockade, deliberately keeping their main force further out, hoping for a breakout attempt resulting in the French and Spanish fleets being caught and defeated. Maintaining either type of blockade was tough. Ships were at sea for months, communications entirely by line of sight, and if an escaping fleet avoided detection, it might not be found again for weeks. But the blockades worked sufficiently well that there was only one major escape. In March 1805, Admiral Pierre-Charles Villeneuve's Toulon fleet evaded Nelson, who was positioned to protect the Italian islands and eastern Mediterranean, by sailing west. Villeneuve's orders were to collect the Spanish from Cartagena and Cadiz, cross to the West Indies and join with the French fleet there. He was then to re-cross the Atlantic, break the British blockades of Ferrol and Brest, freeing the ships there and sailing triumphantly to Boulogne, where Napoleon was waiting with the *Armée d'Angleterre*. Ideally, this odyssey would drag part of the Royal Navy across the Atlantic in chase, improving the odds that the massed Franco/Spanish fleet could fight its way up the Channel. It looked complicated enough on paper; the reality was worse. When Villeneuve reached Martinique in May he discovered the French West Indies fleet, with which he was supposed to rendezvous, had already sailed for Rochefort. He also learned Nelson was in pursuit; that was part of the plan, but Nelson had sailed faster and was already near Barbados. Napoleon had ordered Villeneuve to avoid fighting, as his primary objective was to retain sufficient force to control the Channel. Unwilling to risk a confrontation in the wrong place, Villeneuve therefore turned back across the Atlantic. By chance, his fleet was spotted by a frigate sent home by Nelson to report on his position and intentions, which gave the Admiralty time for countermoves. A British fleet deployed west of Cape Finisterre; on 22 July Villeneuve's Franco/Spanish fleet of twenty ships of the line met fifteen under British Vice Admiral Sir Robert Calder. The action was tactically indecisive, with both sides severely hampered by fog, but it was the moment Napoleon's invasion plans began to die. Villeneuve headed to Vigo for repairs. Briefly emerging again in August, he tried to unite with the Rochefort fleet, but the two missed each other. Concerned that he would be outnumbered if he tried to reach the Channel, Villeneuve turned south and sailed to Cadiz. It was the safe move - by then Nelson had returned from the West Indies and joined with the Channel fleet; perhaps forty British ships would have been waiting for Villeneuve had he pressed on. Even if Villeneuve had beaten them - and the difficulty of that would be demonstrated less than 3 months later - the chances that afterwards his force would remain sufficient to guard an invasion are slim.

Villeneuve's decision to sail away from the Channel despite a raft of increasingly pressing messages from his Emperor was the death knell for Napoleon's plans to invade Britain. But they had come very close to enactment. At the beginning of August, Napoleon was at Boulogne with his assembly ports stuffed with invasion craft. 90,000-plus men had their orders and had rehearsed embarkation plans, which could reputedly be completed in as little as two hours. Everything was ready. But neither Villeneuve's nor any other French fleet could reach him, and in practice none seriously tried, hampered by an inability to combine and unwillingness to confront their opponents at less than full strength.

The 3rd Coalition was now beginning to stir, with the Russians and Austrians threatening eastern France. Unable to ignore this and unable to force his navy to the Channel through willpower alone, on 25 August the Emperor gave his invasion force a new name, a new mission and new orders. They began to march south-east heading, ultimately, for a small town in what is now the Czech Republic called Austerlitz. Napoleon stayed on the Channel coast for a while to help disguise his army's movements but soon followed. The next time he saw the English coastline, he was off the coast of Devon, under vastly different circumstances.

With the march of the renamed *Grande Armée* into central Europe, the war's focus returned to the heart of the continent. As Jack predicted in late 1804, the British government now sought to intervene militarily on the European mainland, but the next expedition would not be to Swedish Pomerania or Portugal and the 23rd would participate. The expedition he and his father had speculated about was initially sent to Malta, with a view to the defence of Sicily. With the invasion threat lifted, however, the British focus returned to northern Europe; specifically, Hanover. Britain's ties to Hanover included the Royal Family and the King's German Legion. Initially comprised of German citizens who enlisted for Britain after Hanover's surrender to France in 1803, the KGL was an important part of Britain's army: some 14,000 men providing five regiments of cavalry, ten battalions of infantry and six batteries of artillery. With Napoleon now heading for Austria, the opportunity to reconquer Hanover in cooperation with Russia and perhaps Sweden seemed a realistic goal. Prussia too might be persuaded to side with the Allies rather than maintaining its delicate neutrality, veering between cooperation with Napoleon and with his enemies. Freed from defending England, the British army now represented a well-trained 'disposable force' for expeditionary missions. Some 11,000 men embarked at short notice for the Elbe, with more intended to follow. The KGL was a large element, ready to fight for their homeland. The rest of the initial force comprised the Brigade of Guards, the 95th Rifles and Major-General Edward Paget's brigade of the 4th, 14th and 23rd Foot.

In October 1/23rd marched to Ramsgate via Deal and embarked. The short notice move meant there was no time to even draft in reinforcements from 2/23rd, though the 1st Battalion was already 726 strong. There was insufficient room on the transports for all officers to take horses, which would instead be bought locally after landing. This caused a problem for Jack. Having dithered about whether to sell or keep his mare, he now had to dispose of her rapidly; potential buyers of course knew this. By the time he found a better solution he had been prevented from marching with his battalion; when he caught up, the troops were already embarked, and the weather was too bad to join them. Returning to Deal, he collected supplies and awaited better conditions.

Deal, [2]7th Oct 1805[2]

Dear Mother,

I this morning received yours of the 24th. I have had a great deal of trouble about my horse, and have endeavoured to sell her for half her value with the bridle and saddle, but immediately as I said I would take [£]20 which was offered, they said no. There's [£]17 if you chose to take as they had progressively gone down in this kind of way, endeavouring to detain me till I should be almost obliged the give her away.

I had this morning determined to ask you for Charles, considering the expence of fetching as her purchase money as she was of no value here. I fortunately at last found out that the London waggoner would take her up, deliver her to Rupert's people who are to give her to Uncle Pinhey. Had I discover'd this before we went to Ramsgate, I should have sav'd myself a great deal of trouble and anxiety. The bridle and saddle I take with

---

2 In the original transcripts this letter is dated 7 October 1804. Yet it describes the embarkation for the Weser expedition, so must have been written in 1805. The letter must have been written after 24 October, as it references one of that date. The correct date of the letter is 27 October 1805 - the following day was Monday, as Jack states.

me – you have her with a halter only, and are to pay her keep from tomorrow (<u>Monday</u>) this may amount to not more than £4.0.0.

We are embark'd on board transports. Bury, Dalmer, etc., with myself are on board the Laurel. I was obliged to ride round from Ramsgate to this place and now it blows so very hard that there can be no communication with the poor fellows on board. Officers have nothing to eat as we were to take in our stock at this place - I shall carry off a leg of mutton and some bread to them when possible.

You must pay the keep of the horse which is on the road on receiving her. I will repay you I hope. I think she will carry you very well, not now too fiery. Let me know what you intend doing with her. I owe Ireland for a regimental coat. I will pay him when they give me the £2.10.0. for embarking. This is all I owe in the world, I believe, except some five-shilling accts. in the Regt.

Sutton of ours has join'd from the Staff. Abercrombie did, but return'd when Moore was order' d to go. I know not what Cortlandt is to do. Offley is in Newfoundland still. Jenkings of the 11th D[ragoon]s has my seal chain and medal, he is coming into Devon and will deliver it to someone or other.[3] You remember our meeting them at Tiverton some time ago. I am quite ashamed of myself. I have been marching and riding from daylight till very late for four days in the same clothes and now my unfortunate old regimental coat is out at the elbows.

There is good news from the Continent. I will write you once again before we sail.

    I remain yours,
    J. HILL

Aboard ship, army officers usually provided their own food, or 'sea stock', which Jack needed to acquire. Private soldiers were fed while at sea, but in the bureaucratic way of the army, a deduction from pay covered the cost; a different amount was deducted for food provided while deployed on land. Regimental pay records preserve all this detail, through a note added by the Regimental Agent which reads:

Those men from whom a deduction of 13s/10½d is made appear to have been on board ship 27 Days at a Deduction of 6d a day,

---

3 Thomas Jenkins, Jack's former Blundell's schoolmate, whose regiment had been camped near the 23rd at Eastbourne (see Chapter 4). The medal is presumably that from the Egyptian campaign of 1801 - the only one Jack had received at this point.

3 Days on the Continent at 1½d a day & 1 Day on Shore in England at full pay.

Those from whom 14/3d is deducted 28 Days on Board Ship, 2 Days on the Continent and 1 Day on Shore in England

Those from whom 15/- is deducted appear to have been 30 Days on Board Ship & 1 Day on Shore in England[4]

Inevitably poor weather meant the first transports only reach Cuxhaven on 17 November. The fleet's route was close to Ameland; perhaps Jack spotted it as they passed. We do not know his feelings about another rough passage across the sea that nearly drowned him six years before; his letter above is the only one of his that survives from this period and few contemporary accounts survive from this expedition. One contemporary did not receive any mail after he left, commenting 'I am not surprised at it. About three letters have been received by the whole regiment since we have been out'.[5] Mail to and from Britain was routinely lost in a complex postal system and atrocious North Sea conditions. After landing, the 23rd endured 'a severe and fatiguing march' before camping on the banks of the Weser about a day's march outside Bremen.[6] The terrain reminded veterans of the Helder: low-lying, waterlogged soil cut by drainage ditches and difficult marching. An officer who came the same way weeks later told his sister 'our march to this place was really an undertaking. It is not sloppy mud, but a sort of clay...I was often in danger of leaving my boots behind me.[7]

The 'good news from the Continent' Jack mentioned in his letter from Deal was a report that the King of Prussia had agreed Russian troops could cross his territory, rather than to sail to Hanover, speeding their arrival in theatre. *The Times* called this a 'mortal offence to the vindictive *Corsican*'.[8] Even better news soon arrived. While the army were crossing the North Sea, William Hill and the Royal Navy were engaged in the most significant battle in their history. On 4 November Lieutenant John Lapenotiere, Devonian commander of HMS *Pickle*, landed at Falmouth carrying despatches reporting victory off Cape Trafalgar on 21 October. After a breakneck 37-hour journey Lapenotiere

---

4 TNA WO 12/3969 *Regimental General Muster books and Pay Lists, 23rd Foot, 1805*

5 *Letters and Journals of Field Marshal Sir William Maynard Gomm, G.C.B.* Francis Culling Carr-Gomm (ed) 1881. Gomm, of the 9th Foot, wrote this after his regiment returned home.

6 Broughton-Mainwaring, *Historical Record* and Cary and McCance, *Regimental Records*

7 Gomm, *Letters*

8 *The Times* Issue number 6561, Saturday, October 26, 1805

arrived at the Admiralty at 1am on 6 November. The next day newspapers printed the report of Vice Admiral Cuthbert Collingwood, his first words noting not the battle outcome, but 'The ever-to-be-lamented death of Vice Admiral Lord Viscount Nelson, who, in the late conflict with the enemy, fell in the hour of victory'. *The Times* devoted almost its entire front page to the despatches, nudging to a single left-hand column the advertisements normally featured, for things like the display of 'Gerrard Dow's celebrated PICTURE of the DOUBLE SURPRISE' at the National Gallery; a fine mare to be sold at auction for 40 guineas (underlining the poor offer Jack had for his); a reward for the finding of a lost, half blind old Pointer dog called Basto; and, by poignant coincidence, the publication of a new full-length painting of Nelson by John Hoppner commissioned by the Prince of Wales.[9]

Trafalgar brought both national celebration and sorrow; Nelson was the nation's hero. Like Abercrombie, he fell in the hour of his greatest achievement, but as Collingwood added ominously 'such a battle could not be fought without sustaining a great loss of men…I fear the numbers that have fallen will be found very great, when the returns come to me'. For the Hill family, this meant anxiety about William, now junior lieutenant in HMS *Achille*, a 74-gun ship of the line. John and Margaret Hill waited for the lists of casualties to be published; killed or wounded officers were always named individually. *Achille* was in Collingwood's line during the battle and attacked four separate ships, the Spanish *Montañés* and *Argonauta*, then her French namesake *Achille* and finally the *Berwick*. Despite the close-range intensity of these fights, HMS *Achille* suffered relatively light casualties: one midshipman and twelve other ranks killed, fifty-nine wounded. William was completely unharmed. After the battle, HMS *Achille* carried French prisoners to Plymouth, to be incarcerated in hulks or, later, in the newly built Dartmoor prison. William must have taken the opportunity of being close to Hennock to see his family, no doubt greatly relieved he was unscathed.

Tucked into the edition of *The Times* reporting Trafalgar was also a report that French troops in Hanover were now besieged in Hameln. The recapture of Hanover and the liberation of Holland was excitedly forecast, based on 'this satisfactory information' which was 'in too authentic a shape to admit of any doubt'. The paper also, however,

---

9 *The Times* Issue number 6572, Thursday, November 7, 1805. Dutch artist Gerrit Dou's '*The Double Surprise*' depicts 'a young maid being caught by an elderly man in the act of drinking some wine from a barrel in a wine-cellar, the man holding a candle and placing his arm around the girl's shoulder; at the same time an elderly woman walks in the basement and sees her husband with the young girl'. https://www.britishmuseum.org

carried news that undermined its forecast; noting with incredulity the surrender, on the day of Trafalgar, of Austrian General Mack to Napoleon who, through a series of rapid manoeuvres, surrounded him at Ulm. Almost Mack's entire army was captured either at Ulm or as the French approached. From the Channel coast Napoleon had marched his army across Europe, crossed the Danube and effectively eliminated an Austrian force of some 60,000 men with barely a fight, and the 'vindictive *Corsican*' was not yet finished.

Back on the Weser, the Prussians were nowhere near as decisive as *The Times* suggested. Partly to encourage them, in early December a second wave of some 12,000 British troops was sent, the entire force now under the command of Lieutenant-General Lord William Cathcart. Cathcart was due to be appointed as ambassador-extraordinary to the Russian and Prussian courts, but his diplomatic skills would be tested by seeking to launch a military campaign alongside their troops. The British second wave suffered a far worse journey than the first; some transports were driven back by storms and hundreds of men were lost in shipwrecks. By the time Cathcart and the survivors arrived, events to the south had undermined their prospects. After Ulm, Napoleon captured Vienna, then lured the remaining Austrians and their Russian allies, around 85,000 men in total, into battle. On 2 December, he comprehensively defeated them at Austerlitz, knocking Austria out of the war and sending the Russians rapidly back to their own country. Prussia havered, terrified by the prospect of a triumphant Napoleon swinging north to attack them. With the 3rd Coalition crumbling around him, Cathcart's position became untenable. He concentrated his forces, removing the KGL and two British battalions from Hameln, where they had been assisting a Russian siege: a few small skirmishes there were the only action any British units saw during the entire campaign. The Russians concluded a local armistice with the French, effectively ending their participation in the operation. The British were now on a politico-strategic hook. If they withdrew, the Prussians and Russians would blame them for ending the Coalition; but the British force was largely useless without allies and vulnerable should French attention turn towards Hanover. London passed the buck, giving Cathcart full discretion to act as circumstances dictated: stay if it were safe, or leave if his army was at risk.

With no fighting and little marching, Jack and the rest of the army were relatively comfortable: 'the people are subject to the King, and therefore well disposed to us...Provisions of every description are cheaper than in England' said one officer.[10] The winter weather

---

10 Gomm, *Letters*

was, however, cold enough for Cathcart to be concerned about the rivers freezing and impairing his escape. When it turned less cold, everything thawed to mud. The British moved inland to occupy Bremen, while also preparing contingency plans to depart. Jack and the 23rd were stationed at places the regimental records call 'Ostendon, Lisajenhonjen and Hasted, with its headquarters at Leesam near Bremen.'[11] They were close to the old battlefield of Minden where in 1759 the 23rd alongside other British regiments attacked and broke lines of French cavalry to win the day; infantry successfully attacking cavalry is close to if not unique in the annals of warfare. To be a 'Minden Regiment' was significant; Jack and his colleagues surely found an opportunity to visit the battlefield.

By mid-January, Prussian preference to do a deal with Napoleon, not fight him, was clear. The collapse of the 3rd Coalition, which had taken so long to construct took a toll on British Prime Minister William Pitt, who had worked himself to exhaustion. Within weeks, he was dead. Britain had lost two of its major figures of the age, Nelson and Pitt, within 3 months. Pitt's successor, William Grenville, issued orders to bring the British troops home from the Weser. By now they totalled some 25,000 men, the KGL having spent their time profitably recruiting fellow Hanoverians. The 23rd stayed in position until 13 February, then marched back to Cuxhaven and embarked for home on the 15th. They reported a strength on departure of 746 men; an oddity of the Hanover campaign is that, like the KGL, the 23rd were stronger when they left than when they arrived.

The Hanover (or Weser) expedition was a major effort for the British army. Of the many expeditions Jack had by now participated in it was the second largest, after the 36,000 deployed to the Helder. It far outstripped the Egypt (15,000) and Ferrol (13,000) expeditions, let alone the Ostend raid (1,400). Only 15,000 British troops would deploy to Portugal in 1808 at the start of British involvement in what would become known (in their country) as the Peninsular War. While the latter was subsequently reinforced, there were plans to do so with the Hanover campaign, had it succeeded. The British force spent three months encamped on foreign soil, potentially posing a significant threat to the northern boundaries of the French empire. Or at least they could have if their allies had been more single-minded and co-operated. The campaign was also notable for having amongst its leaders some of the military personalities who would become key figures in later enterprises, including one Major-General Sir Arthur Wellesley who, after finding

---

11 'Leesam' is presumably Leese, on the Weser about 45 miles beyond Bremen towards Hanover, while 'Hasted' is Haste, about 20 miles further on. Cary and McCance, *Regimental Records*

fame in India was serving in only his second European campaign. Yet the expedition receives little mention in many histories. The two early official histories of the 23rd devote just one or two paragraphs to it, while two later ones include a paragraph and half a sentence, respectively. It is barely mentioned in many works on the period, and not at all in most. The exception is Fortescue, who devotes 10 pages to the campaign, mainly relating its complex international context. While noting that the British government of the day 'argued that the expedition to the Weser might simultaneously answer a number of ends' - encouraging the Prussians to join the 3rd Coalition, securing Hanover, recovering Holland and enabling significant recruitment to the KGL - Fortescue concludes that the whole effort was 'an egregious farce'.[12] He had the advantage of hindsight, however, and his conclusions reflect how the campaign turned out, rather than fairly assessing what it could have achieved. Histories should certainly reflect as best they can what happened, but not at the price of assuming those who did the planning at the time had knowledge learned only afterwards. Ultimately, perhaps the main reason for the lack of coverage of the Hanover expedition is, as another author succinctly put it: 'It is not unnatural that the expedition should be so little known...it had no fighting'.[13] Yet military operations are not all about battles, the Napoleonic Wars not excepted. Napoleon's capture of Mack's army at Ulm is hailed by military experts *because* it was achieved with almost no combat. To be fair, that campaign was a major strategic success while the 3rd Coalition's contemporaneous effort in Hanover was the exact opposite; undermined indeed by Napoleon's success in Central Europe, at Ulm and Austerlitz. Perhaps the whole affair is best summed up by two American authors who almost 200 years later wrote:

> the Allies' diversionary operations had trailed miserably away. The French had evacuated Hanover, except for a few garrisoned towns. Prussia, which had long lusted for Hanover, immediately occupied it. Gustavus IV, the insane King of Sweden, withdrew his contingent in anger over Prussian interference. The British largely confined their activity to enlisting Hanoverians - which incensed the Prussians. The Russians came late and proved useless. The French Garrisons held out.[14]

---

12 Fortescue, *History* Vol. V
13 *Gleanings From the Cathcart MSS Part V – The Younger Pitt's Last Venture: The Expedition to Hanover, 1805-1806. Journal of the Society for Army Historical Research Vol. 30 No. 121*. C. T. Atkinson 1952
14 *A Military History and Atlas of the Napoleonic Wars* Brigadier General Vincent J. Esposito and Colonel John R. Elting Revised Edition 1999

Or, as a another put it, Cathcart's army 'had enlisted a few hundred recruits for the King's German Legion, they had offended the King of Prussia, but they had not caused Napoleon a moment's worry'.[15]

The Hanover expedition was also a dress rehearsal for one just over a year later, with the same size force, same overall commander and many of the same personalities and regiments, though next time there would be no allies, which probably helped foster success. Before that, however, 1/23rd sailed from Cuxhaven for Harwich. They were based at nearby Woodbridge for the next three months, then in June moved to Colchester. The barracks there was built in 1794 after petitions from local innkeepers, on whom the burden of accommodating troops waiting to embark at Harwich previously fell. The barracks had been progressively expanded and when Jack arrived in June 1805 it could accommodate over 7,000 men and 400 horses. The battalion stayed at Colchester for a year. They were a core part of Britain's 'striking' force, which could comprise as many as two divisions of cavalry, almost 10,000 strong, four battalions of Guards and up to forty line regiments, perhaps another 40,000, plus artillery and support arms. A small force by continental standards, it was at the same time too large to be deployed simultaneously as insufficient transport was available. Still, the generation of an army of this size since the lows of ten years earlier was a clear success.

The soldiers were also learning the realities of campaigning and combat, even if some lessons came the hard way. By summer 1806, Jack was one of a core group of younger but experienced officers who were beginning to replace the battalion's older guard. George Mackenzie, who had kept an eye on young Jack in the early days, retired that May; Francis Offley purchased Mackenzie's majority in the 2nd Battalion. Thomas Bury, who was there when Jack first joined, retired about a year later, while George Bradford, who had enticed Jack into the regiment, had transferred to the 58th in 1803 and would retire in 1810. As Jack marked ten years in the army, still less than thirty years old, he had participated in a dozen actions, five amphibious landings (three of them opposed) and three campaigns across three continents. He had survived all these largely unscathed despite close calls, including being extremely lucky to be alive after the loss of the *Valk*. Voyages to operational theatres had seen him at sea for almost a year in total, he had been a prisoner of war for nearly six months and experienced serious boredom and homesickness on the south coast of England while waiting for an opportunity to defend his homeland. That never came, but he had spent the time training his men to be ready had they been

---

15 *Wellington as Military Commander* Michael Glover 2001

needed. Jack was not untypical; their individual stories varied, but many of the officers whose names appear near Jack's in the book recording the 'Succession of Officers' of the 23rd' had been through much the same: Henry Elllis, Francis Offley, William Keith, Thomas Pearson, Jacob Van Courtlandt and Thomas Dalmer.[16] Their shared experience underpinned the effort these young officers had made to master their art, especially during their long home service while Napoleon threatened invasion. They were leaders in an increasingly effective army that was far more capable than when they joined, would over the next decade be thoroughly tested and, largely, would prove itself more than capable. As historian Rory Muir put it:

> Wellington's [later] success in the Peninsula owed much to the years 1803-5 when most of the British army was concentrated at home, and was able to train without the disruption of frequent expeditions overseas...Men, and particularly officers, gained valuable experience, and a sense of collective identity and camaraderie which extended beyond the battalion or regiment to the whole corps.[17]

Grenville's government, the so-called 'Ministry of All the Talents', built on this solid platform, further improving recruitment with short service enlistments introduced. Recruits could sign up for renewable periods of seven years, rather than life. The Militia was reduced and the Volunteer force replaced by a plan to train all eligible men every few years. In time, these measures would help generate a more reliable stream of recruits for the regulars, trained through their second battalions. For the 23rd the evidence came in February 1807 when 257 men were drafted from the 2nd Battalion to the 1st, whose strength was now close to full establishment; at almost 1,000 men by far the largest it had been since Jack joined. The regiment also shuffled its Field Officers: Evan Jones assumed command of 1/23rd from James Losack, with Henry Ellis promoted to command the 2nd Battalion; Majors Francis Offley and Thomas Pearson returned to 1/23rd with Charles Sutton and Thomas Bury succeeding them in the 2nd. Bury retired in November; his majority would normally be offered to the most senior captain, William Keith. But it was Thomas Dalmer, with a captain's commission junior to Jack's, who purchased Bury's majority. Presumably none of Keith, Jacob Van Courtlandt or Jack, all three with earlier seniority than Dalmer, could afford it (as the vacancy arose from Bury's selling out, not from a promotion or death, the rank had to be sold to provide funds as Bury's pension). Dalmer, who also had good 'interest'

---

16 TNA WO 76/218 Twenty-Third Regiment or Royal Welch Fusiliers Succession of Officers Commencing 1790. Jack is entry no. 80.
17 *Tactics and the Experience of Battle in the Age of Napoleon* Rory Muir 1998

having served on the Duke of Kent's staff in Gibraltar, could and so leapfrogged Jack in rank and in the overall promotion stakes, with consequences for both men's later careers. A disappointed Jack took leave for a few months, as he had also done in the autumn of 1806. Another transferee into 1/23rd at this time was 2nd Lieutenant Thomas Browne who would assiduously keep a journal of his overseas deployments that provides invaluable insight into life in the regiment, the campaigns that he and the 23rd participated in and the personalities and foibles of his colleagues, including Jack. But we will come to that later.

With such a force at its disposal the government wanted only somewhere to use it. Yet though of impressive scale by national standards, the British army remained too small to act directly against France without allies, who were in short supply. Austria was a spent force after Ulm and Austerlitz. Prussia, after vacillating about which side to join, ultimately summoned the courage to go to war with France, sparked in part by rumours that Napoleon had offered to restore Hanover to British rule in any peace settlement (though tentative soundings on this proved futile). Had the Prussian decision come a year earlier, they could have combined with the Russian, Swedish and British forces on or near the Weser and perhaps represented more of a challenge to the *Grand Armée* who were triumphant, but exhausted and isolated in central Europe with long lines of communication back to France. But by late 1806 those possible allies were gone and Napoleon's army was refreshed, concentrated and ready to fight again, under a leader at the height of his strategic and operational genius. The campaign of 1805 is often considered Napoleon's greatest, but that of 1806, in which he invaded Prussia, destroyed much of the Prussian army in a single day at the twin battles of Jena-Auerstadt and occupied Berlin in less than a month, runs it close.

The Austrians and Prussians had been beaten into submission and Sweden had signed an armistice with France, leaving Russia as Britain's only significant potential ally. Disputes over British financing and perceived reticence to attack the European mainland, however, soured the relationship. After destroying the Prussians, Napoleon pressed on through Poland and in February 1807 met the Russian army at Eylau. The armies fought each other to a standstill and while the stalemate punctured French momentum, it was only a temporary halt. In June Napoleon caught a Russian army 50,000 strong on the wrong side of the river at Friedland and won decisively. Unable to challenge Britain's naval supremacy after Trafalgar and unable to come to grips with the British army on land, Napoleon turned to economic warfare, imposing a Europe-wide embargo on British trade, the so-called 'Continental System'. This was cemented by the Treaties of Tilsit in July 1807, through which Russia and France were allied and Prussia was humiliated through a massive loss of territory and painful financial levies.

Britain's response to the Continental System was to blockade French ports and impose its own restrictions on trade with France, including by neutral countries. One such country was Denmark, who were seeking to walk a tightrope between France and Britain but coming under pressure from Russia to join a 'maritime league' against Britain, partly encouraged by British insistence on the right to stop, search and impound any vessel of whatever flag, if suspected of carrying goods for France. Denmark, whose territory included that of modern Norway and Iceland, was an important trading nation. Her unwillingness to comply with the Continental System offered a route for British goods into Europe. Of particular significance to both the French and British, however, was the Danish fleet which in 1807 comprised some 18 ships of the line, a similar number of frigates and sundry smaller vessels. Most were in good condition though unready for sea, being unrigged, unprovisioned and unmanned; the British government worried that Denmark's fleet could fall into French hands, either voluntarily on the part of the Danes or otherwise.

On 2 July the 23rd received orders to be ready for immediate embarkation. They marched to Harwich and two days later boarded transports ready to cross the North Sea - again as part of a force of some 25,000 men, and again under Cathcart's command. The army formed three divisions: left, right and reserve. The 23rd were brigaded with the 4th Foot, under Major-General Grosvenor, in the left division, under Lieutenant-General Sir David Baird. This time the journey was relatively easy. Thomas Browne recorded that from departure on 1 August they made landfall on the 6th, despite 'foul and scanty' winds.[18] The fleet assembled in the narrow straight between Denmark and Sweden, off Kronborg Castle. An officer recalled the scene: 'I went upon deck, and was quite surprised at the beautiful sight which met my eyes. About 400 English ships of war and transport vessels had gradually collected together, and Helsingoer and Helsingborg lay completely in view'.[19] They stayed for a week, causing a stir onshore: 'The Danes were astonished to see such a fleet of men of war and so many transports casting anchor in their harbour...During the few days the fleet remained at Elsinore, we received much attention from the Danes; little did they suspect that we should prove such bitter foes'.[20] Bored soldiers fished for mackerel, while Browne and another officer

18 *The Napoleonic War Journal of Captain Thomas Henry Browne 1807-1816* Roger N. Buckley (ed.) 1987
19 *Journal of an Officer in the King's German Legion* John Frederick Hering 1827
20 Cadell, *Narrative of the Campaigns of the Twenty-Eighth Regiment* 1835

of the 23rd rowed to Helsingborg, in Sweden, to visit the theatre. Diplomats sought to persuade the Danish government to surrender its fleet; the Danes, unsurprisingly, refused. On 15 August the fleet sailed south down the Danish coast. At about 4am on the 16th Jack, the 23rd and the main British force landed on the Zealand coast near the village of Vedbæk, about 15 miles from Copenhagen. Browne recorded the picturesque scene:

> it was a beautiful morning. The boats filled with troops, assembled alongside the respective Ships, and on a gun being fired from the Admiral and a flag hoisted at the Main, the whole pushed off at once for the shore. They kept in line as they rowed, in every tenth or twelfth boat, the colours of a regiment uncased and blowing with the breeze…When the boats touched the shore the men leaped out, and immediately formed themselves into companies, and regiments, loaded their firelocks, and fixed bayonets.[21]

This was Browne's first such landing, but veterans of the Egyptian campaign recognised the disciplined approach and rapid organisation onshore. Unlike in Egypt, and despite there being defensible ridgelines in the Royal hunting grounds between Vedbæk and Copenhagen, there was no resistance: 'We received no opposition; we only saw a few dragoons at a distance. The army advanced about four miles this evening, and that night we lay upon our arms in a barley field.'.[22] The 23rd halted in the grounds of the Charlottenlund palace where, in readiness for a Danish attack, the men lay on their arms overnight. The closer they got to the city, the more they were alert for Danish raids, with alarms called regularly, especially at night. One such alert had a significant personal impact for Jack, when in the confusion he found:

> a soldier mistaking me in the dark during an alarm, and wounding me in the right side with his bayonet.[23]

Jack had suffered his first combat wound, from his own side. The injury must have been painful and, given medical standards care of the time, potentially dangerous. He came down with a fever and was:

> confined to my bed for three weeks in consequence.[24]

---

21 Buckley, *Browne*
22 Cadell, *Narrative*
23 Hill 1816 *Statement of Services*
24 Hill 1816 *Statement of Services*; the fever is mentioned in a letter to William dated 24 July 1808 (Chapter 7)

On the 18th the 23rd moved into position a couple of miles further towards Copenhagen, with the rest of Baird's Division forming the left of the British line, resting on the sea. Copenhagen was gradually surrounded on the Zealand side, and the city called to surrender. This was not to be a conventional siege, not least because as weather gradually worsened over the coming months resupply and/or evacuation would become difficult. French or even Russian intervention could also not be ruled out. Additionally, the besieging lines did not extend to the island of Amager so the city, by far the largest in Denmark at around 100,000 inhabitants, could easily be resupplied. Diplomatic efforts simply pressed the Danish to capitulate or face attack; the Danes bravely declined. All the while the British dug artillery positions and Danish artillery and raiding parties tried to disrupt them. For the British troops close to the shore 'the greatest annoyance was from the fire of Danish Gun boats'.[25] As the weather worsened, the British moved closer: on 28 August Browne noted 'our advanced posts pushed forwards, along the whole line, and drove the enemy's picquets out of the suburbs, which we occupied, that our troops might have cover'. Jack, recovered from his fever but still waiting for his wound to heal, was unable to remain idle. He took to visiting his colleagues on the front line. Lieutenant John Harrison recalled that on 26 August 'I went with Lieut. Corfield in a wagon belonging to Capt. Hill (who came to pay us a morning visit. He accidentally received a wound soon after landing which prevented him from doing duty) to our old Quarters to procure some materials to make a hut'.[26] On 2 September one of the houses in which the 23rd were billeted caught fire. Remarkably, the Danes sent fire-fighters from Copenhagen under a flag of truce and, by pulling down the houses either side and pumping water from nearby, stopped the fire spreading, while the men of the 23rd watched admiringly. Browne noted 'I never saw so complete a security against the effects of fire, and we could not help bestow our warmest applause on this Danish fire corps when it returned to the city'. The firemen soon had greater challenges; at about 7.30pm the same day, the British bombardment began; shells and new-fangled artillery rockets rained into the city. There was no attempt to breach the city walls; this was a terror bombardment, as controversial at the time as it has been for historians since: 'the town was in a blaze; the flames spread far and wide, and communicated to that beautiful building the Freikerke; in a short time its magnificent and lofty spire was enveloped in a sheet of fire, and

25 Broughton-Mainwaring, *Historical Record*
26 RWF Archives object 7198. Letters of Col J C Harrison 23rd Foot, 1807-37. Harrison, who joined the 23rd as 2nd lieutenant in March 1805, would go on to command the regiment. Corfield, a Devonian and 2nd Lieutenant in Jack's company, joined in December 1804.

in the space of an hour, fell in with a tremendous crash, which was heard for miles around; the light that issued from the ruins completely illuminated the surrounding country'.[27] The onslaught continued for three days; during occasional pauses large numbers of civilians fled to Amanger. Danish artillery responded, causing a few casualties, including Lieutenant George Jennings of the 23rd, hit by a roundshot and killed outright.[28] On 5 September, the Danish authorities sought terms of capitulation. Rapidly agreed, the principal condition was the complete surrender of the Danish fleet; British forces would then depart entirely. British troops moved into the city, took possession of the dockyard and began readying the Danish ships to leave. Some officers meanwhile visited the town:

> In the course of a few days, when the necessary arrangements were made, and things became a little quiet, officers with passes, were allowed to go into Copenhagen. The sight was truly awful; 305 houses were burnt to the ground, and one church. The devastation and melancholy that reigned in that unfortunate city, it would require an abler pen than that of a soldier to describe. Parents were seen mourning for their children, and children for their parents. In several instances the murderous shells had forced their way into the very cellars, and destroyed mothers with their off-spring at their breasts. Many were the brave hearts in the British army that deeply sympathized with the sufferers, and would have come forward to their assistance with that liberality for which they are so proverbial: but the Danes are a proud fine people, and bore their misfortunes without a murmur.[29]

In six weeks, the dockyard work was done. Sixteen ships of the line, nine frigates, fourteen sloops and thirty-one other smaller vessels, plus all naval stores were taken across the North Sea by scratch crews of British sailors and soldiers. Not all made it, as the inevitable storm blew up and some were abandoned. On 18 October the 23rd embarked for home, though bad weather meant they did not sail until 3 days later, transported aboard the *Brunswick*, *Surveillante* and a captured Danish ship, the *Heir-Apparent Frederick*. After yet another stormy crossing of the North Sea they landed at Yarmouth and returned to Colchester barracks. By the end of October, the entire British force was on its way home. About 2,000 inhabitants of Copenhagen had been killed, mostly during the bombardment, and significant parts of the city destroyed or

---

27 Cadell, *Narrative*
28 Jennings had joined the 23rd in December 1805.
29 Cadell, *Narrative*

damaged. 'To have war in your own country', concluded John Harrison, 'is a most dreadful thing. With what cheerfulness the English ought to pay their taxes to keep them from such a burthen. I never saw such destruction. I am told that 20 thousand people are left homeless. What few houses are remaining in the suburbs are completely riddled by cannon shot.'[30] Having been neutral before the attack, the Danish government unsurprisingly now formally declared war on Britain. In response and following much criticism at home, the *London Gazette* published an extraordinary 'Declaration' in the name of the King. 'His Majesty', it said, 'owes to himself and to Europe a frank Exposition of the Motives which have dictated his late Measures in the Baltic'. Over two pages, the Declaration victim-shamed the Danes for not surrendering their fleet and for showing a tendency to sympathise with France, forcing the British to attack them. It claimed every effort had been made to acquire the Danish fleet through co-operation rather than coercion, but that ultimately 'it was Time that the Effects of that Dread which France has inspired into the Nations of the World should be counteracted by an Exertion of the power of Great Britain, called for by the Exigency of the Crisis, and proportioned to the Magnitude of the Danger.'[31] It was far from a convincing self-justification; there was condemnation in Parliament and the press. Any risk of the Danish fleet falling into French hands was, though, unquestionably now removed. Prize money was awarded to all engaged on the expedition: Browne recorded that he received £97; Jack, a more senior officer, got slightly more. Another benefit Jack did not realise at the time was he had faced his last storm-tossed crossing of the North Sea. He would not, however, have long to wait for a far lengthier voyage. Having lost the Danish fleet, Napoleon turned his attention to the only other significant naval force beyond his orders, that of Portugal. The Portuguese had also been unwilling to comply with the Continental System and with his Eastern front secure following Tilsit, Napoleon now sent 30,000 men under General Junot west through Spain (still at least nominally his ally) and invaded Portugal. By November 1807 Lisbon was captured and Napoleon was master of continental Europe.

---

30 RWF Archives object 7198
31 *The London Gazette Issue Number 16072* September 26 to September 29 1807

CHAPTER 7

ACROSS THE ATLANTIC

'North America, appointed to the Light (Rifle) Company.'

Memorandum to the Duke of York, 1823

Copenhagen was not the most challenging campaign for 1/23rd, and on returning they received a further draft from the 2nd Battalion, bringing their strength to over 1,000 for the first time during the war. With the 4th, 7th and 28th Foot also based in comfortable Colchester, garrison activities such as guarding were shared between the regiments. Browne recorded 'we had little to do, as the weather was too wet & cold for drills, and the garrison was so large, that duties were light'.[1] That was his perspective, but a reorganisation made Jack busier than most as he took command of the 23rd's Light Company. The light and grenadier companies were a regiment's elite. The 'light bobs', as they were known, were specially trained to skirmish ahead of the battalion and often employed on tasks needing greater flexibility and intelligence. On parade, the Light Company always stood on the left and the Grenadier Company the right of the battalion line; they were thus together called the 'flank' companies or 'flankers' (the others being 'battalion' companies). Jack's new role meant more work, but it was a recognised honour to command a Light Company.

With light duties and no further deployments anticipated, selected officers, plus ten men from each company were allowed leave. Jack argued his case to go, as he excitedly told his mother.

3 Decr. [1807]
Colchester

My Dear Mother,

No answer arriving to supersede the orders, I have already [given directions] to my servant. He starts tomorrow for Devon. 8

---

1 Buckley, *Browne*

days after, he arrives at Exeter with my horse. I shall follow in the coach. Ever since I landed I have been hard at work writing but fear it will require two days more here. The Thursday from this at farthest I shall commence my western tour. Don't grumble, you sad rogue. Your wishes set my wits at work and I have set aside two others who claimed it before me, this day in an assembly of the capns. I carried my point. I go from hence to town with Col. Jones; should he be detain'd by business, I shall not delay.

I calculate being in Exeter near about the time my servant will be and my time is now so short that I cannot afford to be 7 days on the road. Remember me to all at home and believe me that I cannot scarcely bring myself to eat, drink or sleep - the anticipated happiness of seeing you runs away with me. Not expecting to leave this winter, I had got plenty of business thrown on my shoulders. I have this day employ'd another clerk and hope I shall not be delay'd. The next communication I hope to have with you will be under our paternal roof at Hennock.

Believe me ever your
J. HILL

Evan Jones was travelling to London to step down from command and retire. His successor was Lieutenant-Colonel Henry Walton Ellis, who Jack had shared quarters with on the Isle of Wight and fought alongside since the Helder. When Ellis assumed command of 1/23rd he was just 25 years old, and yet an experienced veteran. He would remain battalion commander for the remainder of the Napoleonic Wars. Jack presumably finished his work in good time as he departed Colchester on 6 December, arriving in Hennock in plenty of time to catch up with friends and relations and enjoy Christmas at home. He finally had his long-sought reunion with William, who was between ships: he had left HMS *Achille* in July 1807.

World events conspired to cut Jack's leave short. In June 1807, off the Virginia coast, HMS *Leopard* encountered the United States' ship *Chesapeake*. Pursuing the Royal Navy's aggressive search for goods bound for France or deserters from British service, *Leopard's* captain asked to send a party aboard. When permission was refused, *Leopard* fired a broadside into *Chesapeake*. The US government protested strongly, imposed an embargo on trade with Britain and closed all US ports to exports. US President Thomas Jefferson wanted to avoid war, but as tensions rose the British government decided to reinforce Canada against a possible American invasion, turning again to its 'disposable force'. Consequently, on 16 January, while those officers of the 23rd still in Colchester enjoyed what Browne called a 'laughing careless life' in the mess, orders arrived stating 'The 23rd regiment will march in three divisions, to Portsmouth for embarkation, for foreign service. The 1st division will move...on 17th and the remaining divisions on the 18th and 19th...All officers and men on leave of absence, to join the regiment at Portsmouth'. The first elements were required to march next morning; as Browne put it 'the very wind, as it whistled round the corner of the mess-house, seemed to laugh at us. The mess broke up... There were about fifteen Officers and 100 men on leave of absence in all parts of England, Ireland and Wales. Letters were written, ordering them to Portsmouth immediately'.[2] One letter went by post chaise to Hennock, creating as big a surprise when it arrived as the new orders had in the mess. Fortunately, Portsmouth is almost the same distance from Hennock as from Colchester, and Jack only had to get himself there, not his entire company. Still, he had to hurry; the orders were for immediate embarkation, and he dare not miss the sailing. What he would miss was the family gathering at Ashprington for the Christening of Jacob and Caroline Ley's son John. It was frustrating timing, but he made it to Portsmouth in time; Brown recorded that when the regiment sailed not a man was missing.

Aboard the six ships allocated as transports, conditions were far from the comfort of Colchester: 'We were eight Officers and 200 men on board, besides her crew. The cabin was very small, and we slept in wooden partitions, just long enough for one, fixed one above the other. There was a table in the middle of the cabin, fastened to the floor, and round it, just room for a wooden chair, which it was necessary to move, to enable us to step into our berth. This whole cabin was the most uncomfortable that can readily be imagined'.[3] While still in Portsmouth harbour, Jack's Jonah-like luck continued: the boat carrying him out upended, tipping him into the water, then his ship caught fire, destroying some of his company's sea stock. The fire was extinguished, but anyone who knew Jack's maritime history must have been nervous to be aboard with him. By 23 February 1808 the battalion, with the 7th, 8th and 13th Regiments, General Houghton, military commander of the expedition, and Lieutenant-General Sir George Prevost, new Governor of Nova Scotia, were embarked. Accompanied by the frigate HMS *Penelope* and the sloop HMS *Banterer*, the convoy departed. After a few days of contrary winds, the fleet passed along the southern English coastline, Jack looking to spot landmarks. Their voyage, to Halifax, would take two months; Jack would not see home again for nearly seven years. Now in his brother's

---

2 Buckley, *Browne*
3 Buckley, *Browne*

environment, as the convoy approached the Azores Jack wrote to him. The frigate HMS *Undaunted* would eventually take the mail home; another opportunity to write was unlikely before they reached their destination.

20th West Longitude, 37 Latitude
24th Feb. 1808

My dear William,

From the date of this you will say we have been rather fortunate in our passage thus far considering we have had no gales nor scarcely a foul wind since we took our departure from the Lizard. We have missed one of our transports with a comp^y. & half of the B[attalio]n on board. We know not what is become of her as we have not had any bad weather; we are afraid she has been taken in the chops of the channel. The odds are that had I not been in a Flank comp^y., I might have been in her as a junior officer has the command of her. I have my mother's letter before me dated 20 days since, you were then at Caroline's. I hope the Ball went off as gay as the Christening. It was a Mrs. Ros Kelly from the N. of Devon who made the mistake between you and me. However, as a punishment we got a most confounded ducking by the boat upsetting at the mouth of Portsmouth Harbour for gossiping. I was in hopes of putting into Ply[mou]th for a few days as the wind was not very fair for us as we approached the Eddy stone. I us'd your tall glass in looking over the Devonshire hills; the clump of firs near John Edwards' caught my eye as we were off Dartmouth. I intended to have put Mr. Bounce in a state of requisition for a North American trip; as it is, we are now going out with about 12 dogs and not a shooting one among them. I have supplied myself with 150-lb. [of] shot and 12-1b. [of] powder, 300 flints, 5 scarlet jackets and one coat, Flannels and blue cloth in abundance.

In case you answer this and direct Halifax, the odds are that it will be waiting for us by the time we arrive [if] the Rochfort squadron does not get hold of us. The weather now is very fine, so that we are not so impatient for getting into the trade winds as we otherwise might be. 3 or 4 such days as this will in all human probability bring us in among them, a brig and sloop have just left us for the Azores westward about 180 miles at a rough guess. The ream of paper I bought is not of the best quality I perceive. This will serve my father to puzzle over in case of a lack of newspapers - he must get one of his sailors to explain. Say to my mother I am much obliged for her last long one giving a description of your proceedings at Ashprington.

Remember me to all and believe me yours,
J. HILL

I have not yet begun to try for the bonnitas, as I do not imagine we are sufficiently to the southward. In Portsmouth Harbour, in spite of a very large fire in our stores, we were one night forced to put on near all the clothes we could muster, now we are without fires these four days, and all the windows open. Mention in your next what weather you had soon after we left England. As we passed down the Channel, Cornwall was covered with snow, Devon did not appear to be so, which rather surprised me. I saw Dartmouth, Plymouth and Pendennis Castle. I was below and occasionally asking where we were, they said by the reckoning off Dorsetshire, so that I lost my peep at Haldon and Torbay. I was annoy'd at their stupidity in not knowing where they were, most of our fellows being colliers, they knew nothing of the western coast.

We should have run down our latitude in Madeira had there not have been some S. in the wind, but I hope we shall soon get into the Trades. We have had two very heavy swells, one yesterday which has not yet subsided. The wind has not obliged us to take a reef in our top sails. The greater part of the time we have had our top gall[an]^t set. I lament now I forgot to steal one of your Hamilton Mores and have endeavoured to suck up a little information, however, I have been so extravagant as to buy a couple of charts one of the Atlantic and another of the coast of N. America; we continue to prick off our reckoning and learn by having pirated in the Copenhagen business the conversation signals. As well as the old numeral ones, we learn from the frigates every day their communications on the day's works.[4]

You may perhaps hear from me again from Bermuda. Say how Linquo gets on and if you have succeeded in selling my mare. If you do you had better throw [the equipment] to the fund for horse flesh for the [chance] to get a good exchange.

The transport ship that had gone missing was the *Harriot*, on board which were the companies of Captains Jacob Van Courtlandt and John Leahy. The ship was slow and may simply have slipped behind, as the weather was fair. Browne only noticed the *Harriot* missing after a storm on 2 March; Jack was aware of its absence a week earlier. *Harriot* took almost six weeks longer to reach Halifax, another reason for Jack to be

---

4 John Hamilton Moore's navigation textbook *The New Practical Navigator and Daily Assistant*, first published around 1772, was the most popular work of the day on the art of navigation.

pleased he was not aboard her. 'Bonnitas' are presumably bonito, a large tuna-like fish, while the Haldon hills are a prominence south-west of Exeter (and visible from Hennock). On one of the highest points is the Haldon Obelisk, built in around 1742 as a landmark for shipping and perhaps what Jack was hoping to see.

The convoy passed the Azores on 26 and 27 February. As they did, they were approaching an important day for the 23rd Foot, whose mess rules noted it was 'the established custom of the Regiment to commemorate the first of March in honour of St. David (the tutelar Saint of Wales)':

> The custom of the corps is, that on that day, immediately after dinner, when we are in barracks, one of the little drum-boys, rides a large goat, with which the regiment is always provided, round the Mess-room, carrying in his hand a dish of Leeks. Each Officer is called upon to eat one, for which he pays the Drummer a shilling. The older Officers of the regiment, and those who have seen service with it in the field, are favoured only with a small one, and salt. Those who have before celebrated a St. David's day with the regiment, but have only seen garrison duty with it, are required to eat a larger one without salt, and those unfortunates, who for the first time, have sat at the Mess, on this their Saint's day, have presented to them the largest Leek that can be procured, and unless sickness prevent it, no respite is given, until the last tip of its green leaf is inclosed in the unwilling mouth; and day after day passes by before the smell and taste is fairly got rid of. This may be a nasty way of making a Welsh Fusileer and so it is.[5]

Being at sea on 1 March 1808 did not prevent this important custom being honoured, although on this occasion without the full glory of the normal ceremony: there was no goat (always left behind when the regiment went overseas), not enough space to gather everyone together, nor any leeks. Instead, noted Browne 'we had every thing dressed in Onions, and drank an extra glass of grog on the occasion'. St. David no doubt appreciated the effort.

Over the next three weeks the Atlantic offered stifling heat, favourable winds, dead calms and storms, the latter slightly damaging some of the transports. The officers and men amused themselves playing cards, watching birds, dolphin, flying fish and turtles, and occasionally catching some of the latter two. The officers were sometimes rowed from their own transports for collective meals aboard

---

5 Buckley, *Browne*

the *Lord Collingwood*, the headquarters ship, enjoying music from the regimental band while some of the soldiers danced until after midnight. On 21 March, HMS *Penelope* spied Bermuda; the ships carrying the 13th Foot, who were to be stationed there, sailed into port. The rest of the convoy sailed on until on 5 April, when the signal 'land discovered' was hoisted. Jack and his colleagues had learned the signal flags, so no doubt understood the good news immediately. The weather turned cold, snow and fog encumbered their progress and the last of the ships (except the *Harriot*, still some way behind) did not finally anchor in Halifax harbour until 8 April. Browne called Halifax 'a neat town containing about 5,000 inhabitants exclusive of the garrison, which is usually from one to two thousand men. The houses are of wood with few exceptions, the government house is a fine stone building, with a handsome lawn in front'. It took some days to make all the arrangements for landing, but on the 13th the troops went ashore. Or at least those who were to be based in Halifax itself did. The 23rd was to be headquartered not there but at Annapolis Royal, further around the coast on the Bay of Fundy. Before they set sail again, however, the 23rd's officers decided to host what Jack called 'a very dashing ball' for the residents of Halifax; it cost each of them £5, equivalent to almost £400 today. This may have impressed the locals, but with hindsight Browne said 'when sober reflection came over us, we could not help asking ourselves what on earth we had given it for'. Most officers then re-embarked and sailed for almost another week to the western shore of Nova Scotia, arriving on 16 April. A few days later, Jack wrote home, not overly impressed by his new surroundings.

> Annapolis Royal on the Bay of Fundy,
> Nova Scotia
> [undated, c. 20th April 1808]

My Dear Mother,

I wrote you from off the Western Islands.[6] We have been in this country some weeks, but came round from Halifax by water here last Sunday after being 5 or 6 days in the passage. The Packet has arrived at Halifax, but I have not heard from you, perhaps the letters may remain at H[alifa]x, and may yet come round.

The Barracks here are very comfortable, we have only 3 Comp^{ys}, the two flankers and one B[attalio]n. Col. Ellis commands at this post. When I hear from you I will answer all your queries.

---

6 The Azores

We have but a short time to write to save the pacquet.[7] You may say to Charles Mackellar who offered me letters of introduction to a relation of his here, that 6 months' residence in French Prisons introduced me 10 years ago to him.[8]

From what I have seen of this province it is miserable. Lustleigh-Cleave only add pines for furze.[9] The soil granite, the trees appear like the stalks in a wheat field, at this time you would not know the hard timber forest from a heath except the patches clear'd away shews you their altitude. I have been so much out of the habit of writing that I want one of your letters to shew me the way. The natives, or, rather, settlers are very civil to our Corps; we return'd it by giving them a very dashing ball at H[alifa]x. The ladies have all set to work to get us from off the outpost duty. Now that we have been at the trouble of getting here I wish they may allow us to remain to gather our crops. One having turned Cap^n. of Gardeners the other superintends the boats. Tomorrow I recommence work to finish a fishing wear that is left dry at low water which will supply our men with a very necessary reinforcement to their scanty rations of salt meat. We have been standing out and near starving ourselves because we will not pay 7d. per lb. for meat of a miserable quality. Fish is cheap as my servant bought for the mess 16 or 18 cod of 4s.6d., 21 lobsters for 3[s].6[d]. Not Price, I have dismissed him and taken a very superior one from the Lt. Infantry.

I wrote Caroline from off the Western Islands. Remember me to my Father, brothers and her. Aunt and the turkies have not so many foxes at Hennock as we have here. I have been through the Woods with a Gun and a fishing rod, the former is almost useless at this season. We can take a good dish of trout and by going in the boat allow'd by G[overnmen]t. here, can nearly fill her by going 8 miles from hence.

Yours,
J. Hill

Having told his mother he had forgotten how to write, a few months later Jack repeated this claim while asking William to forward a long message to India in support of their cousin, John Pinhey, who had enlisted as a private soldier.

---

7 Have letters ready for the transatlantic mail-boat.
8 Captain John McKellar RN was also captured at Ostend in 1798. In 1810 he was Governor of the Naval Hospital in Halifax; he would end his career as a full Admiral.
9 Lustleigh Cleave is a steep-sided wooded valley, about 4 miles west of Hennock.

12th June, 1808
Annapolis, Halifax

My dear William,

I have been so much out of the habit of receiving letters that I have nearly forgotten how to write. I heard in the last letter of your gaiety at the Christening at Ashprington, while I was at Portsmouth, not having heard since I cannot allude to any posterior occurrence. Let me know how many partridges you kill on the next 1st Sep. I may receive it by Nov. and take till next Spring to ascertain whether a packet goes or not in March and April, and in case it should, I may write you the 2nd Wednesday of May, 1809. Should I be enabled to send it by a private hand, I will as you may depend upon it the public conveyances are unsafe and letters sent that way not above one in hundred arrive safe.

I was fortunate here to purchase a boat 20 feet keel complete in sails and oars, not an iron nail in her and about 1/2 -Doz. lines for £7.17.0. When the tides or wind serve we go down to the entrance of the bason 18 miles distant and generally bring home very large quantities of fish, cod, Haddock, Halibut, Scate, Pollin, etc. I have now got a pony, 4 cats, 2 ducks but not yet a dog. I should much like to have brought out the one Mr. F. Parker gave me. There is a road running parallel with the river on whose banks all the clearances are made, the instant you get into the woods you are something like a mouse running in one of your harvest fields among the corn. Tell my father the soil is granite for the most part near the entrance a basalt, some knowing ones here took the trouble to pack up in bands near a ship load of scoria and brought it from 40 miles here. I have not been at the place but will go, great part was sent to England but producing much gold or silver the rest left here. There is one singularity in it, it has flown over a stratum of sea shells, their impressions are left very perfect the calcined substances the water, I imagine, has dissipated.

We have a Fox tame, the prettiest thing I have seen, 3 Porcupines. Our Bear has run away with a variety of other brutes comprising our menagerie. The vegetables and birds are totally different from yours, except the martin and crow. When I have got a letter of yours before me, I will write a better one than this. Remember me to all at home. I hope to hear a good report of you all, particularly Fred.

Yours,
J. HILL

William, you must copy this, enquire more about John Pinhey. Write in my name to Humphreys, surgeon, 56th Regt., India. I think while deciphering this, you will not miss the following packet.

Yours, J. HILL.

My dear Humphries,[10]
I am requested by some of my Devonshire acquaintances to write you on the subject of a man belonging, I believe, belonging [sic] to your 2nd Bn. He enlisted --- his name ---. In case he should have behaved well and is a corporal or sergeant by his own good conduct, I wish you to inform me what his general conduct has been, etc., etc.

We are, you perceive by the date of this in N. America, our 2nd Bn. in Ireland. This Bn. is scattered in a dozen different detachments. Ellis, Offley, Power and Wynne are with us here, the others you do not know.[11] Pearson is at Halifax, Jacob Cortlandt is there also and married. He has been near 3 years away on the Staff, and near that time married. Mrs. C. for the 1st time now promises to give him a son and heir to his unclear'd American property. Jones is the same. Ellis turns out a very superior officer. Offley is not quite so violent as formerly, he has turn'd a great farmer here for the mess, we have 40 sheep, Bullocks, etc.

In this quarter of the Globe, our Communications with Europe are not so frequent or regular as one might imagine. We are 150 miles from Halifax, and letters are near a fortnight in coming up sometimes, so that it is a mere chance if we succeed in saving the following Pacquet.

As is usual, the contrast between the women here and England is so great that I really think that Offley himself would marry, was there anything worth having. Fishing at present and shooting in winter with an hour and half drill before 8 every morning, is all we have to do here. We have fortunately a very good collection of French Books with us, but few English. A good band which we shall make if we do not go to the West Indies, a very capital [group]. I have ordered a lot of instruments [from] Field and Fiddles for concerts by the desire of Col. Ellis, that will make £100 or two look

10 Richard Humphrey was regimental surgeon when Jack joined the 23rd. He transferred out in 1803. Jack previously mentioned him in a letter from Malta (see Chapter 3).
11 George Power was the current regimental surgeon; he joined as Assistant Surgeon in 1801; Henry Wynne had been Adjutant since 1806.

foolish. We have now a German as master and pay him 3s. a day extra. Burgess turns out a very bad quartermaster, eternally drunk.[12] He will have to leave our 2nd Bn. Bowman is with us, his health begins to give in, he is so valuable a man that his loss would be a very severe stroke on us.[13] Wynne is the A^d. [Adjutant] of as much use as nobody. I saw Harding the other day.[14] He is again married, I believe. I have been writing George Mackenzie this day, he is also married. Dawson West has been, but I believe she did not like so much fiddling and Doctors Commons settled the affair at last.[15] Godfrey Macdonald, you know I suppose, married the woman he had at Battle, Keith saw them the other day surrounded with children of four sorts and with as great a variety of violincellos.[16] Remember me to Col. Skinner Smith.[17] J. Leary is dead.[18]

The mention of the West Indies in Jack's draft letter to Humphrey shows that rumours were circulating within weeks of the battalion's arrival in Nova Scotia. Browne confirms that 'rumours had been for some time in circulation of an intended attack against the French possessions in the West Indies, but they were repeated and contradicted so often, that we began to pay little attention to them, and perhaps the less, as there was no particular disposition in the Regiment for West Indian service'.[19] Tensions over British interruption of American

---

12 Samuel Burgess was appointed Quartermaster of 2/23rd in March 1805; he was replaced by QM George Sedley on 14 April 1808.

13 John Bowman was regimental Quartermaster Sergeant. In the 23rd's Monthly Return for September 1809 he is listed as having died on 20 August 1809. TNA WO 17/126 *Office of the Commander in Chief: Monthly Returns to the Adjutant General 23rd Foot 1806 - 1812*

14 Henry Harding rose through the ranks to Sergeant-Major and was commissioned 2nd lieutenant in October 1799. He retired and sold his commission in March 1804.

15 James Dawson West joined the 23rd just before Jack, in June 1796 as a 2nd Lieutenant. He transferred to the 60th Foot in August 1799. 'Doctors' Commons' was a body of law practitioners known parochially for dealing with 'wills, wives and wrecks'; presumably they legally resolved the West's marital problems.

16 The Hon. Godfrey MacDonald joined the 23rd in April 1797 as a Captain. He transferred to the 55th Foot as a Major in February 1802. By 1808 he had joined the 1st Foot Guards. He married Louisa Maria La Coast on 29 May 1803.

17 Philip Skinner ('Skinner Smith') joined the 23rd as a 2nd Lieutenant in 1782. In 1798 he was interred in Lille after Ostend, when senior Major in the regiment. He transferred to the 56th Foot in December 1799 as Lt. Colonel.

18 James Leary was a private in Jack's old company. He died soon after the battalion arrived in Nova Scotia.

19 Buckley, *Browne*

shipping continued to bubble, but the immediate crisis was subsiding, and thoughts turned to what could be done with the veteran battalions based in North America. Deployment to the West Indies remained unwelcome to the soldiers enjoying a healthy lifestyle of hunting, fishing and farming, interrupted only by occasional drill and inspection. Lieutenant Thomas Farmer shared Jack's opinion of the quarters at Annapolis, calling them 'the most comfortable I have yet been in'.[20] Things were inevitably not as good for the men as for the officers, though even a ranker's life was not tough for those who made the best of it. Richard Bentinck joined the 23rd as a teenager in early 1807 and became a drummer; over sixty years later, he reminisced about his experiences.[21] The recollections of an older man about events in his youth need to be read cautiously, but nonetheless offer a useful enlisted man's perspective. Bentinck recalled Nova Scotia 'was very pleasant for the men. Those of good conduct could at any time get leave to go fishing or have hunting excursions; fish swarming in the rivers and plenty of wolves, deer and rabbits in the woods to be had for the killing'. For some, however, the attraction of the American border was greater. Bentinck claimed 'many soldiers deserted. On a narrow river which divided the two territories, ferry boats were kept at certain places and the ferryman were quite as willing to take over a deserter as they would anybody else...but the punishment was terrible if he chanced to be caught'. The 23rd offered public rewards in the local newspaper for any deserters returned.[22]

When the mail packet finally arrived with letters from home, Jack wasted little time in replying.

[4th] July, 1808
Annapolis Royal, North America

My Dear William,

It is with some pleasure that I have at last the pleasure of answering a letter from Hennock, yours of the 24th April came to hand about the last day of June. The transport of ours that was missing has at last arriv'd safe at Halifax, I have not heard any reason assigned for her parting convoy.

My letter dated in F[ebruar]y was cruising with the Undaunted off the Western Isles for a month before it began to steer N.E. I am

---

20 RWF Archives object 5257b. Letters of Capt. Thomas Farmer
21 Jonathan Crook [ed.] *The Very Thing: The Memoirs of Drummer Richard Bentinck, Royal Welch Fusiliers 1807 - 1823*. 2011
22 Fix Bayonets! A Royal Welch Fusilier At War 1796 – 1815 Donald E. Graves 2006

very sorry to hear that the surgeons made so bad a setting and cure of Mr. Linquo's leg. In my last letter I gave you the heads of one that you must write Mr. Humphries, surgeon of the 56th 1st Bn. in India respecting J. Pinhey, also enquire if he is enlisted for 7 years or life, if his conduct has been such as to get him made a Non-Com[missione]d officer and in case it has, whether any interest at home would be useful to get him a Commission in some of the Native Corps, send it to James Wilmot. I fear he is in the 2nd, Humphries in the 1st Bn.

As we are situated on the banks of a fine river, our boats are in the greatest requisition. I am now tired of giving fish away and have lain my hands on the salt from the pork casks and am filling them with cod to see how many I can scrape together before I distribute them. The weather some short time ago was very warm, so much as to confine us at the middle of the day. Lately I do not think it has been at all disagreeably so. All the birds at this season have gone and hid themselves in the woods to lay. I understand in a short time we shall have plenty of plovers, partridges and ducks, etc. Tell the mineralogist there would be nothing new in seeing the productions of this part, but to the botanist this would be a greater treat; the rarity here is to find anything like English vegetables, the strawberry, rasberry and gooseberry grow wild here, the former in some situations as would astonish you completely superseding the necessity of a garden.

I shall endeavour to make a collection of the seeds of the timber and shrubs here and send them home. I am in hopes that you may procure some good spaniel from Linquo. I have sent home for a Bugle in a double capacity useful either against the partridges or any other more formidable enemies. We are now learning the military calls so that discovering an enemy or a partridge may be the same. Keeping a reconing [sic] in the woods with a pocket compass is rather more perplexing than I thought it would be at first. I found this out going into a ravine N.E., having to return S.W. we were near a mile out when we came back to the river. The object was to procure ice which is lodged there all the year round in which we did not succeed, we must next time hire a guide and blaze the trees with a hatchet to find it out again.

From your not mentioning Caroline I imagine everything is right in that quarter. With respect to the mare, you suspect her wind.[23] I did also within a few weeks I had her, in consequence of her not being able to keep at speed for any length of time, she never

---

23 Breathing!

would do it, either her own violence or her own fleetness winded her, particularly if there was the least ascent. In riding down hill hard you must take care, her spirit will induce her to undertake it and her feet fail her.

Remember me to Caroline when you write her. Ley, the little ones and ladies you must not forget. Should any of the troops leave this part of the world, I think we will remain from our being so detached.

4th July
Remember me to all, yours,
J. HILL

Receiving mail from home was always welcome, though delays and misdirections were frustrating. Meanwhile some took advantage of free labour by soldiers to work the land.

Annapolis
24th July, 1808

My Dear Mother,

The letter you wrote a few days after William I did not receive till a fortnight later in consequence of its having been mis-sent into the other province and from thence had to come back again. I wrote my brother about a fortnight since. I know not what pacquet this may go by, perhaps the same or it may remain a month nearly at Halifax. We have not yet rec'd the pacquet that leaves your country at the commencement of June. We are of course asking every week if the mail from England has arriv'd, and in case of none scarcely take the trouble to go to the post office. I was rather surprised last post day to see your writing, till I saw by the post mark where it had been rambling.

The politicks in this part of the world are that we are not to have an American war. How this will affect our destination I know not, but I hope it will not take us out of this part of the world. The next arrival from England will say what Regts. stay here. Sir G. Prevost has delayed his tour round the provinces till the next arrival from England. From the reports we have receiv'd here of Bonaparte's insolence to the Americans, we imagine the American Government will not be so hasty in their future proceedings with us, but still there are many serious objects to be considered before a final arrangement is made, as I hope our Government will concede nothing except in the affair of the Chesapeak.

This climate at this season is very warm and at the same time very damp. We have had several cases of agues. I have not had any symptoms of it. I have taken care as I did get it in Zealand for a fortnight. Flannel is highly necessary as rheumatisms are very common, none very severe as yet. We have had a great deal of heavy rain. The potatoes and grass are very fine. Wheat they import or, rather, flour from the States. Rye and maize thrive best here, barley is not frequent. A man up this river has lost a very large tract of barley by the grasshoppers, about 4 having attached themselves to each ear, and have left nothing but the beard remaining. You cannot at this season go into the woods, the flies bite so very severely, the musquito is not half so bad as two or three other sorts. We are extremely comfortable here among ourselves, I am afraid they will not allow us to remain so, I do not wish to change just yet - and then for Canada.

The Burringtons were talking of their having some grants of land in this part of the world, if they will point out the province and other particulars, I will make enquiries in the registrar courts. Some late laws and acts of parliament have been severe on people who have not improved the lands allotted them. Now the grants are small and in case in 5 years you have not a certain portion clear'd and in ten a log-house and so many head of cattle, it reverts to the crown. Offley, Ellis, and Thornhill amongst them have purchased a small farm of about 16 acres for £110.[24] There is now hay and a nursery [worth] about £35 on it. The manure from the Fort and labour from the soldiers who are employ'd now in making proper fences will make it a valuable tract. You cannot get people to work for you here, when by making an application they may get 50 acres for themselves and with prudence render themselves independent; labour is on an average 6 (six) shillings a day, to hire a man constantly, often two dollars for a short job.

Remember me to Caroline when you write, with love to all of you at home.

I remain yours,
J. HILL

Jack would get his wish to stay in Nova Scotia, but only for a few months. By the time he next wrote home he was in Halifax and the battalion was making ready to embark.

---

24 Edward Thornhill joined the 23rd as a 2nd Lieutenant on 17 April 1806. He transferred to the 45th Foot as a Captain in February 1810.

23rd October, 1808
Halifax, N.S.

My Dear Mother,

We still continue in this part of the world, everything is ready for our removal at three days' notice. Of course we are full of speculation but cannot divine what may be our future destination. I think my last replied to your kind enquiries and I believe I have answered them all. I have not heard from you since writing the last and consequently shall not make any comment. Now I want you to get some books for me to which I have subscribed, the first the narrative of Mr. Whitelock's business. I have paid George Mackenzie for this last Decr.

The next I have not paid for, but you must put yourself to the expense. Poems by Felicia Dorothea Browne printed at Liverpool by Harrison. I think the latter will please you; her two brothers are Lieut^s. in the Regt. I was of course obliged to put my name down for 10 or 12 shillings, they have turned up trumps, being infinitely superior to Mrs. Bayfield; indeed, I have not looked at them for more than five minutes and like them.

The last pacquet brought me a letter from Caroline I have now so little to say that I think it scarcely worth while to put her to the expense of postage to tell her I am well and often think of you all.

I shall constantly keep £50 by me to be in readiness to go to Europe should peace or any opportunity occur of again traversing the Atlantic. We have been very busy since we have been in this garrison. Every exertion has been made and the troops are in very high order. I should miss the opportunity should I write any longer, we have nothing new in this part of the world.

I am obliged to finish during dinner writing under the table not to allow the president to see me.

Remember me to all.
Yours,
J. HILL

The book Jack subscribed to through George MacKenzie was 'A Narrative of the Expedition to, and the storming of Buenos Ayres, by the British Army, Commanded by Lieutenant-General Whitelock' by 'An Officer Attached to the Expedition'. Published in London the previous year, the narrative claimed to be 'without any flourishing or prolix declamation on the calamities of war, the effects of courage, or the pursuit of wealth and fame'. Jack had both professional and personal interest in the disastrous expedition, having been under Whitelock's command in Portsmouth in 1803. The other book was the just-published first collection of works by Felicia Dorothea Browne. Browne, who became Mrs. Hemans after marrying in 1812, would produce another 18 books during her lifetime and was highly regarded by her contemporaries Shelley and Wordsworth. Her patriotic poems on political and military affairs were particularly popular. She is largely forgotten today, except for the opening line of her most famous work, the poem *Casabianca*, published in 1826. Casabianca was the name of the captain of *L'Orient*, the French flagship at the battle of the Nile; he and his 12-year-old son Giocante, who was aboard, died when the ship exploded. Its (now much parodied) first line is 'The boy stood on the burning deck...'.[25]

The battalion was brought to fighting pitch through drilling and exercising in Halifax. The light company was issued with rifles; probably Baker rifles, the British army's specialist light infantry weapon. Rifles had a spiral-grooved barrel that spun the bullet for greater accuracy. A rifle was slower to load than a smooth-bore musket, but it was ideal for the skirmishing role of Jack's light company. Riflemen often fought in pairs, in extended order with yards between each pair. A rifle-armed soldier would select his target and aim at it carefully. Picking off officers, or enemy artillerymen, was often a key task. They had more scope for individual initiative, which in turn made the role of a rifle company officer more challenging. When fighting in line, as in a battalion company, men stood shoulder to shoulder and command and control was a relatively straightforward process of giving orders that NCOs ensured were fulfilled. In extended line this was infeasible, as the length of a skirmish line impaired voice communication, especially in the din of battle. An officer therefore had to move constantly amongst his men, who would be trained also to respond to commands from a bugle or whistle. This is why, aside from its use while hunting partridge, Jack sent for a bugle in July; bugle calls carry further and different calls can signal different orders. Being a Light Company officer was hard and dangerous work. One recalled 'it is really hard work to make them preserve their proper extended order, cover themselves, and not throw away their fire; and in the performance of this duty, an officer is, I think far more exposed than in line fighting'.[26] Training his company to use their new weapons effectively, and other preparations for embarkation, made this the busiest time Jack had since he arrived in Canada. The reason for the effort soon became clear.

---

25 *Fugitive Poems* by Mrs. Bayfield, which Jack considered inferior work to Felicia Browne's, was published in 1805.
26 *Recollections of the Peninsula* Moyle Sherer 1824

'*your Humble Servant*': Lieutenant Colonel John Humphrey
Edward Hill CB, Royal Welch Fusiliers

'the mineralogist':
The Reverend John Hill,
Vicar of Hennock

*'The English Churches are mere Barns when
compared with the magnificent edifices
dedicated to the supreme Being...in
Valetta.'* St. Mary's Church, Hennock, Devon

*'Mr K gave me a knife for keeping the boys so well in house during
Easter':* Blundell's School, Tiverton as it looked when Jack attended
(Reproduced by kind permission of Blundell's School)

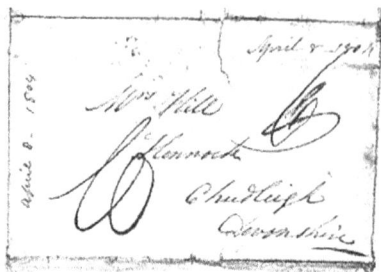

'Mrs Hill, Hennock, Chudleigh, Devon'.
The address on one of Jack's letters

'My Dear Mother'. One of Jack's many letters home

'Twenty-four saved out of near five hundred men, women and children on board': The unveiling of the memorial to the loss of the *Valk*, Ameland 10 November 1999. Lieutenant Edward Hill RWF, Jack Hill's great-great-great-grandson salutes *(Ed Hill)*

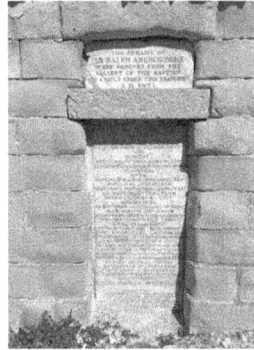

'Under Sir Ralph Abercrombie, and landed in Abukir Bay'. The tomb of Sir Ralph Abercrombie in the baston of Fort St. Elmo, Valletta, Malta

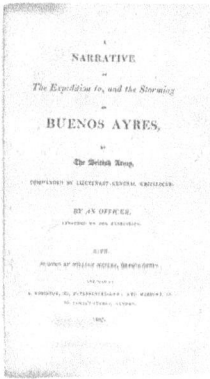

'Now I want you to get some books for me to which I have subscribed': Two books requested from home by Jack during his time in Nova Scotia

'the lustre of the capture of Martinique the prisoners and eagles sent home': The Eagle of the 82nd Ligne Regiment, captured after the attack on Martinique *(RWF Museum)*

CHAPTER 8

EXPEDITIONS AND EAGLES

'West Indies with the Advanced guard on the heights of Serrurier and at the final capture of Martinique.'

Memorandum to the Duke of York, 1823

While professing their enjoyment of comfortable lives, the officers of the 23rd were wearying of their backwoods posting. There were tinges of jealousy when news arrived that their second battalion, supposedly a recruiting and training unit for them, had been sent on operations. Yet an expedition to the disease-ridden Caribbean was probably not considered the ideal way to defeat the ennui.

Halifax, 29th Nov., 1808

My Dear Mother,

We are embarking at this place to sail in a few days on a West India Expedition. Sir G. Prevost goes with us; it is imagined we shall return here in the spring, as the heavy stores and one Captain are left behind. Many are the speculations. Martinique, Cayenne, and the City of St. Domingo are mentioned; however, the object of attack is a profound secret, perhaps wishing to keep our neighbours on their guard and put them to expense. They [the Americans] really have been flattering themselves that Europe could not do without them, but have now found England has not given them much satisfaction and that France has not condescended to pay any attention to them, things remain in much the same state as when we came here. They are gradually increasing their militia, and tell us they would turn us out of this country and the Canadas in two months. A body of troops has been collected at the Barbadoes which we are to join, the Spaniards have collected some troops at Porto Rio, this looks like St. Domingo. Sir J. Craig does not like [that] the Province should be left with only one small regular Regt. The 7, 8 and 23 are to return, the 13th remains in the West Indies, should the American business not be settled we shall be back here by the time the frost goes away, winter they think will in the meantime keep this part secure.

You omitted writing me by the last packet, which sailed in October from England, this is of more importance than you first imagined, as the chances are we shall not hear of you again till April. They have given the Regt. 100 Rifles, this has taken up a great deal of my time and money, we have been extremely busy since we came from Annapolis, what with one thing and another, I have had very little time to myself.

I saw by the last papers our 2nd Battn. is in Spain, we at one time thought they were in the West Indies. I am happy to see by the appointment of a corps of Cavalry, they are not likely to be there. We shall be kept afloat to act on any point North of the line.[1]

I have sent you some seeds collected. I shall get this sent by the mail and hope you will get it safe. I am extremely busy and can only add remember me to all.

Yours,
J. HILL.

I will write again in a few days. Carne assisted me in packing the seeds.[2]

After suppressing Portugal Napoleon had forced the abdication of the King of Spain, installing his brother Joseph on the Spanish throne. On Dos de Mayo (2 May) 1808, the Spanish population revolted; what Napoleon was to call his 'Spanish ulcer' began to irritate him. The British Government saw an opportunity to intervene in support. With several of their best regiments, including the 23rd, on the wrong side of the Atlantic, a new expeditionary force largely drawn from units based in Ireland was placed under the command of Lieutenant-General Sir Arthur Wellesley and sent to Portugal. After winning battles at Roliça and Vimeiro, Wellesley was superseded in command by Sir Hew Dalrymple and Sir Harry Burrard. Burrard had recent active experience, having like Jack been imprisoned in Lille after Ostend and participated in the Helder and Copenhagen campaigns; Dalrymple was a good diplomat but had seen no action since 1793. Neither were stellar soldiers. Following Wellesley's victories, Dalrymple promptly agreed the Convention of Cintra with Junot, allowing the French army, its equipment and a good deal of Portuguese loot to be taken back to

---

1 the Equator.
2 This may be the same Carne mentioned in Jack's letter of 11 January1804. From the content of this and other letters the Carnes were clearly acquaintances of the Hills; Carne was also Fred Hill's middle name.

France - by the Royal Navy. A Russian fleet in Lisbon harbour was also allowed to depart, despite Russia and Britain being at war. The granting of such generous terms to a defeated French army was met with disbelief in Britain. Dalrymple and Burrard were recalled, Wellesley returned to Ireland and all three faced an inquiry. Wellesley was ultimately absolved; Dalrymple and Burrard never again saw active service. Meanwhile Sir John Moore took over command of the British troops in Iberia and reinforcements, including 2/23rd, were sent to Coruña. By October Moore was advancing into the interior of Spain. Unfortunately, so was Napoleon who took personal command of a significantly reinforced French army and quickly destroyed the Spanish forces Moore had been sent to support, leaving Moore and his army isolated and facing a far greater challenge than either he or his government had expected. Moore was forced into a long and arduous winter retreat to Coruña, with the French army on their heels.

Back in Halifax, the convoy carrying Sir George Prevost, the men of the 7th, 8th and 23rd and a detachment of artillery, was ready to depart. Most remained unsure of their destination but were sure that the plan was ultimately to return to Halifax; Jack's guess that they might be back in April was to prove remarkably accurate. The clue was as he noted: their heavy stores were not going on the expedition. The battalion also left 110 men, whom Browne called 'the weakly men of the Regiment', under the command of Captain Jacob Van Cortlandt, supported by 'Lieutenant Griffith who was an old and infirm Subaltern, and Lieut. Treeve, who was only just recovered from a severe indisposition'.[3] The West Indies had its health risks, but there was one significant advantage to going there: they would miss wintering in Halifax. The convoy waited until 6 December for favourable winds, then started south. A few days out Jonah Jack struck again when they encountered heavy gales. The ship Browne was in was struck by lightning; he and more than a dozen others on deck were knocked down, with one soldier killed outright. On the 21st the fleet crossed the Tropic of Cancer, accompanied by ceremonies with sailors dressed as Neptune, Christmas Day at sea saw fine weather, dancing and singing and on 29 December they anchored in Carlisle Bay, Barbados. Vendors from the island immediately surrounded the ships offering fruit, beer and milk for sail. The contrast between the crystal-clear waters and palm-fringed tropical island in front of them with 'the rugged and leafless shores of North America' was striking.[4] As was the medical

---

3 Buckley, *Browne*. Thomas Griffith joined the 23rd in May 1805. Treeve joined in July 1805.
4 Buckley, *Browne*

staff's imposition of strict rules to reduce exposure to the risk of disease, heat stroke and other menaces. Ellis toured each of the ships in turn to lend his authority to the doctor's orders: the men were to go ashore only once a day, just before daybreak, to bathe in an area of sea fenced off from sharks. They then would return to the ships and stay there until the exercise was repeated the next morning.

Officers had more liberty but were told to avoid going out during the hottest part of the day and 'the damp of evening'. Like high-spirited young men throughout history, these cautions they promptly ignored, with 'the hottest sun of noon-day' according to Browne being routinely when the officers went ashore. In the evenings, they frequented a hostelry called Nancy Clarke's for dinner and plenty of drink, then repaired to other hotels for dancing (possibly a euphemism for other nocturnal activity). They still didn't take the hint when Nancy herself offered to show Browne 'plenty of 23rd' in the local cemetery, the legacy of the regiment's postings in the 1790s. Within a week of their arrival, one of Jack's junior Light Company officers, Lieutenant Samuel Corfield, 'a fine healthy, active young man', became ill suddenly and died.[5] Corfield, a married man from Somerset, was 26 - just four years younger than Jack. The next day Lieutenant Robert Hall also became sick and was rapidly shipped off to Nevis, where he had relatives. He fortunately recovered, rejoining the battalion in September 1809, travelling via New York to Halifax on the Packet ship.[6] Two of their number falling ill in quick succession, said Browne, 'recalled us a little to ourselves, and prudence for a short time'.[7] But their behaviour did not completely change and next to fall sick and die were a Captain and a Lieutenant from the artillery. The message sunk in more clearly now and the officers resolved to behave themselves for the rest of their stay in Barbados, though they couldn't resist an occasional visit to Nancy Clarke's and throwing at least one formal ball. While awaiting the arrival of the 13th Foot, last seen when dropped off in Bermuda the previous year, it became clear their target was Martinique. It was hardly a significant objective, but there was strategic merit in capturing Martinique, Guadeloupe, and the few smaller last French West Indian possessions. If French presence in the Caribbean was eliminated and conflict with the USA avoided, thousands of British troops could be brought home as reinforcements for Europe.

---

5 Buckley, *Browne*

6 Corfield, a Devonian, joined the 23rd in December 1804 as a 2nd Lieutenant. Hall joined in January 1806, also as a 2nd Lieutenant. TNA WO12/3972 *Regimental General Muster books and Pay Lists, 23rd Foot, 1808 & 1809* details his absence and return. His health may never fully have recovered as he retired in April 1811.

7 Buckley, *Browne*

During celebrations for the King's birthday on 18 January, the announcement to embark was made. The British force of more than 12,000 men was perhaps twice the number of French regulars and militia holding Martinique. The 23rd were assigned to a 'Fusilier brigade', under Brigadier General Daniel Hoghton, with the 7th Foot (the Royal Fusiliers) and the 1st West India Regiment. On 28 January, Prevost's force sailed; it was a short trip, and just two days later the troops were being landed on the French island. The plan was for a two-pronged attack. A first division, over 6,000 men with the 23rd amongst them, landed at Baie Robert on the north-eastern coast. They were to advance inland, approaching the island's capital, Fort Royal (now Fort-de-France), from the north. A second division under Major-General Sir Thomas Maitland sailed to the west coast, threatening the capital from the south. Landing unopposed, Hoghton's men marched overnight across the island. It was another tough trek for Jack and his fellow soldiers, over steep hills. Artillery horses had to be left behind; they were unfit to be used so soon after coming off their transports. The guns were instead man-handled along 'roads [which] were in such wretched condition from the rains that it was one o'clock in the morning ere they accomplished a distance of five miles'.[8]

The next day, 1 February, they met their first resistance as they approach Morne Bruneau, a mountain in the centre of the island. Jack's rifle company had a key role in overcoming it. Hoghton reported:

the Column was scarcely in Motion before a considerable Body of the Enemy's Regular Forces...was discovered very advantageously posted on the Declivity of a Hill, with the River Monsieur in their Front, and One or Two Field Pieces on their left. Having reconnoitered [sic] their Position, I determined to attack them, although the Light Artillery attached to the Brigade could not be brought up. The Honourable Lieutenant-Colonel Pakenham, with the Rifle Company and Grenadiers of the 7th and the Rifle Company of the 23rd, was directed to turn the Right, and Major Campbell with the Light Battalion the Left of the Enemy's Position, whilst I proceeded to attack them in Front with the Battalion companies of the 7th, and the Grenadiers of the 1st West India. The result proved in every Respect such as was to be expected from the Bravery and Discipline of the Troops which I had the Honour to have placed under my Command. The Enemy were driven back from every Part of their Position with considerable loss, and retired in the greatest Disorder'.[9]

8 Broughton-Mainwaring, *Historical Record*
9 *The London Gazette* Number 16240 Saturday March 25 to Tuesday March 28, 1809

Hoghton's tactics were well considered and worked quickly. The accuracy of fire from the rifles of Jack's company and those of the 7th on the French flank must have been galling. The French were unable to respond effectively with their shorter-ranged and less accurate smoothbore muskets. The pass gained, Pakenham's force pushed on towards the heights beyond, another steep hill called Morne Surey.[10] The main body of the 23rd, in two wings under Ellis and Pearson, came up in support. They found another strong French force but, said Hoghton, 'Notwithstanding such formidable Obstacles, Lieutenant-Colonel Pakenham, seconded by the Exertions of Lieutenant-Colonel Ellis, Majors Pearson and Offley of the 23rd, and the determined Bravery of the whole Detachment, after repeated Attacks, at length, by a very spirited Charge, compelled the Enemy to take shelter under the cover of their Redoubts, and established his position on the Heights'. Taking this high ground was vital; it was just over two miles from the main strongpoint on the island, Fort Desaix, which protected the capital. As light faded, the officers and men of the 23rd made fires, cooked their provisions, and settled down for an uncomfortable night amongst the sugar cane, being soaked by rain. On 2 February, the redoubts the French had withdrawn into needed to be cleared. Pakenham tried with the 7th but had to fall back after an expensive assault. Ellis was asked if the 23rd could do the job, to which he reputedly replied 'I will take the flints out of their firelocks and they shall take them.'[11] Wiser councils prevailed, however, and the assault was paused to see if the French intended to hold their ground. They did not, withdrawing overnight into Fort Desaix itself.

There was no need to attempt to assault the fort itself, which was now surrounded. Over the next week or so, heavy artillery came up and batteries were constructed. Artillery fire from the fort and some skirmishing continued, in which Jack's riflemen again proved invaluable. The French also launched occasional sorties to try to disrupt work on the British batteries. On the 13th, the British had the novel experience of a couple of minor earthquakes, not infrequent on the volcanic island. On 19 February the British bombardment began. The French held out for five days under fire from over 40 British cannon until on

---

10 English-speakers had difficulty with the name of this hill. It was variously spelled as Surrurier (by Jack in his 1816 *Statement of Services*), Sourriré (Browne in his Journal), Surrarië (23rd Foot monthly returns), Surirey (Prevost and Hoghton official reports), Sourier (Fortescue, *History*) and even Sowrier (on the plaque placed in St. Georges church in Halifax, N.S. in memory of a corporal and two privates of the 23rd Grenadier company killed during the assault). Morne Surey is its spelling on modern maps.

11 Broughton-Mainwaring, *Historical Record*

24 February they surrendered unconditionally. The next day the 7th and 23rd marched into the fort and formally took possession; the King's Colour of the 23rd was raised on the ramparts. Browne recorded 'the inside of the work presented a shocking spectacle of ruins, and blood, and half buried bodies, and was literally ploughed up, by the shells we had thrown into it'.[12] Damage to the roof of the fort's powder magazine was apparently significant in the decision to surrender, for another shell landing on it would blow the place apart. Aside from the fort, garrison, and island another significant prize was won as the defeated French 28ème and 82ème Ligne were required to hand over their Imperial Eagles - the first the British had ever captured. The symbolic equivalent of a British regiment's Colours, Eagles were sacred, handed to each unit by Napoleon. Sent home and laid before the Prince Regent, they were displayed in St. Paul's Cathedral and then the Royal Hospital, Chelsea. Over 100 years later they were formally presented to the 7th and the 23rd. That of the 82ème Ligne is now displayed in the Royal Welch Fusiliers Museum, Caernarfon.

Trophies were valuable, as was Martinique, which remained in British hands until 1814, but there was a cost. Total British losses were around 100 killed and 400 wounded or missing; French casualties may have approached 1000, plus the capture of their entire garrison. Some 155 French officers and 5,000 men were transported to France for exchange. They seemed happy to have survived and be leaving their pestilential post. Browne recorded that they 'were seen laughing and singing & dancing on the decks...we could hardly refrain from envying their happy frivolity'.[13] Their joy dampened, however, when on arrival off France Napoleon refused to exchange any British prisoners; the Martinique captives were therefore taken to Britain, where most were destined to spend the rest of the war, the officers on parole in towns around the country (including Tiverton, where the first French prisoners had arrived in 1797, the year after Jack left Blundell's), the men on prison hulks in places like Plymouth and Portsmouth.[14] Some were almost certainly sent to Dartmoor prison, constructed specifically to take prisoners captured during the Napoleonic Wars, which received its first inmates in May 1809. They are unlikely to have appreciated it, but they saw Devon well before Jack would again.

Official records show the 23rd had twenty men killed, with 100 men plus Surgeon George Power and Lieutenant Thomas Roskelly wounded.[15] This is inaccurate, however, as Browne's journal records

12 Buckley, *Browne*
13 Buckley, *Browne*
14 *Prisoners of War in Britain 1756 to 1815* Francis Abell 1914
15 Roskelly joined as a 2nd Lieutenant in July 1807.

that he was wounded in the week before the surrender by a musket ball through his left arm which put him in the field hospital and nearly caused the limb to be amputated (Browne claimed he persuaded the surgeon not to operate because he was learning the flute!). Thomas Pearson was also injured, hit in the leg by a piece of canister. The wound was not serious but was enough to remove him from duty for the rest of the campaign.[16] Sickness also took a toll. Between 1 and 27 February, the field hospital in Martinique recorded its admissions from the 23rd as eighty-eight from gunshot wounds, nine from fevers, forty-four from 'fluxes' and three other casualties. Fifty-two of these had been discharged cured while six had died (five of wounds, one of flux); the rest were still in hospital at the time of the return. The regiment's monthly muster showed a total of 736 private soldiers present, with 104 sick and twenty-three dead; the total for all ranks was 975. It had been a lightning campaign; the final despatch noted 'the enemy capitulated on the night of the 24th...in twenty-seven days from the period of our departure from Barbados'.[17] The battle honour 'Martinique' was eventually awarded to the regiment; after Egypt the second such honour Jack had played his part in winning.[18]

Guadeloupe and some other small islands were still to be captured, but the 23rd re-embarked and set sail for Halifax with the rest of Prevost's division on 9 March. In relatively calm sea, the fleet anchored off St. Kitts to replenish supplies. The garrison on St. Kitts was provided by the 25th Foot, who Browne described as 'old friends of ours'; they invited the 23rd's officers ashore for dinner in the regimental mess.[19] Browne noted 'the meeting of two old Regiments who had seen hard service together, was not likely to take place without copious libations to Bacchus, and this meeting was certainly one of the most distinguished of the description. It was followed up by a similar invitation for the next day, which was also accepted, and celebrated pretty much in the same manner'.[20] The frivolity was costly: disease began to spread through the battalion, and several died before the ships weighed anchor

16 Graves, *Fix Bayonets!*

17 *The Capture of Martinique, 1809* W Y Carman. Journal of the Society for Army Historical Research Vol. 20, No. 77 (Spring 1941)

18 The honour was not formally awarded until 1816. It was later amended to read 'Martinique 1809', to distinguish it from actions there in 1762 and 1794.

19 The 25th were in the Helder in 1799 and in Egypt in 1801. They had spent much of their time since in the West Indies, inevitably suffering severely from losses to disease. Their flank companies had participated in the capture of Martinique.

20 Buckley, *Browne*

again on 21 March with some twenty-five more lost on the voyage north. The next day they paused again off the Virgin Islands and many took advantage of the packet from St. Thomas to write home, though unfortunately for his family and for us, Jack's letter did not make it. On the 25th, having left the West Indies behind, a sail was spotted; signal exchanges proved it friendly. The ship brought news of the disastrous retreat to Coruña, the battle there and the death of Moore. After the triumph of Martinique, the mood turned gloomy. The 23rd had fought alongside Moore in Holland and under him in Egypt; he led Jack and his men up the sand-hills at Aboukir Bay and through the testing battles of the advance to Alexandria. Like Nelson and Abercrombie, Moore died a hero at the moment of victory, as his army held off the French long enough to embark in transports and escape. The officers of 1/23rd wondered how well the 2nd Battalion had fared. The retreat to Coruña had been hard, over freezing mountains and there were bound to be casualties.[21]

The Atlantic weather matched the gloom. On 7 April a tremendous storm damaged numerous ships. Continuing north, decreasing temperatures finished off some of the sick. Offloading the most poorly in Bermuda was considered, but Prevost ordered the fleet on. Browne, on the hospital ship, thought 'many valuable lives were undoubtedly lost' by the decision.[22] On the 12th they spotted the coast of Nova Scotia, but thick fog and foul winds prevented them entering harbour until the 16th. There they learned they had missed the worst winter the town had seen in 20 years; the sick they had left behind had suffered accordingly. The battalions were, however, welcomed back as conquering heroes. The Nova Scotia Assembly passed a Resolution granting 200 guineas for a sword or piece of plate to be presented to Sir George Prevost 'as a Testimony of the High Opinion entertained by the House of His Excellency's Conduct at the Capture of the Island of Martinique from the French'. The officers and men of the regiments would eventually be awarded prize money; in 1813 Jack received £25. The 23rd enjoyed the social side of returning, but the unit was in a poor state. As the surgeons worked to help the sick and wounded recover and the healthy settled back into their quarters, Jack caught up with mail that arrived after he left.

---

21 Moore's army of around 16,000 men suffered more than 1,500 casualties, and over 5,000 sick. 2/23rd escaped relatively lightly, though still lost over 200 men in the campaign, mostly from illness or capture. They provided a rearguard during the embarkation, being the last unit to leave Coruña. Captain Thomas Fletcher locked the town gates as he left and took the keys with him, which are now exhibited in the RWF Museum, Caernarfon.

22 Buckley, *Browne*

My Dear Mother,

I received on my return here a letter partly written by you and my father, and also one from William. I was much gratified with both, but particularly with the very long one. There were some questions proposed for my answering, but I have misplaced the letter and cannot at present recollect. Do repeat them in your next. My writing desk I recovered, my seal and chain never.[23] Some doubts were entertained as to the correction [sic] of my statements as to the fossils I have seen here. I call'd again to mind what I asserted and am convinced I am not mistaken.[24]

You will of course receive my communications from Martinique and the other West India islands, and I will resume from the period when I wrote you last off St. Thomas.[25] Our passage on the whole was good, but we had one of the most severe squalls and three days' thunder and lightning I ever in my life beheld. We were 3 days off this coast before we got in which was on the 16th of this month, we are at present in the town and have very comfortable apartments. It is at present proposed that we take the outpost duty again in July, but I am afraid we shall not go again to Annapolis. As you know, I am not much an admirer of garrisons. The state of our Regt. at present is deplorable, the dysentery or a complaint something like it has got among the men and we have 320 sick, the Expedition has cost us near 70 men buried since we left this last winter. The sick we brought back either very shortly died or recovered, the principle [sic] part which have fallen ill since, in my opinion have caught it by infection, not, as some of the wiseacres say, owing to new rum bought in Halifax. My company never were so sober. I do not think, and the Sergeants tell me the same, that [more than] five have been drunk since we landed, and that, under the temptation of having it for nothing, as every one tried who should give them drink, the people being so glad to see us back again. The men themselves are cow'd, it has not as yet cost us any lives, but our men are so much reduc'd that it will take some time to get a healthy appearance in their faces again.

---

23 Presumably the items sent home with Thomas Jenkins before the Hanover expedition. These must have reached Hennock, as they included Jack's Egyptian medal, which is today in the RWF Museum.

24 See letter from Annapolis of 12 June 1808.

25 Unfortunately, these letters did not make it home, as Jack will explain later.

People are rather mistaken if they imagine we have escaped a winter, in fact, we have experienced two, at this moment a N.E. is blowing a gale, and I cannot venture to put my nose out a-doors, the bason above the Harbour is still frozen over in parts, the lakes are still covered with ice. Here we come, from a sun within 14 degrees of being vertical to very severe frost. I know not which was the most perplexing, but I think going into heat. I am, thank God, very well, but a few of the officers are unwell, only one has fallen sick since we have returned, but 20 of my men have. The increase of the sick occasioned by the rapid transition was from 90, including our wounded, except 30 left in the West Indies, to 320. Thus you see how this Bn. is frittered away.

Boulderson is expected from New York. Wm. Carne is much grown, Grassie, who is one of the partners, I understand wishes to be introduced to me. Wm. C. has dined with us about a dozen of times, and has never committed any excess, he has often breakfasted with me and Thornhill. Grassie has, I think, taken offence at this, wherefore I know not, as if he is not pleased with Carne, I know not where he will get a better, or whether he does not wish him there least Mr. Carne should come into the same markets with their house, I know not, but certainly should he have the delicacy to say to me I do not think it proper Carne should come and see me (three or four times at farthest since I landed). I shall certainly give him up the possession of my rooms after thanking him for the compliment he has paid me, and I think he has given one solitary dinner to William, who boards and lodges somewhere in the town. Grassie called or, rather, left his card twice with Bromley the Pay Master, and has ridiculously made apologies for not asking him to dinner.[26]

The Military rules are now so extended that they completely form a society of themselves. I know no one of the town. Grassie said to Bromley he could not call, but wished to be introduced as he had something to say to me, this was at the Ball given by the Inhabitants to Sir George, and the three Regts. etc., etc. returned from the Expedition. I had din'd at Government House and came in among the suite of the big ones. This civility does not originate from any of Mr. Parker's letters as one of his staff with whom I have been in the habit of fishing in the harbour would perhaps have hinted.[27] The first dinner he gave was to the field [officers] the

---

26 Walter Bromley enlisted as a boy soldier and was appointed Quartermaster in Jun 1800. He had become Paymaster of 1/23rd in May 1807.

27 This may be Benjamin Parker, who came to Nova Scotia after US independence and became a prominent merchant figure in the town of Liverpool, down the coast from Halifax.

next to the flank officers of the Regts. [He] gave yesterday a superb dinner to the navy, the field officers of the other two Regts. [plus] Cortlandt and myself of the 23rd. Pearson, I believe, had some unpleasing correspondence with him last year, while we were at Annapolis, this accounts for his shyness to them.

I hope the lustre of the capture of Martinique the prisoners and eagles sent home, will counter-balance the 1st Spanish Campaign. The transport still continuing attached to our troops, the reports of the Continental war spreading, make us look with impatience for the dispatches from Europe, but I think if they wait till they receive a report of the present state of our Battalion, they must then see the necessity of giving us a few months' repose. Anything except the West Indies. They told me in the West Indies that Wm. was made Master and Comm[ande]r. I fear you will not be enabled to confirm this good news.

The American affairs are settled, we expect to leave this [posting], and that some young Regt. will do the Garrison duty of this place. This has altogether altered my plans, I shall keep in constant readiness to move, I should not be surprised if we were in August next in Plymouth or Falmouth. This, of course, depends on our European news. It will determine whether we are to go into another quarter of the Globe to seek enemies, or peaceably sit down in the North American Garrisons.

I am really too lazy to write to Caroline; since I commenced my letter I have got a cold in my head and am too stupid to do anything. Boulderson and Carne dine with me. This is Thursday, the packet sails Saturday evening, 6th May. Remember me to all at home and also to Wm., Caroline and Fred when you write them. I think I shall write Wm. tomorrow, but I do not know the station of the ship.

Believe me ever yours most sincerely,
J. HILL

The most westerly large port in Britain, Falmouth was home of the Government packet service since 1689. By the early 1800s, some 40 packet ships operated from there, taking mail around the world. The Bouldersons had sailed packets between Falmouth, New York, Halifax and Quebec since 1759. Three generations of John Bouldersons succeeded each other as captains of their vessels. In 1808, Jack was probably dining with John Boulderson III, who four years later became the last captain of the Boulderson's packet when his ship was captured by an American privateer during the War of 1812. In 1805, John Boulderson III married Mary Anne Carne; William Carne (born 1792) was her brother. Grassie & Co were shipping merchants in Halifax.[28] The person seeking an introduction may have been George Grassie, one of the owners. Carne may have been Grassie's employee, which was perhaps why he was unhappy about the amount of time Carne was with Jack. The ball Jack mentions was a couple of evenings before, at the Masonic Hall. Sir George Prevost and his wife were guests of honour, and Jack presumably arrived with the official party, having dined at Government House beforehand. The ballroom 'was decorated with laurel, and filled with transparencies of Battles fought and breaches mounted, and every other description of military honour'.[29] The bands of the 7th and 23rd provided music; the festivities continued past midnight. Food included a pastry model of Fort Desaix, presumably initially looking as it did before the British bombardment, and following its consumption, after.[30] Browne said 'the entertainment went off capitally'. Even if Jack's company 'never were so sober', as he claimed, their officers could probably not claim this as they staggered home to their quarters, wrapped in fur coats and hats against the cold.

Fortunately, those quarters were well heated. Browne recorded 'we kept up enormous fires in our rooms, as the allowance of fuel, which is wood, was more than any Officer could possibly burn'. The living was clearly good, with wines in ready supply thanks to Royal Navy interceptions of ships supplying French West Indian outposts. Browne was Jack's neighbour in Halifax, in his diary anonymising him as 'an Old Captain of the Regiment' (Jack was 30 years old; Browne 21, but there was only one captain who had survived a shipwreck on returning with the regiment from Holland):

My Barrack room was next to that of an old Captain of the Regiment, who had been with it in Holland, and in returning to England, the Transport in which he was embarked, having on board the Grenadier company & the band, was unfortunately wrecked, and very few were saved. This Captain was thrown on the Beach where he was violently struck on the head, by the butt end of a piece of floating timber. To this misfortune we attributed many singularities, for which he was remarkable. Going into his room one morning, I was surprised to see all his clothes and every thing else belonging to him, spread out upon the Floor, a sort of Alley being left from the door to his bed. On my smiling at this arrangement he very calmly pointed out to me the great advantage

---

28 https://nmmc.co.uk; *Boulderson Family of Falmouth, Cornwall, England* John Raymond 2022; *History of Halifax City* Dr. Thomas B Atkins 1895

29 Buckley, *Browne*

30 *Nova Scotia Gazette* 2 May 1809, quoted in Graves, *Fix Bayonets!*

that it had, over the usual custom of keeping things in boxes & portmanteaus. 'Now', says he, 'when I come into my room & want something I have only to look round about me and see at once where it is, whilst you, I daresay, are poking half an hour or more in your box, and perhaps don't find it after all.' The Captain was quite serious, and satisfied that his wardrobe was better placed on the floor of his barrack room than it could possibly have any where else. It was indeed a curious piece of Mosaic work, composed of coats, waistcoats, fishing rods & stockings, boots and swords, shoes and sashes. He told me also that there was another advantage attending this plan of his, which was, that he could count at any time, in about ten minutes, the number of things he had in the world - that he then possessed 307 things, counting every pair of boots and gloves as two things. I could have split my very sides with laughter, but that he was so grave about it, and a man at all times sensitive to ridicule. His eccentricities affected every thing he did, except his military duties, in all of which he was as correct as any Officer of the corps, & exceedingly beloved by the soldiers of his company.[31]

Jack's 'eccentricities' may have resulted from the *Valk*; this was certainly a novel way of keeping belongings. Having suffered past calamities with his baggage, losing everything on the *Valk* and then his servant selling what he left in Gibraltar, perhaps keeping his possessions this way was a measure of paranoia. Browne also recorded another quirk:

His mode of keeping accounts with his brother Officers, partook of his general habits. For instance, had I met him in the street and borrowed a shilling from him, he would immediately walk to his barrack room, and write upon the wall, with a piece of red chalk, with which he was always provided, in large characters 'I have just lent Browne a shilling' adding the date. If in the course of the week I repaid him the shilling, this was again a walk to his barrack room, and the piece of red chalk, recorded, underneath the former memorandum, 'Browne has just repaid me the above,' and should a delay of more than a week take place in the repayment, it was not unusual to see ones name in red letters on his wall 'To remind Browne of this debt.' As on leaving barracks, Officers are obliged to pay for any damage they may have done to their rooms, my friend the Captain had always a bill to discharge for the fresh white-washing of his room, which he invariably did without the

---

31 Buckley, *Browne*

least dispute. I believe his room was not unfrequently shewn as a curiosity to the Regiment taking our place in the barrack. [32]

Since Jack had moved to new barracks, billets or other accommodation frequently, he must have racked up hefty redecoration charges over the years. A notebook might have been better for keeping track of debtors, but then his letters routinely admit his habit of losing correspondence while the walls of his room were as easy to find as his belongings on its floor. Someone with so many experiences, and violent ones at that, may well have developed peculiar ways of doing things. If he was sensitive to ridicule it is to his credit that a more junior officer considered him 'as correct as any' and 'exceedingly beloved by the soldiers'.

The impact of Martinique lingered for weeks. Prevost inspected the 23rd on 14 June; they still had more than 120 sick. Health improved with the weather, but the mail service remained unreliable.

21 May 1809
Halifax, N.S.

My Dear Mother,

I wrote you a short time since by Boulderson's pacquet. We have not received any letters directed to us N. Scotia. The last information I had of your domestic proceedings was dated 22 Novr.

We are now as usual in an unsettled state, as we imagine the American business being settled, we may possibly be withdrawn from this part of the world and do not feel inclin'd to make any arrangement that cannot be speedily carried into execution. Do let me know the prices of Blue, Scarlet and White cloth in your part of the world.

We have had the summer break on as all at once. A week ago, the cold very great, now the summer has set in, and we are again in a stew, our men are getting more healthy, not more than 100 on the sick report. I cannot make it out, but I find it very difficult to write when I have not one of your letters before me. Your last long one from you and my father were delivered while we were on board the transport in the harbour, and by some ill-luck lost or mislaid.

23 May. I have nothing more to say to you. I believe from what S[ir]. G. Prevost said to Keith and Ellis the other day that had he anything to give away on the Staff, I should be the first. In consequence of the Flankers in Martinique, we must remain in

---

32 Buckley, *Browne*

suspense till the next packet, for news from you, and before we can be enabled to make a guess what will become of us.

Remember me to all, and believe me ever yours,
J. HILL

On returning to Halifax the 23rd received news of an unwelcome decision by Horse Guards, concerning the important matter of hairstyles. Like all members of the British army, the officers and men of the 23rd wore long hair styled into a plait, or queue, for officers and rolled into a ball ('club') for the men. This was a longstanding tradition, beloved not least by the men's wives, some of whom accompanied their husbands on deployment. It was the wives who tied the queue or club ready for duty, earning extra money for this hairdressing. But in 1808 new dress regulations announced hair was to be worn short. The order arrived while the 23rd were in Martinique, but it was waiting when they returned: the queues and clubs had to go. The full story of how the battalion reacted was recorded by Thomas Browne:

I have mentioned the custom of Fusileer Regiments wearing their hair in a small plait behind, and fastened with a little comb to the top of the head. This remark is applicable to the Officers only, with whom it was a very favourite distinction, as differing from the pig tails worn by the rest of the army. Powder was also used, & the hair at the sides of the face, which we called the side locks, was not allowed to grow longer than an inch, & was frizzed and rubbed up with the palm of the hand, before the powder was dusted into it. This mode of decorating the flanks of the human countenance was also the regulation with regard to the men, but they were not allowed the plait behind. Their hair was permitted to grow about a foot long, when it was turned up in a single roll which we called a club - this was clasped by a polished leather strap about half an inch wide, in the centre of which was a platted Grenade, the whole well greased and powdered. It may well be imagined, what a tedious and troublesome operation all this was, and how much of the Soldier's time was needlessly occupied in this formidable preparation for parade. The talents of the women were very conspicuous in this head dressing of their respective husbands, and as the Officers of companies were always well pleased when they saw a smartly frizzed pate, the credit of their good humour was naturally given to the wife who had operated so successfully. The wife in her turn, held up her head the higher, from the Captain's favor to her husband, produced by his handsome side-locks; and the estimation in which the women were held by the soldiers, was not by any means derived from beauty or good conduct, but was proportioned to the degree of approbation bestowed upon the heads which they had dressed, and as casualties are frequent in Regiments so strong as they were at this time a woman of first rate talents in this department, was not unfrequently bespoken by one or two candidates for her hand, in case of misfortune to her actual lawful Lord.

It was about this time that a general order was issued from the Horse Guards, for the discontinuance of the use of powder in the hair of the soldiers, and directing that their heads should be closely cropped. It is natural to suppose, that an order of this description, would have been received by the men most gratefully, and that the Officers would also rejoice at being permitted to disencumber themselves of so useless an appendage. No such thing, the order was obeyed in sulky silence by the Officers, and particularly by those, who had been distinguished, by a luxuriant plait. The Colonel himself, who was one of these, was by no means pleased with the measure. We were seated at the Mess table, when the matter was talked over, and having perhaps taken an extra glass, by way of softening our vexation, one of the Officers proposed, that we should, then and there, cut off each other's plaits with a carving knife, and make grand friz of them, in the fire. The first part of the proposition was acceded to, and I can vouch for its having been a rough and painful operation. The question of burning and frizzing our precious locks, was of a much more serious nature, and acceded to only by one or two old Subalterns whose heads time had taken its usual liberties of thinning and bleaching. The rest of us wrapped up our discarded tails in pieces of brown paper or pocket handkerchiefs, and carried them to our barrack rooms. I do not think it would be hazarding much to add that more of these tails could have written a curious history had the power been granted it, of the division and distribution of its after days.

With the men the scene was far different, and the row which this order produced in the barrack yard amounted to very little short of mutiny. The women assembled in groups of three and four, which after their respective stormy discussions joined each other and added to the uproar. They swore by every oath that a soldier's wife has no difficulty in uttering that the order should not be carried into execution, and that they would murder the first operator who should dare to touch a hair of their husband's head. They felt at once, that should the barbarous decree be carried into execution, they descended more than one step in the scale of female perfection, and that widowhood would inevitably be their lonely portion, in case of that event to which some of them looked forwards with complacency, & perhaps there were not wanting those who would rather have parted with their husbands heads, than that their claims to preservation of caste as wives should be weakened by this cruel docking innovation. Things were in this state of ferment when the Adjutant waited on the Colonel to report the state of confusion which prevailed in the barrack yard. He went there immediately and ordered out the first company. The Regiment not giving the garrison duties that day, he ordered a roll call of the company to see that every man was present; which was the case as it was near the dinner hour. Having ascertained this he desired them to take open order, and sending for benches from the barrack rooms had them placed behind each rank, and commanded the men to sit down. This they did in perfect silence, he then ordered off their foraging caps and sent for half a dozen hair cutters, of which there are always plenty in every Regiment. They were set to work and in less than ten minutes, nothing remained but the stump of the favourite club. The benches were then removed, ranks closed, and the company dismissed. The women assembled in groups and cursed and muttered, but the eye of the Commanding Officer subdued every other indication of mutiny, as he would inevitably have turned out of barracks, any of these heroines whose voice he could have distinguished. Company after company underwent the same process, and it was droll enough to see the men as they were dismissed to their barrack rooms, applying their hands to the backs of their heads, to ascertain if it were a dream or a reality. The Soldiers however soon became reconciled to this great improvement, and the Officers quickly perceived its good effects from the cleanliness which it produced. The women, I daresay, soon discovered some other foundation on which to build their hopes of perpetual wifehood, and in a few months, all the heads of the Regiment were as quiet on the subject as if such a thing as a club had never been heard of. [33]

So ended the old tradition. But in the inimical way of the British army (and perhaps encouraged both by the Atlantic Ocean separating them from Horse Guards and that extra glass), a new and unique one started for the Royal Welch Fusiliers. For reasons unknown, the officers decided to retain the ribbons which formerly tied their hair and to attach them to the rear collar of their uniforms. Whose idea this was and why Ellis, so firm in ensuring compliance with the cropping order, agreed is lost to history. But using an old slang term for a wig, the ribbons became

---

33 Buckley, *Browne*

known as 'the Flash'. The affectation was unquestioned by higher authority for well over twenty years until an inspecting officer declared it an unauthorised addition to the uniform. The regiment appealed directly to the King and in 1834 William IV approved the RWF wearing the Flash 'as a peculiarity whereby to mark the dress of that distinguished regiment'. It has been worn by Royal Welch Fusiliers ever since.

When personal mail arrived, inevitably multiple letters came together. This overcame Jack's writer's block, as in response he produced one of his longest letters yet:

Halifax
15th June, 1809

Dear Father,

I have now before me your letters of Nov. 29th, '08 and 26th April, '09, each celebrating the capture of a Frigate by William's late ship the Amethyst, I am very happy indeed that it has been the means of his getting promotion without being under obligations to anyone but the routine of the service. I imagine that from his having been at Court, you are now looking out for a Command for him. As for myself, I believe from what Sir George Prevost said to Col. Ellis, tho' he would not give me promotion, he would, had he it in his power, place me on the staff here. Macdonald and myself between us lost 50 flankers killed and wounded, you may easily guess we must have been in the thick of it.[34] Sir G. in consequence has given Macdonald a grant of land near Picton, his clan have emigrated in great numbers from the Highlands and have settled there, they wish him to come among them and have volunteered to clear between 50 and 60 of very fine meadowland in the twelvemonth. It is particularly valuable from being in the middle of a cultivated country, some people of less interest have been repeatedly refused it.

This morning when I was going to the office to inquire after the Ireby grant, some of them began to inquire if I intended to follow the example of my brother flanker, and I had some difficulty in persuading them to the contrary. You have not been very explicit in saying in what year the grant was made to Capn. Ireby, if it had been survey'd and register'd, its boundaries, if the stipulations had

---

34 Colin MacDonald joined the 23rd in July 1794 as a lieutenant and was promoted Captain in January 1805. One member of his family who later emigrated to Canada was John A. Macdonald, who in 1867 became the first Prime Minister of Canada.

been complied with as to clearing some portion and of erecting a block house on it, if the quit rent of about 6d. a year had been paid.[35] If all these things have been neglected, after 10 years it escheats to the crown. The value of Lands in that county unclear'd is about 6 shillings an acre, 12 years ago not worth as many pence. An instance has been known here of a man selling his estate of 500 acres for a dinner of Codfish and a glass of grog. That portion of the province is by far the finest. Property here is enhancing extremely in value. I shall not be able to get an answer from the officer here respecting Mrs. B. for some days, and the Hussar sails the day after tomorrow, Tuesday next we go again to the outposts.[36] I shall have the charge of a Depot of French prisoners, 400, a few miles from hence. Should we remain here till the autumn and the property not have reverted to the Crown, I will go down there, or rather, as they say here, <u>through</u> the woods, I suppose they mean, and again visit that part, which principally about Aylesford in a red sandy flat soil, at Windsor 40 miles from hence there is an abundance of Gypsum cliffs and pitts, ship'd for the States and paid for in corn by the farmers who use it as a manure. On this soil it does not at all answer, very little corn is raised here, it mostly comes from Canada or the States.

Of the West Indies I gave you as good an account as I was able in some letters from that country, but one very long one, I fear, has shared a very melancholy fate, the ship having been burnt at sea in consequence of some rum taking fire, one boat full of people was picked up, and brought to Picton, the other has not been heard of.

Barbadoes is situated on a coarse Bath or Portland stone, like Malta and the shores near Alexandria, there are a number of sparry pebbles on the beach penetrated by some marine insect. You have a specimen brought from the W.I. by W[illia]m. St. Keith to the S.E. is limestone, to W., where Brimstone Hill Fort and Barracks are situated, is a white isolated Hill. I was very unwell there and, not like venturing a ducking in the Swiff as I had had a plentiful allowance of calomel, I cannot say whether or no it was calcareous and approaching to chalk. S. Thomas again is limestone. Martinique is composed of a rich fertile soil with detached water worn masses of Granite, Basalt and a hard textured grit stone, nothing regular in

---

35 This seems a different holding from that of the Burringtons, mentioned in the letter of 24 July 1808. Presumably Jack's father had mentioned the Ireby holding in a recent letter.

36 This may have been the former HMS *Hussar*, a sloop captured from France in 1798 and sold into private ownership in 1800. If so the ship was presumably acting as a packet at this point.

its strata. There are mountains in the center of the island, the most spired of any I ever yet saw. Of what they are composed I know not and I believe scarcely a negro has been on their top from their steepness, snakes, and other difficulties.

Nova Scotia in the neighbourhood of Halifax, appears like the ridge of some high land emerged from the sea, composed of Shistus and Granite principally, the Shistus varies in its appearance, in many places particularly the N.W. arm of H[alifa]x. Harbour, it is tinged with iron, in some it is nearly slate (back of the dockyard). The surface of the country, though undulating, never presents anything mountainous, the coast studded with islets which furnish so many good harbours.

The slag you alluded to I had only specimens of I had not the opportunity of inspecting the country which produces that species of ore. The Bishop of Nova Scotia showed me the specimens of the black lead ore brought from Cape Breton, in [the] mouth of St. Lawrence. Limestone is not found in this province. The River St. John, New Brunswick, the other side the Bay of Fundy, has its banks and cliff limestone, furnishing, I understand, some of the most beautiful scenery in N. America. The Gypsum, as I before said, shews itself at Windsor at the very southernmost part in the Bay of Mines which is situated at the bottom of the Bay of Fundy 40 miles from here. The lay of the Shistus is nearly due North and South. I mean that in case you struck them in their beds E. and W., you destroy them as slates, but I do not mean to say that it is altogether slate. You have a Shistus near Ashburton very like this.

Melville Island, 25th June.

I am here with my riflemen doing duty over the French prisoners. I have as good a house as I could wish ever to have. The choice of officers is one of the privileges allowed flank companies. I have Thornhill and Collins with me.[37] Corfield's vacancy is not fill'd up, the Regt. being detach'd. I have obtained one of the best quarters, though we are forced to keep a good look-out over our neighbours. I have just put sticks to my peas, and the fruit has just set, the potatoes coming above ground. By this tho' we are S. of you we are much later.

I am sorry to hear of Mr. Crocker's ill state of health. Should William not get a ship soon I expect a letter from him next packet.

---

37 George Collins joined the 23rd in May 1806 as a 2nd lieutenant and had been promoted lieutenant in June 1807.

Government had not learnt, when the last sailed, that we had got back to this place. We are still waiting to know what they will do with the surplus of troops. One of the Regts. may go to England and one to Canada, and one, I think, here. I hope this division of troops may be broken, up as we do not want to go down to Guardaloupe next winter.

Carne was to have spent this day (Wednesday) with us, but the rain has prevented him.

28 June

I am going into the gay town of Halifax to put my letter in the post office. You may expect news from any place except a corner of the American woods. Remember me to all at home.

Yours,
J. HILL

As a lieutenant on HMS *Amethyst*, a 36-gun frigate, William participated in the capture of the French ships *Thétis* in November 1808 and *Niémen* in April 1809. *Thétis* had been carrying troops to Martinique that Jack could have faced had they arrived. Her action with *Amethyst*, off the west coast of France, was tough; both ships fired repeated broadsides at each other and both lost masts before *Amethyst's* crew boarded and captured *Thétis*. The casualties were significant on both sides - nineteen killed and thirty-five wounded on *Amethyst*, fifty-two killed and 102 wounded on *Thétis*. As Captain, Michael Seymour recorded in his report, William was 'happily preserved to add Lustre to His Majesty's Service'.[38] *Niémen* was carrying stores to Mauritius when spotted by the Royal Naval detachment watching the Gironde estuary. After a chase, *Amethyst* caught her and broadsides were exchanged; *Niémen* caught fire and two of her masts fell. *Amethyst* was also seriously damaged, and it was only when another British frigate, HMS *Arethusa*, arrived that *Niémen* surrendered. She lost forty-seven killed and seventy-three wounded; the toll on *Amethyst* was eight killed and thirty-seven wounded. Seymour noted 'the great Exertions and Experience of the First Lieutenant, Mr. William Hill...I am particularly indebted for'.[39] Jack was correct to guess that William would be promoted following these actions; the 1st Lieutenant of a ship which captured another customarily received immediate promotion and

---

38 *The London Gazette* Issue no. 16201 Tuesday November 15 1808
39 *The London Gazette* Issue no. 16246 Tuesday April 11 1809

William's commission as Commander was dated 6 April 1809, the date of the capture of *le Niémen*. He was initially ordered to Plymouth to command the *Colombe*, a 16-gun Brig captured in 1803, but the Admiralty decided not to commission her into British service. William therefore went on half pay to await a different appointment. He would wait over 3 years: mass promotions following Trafalgar meant the Royal Navy had fewer ships than captains.

Melville Island, originally called Kavanagh Island, in the north-western arm of Halifax harbour had held French and Spanish prisoners since 1794. Initially a hospital, it was bought by the British government in 1804 and renamed Melville Island after First Lord of the Admiralty Henry Dundas, Viscount Melville. When Jack took charge there, a new barracks and prison had just been finished. Being close to the mainland (and soon to be joined by a causeway), escapes were not uncommon, hence the need for Jack and his men 'to keep a good look-out over our neighbours'. His detachment comprised his light company less the sick: the regimental monthly return of 25 June, when he wrote the end of his letter above, records '3 officers [Jack, Thornhill and Collins], 3 sergeants, 3 corporals, 1 drummer, 69 privates' at Melville Island.[40] It was not an isolated post - in fact the locals were attracted to buy craftwork the prisoners produced: stockings and mittens, model ships, snuff boxes, cutlery and even specially-commissioned items.[41]

Yet life was far easier in 'the gay town of Halifax' than on outpost duty and the officers were pleased when the rotation of companies brought them back to the town. They and their red coats were considered an asset at any social function, so there was always plenty of entertainment, from dining at Government House or the home of a rich merchant to visiting the town theatre or the waxworks (star attraction: a depiction of the death of Nelson). Summer might see picnics, hikes and sailing; winter sleigh-rides. The battalion's Paymaster, George Bromley, later wrote of Halifax: 'The gayest season is in winter. The first fall of snow is hailed as the commencement of amusement. Sleighs built, decorated and trimmed in all the different shapes and forms that the fancy of the owners can devise immediately make their appearance; some driven with four horses, and some with two, either abreast or in tandem. So long as the snow continues on the ground this amusement is prosecuted with great eagerness and spirit.'[42] Jack did not enjoy such metropolitan delights for too long though; by September he was back at Annapolis Royal, bored and keen for news from home.

---

40 Cary and McCance *Regimental Records*
41 Graves, *Fix Bayonets!*
42 *A General Description of Nova Scotia* Walter Bromley 1825

My Dear Mother,

I wrote my brother Wm. about a month since. The paquet that left Falmouth in the beginning of August has not yet arriv'd. Being at a distance from Halifax I cannot so exactly know the sailing of the pacquet, but fear that sometimes you will not hear as regular, as two of my epistles may cross the Atlantic in the same conveyance. Our neighbours are status quo, nothing decided as to peace or war. A proposition has been made to Government by Sir Beckwith and Admiral Cochrane to attack Guardaloupe, provided 1200 men can be spared for a short time from the provinces. In case it is acquiesced in, 400 per Regt. will go, the Flankers, of course.

Our Regt. is divided as I told you in my last, and likely to be more so, so says Sir G. Prevost, this alluded to some companies of ours going over to New Brunswick, the pacquet will decide this. We have been unusually long without intelligence from Europe, this, when so many great events are passing, redoubles our curiosity. We have supplied ourselves with an abundance of game. I wish you could partake of it without the trouble of crossing so large a sheet of water.

The explanation given of Ireby's Grant is not sufficiently explicit, they must be more particular to name, Bank, when granted, and what part of the province. I have got from the Bishop of this province some specimens of plumbago, or lead ore which you may desire, I will pack it up one day and send it [via] Carne for you. We begin to smell winter already. The last was the hardest for twenty years. I have answered your last and much wish I had your August letter before me. Thursday next may bring it. Remember me to Caroline when you write or see her. I flatter myself you are all well at home, and when this is put into your hands you will smell winter also. We are very snug and comfortable here and should not mutiny should they order us to remain the winter.

Wm., I suppose, will find some difficulty in getting a ship yet awhile. Will not the grand expedition do something for him? The West India fleet has arrived at Halifax to refit the ships and recruit the health of the crews. The men that our 2nd Bn. ought to have sent were countermanded while at the Isle of Wight, and are going with the grand expedition with the 2nd Bn. We are very short of officers.

I am anxiously looking out for a letter from you. Remember me to Father, William, and Aunt. I hope the foxes have not prayed on her turkies.

Believe me ever yours,
J. Hill

The 'grand expedition' was the largest Britain had yet assembled during the war, over 40,000 strong. Having recovered their strength after Coruña by not sending drafts to the 1st Battalion, 2/23rd again participated, part of the 'left wing' under the overall command of the Earl of Chatham. The plan was to deny the use of the river Scheldt to France, destroy naval assets in Antwerp, and tangentially support Austria, now part of a 5th Coalition, back at war with France and recently victorious over Napoleon himself at the battle of Aspern-Essling. Napoleon defeated the Austrians at Wagram before the expedition sailed, but the other objectives were deemed sufficient to justify continuing. Landing on Walcheren island, near Antwerp, on 27 July, the expedition quickly became a disaster, due not to the enemy, but to disease. What became known as 'Walcheren fever', largely malaria but combined lethally with dysentery, typhus and typhoid, spread rapidly through the army. By the end of August, 244 of 398 men in 2/23rd were declared sick; there were barely enough men for duty. The battalion was ordered home, with most too ill to march and carried in wagons to transport ships. By the end of October, the entire expeditionary force followed. Austria signed another peace with France and Britain had dissipated a large force on another futile expedition. Some 4,000 died before they left Walcheren, while of the 35,000 who returned to Britain, 11,500 were sick; the government built six new hospitals to take them. Many of the survivors 'carried ruined constitutions to their graves'.[43] A national scandal followed which helped bring down the government. The officers of 1/23rd, languishing in Nova Scotia, were envious of their 2nd Battalion seeing action, but with hindsight they were lucky. Participation in the retreat to Coruña and the Walcheren expedition meant their colleagues experienced two of the biggest disasters British troops suffered during the war. Meanwhile a French army led by Marshal Jean-de-Dieu Soult invaded Portugal from the north and captured Porto by the end of March 1809. The following month Arthur Wellesley returned to Lisbon to command British troops that had remained there when Moore evacuated the rest of his army from Coruña. Wellesley was joined by William Carr Beresford, a British general recently appointed to command the Portuguese army. Beresford introduced major changes to Portuguese training, regulations and ways of fighting to parallel those of the British army enabling the two armies to be unified under Wellington's overall command. Moving north, in May they surprised and defeated Soult at Porto, then marched into Spain where, alongside Spanish troops, in July they defeated another French army, under Marshal Jean-Baptiste Jourdan, at Talavera. The

43 Cary and McCance *Regimental Records*

successes made Wellesley a national hero and earned him a new name: Viscount Wellington. But his army was exposed in central Spain and to avoid being cut off he took his men back to Portugal. The retreat caused disappointment in Spain and at home. Many questioned whether Portugal could be defended; if not, Wellington's force should be withdrawn - after the disasters of the retreat to Coruña and Walcheren, Britain could ill-afford to risk more of its already-small army. Wellington's command may have been saved only by his own reputation as the government decided to back him, for now.

Back in Annapolis, if there was little intelligence of these affairs, there was at least news of an old friend.

12th Oct. 1809

My Dear Mother,
    Your letter of July 23rd is this moment put into my hand and in great haste I answer it, as the post brought orders for one of our officers to set off himself for Europe, being promoted, and the ship was expected to sail this day from Halifax for Europe, there is danger of his loosing his passage. My horse will take him forty miles out of the 130.[44]
    You mention in the 23 July [letter] Major Bradford and Mrs. Hole's ill state of health. An intermediate letter of mine to W[ilia]m, inclosing one for Fred, has since made me think an hundred times whether it was not too severe a dose - now I think not. Enquire will it be advisable to write John Pinhey or not, turn this in your minds.
    We stay here, it is most probable, [for] the winter. There are reports respecting Guadeloupe, but certainly no order has come from home, as 3 of our companies go to the frontier in the other province. We have manoeuvered to get out of this, the Qrs. not being so comfortable. You did not mention Caroline, I take it for granted all well. At this place we do not hear when the pacquets sail for England, so that it is all a lottery whether we hit it off so as not to have two letters go in the same vessel. I hope you do not keep too much at home, will not a little amusement dissipate low spirits? I would much like to be with you, particularly as my old friend George Bradford is in the neighbourhood. Tell him when an opportunity offers I shall follow the same line of march, if it be

---

44 The officer was Surgeon John Griffiths, listed as 'Promoted to the Staff in Portugal' in the November 1809 Monthly Return. TNA WO 17/126

possible. This is among ourselves, it is not impossible he may get promoted. Bradford must often smile when he sees the changes in this corps. George Mack. has made the best bit of it.

I am getting a partridge and Woodcock of this country stuff'd, which I will send home for you to see the difference. I would send them but I fear the duties. I was going to collect the woodpeckers. I have one very fine fellow on my chimney-piece to see how they keep, one of our men does it very well.

Remember me to Caroline, William, in fact, to the whole of your domestick roll and believe me ever yours,

J. Hill.

I flatter myself if there's any luck this will have a short passage. Bradford as a soldier would like this place.

The three companies sent to Saint John, New Brunswick were commanded by Major Thomas Pearson. They arrived on 23 October. Jack had avoided the deployment, but Pearson had an ulterior motive to take it, despite the discomfort (Browne, who also went, called Saint John 'a miserable looking place'). Pearson had caught the eye of Anne, daughter of loyalist veteran of the American War General John Coffin. The Coffins lived in Fredericton, New Brunswick's capital, 100 miles away from Pearson's outpost but he would seek an excuse to pay respects on the General - and his family. An invitation to a ball in Fredericton duly arrived; Browne noted naïvely that none of the officers thought it worth a round trip 'except the Commanding Officer himself'.[45] Perhaps from sheer boredom, Browne decided to accompany Pearson on the trip; they set off up the frozen river by horse-drawn sledge, covered in bearskins. A freezing journey of 10 hours enabled Pearson to see the object of his affection, returning the next day.

Jack's letter of 12 October suggests he was contemplating transferring to seek promotion. Others had set the example: this was the 'line of march' of not only George Bradford, but of Charles Sutton and Francis Offley, both of whom transferred to the Portuguese army on promotion at around this time. No further promotion came Bradford's way, however, who within a year retired to Bishopsteignton in Devon. Perhaps he had already acquired property there, as Jack's mother had said he was 'in the neighbourhood' (Bishopsteignton being 8 miles from Hennock and only three from Bradford's family in Ideford). Perhaps Jack's thoughts of leaving his beloved regiment were

---

45 Buckley, *Browne*

prompted by the melancholy of winter's approach. Being back at Annapolis Royal, away from the distractions of Halifax, missing the action in Europe and anxiety about his family, who he had not heard from for four months, all added to his gloom.

Annapolis Royal,
19th Nov. 1809

My Dear Mother,

The Parson is gone to be married. I have nearly the whole day to myself as there is no Divine Service. I have been like the sailors, reading all your old letters ever since we came to this country. Your last that I have received is dated July 23rd. You will perceive I have not received any very recent letter from you. Indeed, the last pacquet not bringing me any has made me lately feel uneasy on your account. You will not receive my letters so regular, in consequence first of our being here, 2nd, winter setting in which in a great measure stops our communications with Falmouth. I hope I may save the last pacquet that will sail for Europe about the end of this month. Your last mentioned Mrs. Hole's illness. I hope she may be spared a little longer, but I am afraid to flatter myself.

I have since that replied to it and also [sent] another letter to my old friend Major Bradford. William has had a letter since that with an enclosure. I hope you will in your next inform me of your being all well. The winter has thus far gone on, and from our being again sent to the outposts, there is no idea of our going to Guadeloupe.

We have been tantalized this morning by being told a sloop of war has arriv'd from England at Halifax with good news, but I still flatter myself she may bring us some letters. Tho' William can not get a ship I hope he will pass his time very pleasantly at Hennock, and I think George Bradford will add to your circle of acquaintance. Tell my father my chimney-piece is well stocked with various specimens of ore. He may divide it with the Professor of Mineralogy of the States University to whom part will go through Dr. Power. The Bishop of Nova Scotia has given me a specimen of plumbago, or rather, as he thinks of [it] lead ore, which it is I will not venture to affirm, and there is too little to try, by Mr. Parkinson's assistance, which it is. I should not be surprised if it turned out akin to your Hennock blacklead, at least it has not the inflammable properties of plumbago.[46] This country in some parts so completely abounds

---

46 Plumbago is now known as graphite.

with Iron that the compass used in the woods ceases to point to the North.

20th Nov. I have not heard from Caroline for some time, I intend writing her next week, we begin now to smell winter.

26th Nov. We are still without any letters from you. I must say I am every day more anxious. I have nothing of any consequence to give you in way of news or information. We have just heard of the ministers fighting. The American house has now just about commenced their session, so that we know not how they will talk to Mr. Jackson. Our books are now our only resources. I shall steal some lessons from an old German engineer officer here. While sitting round our large wood fires, like the Swiss, home is generally the subject, and the Atlantic presents itself precluding a few months' leave taking us home.

We have had a four days' extremely bad weather, wind and snow which left several feet in depth. Now rain has come on and it is thawing. Like Europe, they do not expect any very severe weather till the days lengthen. Carne has been very civil in forwarding the Cornish weekly papers to me. I think you may receive this about New Year's day. Our communication with Halifax by water is nearly at an end, the expense of land carriage in this Q[uarte]r is very great. I shall keep a few months longer.

Remember me to all at Home, to Caroline's when you write or see them. Tell William he must write me when he can spare time. Frederick owes me a letter.

Salter has succeeded Bartholomew. I think either [they] or Carne told me so. If you see G. Bradford tell him I know him too well to expect him to write, you must transmit any message he may give you. Do not let so long an interval elapse between our letters.

Yours,
J. HILL
27th Nov. 1809

Francis Jackson, one of the negotiators with Denmark before the bombardment of Copenhagen, was appointed as 'His Majesty's Envoy Extraordinary and Minister Plenipotentiary to the United States' on 26 May.[47] His predecessor, David Erskine, had been recalled after George Canning, the Foreign Secretary, objected to terms Erskine had negotiated after the *Chesapeake-Leopard* incident. Jackson would be received badly in America, partly through his 'intransigence and haughty

---

47 *The London Gazette* Issue No. 16620 Tuesday May 23 1809

attitude'.[48] Britain assumed the US would not want war because of the detriment to its trade interests; hostilities were avoided in 1809, but relations continued to decline until the US eventually declared war in June 1812. As for 'the ministers fighting', there were many internal disputes in the first half of 1809, including on the cost of the war, whether to reinforce in Portugal or withdraw, the proposals for what would become the Walcheren expedition and a scandalous allegations of the Duke of York's former mistress, Mary Anne Clarke (the scandal being not that the Duke had a mistress, but her claims of bribery in the sale of army commissions). York resigned in consequence in March. But Jack refers to the extraordinary duel fought between George Canning and Robert Stewart, Lord Castlereagh, the Secretary of State for War. The two had been increasingly at odds over foreign and military policy, and Castlereagh discovered Canning had been plotting to remove him from the Cabinet. Castlereagh challenged Canning to a duel; they met on Putney Heath on the morning of 21 September. Castlereagh was a good shot; Canning not. The first shots both missed, but in a second round Canning was hit in the thigh; drawing blood settled the matter. Canning recovered and both continued their government careers, though in Castlereagh's case not until 1812. What professional soldiers made of this when reading of it on the shore of Nova Scotia, we sadly have no insight into.

We also do not know how quickly Jack received news to salve his fears of November. The next surviving letter is one he wrote more than 6 months later. He may have received nothing in the meantime; if so, he endured an anxious winter. In June, however, important news arrived of Europe and of William.

Halifax, June 19, 1810

My Dear Mother,

I receiv'd yours of April 26 a few days since, announcing William's marriage to Miss Upton. You must say every requisite pretty thing to them for me. I would do it myself but the rheumatism will scarcely allow me to finish this, I fear.

The two Regts. of Fusiliers here are under orders to go to Europe, so that in two months' time I may be on the same side of the Atlantic as you. What may be our destination in your quarter of the globe I know not. We understood here Bradford had sold out of the army. I am sorry to hear of old Farmer Edwards death. You may keep the spyglass till I return, perhaps to England in case the

---

48 *Britain and the Defeat of Napoleon 1807-1815* Rory Muir 1996

Spanish business should be finished. I should not be surprised if we cross'd the Atlantic before Wm. Carne who is now in the States.

The old mare, you say, is better than when I left England. Fred wrote me some time since, but really not knowing where to direct him, I have not answer'd it, you must say from me that when I have a direct channel of communication open I will write.[49] I am happy to hear our relative in the 56 is mending his ways.[50] I am very sorry to hear so bad an account of your crops. So Miss P. Parlby is married at last. I will retain the minerals till I return.

The Americans are getting into better humour, you must buy flour from them. I understood Sir G. Prevost either did or does intend giving me a situation on the Staff here, but our being under orders for Europe will [make] it quite out of the question. There is some American news in town of their having again lain on the embargo. From the government being so democratic, and the mob changing their opinions so often, there is no knowing what they would be at. Scarcely one thing blows over in India before we hear unpleasing things from Canada. Sir F. Burdett is also making a bustle with you at home.

I hope the failure of the crops will not make our neighbours in the West discontented. I should imagine by the time you receive this some affairs of great importance will have taken place near Lisbon and Cadiz.

22nd June, 1810

An order was given out last night for the 98th who were going to relieve our outposts to be disembark'd and sent to Europe, Portugal or Cadiz. Sir J. Warren's Flag-ship takes part (the Swiftsure); he must a shift his Flag.[51] They embark Tuesday and will not delay an hour, we wait for transports from England, who we shall follow. We are now in a state of activity to get ready.

I do not know where to direct to William and his wife. I will write by the pacquet which will go in a few days. I was thinking of bringing home some furs for you, but as we do not go to England I shall reduce mine to a soldier's kit. Remember me to all our friends in Devonshire. Fletcher, I see, is in Portugal.

3 weeks' easterly wind with a continued fog has been trying every weak point in my frame. I am in hopes Newfoundland will

49 Fred, now 16, followed William into the Royal Navy
50 John Pinhey, Jack's cousin, had joined the 56th Foot.
51 Admiral Sir John Borlase Warren was now naval commander-in-chief of the North American station, based in Halifax.

have expended all its fogs in a few days and I shall get rid of rheumatism. Tell Fred I shall perhaps be near him.

Excuse this short epistle but say something fine to Major and Mrs. B. as well as in my former I have desired you to Mr. and Mrs. Wm. H. Tell Aunt I did expect that an event of this kind would have got some of my queries in a former epistle solved. I shall almost give up making any future enquiries, on this head, from her, not knowing who may be next on the roster.

Yours ever affectionately,
J. HILL

William married Rose Pitts Upton, from Ashburton, at St. Mary's in Hennock on 23rd April 1810, an event seemingly subject to long-range speculation between Jack and Aunt Peggy. Perhaps she had been wondering if Jack was 'on the roster' with a young woman of Halifax, for whom there was often the possibility of a future husband with a splendid red coat. There is however no evidence of Jack having any liaisons at this stage, though some of his brother officers did fall for the locals: Lieutenant Henry Blanckley married Elizabeth Foreman and Major Thomas Pearson married Ann Coffin at her home near Fredericton on 2 July 1810. Sir Francis Burdett's 'bustle', was about Walcheren. Burdett was a reformist MP and opponent of the war. During stormy debates in the House in February, government supporters moved to clear reporters from the gallery. Condemned as an attack on the press and freedom of speech, this led to John Jones MP being charged with breach of Parliamentary privilege and jailed. Burdett took up Jones' cause and in April was himself threatened with arrest; rioting supporters attacked the homes of government Ministers. Burdett was arrested at home, sent to the Tower of London and not released until June. Meanwhile poor harvests in 1809 and 1810 pushed prices up and increased pressure on banks (some of which failed) and trade, already suffering from Napoleon's Continental system and the American embargo. Presumably by 'our neighbours in the West' Jack means Ireland, where further uprisings remained likely.

Assuming Jack's letter travelled for two or more months, 'affairs of great importance' had indeed taken place before it reached Hennock. In January 1810 French armies rapidly conquered Andalucía and besieged Cadiz. Ostensibly demonstrating French power, the longer-term consequences of this ultimately helped turn the war against Napoleon as increasing numbers of French troops were tied down trying to control conquered territory; some 70,000 men were committed to internal security in Andalucía alone. Supplied by sea, Cadiz held out, while the time taken to conquer Andalucía and a French assumption that they need not hurry to retake Portugal played into Wellington's hands. Poised on the Portuguese border, every month he did not have to face a French onslaught gave time to train his troops, for reinforcements to arrive, and for defenses to be prepared. Jack noted 'Fletcher, I see, is in Portugal'; his friend Colonel Richard Fletcher, now Wellington's Commanding Engineer, was doing excellent work while the Emperor dallied.

In April Napoleon appointed Marshal André Masséna to command the *Armée de Portugal*, some 130,000 men of which around 86,000 were available for operations. With Austria subdued, Prussia reduced and Russia an ally, Napoleon had intended to command this army himself. History may have been different if he had; at the very least, Wellington would have met him in the field five years earlier than he did. But another appointment that month took precedence: Napoleon's new wife. Having divorced the Empress Josephine in December 1809, he married the 18-year Archduchess Marie Louise of Austria. It was not a love match. Napoleon wanted to keep Austria out of the war and legitimize his rule by marrying into one of Europe's oldest dynasties. He also wanted an heir, and Marie Louise's fate was to be the means for this (he reputedly said that he had 'married a womb'). Napoleon successfully began a line of succession with a son born in March 1811, but his appointment of Masséna was to be less fruitful. Masséna's track record made him arguably the best available, but he did not have the same authority as the Emperor to force his subordinate commanders, Generals Junot and Reynier and especially Marshal Ney, to act coherently. Napoleon's orders to Masséna proposed a measured campaign, first capturing the border fortresses of Ciudad Rodrigo and Almeida, astride the road into northern Portugal, then preparing 'to march methodically into Portugal, which I do not wish to invade until September, after the hot weather and in particular after the harvest'.[52]

The British government now had a choice of reinforcing Wellington's army or withdrawing it; they decided to reinforce. Wellington had asked for his army to be increased to 35,000, but the debilitating effect of Walcheren meant there were few new units available at home. Instead, drafts were sent to fill the ranks of regiments already in Portugal and regiments in overseas garrisons were readied to move. Edward Pakenham, who had led Jack and his riflemen up the Surey heights, left Halifax for Portugal on promotion to colonel; he 'faithfully promised that he would spare no exertion to induce Sir Arthur to ask for the two Fusileer Regiments & thus have them emancipated from the inactive scenes of a garrison life in North

---

52 Quoted in *Wellington Against Massena: The Third Invasion of Portugal 1810 – 1811* David Buttery 2007

America…We were all fond of him, & looked forwards with sincere delight to service under his command'.[53] Packenham was well placed to deliver: Wellington was his brother-in-law. The 7th got their orders and sailed, but the 23rd did not; the mail packet they expected to bring them was late.

Halifax
July 3lst, 1810

My Dear Mother,
The non-arrival of the June pacquet at this period throws us all aback. I replied to the letters received by the May conveyance, some time ago. I then told you we expected to go to Portugal. The 7th Regt. is there by this time, you will know our destination by looking in the papers and seeing if any Regts. are sent out here, in case they are we shall quit this part of the world.

I said as many fine things (or did I get you to say for me?) to Mr. and Mrs. W. H. as I possibly could. You may say them ever again. What with not knowing wether we are to go or stay, our situation is not very pleasant, as in this country, it is in the summer one must prepare for winter. I have not answered Frederick's last letter, the fact is that I must write through you as I know not where to direct. Carne is at New York, I believe. Your last letter is dated about 22 Ap^l. The Penelope which will take this sails tomorrow for England, 1st Aug., so that we have been 3 months without any official news, we have rumors in abundance. You must remember me to Caroline. I ought to write her, but there is nothing worth the postage as you know no one in this part of the globe.

We are to be reviewed 2 August and are consequently busy preparing. Major Bradford, I see, has sold out. We remain statu quo. Pearson has got married to a daughter of Genl. Coffin's. In case we go to Portugal it is likely we may have some changes in this Regt. Offley purchases a Lieut. Colcy. immediately. I know not who will get the Majority. Sutton may likewise get a Lieut. Colcy. which will provide for Keith. Pearson by this last step of his will remain a long time in the Regt. as I know not how it will be relish'd at home. I do not think I shall get anything in this country.

We are anxious to know how affairs go on in Portugal. I have little doubt but that we shall gain the first 3 or 4 battles, but when it is reduc'd to expenditure of men, the French can certainly afford it much better than we. There are hopes as long as the Allies stick

---

53 Buckley, *Browne*

by one and another, but the instant a quarrel, or perhaps bickering [begins], the enemy will get the upper hand. Bonaparte begins to have a few more rational ideas than formerly, peace will be as dangerous to him as to us, as I believe their government will not bear looking into, and even in a state of peace he would be forced to amuse the military with the prospects of future wars. We have had no American news lately.

Remember me to all our relations. Tell Wm. I will write him when he becomes a quiet settled character. I shall hardly know any of Caroline's boys when I may come back, they will be so much grown. I am happy to hear our friends in Exeter have had good accounts from India. Pray, what is become of the Nabob Abraham? Does he still stick to "have a wife and rule a wife"? Tell Aunt I despair of ever having a letter from her as she would not tell me Wm. was in love. Say I left all my poultry behind at Annapolis, but we brought 4 Foxes with us. I will send her one home provided she will keep it. Tell my Father be must let me know how the farm gets on.

Believe me ever,
Yours,
J. Hill

The 2 August review went well; Prevost reported 'Unanimity and good understanding prevails in this corps. The regiment is a good serviceable body of men, with a general appearance of health, though many are under the fixed [height] standard. The officers mess together, and the regimental mess is established on a proper system of prudence and moderation'.[54] Unwilling to continue waiting, officers with means took steps to reach Portugal. Sutton was promoted to Lieutenant-Colonel of the 9th Portuguese Infantry Regiment, in August 1809. Offley joined Marshal Beresford's staff, also as a lieutenant-colonel; he would also later command a Portuguese regiment, the Loyal Lusitanian Legion. Pearson stayed with the battalion for now, but lobbied Horse Guards for promotion.[55] Blatant self-promotion was considered poor form, hence Jack questioning how the move would 'be relish'd at home'. 'Good accounts from India' via Exeter suggests encouraging news of John Pinhey in the 56th Foot, while the 'Nabob Abraham' was Thomas Abraham of Gurrington, near Ashburton, who was employed by the East India Company; what the specifics of his peculiar views on wives was, is unclear.

---

54 Cary and McCance *Regimental Records*
55 Graves, *Fix Bayonets!*

Another month passed with no news either from Horse Guards or Hennock. Jack longed for information.

Halifax
30 Aug. 1810

My Dear Mother,

We have been daily expecting to see the transports arrive that are to take us to Europe, hardly knowing wether we are not likely to be home as soon as the pacquet. One hardly knows what to write, we are in this Garrison with not very much to do.

I have been writing William and directed it Hennock. Carne will be here in the next pacquet from New York, I believe. I find you have all been rambling a great deal lately. Mr. Pinhey at Bath, Aunt P. has got another pet. I am sorry to say I have not written Caroline lately; however, I have desir'd Wm. to write her for me as one letter from this place now is quite enough. We have not a word of any news here. The passages from Europe have been this year remarkably long, our last [up]dates from Spain and Portugal 2 months old.

I have not answered Fred's letter because I know not exactly where to direct to him. Remember me to him when you write. So, I perceive several of our old villagers have dropt off. Pray, how does the Farm get on? My Father ask'd for a newspaper writing half an hour after he saw you in Exeter, and did not say if my Aunt and the Foxes agreed tolerably well. From there being no complaint, I imagine the hounds were successful last spring. Pray, how does the Farm? Where are Mr. and Mrs. Salter and Mr. and Mrs. Jones; except one looks over the roll one does not remember half. You did not tell me how Humphrey did, and not once did you mention if the other young ladles are likely to get married. You must mention how our acquaintances in Totness get on. There is not a person that you know here since Carne is gone away, except me. I have written you a very short letter, but however, you must not follow such an example. This Climate is nearly as warm as the West Indies.

You have not mentioned how the Burringtons are in the last two or three letters. Pray, what become of the Dosneths, is the old lady still alive? One of the Lady de le Poles is dead. Is it the young or old? Remember me to all our friends and acquaintances. I wish I could get among you again.

Believe me ever yours most affectionately,
J. HILL

Jack was not alone in the misery of his uncertainty; Browne recorded 'the next English Packet might possibly condemn us to North American service for years to come, we were really quite in despair, & it is not possible to describe the intensity of our feelings as the usual time for the arrival of the Packet drew near. We were kept too, in that state of doubt, which prevented our making any arrangements of Mess, or Barrack rooms, of a permanent or comfortable nature, and this inconvenience, added to our other disquietudes, made us sulky and ill-tempered'.[56] But then 'the well known signal from the Citadel announced the packet in sight, and down we flew to the shore, as tho' it had been possible to see our destiny written on her very top-sails…it is needless to say for what, or how many bottles of wine were drunk at the Mess that evening, to assist us in getting off a stock which we did not choose to leave behind us'.[57] So much for Prevost's report that 'the regimental mess is established on a proper system of prudence and moderation'. The 23rd were ordered to Portugal; the men cheered when told. On 6 October the transports appeared, and Jack dashed off his last letter to Hennock from Nova Scotia.

6th October 1810

My Dear Mother,

We embark about the middle of next week for Portugal, you will learn if the fate of that country has been previously decided. There was at one moment an idea that we might be sent to the Mauritius.

Carne is still in the States, Mr. Malone is dead somewhere near Boston. I have not heard from any of you for a length of time. My last letter I wrote did not go about a fortnight since. We may be in Portugal at the moment you receive this, so that you may write me there. Of course, we are now busy and I want one of your letters to reply to. I have not answered Fred's last letter to the Med[iterranea]n, as it must go through London. I thought it was as well to write through you so that you must say my reasons. I want to know what is become of Wm. and his wife, tell him Mends is Sir J. Warren's first Lieut. I believe his Com^m. is come or coming out as Commander.

I go on board the Regulus - Man of War fitted for troops. In this quiet, out-of-the-way place we have nothing new, that principally comes from Europe. Bonaparte has thrown us into an

56 Buckley, *Browne*
57 Buckley, *Browne*

awquard [sic] predicament with the Americans, for people can have no right to prevent the Americans going to France with their own produce. In case we did, it would strengthen the French Party in the States. Remember me to your circle of friends and acquaintances.

Believe me yours ever,
J. HILL

After weeks of inactivity, everything now buzzed. Companies were allocated to the two ships: *Regulus*, on which Jack and his Light Company travelled, and the larger *Diadem*. Stores and supplies for the journey were loaded, 'Bills were collected and I believe paid, farewells were said to Sweethearts'.[58] Jack collected his belongings from the floor and no doubt had its walls whitewashed to erase his financial records. Prevost made one final inspection and issued glowing praise of the battalion. The people of Halifax published a tribute saying the battalion's conduct had 'endeared them to all ranks of people in the Province'.[59] The officers and men of the 23rd may have wanted to leave, but Halifax had enjoyed their presence; most of the officers would have admitted with hindsight that theirs had been a comfortable and largely enjoyable stay. Leaving twenty sick men behind in Halifax, on 10 October, 814 officers, NCOs and men of 1/23rd embarked for Lisbon.

---

58 Buckley, *Browne*
59 Graves, *Fix Bayonets!*

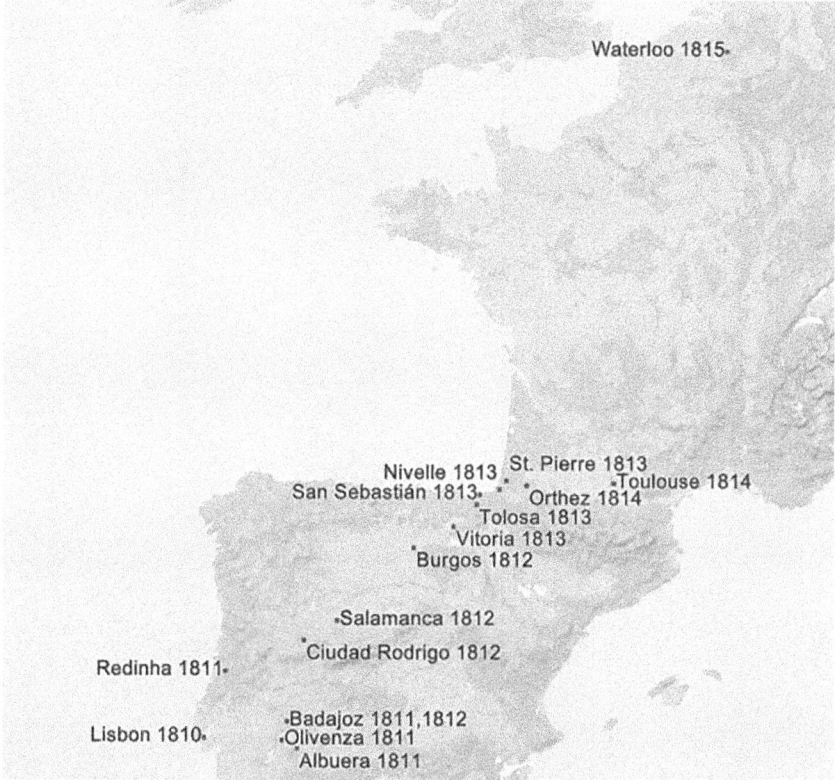

Map 2: The Marches of Jack Hill 1810 – 1815

CHAPTER 9

PORTUGAL & PAIN

'Portugal, joined the army in the lines of Torres Vedras.
Spain, at the first siege of Badajos'

Memorandum to the Duke of York, 1823

Regulus and *Diadem* sailed on 12 October. Fair winds meant the crossing took less than a month, though as usual Jack's voyage was not without its excitements. On 16 October several waterspouts appeared during a storm. Browne, on *Diadem*, recorded that *Regulus* fired at one of them and collapsed it, an impressive piece of shooting. By the 29th the ships passed the Azores and on 10 November Jack and *Regulus*, with *Diadem* a couple of days behind, entered the mouth of the River Tagus, passed Belém Tower and anchored close to the Praço do Comércio in the centre of Lisbon.[1] There the officers and men of the 23rd kitted themselves out for the campaign: camp kettles for cooking, canteens and cutlery, and mules to carry baggage. Once equipped, after a few days the regiment took their place in the army at Azambuja. Jack started a letter home confirming his safe arrival in Lisbon, finishing it in Azambuja.

Lisbon, 11th Novr., 1810
Direct 4th Dn. after 23rd Regt.

My Dear Mother,
We arriv'd here yesterday after a 4-weeks' passage, we are so short [of] time that I cannot give you correct political news. The people here seem to think Massena has got himself into a scrape. They are in high spirits. They do not seem to be very much in a hurry in sending the troops to the army, distant from hence 24 miles. The French are within 30 miles of this place. Lord

---

1 Cary and McCance *Regimental Records* incorrectly records the dates as sailing 10 November, arriving 11 December; both Jack's letters and Browne's journal confirm the voyage was a month earlier.

Wellington has an equal army in front. The Spaniards a considerable corps in the rear, their communication is cut off.

Azambuja, 21st Nov.

We march'd in here last night and did expect to go on this morning towards Santarem, in which place the French Army is. I hardly know enough as yet to give you any idea of the position of the army. You may by reading the opposition and ministerial papers form an opinion for yourselves.

Massena, I understand, is not in good health. The French yesterday and this morning wish'd to blow up the bridge near Santarem, I should imagine to keep us more at a distance - this and their retiring from Sobral and its vicinity, may induce one to imagine they have given up offensive measures.

The country is dreadfully ravag'd, I saw nothing except a few pigeons left about the villages; the floors and rafters taken out either to burn or make huts. All the inhabitants had retir'd before our army, so that what a few months before had been a fine country is literally now a desert, with the exception of the roofs of the houses. Our supplies are all brought from Lisbon to which place our shipping conveys it. I know not from what quarter the French Army is victualled, but I should imagine that the country is so much exhausted that they must subsist with great difficulty. Lord Wellington is very high in estimation; his manoeuvres and operations have been masterpieces. The lines to which the Army retir'd are formidable indeed, in fact, the country near Lisbon is a continuation of entrenched positions.

I have not heard from you for many months. I understand there has been much promotion in the Navy. Pray, will this give Wm. employment or a ship? Where is Fred? I want to hear of Caroline. I have not seen Fletcher. Archdale sought me out in the line of march the other day and enquir'd after you all, he mention'd Raymond's having settled in the North of Devon.

We march'd from Lisbon for the left of our position in the lines of Sobral, and have made the traverse to the banks of the Tagus, this is the first halt we have had. The dysentery has got among our people. We disembarked at Lisbon from the Regulus, 44 with only 3 men sick out of four Companies. The Diadem had outside 20. Tell Wm. we attribute it to never allowing men to dine between decks. The smell of the meat never tainted the air below. Our fellows [are] like plowmen, the others like tailors. Our mules have suffer'd from our people not knowing yet how to pack them, I have not a West Country brute with me to teach them; this is not the first time in my life I wanted to profit by their experience.

I know nothing of the affairs of Spain, and as the husband in Marlborough's Army desir'd the wife to send him out newspapers to let him know what he was doing, so it is with us, we know not what we partially see and do, the effect it has on the general whole. We only find out by the final results.

Remember me to all our circle of friends and relatives. Write me soon and believe me ever your most affectionate Son,

J. HILL

The 23rd joined an army that by November 1810 comprised almost 43,000 men, by far the largest force which Jack and his colleagues had been part of. As recent arrivals, it is unsurprising that Jack thought newspapers might offer a clearer view than him of the military situation. His commentary was accurate, though, no doubt based on insights from officers who had been there longer. Massena had 'got himself into a scrape', the country was 'dreadfully ravaged' and, most telling, his comments on Wellington and 'The lines'. Masséna had captured Ciudad Rodrigo in July and Almeida in August. Almeida fell when a magazine exploded, killing 800 Portuguese defenders and destroying the middle of the town. The effects of the blast remain visible today; the French defenders of Fort Desaix in Martinique wisely surrendered before suffering a similar fate. Masséna marched into Portugal, attempting to bypass Wellington's army and place his own between the British and the Atlantic. But Wellington moved his army further north and took position on the heights of the Serra do Buçaco, a steeply sloped ridge about 1,800 feet high. The position rendered cavalry useless and French artillery could barely touch the British lines so far above, while the British could fire down on attackers. It was a formidable obstacle, well-chosen for defence. Masséna attacked on 27 September and was roundly defeated, losing 4,500 men to Wellington's 1,250. Buçaco also gave a literal baptism of fire to the renewed Portuguese army, who passed the test admirably. Wellington now had a tested, integrated army that would be the key to success over the coming years.

Masséna again manoeuvered to flank the allies, but now the genius of Wellington's defensive strategy for Portugal was revealed. The measured French advance, capturing the border fortresses and fighting at Buçaco had granted the allies time. It was unsurprising that Jack had not seen Lieutenant-Colonel Richard Fletcher; he was a very busy man. Under Fletcher's oversight, Wellington had ordered the construction of the Lines of Torres Vedras, one of history's most impressive defences. Lisbon sits on a peninsular around 30 miles wide, with the River Tagus to the east and the Atlantic to the west, and hilly terrain to the north. The Lines of Torres Vedras made brilliant use of this geography. The hills were capped with 152 redoubts and forts, mounted with cannon, close enough to support those either side, stretching all the way from the Atlantic shore to the west bank of the Tagus. There were three lines of works, the second line five or so miles south of the first and a third, much shorter, covering São Julião harbor west of Lisbon, where the British army could embark and escape, if all went wrong. The first line alone comprised sixty-nine emplacements mounting 319 pieces of artillery.[2] If that line was breached, the allies could fall back to the second and force the attackers to try again. The hills had been regraded to be steeper, woods were cleared to improve lines of fire, approach roads were destroyed, trenches were dug and lines of stakes and other obstacles established, including damming streams to flood likely attack routes. All would slow an attacker down and 'made the prospect of enduring the fire of the forts and marching past them bleak'.[3] It was a huge endeavor by Fletcher, his seventeen engineers and some 7,000 hired Portuguese workers; remarkably it took just a year to complete. The earthworks were manned by Portuguese militia, with the regular army held ready to respond to any enemy breakthroughs. Roads behind the Lines were improved and a semaphore signaling system installed; communications from one end to the other took only seven minutes, enabling troops to be quickly sent where they were needed. Royal Navy gunboats patrolled the Tagus, to bring extra firepower against any attacks near its banks and prevent any attempt to bypass the Lines via the river. Most significantly, the countryside for miles to the north was stripped of everything that could sustain an army. Perhaps 300,000 Portuguese residents moved from their homes and farms to the countryside around Lisbon, within the Lines, their livestock and crops either brought in with them or destroyed. Food was provided by Portuguese and British authorities, the church and charities, but still by some estimates as many as 50,000 still died during the winter that followed.[4] It was an act moved by desperation to prevent Portugal falling to the French and prompted Jack's observation that 'a fine country is literally now a desert'. The goal was that Masséna's army should be neither able successfully to breach the Lines nor sustain themselves for long in front of them.

As Masséna outflanked the Buçaco position, Wellington pulled his men back into the Lines, where his Anglo-Portuguese army was joined

2 *The Lines of Torres Vedras: The Cornerstone of Wellington's Strategy in the Peninsular War 1809-1812* John Grehan 2000
3 Buttery, *Wellington Against Massena*
4 *The Spanish Ulcer: A History of the Peninsular War* David Gates 1986

by some 8,000 Spanish troops. On 11 October, Masséna's army approached. From the Commander to the lowliest private soldier, they were stunned by what they saw. Intelligence had told of defensive works being prepared around Lisbon, but Masséna had no idea of their scale and sophistication. After scouting them himself he concluded 'the enemy is dug in to his teeth. He has three lines of works that cover Lisbon. If we seized the front line of redoubts, he would throw himself into the second line...I have already visited the line three times to the right and left and I see great works bristling with cannon...I do not believe this is the moment to attack the enemy.'[5] After initial probes, Masséna concluded he could do nothing without reinforcements and sent messages to Napoleon, over 1,000 miles away in Paris, requesting them. Meanwhile, he needed to feed his army as they sat in the 'desert'. Eventually he pulled back towards Santarém and there remarkably, by discovering food which had been stashed away rather than destroyed and by sending foraging parties out ever wider for supplies, Masséna held out. Wellington was both annoyed so much food had been found and amazed at French resilience. Still, by the time Jack and the 23rd arrived, sickness, desertion and securing communications to Spain and beyond had reduced Masséna's army to around 40,000 effectives. Wellington's army, conversely, was well supplied by sea through Lisbon and receiving reinforcements like the 23rd. As Masséna pulled back, Wellington pushed his troops forward to maintain contact between the two armies.

On arriving in Azambuja the 23rd received welcome news: Pakenham had delivered on his promise and they were brigaded, under him, with the 1st and 2nd Battalions of the 7th Foot, and a company of Brunswick riflemen. The Brunswickers were established in 1809 by Freidrich Wilhelm, Duke of Brunswick, after the Prussian defeat at Jena-Auerstedt, where his father was killed. After Wagram, Brunswick took his men to Britain where they were added to the British army; they would fight throughout the Peninsular War and at Waterloo. The lead of the company attached to the Fusilier Brigade, Captain Friedrich von Wachholtz, left a diary full of insights from this time.[6] The inclusion of a dedicated rifle company in the brigade meant Jack's light company surrendered the rifles they had carried in Martinique and reverted to carrying the Brown Bess.

This new Fusilier Brigade was far stronger than the one of Martinique; 'it is said to be the finest in this Army', wrote Lieutenant

5 Quoted in Grehan *Torres Vedras*
6 *Auf der Peninsula 1810 bis 1813. Kriegstagebuch des General Friedrich Ludwig v.Wachholtz (On the Peninsula 1810 to 1813: The War Diary of General Freidrich Ludwig von Wacholtz)*, H.L. von Wacholtz (Ed.) 1906

Thomas Farmer of the 23rd to his brother, underlining the words with pride.[7] It was part of the 4th Division, under Major-General Galbraith Lowry Cole, alongside James Kemmis' brigade (27th, 97th and 40th Foot) and William Harvey's brigade (11th and 23rd Portuguese Infantry). The 23rd was the newest arrival but were as experienced as any. An inspection return showed the 23rd contributed significantly to the 4th Division's fighting strength: fifty officers, fifty-four sergeants, twenty-two drummers and 1,000 private men. The 23rd moved a few miles northwest to Aveiras de Cima and there the entire 4th Division, perhaps 6,000 men in all, was paraded for review by Wellington. Von Wacholtz described the event:

> The bugles gathered us on a windmill hill close to the village; there a square was formed, into which General Cole and Colonel Packenham rode. The former, our divisional commander, is a tall, serious-faced man between about 40 and 50, the latter a young man, barely in his 30s, but endowed with one of those physiognomies that captivate us, or at least me, at first glance... [Afterwards,] We were sitting in our quarters in great repose toward dusk, when the bugles sounded again. We immediately packed up and advanced to the windmill hill...we found the other regiments of the brigade and stopped. After half an hour General Cole's order to move back came; it had been a rehearsal. Unfortunately, on the way back, we were soaked to the skin by the pouring rain.[8]

There was to be another special role for Jack's Light Company and von Wacholz's riflemen. According to General Orders:

> The light infantry companies belonging to, and the riflemen attached to each brigade of infantry, are to be formed together, on the left of the brigade, under the command of a Field Officer or Captain of light infantry of the brigade, to be fixed upon by the Officer who commands it. Upon all occasions, in which the brigade may be formed in line, or in column, when the brigade shall be formed for the purpose of opposing an enemy, the light infantry companies and riflemen will be of course in the front, flanks, or rear, according to the circumstances of the ground, and the nature of the operation to be performed. On all other occasions, the light infantry companies are to be considered as attached to their

---

7 RWF Archives object 5257b.
8 v.Wachholtz, *Auf der Peninsula*

battalions, with which they are to be quartered or encamped, and solely under the command of the Commanding Officer of the battalion to which they belong.[9]

The light companies of the Fusilier Brigade, from both battalions of the 7th, 1/23rd, and the Brunswickers, were therefore combined into what was called a 'converged light battalion' and placed under the command of Major Thomas Pearson of the 23rd. They would act as a unit, tasked to lead advances and provide covering parties. In battle their job was to counter enemy light troops, protect flanks and cover any withdrawals. In short, Jack could expect to be wherever the action was hottest.

1811 started with command changes: Pakenham took a position on his brother-in-law's staff, replaced at the head of the Fusilier Brigade by Major-General William Houston. Houston did not stay long, however, leaving to command a new 7th Division and replaced by a fusilier - Lieutenant-Colonel Edward Myers, previously commander of the 1/7th Foot. Meanwhile the army remained alert for any attack, but routine was soon established. Browne (also now in a staff position) recorded 'the Troops were always under arms before day light, with their Commander ready to direct their operations, in case of a general attack; and thus matters went on day after day, and week after week…the enemy…began to amuse themselves, and act plays, and invitations were sent to Officers of our Staff, to go in, and witness these spectacles, with the assurance of perfect freedom of return. Several were exceedingly well disposed to accept these invitations, but Lord Wellington would not permit it'.[10] Bentinck similarly remembered 'the hostile sentries were almost within musket shot of each other, but after the first duty, by tacit understanding, ceased to punch bullet holes into each other'.[11] Despite the fraternising, there were occasional French raids and during one, on 19 January at the village of Rio Maior, Captain James Mercer and three men of the 23rd were mortally wounded. Wellington reported 'The Enemy…drove our Picquets through the Town of Rio Mayor on 19th Instant, with a strong body of Cavalry and Infantry; but retired again immediately'.[12]

Otherwise both armies stayed put over a wet Portuguese winter. Jack had a chance to pursue his favourite pastime of culling the local game. In February Lieutenant John Harrison wrote home to his father:

---

9 *General Orders, Spain and Portugal April 27th to December 28th 1809. Vol. I*
10 Buckley, *Browne*
11 Crook, *Bentinck*
12 *London Gazette Issue 16451 5th February 1811.* James Mercer joined the RWF as a 2nd lieutenant RWF in September 1805 and was promoted lieutenant in July 1806.

Hill is the same sterling fellow as ever, his great delight is poking after a few partridges and cocks, which bye the bye are very plentiful in the neighbourhood, but as my mother says, what's a recruiting party without a Drum and Fife, and what's a partridge shooting without dogs which is the way they are obliged to sport here. And as the Irishman says, if it was not for the honour of the thing they might as well stay at home, as they generally return without a feather, and are rewarded with a good soaking'.[13]

Jack was no doubt missing Linquo.

By March the weather improved, but Masséna's situation worsened. Napoleon had sent reinforcements under command of General Drouet, helping to keep communication to the Spanish border open but providing insufficient additional strength to attack Wellington and 8,000 more mouths to feed. Marshal Soult was ordered to move north from Andalucía and potentially offer a diversion by attacking the Spanish city of Badajoz, guarding the southern border with its Portuguese counterpart, Elvas. What the Emperor did not do was give Masséna overall command of French forces in the Peninsula, which might have enabled him to coordinate them more effectively. With little food, no hope of attacking and ineffective command and control, Masséna began to retreat towards the Spanish border. Not wanting to leave part of his army exposed to attack he moved carefully, filling his former positions with dummy sentries made of straw to deceive onlookers. Wellington followed. On 5 March the Fusilier Brigade moved forward to Cartaxo; on the 6th they marched 9 miles further to enter Santarém; then next day another 18 miles to Golegã where 'we found boiled beans left by the enemy, who had quitted in the morning.'[14] Another 16 miles brought the regiment to Tomar during the evening of 8 March, again just missing the French: 'so close did we follow them up, by hard and long marches over the worst road in the world'.[15] Wellington felt the French had retreated far enough that he could release a force under Beresford, including the 4th Division, to try to relieve Badajoz from Soult's pressure. But a day later he found that at least part of the French army had stopped at Pombal, and the 4th Division was recalled to Wellington's main force.

The 4th Division therefore marched nearly 30 miles back north, reaching Pombal on the evening of 11 March, by when a small

---

13 RWF Archives object 7198.
14 Letter by an anonymous 'officer of the 23rd' quoted in Cary and McCance *Regimental Records*
15 Cary and McCance *Regimental Records* (anonymous 'officer')

engagement had already taken place. Pombal was in flames, the French had retreated again, and a rearguard under Ney held high ground before Redinha. Marching through Pombal, the men of the 23rd covered their ammunition pouches to avoid sparks setting off their powder. On the morning of the 12th Wellington probed Ney's position but waited until more troops were at hand to attack. When the 4th Division arrived, Wellington formed his troops into lines some 3 miles across, with the Light Division on his left, the 3rd Division on his right and the 4th Division in the centre. Jack's light company, in Pearson's composite battalion, were in front, acting as skirmishers ahead of the advance. A soldier of the 2/7th recalled the orders to the Fusiliers as they took their position: "form close column'; 'prime and load'; 'fix bayonets'; 'shoulder [arms]'; 'slope [arms]'; 'silence'; 'steady'; 'deploy into line".[16] At about 2pm on 'a signal of three guns fired by the artillery the whole advanced in superb order, extending far beyond Ney's army upon both flanks.'[17] It was a magnificent sight: 'suddenly a most splendid spectacle of war was exhibited…in a few moments thirty thousand men, forming three gorgeous lines of battle, were stretched across the plain, bending on a gentle curve, and moving majestically onwards'.[18] Even the participants were impressed 'to have seen us deploy and march in line, as we did, you would have been highly pleased. I never saw better. The troops in the highest spirits.'[19] Another added 'fortunately all the shot from their canon went over us - we did not loose [sic] a man'[20] But Ney only wanted to delay Wellington, not fight him and as the Light and 3rd Divisions outflanked both ends of the French formation, he fell back about 5 miles to a position near Condeixa.

The next day was almost a repeat. Wellington drew his men up in the same formation, and as the 3rd Division approached Ney's left flank, he set fire to Condeixa and moved rapidly off again, this time eastwards to Casal Novo. The manoeuvering by Wellington's men on both days was impressive and, while not entirely bloodless, the engagements demonstrated the impressive military machine he commanded. Ney's move east meant there was now no prospect of the French standing at Coimbra or moving north to threaten Porto, as Wellington had thought they might; instead, they were inexorably heading out of Portugal. Wellington again attempted to outflank them,

16 *Rough Notes of Seven Campaigns in Portugal, Spain, France and America During the Years 1809-10-11-12-13-14-15* John Spencer Cooper 1869
17 Fortescue, *History* Vol. VIII
18 *History of the War in the Peninsular and in the South of France, from the Year 1807 to the Year 1814 Vol. III* 2nd Edition 1833 W F P Napier
19 Cary and McCance *Regimental Records* (anonymous 'officer')
20 RWF Archives object 5257b.

sending the 4th Division southeast towards Espinhal. It was tough going: 'our division...was detached over the mountains to the left of the enemy, and had as hard a march as ever we experienced...We had to climb the most difficult places, and what with the heat of the weather, and being without provisions, I was nearly exhausted'.[21] Further north the Light Division, advancing towards Casal Novo, attacked without waiting for support and engaged in a sharp fight on 14 March which, with the 4th Division moving around their left flank, forced the French to fall back again. The 23rd reached Espinhal around 6pm that evening and found a welcome sight: 'every oven was full of Indian corn [maize] bread which was very acceptable ...the enemy had even cut wood for our fires, and brushwood to hut themselves, which fell to our lot'.[22] The rugged territory forced Masséna to destroy much of his heavy baggage (and the animals that pulled it) and as he continued eastwards Wellington decided that he could again release the 4th Division to Beresford. On 16 March the 4th Division turned south; by evening the next day they were back in Tomar, having left less than a week before. Ahead of them was a march that would stay in the memory of many.

Crossing the Tagus via a temporary bridge of boats at Tancos, almost 12 miles due south of Tomar, the column 'halted for a night on a rising ground nearly two miles from where we crossed. Our places of halting were always called by the name of encampments, but they little deserved that name, as, from the difficulty of transporting equipage, not more than six or eight tents appeared in an encampment of as many as thousand men. When obliged by fatigue to lie down, we wrapped our blankets about our bodies, placing our knapsack for a pillow. When in the neighbourhood of an enemy, no one was permitted to take off his belt till clear daylight, before which time we always stood to our arms for about an hour'.[23] The rest of Beresford's detachment meanwhile advanced from Abrantes, where they had waited while Wellington was chasing Masséna. Beresford's task was to relieve Badajoz, but a week is often as long a time in war as in politics. Wellington thought the Spanish defenders of the town could hold out for at least a month and told them help was coming. Unfortunately, Governor Menacho of Badajoz was killed during a sortie against the French lines outside the city; his successor quickly decided to surrender. The unexpected loss of Badajoz would vex Wellington for a year, starting with Beresford now marching to recapture the town, a much more difficult proposition than relieving it. Beresford would not

21 Cary and McCance *Regimental Records* (anonymous 'officer')
22 Cary and McCance *Regimental Records* (anonymous 'officer')
23 *Recollections of the Late War in Spain and Portugal* J. Emerson in *Peninsular Sketches by the Actors on the Scene Vol. II* W H Maxwell (Ed) 1845

immediately have to face Soult, as after the surrender he rapidly returned to Andalucía, leaving around 11,000 men in Badajoz. With no need now to hurry, Wellington suggested that Beresford mop up a couple of smaller fortresses first, starting with Campo Maior.

The 4th Division caught up with Beresford's rearguard at Portalegre on 22 March having 'made an admirable march, a hundred and ten miles of mountain road in six days'.[24] It was hell for those involved, 'over hilly stony roads with not a mouthful of bread. Great numbers of men unable to keep up remained on the roads or in the fields during a wet night...the column...suffered dreadfully from hunger, thirst, little shoes and blistered feet'.[25] The countryside was devastated: 'The country through which we passed on this day exhibited a fearful scene of desolation from the excesses of the enemy, by whom it had been occupied the preceding winter. Neither man nor beast was to be seen, though, from the ruin of the houses and olive plantations, it had evidently been inhabited until lately'.[26] By the time they reached Portalegre the entire 4th Division was in a state; the men still present were bare-footed and some six hundred were straggling somewhere behind. Cole estimated they needed fourteen thousand pairs of shoes. Indeed, both the 4th and 2nd Divisions needed reequipping before they could proceed. They had also outmarched their supplies: 'our being without provisions was not owing to any neglect; the rapid marching was the sole cause. A ship biscuit lasted me four days, when I was necessitated to eat boiled Indian corn: it was the same with the men'.[27]

To allow provisions to catch up the 4th Division paused in Portalegre for two days. The rest was much needed: they had marched over 200 mountainous miles in 18 days, almost half of it since they left Espinhal, less than a week before. At Portalegre they received new locally made footware, but a combination of its poor quality, the state of the men's feet and no socks meant some preferred bare feet. The shoes 'were very clumsy, and of a dirty buff colour; and as many amongst us were without stockings, their rough seams soon made the wearers hobble like so many cripples'.[28] Thomas Farmer wrote home 'Our march has been a very severe one, I have not a shoe or stocking to my feet, nor a farthing to purchase them. The whole of the Division are in the same way. We have sometimes been without food two or 3 days'.[29]

---

24 Oman, *History Vol. IV*
25 Cooper, *Rough Notes*
26 Maxwell, *Sketches*
27 Cary and McCance *Regimental Records* (anonymous 'officer')
28 Maxwell, *Sketches*
29 RWF Archives object 5257b.

So replenished, the 4th Division resumed their march, first towards Arronches and then to Campo Maior. Beresford led some 18,000 men, including the 2nd and 4th Divisions, a Portuguese Division, two brigades of cavalry and artillery; by far the largest force he had commanded. Major-General Rowland Hill should have been in command but had returned to Britain on sick leave; Beresford's seniority made him next in line. On 25 March the 4th Division arrived at Campo Maior, north of both Badajoz and Elvas, the latter still in allied hands. Three weeks of almost continuous marching with bad weather and poor supplies told in the 23rd's numbers. A muster showed they had present only thirty-two officers, twenty-five sergeants, thirteen drummers and 503 rank and file, almost half their numbers before leaving Aveiras de Cima. Some stragglers were trying to rejoin them, but there were also over fifty men sick back in Lisbon; others had deserted or died on the roadside.

The weather on 25 March was wet; unfortunately, so was Beresford's performance in one of the most controversial affairs of the war. The minor clash outside the walls of Campo Maior was largely a cavalry affair, and neither Jack nor any of the 4th Division was involved: they were perhaps two miles back, on the road from Arronches. But a brief description of events is worth including, because it foreshadowed others that definitely involved Jack and his men a few weeks later. Beresford's cavalry, under the command of Brigadier General Robert Ballard Long, approached the town. They spotted, and were spotted by, a small French force of around 2,400 men under the wonderfully named General Marie-Victor-Nicolas de Fay Latour-Maubourg, who had been tasked with rendering Campo Maior defenceless by destroying its walls and removing its guns. The appearance of a large enemy force was a genuine surprise to Latour-Maubourg, who had no idea Beresford was nearby. He rapidly placed his men, guns and stores on the road to Badajoz, about 10 miles away. Long attacked with his light cavalry. The 13th Light Dragoons broke part of the French cavalry, pursued them to the walls of Badajoz and supported by Portuguese units, captured no less than 16 guns, ammunition and large amounts of stores. Unfortunately, Long's heavy cavalry, which should have followed, were halted by Beresford, despite Long's pleading. Beresford could not see the result of the 13th Light Dragoons' charge because of the undulating countryside; he inexplicably chose to believe a false report they had been annihilated. Protected by the guns of Badajoz, Latour-Maubourg's troops marched unmolested into the fortress. In the absence of their supports, the 13th Light Dragoons abandoned the captured guns, which the French swiftly recovered. What could have been a major success, the probable capture of the entire French force, was instead a farce, caused by Beresford's mistake. Thomas Farmer wrote home that 'The Marshall is very much blam'd by the whole of the army'.[30] That the Dragoons were highly successful, and bested their French opposite numbers on the day was in no doubt. Fortescue later remarked 'I know nothing finer in the history of the British cavalry'.[31] But Beresford claimed they had lost control, blamed Long for not managing them properly and reported this to Wellington, who formally censured the Dragoons. The row flared for years thereafter.[32]

Campo Maior was occupied and Beresford's army moved to the Portuguese fortress of Elvas, across the Guadiana river from Badajoz. Most of the army marched on 26 March, the still-recovering 4th Division lingering at Campo Maior another day.[33] On reaching Elvas, von Wacholtz rejoined from leave: 'my arrival visits were unfortunate, for I found Brigade Colonel Meyers, Major Pearson and Captain Sympher, who commanded our artillery...not at home, just the brigade-major and Captain Hill'.[34] As usual, Jack was at his post. To approach Badajoz the army needed to cross the Guadiana; the huge fortress sits on a prominence of the river's south bank, where a tributary, the Rivillas, joins. The bridge into the town from the north bank was fortified at both ends and controlled by the French garrison. Beresford therefore moved south to fords at Jeruminha where he had been led to believe pontoon boats could build a temporary bridge. Unfortunately, the river was swollen, unfordable and he had only about half the number of boats needed to span it. By the time the 4th Division reached Jeruminha on 1 April, after another twenty-mile march, engineers were building trestles from each bank to narrow the gap. Work on the trestles completed late on 3 April; the troops readied to cross the next day. But overnight a flash flood further raised the river, sweeping the trestles away. The engineers began again, this time constructing 'flying bridges', two large rafts to be hauled across. Each could carry 100 men, but with thousands plus cannon, horses, ammunition and other stores all needing to cross, it would be a painstakingly slow process. To add capacity, wine casks from the neighbourhood were gathered and lashed together with the pontoon boats to make a narrow floating bridge described as

---

30 RWF Archives object 5257b.
31 Fortescue, *History* Vol. VIII
32 Beresford was castigated by historians, including Napier, for his performance at both Campo Maior and Albuera; he later sought to defend himself. Balanced analysis can be found in *Galloping At Everything: The British Cavalry in the Peninsular War and at Waterloo 1808-15* by Ian Fletcher (1999) and *Albuera: Wellington's Fourth Peninsular Campaign, 1811* by Peter Edwards (2008).
33 Edwards, *Albuera*
34 *v.Wachholtz, Auf der Peninsula*

'not very substantial, but, upon trial, found capable of admitting infantry to pass in file.'[35]

It took three days to get the bulk of the army across. After their recent exertions Jack and the sore-footed 4th Division may have enjoyed an enforced rest on the banks of the Guadiana, but to Beresford it was a frustrating delay, with risk of a French attack before all were across. Fortunately, the French did not try; though every day's delay gave the defenders of Badajoz, under the competent General Armand Phillipon, time to repair and improve the town's defences. Once the whole allied force was across, Latour-Maubourg decided not to risk trapping his cavalry inside Badajoz, where they would be largely useless. Instead, leaving a garrison of 3,000 under Phillipon, he marched south to a point from which he hoped he might both disrupt the forthcoming Allied siege and connect with Soult's army, who he expected to return to relieve the city. Latour-Maubourg left another 400 French soldiers in the small fort of Olivenza, not far from the allied crossing point. Olivenza was not strong; Beresford called its garrison to surrender as he approached on 9 April. Surprisingly, they refused. This was little more than a nuisance, but even such a small force threatened the brittle allied communications across the river and could not be ignored. Cole's 4th Division was assigned to deal with the problem.

There were three basic ways to capture a fortress, whether a huge one like Badajoz with strong, modernised defences, or a small, antiquated one like Olivenza. The first was to surround it, cut it off from outside help and starve the garrison out. That required time which, with the probability of Soult marching up from the south to intervene, was not available. The second was to breach the walls with cannon, usually accompanied by digging trenches, or saps, to allow infantry close enough to assault through the breaches. This also took time, needed the right artillery and might be costly in lives, though a town's defenders might surrender once their walls were breached, rather than face an assault. The third - quickest, less sure and potentially more costly - was to storm it: launch a direct attack, preferably against a weakly-defended spot and possibly using ladders to scale the walls. Olivenza had 400 men defending a mile of walls. Even after hard marching, the 4th Division were more than capable of taking it by storm. Beresford, though, decided first to breach the walls. Why, when time was not on his side and the real target was Badajoz, is another controversy that dogs his reputation, especially as the artillery needed was still in Elvas. Perhaps he did not want to spend his men's lives storming a minor target. Perhaps he considered the 4th too weary; they

---

35 Benjamin D'Urban, Beresford's Chief of Staff, quoted in Oman, *History Vol. IV*

could rest further while the guns did their work (though he had other troops at hand who could have been given the task instead). Perhaps he considered Olivenza a rehearsal for the main task; his army had little experience of attacking fortresses, especially in Europe.[36] The guns were sent for, along with their accompanying Portuguese artillerymen, all transported over the rickety Guadiana crossings. It took nearly a week, until 15 April, for the first shots to be fired.

Pearson's Fusilier Brigade light companies went forward to cover the artillery batteries, putting Jack again in the heart of the action. It was dangerous work, as one soldier recalled:

> here a fit of ill humour cost one of our company his life. His name was David Wilson a handsome young Irishman. For some fault, a lieutenant ordered him an extra tour of duty. Accordingly, when the time came for relieving a small firing party that was placed under the wall to draw off some of the fire from our battery, he was sent along with others to that post. In that dangerous place it was necessary to keep close under cover, instead of which, David stood bolt upright before the enemy, and was shot right through the heart. An officer asked, 'who will volunteer to fetch the body?' Four of us volunteered, but we found it no easy task, as the place was quite exposed to the enemy's fire. At last we made a dash, threw the body into a great coat, and ran down an open sewer full of filth. A shower of balls came whizzing, but no harm was done, except a man's neck being grazed by a ball.[37]

Von Wacholtz had a similar experience when his riflemen took their turn: 'I had just advanced a little in the darkness...when the first shots were fired, probably by the sentries. We all lay down. Soon after we got a strong volley and a couple of cannonballs, all of which were aimed very well, so that one of them took a good bit off my sergeant's head'.[38] At least the danger was short lived: within about 4 hours a breach appeared and at around 11am a white flag appeared over the town; Olivenza had fallen. While Olivenza occupied the 4th Division, Beresford did not march directly to Badajoz but, aware that moving the artillery and preparing the siege there would take time, he took the rest of his army southeast towards Zafra. The speed of Olivenza's fall saw Cole's men soon follow; the 4th Division marched 30 miles to Santa

---

36 Wellington had besieged fortresses in India, and the British captured Montevideo in 1807. But neither were strongholds on European lines and in any case even Wellington was not at this point with Beresford's detachment.
37 Cooper, *Rough Notes*
38 *v.Wachholtz, Auf der Peninsula*

Marta on the 15th and 20 miles further, to Zafra, the next day.[39] Beresford had taken his army so far from their objective in order to push Latour-Maubourg further away from Badajoz, reducing his ability to interfere with the siege. He also wanted to connect to Spanish forces in the area; remarkably the Spanish commanders agreed to place themselves under Beresford's command if Soult threatened. Reinforcements also arrived from Lisbon in the form of a brigade of the King's German Legion. Beresford therefore potentially had at his disposal a truly international British-Portuguese-Spanish-German force that, in total, would amount to 35,000 men. He would need it.

Back at Badajoz the engineers, under the command of Richard Fletcher, were considering how best to attack the fortress. Fletcher determined that they should first capture one of four outlying defensive works, Fort St. Cristóbal. St. Cristóbal overlooked the town from high ground to the north. If taken, Badajoz itself would be vulnerable, and the siege might be over quickly. Wellington personally endorsed the plan; having pushed Masséna into Spain, he made a flying visit to see Badajoz himself on 22 April. Wellington gave Beresford detailed orders on how to conduct the siege and told him what to do if Soult threatened. A small village about 16 miles south of Badajoz was strategically situated at a junction of the roads Soult would probably use with those the Spanish could use to join Beresford's army. It stood on a range of low hills that, with careful troop positioning, offered good defensive ground. Described as little more than 'a street of mean houses, with a church', the place would have reminded Jack of Hennock.[40] Nearby ran a small river with which the village shared a name: La Albuera.

Wellington rejoined the main army on 25 April. Beresford moved his infantry towards Badajoz over the next few days, leaving cavalry to patrol south and watch for signs of a French advance. On the day Wellington rode north, the 23rd were at Valverde, strengthened by an intake from the 2nd Battalion of nine officers, five sergeants and 198 men. One of the officers was Lieutenant George Brown, brother of diarist Thomas. All were new to the 1/23rd, but the intake knew something of marching and fighting; some had survived both Coruña and Walcheren. George Browne was one of those, as were John Enoch, Samuel Thorpe and William Whalley. Another newcomer was 2nd Lieutenant Revis Hall, who Jack took special note of; he was from Topsham, only 13 miles from Hennock. The most junior 2nd Lieutenant in the battalion, Hall assumed the honour of carrying the King's Colour; he was 16 years old. From Valverde the 23rd moved to Badajoz, but didn't stay long. The 4th Division were sent 40 miles east to Mérida, to

---

39 Edwards, *Albuera*
40 Sherer, *Recollections*

secure the bridge there as a more robust crossing of the Guadiana. Jack and his weary colleagues marched again, Sergeant Cooper of the 7th Fusiliers recalling 'we suffered much, as the rations were insufficient. Many a meal was made of fried bullock's blood; and that man was counted happy who possessed a little salt'.[41] The officers' food was inevitably better, though at least von Wacholtz still found cause to complain: 'In the evening I dined at Meyers; General Cole and all the commanders of the 4th Division were there. The dinner was tolerable enough for the campaign; but we sat so close together, and it went so quickly in the English way, that I could hardly eat my fill'. He was cynical too about a parade held that day: 'The division drilled for a few hours today and then made a parade march in front of General Cole, probably in honour of his beautiful landlady, who was looking on'.[42] The Division stayed in the Mérida area until 6 May, when they were ordered back to Badajoz, arriving the next day and camping where there was wood and water available, about 4 miles from the siege lines.[43]

Fletcher reported on 3 May that everything was ready for siege operations to begin; it took another five days for the infantry to take their places in the lines surrounding the fortress. On the night of the 8th the labour finally started. Each regiment spent twenty-four hours at the front, either digging or guarding. For the men of the 23rd, that meant an 8-mile round trip whenever their turn came up, with hard work for their pleasure when they reached the front. Unfortunately, Fletcher's plan began to unravel almost immediately: solid rock was found inches below the surface. Protection therefore had to be provided above ground by positioning gabions, wicker baskets filled with soil and stones, as cover from the guns of Badajoz. Phillipon was an aggressive commander, sending sorties out to attack the batteries which therefore had to be defended. Light troops usually drew this duty and Jack recalled later that he:

> Commanded the three Fusilier Light and Brunswick Rifle Company by order of Sir William Myers at the first siege of Badajoz[44]

Which suggests that at least occasionally he took Pearson's place at the head of the composite light battalion. The cannon the allies had were poor: some antiques 200 years old, of various calibres, and many so worn that the balls fitted poorly, making them inaccurate. All the while

---

41 Cooper, *Rough Notes*
42 v.Wachholtz, *Auf der Peninsula*
43 RWF Archives object 7198.
44 Hill 1816 *Statement of Services*

communications to Elvas were at risk from the Guadiana. A new flying bridge was being built on a more direct line between the two fortresses, but when the river rose again, work had to be stopped; the cask bridge at Jeruminha was swept away. Temporarily, the bridge at Mérida was the only link between Beresford in the south and Wellington in the north. It was a risky position to be in.

Inside the walls of Badajoz, Phillipon put the residents under curfew between 8pm to 5am and ordered them to stay away from windows in daytime. Gatherings of more than seven people were banned. Anyone not complying with these instructions could be arrested or shot.[45]

Outside the walls, siegework was highly unpopular: an officer described the nature of the daily grind that Jack and his Light Company also experienced:

> the duties of a besieging force are both harassing and severe; and I know not how it is, death in the trenches never carries with it that stamp of glory, which seals the memory of those who perish in a well-fought field...[we] struggled only with privation, hardship and disease.[46]

News came through that Wellington had finally fought a major battle with Masséna in the north, at Fuentes d'Onoro, and won. Masséna was recalled, and his army retreated deep into Spain to recover. Any sense of missing out by the officers and men of Beresford's force would not last long; they would have an opportunity to 'perish in a well-fought field' soon enough.

On 13 May the army was ordered to make ready to march. One recalled 'reports soon began to circulate, that Soult was moving rapidly...that the siege was to be immediately raised; and that a battle might shortly be expected'.[47] The reports were accurate; Soult's advanced guard was already near Zafra. Following Wellington's plans, Beresford determined to march south, rendezvous with the Spanish and offer battle. He didn't have much choice; not to have moved would have meant facing Soult close to Badajoz, with the guns of the fortress and the river behind him and poor lines of retreat if things went wrong. The race for Albuera had begun, though John Harrison of the 23rd was surprised both by the rumours and that his regiment did not immediately march: 'this so unexpected and sudden piece of information, you may

45 *"At dawn, great firing was heard": A Spanish Eyewitness to the Sieges of Badajoz, 1811.* João Centano and Donald E. Graves 2006.
46 Sherer, *Recollections*
47 Cooper, *Rough Notes*

easily suppose, excited our astonishment not a little. This did not prevent our taking the duties...we had orders to move at a moment's notice [and] to our no small astonishment remained in this unpleasant uncertainty all day the 14th, that night and the following day, during which time our poor fellows were exposed to dreadful weather, and not more than a blade of grass to cover them'.[48] The 23rd did not move immediately because the 4th Division was ordered to cover the removal to Elvas of the artillery and other siege items so laboriously brought up just weeks before. As one of the regiment's histories rather immodestly put it, this was 'so completely effected, that not a single article fell into the hands of the enemy'.[49]

The first siege of Badajoz was over; it cost Beresford 733 men, all but seven from regiments of Kemmis' brigade working in the trenches near St. Cristóbal.[50] To add to Kemmis' woes, the Guadiana rose again and trapped most of his men north of the river. Save their regimental light companies, acting on the south bank as another converged light battalion alongside the Fusiliers, Kemmis' brigade faced a long, forced march via Jeruminha before they could rejoin Beresford. The rest of Cole's Division - Myer's Fusilier Brigade of 1/7th, 2/7th and 1/23rd; William Harvey's Brigade of the 11th and 23rd Portuguese Regiments and the Loyal Lusitanian Legion; divisional artillery; the company of Brunswick riflemen and Kemmis' detached light companies of the 2/27th, 1/40th and 97th had no such problems. With the siege stores safely in Elvas, this mixed bag of different nationalities, battalions and fragments, just over 100 officers and 2,000 men, left the outskirts of Badajoz in the early hours of 16 May to march 16 miles to Albuera. By the time they arrived, they literally were marching to the sound of the guns.

---

48 RWF Archives object 7198.
49 Broughton-Mainwaring, *Historical Record*
50 Edwards, *Albuera*

CHAPTER 10

THE FATAL HILL

'Commanded the three Fusilier Light and Brunswick Rifle Company…
during the latter part of the Battle of Albuera'

Statement of Services, 1816

It took nearly two weeks for news from Spain to reach those at home. The *London Gazette* of 28 May contained the briefest of reports 'On 16th Marshal Soult attacked the Combined [British/Portuguese/Spanish] Army at Alboera [sic], and, after an obstinate Action, was repulsed with great Loss, abandoning his Wounded, and retiring to a Position in Sight of the British Advanced Posts. The Loss on the Part of the Allies is not specified, but understood to be very severe'.[1] The news was repeated in newspapers across the land, the last sentence sending a chill through every family member who had a loved one with Beresford's part of the army. For the Hill family in Hennock, there was a clue on what 'very severe' might mean: the Gazette said Major-General Hoghton, and Lieutenant-Colonels Myers and Duckworth were killed; Major-Generals Cole and Stewart wounded. The Hills knew Jack was in Cole's Division and Myers' Brigade. If his two most senior commanders had been killed or wounded, everyone below them, Jack included, must have been in the thick of things. But there was no fuller list of officer casualties yet; all the Hills could do was wait anxiously, scan the daily newspapers for more detail and watch for word that would tell them the fate of their eldest son.

About a fortnight before, 1,000 miles south of Hennock, on 15 May, William Carr Beresford, Marshal of the Portuguese Army and commander of the southern wing of Wellington's Peninsular army, rode into the largely deserted Spanish village of La Albuera. The road he had travelled from Badajoz continued in front to the south-east. It crossed a gently rolling plain dotted with olive groves and woods, heading

---

1 *The London Gazette* Issue No. 16489 Saturday May 25 to Tuesday May 28, 1811

towards Santa Marta, Zafra and ultimately Seville. He knew that road, having travelled on it as far as Zafra only the previous month. He also knew that Marshal Jean-de-Dieu Soult, *Duc de Dalmatie*, was leading an army of some 25,000 men up that road towards him. Soult and his army were marching to relieve Badajoz from the siege Beresford had been undertaking for the past few weeks; in that respect he had already partly succeeded. Beresford could not risk becoming trapped by the rivers Badajoz stood on, as he would if Soult advanced unchecked. He had therefore marched his own army to Albuera to meet the oncoming Marshal; both men knew a battle was coming.

To Beresford's left, as he looked south, ran the road through Talavera la Real to Mérida, where the Guadiana could be crossed. If things went badly in the coming fight, that was one possible line of retreat. To his right ran the road to Valverde, past Olivenza and then on to the other possible crossing at Jeruminha. All the roads came together at Albuera. If Soult was to reach Badajoz, he had to come through here. Holding this point was critical to the defensive battle Beresford intended to fight. The village itself nestled between a river of the same name and a line of low hills running north to south. He deployed his troops on those hills as they filed in during the afternoon. Beresford considered the British infantry already with him, Stewart's 2nd Division, the most reliable part of his available force; he posted them immediately behind the village. He placed Victor von Alten's Brigade of KGL in the village, defending the two bridges over the Albuera river. Those bridges Beresford thought critical; they were on the direct route to Badajoz. Soult was bound to focus on capturing them. On the hills to the north, his left, he placed a Portuguese Division under Major-General John Hamilton. On those to the south he placed his Spanish allies, under Generals Joachim Blake and Francisco Castaños - or at least he would have done if Blake had arrived yet. The Spanish general and his troops were due to come in via the Valverde road and arrive by noon, but they were late. Beresford sent messages to hurry them up and for Cole to leave Badajoz and bring his 4th Division as quickly as possible. Beresford had in mind that Cole's men would defend the routes the allies needed to retreat by. To either end of his line went cavalry - Portuguese to the left, British and Spanish to the right. Across the plain, Soult had ridden ahead of his army and scanned the allied troops as they deployed. The hills meant he could not see the whole of his opponent's line, but he knew that they were not yet all in place - Cole, he thought (rightly) was still at Badajoz and Blake also appeared to be missing. Soult could see that there were troops in the town. He thought he saw an opportunity; as his forces marched in, he deployed them on the plain, ready to strike in the morning.

Back towards Badajoz, Jack, the 23rd and weary 4th Division were engaged in a night march. Sergeant Cooper of the 7th recalled:

after marching till daylight appeared, we halted and put off our great coats. Everyone was complaining for want of rest and sleep. Having marched a few miles further up a valley we heard distant sounds, and though they grew more frequent, yet we did not think that they were the noises of a battle field, as we were quite ignorant of any enemy being near. But so they proved, for in a few minutes the words, 'Light Infantry to the front', 'trail arms', 'double quick', were given. We then knew what was astir. Being tired, we made a poor run up a steep hill in front; but on reaching its summit we saw the two armies engaged below, on a plain about three quarters of a mile distant.[2]

As Jack led his light infantry company to the top of the slope he could see the smoke of battle. To his right front, cresting a ridge of hills, were the 2nd Division, mixed in with Spanish troops, the colours of the regiments flying above them, engaged with a mass of French infantry. More concerning was that to the right of that fighting, French cavalry was moving towards the rear of the ridge. It looked, he said later, as though everything was going against the allies.

What had already happened by the time the 4th Division arrived was a mixture of deception, opportunism, poor judgement, mistakes, obstinacy and resolution that would render the battle of Albuera one of the most controversial of the war. When Blake's Spanish troops finally arrived at around midnight - coincidentally at about the same time the 4th Division was beginning its march from Badajoz - they took position not to the right of the 2nd Division, but in front of them. At daylight the error was discovered; they began moving towards their correct place, extending the allied line to about 3 miles along the hills. They were not yet fully in position when the French began to advance. At around 8am, a large formation, perhaps 10,000 men, headed across the plain. The French were marching directly towards Albuera, just as Beresford anticipated. Seeing a possible opportunity to attack the French advance in the flank, about half of Blake's Spanish units, who had not yet moved to their proper place on the right were told to wait. A brigade from the British 2nd Division moved towards the village to strengthen its defences. All were sensible steps aimed at strengthening the allied line near the bridges outside Albuera. Unfortunately, Beresford had fallen for a ruse and done exactly what Soult wanted him to; the French advance was not what it appeared. Southwards, beyond the allied right, sheltered by folds in the land and woods, another French column advanced. About 8,400 infantry and over 3,000 cavalry swung out like a boxer throwing a left

---

2 Cooper, *Rough Notes*

hook aiming to attack the right end of the allied line; they were heading for precisely the place where the other part of the mis-placed Spanish troops were still deploying, facing east. William Beresford had little luck that morning, but one bit he did have was that the French 'left hook' was spotted: late, but still in time for him to issue rapid orders for the Spanish to turn and face south. One brigade, headed by General Zayas, managed the manoeuvre in time. But Blake, convinced that the main attack would be on the village, refused to move the rest of his troops. In response, Beresford directly ordered other Spanish units to move to their compatriots' support; one benefit of his being placed in command over everyone else on the field. He also ordered the 2nd Division to move rapidly a mile to their right and fall in behind Zayas' men. By the time they got there the Spanish were facing horrendous odds, a French force over 500 yards wide and around forty ranks deep, the widest French formation anyone in Spain had seen.[3] The Spanish stood their ground magnificently in the face of this and managed to stop the massive French advance in its tracks. The two sides slugged it out for at least half an hour before the lead brigade of the 2nd Division, under Sir John Colborne, begun to approach. This was what Jack and his colleagues in the 4th Division could see in outline as they climbed the hill behind Albuera: a huge mêlée of infantry about a mile or so away, wreathed in smoke with both sides standing their ground and pounding away up close. Colborne's men had marched up in column, the fastest to move across a battlefield. But to fight they needed to deploy into line. As they did so, two bad things happened. First the skies, which had been gloomy all morning, blackened and the heavens opened. Over behind Albuera, Cooper recorded the 4th Division 'lay down in a storm of hail and rain', while von Wacholtz recalled 'we ducked into some low bushes and sheltered ourselves as best we could'.[4] For those fighting on the hill in front, loading and firing their muskets became next to impossible; gunpowder does not react well to water. The second bad thing was that the French cavalry, who had been manoeuvring to get behind the entire British line until the 4th Division appeared in the nick of time over the crest before them, now saw an even better target: an unprotected line of infantry with weapons rendered almost useless by rain. 1,000 French riders dug their spurs into their horses and charged.

The British battalion immediately ahead was the 3rd Foot, the Buffs. They could see little through the downpour and the choking cloud of smoke around them. They were also focussed on the French infantry to their front who were trying to kill them and their Spanish allies. As a recent historian put it 'there can have been few eyes…idle enough to

---

3 Edwards, *Albuera*
4 Cooper, Rough Notes; v.Wachholtz, *Peninsula*

peer around through the swirling smoke at the blotted-out landscape, and the thundering beat of a thousand sets of steel-shod hooves would be lost in the continuous hammering of the cannons'.[5] Caught in the open, the Buffs had no chance. Some of the French cavalry were lancers, carrying 9-foot-long poles tipped with a steel point that easily outreached the infantry's bayonet-tipped muskets. Twenty of the Buffs' twenty-seven officers, and 623 of their 728 men were killed, wounded, or captured in maybe five minutes. The 80% casualties the Buffs suffered at Albuera was the worst incurred by any British battalion in the entire Peninsular War. When the Buffs' men and Colours were cut down, the French cavalry moved on to the next battalion, 2/48th (Northamptonshire). In minutes they too had lost both Colours, twenty-three out of twenty-nine officers and 320 out of 423 men. Coming up behind the Northamptons were the third unit in Colbourne's column, 2/66th (Berkshire). Their fate was much the same: both Colours, fifteen of twenty-four officers and 257 of 417 men lost. Behind the Berkshires were 2/31st (Huntingdonshire); arriving last and seeing what had happened ahead of them, they were able rapidly to form square, the traditional defence of infantry against cavalry. As proof of the effectiveness of such a formation, 2/31st suffered far less - though still had twenty-nine men killed, and seven officers and 119 men wounded from their strength of nearly 420. Disorganised by their success and with tired horses, the French cavalry now withdrew. They had done their work well; Colborne's brigade had effectively ceased to exist.

It was now about 11am. The fighting at Albuera had already been some of the most ferocious of the entire war, but the battle was far from over. Along the hill where Colborne's men had met their fate now came the 2nd Division's two other Brigades, under Daniel Hoghton and Alexander Abercromby. Jack had a connection to both commanders. Now a Major-General, Hoghton had led the first incarnation of the Fusilier Brigade across the jungle of Martinique and up the Surey heights, where Jack's riflemen had fought with such distinction. Abercromby, son of Sir Ralph who had died at the head of his army in Egypt, had joined the 23rd in Egypt and had been one of Jack's fellow captains while they were guarding the south coast of England in 1802-4. Now a Lieutenant-Colonel, he led 2/28th into the field but took over the Brigade when its commander, William Lumley, moved to command the British cavalry on the morning of the battle. The arrival of two British brigades might have been decisive, except that more French troops also reached the top of the hill at about the same time. A second bloodbath ensued on the same patch of ground. Including the survivors of 2/31st,

5 Edwards, *Albuera*

seven British battalions, perhaps 3,500 men in total, faced some 7,000 French soldiers, both sides supported by artillery. Something unusual now happened: Fortescue called it 'a duel so stern and resolute that has few parallels in the annals of war'. The two sides simply stood and fired repeatedly into each other, with little attempt to manoeuvre. The British were in line, two ranks deep, their breadth gradually contracting towards the centre as men fell and survivors closed the gaps. The French were in column, a narrower formation but one whose gaps filled up from behind. Moyle Sherer, fighting in the British line, later noted: 'the best soldier can make no calculation of time, if he be in the heat of an engagement; but this murderous contest of musketry lasted long'. The stalemate probably went on for at least an hour. Hoghton's brigade, on the right of the line, had the worst of it. Hoghton himself was killed; his 'three battalions, 29th, 1/48th and 1/57th absolutely died in line, without yielding an inch'.[6] As Colonel William Inglis of 1/57th lay severely wounded he called on his battalion to 'die hard', thus bequeathing the nickname it would proudly carry for decades. Hoghton's brigade lost over 1,000 men out of around 1,650; they were running out of soldiers and ammunition. The French were suffering too, but on hills to the south of Albuera the allied army was perilously close to defeat.

Behind the village, observing the chaos through the smoke and rain, stood Lowry Cole and the 5,000 men of his 4th Division. Watching their colleagues being slaughtered on the hills to the right was nightmarish and frustrating. Cole later wrote 'the issue at one time was very, very doubtful. So severe a combat has not, I believe taken place in this war'.[7] Even the private soldiers could tell things were not going well: 'The day was apparently lost, for large masses of the enemy had gained the highest part of the battle field, the numerous cavalry and artillery ready to roll up our whole line.'[8] One of Cole's staff commented 'General Cole continued anxiously to watch the progress of the contest…impatient with being compelled to withhold support under an evident demand for succour'.[9] Cole had been firmly ordered by Beresford to guard the line of retreat and not to move without express orders. Cole sent an aide to Beresford seeking permission to move up and support the allied troops dying in front of him. But Beresford had his mind on the prospect of defeat and had begun to issue orders to withdraw. If he had had his way, the outcome of Albuera would have been very different, but the fate of the battle was taken out of Beresford's hands, by a collective act of insubordination.

6 Oman, *History Vol. IV*
7 *Memoirs of Sir Lowry Cole* Maud Lowry Cole and Stephen Gwynn (Ed.) 1934
8 Cooper, Rough Notes
9 Quoted in Edwards, *Albuera*

As Cole sat on his horse becoming more and more tetchy at his inability to act, a horseman raced towards him. The rider was a 26-year-old major on secondment to the Portuguese staff, Henry Hardinge. Hardinge's actions that day might have prematurely ended what would instead become a rise to the very top: by the end of his career, he was a member of the House of Lords, Governor-General of India, Commander-in-Chief of the British Army and a Field Marshal. Hardinge had seen that Hoghton's brigade was nearly spent. He rightly assessed (as had Cooper, and no doubt Cole) that if they collapsed entirely, the French infantry would swing around on Abercromby's men, push them beyond the town, and the day would be lost. Without consulting Beresford, Hardinge took it upon himself to ride to the 4th Division and press Cole to intervene. He found a receptive audience. Cole gave the orders for his division to form up. The order was passed through the Division: 'Fall in Fusiliers'.

Jack had his light company spring to their feet. Their role would normally be to get out in front of the battalion and fight independently, tackling enemy skirmishers and softening up the opposing line before the main body of troops arrived. But Cole required something different. In Napoleonic battles, the opportunity to use infantry, artillery and cavalry together was tactical nirvana. That was exactly what Soult was doing: his infantry and artillery were on the ridge in front and his cavalry, having already intervened to devastating effect once, were gathered in a threatening mass over towards Cole's right. Cole therefore had serious tactical problems to overcome. First, he had about a mile of exposed ground to cover before reaching his objective, the hill where the Spanish and the 2nd Division were suffering. Speed was essential; to get there quickly meant moving his battalions in columns. But in a column, only the front ranks and those at the side could fire their weapons. He could have formed his regiments into line, but lines moved more slowly because they were more difficult to control. When they got close enough, the troops would have to change formation to face the enemy in line, as a line meant every gun could brought to bear; firepower would matter at the top of the ridge. Changing from column into line was exactly the manoeuvre Colborne's men had been performing when they were caught by the French cavalry; the same cavalry who were now waiting for another opportunity to catch infantry as they were changing formation. This was a significant risk; as Oman put it 'the proposal that he should advance across open ground in face of 3,500 French cavalry, without adequate support of that arm on his own side, was enough to make any man think twice'.[10]

---

10 Oman, *History Vol. IV*

Cole's second problem was that when he got to the top of the hill, he needed the left of his division to arrive first, joining the right of the 2nd Division, where the fighting was hardest. He had absolute confidence in the Fusilier Brigade to be able to do that, so he would form them on the left. But the Portuguese troops in Myers' brigade, who would therefore have to be on the right, were untried in battle. He could not risk exposing them to the lurking French cavalry. His solution lay in the General Order concerning light troops: 'light infantry companies…are to be formed together…when the brigade shall be formed for the purpose of opposing an enemy, the light infantry companies and riflemen will be…in the front, flanks, or rear, according to the circumstances of the ground, and the nature of the operation to be performed'. Cole ordered Major Thomas Pearson to re-form a larger version of his 'converged light battalion'. This time it would comprise not just Jack's Light Company of the 23rd and those of the two battalions of the 7th, but also the three detached light companies of 2/27th, 1/40th and 97th from Kemmis' brigade, Portuguese companies from Myers' brigade and the company of Brunswick riflemen. In total, this scratch battalion comprised some 400-500 men. They would guard the Division's most vulnerable point: the extreme right of the formation where the French cavalry lurked. The 'light battalion' would march off in column, like the rest of the Division. But instead of forming line as they approached the enemy, they would form square. Then their job would be to protect the entire 4th Division line from cavalry attack. The light battalion square would not be able to take position and hold it, they needed to keep advancing alongside the rest of the Cole's line. Advancing in square was one of the most difficult manoeuvres soldiers could undertake; it says much of Cole's confidence in Pearson and the men under his command that he believed they could do it.

With a relatively small number of Spanish and British cavalry and horse artillery positioned behind and further to the right, and a mirroring formation of Portuguese cavalry, together with the Loyal Lusitanian Legion in column on the left, everything was ready. From left to right, Cole's formation was: the Loyal Lusitanians (about 650 men), 1/7th Royal Fusiliers (700), 2/7th Royal Fusiliers (570), 1/23rd Royal Welch Fusiliers (730), 11th Portuguese (1,150), 23rd Portuguese (1,200), Pearson's composite light 'battalion' (4-500). Slightly after midday Cole gave the order for the mile-wide formation of some 5,000 British, Portuguese and German infantrymen to step off and begin an advance into history.

On probably 5 or 6 June 1811, the rural tranquillity of Hennock was disturbed by the clatter of hooves. The sound of horses was, of course, entirely normal in the village. There was though, a sense of urgency this time as the horse and rider, having climbed the hill from Bovey Tracey, pulled up outside the door of the vicarage; the rider dismounted and knocked loudly on it. He bore a letter with a hastily scribbled covering message, bearing the instruction:

Mrs. Jones, Bovey – Mr. Pinhey is requested to read this, and send it up immediately afterwards to Hennock.

W. Hill

The covering note was from William Hill to his father. It read:

Revd. Hill
Hennock,
Chudleigh

I have this morning received the joyful news of our dear John's wellfare after the late most dreadful occurrence at Albuhera - This account in some particulars corresponds with the Gazette extra d[eliver]y, a small part of which I have seen. You I suppose will receive it from Mr. Garrett tomorrow. The French loss according to Lord Liverpool's letter to [the] Lord Mayor is 9,000. I mention this as John says nothing about it.

Mr. Corkey is good enough to let his boy ride over so far as Bovey with this and I shall request Uncle Pinhey to read it and send it up to you immediately.

Mr. Ley was here yesterday all very well. My wife sends her love.

Attached was a letter containing the news the entire Hill family had been waiting anxiously to receive.

22nd May, 1811
La Albuera

I wrote immediately after the last action to inform you I had escap'd unhurt. This thank God was necessary to quiet your apprehensions when not one half has that good fortune.

We had previously to the 16[th] gradually withdrawn our mortars and heavy cannon, anticipating some efforts that would be made to relieve that place [Badajoz]. Between 12 and one of the morning [of the]16[th] we march'd from our trenches before Badajos, in front of which I had been with my Com[pan]y as a covering party three days previous, and during the dark in which we decamp'd left four of our sentinels under the walls, whom we could not find among the com[pany] however, they have made good their retreat. Three leagues from Badajos we join'd the 2nd Div. of the army which was at that moment engaged in a cannonade with the enemy - The lines were soon formed, our Divn. on the right.

The light Com[panies] were found on the right of the Portuguese in a hollow square. With this to cover its right, the line moved on to carry some heights on which the enemy had posted Artillery, Cavalry and sharp shooters. As our line approach'd, their infantry crown'd the heights in columns, afraid as the prisoners inform'd me to deploy in consequence of the superiority in cavalry we had manifested in the affair of Campo Major.

From the square on the right in which I was, (which outflank'd their infantry, but in return was outflank'd by the enemy's cavalry) I conceive the depth of each of the columns was 9 Ranks. The distance of the enemy's second line or column (which you please) was about 60 yards. In their rear again some cavalry was found. Anxiously looking to the left to see how our Regt. got on we saw them gradually ascend the slope which brought them to a ridge commanded by another still higher which the enemy occupied, distant about 60 yards. Here a most heavy destructive fire of musketry was exchang'd, the infantry mutually advancing. At last the enemy halted. Our people continued advancing, and we had the satisfaction of seeing our Regt. on the summit of the hills which their [the French] two lines or column had been unable to maintain themselves.

I have been speaking of our Regt. [which] in consequence of its being on the right of the Fusilier brigade was nearer me and less cover'd with smoke, the other two Fusilier Regts. were in line with them to the left, and at the same moment carried the heights oppos'd to them. The Fusilier Brigade [before they] arriv'd on the heights were attack'd in front by cavalry who receiving the fire of one of our companies put themselves in order and prepar'd to charge thinking the whole unloaded. The spurs were in the horses' sides, they were coming on, the Grenadiers then fir'd on them about 15 paces distant and the file fire recommenced from those who had first fired, when they went to the right about and galloped off. During this some small parties of cavalry had got in our rear and took prisoners [of] the wounded [as] they were getting from under the fire.

On the left the British suffered most amazingly, I do not hesitate to say that at one moment I thought it would have been the most fatal to our arms, I had ever seen. As we went into action the red coats were retiring pursued by the cavalry. The Ground was perfectly open, there was no position to retire to, and the enemy was very superior in Cavalry. The regular Spanish troops at this moment came up and took their places on the left which had been occupied by the British, their conduct was extremely good, their loss 2/3rds of what they brought up to that point. One of their Gen[era]ls (I think Blake) had the whole of his attendants, one excepted (his A[djutan]t Gen[era]l) killed or wounded and Blake himself had his horse shot under him.

British	kill'd 886	Wounded 2705	Missing 547	Total 4138
Portuguese	102	252	26	380
				4518

You may add to this at least 1700 Spaniards. I know from one of the A[djutan]t Gen[era]ls that their regulars on the left lost above 900. Their light irregular troops continued [to] scrimish till nightfall and their loss in cavalry must have been great, as when they retir'd pursued by the French cavalry the fire of the infantry could no longer be witheld, without endangering their being broken both by the flying and pursuing parties. The alternative was dreadfull and from the state of our left it was nothing but the steady determin'd attack of the Infantry on the right that sav'd the day. Had they been broken we should have been annihilated. Our Cavalry were not engaged generally.

The enemy was superior in numbers to ours. We have lost a howitzer and taken one some say two French pieces. Some of the Regts. on the left lost their colours. Of this the French will say enough. The wounded French officers say the late affair was more severe than Barrosa. They must have been epicures to take a second drubbing – Lord Wellington is here, we shall in a few days receive very strong reinforcement.

Whether Badajos will detain us I know not - the enemy is retiring on Seville. The Portuguese behaved very well, a Brigade of theirs was between us and the Fuz[ilier] Battalions. Their steadiness with so great a number of cavalry in their neighbourhood does them great credit. We are laying on our arms or three leagues east of Merida.

Send on to Hennock,
Yours,
J. HILL

Cole's unauthorised advance of his division had taken place in the nick of time. About halfway to their destination, at around the point where the ground began to slope more steeply upwards, Cole gave the order for his battalions to deploy from column into line. It was, he later said, 'a manoeuvre always difficult to perform correctly even in a common field day,' never mind under incessant fire from French artillery, who by then had them in their sights.[11] Cooper remembered: 'The line in this order approached at quick step the steep position of the enemy; under a storm of shot, shell, and grape, which came crashing through our ranks'.[12] On the far right, the column of light companies formed their hollow square while under fire, as von Wachholz recalled:

> We advanced calmly, however, with a few guns in front of us and a strong column of enemy cavalry opposite us...A few times I thought they would charge us; only our cavalry next to us, which by the way did nothing at all, the artillery and even our square, as I later learned from some prisoners, kept them in respect; I wasn't afraid for us Englishmen [sic], we would have received them properly with our bayonets; but the front and by far larger part of our square consisted of Portuguese, who could only be kept in order and closed with a lot of shouting. That they weren't very wise either was shown by a cannonball that went diagonally through our square, took the legs off a few people in front, punched the officer marching in the middle next to the flags in the chest, and then continued on its way without further ado. Where the gap had been created by the wounded in front, they did not really want to close them together again and always believed that the following cannonball would have to come to the same spot. [13]

As the rest of Cole's formation moved into line, the denser target offered by the light infantry square would have been tempting to the French gunners, but artillery was far from the only danger Jack and his

---

11 Cole, quoted in Edwards, *Albuera*
12 Cooper, Rough Notes
13 *v. Wachholtz, Peninsula*. Most histories refer to Cole's composite light battalion as British, but it was of mixed nationality: Von Wacholtz, who was in it, states clearly that Portuguese soldiers participated. Oman says Cole's light battalion was 'made up of the nine light companies of all his regiments, British and Portuguese'. If Oman is correct, those companies were from 1/7th, 2/7th,, 1/23rd, 2/27th, 1/40th, 97th (British); 11th and 23rd (Portuguese); and the Brunswicks (German), though Portuguese line regiments had no light companies, and the Loyal Lusitanian Legion, the other battalion in Harvey's Brigade, was deployed on the left of Cole's line. Wacholtz interestingly also refers to the formation having flags. It is not clear what these were. Regimental Colours would have remained with their parent battalions; those in the light battalion square may have been marker pennants.

colleagues were in. Now the French cavalry saw their chance. As Jack put it, 'the spurs were in the horses' sides.' Cooper remembered the same incident: 'the French cavalry made a charge at...our front. Immediately a volley from us was poured into [them]...This checked the French'.[14] From Jack's description of this incident, the front company of the light battalion square fired the first volley, with 'Grenadiers', perhaps the right company of the 23rd Portuguese, who were closest to the square, firing soon after. The cavalry seen off, Cole's division now had to climb the hill. Cooper again: 'we began to climb its slope with panting breath, while the roll and thunder of furious battle increased. Under the tremendous fire of the enemy our thin line staggers, men are knocked about like skittles; but not a step backward is taken'. The advancing line, marching on steadily to the beat of the drummers with each battalion's Colours flying overhead was a magnificent sight. Moving 'with an élan, but regularity of formation, never excelled on the battlefield, the Fusilier brigade moved against the enemy'.[15] As they climbed, the smoke cleared enough to show they were not the only infantry who had just joined the fight.

Soult had seen Cole's division move forward. He knew their joining the fight on the hill would be decisive if he did not act; he had one final move of his own available. Some 5,000 infantry under General Werlé, part of the decoy attack on Albuera, had not yet been engaged. As Cole marched, Werlé was ordered to move to his left and climb the same hill from the French side. They were closer than Cole's line; marching in column all the way to the top, they arrived first. With the 4th Division coming up, Werlé's men tried to deploy into line, but Cole's men opened fire as soon as they saw French uniforms lining the ridge. For the second time in the battle two opposing sets of troops poured fire into each other. This time, however, neither side simply stood still. As Jack described, while keeping up 'a most heavy destructive fire of musketry' both sides also kept pushing forward, the French continuously trying, but failing, to get into line and so bring more of their muskets into action. The scene was again chaotic: 'The orders were 'close up'; 'close in'; 'fire away'; 'forward.' This is done,' said Cooper.[16] Ingrained moves by every man in the line kept the pressure up from both sides. Officer after officer fell, French and British alike. Cole was wounded; Myers was killed. At the head of the 23rd, Henry Ellis was shot painfully through the hand and had to leave the field. The hierarchy of command meant that as Ellis departed, Major Thomas Pearson now had to be called back from the light infantry square to take charge of his regiment.

14 Cooper, Rough Notes
15 *Battles of the British Army*, Charles Rathbone Low 1890
16 Cooper, Rough Notes

Pearson passed control of the light battalion to the next most senior officer in the formation: Captain Jack Hill. It was Jack's first field command; he could not have acquired it in more trying circumstances.

The struggle on the crest lasted maybe half an hour. Soldier after soldier, officer after officer fell. But still the opposing lines kept pressing closer. 'The whole field behind our line was covered with red, retiring wounded' said von Wacholtz:

> it was a terribly beautiful scene to see both fire-breathing lines so close together, and death roaring terribly beneath them. But the beating of the anxious, expectant heart rose even higher when suddenly a dull, louder and finally horrible hurrah rose in our line and our brigade rushed at the enemy column with the bayonet. Soon the short distance was covered, the enemy saw the long bayonets, the towering Englishmen at 15 paces in front of him, his first ranks began to dissolve, the others followed, and in two seconds he fled with the greatest disorder and speed.[17]

The French, already suffering from the firepower in front of them, and faced now with a roaring, charging mass of bayonets, broke. Jack's light battalion had held off the French cavalry, Cole had captured the hill, and Beresford had won the day.

When the news of Albuera reached Britain, the story of the struggle and the level of slaughter inspired numerous poets to reach for their pen. They included Byron, who called it the 'glorious field of grief' and Felicia Browne who wrote of 'the dead and dying on Albuera's plain' (unable to resist rhyming the last word, of course, with 'Spain').[18] The attack of the Fusilier Brigade, and their Portuguese allies, also inspired some of the most famous lines ever written by a military historian. William Napier, himself an officer in Wellington's army, published his history of the Peninsular War between 1828 - 1840. In seven volumes it was (and is) a monumental piece of work. Napier was strong in his opinions and flawed as a historian; he was not at Albuera and did not visit it, so his narrative relied on what he was told by others. Napier's description of the advance of the Fusiliers at Albuera has, however, been quoted innumerable times in other histories. Jack Hill played a leading role in that advance and as this book borrows its title from one of the sentences, it would be incomplete without it:

---

17 *v.Wachholtz, Peninsula*
18 Byron, *Childe Harold's Pilgrimage*; Felicia Dorothea Hemans, *English Soldier's Song of Memory*

Such a gallant line, issuing from the midst of the smoke, and rapidly separating itself from the confused and broken multitude, startled the enemy's heavy masses, which were increasing and pressing onwards as to an assured victory: they wavered, hesitated, and then vomiting forth a storm of fire, hastily endeavoured to enlarge their front, while a fearful discharge of grape from all their artillery whistled through the British ranks. Myers was killed, Cole, the three colonels, Ellis, Blakeney and Hawkshawe, fell wounded, and the fuzileer battalions, struck by the iron tempest, reeled, and staggered like sinking ships. But suddenly and sternly recovering, they closed on their terrible enemies, and then was seen with what a strength and majesty the British soldier fights. In vain did Soult, by voice and gesture, animate his Frenchmen; in vain did the hardiest veterans, extricating themselves from the crowded columns, sacrifice their lives to gain time for the mass to open out on such a fair field; in vain did the mass itself bear up, and fiercely striving, fire indiscriminately upon friends and foes while the horsemen hovering on the flank threatened to charge the advancing line. Nothing could stop that astonishing infantry. No sudden burst of undisciplined valour, no nervous enthusiasm, weakened the stability of their order, their flashing eyes were bent on the dark columns in their front, their measured tread shook the ground, their dreadful volleys swept away the head of every formation, their deafening shouts overpowered the dissonant cries that broke from all parts of the tumultuous crowd, as slowly and with a horrid carnage, it was pushed by the incessant vigour of the attack to the farthest edge of the height. There, the French reserve, mixing with the struggling multitude, endeavoured to sustain the fight, but the effort only increased the irremediable confusion, the mighty mass gave way and like a loosened cliff went headlong down the steep. The rain flowed after in streams discoloured with blood, and fifteen hundred unwounded men, remnant of six thousand unconquerable British soldiers, stood triumphant on the fatal hill![19]

As a factual account of a military engagement, Napier's prose has considerable problems, as many have pointed out.[20] As a piece of heroic literature, however, his narrative is unsurpassed. US President Theodore Roosevelt, no mean soldier-historian himself, later said: 'No poet can

19 Napier, *History*
20 For example, in *The Face of Battle* John Keegan, 1976; Keegan concedes the passage was 'a very remarkable achievement', but asks: 'Just what does it tell us about the Fusiliers' advance; and is what it tells us credible'.

ever supersede what Napier wrote...of the British infantry at Albuera'; Roosevelt is the only man to have won both the Congressional Medal of Honor and the Nobel Peace Prize, so might be considered a decent judge.[21]

The detail the Hills and other families across the country waited for was published in a Special Edition of the *London Gazette* on 3 June. Over the next few days newspapers across the country reprinted Beresford's sombre dispatch. Albuera was a victory bought at an exceptionally high price. In the *Exeter Flying Post* the list of officers killed and wounded alone took up an entire column.[22] To the great relief of John and Margaret Hill, Jack's name was not among them. Then the letter forwarded by William confirmed he was unhurt. The far right of the line had avoided the worst of the carnage, though von Wachholtz's recollections show they still took casualties. The numbers the light battalion companies lost are subsumed within those of their parent battalions, except for the three from Kemmis' Brigade, the only part of that formation on the field. These three companies suffered one officer and five men killed and another fourteen men wounded.[23] As Kemmis' men comprised roughly a third of the composite light battalion, if casualties were similar across the other units, the whole formation lost around 60 men, perhaps 15% of its strength. Had the French cavalry charged the end of Cole's line, the light battalion square would have been required to hold firm to avoid disaster; the deterrent effect Cole achieved by placing some of his best men in such a vulnerable position worked. In the middle of the line, the main body of the 23rd saw Captain Frederick Montagu, who had been acting as Brigade Major, and Lieutenant Revis Hall, who arrived just a month earlier, both killed outright. A sergeant and seventy-three men were also killed. Henry Ellis, Captains William Herford, Alexander Macdonald and William Stainforth, Lieutenants Gordon Booker, Robert Castle, Isaac Harris, John Harrison, Henry Ledwith, Robert MacLellan, Samuel Thorpe and Richard Treeve, twelve sergeants, a drummer and 232 men were wounded. Another sergeant and 5 men were missing. Robert Castle later died of his wounds, as did Alexander MacDonald, who had led the Grenadier Company alongside Jack and his riflemen up the Surey heights in Martinique; MacDonald never would farm the land in Nova Scotia Sir George Prevost granted him in reward for that action. Stainforth's company lost all its officers and sergeants; by the end of the battle those left were being led by corporal Thomas

---

21 *History As Literature* Theodore Roosevelt in *The American Historical Review Vol. 18, No. 3* 1913

22 *Trewman's Exeter Flying Post* June 6, 1811

23 Fortescue, *History* Vol. VIII

Robinson.[24] Thorpe was lucky that, left on the field for dead following two serious wounds, he was later found by two soldiers who noticed him breathing and carried him back to camp.[25] The battalion's casualty rate of 46% only seems relatively low when compared with the other battalions of the Fusilier Brigade, the 1/7th (50%) and 2/7th (62%), or with the utter devastation of the 2nd Division.

The battle ended around six hours after it started. In total the British lost 4,160, the Portuguese 1,300, the Spanish 1,370, the French perhaps 8,200 (Soult claimed only 2,800 in his report; a flagrant deception). Most of the dead, and many of the wounded for the next few days, lay together in an area roughly half a mile square. Exhausted, the men on both sides rested and tried to recover. Then the skies opened again and soaked them all, living, wounded and dead. Bentinck recalled 'our provisions came late in the evening and our Corporals went to fetch them. When they asked them how many they had they did not exactly know but they told them a great deal more than there was. So that we all had enough. We kindled the fires with the broken stocks of the rifles and the broken gun carriages. We made ourselves very comfortable amongst the dead'.[26] Cooper had similar recollections:

> We lay down at night among the mire and dead men. I selected a tuft of rushes and coiled myself up like a dog, but sleep I could not, on account of hunger and cold. Once I looked up out of my wet blanket, and saw a poor wounded man stark naked, crawling about I suppose for shelter. Who had stript him or whether he lived till morning I know not. Before daylight we were under arms shivering with cold, and our teeth very unsteady; but the sun rose and began to warm us. Half a mile distant were the French, but neither they nor we showed any desire of renewing hostilities. A little rum was now served out, and our blood began to circulate a little quicker. We then rubbed up our arms and prepared for another brush; but nothing serious took place.[27]

The two sides watched each other for the whole of that day. The wounded who survived the night but had not made their own way to the surgeons were recovered; the dead were collected. Beresford made ready to retreat should Soult renew his attack but received a welcome reinforcement when the main part of Kemmis' brigade tramped in, to be

24 Cary and McCance *Regimental Records*
25 *Narrative of Incidents in the Early Military Life of Major Samuel Thorpe, KH* 1854
26 Crook, *Bentinck*
27 Cooper, Rough Notes

stunned at what they found. In the early hours of the 18th Soult began to move his men, able and wounded, away towards the southeast. The same day Jack sat down and wrote his first letter about the battle to his mother. He wanted his family to know he was alive. The vagaries of the mail service meant this letter arrived after that he sent subsequently to William. Written two days after he led the light battalion in by far the biggest battle of his life, his exhaustion and numbness are tangible.

18 May, 1811

My Dear Mother,

Thank the Almighty that He has again saved your son unhurt in the tremendous battle of the 16th, the papers will give you the details. Our Regt. went into the field, counting the men with the mules in the rear, about 560, our return of killed, wounded and 16 missing, the latter of which we have now all accounted for amounted to 310, which included 14 officers.

Ellis is wounded not dangerously, part of his hand carried away. Montagu whose friends live near Caroline and Hall the son of the Col. at Topsham, are among our killed. I cannot say enough for the brigade and Battn. They charged two lines, one behind the other about 80 yards and in their rear cavalry and succeeded in gaining the heights.

In the early part of the day I thought every thing was going against us. A portion of the British Infantry was put into confusion by a charge of cavalry after some of the regt. had made a 2nd Charge on the French Infantry. The Spanish Infantry, regulars, behav'd very well; the Portuguese in our Division were as steady as rocks. Yesterday was employ'd by both parties in taking care of the wounded.

The French retreated last night and this morning our troops commenced the pursuit by attacking their rear guard. I will write a longer letter soon, and in the meantime desire you to communicate to Caroline and Wm.

Yours,
J. HILL

The Spaniards have lost about 1500 men, the Portuguese not so many. The Carnage was without exception far more terrible than any I ever before have seen. Our inferiority in Cavalry sav'd the French army from destruction.

Had we succeeded in a charge of that arm when the infantry was driven from the hills, it must have been the case. This will account for our not having taken many prisoners. The ground is much like Salisbury Plain. The French took post behind a small river that ran parallel with the lines of operations & after their defeat remained there yesterday employed as above mentioned.

On the day after Jack wrote, the exhausted Allies moved east to Almendralejo, covering any attempt by Soult to return north. There was a small clash at Usagre, mostly between cavalry, following which both sides moved further apart, the 4th Division retracing its steps ultimately back to Torre de Mouro, near Campo Maior in June. Then the recriminations began; many officers thought Beresford had bungled his initial deployments, been slow to see the threat emerging on his right, focused too much on possible retreat and nearly lost the battle in consequence. Wellington, though publicly supportive, thought similarly and was privately damning, while also blaming the Spanish for moving too slowly when Soult's real attack was discovered. Even Beresford himself was downcast, writing to Wellington gloomily: 'We have by beating him [Soult] escaped total destruction which must [otherwise] have been the consequence and I am very, very far from feeling happy after our Triumph...The Great Gallantry of our brave British saved the day, which was at one time in a most perilous situation but our loss has been enormous'.[28] His official dispatch was similar in tone; Wellington called it 'whining', set it aside and directed Beresford's ADC and his own staff to produce a more positive version, fearing the reaction to the scale of casualties if underpinned by such pessimism - he reputedly said 'This won't do - write me down a victory'.[29] The Fusiliers' thought even the more positive version did them insufficient justice. Much of the report focused on Stewart's 2nd Division; ignoring that Beresford did not order Cole's crucial move the dispatch reported 'Major-General Cole, seeing the attack of the enemy, very judiciously bringing up his left a little, marched in line to attack the enemy's left, and arrived most opportunely to contribute, with the charges of General Stewart's division, to force the enemy to abandon his situation and retire precipitately and take refuge under his reserve; here the fuzileer brigade particularly distinguished itself.' The Fusiliers were convinced their intervention had won the battle; to have this described merely as an opportune contribution was to them damning with the faintest of praise. Edward Packenham, still proud of his association with the Fusiliers, told Wellington 'After all I told you of the Fusiliers' Conduct you must have been surprised to peruse the dispatch of Beresford. In

28 Beresford to Wellington 17 May 1811, quoted in Muir, *Wellington* additional commentary
29 Muir, *Wellington* additional commentary

truth there never was an official detail which more completely failed to put the Authorities, to whom so ever it might be addressed, in possession of both the circumstances and fact of the Affair'.[30] Stewart of the 2nd Division acknowledged Cole's intervention had 'secured the victory'; Hardinge told Cole 'the Fuziliers exceeded anything the usual word gallantry can convey, and your movement on the left flank of the enemy unquestionably saved the day and decided the victory'.[31] Oman later concluded 'the real hero, most undoubtedly, of the whole fight was Sir Lowry Cole, who showed as much moral courage in striking in, on his own responsibility, at the critical moment, as he did practical skill in conducting his two brigades against the enemy opposed to him...it was a great achievement and the General was worthy of his soldiers, no less than the soldiers of their General'.[32] Beresford commissioned a sergeant from each of Hoghton's regiments, but didn't extend the honour to the Fusilier Brigade until Cole directly asked him to do so a month later, sarcastically telling Beresford 'I trust you will not conceive I am assuming too much in claiming for the Fuzileer Brigade a similar mark of your Excellency's approbation of their conduct on that day, which I may venture to assert was as distinguished for gallantry and steadiness as that of their rivals'. Beresford conceded, replying he was pleased 'to have an opportunity of testifying to that Brigade my approbation of the excellent conduct on that day on which in the noblest sense of the word it can be said to have rivalled the best'. Sergeant David Scott of the 23rd was duly promoted to an ensigncy in the 11th Foot.[33]

Despite the disquiet about Beresford's performance, the House of Commons passed a motion of thanks to him and the army. But Beresford was shuffled temporarily into non-combat duties, relieved by a fit-again Major-General Rowland Hill. Fortescue's summary is damning: his 'haunting solicitude for the means of running away, nervous persistence in looking to the rear instead of the front, vitiated every step which Beresford took during the day'. A more recent historian noted Cole's decision to attack was taken 'in the face of Beresford's breakdown and refusal to give any useful orders'.[34] The 23rd, with all the British regiments present, were eventually granted the mis-spelt battle honour 'Albuhera' to add to their regimental Colour. They and everyone else that was there deserved it: Albuera was hell. There were more casualties in that single day, mostly incurred on that 'fatal hill', than in any other clash during the Peninsular War. Other

---

30 Muir, *Wellington* additional commentary
31 Quoted in Cole and Gwynn, *Memoirs*
32 Oman, *History Vol. IV*
33 Cary and McCance *Regimental Records*
34 Muir, *Tactics*

battles - Talavera, Salamanca, Vitoria - involved more troops and are probably better known today. But for most who survived Albuera, nothing would rival it until Waterloo, and even there, nothing happened like Albuera's sheer bloody-minded refusal by the infantry of both sides to give an inch. Nor during the rest of the Peninsular War would there be another disaster for the British to compare with that befalling the 2nd Division on 16 May 1811. Cole's accurate verdict was: 'So severe a combat has not, I believe, taken place in this war...I certainly never saw anything like it and I hope I never shall [again]'.[35] Wellington's concluded 'I think this action one of the most glorious and honorable to the character of the troops of any that has been fought during the war'.[36] The sense of his remark is remarkably like that of Beresford's opponent on the day. Of the British, Portuguese, Spanish and German soldiers who had faced his equally brave Frenchmen, Soult reputedly said 'they could not be persuaded that they were beat...they were completely beat, the day was mine, but they did not know it and would not run.'[37]

---

35 Cole and Gwynn, *Memoirs*
36 Wellington to Admiral Berkeley on 20 May 1811, quoted in Muir, *Wellington* additional commentary.
37 Quoted in Edwards, *Albuera*

CHAPTER 11

A NEW ROLE

"Appointed to do duty with Portuguese troops. Major 2nd Battn.
With 5th Cassadores before Ciudad Rodrigo, Badajos,
Salamanca, Madrid and Burgos."

Memorandum to the Duke of York, 1823

Albuera left the Fusilier Brigade in a bad state. Both battalions of
the 7th had lost half their men, leaving them so understrength that the
two were combined; the 2nd Battalion men were absorbed into the 1st
Battalion, its officers sent home to recruit and resurrect their unit. The
23rd's lightly wounded trickled back into the ranks, but a month later
they could still field only twenty officers, nineteen sergeants, nine
drummers and 327 men fit for duty against a nominal complement of
around 1,000. No less than thirteen officers and 232 NCOs and men
were having their wounds treated in rear areas; most were sent back to
Lisbon for care. After Fuentes d'Onoro the *Armée de Portugal*, now led
by Marshal Marmont, withdrew into Spain to recover. Wellington
therefore felt sufficiently secure in the north to leave a screening force
there and reunite the two parts of his army around Elvas for another
siege of Badajoz. The difficult work this time was mostly undertaken by
the 3rd and 7th Divisions, while the survivors of Albuera sought to
recover. But Wellington fared no better than Beresford and by mid-June
this attempt was also called off. The allies pulled back across the
Guadiana on 17 June; Badajoz would have to wait for another day. The
strategic stalemate that followed, in the heat of summer, precluded
major movements by either side and Wellington ordered his army into
cantonments. On 18 July, the 4th Division were ordered to move to
Estremoz and then on northwards to Pedrogão, while Wellington
contemplated his next move.

Despite its losses at Albuera, the 23rd had a full complement of
field ranks: Ellis was recovering, while its four majors - Pearson (in
acting command of the Fusilier Brigade), Sutton, Offley (both in
Portuguese service), and Dalmer (with 2/23rd, but shortly to return to
1/23rd) - were fit and well. Even should a vacancy arise, van Courtlandt

and Keith were ahead of Jack on the captains list and had first refusal. For the third most senior captain, no early promotion within the regiment was likely; it was time to look elsewhere. Fortunately, an obvious avenue was at hand. To help reconfigure the Portuguese army, William Beresford had appointed British officers into some senior Portuguese positions, including command of brigades and regiments. By 1811 over 200 British officers served in the Portuguese Army; in total some 350 would serve during the war. Charles Sutton had joined the Portuguese army in 1809 and Francis Offley followed in 1810; both may have discussed the potential benefits with Jack. One was that transferring officers stepped up in rank on brevet promotion; a captain in British service became a major in Portuguese service. They did not lose seniority in their substantive regimental rank, so retained promotion opportunities in their parent unit remained. Indeed, performing at more senior level made it likely the higher rank would also be achieved in the British army.[1] In addition, pay for Portuguese service was in addition to that received from King George. Transferring to the Portuguese army therefore brought higher rank and double pay. Having performed well at Busaco, Fuentes d'Onoro and Albuera, the Portuguese infantry was considered fully integrated with and just as capable as the British and German troops they fought alongside. With twenty-four line regiments, twelve light infantry battalions known as *Caçadores* ('hunters'), twelve cavalry regiments and four artillery regiments, the Portuguese comprised almost half the army Wellington commanded in the Peninsular, or a third with Spanish troops included.[2] Service in the Portuguese army was therefore a tempting option; Jack determined to pursue it. He wrote home to tell his brother of his plans. William, apparently living with Caroline and Jacob Ley at Ashprington at the time, quickly passed the note on to his parents.

Thursday Morning, 11th August 1811

My Dear Mother,

I have just received this short letter from John - the date of it, although omitted, must be very recent, it is in answer to that sent out through Sir Mich¹. Seymour in a parcel to Captⁿ. Hamilton the

---

1 Brevet promotions meant officers commonly held rank in the army higher than that held in their battalion.
2 *In the Words of Wellington's Fighting Cocks: The After-action Reports of the Portuguese Army during the Peninsular War 1812-1814* Moises Gaudêncio and Robert Burnham 2021

other day when I was at Plymth.³ I hope he may succeed to the whole extent of his wishes. We are just going to set off for Crockernwell & next week go on to Exeter. My wife sends her best love to all and believe me affectionately,

William Hill
Ashprington

The letter William forwarded read:

Capn. W Hill R N
Ashprington
Devon

I received yours of the 22nd June to 2 July jointly written by other parties and am so much obligd. for it as I had not heard of you for some time.

I am at present at Genl. Cole's forwarding my getting a majority in the Portuguese - it will end most likely in my getting a brevet in the British army.⁴ The Gen¹. promises if possible that I shall be in the same division in which I am. I shall hence be constantly with my own Reg^t. & get a dollar or two a day, a more respectable rank & chance of being confirmed in a year. We have been overlooked in the Albuera business. Lord Wⁿ. will yet get something for Keith.⁵

Yours
J Hill

The comment 'we have been overlooked in the Albuera business' indicates festering Fusilier resentment in the aftermath of the battle. The grudging official dispatch aside, there was little official recognition for having, in the Fusiliers' view, snatched victory from the jaws of

---

3 Sir Michael Seymour was captain of HMS *Amethyst* and recommended William's promotion after the capture of *Le Niéman* in 1809; he was now commanding *Le Niéman* in RN service. It is less clear who Captain Hamilton was; nobody with that surname seems to have held the rank of captain in August 1811 (https://threedecks.org). It may be Gawen William Hamiliton who, while he did not promote to captain until December of that year, was at the time Commanding Officer of HMS Onyx, a sloop serving on the Cadiz station; William could have been using the title captain honorifically. Both Seymour and Hamilton were Irish, perhaps the connection between the two.
4 Cole's HQ was at Pedrogão.
5 William Keith was gazetted Major in the Army in July 1811.

defeat. Cole had pressed for sergeants to be promoted; recovered from the wound he received and back in command of the 4th Division, he determined also to do what he could for his officers, and one thing he could easily do was endorse applications for Portuguese service. Jack's recommendation for brevet promotion to major in the Portuguese army was approved; ironically this put him back under the command of Beresford, who the Fusiliers blamed. A few weeks later, on 1 September, a General Order from the Adjutant General's Office in Fuente de Guinaldo included the notice:

> Memorandum – Captain Hill, of the Royal Welch Fusileers, is to place himself under the orders of Marshal Sir William Carr Beresford[6]

Just over a week later, on 9 September 1809, from the Headquarters of the Portuguese army at Cintra, came an Order of the Day:

> By a decree of 30 August 1811, a promotion is declared...Major of the 5th Caçadores battalion, Captain Hill, officer in His British Majesty's army[7]

British first names were translated in the records of the Portuguese army; the new Major João Hill, as he would now be officially known, would have welcomed the recognition of his experience as a light infantryman in his assignment to the 5th Caçadores. The Caçadores, light infantry battalions, had first been raised in 1808, recruited from various provinces of Portugal. The men of the 5th originally came from the Alentejo region in the south of the country, but from December 1809 they started to be conscripted from Trás-os-Montes, a northern mountainous province, since the Alentejo was thinly populated and overburdened; by 1811 most of Jack's men were probably from there. Many were from farming and hunting stock, with pre-war lifestyles very familiar to a Devonian. Like most Portuguese soldiers they were conscripts, but they made good soldiers; 'humble and good willing men but at the same time hard and fierce fighters...showing a great endurance'.[8] Wellington would later call them 'the fighting cocks of the

---

6 *General Orders, Spain and Portugal. January 1st to December 31st,1811 Vol. III* 1812

7 *Collecção das Ordens do Dia Guilherme Carr Beresford, comandante em chefe dos exércitos de S. A. R. o Príncipe Regente Nosso Senhor.* 1811 Translation by Moises Gaudêncio

8 *The Portuguese Caçadores, 1808 – 1814* Sérgio Veludo Coelho 1995

army.'[9] A Caçadores battalion was slightly smaller than a British one; when Jack joined they normally had six companies of 112 men each. With battalion staff that made each around 695 strong at full complement. Some were sharpshooters, armed with Baker rifles, but most carried smoothbore muskets.[10] The 5th Caçadores wore dark brown uniforms, with red facings, intended to help provide camouflage for their primary skirmishing role. For his new role, Jack took off his red coat: regulations required British officers to wear Portuguese uniform, which he had to use his own money to buy.[11]

Jack's memorial plaque in St. Mary's, Hennock states that he was a member of 'the 4 Portuguese Regt. of Cacadores, which he formed'. This posthumous plaque was written by someone unfamiliar with the details of Jack's Portuguese service. When Jack joined the 5th (not the 4th) Caçadores they were an experienced unit, having been at Buçaco and Albuera. Cantoned at Pinhel with the 13th Infantry Regiment, the two units were brigaded under the command of Brigadier General Thomas MacMahon on 12 August 1811.[12] In September another Portuguese regiment, the 23rd Infantry, joined them at Pinhel, turning MacMahon's formation into a typical Portuguese brigade of two infantry regiments and one Caçadores battalion.[13] Jack was one of the more senior members of the new brigade on its establishment and no doubt played his part in its early development; this may be the half-remembered fact to which the author of the memorial plaque referred, over 25 years later.[14] Cole's promise that Jack would remain in the same division turned out to be undeliverable; he was not to be 'constantly with' the 23rd, though he did visit them as often as he could. He naturally wanted to stay in touch with his friends in the battalion, keep abreast of how his peers were doing, and stay in the mind of those who could help his career. The monthly pay of a major in the Portuguese army was 38,000 réis (the Portuguese currency) plus 12,000 réis in

---

9 Quoted in Haythornthwaite, *Armies*

10 In 1813 Captain John Dobbs took command of a company in the 5th Caçadores, recalling: *'The company consisted of 120 men; one half were armed with rifles, the other with muskets and bayonets.'* Recollections of an Old 52nd Man John Dobbs 1859. See also Moises Gaudêncio: https://www.napoleon-series.org/military-information/battles-and-campaigns/were-the-portuguese-cacadores-armed-with-baker-rifles

11 Moises Gaudêncio https://www.thenapoleonicwars.net 25 October 2021

12 *Collecção das Ordens do Dia*

13 *Arquivo Histórico Militar* (the Portuguese military archive). PT/AHM /1/14/239/2 ms 26

14 Though the mistake is not repeated in the posthumous record of Jack's service written by his son, which refers correctly to the 5th Caçadores. Hill, *Colonel Hill (CB) Services*

allowances, a total of 50,000 *réis*, or a little over £15 a month. Jack received this *in addition* to his pay at his substantive rank of captain in the British army, which was about £16 per month.[15]

The 5th Caçadores had been commanded by Lieutenant-Colonel Michael McCreagh since November 1810. McCreagh, who served in the West Indies for most of his early career, was one of the first group of British officers appointed to Portuguese service. When Jack joined his battalion McCreagh was twenty-six years old, three years younger even than Henry Ellis; seven years younger than Jack, who was at least used to having a younger boss. Caçadores battalions had a single major; Jack was McCreagh's second in command. Few accounts of McCreagh survive; his obituary claimed he was 'universally beloved by his fellow-soldiers'.[16] Obituaries cannot always be trusted, but there is some support for this in the recollection of a near-contemporary officer who joined the 5th Caçadores after McCreagh left. He tried to stop the men of the battalion singing and was told they did it because McCreagh 'always liked to see the men merry on the line of march'.[17] That said, by the time Jack and McCreagh parted company two years later their relationship was less than perfect. Below Jack were six captains, four Portuguese and two British. All the former were settled in their roles: Captains Francisco José Lobo, Tiago Pedro Martins, Francisco de Paula de Mendonça Arrais and Dom Francisco Xavier da Silva Lobo all joined on 21 January 1809, the date they were appointed to the Caçadores battalions after they were first organised in late 1808. Captain Henry Perry, late 28th Foot, had joined them in March 1810, while Captain Thomas Lalor was a more recent recruit, from the 43rd Foot in March 1811. There were also six lieutenants, all of whom had also been with the battalion from the start, six ensigns, an Adjutant, Paymaster, Quartermaster, Chaplain, Surgeon and an Assistant Surgeon. All these were Portuguese, contrary to the impression given in some histories that the Portuguese army was largely officered by the British. Many of these officers were young men at the start of their military careers, in contrast to their new major who had been a soldier for fifteen years. Some would eventually enjoy higher rank: Captain Tiago Pedro Martins and Lieutenant Manuel Joaquim Meneses e Melo would both ultimately become brigadier generals, as would Captain José Figueira de Almeida, who joined later.

---

15 The British army was paid with Spanish silver dollars, of which 4.5 = £1. Jack's combined British and Portuguese salaries, about £31 per month, or £1 per day, would therefore be paid as 4.5 dollars per day, which is exactly what he suggests it would be in his letter of 18 Oct. 1811 (below)

16 *The Gentleman's Magazine Volume II* January to June 1835

17 Bunbury, *Narratives*

As Portuguese brigades were at the time unnumbered, the brigade was known as 'MacMahon's brigade' (even though MacMahon himself was often on leave). At least at more junior levels, nationalities at each level of command were supposed to alternate, but this was often not applied and the 5th Caçadores had a succession of three senior British officers: MacMahon, McCreagh, Hill. Usual practice in Wellington's army was for Portuguese brigades to be incorporated alongside British brigades in dual-nationality divisions, but the brigade Jack was now helping to form, and one other, would remain independent for the rest of the war.[18]

The focus of much of Jack's initial period in the Portuguese army was helping to turn three unfamiliar units, some 1,900 men, into a coherent fighting formation. The armies went into cantonments for the second part of 1811, which should have given Jack and his fellow officers time to give the brigade a sound footing, establish proper administration and ensure it was well-trained. Despite the announcement of his appointment in August, however, Jack's Portuguese service record for the 5th Caçadores shows him arriving with the battalion only on 8 November 1811.[19] His next letter (below) shows that on 13 October he had been in Lisbon for a fortnight. He was probably ordered to travel to Lisbon before joining them, to acquire his Portuguese uniform and other equipment and while there to collect items the battalion needed from the Lisbon Arsenal, the main military depot for the Portuguese army. It was routine practice for shoes and uniforms etc. to be requested from the Portuguese Quartermaster General's department, who would then order the Arsenal to furnish the articles to one of the unit's officers.

But while Jack was away there were unexpected developments. The dispersal of Marmont's troops across northern Spain encouraged Wellington to move his forces to surround Ciudad Rodrigo. He did not plan to besiege the town, just blockade it and cut off supplies to its French garrison. McMahon's brigade moved up, reaching Rendo by 27 August, though as a new unit they were kept in reserve. In response to Wellington's blockade, Marmont concentrated his forces. Wellington pulled back from Ciudad Rodrigo rather than force a battle, but Marmont decided to press him. He clashed with the retiring 3rd Division at El Bodon, on the day the 5th Caçadores reached Rendo, then came up against the allied rearguard, provided by the Fusilier Brigade, at Aldeia de Ponte. The Fusiliers' job was to delay the French advance while the allied army established a defensive position further back. The action was 'a trifling affair', but was costly for the 23rd Foot,

18 *The Portuguese Infantry Brigades, 1809-1814* S G P Ward. Journal of the Society for Army Historical Research, Vol 53, No. 214 1975
19 *Arquivo Histórico Militar* PT/AHM/1/14/340/04 ms 64-65

who lost three killed and fifteen wounded.[20] One of the dead was Jacob van Courtlandt, who had served with Jack from Ostend to Albuera. His loss was deeply felt; John Harrison recalled 'he was struck on the lower part of the belly by a canon shot, and retained his perfect senses for an hour when he died, quite resigned. His expressions were very touching. He desired Ellis to tell his wife his last thoughts were of her and the dear children, that he knew his fate would break her heart and that he should soon meet her in heaven.'[21] Another Welch Fusilier recorded 'none can be more truly lamented than our excellent friend Capt. Van Cortlandt…his death has thrown a gloom over all friends here, for I believe there are none who do not sincerely lament him".[22] Another casualty was Major Thomas Pearson, seriously wounded in the leg and almost captured when his horse was killed and he was trapped under it. Pearson survived and was rescued (despite some apparent reluctance from the men of the 23rd to do so, due to his unpopularity).[23] He was lucky not to lose his leg, but the injury was sufficiently serious that he had to go home. Pearson did not return to the Peninsula; early in 1812 he was appointed to a staff post in Canada, reuniting him with his wife and her family.[24] Captain James Cane (whose name was incorrectly recorded as Payne in the official returns) was also severely wounded.

At Albuera the 23rd had lost three captains dead or wounded; two more and a major had now suffered a similar fate. If battle losses were not enough, William Keith, brevet major but still serving as the battalion's senior captain, contracted a fever, possibly in the unhealthy climate along the banks of the Guadiana, and died before September was out.[25] Thomas Dalmer was at that point ordered back to the 2nd Battalion, taking another major away from the 1st Battalion and Major Francis Offley found his career in jeopardy. In Nova Scotia in 1808, Jack had described Offley as 'not quite so violent as formerly', but his temper flared at the end of September 1811. Offley, it was alleged, had used 'violent, intemperate, and threatening' language in a dispute with Portuguese officers over the use of an area of camp for grazing mules and horses. As tensions rose on both sides, Offley drew his sword and appeared to be trying to provoke a dual. One of the Portuguese officers struck him. Things calmed down, but Offley was charged with four

---

20 RWF Archives object 7198
21 RWF Archives object 7198
22 Quoted in Cary and McCance *Regimental Records*
23 Crook, *Bentinck*
24 Pearson would limp for the rest of his life. His full biography is Graves, *Fix Bayonets!*
25 RWF records say Keith died in Devonport, suggesting he was repatriated before he died.

offences including unmilitary conduct. He was ordered to face a court martial on 15 October. Once he joined the 5th Caçadores Jack would no doubt have visited his colleagues in the 23rd as soon as he could; he surely felt personally shocked at what had happened to so many of them in such a short time.[26] Van Courtlandt, Keith, Offley and Pearson had all joined at about the same time as Jack. They had been his companions in arms for 15 years; the battalion must have a felt different place in their absence. As with the loss of the Valk all those years ago, however, the ill-luck of friends was Jack's good fortune; Van Courtlandt and Keith's deaths placed him top of the 23rd's captain's list. Moreover, Pearson's departure, Dalmer's re-assignment and Offley's troubles meant the battalion needed new majors in Portugal. It was time for strings to be pulled again.

Lisbon, 13 Oct. 1811

My dear Father,

I have again drawn for £25. This will complete my equipment, I hope to repay you within a twelvemonth.

Now you and I must look about ourselves. Keith is dead of a fever and Cortlandt killed in the late affairs, this brings me to the top of the cap[tai]ns. You have lately been asking Gen. Grenville for something I think I said it was to little purpose your asking for anything except what came in succession. Now the chances are these, Pearson now Lt.-Col. in the army, and having married in America, wishes to get the situation of Inspecting Field Officer, he will then get station'd near Genl. Coffins. Genl. Grenville has promised to use his interest for him, being wounded and Lt.-Col. in the army. I think he may get it, this would leave an opening for me. Another chance I have is Sutton's getting something, who is also Lt.-Col. in the army, his interest is very good now.

What I wish you to do is merely this, get your friend merely to say as I am Senior Capn. he hopes Genl. Grenville would use his interest to get me the first Majority without purchase that may become vacant in the 23rd, my being in the Portuguese service is an additional recommendation, and in case I should get a Majority in my own corps, I may go back to the 2nd Battn. or in a short time get a Lt.-Colcy. in the Portuguese service. I flatter myself I can get all the necessary recommendations here as some degree of interest was requir'd to get what I have. Do not say a word about purchase.

---

26 In a letter from Lt. John Harrison to his father of around this time, Harrison mentions that he had received a letter 're-directed by his friend Hill'. RWF Archives object 7198.

As it was mention'd by Genl. Grenville, you had lately signified an intention to that effect, what you have been doing I know not as I have not received any of your letters for the last 10 weeks, this is in consequence of my being in the rear, and all my letters are with the army. They say if this man has money why does he not risk it, now a man with less than 10,000 has little right to purchase a step in my situation, it is when young in the rank it is worth while. You will write Greenwood and Cox that any sum I may overdraw on them for, you will pay. You may depend I will only ask for what is requisite and scramble through the army without putting you to any unnecessary expense.

I have not done so much in this last fortnight for the 5th Cacadores as I could wish, but I believe I have put all in train to get what we want from the Arsenal. The general idea is there will be some quiet for a few months. It is a long time since we heard from England. The idea here is not in favour of the Spaniard who is making no progress in shaking off entirely his pride or ignorance. Balasteros has given another specimen of his abilities as a partizan.

Our Division, 4th, is exactly where they were previous to the movements of the enemy in revictualling Ciudad Rodrigo. The Gallican army is in some force. Ld. Wellington will oblige the enemy to keep a strong corps oppos'd to him in order that detachments may not be sent to attack the Spanish parties.

Give my love to my Mother and Aunt. I will write Wm. soon.

Believe ever your
J. HILL

Jack's report of British views on their Spanish Allies reflects a common uncomplimentary perception. His noted exception, General Franciso Ballesteros, was active around Algeciras helping to keep French forces tied up there. Jack was still in Lisbon a week later, when he wrote again about his prospects, this time to William. He recognized that what seemed a hopeless situation in August had reversed itself in just two months:

Lisbon, 18th Oct. 1811

Dear William,
I have not written you for some time and now have to tell you I am trying to pick up chips, as the work seems slack just now.

Since I made the application to get the Majority of the 5th Cacadores, our senior Captain then is dead of a fever and the 2nd,

Cortland, kill'd by a round shot. Offley, our 2nd Major, has got himself into a Devil of a scrape, which is most likely to break him.

From my situation as senior Captain and getting a majority in my own corps, it is possible I might be ordered to the 2nd Bn. which if they do not do I shall become a candidate for a Portuguese Lieut.-Colcy.

Imagine out of our Capn^s., we have 4 underground and two so badly shot through the lungs that neither are expected to live long. There are [now] only two of the Capn^s. we brought from America, who command the flank Compy^s. We have our four Majors here.[27] Pearson is going home shot through the thigh. Col. Ellis has recovered and rejoin'd. Dalmer is ordered home, he went to Oporto and through Coimbra & will come here to get a passage.

Everything seems quiet just now. I think the campaign might as well be considered at an end and certainly we have lost many of our best officers. Balasteros has been doing something again, the particulars I know not. We have received 450 men from our 2nd Bn. and cannot now bring that number into the field.[28] Every day adds to our strength as the fever cases are much fewer. The dog days cut the army up very much.

When you go to Hennock tell my Mother I received her very amusing letter of the 20th Sept., there is one before that which I have not got. I should like to have it as it contains some correspondence between my Father and Gn^l. Grenville. You must among you treat this latter gentleman and get his promise that no one shall be put from another Regt. over my head. In this, not a moment must be lost. It would be indelicate it is uncertain what may be the result of the Court Martial. But it is look'd on in a very serious point. You are well aware of the situation I am placed in, as I said to my Father, we cannot sleep or act on it, but must be completely on the alert.

My equipment here which has cost me near £200 would in some degree be useless if I was to succeed to anything in my own Corps and be ordered home. If I stay a few months at best, I shall well be enabled to repay £85 I have had from home.

I am detain'd here day after day getting things from the Arsenals, but they are requisites of the first importance and I must do it. My baggage has been packed this week and [the] great part [is] in Coimbra. In a great town I am without society and have nothing but books to amuse me. The only theatre worth going to - the Opera - is shut, I was once at one of the 2nd rate ones, that was

27 In order of seniority the majors were Pearson, Offley, Sutton, Dalmer.
28 198 in March and 246 in September. Cary and McCance *Regimental Records*

sufficient, I have been living with our Quarter Master, he is gone up and took up my tea, sugar, etc. so that I have little now except my blankets, portmanteau and canteens [as] my establishment, 3 horses and a mule which is the great incumbrance as up the country they cost us nothing more than 2½ Drs. a day. My pay I can [not] say exactly but about 4½ Drs a day, so that if I find Col. McCreagh not expensive I shall do very well. I am the senior Major which gives me something more than if I was a supernumary.[29]

Say everything to my sisters. I hope that happiness may be granted to me of seeing you all one day or another.

I remain, my Dear Wm., Your
J. HILL

It is notable that in this letter, written only five days after he had asked his father to press his case with General Grenville, that Jack talks of 'my situation as senior Captain and getting a majority in my own corps'. This strongly implies that Ellis had told Jack he was recommending his promotion (and why he was keen for his father not to mention purchasing the rank). Indeed, Jack's mind had already moved on to the wider benefits of obtaining his majority, namely a possible posting to 2/23rd in Britain or, if he stayed in Portuguese service, the 'one up' rule meaning that as a British major he could have a Lieutenant-Colonelcy in the Portuguese army. Suddenly Jack's prospects looked far brighter than they had in August. As for Offley, Jack was more accurate in his assessment than less experienced officers. Lieutenant John Harrison, who had just rejoined the regiment after being shot in the leg at Albuera, wrote home to his father that Offley 'was likely to extricate himself in an honourable manner'.[30] The court martial accepted Offley had been provoked and cleared him of some charges, but found him guilty of unmilitary conduct. His sentence was suspension from rank and pay for six months from 1 January 1812. The sentence was confirmed by Wellington; 'Prisoner Major Offley', as he had been known throughout the proceedings, was to be sent home in disgrace.[31] From having four majors in Portugal, 1/23rd had now lost three - Pearson, Offley and Dalmer - within the space of weeks while the fourth, Charles Sutton, remained in Portuguese service.

---

29 This is a misstatement or misunderstanding; Caçadores battalions had only one major. Nor was he senior major in the brigade; that was Major John Rolt of the 13th Infantry.
30 RWF Archives object 7198.
31 *General Orders, Spain and Portugal January 1st to December 30th 1812. Vol. IV*

After Aldeia da Ponte, Marmont declined to attack Wellington's army again and withdrew into Spain. Each side remained wary about possible moves by the other, but Wellington and the various mutually uncooperative French commanders took the risk of dispersing their armies to resupply and recover. The allies returned to cantonments; MacMahon's brigade was near Pinhel, where it is likely that Jack finally joined them. They remained there until November, with the units dispersed to several villages located between Pinhel and the Douro, along the Côa river.[32] Wellington remained intent on again striking into Spain, starting with the two fortresses that guarded the main cross-border routes, Ciudad Rodrigo in the north and Badajoz in the south. The opportunity he was awaiting came sooner than expected, following some ill-advised remote interference by Napoleon. While French forces remained within a few days march of concentrating against him in northern Spain, Wellington's ability to attack either fortress was constrained; any siege could be disputed by a French army exceeding the size of his own. But in October orders arrived from Paris for Marmont to detach some 15,000 men to help besiege Valencia, tilting the balance of forces along the Portuguese-Spanish border in the allies' favour; Wellington quickly moved to take advantage. Despite bad weather, at the beginning of January 1812 the allies marched through snow and sleet to encircle Ciudad Rodrigo. Jack later recorded that he 'commanded the 5th Caçadores at the commencement of this campaign'; McCreagh must have been indisposed or temporarily assigned to some other role (his Portuguese service records show him with the battalion). The 5th Caçadores moved southwest from their positions on the Côa to Reigada, a small village near the Spanish border.[33]

The units assigned to besiege Ciudad Rodrigo were the 1st, 3rd, 4th and Light Divisions and the other independent Portuguese brigade, commanded by Brigadier-General Denis Pack. The remainder of Wellington's force was deployed to screen the approaches to the town, watching for any French attempt to intervene and protecting the army's line of retreat. The 5th Caçadores guarded the bridge over the Águeda river at Barba del Puerco. Like any siege and storm of a major fortified city, the capture of Ciudad Rodrigo was a bloody affair. It cost the allies around 200 killed and almost 1,000 wounded. The 2,000 defenders lost about half as much. By the standards of the day though the operation was rapid, surprising even Wellington himself. The city fell after a night assault on 19/20 January, less than two weeks after the siege started.

On the 20th, Jack received a new brigade commander. Brigadier-General Thomas Bradford, most recently of the 82nd Regiment, was

---

32 *Arquivo Histórico Militar* PT/AHM/1/14/239/05 ms 6
33 *Arquivo Histórico Militar* PT/AHM/1/14/239/05 ms 6

appointed on 20 January 1812. Bradford was a year older than Jack; he had become an ensign four years before him, in 1792. Much of Bradford's military career had been in the militia; he joined the regular army in 1809, by which time he been a brevet Lieutenant-Colonel for eight years. Bradford was a good example of how purchase accelerated a career and reputedly 'a terrible fire-eater, and always anxious to get the regiments of his brigade engaged.'[34] This was not a recipe likely to impress an experienced regular officer like Jack Hill. Oddly, the Portuguese Order of the Day announcing Bradford's appointment stated the brigade was composed only of the 13th and the 24th Infantry Regiments. The 5th Caçadores was not mentioned. There is no record of the 5th Caçadores being detached from the rest of the brigade (at that point or any other), in which case this was an administrative lapse that would not have gone down well with the Caçadores officers.

In mid-February Wellington turned south towards his next target, the far more difficult proposition of Badajoz, which he and Beresford had between them already failed to capture twice. While the main part of his army moved directly south towards Elvas, the now-renamed Bradford's Brigade took a circuitous route, via Coimbra. Perhaps this was to continue the reprovisioning that Jack had been engaged in the previous October. In the Portuguese Military Archives is a campaign book left by Bradford's aide de camp, Lieutenant Manuel Isidro da Paz. In it, da Paz, a gifted officer, sketched a series of maps showing the brigade's itinerary from the middle of February 1812, when they started their movement. He also included sketches of the scenery and some of his colleagues.[35] The brigade first marched 120 miles to Coimbra. After about eleven days there, on the 29th they marched south, the 5th Caçadores moving via Ega, then on successive days to Ranha, Leiria, Seiça and Tomar, which Jack had marched through with the Royal Welch Fusiliers a year before. On 5 March they continued to Tancos and then Abrantes, where they halted for a day. In the week since leaving Coimbra they had marched around 115 miles. There was more to come, though the next part of their route was taken at a more leisurely pace. They left Abrantes on 8 March, crossed the Tagus, and halted at Ponte de Sor. The day after they marched to Chancelaria where they remained for five days, marching on 15 March to Fronteira, on the 17th to Monforte, Barbacena the next day and arriving at Vila Boim, a few miles from Elvas, the day after. Their march was close to

34 Bunbury, *Narratives*
35 *Arquivo Histórico Militar* PT/TT/CF/212. I am much indebted to Moisés Gaudêncio for bringing this fascinating record to my attention and for his significant help in interpreting its contents.

300 miles long since leaving Barba del Puerco; the direct route would have been just over half that.

Bradford's Brigade was unsurprisingly one of the last formations to arrive in the new theatre of operations. Assigned to the reserve, by the end of the siege they were camped in woods to the west of Badajoz. Wellington again wanted his most tried and tested units for main operations, which this time fell to the 3rd, 4th, 5th and Light Divisions. For this third attempt to capture Badajoz within a year, Wellington had more men, better and more artillery, and an army that was learning painfully and rapidly how sieges were best conducted. Saps were dug, batteries placed, battering completed, breaches in the towering city walls made and deemed practicable. On 6 April the assault went in; Jack's former colleagues in the 4th Division attacked the breach in the Trinidad bastion. It was chaos. Ditches under the walls were full of water; many drowned. Those that made it to the breach faced an 'inferno of bursting shells, grenades, and powder barrels'.[36] The 23rd lost three officers and over fifty men killed or missing; seventeen officers and almost 100 men wounded. Ellis, inevitably leading from the front, was wounded yet again, as was Captain William Potter, made brevet major in the absence of anyone substantively of that rank with the battalion; Potter died of his wounds soon after. Jack, following events from afar, may have wished he was involved, but moving to Portuguese service meant he missed both Aldeia da Ponte and the assault on Badajoz; either may have cost him his life.

While the 5th Caçadores were slowly making their way towards Badajoz, back in England General Grenville wrote to Sir Hugh Torrens, the Military Secretary:

11 March 1812

...it may escape your memory that I spoke to you yesterday very strongly in favor of Capt. Hill in the 23d Regt. RWF, recommending him to succeed to the majority in the 23d Rgt. vacant by the appointment of Brevet Lt. Col. Pearson to a Staff employment in N. America; I beg leave to trouble you with these few lines to desire that you will have the goodness to bring my recommendation of Capt Hill before the Commander in Chief & hope that His Royal Highness will approve of Capt. Hill's succeeding to the Majority...[37]

36 Cary and McCance *Regimental Records*
37 TNA 31/342 *Memoranda of appointments, promotions and resignations: 5, 12 March 1812*

The Duke of York approved and Jack's majority in the 23rd, vice Pearson, was gazetted on 14 March.[38] After the anxiety when awaiting promotion to captain nine years before, his next step came almost unremarked. Already holding the rank in Portuguese service perhaps reduced the tension; he also knew the 23rd needed majors, that he was first in line and that Ellis wanted him to have his majority, without purchase. Jack now held field rank in his own regiment and was formally appointed to 2/23rd, back home in Britain. But this appointment was nominal; he stayed with Wellington's army. Leaving for Britain would be against the Commander's express wish that experienced men stay in the Peninsula: 'I am desirous, if possible, not to reduce this army in old soldiers. One soldier who has served one or two campaigns will render more service than two recently sent from England' and 'I prefer having one officer or soldier who has served one or two campaigns to having two or three who have not.'[39] The fighting season was underway, Wellington was already preparing his next offensive, and experienced officers were encouraged, if not ordered, to stay in theatre. Jack presumably could have rejoined 1/23rd, but as a senior officer in a brigade yet to see action, perhaps his presence with 5th Caçadores was deemed more important, not least as cover for McCreagh's absences. By remaining in Portuguese service Jack of course also continued to earn 'double pay' and should now be entitled, as a British army major, to a Lieutenant-Colonelcy in Portuguese service. Probably for a combination of all these reasons, Jack therefore stayed with his Caçadores.

After Badajoz the army's next target was Marmont's *Armée de Portugal*, but Wellington knew that if Marmont was reinforced by other French forces elsewhere in Spain, he might be outnumbered. He therefore encouraged allied manoeuvres elsewhere to prevent that happening. In Andalucía Ballesteros continued to fight; in the north, two Spanish armies supported by a British naval and marine squadron under Jack's former dining companion Sir Home Popham pinned down French forces there, while plans were developed for an expedition to land on the Spanish east coast using British troops from Sicily. Wellington also left about 18,000 men of his own army near Badajoz under General Sir Rowland Hill to guard his southern flank should Soult again move north from Andalucía. Hill also destroyed a key bridge at Almaraz, which meant a far longer march would be needed to unite French forces than for Wellington and Hill to do the same. In addition to all this, Spanish partisans, commonly known today as

---

38 *The London Gazette* Number 16583 Saturday March 14 1812
39 *The Despatches of Field Marshal the Duke of Wellington.* Wellington to Bathurst 27 January; Wellington to Bunbury 2 February 1813

guerrillas after the 'small war' they practiced behind enemy lines, continued their insurgent campaign, pinning down thousands of French troops, capturing supplies and disrupting communications. As one historian put it 'it is hard to see what more Wellington could have done to ensure Marmont's isolation in the [forthcoming] campaign'.[40] In April, Wellington took the bulk of his army back towards Ciudad Rodrigo. Bradford's Brigade marched from their bivouac west of Badajoz to Elvas on the 10th, staying there until the 13th, when the 5th Caçadores moved to Arronches and the next day to Portalegre. On 15 April they marched to Tolosa, then on successive days to Nisa, Cebolais de Baixo (crossing the Tagus at Villa Velha) and Castelo Branco where they halted for a day. Heavy rain set in soon after they left Badajoz and the resulting mud made for a slow and unpleasant march. On the 20th, they moved again, to Lardosa, then Vale de Prazeres, Capinha, Sabugal and Aldeia da Ponte, where they again stopped for a day. Jack would no doubt have taken the opportunity to examine the scene of the 23rd's combat of the previous August; perhaps he found and visited the grave of his old friend, Jacob van Courtlandt. On 26 April, the march resumed, via Malhada Sorda, Castillejo de Dos Casas, Vilar Torpim, Almendra and finally, on the 30th to Muxagata. After marching over 300 miles since leaving Elvas, most troops were now given time to recover and allow their supplies to catch up. The two infantry regiments in Bradford's Brigade went back into the cantonments they had occupied on the Côa, but the 5th Caçadores needed re-equipping again so early in May they marched another 100 miles to Porto. There they remained until the beginning of July.[41]

In late May the allies concentrated near Ciudad Rodrigo, advancing into Spain on 13 June. Over 50,000 strong, they crossed the river Agueda heading for Salamanca. The army divided into three columns marching in parallel across a front ten miles wide. Bradford's Brigade, less Jack's 5th Caçadores, were in the left column. By the 16th they were in sight of Salamanca and took possession of the city on the 17th. The French had left behind a small garrison in three fortified convents, but these were not a serious threat and were, eventually, overcome. In response to the fall of Salamanca, Marmont began his own manoeuvres, seeking either to bring Wellington to battle or cut his line of retreat to the Portuguese border. Wellington slightly outnumbered Marmont and was keen to fight him but wanted to choose his ground and invite a French attack. Marmont, knowing the futility of attacking Wellington with his army in place (such

---

40 *Salamanca 1812* Rory Muir 2001
41 *Arquivo Histórico Militar* PT/AHM/1/14/239/05 ms 6

as at Buçaco), declined to accede. The result was a month of chess moves by both armies, often in baking heat across the dry plains of central Spain, as each move by Marmont's army was countered by one from Wellington's. The first of these was on 19 June, when a strong French force approached the allies' position. Wellington formed his troops for battle, Bradford's Brigade on the right of the line. Marmont similarly formed his army and as evening fell the allies assumed he would attack at first light; they slept in their lines ready for the first signs of French movement. But no attack came the next day, nor the one after. The armies faced each other for two days, neither commander apparently willing to start proceedings. Wellington sent the 7th Division forward but could not provoke a French response. Instead, on the 23rd Marmont withdrew his troops to defensive positions six miles back. The day convinced him Wellington would only fight on the defensive; that perspective would influence his approach over the next month.

With occasional probes and skirmishing, the armies stayed put for another week, until Marmont fell further back to the river Douro. Wellington had secured Salamanca and pushed Marmont's army back but had not fought the decisive battle he wanted. He decided to await the next French move and monitored the crossing points of the Douro. By 7 July Bradford's Brigade had moved to the left of the army, charged with holding the fords at Pollos. It was probably here that Jack and the 5th Caçadores rejoined, having marched 200 miles from Porto. On the 16th the French began to move westwards along the north bank of the river. Wellington moved his army to cover this development, with Bradford's Brigade ordered to Castrillo, around twenty miles to the south-west. But as the allies reached their new positions, it became clear that the French move was a feint, designed to shift Wellington's army westwards and expose his line of retreat. The allies hastily shifted back eastwards, with some sharp fighting breaking out as parts of the armies closed on each other. Wellington resumed a defensive position and by the 19th another stalemate seemed about to begin. Instead, further manoeuvres followed, which nobody who participated in would ever forget.

On the morning of 20 July, the French army began to move south-west, again looking to turn Wellington's right flank; Wellington again mirrored the movement. Before long the two armies began to march in parallel, in full view of each other. This continued all day. Thomas Browne noted 'the sight of two well-equipped armies of nearly 50,000 each, marching in two parallel lines within artillery range...was the most beautiful & magnificent military spectacle that could be witnessed...the day was beautiful - a bright sun & a gentle breeze to which the colours of the British floated as they moved below, whilst the Eagles of the French were glittering above...the order was as regular as if at a review. Each watched his adversary most jealously for a fault which neither could discover.'[42] Marmont himself later recalled that in his long service he never, before or after, saw such a magnificent spectacle.[43] Wellington's army was again in three columns, with Bradford's Brigade this time in the centre. Impressive and memorable it may have been, but it was still 'a most fatiguing day - the British army had marched, practically in battle formation, not less than four Spanish leagues.'[44] On the 21st the allies reoccupied the position at San Cristobal they had held a month before. For all involved it had been a tiring and ultimately frustrating period. Marmont had forced Wellington to move his army around the area north of Salamanca; Wellington had been equal in his responses. Both waited for the other to make a mistake. The next day it happened.

The evening of 21 July 1812 saw both armies encamped outside Salamanca in a horrendous thunderstorm that scared horses and soaked everyone. But dawn broke to a cloudless sky and bright sunshine, raising temperatures and drying soldiers and ground alike. The French began moving south and westwards again, and again Wellington responded, shifting the balance of his troops more to his right and ultimately adopting an L-shaped formation with most of his army facing south. Jack and Bradford's Brigade were moved from their previous position on the left to a more central position near a village called Las Torres, some three or so miles south of Salamanca. Their role, with the British 1st and 7th Divisions and a brigade of Spanish troops, was to provide a central reserve, available to support wherever needed should a battle ensue. Once in their new positions, the troops in the reserve waited while French artillery began a bombardment. They were not immune from this, as a soldier of the 79th Regiment, positioned to the left of Bradford's Brigade, recalled: 'the roaring was like one continued peal of thunder...[the] reserve received general orders to cook which we set about with a dispatch...we were in great danger at the camp kettles, as both shells and shot were coming thickly and rapidly from the enemy amongst us...I took care always to lie down flat on the ground, whenever I could perceive a shell coming in my direction'.[45]

The battle that took place in the afternoon and evening of Wednesday 22 July 1812 would be remembered as one of Wellington's most memorable victories. As the French continued their march south, by mid-afternoon a gap began to appear between two of their divisions,

---

42 Buckley, *Browne*
43 Quoted in Oman, *History Vol. V.*
44 Oman, *History Vol. V.* Four Spanish leagues is about 10 miles
45 Robert Eadie, quoted in Muir, *Salamanca 1812*

leaving the leading one unsupported. Wellington saw an opportunity and attacked. By coincidence, almost at that moment, Marmont was seriously wounded by a British artillery shot; his successor in command, General Bonnet, was also wounded soon after. The third in line, General Clausel was a capable officer, but a double change of French commander just as the allied attack developed contributed to the chaos in the French lines that followed. First attacking on the right with the 3rd Division, Wellington then attacked in the centre with the 4th, and 5th Divisions, who Bradford was ordered to support. Bradford moved his brigade up as rapidly as he could, but in the event neither Jack, on the right front of the brigade with his Caçadores, nor any of Bradford's units were closely involved in the action, because as the three British divisions pressed, the entire French left collapsed. The rapid destruction the infantry inflicted was followed up by a decisive British cavalry charge that probably passed within feet of Jack and his men and scattered what French resistance remained. The speed of events meant that by the time they were in position, Bradford's Brigade had nothing to attack. Browne noted: 'the vigour & ardour of the 3rd Division having formed its front upon the enemy's flank, gave Bradford & the 5th Division great assistance.'[46] It was more than 'assistance'; it was the complete destruction of their target. Bradford was mentioned in Wellington's despatch after the battle in a long list of senior officers to whom he was 'much indebted'. But the 'fire-eater' Bradford cannot have been pleased to be almost unengaged, despite being in the heart of the allied line during one of the most significant battles of the war. Afterwards, he reported glumly 'I have every reason to be satisfied with the conduct of all officers and men of my Brigade in the action of 22 July, but on this occasion none of them had the opportunity to distinguish more than another.'[47] The 5th Caçadores suffered just two men killed and one wounded, probably caused by French artillery rounds as they waited for orders to go into action.

No such fortune favoured Jack's Welch Fusilier comrades. Attacking with the 4th Division, Thomas Dalmer was wounded while leading a composite battalion of light companies; the job Jack may well have had if he had stayed. Dalmer would eventually recover, but Francis Offley, just returned from his 6-month banishment, was not so lucky. After any battle the field was quickly covered by camp-followers and locals seeking loved ones and/or the opportunity to loot the possessions of dead or wounded. Salamanca was no different, and Browne relates the dreadful story of Offley's probable fate:

---

46 Buckley, *Browne*
47 Gaudêncio and Burnham *Fighting Cocks*

The character of the women, Wives of British Soldiers, who in spite of orders, threats, & even deprivation of rations, had forced themselves in numbers, (from the depots in the rear, appointed for them), to the sides of their Husbands, now began to exhibit a fearful and melancholy change. All ideas of conduct or decency had disappeared - plunder & profligacy seemed their sole object, & the very Soldiers their Husbands evidently estimated them in proportion to their proficiency in these vices. They covered in number the ground of the field of battle when the action was over, & were seen stripping & plundering friend & foe alike. It is not doubted that they gave the finishing blow, to many an Officer who was struggling with a mortal wound; & Major Offley of the 23rd Regiment, who lay on the ground, unable to move, but not dead, is said to have fallen a victim to this unheard of barbarity. The daring & enterprize of these creatures, so transformed beyond anything that we have heard of in man, is not to be described.[48]

One man may have thought Offley's dreadful fate represented some kind of justice. Captain Barralier of the 71st Foot was also seriously wounded during the battle. Unable to move, he lay where he fell and as the battle ebbed and flowed later found himself near the 23rd:

The regiment halted close by me, and I called out to the officers, that I was an officer of the 71st Highland Light Infantry, and begged to be removed from the field. It was the 23rd Welch Fusiliers, and several of the officers came up to me. They returned to the regiment, and a few minutes after a field officer and four or five other officers stood beside me. I told them who I was, and entreated to be removed, but I had the mortification of seeing the field officer face about, and call out Forward. The officers and men called out shame, but the regiment moved to the front. Thus was I, a Captain in the same division as the Welch Fusiliers, left as a dog to perish for want of aid, by a man who could have had no feelings for a fellow creature. This was Brevet Lieutenant-Colonel Offley, who, I afterwards heard, very shortly met with his death.[49]

Barralier, Dalmer and the ill-fated Offley were among perhaps 5,000 allied casualties in the battle of Salamanca. Because they did not engage the enemy, Bradford's Brigade had among the lowest casualty figures in the army, just twenty-one of nearly 2,000 men. The 4th Division lost

---

48 Buckley, *Browne*
49 Barralier, quoted in Muir, *Tactics*

659 from around 6,700. French losses were probably over 12,000, well over half prisoners captured as their left wing collapsed. Wellington's victory shattered both the *Armée de Portugal* and the myth that he could only fight defensively. It also increased his army's sense of superiority over their opponents. In Britain, the Archbishop of Canterbury wrote a prayer of thanks to be read in every church in the land. No doubt at St. Mary's in Hennock John Hill, after confirming his son was not among the casualties, spoke with gusto the words: 'Gracious God accept we implore thee the Praises and thanksgiving of a grateful Nation for the Successes thou hast repeatedly vouchsafed to the allied army, in Portugal and Spain...Continue we pray thee, thy favor and protection to our Captains, and Soldiers, and allies'.[50]

For a week the allies pursued the defeated *Armée de Portugal*, keeping it under pressure and preventing it being reinforced from Madrid by King Joseph, Bonaparte's brother. The 5th Caçadores were under Jack's command as McCreagh was recorded as absent on sick leave from 24th July. McCreagh may, in fact, have been indisposed during the battle of Salamanca, as in his 1816 *Statement of Services* Jack recorded that he commanded the battalion during the battle; McCreagh later received medals for Salamanca, suggesting he was formally with the battalion that day, but he may not have been on the field. According to Lieutenant da Paz's record, after the battle Bradford's Brigade moved to Alba de Tormes, where it remained on 23 July.[51] Over the following days the allies moved north-east, the 5th Caçadores marching via Peñaranda de Bracamonte, Cisla, Salvador de Zapardiel, San Vicente del Palacio and Olmedo until on 1 August they reached Cuéllar. Wellington now decided to let his army rest for a few days to recover from yet another fatiguing march. Bradford's men bivouacked on the banks of the river Cega near Fuente Pelayo from 2 to 4 August. In the month of July 1812, from starting in Porto the 5th Caçadores had travelled over 300 miles, participating in one of history's greatest battles along the way.

Now in central Spain, Wellington had choices for his next step. He could continue pursuing the *Armée de Portugal* northwards, towards Burgos, but an alternative beckoned. Leaving a small rearguard to cover any unexpected French advance from the north or east, he took five divisions, the two independent Portuguese brigades and most of his cavalry and artillery to seize Madrid, around 100 miles to the southwest. The march commenced on 5 August, passing through Segovia on the 7th and then crossing the Sierra de Guadarrama. Bradford's Brigade

---

50 National Army Museum Study collection, Accession Number NAM. 2004-07-18-39
51 *Arquivo Histórico Militar* PT/TT/CF/212

was in the rearguard of the advancing army. It took two days for the 36,000 allies to pass Segovia; as Oman put it 'the necessity for moving the whole army by a single mountain road - though it was a well-engineered one - caused the column to be of an immoderate length, and progress was slow'.[52] The troops passed the Royal Palace of San Ildefonso, which Browne, channelling his poetic sister, described as 'beautiful...most romantically situated, at the foot of the Guadarama mountains'. As they approach Madrid, Joseph abandoned it, leaving a small garrison in El Retiro, the royal summer palace at the edge of the city, which was soon forced to surrender.

On 12 August Wellington and his army entered the capital. The scenes were unforgettable, as Browne recalled:

> The windows & balconies were filled with people, principally females elegantly dressed, repeating the acclamations of their friends below in the streets, Garlands & tapestry were suspended from all parts of the houses; the stirrups of the Officers, as they rode along, were taken hold of, & they were gently stopped to be saluted with every possible expression of good will & joy. Many were taken into the ice and lemonade shops by the rejoicing citizens of this delivered capital, & made to partake abundantly of these delicacies, nor would any money be received in payment. The inhabitants contended with each other, who should take the British Officers into their houses, nor would there have been any need of the usual process of issuing billets, but for the necessity of the address of every Officer being known at Head Quarters. For three successive nights the city was brilliantly illuminated, & British Officers were seen in all directions with Spanish Ladies leaning on their arms, who were pointing out to them, the different habitations of their Grandees by the light of the lamps. Priests & Monks too joined in this festive scene. Portuguese & Spanish Officers also, mixed abundantly in it, & the whole presented one of the most curious & interesting spectacles I ever beheld. The whole city was in a sort of confusion of joy for several days.[53]

Another officer put things more pithily: 'Few of us were ever so caressed before, and most undoubtedly never will be again'[54]

A year and a half before Jack had arrived in Lisbon with the Portuguese capital under serious threat. Now he was in a triumphant army that had marched and fought its way to the other Iberian capital.

---

52 Oman, *History Vol. V*
53 Buckley, *Browne*
54 J. Leach of 95th Foot, quoted in Muir, *Salamanca 1812*

As the British, Portuguese, Germans and Spanish settled down to refresh and re-equip, the officers took full advantage of opportunities to visit palaces, museums and theatres, hunt in the surrounding countryside (which Jack would certainly have enjoyed) and relish distraction from the war. The allies laid on entertainment: 'Ld. Wellington gave frequent large dinners to the Spanish Generals, & Guerrilla Chieftains, inviting always a proportion of British Officers to meet them. Several balls were also given by him, at which the beauty of Madrid was assembled, & it almost appeared that we were at Madrid for the sole purpose of amusing ourselves'.[55] The Spanish organised a bull fight, which Wellington and almost every officer of the army attended: one recorded that 'each of the officers had a ticket for the boxes...the place was completely full', but he was unimpressed, calling it 'this scene of blood...I shall see no more'.[56] It is reasonable to assume Jack attended too, though what he made of it we will never know, as none of his letters from this time survive.

Seizing Madrid had both political significance and the strategic benefit of threatening Soult's main route of communications to France. If Wellington was reinforced by the troops he had left under General Hill near Badajoz, the French army in Andalucía was in danger of being overwhelmed. Soult was therefore forced also to abandon his siege of Cadiz and retreat westwards towards Valencia to join Joseph. But the mathematics of this gave Wellington a dilemma too. Once Joseph and Soult combined, they would together have sufficient strength to try to retake Madrid. Meanwhile, the *Armée de Portugal*, still to the north under Clausel, had recovered sufficiently after Salamanca to return south towards Valladolid and again pose a potential threat to Wellington's communications with Portugal, where most of his supplies still came from. Once he knew Soult was moving eastwards, therefore, Wellington's eyes turned back to Clausel. To protect Madrid, he ordered Hill to move up to the Spanish capital while Wellington himself took just over half of his army north. Bradford's Brigade were one of the units selected to go. Having enjoyed just a couple of weeks in the Spanish capital, the men in Wellington's detachment retraced their route across the Guadarrama mountains, getting used again to the rigours of the march. One officer described the experience that he, Jack and everyone in the army shared:

> a splendid sight it was to see so grand an army winding its way zig-zag up that long pass, as far as the eye could see from the top step, in the far distance. The old trade was going on, killing and

---

55 Buckley, *Browne*
56 Glover, *Hennell*

slaying, and capturing our daily bread. When we got on to the plains on the other side, and crossed the Tormes, we expected some rest, a bit of sleep, and better rations, or some improvement in the foraging department; but things got worse and worse...It must be remembered that the British army had no tents, it was all bivouacking, i.e., lying out on the sod in all weather, like any other wild beasts, and always up and armed ready for anything one hour before daylight, and never dismissed until we could see a white horse a mile distant. This was always a very long hour, just unrolled from one's blanket to stand shivering in the early chill of a drizzly morning.[57]

By 31 August Bradford's Brigade was at Orbita. They reached Olmedo by 4 September, Valdestillas on the 5th and Boecillo on the 6th.[58] Crossing the fords of the Duero again, they found most of Clausel's army drawn up between Valladolid and the heights of La Cistérniga, to the south-west of the city. Wellington planned to attack the next day, but by dawn the French were gone, leaving only a small rearguard. McCreagh was finally sufficiently recovered to resume command of the battalion; Jack later recorded that having 'commanded the 5th Cacadores at the commencement of this campaign, at the Battle of Salamanca and Madrid' he was 'superseded in the command after the capture of Valladolid'.[59] This was the way of things in the army, but the tone of his comment, written over three years later, suggests he was not happy to revert to second fiddle. British cavalry, Bradford's and Pack's Portuguese Brigades and the 6th Division were sent after the retreating French army, moving through Cabezón on the 9th, but whenever they caught up, the French retired again. The pursuit continued along the line of the Pisguera river through Dueñas on the 11th, Magaz and Torquemada on the next two days and then followed the Rio Arlanzón through Quintana arriving at Villodrigo on the 15th. On 16 September the main army was joined by Spanish troops, while Jack's Caçadores and the rest of Bradford's Brigade were again further forward, camping overnight in the rain at Pampliega then continuing to Celada. There they found the French again drawn up in position; it seemed the opportunity Wellington had been looking for to

57 *Rough Notes by an Old Soldier, During Fifty Years of Service* George Bell 1867

58 Details of the army's movements in this paragraph come from *The Diary of a Cavalry Officer in the Peninsular War and Waterloo Campaign 1809-1815* William Tomkinson 1895

59 Hill 1816 *Statement of Services*. McCreagh's records in the *Arquivo Histórico Militar* show he returned from sick leave on 5 September.

strike. The baggage was sent to the rear and at 4am the allied army formed up ready to attack. Wellington's orders were:

> Brigadier General Bradford is to ascend the heights on the right of Torrepadierna with his brigade and is to turn the left of the enemy by the hills. Colonel Delancey will instruct him regarding the route he is to follow and Brigadier General Bradford is not to begin his movement till he will see the troops in motion in the centre. One squadron of the 11th and one squadron of Major-General Bock's Brigade and the cavalry under Don Julian are to attend the movements of Brigadier General Bradford's Brigade.
>
> One division of Spanish infantry are to support Brigadier General Bradford and are to be posted by Colonel Delancey on the heights near Pampleiga so as to cover the bridge of the latter place.[60]

But daybreak again revealed the French had gone, leaving their campfires burning to disguise their movement.[61] After some small rearguard skirmishes, Clausel finally took his men beyond the fortified city of Burgos, in which he left a garrison. The allies reached the outskirts of Burgos on the 18th. Since they left Madrid, the allies had marched another 200 miles.

'The castle of Burgos commands the passages of the river Arlanzon in the neighbourhood, and the roads communicating with them, so completely that we could not pass the river till the 19th, when we effected that operation in two columns, the 5th division and Brigadier-General Bradford's Brigade above, and the 1st division and Brigadier-General Pack's brigade, and Major-General Anson's cavalry, below the town' wrote Wellington in his despatch on the investment operations.[62] As the allies surrounded the city, Bradford's Brigade, with the 5th and 7th Divisions, was posted near Ibeas, covering the approaches to Burgos from the north and west. This was the road Clausel had taken and, unbeknownst to the allies, where he would soon be joined by troops from the *Armée de Nord* under General Cafarelli plus further reinforcements from France led by General Souham, who would take command of the whole force. Wellington had failed to further damage Clausel's army, but he felt now he could seize Burgos, a highly strategic town commanding the main road to France. He failed at that too, from a combination of having insufficiently strong artillery to reduce the walls

60 *The Correspondence of Major General William Henry Pringle* The Waterloo Association 2021
61 *Wellington's Worst Scrape: The Burgos Campaign 1812* Carole Divall 2012
62 *The London Gazette* Number 16652 Saturday 3 October, 1812

quickly; too few engineers to direct allied efforts; and an impressive opponent in General Dubreton, the French Governor of Burgos. Horrendous weather rendered the surrounds of the castle a sea of mud, further impeding operations and undermining morale. Wellington said his troops 'have lately, in several instances, behaved very ill...they are not in the style they were'.[63] Wellington put this down to lack of pay, a perennial problem his army suffered during the Peninsular War; food and other supplies were short too and the unpopularity of siege work did not help. A soldier who was present remembered:

> we came within sight of the Castle of Burgos, and we began to anticipate, not with much pleasure, all the inglorious toils, and arduous and fatiguing business of a siege, - the most disagreeable military duty a soldier has on service, digging and delving in dust and dirt like ploughmen, to shelter ourselves, ere morning's dawn, from shot and shell whizzing about our ears at each moment, killing or mutilating our next neighbour. No excitement, as in a general action, by the immediate prospect of getting at the foe, your only hope that you may get through your twenty-four hours in the trenches unscathed, back to your bivouac to eat, drink, and sleep till your turn in the batteries comes round again, varied by the storm of an outwork or a sortie of the enemy, to either of which occurrences the soldier looks forward as something to enliven and break in upon this routine of his daily labours.[64]

The rain soaked everyone and everything; at night the temperatures dropped uncomfortably and there was no shelter from either the wet or the cold for men and officers alike. A British soldier posted in the same area as Jack later wrote:

> We were almost naked...we were nearly out of all the necessaries so essential to our comfort; such as stockings, shoes, shorts, blankets, watchcoats and trowsers; and, what was worse than all, it now began to be very cold, for when the rain ceased, there was a frost every night, so that we were nearly perished...hunger often caused us to do things, which we should have been ashamed to do, if we had plenty: but this was not the case, for we have often been working and watching the enemy eighteen hours out of the twenty-four, having only the same scanty allowance, and sometimes not that.[65]

---

63 Quoted in Divall, *Burgos*
64 'A Field Officer' *Four Years*
65 *The Vicissitudes of a Soldier's Life* John Green 1827

The poor morale occasionally revealed itself. On 3 October the Adjutant General's Office issued a General Order in the wake of bad behaviour by some of Jack's men:

1. The Commander of the Forces noticed in General Orders on the 1st instant, the complaints he had received of the working parties, and he is concerned to have again to notice, that he has received complaints of the working parties ordered for last night.

2. The whole of the working parties ordered for the trenches, from Brigadier General Pack's, and Brigadier General Bradford's Brigades, from six to twelve o'clock last night, absented themselves from the trenches.

3. The Commander of the Forces desires that Ensign Antonio de Gouvia Cabral, of the 4th Regiment of Caçadores, and Ensign Jose Carasco Guerra, of the 5th Regiment of Caçadores, may be put in arrest, and that the Non-commissioned Officers and soldiers composing these parties from General Pack's and General Bradford's Brigades, may be employed at working parties for six hours, during the twenty-four hours of the next four days, and that during the remainder of the twenty-four hours of the same four days, they may be kept at their arms in front of the encampment, fully accoutred, and in readiness to turn out at a moment's warning.

4. The Commander of the Forces is concerned likewise to have to notice, that the working party ordered last night for the commanding Officer of the Artillery, did not perform their duty.

5. All the Officers, and the whole of the Portuguese detachments absented themselves, and of course when such an example was set by the Officers, much was not to be expected from the soldiers.

6. The following Officers are to be put in arrest for quitting their duty without leave, on the night of the 2[d] instant, viz. Captain Francisco Jose Lobo, 5th Caçadores, Lieutenant Charles Holle, 1st Line Battalion King's German Legion, Lieutenant Maximiano Gomes de Silva, 1st Portuguese Infantry, Ensign Jose Ignacio de Vasconcellas, 5th Caçadores.[66]

---

66 *General Orders, Spain and Portugal, Vol. IV January to December 1812*

This ill-discipline did not reflect well on either McCreagh or Jack as the senior officers of the 5th Caçadores. But worse, the consequence was to prove fatal for some of their men. On 7 October, the fourth day of their punishment, they were the target of a sortie by the defenders of Burgos, looking to disrupt the works. One of the 5th Caçadores' British captains, Henry Perry, was killed. A week later McCreagh sent a report to Bradford about the incident, in which Sergeant Gaspar de Brito of Jack's regiment perhaps redeemed a little of the battalion's honour by his 'very gallant and exemplary behaviour...when engaged in repulsing the sortie from the castle of Burgos':

> The particulars of his distinguishing himself so highly in instantly collecting that portion of the working parties of the 5th Caçadores consisting of fifty men which were under his immediate command after Captain Perry fell, his twice charging up the glacis and establishing himself in spite of the superior numbers of the French assisted by a destructive fire from their ramparts, have been reported to you by officers who were witnesses of his conduct, and if their assertions required further confirmation the testimony of the soldiers engaged may be deemed worthy of attention, who all with one accord declare his inspiring words and behaviour, with his personal example of bravery, to have animated all around him.
>
> Sergeant Gaspar de Brito is I understand of respectable parents in Serpa. He is nineteen years of age, has served in this battalion four years with the best character and is highly respected by his comrades. In full confidence that he will do credit to my recommendation and approve himself every way worthy so distinguished a mark of His Excellency's approbation I beg leave to recommend him for an Ensigncy in this battalion in which there are at present five vacancies.
>
> I have the honour to be Sir your very obedient servant

M. McCreagh
Lieutenant Colonel 5th Caçadores[67]

Sergeant de Brito received his promotion. A report by an officer from another of Bradford's regiments, Ensign Barbosa of the 13th Infantry, gave more detail of what happened:

---

67 Gaudêncio and Burnham *Fighting Cocks*

I report to Your Excellency that in the 7th instant about midnight I was ordered to go with the working party for Burgos's castle. The party was composed of 4 subalterns, 3 sergeants and 110 men, all under the command of Captain Henry Perry, 5th Caçadores, who according to orders, sent 44 men, 1 sergeant, and 1 subaltern to work on the trench. Of those a sentry was placed in front being both sides covered by the fire of the German troops of the British army from the parapet; the rest of the party remained in the esplanade in front of the breach; from those 12 men and 1 sergeant were ordered to bring the working tools. At the moment that the men joined, the sentry in front of the trench shouted to arms and to which followed a great outcry all around the parapet. The enemy, taking advantage of the darkness of the night, attacked us in great numbers and immediately took some of the workers. Our brave Captain Perry and the other officers on the esplanade directed our people against the enemy at the breach and suddenly face-to-face with the enemy, under its illuminating fire, our captain ordered to fix bayonets and fire. In this instant he received a musket ball in the chest and then was bayoneted, the same fate had befallen Major Cocks who was the senior officer of the day.

At this time the Germans who occupied the breach's parapet and fired from it, seeing the enemy moving through the parapet turned around and showing their bayonets pushed my men (under my command after the captain's death) aside and ran away through the esplanade. By this the enemy became master of the breach and all our people were in great confusion. In this moment I received two blows from a musket and fell surrounded by the enemy. I recovered and escaped to our side where, with Ensign Francisco Alexandre Lobo, 5th Caçadores, shouting to the men, we were able to regroup most of them and charge the breach two times but we were repulsed by a continuous fire of grape and hand grenades. We tried a third time and were joined by a captain from General Pack's Brigade and some soldiers from the 1st and 16th Regiments (the captain's regiment) and successfully expelled the enemy from the breach. Our loss was 43 or 44 dead and wounded. We continued to defend the breach keeping a steady fire. By 5 o'clock in the morning some British officers appeared and one of them asked for the senior officer. I told him that he was dead, and my men were tired, and the parapet needed reinforcements. The British officer told me that in the village below was the 12th British Regiment and sent me to call them. I found a British sergeant and conveyed the order. After about 20 minutes a British reinforcement arrived. I finally was relieved and gave the orders for the dead to be buried and the wounded collected.

Camp of Ibeas 17 October 1812

Jeronimo Soares Barboza
Ensign[68]

On 18 October a final attempt was made to take the castle by storm, aimed at breaches made through a combination of artillery and mines dug under the wall, filled with powder and exploded. The assault failed. Wellington was by now receiving intelligence both on the size of Souham's force and that Joseph and Soult had combined and were moving on Madrid. Souham had some 50,000 men at hand; Joseph and Soult some 60,000. Both French forces were larger than the portion of the allies facing them: Wellington in the north had perhaps 35,000; Hill in the south had around 36,000. Both Burgos and Madrid would have to be abandoned, and the allies reunited. On the 19th, however, Wellington formed his army in the area between Ibeas and Sotopalacios to see if Souham would attack, confident that if he did, the allies could strike a blow that would provide time for an orderly retreat. Souham prepared to do so, but orders from Joseph arrived telling him not to risk a major engagement as the movement on Madrid would force Wellington to abandon Burgos without further French losses. Joseph was right; the timing of his orders prevented what might have been a significant encounter in the north, rather than the brief skirmish that ensued.[69] Lieutenant da Paz wrote in his notebook that the French made what he called 'a strong reconnaissance' at about 5pm on the 20th, which was repulsed as far as Quintanapalla.[70] Bradford's Brigade then moved to their left, taking position on the heights of Atapuerca at dawn on the 21st. That night, Wellington gave orders to raise the siege. The troops lit campfires and stealthily moved off. At 9pm Bradford's men left their ridgeline and joined the more southerly of two columns. Theirs was the trickier route as after passing through Villafría they had to cross the bridge in Burgos, right under the French guns in the castle, which da Paz records Bradford's men did at around 1am in the morning of the 22nd. Silence was ordered so as not to alert the defenders. A man from another regiment recalled:

> There was something peculiarly awful in this night march of so great a body of men - the cautious silence, the dead hour, and the consideration that in an instant the guns of the castle might send death among us. Some of the last troops had a few shots fired at

68 Gaudêncio and Burnham *Fighting Cocks*
69 Oman, *History Vol. VI*
70 Arquivo Nacional Torre do Tombo PT/TT/CF/212

them; but altogether this clever movement was so well conducted, that the garrison were ignorant of it until it was too late for them to cause us any serious annoyance.[71]

Once past Burgos, their march continued all night to Buniel, twenty miles from their departure point, where they rendezvoused with the northern column. After a short rest (da Paz says for two hours) the whole army continued their retreat. Bradford's weary men camped at Celada del Camino, just eight miles further on, the next evening. The march continued on 23 October, towards Torquemada, a further twenty-five miles away. Men began to fall out by the wayside, exhausted. By now the allied departure had been discovered and Souham was in pursuit; his cavalry was being held off by the allied rearguard. Their predicament did not improve the mood among the men:

> The failure of the siege and the retreat disheartened us all…we were retrograding, and an English force is ever a difficult one to manage on a retreat, the soldier's spirit flags, he becomes sulky, growls, and grumbles, because he is not allowed to turn and fight. He had not been broken by defeat, battle and victory had ever been one and the same thing to him, and he cannot be made to understand why he is to retire, and be harassed by forced marches, to get away from a foe whom he had so often drubbed. Under the excitement of these feelings, and perhaps from some slight carelessness on the part of our Chiefs, excesses were committed on this march.[72]

They were retreating through a centre of wine production; many could not resist the temptation of the vaults:

> The soldiers…so soon as their arms were piled, rushed in in crowds, broke open the doors, drank to excess. Some of them were found dead, literally drowned in wine, it having overflowed in the cellars and suffocated the poor wretches who were too drunk to escape. Next morning at daybreak, when we stood to our arms to recommence the march, the scene was one, perhaps, without parallel in the annals of military history; for I scarcely exaggerate when I say that, with the exception of the officers, the whole army

71 *With the 'Thirty-Second' in the Peninsular and Other Campaigns* Major Harry Ross-Lewin 1904
72 'A Field Officer' *Four Years*

were drunk. We at last moved off the ground, although the men, overpowered and stupefied by wine, could scarce totter along, some lay down, and could hardly be persuaded to move. We were in better plight than many of our neighbours. The gallant Guards were far worse off than ourselves, inasmuch as they had bivouacked much closer to the town. We were all, however, bad enough; and in the midst of all this was to be heard the firing of the rearguard, smartly engaged with the enemy.[73]

As Oman understatedly noted 'it was very hard to get the battalions started the next morning'.[74] Bradford's Brigade started from Torquemada at 7am on the 24th, heading for Dueñas, where with the rest of the army they formed a line between there and Palencia, mostly behind the Carrión river. Wellington looked to make a stand and ordered all the bridges destroyed. But a rapid French advance captured the bridges at Palencia and Tariego before they were blown; the allies had to fall back again. Late on the 25th they marched another twenty miles to Cabezón, crossed the Pisguera river and formed along it, with the south of their line at Valladolid. Here they were finally able to rest for two days, with the French frustrated by the strength of the Allied position. Unfortunately for the allies, however, they were soon at risk of being outflanked to the south by the French capture of a damaged bridge at Tordesillas. Before it could be repaired, Wellington shifted again and took up another strong position behind the Duero. Here his luck changed as tensions between the various French armies led to General Caferelli taking his contingent from the *Armée du Nord* back to their regular area of operations; his departure swung the numerical balance back to the allies.

The respite enabled the dishevelled and demoralised allied army to recover a little. They maintained their position until 5 November; Jack and his men bivouacked in Valdestillas, south of Valladolid. General Hill, simultaneously withdrawing from Madrid, was also now nearby. The reunited allied army would be around 65,000 strong; enough to take on either Souham or Joseph individually. But if Wellington fought and defeated one, the other could move to cut his supply lines to the west, and might be strong enough to defeat what remained of the allies after a major battle. Both parts of the allied force were also in poor condition. Hill's retreat from Madrid was as exhausting as Wellington's from Burgos. Some 17,000 men were sick and many more were straggling somewhere behind. The pause in

---

73 'A Field Officer' *Four Years*
74 Oman, *History Vol. VI*

Madrid aside, the army had been on operations continuously since the start of the year; men and equipment were worn out. Wellington decided to retire back to the strong position outside Salamanca they had occupied in June. Starting on 6 November, the allies covered the fifty miles at a more gradual pace, 'and by the evening of the 8th all were safely placed in their old positions...in a semicircle from Aldea Lengua to San Cristobal'.[75] Jack and his Caçadores, with the rest of Bradford's Brigade, were at Aldealengua, watching the fords over the river Tormes at Huerta. The French army, looking also to combine its disparate parts, did not pursue vigorously and the men finally began to recover properly, though continuing bad weather and lack of shelter led to the outbreak of more sickness.

As the French approached, it seemed for a while that a second battle of Salamanca might be fought in the same area as the July clash. On 15 November both armies were drawn up around the old battlefield. Bradford's Brigade was again in the second allied line, this time more to the left. Unlike 22nd July, this day was wet and poor visibility was not the only difference as Soult, placed in overall command by Joseph, was more careful than Marmont had been. This time there was no error for Wellington to capitalise on as the French again sought to move around their opponents. Without such an opportunity and with an army still suffering from the effort of its retreats from Burgos and Madrid, Wellington decided he had little choice but to fall back to the Portuguese border. That afternoon he ordered the army to retreat towards Ciudad Rodrigo, fifty miles to the south-west. As they began to move, the rain worsened, turning the roads into quagmires. 'I shall ever remember those days' said one participant 'we marched several miles up to the ancles [sic] in water, sometimes indeed up to the knees, and continued to move along through mud and mire until night, and then encamped in a place completely flooded with water.'[76] Despite having been in the Salamanca area for a week, supplies again failed – the supply column had been sent on the wrong road and food was short:

> The whole British army was now in full retreat; the rains had set in, the weather had become dreadful, and we were sorely pressed by the enemy; all dreary and desolate, marching and fighting all day, tired and hungry... This was a hard day upon the men, from the heavy rains; many fell out, some sick, others disabled and footsore; hundreds broke down overcome by the great weight they had to carry, in addition to the wet clothes on the back - viz., a knapsack,

75 Oman, *History Vol. VI*
76 Green, *Vicissitudes*

heavy old flint firelock, 60 rounds of ball cartridge, haversack with sometimes three days' rations, wooden canteen, bayonet, greatcoat, and blanket, half-choked with a stiff leather girdle about the throat, and as many cross buff belts as would harness a donkey - it was wonderful how they moved along, and more surprising that they were not all left on the line of march; as it was, the French were picking them up in scores as they dotted the cheerless route.[77]

Straggling and falling out to find food became a serious problem. When some men found what appeared to be suitable prey, they quickly took matters into their own hands. On 16 November General Orders issued a reprimand:

1. The Commander of the Forces requests the General Officers commanding Divisions will take measures to prevent the shameful and unmilitary practice of soldiers shooting pigs in the woods, so close to the camp and to the columns of march, as that two dragoons were shot last night. And the Commander of the Forces was induced to believe this day on the march, that the flank patroles were skirmishing with the enemy.

2. He desires that notice may be given to the soldiers, that he has this day ordered two men to be hanged who were caught in the fact of shooting pigs; and he now orders, that the Assistant Provosts may attend their Divisions on the march, and that they will do their duty, as well in respect to this as other offences.

3. The number of soldiers straggling from their regiments, for no reason excepting to plunder, is a disgrace to the army, and affords a strong proof of the degree to which the discipline of the regiments is relaxed, and of the inattention of the Commanding and other Officers of regiments to their duty, and to the repeated orders of the army.[78]

Some in the army were unimpressed by this:

The Duke made a great fuss about all this insubordination; but it is to be remembered that the line of march from Salamanca was through a flooded and flat clay country, that the troops, ankle-deep in mire, mid-leg in water, had lost their shoes; and with strained

---

77 Bell, *Rough Notes*
78 *General Orders, Spain and Portugal, Vol. IV January to December 1812*

sinews had heavily made their way upon two rations only in five days, feeding on acorns, when Wellington supposed that the commissaries were supplying the army with their usual rations. The great commander, in whom we had the firmest reliance, was unrivalled in skill, vigour, and genius, but could not see at once into the wants and necessities of 70,000 men. The pursuing enemy captured much of our stores and baggage, and our loss of seasoned British soldiers on this retreat, in killed and wounded, and prisoners, according to the returns, came up to 8,000 men. War tries the strength of military framework, and hunger will not resist a pork-chop fried on the top of a ramrod. "The pigs," men said, "had no right poaching on our grounds, and we had a right to our ration of acorns.[79]

On the reprimanded army trudged, along parallel roads towards the Portuguese border. They had marched off as they were formed outside Salamanca; those who had been in the first line took the more southerly route and those in the second line the more northerly. Jack and his Caçadores marched through Aldehuela de la Boveda. If anything, this leg was worse than that from Burgos. 'Our sufferings in this retreat were very great, and great in proportion was our joy at the sight of the walls of Ciudad Rodrigo'.[80] The various units arrived at Ciudad Rodrigo on the 20th and 21st. French cavalry had pressed them much of the way, which meant anyone straggling was quickly captured or killed. Losses from this cause alone were enormous; by the time they reached safety, some 50,000 were found to be missing, and though some ultimately made it back to their units, by far the majority had been lost in the few days since the army left Salamanca.[81] Bradford's Brigade suffered particularly heavily. At Salamanca their strength had been 1,894. On 23 October, shortly after departing Burgos, the brigade had 1,645 men present under arms, excluding officers, NCOs and drummers. A month later, outside Ciudad Rodrigo, they recorded just 881 between all three regiments. The brigade had shrunk by over half in four months, despite being largely unengaged at Salamanca, seeing little action at Burgos and none at all during the retreat. No less than 514 of those lost on the retreat were declared as 'missing'. Oman noted that this was 'much the heaviest percentage in the whole army…they simply sank by the wayside, and died, or suffered themselves to be taken prisoners without attempting to get away'.[82] It was a record of which

---

79 Bell, *Rough Notes*
80 'A Field Officer' *Four Years*
81 Oman, *History Vol. VI*
82 Oman, *History Vol. VI*

none of Bradford, McCreagh nor Jack could be proud, though Jack later suggested that things could have been worse, in that the incentive of marching home kept some Portuguese going, rather than accept their fate in Spain.

The allies waited outside Ciudad Rodrigo for a week, in case the French attacked. But the French had suffered too from the weather and long marches and instead they fell back in search of supplies to sustain them through winter. On 27 November Wellington ordered his army into cantonments. Jack and his Caçadores marched another 100 miles into the interior of Portugal. By 30 November they were at Penças, before taking up winter quarters around Vila Real, in the mountainous Trás-os-Montes region where many of the 5th Caçadores were from.[83] They left with a parting gift, as General Orders announced:

> The Commander of the Forces has directed that those Non-commissioned Officers and Soldiers of the Infantry and Artillery who were present at the siege of Burgos, and those who were present with their Regiments in Spain, between the 15th and 19th of November, as well Portuguese as English, shall receive a pair of shoes gratis from the Commissary.[84]

It was promised that the much-needed shoes would be provided before 1 February. Less positive was a further message Wellington issued on 28 November, in which he castigated the officers of his army for having 'lost control over their men' during the retreat. Downplaying the appalling conditions, he claimed the army had not 'suffered any hardships, excepting those resulting from the necessity of being exposed to the inclemencies of the weather'. He said the marches had been short, there had been long halts, and the enemy had 'little pressed' them. In summary, he believed the army 'suffered no privations which but trifling attention on the part of the officers could not have prevented'.[85] The message was apparently not intended for wide circulation, let alone publication. Yet leaks were as inevitable in 1812 as today; the remarks made the newspapers in Britain. Many officers reacted with disbelief and disappointment at the lack of recognition of what the army had been through. Wellington was unapologetic 'I believe there is no officer in the army who is not aware of the necessity of the adoption of some

---

83 Penças is the location given in the records of the 5th Caçadores in the Portuguese Military archives (PT/AHM/1/14/239/05 ms 6). No such town appears on modern maps.
84 *General Orders, Spain and Portugal, Vol. IV January to December 1812*
85 Oman, *History Vol. VI*

measures to restore discipline; and I am only afraid that those I have recommended are not sufficient for the object.'[86]

For Jack, 1812 had been an exhausting and frustrating year. On a personal level, his majority in the British army was confirmed and, in McCreagh's absence, his secondment to the Portuguese army meant he had commanded the 5th Caçadores through the most successful part of the campaign: Salamanca and the triumphal entry into Madrid. But he was disappointed to lose command when McCreagh returned at Valladolid. Professionally, although he and his regiment had been 'present' at Salamanca and the sieges of Ciudad Rodrigo, Badajoz and Burgos, they had taken little active part in any of the major engagements of 1812 and ended the year seriously understrength. He and his men had marched well over 1,500 miles during the year, suffered hot, cold, wet and dry weather and poor supplies, and ended up close to where they started. The Burgos campaign has historically been considered the only serious blot on Wellington's record during the Peninsular War. One historian said 'the whole operation had been a tragic farce and had served no useful purpose.'[87] The attempt to capture Burgos was undoubtedly a failure, but Wellington's aim initially was to damage Clausel's force enough to prevent him threatening his communications. He did not achieve this because his opponent refused to fight. With hindsight, the attempt to capture Burgos was certainly a mistake. Wellington called it 'the worst scrape I was ever in'; Oman thought 'nothing...was gained by the whole manoeuvre'.[88] But the allies' achievements in 1812 were significant, not least in ending the French occupation of Andalucía; the French never returned to that part of Spain. Contributing to that was the impact of a far more damaging retreat at the other extreme of Europe, as Napoleon lost 90% of his army withdrawing from Moscow. In 1813 Spain would be far less a priority for an Emperor now trying to retain his domination of central Europe; Wellington's army would reap the benefits.

---

86 *Wellington Despatches*. Wellington to Bathurst 10 February 1813.
87 Gates *Spanish Ulcer*
88 Divall *Burgos*; Oman, *History Vol. VI*

CHAPTER 12

TRIUMPH

'Vittoria, Sigura, Tolosa, St. Sebastian (there obtained the rank of
Lieut. Colonel).'

Memorandum to the Duke of York, 1823

In September 1812, William Hill's three year wait for a ship finally
ended when he took command of HMS *Rolla*, a 10-gun sloop. Among
the duties of the *Rolla* was delivering communications and supplies for
the army in Portugal, which raised the prospect of a possible rendezvous
with Jack. It seems, however, that the brothers never managed to be in
the same place at the same time, though it is not impossible that William
carried mail written by his brother. After being frustrated in
correspondence with home for much of the previous year, Jack was
again somewhere a regular mail service could be put in place. General
Orders set out the arrangements with suitable military precision for the
army's various units that were in the same area:

> The 3rd Division will receive their letters at Alvito, the 5th Division,
> Brigadier General Pack's and Brigadier General Bradford's
> Brigades, at Lamego, and care must be taken that the Non-
> commisioned Officers are at the proper places to receive them...A
> post will be despatched from Lamego to Celorico at 6 o'clock,
> A.M...care must be taken by the 3rd and 5th Divisions, and
> Brigadier General Pack's and Bradford's Brigades, to send the
> letters for Head Quarters by this post.[1]

Early in the new year Jack wrote to his mother with reflections both on
the retreat and on Wellington's criticism of his army's behaviour.

---

1 *General Orders, Spain and Portugal, Vol. IV January to December 1812*

My Dear Mother,

I cannot exactly say if I have answered your letter of the 4th Dec., the last I have rec'd, but I am sure I have not yours dated May the 2 1812. In it you mention the loss of D[unclear] and other domestic news. I rec'd it from Mr. Julian who join'd the 23rd while I was on a visit to them.[2] I also rec'd a letter from Mr. White of Plymouth, to whom I am much oblig'd for some powders principally bark, it is a thing I always have had in my baggage. Last summer when going into Spain, I was quartered for a night on the greatest man in a town, his little girl was ill of the ague. I produced my bark & desired them to take half, by some mistake I left the whole there. But returning I was put in another house where they sent their servant to find out if I had some bark, & desir'd me to call on them, when lots of fine things were said because the bark cur'd the ague, two fits only returning. In going away my baskets were filled with fruit.

Col Ellis makes an application through Gen'l Cole to Ld. Wellington for my being sent to a post in recruiting the 2nd Bn. I am waiting the answer. I have heard nothing more from Peter Brown respecting the money, it is some time since I rec'd my British pay. The shirts you sent remain in Lisbon. Mr. Julian marched all the way from Lisbon. He was slightly ill but is now well. Three weeks or a month marching successively had brought it on. You note respecting the retreat Ld. Wellington's letter has appeared in the newspaper. I will make no comment on it but will say what assisted us, in the Portuguese service, in getting out of Spain all that could march is the antipathy the Portuguese have for the Spaniards, with which I am a little tinctured. Nuts for Cobbett, he will crack them in high style. This fellow gave Sir James Craig a pretty disposing on a similar subject.

The day I met the 23rd on the retreat, indeed twice, I shar'd what I had to eat with them as my servant was near me, they had only rec'd their rum for four days no bread, no meat. I said your men are having their privations as soldiers the food & bread omitting. I stay'd & asked them how they got on. I fear Archdale is in a confounded scrape. The court martial is over the sentence not known, he certainly succeeded in bringing the whole of his men

---

2 Richard Julian had been Paymaster of the 23rd since 1803. He joined the battalion in the Peninsula in December 1812.

into Portugal with the exception of two, I understand he caught 16 breaking open a house & stealing wine. The whole of whom he punished without a court martial. The Provost Martial has this power, the Officer Commanding a Regt. has not.[3]

Remember me to Caroline [&] her little stranger. I shall go now again to see Col. Ellis when I shall get the letter from him for Fred to Sir J. Warren. Ellis said he should be happy to recommence his correspondence with the Admiral & that would be a good opportunity. I see by your letter of Jany. the 6 you had not seen my letters sequentially, particularly one written from the banks of the Coa. I think I got here [all] of yours in a lump. You mention the Martinique prize money is paying. I am happy at it, but fear it will not amount to much. Mrs W. you say is with you. Say all the fine things possible to her from me. Wm. while in the Tagus did not receive my letters for which I am very sorry. He would have sav'd what remains of my heavy baggage from destruction, could he have taken [it] out of the transport. I forwarded my letters under cover to Peter Brown with directions to burn them in case he had sailed. It was more than ten days before I got his letter. He promised to write again before he sail'd but I said I could not get the letter.

I have killed only two woodcocks this winter. America spoil'd my shooting, or perhaps want of practice. We shall soon have some good trout fishing, but I am always employ'd on one thing or another. The British service is a sinecure compared with this. I have a weeks work before me in overlooking the Companies, being President of a Court of enquiry - this country being unaccustomed, do not like overt intrusions into their proceedings; This one left his depot of Bullocks taking him in the retreat, not leaving orders to the guard to retire, all were taken, except [a] Corpl. charged with 220 bullocks, some of them were retaken by the Spanish cavalry. I see by the papers Wm. is arrived at Plymouth. You mention Mr. Blake of Ashworth – My Brother mentions Mr & Mrs Parker were to live at Stokelake, Archdale informed me the Honble something had taken some place near you, and described him in good terms. From Sept. to Jany. I see you had no letters from me, I presume that was through Jenkins. I wrote several, but perhaps private letters were not allowed to go, this is most likely the case.

---

3 Lieutenant-Colonel Richard Archdall (not Archdale) was commanding the 40th Foot; Jack had mentioned him in previous letters, including one of 11 November 1810 in which Archdall 'enquir'd after you all'. Court-martialled at Lamego for violent conduct, including unauthorised flogging. and found guilty, Archdall was sentenced to dismissal from service, but was allowed to resign his commission.

28 Feby. We have been without letters from England for some time, and are anxiously looking out to learn what is going on in these eventfull times. Our society in this brigade is imperfect indeed, of the officers who are now left half of them are sick. As for myself, I am getting fat from the meat. As for living I now had much worse fare, though good when compared with things around, our ranks are being filled by new levies, we are busy drilling them. They talk of Lord Wellington reviewing the different divisions of the army. We have various reports respecting the movements of the French armies. By their having sent everything valuable from Madrid, strange as it is we generally get the most correct news from the English papers. The Cortez have formally abolished the Inquisition. [4]

Remember me to all our family circle & believe me most affectionately Yours

J Hill

The 'bark' Jack had received from Mr. White and with which he had helped his previous Spanish hosts was presumably quinine, the bark of the cinchona tree, whose medicinal qualities were valued at a time of few treatments for fevers or 'agues'. This letter also confirms that Jack, like many of his colleagues, had not recently been paid, the shortage of provisions that many had experienced and the ill-discipline of some troops during the retreat. The 'application through Gen'l Cole to Ld. Wellington' to move to 2/23rd was doomed to fail; Jack never would take up the post he formally held in that battalion. Ellis knew Admiral Sir John Borlase Warren from Halifax: Warren was naval commander-in-chief of the North American station while Ellis was there with the 23rd. Presumably Jack wanted a recommendation for his brother Fred as a volunteer aboard one of Warren's ships - Fred would not be commissioned lieutenant until October 1814.

Wellington's army was in poor condition after its retreat. Bradford's Brigade may have lost proportionately more men, but its overall state was little worse than much of the army. Dysentery, rheumatism and other sickness was rife, with at least 18,000 hospitalised. Shelter, food, re-clothing and re-equipping was much needed and would take time. Wellington pressed London for money to pay his men and complained particularly about the length of time Portuguese troops had gone

---

4 The Inquisition was abolished while Joseph Bonaparte was on the throne. The Cortes, the ruling body of Spain based in Cadiz, confirmed the abolition after Joseph fled, hence Jack's use of the word 'formally'. It would be reconstituted when Ferdinand VII recovered the throne in 1814.

unpaid: 'The greatest inconvenience, indeed serious ills, were the consequences last campaign of the deficiency of regular payments to the Portuguese troops, which will be aggravated in the next campaign if some decided measures are not adopted to apply a remedy to the evil'.[5] Although he had reprimanded his officers for their inattention to the discipline of his troops, he was also sure of the root cause of the problems that the likes of the 5th Caçadores had experienced before Burgos: 'in several instances the Portuguese troops behaved excessively ill before the enemy, and this conduct was attributed by the officers to the miserable state in which they were kept for want of pay'.[6] Some money did at last come through, and the allied army slowly recovered, regrouped and reinforced in its cantonments. Meanwhile, the mail service was better again, if not perfect, and Jack took the opportunity of this relatively quiet period to write his longest letter home in many months.

Villa Real
24 March, 1813

I rec'd yours of the 10th Feb[y]. some days since. I have delay'd answering expecting daily to hear from Ellis, he has been harried. I have not got what I wanted for Fred or myself. We have papers to the 3rd March. I presume they were very busy in the Diplomatique department which we shall not know the result till some determination is made on one side or the other. You mention my letter of the 17 Jan[y]. but take no notice of one written about the 10 Dec. about a week after my arrival at this place. I cannot account for this except its having been detain'd, at this I should not be much surprised.[7]

I do not remember commenting on the retreat, the letter you received before that was by a private hand, that of our Sidmouth acquaintance. By the bye, my Dec[r]. letter did say something of Alava's army as having been pent up in a corner and had been of little use to us. I expect to receive the deal box in about a week from this, it is with a friend of mine in Lisbon.

So our Whiteaway acquaintance is dead; well, I have some curiosity to learn what will be the consequences. I am very sorry to hear of Mr. Abraham, the country bankers have done a great deal

5 *Wellington Despatches*. Wellington to Stuart 7 March 1813
6 *Wellington Despatches*. Wellington to Stuart 24 April 1813
7 There are no letters of either date in the surviving collection. The one referred to as '17 Jany.' may be that dated 7 February 1813, as the content of this letter follows on from that.

of harm, it is owing to them that the value of a pound has been forgotten and hence has arisen the difference between it and a Guinea.[8] I am very sorry to have so bad a report from Linridge, a Mrs. Haywood is related to the Brinley of Halifax.[9] Pray, has Joel Barlow been found who set out for Moscow to pay Bonaparte a visit there? I should like to learn his adventures.

The Portuguese are going to give the Russians 15,000 pipes of wine. Our Government should send officers to collect the Portuguese and Spaniards taken by the Russians, but few are left of the 12,000 taken by the French out of this country as many fell in the battle of Aspern.[10] We do not exactly know the result of the Catholick question, if carried the next point of attack will be the tythes, what guarantee have you for the Church of England.

I am not sufficiently versed in the different theories of Geology to be enabled to give you satisfactory answers. There is a new and very highly finished map of Portugal published that will show you the bearings of the Sierras which are various. I went the other day to see some Gothick Pagan curiosities the other day [sic]. There is a Portuguese account of it, I will endeavour to get the book, there is an old Padre about 18 miles who has many things taken out of the Mausolea, there is an isolated rock with steps cut in its sides, on the top vaults for burying their great men in, sunk into the upper surface, over which had been bits of stone with iron bolts, like the locker in a ship's cabbin. There are several inscriptions in Roman letters, the one that had been on the side of the principle rock has been blown off by Gunpowder and carried away as a curiosity. I suppose one of the Graves is about 7 ft. 4, the others about the general run.[11]

---

8 Abraham was an Ashburton banker who was facing financial difficulties; a Certificate of Bankruptcy was issued to him in July 1813. *London Gazette Issue 16755* 20 July 1813

9 Lindridge was a large mansion near Ideford owned by the Templar family. Jane, wife of the Rev. John Templar, died in 1813, perhaps the bad news Jack mentions.

10 Following the French invasion, the Portuguese army was disbanded in 1808. Some officers and men were sent to France to form the *Legion Portugaise* of the Imperial army, which suffered severe losses at Wagram in July 1809 (not Aspern). The survivors participated in Napoleon's invasion of Russia in 1812, taking heavy casualties at Smolensk and Borodino; in the retreat from Moscow the *Legion* literally disappeared from the further losses they suffered. The Portuguese government did not want men captured by the Russians back during the Peninsular war: having fought for France for so long, their loyalty was considered doubtful.

11 This description fits the *Santuário de Panóias* in Vale de Noguerias, near Villa Real, a ritual sight dating to the 2nd and 3rd centuries. The area has large rocks

The materials of this Province are mountainous, Shistus and Granite in great varieties are the most common. Lead, iron, tin, copper, many warm springs, about 10 miles from hence some prodigous mines worked by the Romans. We are talking of visiting them.[12]

The Douro while it waters Spain runs through a continued plain, entering Portugal it flows among mountains. The Tagus is the opposite, low in Portugal, mountainous in Spain. This is what prevents the navigation of the two rivers not being so good as in general other rivers of their size are. Were you here I do not doubt but you would propose a trip from the banks of the Douro to the top of the Sierra Maron which threatened to tumble into its bed and forbid its entering the sea; this would be a bad move as our wine merchant could not make about £25 per pipe on the Douro wine of which porto is Oporto again. Your Devonshire cyder would drink genuine without mixing with Bonaparte's brandy and making 3 pipes perhaps out of 2. The vines are planted as close as your currant bushes and one stem is allowed to retain two spurs. The stump may be 3 feet, the two branches about 2½ ft. In case the vine is weakly only one shoot is left, the earth around their roots must be turned or the grape falls off in juice. The different quality of the grape depends on soil and aspect.

Talking of the Oporto people (English) they brought some dispute they had with the municipality of that city before the House of Commons their cause and their speeches were equally good, the difference was the magistrates wanted to billet English officers only on them according as it came to their turn with the rest of the citizens, ought not the people who derive a monopoly receive their country men who may chance in service to be there. To this they plead we do.[13] I will show how. On coming near Oporto one of the Merchants came out, met us, and invited the English officers to dine with the Company. Bow'd, said yes, din'd - next day dunned for my dinner. Dined a second time, after the

---

carved with Latin and Greek inscriptions; one has a staircase cut into it. Rectangular cavities dug into the rock, which Jack took to be graves, are now thought to be the remains of temples. The book Jack refers to was probably *Memorias para a historia ecclesiastica do arcebispado de Braga, primaz das Hespanhas* by Jerónimo Contador de Argote, published in 1732

12 These are Jales' plateau mines, which the Romans exhausted and abandoned.
13 The British port wine merchants of Porto were worried about moves to end their privileged trading licence. *Hansard Volume 24: debated on Friday 19 February 1813 – Petition of Wine Merchants, Correspondents of the Royal Wine Company of Oporto*

cloth was remov'd, a merchant's clerk came in and delivered a letter, no notice taken of it. A Sergeant came in and deliver'd some paper that required a receipt to prove the conveyance had not exceeded the time order'd and allowed - a long argument, coarse language. I got up and, leaving them, said, Gentlemen, you will excuse my dining with you again. We sat looking at one another during the talk and walk'd off in that manner, knowing our own society among ourselves was much better. The fact is the fear of the French keeps the heads of the houses at home, and the business is done by Clerks and the youngest partners. The class of men very inferior to those we met while in Cadiz coming home from Gibraltar.[14]

The French are marching troops out of Spain. The French tell us their army of observation is at Hamburg. What to observe the Hessians, Hanoverians who are on the French side of the Elbe? From Moscow to Hamburg no halting place, no point d'appui, what a retreat, what a dressing! I should imagine the Hannoverians will change their tune, when I was among them, and possibly, taught by the French Companies as it is on Bonaparte's coin, Dieu protege la France that it was useless to fight against the French for God fought for them, they may join the Russians on the same principal, you may go back to the Bible and get the most instructive lessons to find out causes and consequences. Alexander made a good soldier and general but a very bad God; Bacchus, he died drunk and his servants rob'd the house he had acquir'd by violence. Let us look round us in these awful times in which we live; where is Josephine, the moddle [sic] for her sex, where are the blasphemous compliments paid to Bonaparte when he was in full feather. The Non Nobis of Alexander gives us hopes he is building his Empire on a more solid foundation It is amusing to remember some of the French gasconades. The Minister of the Interior Duke of Cadore, said to the contemptible Americans: "there is some difference with the Court of St. Petersberg, a few French Cannon will soon dissipate it".[15] Bonaparte's invasion of Russia was by no means classick, he ought much earlier to have found out the trap laying for him, that the same system had destroyed several armies before,

---

14 This may refer to a visit to Porto while Jack was in Villa Real, or to an incident when the 5th Caçadores were there refitting in May and June 1812. The latter is more probable as the mention of a sergeant suggests that the battalion was present.

15 Jean-Baptiste de Nompère de Champagny, 1st Duc de Cadore, was appointed Napoleon's Minister of the Interior in 1804, but retired after a quarrel with his Emperor in 1811

his vanity and love of splendid mischief lost him his army, making good the old proverb "quem Deus vult perdere prius dementat".[16] The House of Braganza has ceased to reign but she was the first that commenced the insurrection of Europe and showed the way in which the French were to be resisted. [17]

We are without recent information from America, I should imagine the plot thickens with them. The Canadian operations will cease in some degree in the latter end of the spring, at the breaking up of the frost, the roads require time to get dry. It equally applies to the North of Europe. Were we not so much employed in Europe the Americans would find 20 years of war had produced more science among our military and ministers than existed when by French assistance they became independent. As to the American frigates, I saw them at Gibraltar, they were intended for line of battle but money being scarce, they left them without the other deck. It was an unwise and cruel thing not sending 74s against them, to save an unnecessary waste of life. Sir George Provost by extraction a Canadian independent of his other talents which are great will do everything that is possible on the St. Lawrence. The Black Regts. from the West Indies with a few thousand stand of arms would make the Carolinas and Virginia keep their white population on the alert and form a diversion from Canada. Prince Eugene remarks that people who have seen war are always the last to advise it, that is generally brought about by people who are not to partake of the miserys and exertions that accompany it.

I have been to pay a visit to one of the Officers who sent me some wine of the 1st Class. The farmer here is not content if he can only get 50 Dollars = 40,000 Reis, a pipe. How the English gentry can contrive to bring it to £120 a pipe really is beyond my comprehension. The second and third quality still cheaper. The wine is abundant of a finer quality than most years.

Remember me to all our Relatives and believe ever yours,
J Hill

Jack clearly had time on his hands to write in so wide ranging and philosophical a manner. Speculation about the work of the 'Diplomatique department' reflects uncertainty about how various European powers would react to the French disaster in Russia. Britain sought a renewed

---

16 'Those God wishes to destroy he first drives mad'
17 The Braganzas, the Portuguese Royal family, fled to Brazil in November 1807 following the French invasion. King João VI, the former Prince Regent, returned to Europe in 1821.

combination against France, but at the time Jack wrote he would not have known that Prussia and Austria, who in 1812 had been respectively a French client state and ally, would join Russia and Britain in a 6th Coalition. His comments on French hubris were probably not untypical of the reaction of his peers in the wake of Napoleon's Russian disaster. Similarly typical were dismissive opinions of Americans, whose patience with British naval highhandedness finally ran out when they declared war the year before. Reference to US frigates reflects their success in a series of encounters with Royal Navy frigates; the British government did not commit line-of-battle ships, or '74s', which were allocated to the higher priority of protection of sea lanes and the continued blockade of France. Jack's prediction of what would happen if American troops met Wellington's seasoned veterans is a not untypical conceit by a British soldier; it proved incorrect when a British army including many of Wellington's Peninsular veterans was defeated at New Orleans in 1814. More interesting is his speculation on the response of southern American states to finding West Indian regiments in their midst, which presages a debate 50 years later during the US Civil War, when the Union was considering raising black regiments to fight the Confederacy (which it eventually did, to great military and political effect). Jack had seen British West Indian regiments in action during the Martinique campaign and clearly respected their competence. For the British government, the War of 1812 was an unwelcome distraction, and though it diverted resources that Wellington would rather have had deployed on the Peninsula, as Jack implies unlike in 1776 the US would not this time gain French assistance; the Emperor was too busy fighting for his own throne.

Joseph had succeeded in chasing Wellington out of Spain in late 1812, but the strategic situation in the Peninsular had swung significantly against him since. The winter of 1812/13 saw Wellington's strength grow while, as Jack noted, his opponent's reduced. To recruit a new army to replace that lost in Russia, Napoleon ordered the French army in Spain to be 'plundered both of formed units and cadres of veterans'.[18] These men were soon 'marching...out of Spain' to provide a core for inexperienced units in central Europe, but their loss weakened the army in Spain. Several of the most experienced commanders in Iberia, including Soult, Souham and Cafarelli, were also recalled. Joseph still had almost 200,000 men in Spain, but protecting supply lines, supressing guerrillas and controlling French-occupied areas dispersed his forces. He had only around 40,000, currently posted along the river Tormes around Valladolid, available to counter

---

18 *1813 Empire at Bay - The Sixth Coalition & the Downfall of Napoleon* Jonathon Riley 2013

Wellington's next move. Joseph's brother magnified his problems; Napoleon continued to interfere remotely in a theatre he was out of touch with, his messages often arriving late or not getting through because of guerrilla activity. Many fell into the hands of his opponent, while the friendly local population also provided Wellington with intelligence on French activity. With no need to secure his own rear areas, Wellington could concentrate his army to generate a deployable, unified Anglo-Portuguese force of at least 70,000 men.[19] Appointed Spain's *Generalissimo* in late 1812, Wellington had additional Spanish forces available too, though he was unconvinced of their quality.

In January Wellington wrote to the Earl Bathurst, Secretary of State for War, of his 'expectation that I should be able to give employment to between 150,000 and 200,000 French troops in the next campaign.'[20] He reorganised his army into two wings under his two most capable generals, Sir Rowland Hill and Sir Thomas Graham. Jack and his Caçadores, in Bradford's Brigade, were allocated to Graham. 'Next to Lord Wellington's self, there is no one who will take so good care of us' said one officer of Graham.[21] Wellington planned to bring Joseph to a decisive battle, ideally somewhere in northern Spain. On 23 April he told Graham 'I propose to move as soon as I can after the beginning of the month; and rather think, between ourselves, I shall direct my march across the lower Duero within the Kingdom of Portugal'.[22] Rowland Hill's right wing would march towards Salamanca; Wellington would initially accompany them, to make Joseph assume this was his main thrust. But Graham's left wing, substantially the larger, would concurrently move on a more northerly route, strategically outflanking the French army and forcing them to retreat. Wellington was full of confidence; the goal of his 1813 campaign could not be higher: to end the French occupation of Spain. He told Bathurst 'I do not know whether I am now stronger than the enemy, even including the [Spanish] army of Galicia; but of this I am very certain, that I shall not be stronger throughout the campaign, or more efficient, than I now am; and the enemy will not be weaker. I cannot have a better opportunity for trying the fate of a battle, which, if the enemy should be unsuccessful, must oblige him to withdraw entirely'.[23]

The allies left their cantonments at the end of April and the army concentrated on 1 May. Jack and his Caçadores were already near the army's point of departure so stayed temporarily at Villa Real. But the

---

19 *Wellington Despatches,* Wellington to Graham 7 April 1813
20 *Wellington Despatches.* Wellington to Bathurst 19 January 1813
21 Gomm *Letters and Journals*
22 *Wellington Despatches.* Wellington to Graham 23 April 1813
23 *Wellington Despatches.* Wellington to Bathurst 11 May 1813

opening of the campaign was delayed because the weather, mostly dry through the winter and early spring, turned to heavy rain and delayed the arrival of a pontoon train needed to cross the rivers ahead. The army was ready to wipe away the memories of last November: 'I never saw the British Army so healthy or strong' said an upbeat Wellington 'We have gained in strength 25,000 men since we went into cantonments in the beginning of December, and infinitely more in efficiency'.[24] The advance was finally ordered on 18 May. Graham's wing crossed the Douro, with Bradford's Brigade of around 2,400 men part of its centre column. Detailed routes of march and timings required Bradford's men to head for the area around Outeiro, 80 miles from Villa Real, which they were to reach by the 21st. They would then push on another 40 miles 'in four marches to Losilla', arriving there 'on the 29th... the object of these movements is first to turn the enemy's positions on the Duero, and next to secure the junction of the right of the army with the left, as far up the river as possible.[25] Jack later wrote home listing the route he took and where he and his men camped each night. He wanted his parents to be able to trace his footsteps on a map, adding the comment 'Whenever you cannot find out the places mentioned in the maps, you may conclude we were in some small place to the left of the line running from one place to another'.[26] Progress was good, and by the end of May they were ready to cross the river Elsa. But although fords were identified, the rain had raised the river and strengthened the current. They tried to cross, but the river was impassable for infantry: 'On our arrival within a league of the Esla the ford was found to be impracticable, and we were on our return to Tabara, when we were again ordered up to the ford, two leagues from the place where we received the first order. On our arrival, the Heavy German brigade and Portuguese cavalry had got over, losing seven or eight horses and three or four men drowned. The ford was as bad as possible, and we were ordered two leagues lower down the river. A pontoon bridge was thrown over, by which the infantry were passing.'[27] Jack recorded that he and his men tried the fords on three separate days from 29 to 31 May. But the efforts were proving too slow and costly; Graham's wing therefore marched south and crossed a pontoon bridge that had been thrown across the river at Almendra.

---

24 *Wellington Despatches*. Wellington to Bathurst 5 May 1813

25 *Wellington Despatches*. Wellington to Graham 18 May 1813

26 Letter to his mother dated 26 June 1813. His comment remains apposite today, many places he lists (nor anything spelt vaguely like them) do not appear on Google maps!

27 Tomkinson, *Diary*

The advance now continued rapidly, passing through farmland described as 'one continuous cornfield. The villages are but thinly scattered over the country, so that it appears a difficulty to find hands to cultivate the crops. The land is of the richest quality and produces the finest crops with the least possible labour...the army has trampled down twenty yards of corn on each side of the road (forty in all)...but they must not mind their corn if we get the enemy out of the country'.[28] By crossing the Elsa, Graham's wing had as ordered outflanked the French positions along the Douro. Joseph retired to a defensive position near Burgos, thinking Wellington would again try to capture the town, but Graham moved further north. On 10 June they crossed the Pisuerga near Rezmondo and by the 15th Jack and his men were crossing the Ebro well north of Burgos, near Villarcayo. It was another masterly manoeuvre, forcing the French to retire again, toward the border. 'The triumphant and almost unopposed advance from the Elsa to the Pisuerga, executed in one sweep and at high speed', said Oman, 'was an episode which those who were engaged in it never forgot'.[29] Not least what stayed in the memory was the magnificent countryside. Jack commented 'The passage of the Ebro presented some very extraordinary scenery both in the march down the right and the ascent on the left bank, there was also a lateral march made on that river among a variety of beautiful combs and tremendous passes.'[30] Another soldier recalled:

I shall never forget the beauty of the valley through which this river runs, I had never before seen anything to equal it. About three miles from the bridge by which we crossed, on the top of a mountain, all on a sudden, the valley opened to our view, at one glance many miles of the river were visible, its rich banks ornamented with vineyards. Trees, villages, bridges, all in miniature, as we descended, the beauty of the scene increased as distant objects became more clear.[31]

Another noted 'The country is beautiful; richly-cultivated valleys. And mountains covered with the noblest forests...I can conceive nothing finer than the whole route from the banks of the Upper Ebro across the mountains.'[32] The allies pressed on, Graham's and Hill's wings keeping close enough for mutual support if needed. The terrain became more difficult with 'very hard marches, of four long Spanish leagues on three

---

28 Tomkinson, *Diary*
29 Oman, *History Vol. VI*
30 Letter dated c.2nd July.
31 *The Letters of Private Wheeler 1809-1828* B H Liddell Hart (Ed.) 1951
32 Gomm *Letters and Journals*

successive days, across upland roads.'[33] As they approached France, Wellington knew that Joseph would have to fight soon to avoid the ignominy of being driven out of Spain without resisting. On 18 June Graham's wing bumped into a part of the French army near Osma.

> The 1st and 5th Divisions, with Pack's and Bradford's Brigades, formed in [the] rear of Osma, about two miles. Osma lies in a plain, surrounded on all sides with steep hills, the enemy occupying the foot of them on the Vittoria road, whilst we held those to the right on the Bilboa road, and the valley in the bottom to the opposite range. This range is very steep, and commands the village as well as the position the enemy took up, and over which the light companies from the 1st Division were detached. This movement, with the 4th Division coming up on the hills to our right, caused them to move, after a little skirmishing, from the detachment made to the left, and a considerable cannonade from those on the right, as well as from our guns. As the enemy was moving off, the 5th Division was passed from the valley along the range of hills to the right, and came up with the enemy's rear with their light troops. There was a considerable fire on both sides, but little [damage] done.[34]

Jack described this same incident prosaically: 'march'd twice down and once up the famous passes, under arms and principal marching from 4 in the morn to 11 at night after a stray French division...A wandering French division had that morning first run foul of the Cavalry, next of the 5th Division, after some fighting got away, stumbled on the 4th and light divisions, the latter took all their baggage - what became of the rascals after I never have learnt, some say that they are still in our rear.'[35]

The main French stand would be made along the banks of the river Zadorra, outside the town of Vitoria. Wellington was seeking not just a victory, but a decisive one; he ordered Hill directly towards the French positions, aiming to strike their left and centre. Graham's wing, supported by Spanish partisan troops under Colonel Francisco de Longa, would meanwhile move across the hills north of Vitoria, strike the right of Joseph's line and block the main road to the French border. On 19 June, as Graham's troops approached their starting positions, 'It rained the whole day, which rendered the roads - always bad - almost

---

33 Oman, *History Vol. VI*. Four leagues is about 10 miles.
34 Tomkinson, *Diary*
35 Letter dated c.2nd July.

impassable'.[36] The next day they moved further forward to within a few miles of Vitoria itself.

Wellington ordered the attack on 21 June. Graham's approach was, however, constrained by negatively worded instructions. He was told to coordinate with part of Hill's wing, a column to his right comprising the 3rd and 7th Divisions under the Earl Dalhousie, and not 'to descend into the low grounds towards Vitoria or the great road, nor give up the advantage of turning the enemy's positions and the town of Vitoria by a movement to their left'.[37] But when Graham's troops reached their starting point there was no sign of Dalhousie; Graham sent Bradford's Brigade probing westwards to try to establish contact with them. Meanwhile he also sent part of his force eastwards towards the bridge at Gamarra Mayor, north-east of Vitoria, and Longa still further eastwards to block the main road to France at Durana. Bradford later said that he saw Dalhousie's force advancing towards Vitoria and so moved his men down towards the bridge over the Zadorra beyond the village of Yurre. At around the same time, in the early afternoon, Graham received positive orders from Wellington to 'move forward and press the enemy'. Graham recalled Bradford, but his orders coincided with the movement Bradford was already making, so Bradford's Brigade attacked the bridge at Yurre, crossed the Zadorra, then turned left and followed the road from it to Arriaga. In doing so he flanked the French units who had been defending Arriaga from another part of Graham's force which had crossed the river near Abechuco. 'I conceive [this] may have facilitated the evacuation of it and the capture of their guns as they retired almost immediately', reported Bradford.[38] Another observer believed Bradford's movement had a significant impact on the outcome of the whole battle:

> the 1st Division and Major-General Bradford's Portuguese brigade moved on the high road to Vittoria, Colonel Halkett's brigade of Light German infantry, supported by Major-General Bradford's Brigade, and covered by Captain Duberdin's brigade and Captain Ramsay's troop of artillery, attacked and carried the village of Abechuco, so giving us possession of both passes over the Zadorra. The light battalions charged the enemy on the bridge, and drove them away, taking a howitzer and three guns. The possession of these points completely turned the enemy off the main road from Vittoria to Bayonne...obliging them to take that of Pampeluna,

---

36 Tomkinson, *Diary*
37 *Wellington Supplementary Despatches*. 'Arrangements for the Movement of the Army on the 21st of June 1813'
38 Gaudêncio and Burnham *Fighting Cocks*

which so completely put them in confusions, that by 4p.m. their whole force had passed Vittoria, making off how they could, leaving in the rear of the town all their artillery, ammunition, waggons, money, and baggage, only taking their arms and men's kits on their backs.[39]

Jack's Caçadores were leading Bradford's attack, and his version (see below) confirms this movement.

Writing over 100 years later Sir Charles Oman, critical of what he considered Graham's lacklustre performance, said in his account of Vitoria that Bradford 'could find nothing' when he sought Dalhousie, was ordered to demonstrate 'for a short time' against Yurre and then called back to rejoin Graham at Abechuco. Oman concludes 'it is clear, therefore, that Graham never attacked the Arriaga position at all'.[40] The opinion that blame for the lack of communication between the two wings of Wellington's army fell on Graham was shared by General Charles Colville, leading a brigade as part of Picton's 3rd Division. Colville wrote home after the battle that 'a bad look-out was kept by his [Graham's] people, and though our column, consisting of the 3rd and 7th, saw his very plain as we reached the top of the mountain, they did not see ours, which was to have been the signal for his advance, and I believe consequently he did not march for three hours afterwards.'[41] Fortescue reinforces the impression that Graham's men halted prematurely, writing 'Graham meanwhile had brought up two batteries before Abechuco which, being on the main road, was more easily accessible to guns than Gamarra; and with this to prepare the way for them, Colin Halkett's two light German battalions stormed the tiny hamlet with little delay or loss, and captured four guns. There, however, their success came to an end. The bridge of Arriaga was nearly half a mile from Abechuco, and it does not appear that any serious attempt was made to carry it, for the casualties of the whole of the First Division, including Bradford's Portuguese, did not amount to one hundred killed and wounded. Be that as it may, it is certain that Graham's force was absolutely stopped by one-half...of their numbers'.[42] But neither Oman nor Fortescue had apparently seen Bradford's report of his brigade's movements that day, nor did they have available Jack's letter about the battle. Both clearly contradict the historians' conclusion. Colville's opinion, based presumably on camp gossip, also does not reflect reality. Bradford's post-action report

---

39 Tomkinson, *Diary*
40 Oman, *History Vol. VI.*
41 *The Portrait of A General* John Colville 1980
42 Fortescue, *History* Vol. IX

clearly states that he saw both 'the column of the left [Graham] halted and the Division on the right [Picton's] making progress towards Vitoria'. Communication was thus established, at least to the extent that it was clear the 3rd Division were advancing, which is all Graham needed to know. Bradford reported he then 'descended from the heights and moved upon the bridge below Zurti [Yurre]'. He does not say he returned to Abechuco, nor that his movement towards Yurre was merely a demonstration ordered by Graham (to whom he was writing). Graham's report to Wellington does say he recalled Bradford, but not to Abechuco, and Bradford was probably already moving towards Yurre by the time he received this order. Bradford's comment that 'crossing to the left bank of the Zadora, and from thence upon the village of Ariazo [Arriga]' shows that, contrary to Oman and Fortescue's conclusion, Graham's force did indeed move beyond Abechuco and attack Arriga and that Bradford's men were part of the force that did it, alongside Colonel Halkett's men from the 1st Division, who attacked across the bridge Fortescue refers to after they had taken Abechuco. Graham's own report backs this up, recording that as Halkett attacked the bridge south of Abechuco 'at this critical time Brigadier-General Bradford's Brigade arrived on the right of the chaussée, and supported the attack on the village'. Abechuco is on the other side of the river from the '*chausée*' (the main road through Vitoria to France), thus the village attacked by Bradford and Halkett must have been Arriaga. Halkett's report of this attack, forwarded to Wellington on 24 June, makes no mention of Bradford's flank attack, reserving all the credit to his own men, but does confirm the attack and capture of the guns. This revised version of events at the bridge of Yurre and at Arriaga is fully consistent with Jack's description of the events, in a letter he wrote home a few days later: 'we mov'd towards the level ground, descended the left bank of the river, found a bridge [&] cross'd, brought up our right shoulders on the right bank. On the head of our column approaching the causeway leading into Vitoria on the West Side, the bridge and guns were abandoned by the enemy. This let over the first division whose sharpshooters seiz'd the guns before us'.[43] It is understandable that the two great historians were unaware of either Bradford's or Jack's version of these events, though why they disregarded or misinterpreted Graham's is less obvious. Fortescue's conclusion that there was no attack because of the low casualties incurred fails to recognise that the French did not stay and fight but abandoned the bridge at Abechuco and the village of Arriaga because

---

43 Letter dated c.2nd July

they had been outflanked by Bradford and, with Halkett attacking in front, were at risk of being surrounded.

After capturing Arriga, Graham's advance continued, pursuing the retreating French troops of General Reille. As well as some British cavalry, Oman accepts this pursuit was led by 'the Caçador battalions of Pack and Bradford, and some of Longa's skirmishers who...followed him along the hills on his left, shooting into the retreating masses...The Caçadores and cavalry, however, did not halt until they reached El Burgo [Burgelu], four or five miles further on.'[44] Graham's report of the action confirms the prominent role the 5th Caçadores played in the pursuit: 'the greatest eagerness in the pursuit was manifested by all the different corps. The Caçadore battalions, followed with the cavalry, while part of Colonel Longa's troops harassed the enemy on their flank...the pursuit was continued on the left to El Burgo, when night obliged the troops to halt'.[45] Jack's version of this pursuit (see below) contained not a little pride in his men's efforts.

Vitoria was the crushing victory Wellington sought. The speed and vigour of the allied attack on the French left and centre, while Graham blocked their main escape road, routed Joseph's army who lost some 8,000 men and, remarkably, over 150 guns - all but two they started the battle with. More troops might have been captured, but a large part of the French baggage train, including huge quantities of 'treasure' looted from Spain and including Joseph's own personal baggage, became blocked outside Vitoria and was plundered by allied troops. 'Carriages, wagons, mules, monkeys, parrots, were all left in rear of the town. Everything useful to an army we have taken...The Paymaster-General, with all the military chest, fell into our hands. None of it was saved for the public service; the soldiers took the greater part'.[46] Many soldiers reportedly became very rich in the aftermath of Vitoria; Jack, busy leading his Caçadores after the retreating French, was not one of them. He later reported home 'The money taken will never be known. Some soldiers divided it by each receiving a cap full. I have got nothing except a dog and ½ a piece of linen'. The looting so disorganised Wellington's army that he felt unable to send more troops after Jack's Caçadores in pursuit of the main French army that was now heading pell-mell towards the border. Wellington later severely castigated his men for this, unfairly not excluding from his criticism troops like the 5th Caçadores who did their duty and pursued their foes, despite passing close to where the looting was taking place.

---

44 Oman, *History Vol. VI*
45 *Wellington Supplementary Despatches*. Graham to Wellington 23 June 1813
46 Tomkinson, *Diary*

At Salamanca a year before, Bradford's Brigade had been close to the action, but not seriously engaged. At Vitoria, it seemed for a time that they would play a similar role, sent hunting for Dalhousie's column with Graham constrained by Wellington not to commit until the allied attack developed on his right. But their role late in the day, with Jack and his Caçadores to the fore, redeemed the battle for them and was crucial to the victory. That they did not engage until the French were in practice already under severe pressure from their left meant casualties were light - just five killed and eighteen wounded in the entire brigade.[47] By far the lion's share of these were suffered by Jack's men: all those killed and thirteen of the wounded were 5th Caçadores. The 5th's prominent role ahead of the main body of the brigade was reflected in Bradford's after-action reports, to his Portuguese and British superiors:

To Adjutant General Mozinho
Andoain July 1st 1813

Sir,

I have the honor to request you will be pleased to submit to His Excellency the Marshal Commander in Chief the enclosed paper which, as nearly as I can recollect, is agreeable to the report I made to Sir Thomas Graham commanding the left column of the Army on the 23rd ultimo of the proceedings of the brigade under my command on the 21st at the battle of Vittoria. I have to beg at the same time that you will be kind enough to request the Marshal will have the goodness to excuse the omission I fear I have been guilty in not sooner sending this report to be laid before His Excellency, which arose from the supposition that the representation I made to Sir Thomas Graham would have been forwarded to the Headquarters. I trust this mistake of mine, which I am extremely sorry should have happened, will not prevent His Excellency expressing any feelings of approbation which he may consider the Brigade entitled to, as in justice to them I must bear testimony of my entire approbation of their good conduct on that day and particularly of the 5th Caçadores and the Grenadier Battalion, the former under the command of Lieutenant-Colonel McCreagh and the latter under Major Snodgrass of the 13th

---

47 Oman gives only 4 killed and 9 wounded; this slightly higher total is in the returns contained in Gaudêncio and Burnham's *Fighting Cocks*.

Regiment, whose fortune it was to be more engaged than the rest in the pursuit of the enemy.

I have the honor to be, Sir, your most obedient and humble servant.

T. Bradford

To Lieutenant General Sir Thomas Graham
June 23rd 1813

Sir

I have the honor to report to you that agreeable to your orders, I moved from Vitoriana on the morning of the 21st June to the heights to the left of Guita d'Aribal with a view of communicating between the left column and the 7th Division.[48] Seeing the column of the left halted and the Division on the right making progress towards Vitoria, I descended from the heights and moved upon the bridge below Zurti [Yurre] crossing to the left bank of the Zadora, and from thence upon the village of Ariazo [Arriga], at the period that Colonel Halket's brigade was advancing to the attack of the bridge leading to that place; by this movement the enemy's post was taken in flank which I conceive may have facilitated the evacuation of it and the capture of their guns as they retired almost immediately. I then put myself in communication with the cavalry of General Anson and General Ponsonby's Brigades and continued in support of them till the night prevented further pursuit. I cannot avoid mentioning with what zeal and alacrity this movement was performed by the officers and men of the brigade under my command as to derive any advantage from it, it was necessary to advance in double quick time for near two leagues.

I have the honor to be your most humble servant
T. Bradford[49]

---

48 Guita d'Aribal does not appear on modern maps, but older maps (including that in Oman's *History*) show a small village called 'Gueta de Arriba'. Assuming this is the place, then the heights 'to the left of it' are probably those west of Legarda, from the top of which Bradford may well have been able to see the 3rd Division advancing to the bridge at Tres Puentes, in the valley below and only about five miles away. In 1813 a road led directly from Legarda to the bridge at Yurre; the path of that road (today blocked by Vitoria airport) fits well with Bradford's description of his movements.

49 Gaudêncio and Burnham *Fighting Cocks*. The places referred to by Bradford are Bitoriano ('Vitoriana'), Hueto Arriba ('Guita d'Ariba'), Yurre ('Zurri') and Arriaga ('Ariazo').

There was more work for Bradford and his men to do, however. Blocking the main road to France meant most of the French army retreated eastwards along poorer roads towards Pamplona. Wellington gathered his army and followed them. From Burgelu, where Bradford's men had spent the night, Graham's wing was ordered to 'move by Arzabiaga [Arzubiaga], Audican [Audikana] and Dollo [Dallo] to Salvatierra'.[50] Reports came in, however, that a smaller French column had left on the main road north-eastwards towards Tolosa before the battle began. On the 22nd Wellington's Quartermaster General, George Murray, suggested a force might be sent over the mountains on a road leading from Salvatierra to try to cut this column off before it reached France; 'Probably the two Portuguese brigades and the 1st division had better go', said Wellington.[51] Graham was ordered 'with General Anson's brigade and the 1st division, and Pack's and Bradford's [to] proceed to Villafranca upon the great road from Vitoria towards Bayonne. This corps is to act against the enemy or any of his convoys moving on the great road to France.'[52] As Graham departed, the rest of Wellington's army continued to follow the French main body.

The mountainous 'road' Jack and his men took was a rough, mist-bound, goat-track. Bad weather made the climb worse. Jack reported: '[we] started climbing up the woody sides of a craggy mountain over the worst roads in heavy rain. On the summit we entered the Puorto do Santo Adrian, an immense cave that led us through the mountain to the other side. In it is situated a chapel and a farmhouse'.[53] Another officer recalled 'Such a march I never saw. The road we marched by was old pavé, totally broken up, worse and steeper than any stairs. Our men had not reached their ground before midnight the night before, and torrents kept falling night and day. The ground was so slippery that the men could hardly move, nor could the horses keep their footing. On the summit the road passed through a natural cavern or tunnel, some eighty yards in length; and here a great part of the troops bivouacked, too thoroughly fatigued to go any further.'[54] Jack's men again led the way, Bradford's Brigade and some KGL troops arriving at Segura on the

50 *Wellington Supplementary Despatches.* Arrangements for the Movement of the Army on the 22 of June [1813]
51 *Wellington Supplementary Despatches.* Wellington's approval note on Murray to Wellington, 22 June 1813
52 *Wellington Supplementary Despatches.* 'Arrangements for the 23rd of June' [1813]
53 Letter dated c.2nd July. The Túnel de San Adrian, or Lizarrate in its Basque name, was originally part of the Camino de Santiago.
54 James Stanhope, who at the time was a captain on Graham's staff, quoted in Fortescue, *History* Vol. IX

23rd. Blocking the valley ahead was a French rearguard under General Maucune holding the village of Villafranca [Ordizia], but the rest of Graham's force had not yet arrived. Graham attacked as soon as he had enough troops available, but by then he was too late; the French column he had been sent to intercept had just passed beyond the town. Bradford was sent to the right to outflank the French rearguard, while the Germans and some of Pack's Portuguese went left. 'Bradford's leading unit, the 5th Caçadores, attacking recklessly on unexplored ground, was thrown back at its first assault' recorded Oman 'but the Brigadier, extending other battalions farther to his right, ended by taking the village of Olaverria and pushing his immediate opponents across the river...by three in the afternoon Graham was beginning to outflank Maucune's line about Villafranca, with Bradford's Brigade on his right and Pack's on his left...thereupon the French General, having held his ground for the necessary space of time, made a prompt retreat along the Tolosa road...This ended a rather unsatisfactory day - the French had lost more men than the Allies, but the trap to catch them had failed completely'.[55] The allies suffered 93 casualties in the attack. Oman claimed most of those were in the 5th Caçadores, but Portuguese records show Jack's battalion lost only 12 killed and 19 wounded.[56] Jack's version of his regiment's attack also differs in important aspects from Oman's, suggesting that the 5th was not 'thrown back at its first assault', but rather waited for support that did not arrive, before deliberately withdrawing:

> Near Villa Franca we came up with the French; about 300 were in a valley below us. We extended and attack'd them sharply, drove them across the valley river and up the opposite hills when firing commenced on our left and rear. We halted and hesitated and soon found out the enemy had possession of the heights we came from, still waited, expecting our heavy battal[lion] would charge them down and we should take many prisoners. That not taking place, our left gradually fell back in extended order firing all the time, the men behaved very coolly, and extricated themselves well, out of the scrape. The German light troops came into action on our left, and the village in the valley was secured by our Grenadier companies; again advancing, we enter'd Villa Franca, struck off among the mountains and slept at Billerain [Baliarrain]'.[57]

---

55 Oman, *History Vol. VI*
56 Gaudêncio and Burnham *Fighting Cocks*
57 Letter dated c.2nd July. Fortescue is similarly inaccurate about the attack, apparently mirroring Oman's mistake: 'the first attack of Bradford's Portuguese, which appears to have been carelessly delivered, was repulsed with some loss',

The next day the remainder of Graham's force arrived; he now had some 26,000 men at hand. Further up the valley, drawn up in the area around Tolosa, the French under General Foy had 16,000. On the 25th the allies advanced to Alegia. Tolosa itself had been fortified: 'They make wooden gates for the entrances, and loop-hole the houses on the outside, connecting those which do not join by a wall, which is loop-holed in the same manner. In many instances they pull down the houses on the outside for the sake of the outer wall, which they leave standing. Tolosa was done so, and every town on this route where they had any garrison'.[58] Blocking the entire valley, the French position was a strong one. Graham again sent Bradford to the right, this time reinforced with some KGL troops and the 4th Caçadores from Pack's brigade. Bradford's flanking movement meant climbing steep hills, crossing the valley of the river Lizartza and attacking the French-occupied heights beyond. Their attack quickly stalled. Jack's recollection was of a tough fight:

[we] march'd for a hill in front of Tolosa on which the French had a post. This hill was situated in the angle where the great roads coming from Vitoria to Tolosa and from Pampeluno to Tolosa meet in the latter town. The summit was soon carried by the 4 Caçadores, our brigade also got on the summit, a useless heavy skirmish was kept up for several hours along the woody declivities. We did not crown the height with artillery. Towards the evening Longa appear'd on the French left flank...The Artillery advanced in the center on the great Vittoria road, the enemy's right flank was also attacked. The musketry became very lively, the artillery open'd. Genl. Bradford led on the 24 Port. Infantry on the Pampeluno road, the enemy began to retire, everything advanced. The 24th could not force the gate on the bridge which shew'd marks of hatchets. The French fir'd on their left flank about 40 yards' distance from a colonnade prepar'd for musketry; some troops in the meantime getting in the French rear sent them off and we entered the town. The Brigade has suffer'd in men and officers.[59]

---

though he goes on to give a little begrudging credit: 'Working, however, towards Macune's right flank, Bradford induced him to weaken his centre', enabling other troops to succeed with a direct attack on the village. Fortescue, *History* Vol. IX

58 Tomkinson, *Diary*

59 Letter dated c.2nd July.

Graham's view was less complimentary on Bradford's part of the attack. In his official despatch he reported

> On the right of the chausée and river, Bradford's Brigade, supported by three battalions Kings German Legion, were more or less engaged in skirmishing the whole day, and afterwards advanced by the Pamplona road and the ground on the right bank of the river...the rest of the day was chiefly spent in skirmishing with the enemy's tirailleurs, to give time for the Spanish corps arriving at their destination...General Bradford and the line battalions of the Germans driving in the enemy on their front, by the Pampluna road, and Colonel Longa from the side of the mountains still more on the right, turning and forcing, from very strong positions, all the posted bodies of the enemy on the right of the town.[60]

But in a private letter he told Wellington 'I particularly allude to the conduct of the German line battalions, without saying anything of Bradford's Brigade, and this, I should think, would convey sufficiently that I did not so much approve of their conduct. Many of them, both officers and men, behaved very gallantly, exposing themselves unnecessarily in open ground to the fire of the enemy hid in the woods; but, on the whole, the officers did not seem to understand well what they were about, or how to keep their men in their proper places, and certainly a good number of them kept back altogether.[61] Despite Graham's criticism (which is supported by Jack's comment that 'a useless heavy skirmish was kept up for several hours') Bradford's attack, with the support of the German and Spanish units around him, eventually overcame the stubborn resistance of no less than three French brigades and pushed them back towards Tolosa. His brigade had indeed 'suffer'd in men and officers', with total of twenty-two killed and 126 wounded, of which nine killed and nineteen wounded were from the 5th Caçadores. One of the latter was Captain Dom Franscisco Xavier da Silva Lobo, who Graham's report lists as 'severely' wounded.

The day after the battle of Tolosa, Jack finally found time to write a short letter home. It is unlikely this reached his parents before Wellington's official despatch on the battle of Vitoria was published, on 3 July, though it may have arrived before Graham's report of the fights on the 24th and 25th, which were not published until 20 July.

---

60 *The London Gazette*. Issue no. 16753 Tuesday July 20 1813
61 *Wellington Supplementary Despatches*. Graham to Wellington 2 July 1813

26 June, [1813]
Tolosa

My Dear Mother,
   Events have been passing so quickly around me that I cannot give you any of the particulars of what passed at Vittoria. We took all the Guns and Baggage the French had. I do not think from what I saw the loss of lives on each side was so great as might have been expected.
   Since that we crossed a Sierra and came into this road, trying to cut off a convoy which had got away. We have had some very sharp affairs with the French, our little Bn. is minus very many men, particularly yesterday in the evening when we turned them out of this town. Lord Wellington is in the neighbourhood of Pampeluna.
   Thank God I am well after 40 days' marching. You must read the papers for more details. We were on the left in the Vitoria business, and have been principally engaged in the last affairs. We have halted this day.

Remember me to all our friends,
Yours,
J. HILL

A day's rest in the hills outside Tolosa near the village of Elduain was all the wounded and weary men of the 5th Caçadores enjoyed. As Foy retreated towards France, Graham followed. He had failed to cut off the convoy but wanted to ensure the French column left Spain. The allies marched another 30 miles to Lesaka where on 26 June they halted for a few days, watching as Foy took his men through Irun and into France. In the camp at Lasaka, the 5th Caçadores began slowly to recover after their exertions at Vitoria, Villafranca and Tolosa. On 29 June Bradford's Brigade handed their border watch to Spanish troops, first employing the old trick of lighting numerous fires to make the French believe a larger force was in the area. That done, they retired towards Oiartzun, on the outskirts of San Sebastián, which was still occupied by a French garrison. Soon after arriving, Jack took up his pen and, having gathered his thoughts about Vitoria, wrote home with a longer account of the battle, his part in it and the days that followed. He started, however, with a detailed delineation of the route he had marched since leaving Portugal for what would turn out to be the last time. The sheer length of his list of villages and towns demonstrates how long a journey it had been.

Route of march from Villa Real Trayos montes, to Irun on the frontiers of Spain and France. Villa Real 16 May, 1813, Cadaval 17, Mirandella 18, Villa Nova dospartos 19, Pudenzias 20, Aryozettos 20th, 21, 22, 23, 24, 25. Halted to let the artillery get through the Trayos montes, Serrapico 26, Alkonizes 27, Veya de la Trabe 28 May. Campo di Monquive 29 May, 30 and 31, tried the fords of the Esla, but forc'd to cross the Infantry on pontoon bridge, the Cavalry and Light Artillery fording, by this turn'd the position of the Douro. Val de Perdizes I June, Benagiel 2 June, Cornilla 3, Villa Nova dos Cavalleiros 4 June, Medina del Rio Seco 5 June. Balhovias 6 June, Greta 7, Mariolas de riba 8th, Cabanas 9, Resmondo 10, Villa Bidon 11 and 12; this move made the French blow up Burgos. Camp on the march towards the Ebro, 14; pass'd the Ebro then encamp'd Villa di Cala 15 June, La Serda 16, Bilotta 17, Ordunha on the 18, march'd twice down and once up the famous passes, under arms and principal marching from 4 in the morn to 11 at night after a stray French division. Cantilllana 19, Amiselga 20, Mataaco and about Vitoria 21, Salvaterra 22, Sigura (through the pass of San Adrian) 23, Billerain 24, Tolosa 25; Lesarca or Elduain 26 (on the Pampeluno and Tolosa road) 27th and 28; remained in Lesarca. Andoin 29, Ocarzun 30, having turn'd back after seeing our charge safe into France near Yrun.

I think my last letter gave you all the details to the 12th May. I wrote since that from Elduain-Lesarca on the Pampeluno and Tolosa roads merely to say I had escap'd at Vittoria.[62] I will commence from that period and say what pass'd near us, in the left column. Whenever you cannot find out the places mentioned in the maps, you may conclude we were in some small place to the left of the line running from one place to another. The movements on the 12th united us with a column of Spaniards coming from Espinosa; the junction was made about 3 leagues from that place and also induc'd the French to blow up Burgos [on the] 13th. We mov'd at first as if to turn the heights in rear of Burgos and also Pancorbo, but about the middle of the day desisted our march to the Ebro. The passage of the Ebro presented some very extraordinary scenery

---

62 There is no letter dated near 12 May in the collection; the latest that survives from before Jack left Villa Real was dated 24 March, 1813. The letter written 'from Elduain-Lesarca on the Pampeluno and Tolosa roads' is that of 26 June, in which 'Tolosa' is given as his location.

both in the march down the right and the ascent on the left bank, there was also a lateral march made on that river among a variety of beautiful combs and tremendous passes. The approach on the 18th to Ordunha presented a beautiful valley with the town in its center while the troops issuing from the passage out through the top of the cliff and by the Adit (I believe the mining term),[63] filing through the Zig-Zags down during a thunderstorm made it appear at first view as if they were all mad, or trying to dance a country dance without musick, while on our right by a similar road descended a column of red coats who strongly marked the skill of the Engineering by the choice of the ground by which Carriages only can go down.

We had arriv'd in Ordunha, quarters ready, when an order came to ascend the mountain, by the road the British came. A wandering French division had that morning first run foul of the Cavalry next on the 5th Division, after some fighting got away, stumbled on the 4 and light divisions, the latter took all their baggage what became of the rascals after I never have learnt, some say that they are still in our rear. The Governor of Aragon was reported to be in a similar scrape, his Lordship marching for the passes of the Pyranees, shutting the door and looking around for how many he had caught. [64]

We continued our march from Ordunha, Vitoria, Salvatierra in a straight line over the mountains among the iron mines. I told you in my last I could give you but few particulars of the battle of Vitoria, we are as anxious to learn them as you. We came on the heights that overlook'd a fine valley, I think not much more than 5 miles across in one part but gradually became wider. Vittoria show'd itself the other side of the river a little on our left, the cannonade had begun, up the river on our extreme right, on the right bank of the Zamorra, there was much obstinacy displayed there from the firing continuing for some considerable time stationary. "The tide of war now roll'd down the valley" (Ossian to

---

63 An adit is a horizontal access to an underground mine.
64 Marshal Louis Suchet, Governor of Aragon since 1809, operated largely independently in Catalonia. The comment 'his Lordship marching for the passes of the Pyranees' refers to Wellington's blockading of Pamplona. Suchet and his army did not leave Spain until Napoleon ordered him back to help defend France in February 1814.

wit).[65] Two other divisions join'd in the conflict carrying a bridge on our immediate right.[66]

The French had now taken a position in a small elevated village in the valley, the cannonade was heavy, and stationary here for some time, when firing commenced among the mountains on the opposite side.[67] The French line at this moment was drawn across the valley, their left was generally thrown back, we mov'd towards the level ground, descended the left bank of the river, found a bridge cross'd, brought up our right shoulders on the right bank.

On the head of our column approaching the causeway leading into Vitoria on the West Side, the bridge and guns were abandoned by the enemy. This let over the first division whose sharpshooters seiz'd the guns before us. The 5th D. who had been sent farthest to the left took a village; the enemy recollecting the importance of the post, tried to recover it, employing 20,000 nearly. It would not do, as they had it they thought 'twas well to keep it. Their conduct has been highly spoken of.

Between Vittoria and I believe the Western mountains about ½ past 3, we had on our right a column of British heavy infantry, a column of Dragoons, British heavy and light, 6 Guns, 3 Caçadores corps, some companies of Grenadiers Portuguese, on the left German light troops. When we started to help the French off the field, going over hedges and ditches for near ½ a mile, we found the French infantry and cavalry on a small plain near a wood. The difficulties of the ground prevented the French Cavalry from doing anything, the formation of the Cavalry on our side, the bringing up the guns, the crossing the plain and entry of the light troops into the wood, assisted by the fire of our cannon, was very well executed. Some short time after word was passed along the line "we have taken all the enemies guns". The Rifle man among the trees was at home and went on as fast as his legs could carry him. Near the end of the wood the enemy had form'd. Some light Dragoons dash'd forward, but would not close, and came back

---

65 From Ossian's *Fingal*: '*They came, and saw the tide of battle, like the crowded waves of the ocean*'

66 Graham's two other divisions, the 1st and 5th, were attacking bridges to Bradford's left. This must refer to the attack across the bridges further downstream, to Bradford's right, by the 3rd and Light Divisions, especially as it follows from the comment about the fight 'rolling down the valley', a good description of the effect of the attack by Hill's corps.

67 This may refer to the French attempt to stand around the hills near Arinez, which is indeed in the centre of the valley.

behind the skirmishers who, I was very happy to see, still press'd forward on the enemy's flanks.

The Guns came up and opened with case shot. The French suffered and would have been more punished by the Artillery but the Caçadores still press'd on. The German light troops, seeing the Oxford blues on their flanks, collected and form'd square. An Aide [de] Camp came and said he thought they were mistaking our Cavalry for the French and by this they were thrown right out of the charge. It is well no more serious accident has happened from our frenchyfying our cavalry.[68] The pursuit continued till dark and the troops began mistaking each other, when the bugles sounded the close.

Next morning we got some horses, mules, oxen, sheep, etc. the French could not drive off, and in the evening halted to the front and left of Salvitierra 22 June. The 23rd, we had orders to march to Villa Franca and started climbing up the woody sides of a craggy mountain over the worst roads in heavy rain. On the summit we entered the Puorto do Santo Adrian, an immense cave that led us through the mountain to the other side. In it is situated a chapel and a farmhouse. We continued our march to Sigura and halted within ½ a league of the French, threw out pickets and awaited the arrival of the other troops, which could not keep up with [us,] by which we lost a convoy. To the surprise of the Spaniards, we also brought guns over, but they arriv'd 30 hours too late.

Near Villa Franca we came up with the French; about 300 were in a valley below us. We extended and attack'd them sharply, drove them across the valley river and up the opposite hills when firing commenced on our left and rear. We halted and hesitated and soon found out the enemy had possession of the heights we came from, still waited, expecting our heavy battal[ion] would charge them down and we should take many prisoners. That not taking place, our left gradually fell back in extended order firing all the time, the men behaved very coolly, and extricated themselves, well, out of the scrape.

The German light troops came into action on our left, and the village in the valley was secured by our Grenadier companies; again advancing, we enter'd Villa Franca, struck off among the mountains and slept at Billerain.

On the morning of the 25th, we again came into the great road and Longa went to our right among the mountains, halted for

---

68 The 'Oxford Blues' were the Royal Regiment of Horse Guards, seeing their first Peninsular action at Vitoria. Their blue tunics and crested helmets may easily have been mistaken for French uniforms by units unfamiliar with them.

a short time in a town, march'd for a hill in front of Tolosa on which the French had a post. This hill was situated in the angle where the great roads coming from Vitoria to Tolosa and from Pampeluno to Tolosa meet in the latter town. The summit was soon carried by the 4 Caçadores, our brigade also got on the summit, a useless heavy skirmish was kept up for several hours along the woody declivities. We did not crown the height with artillery. Towards the evening Longa appear'd on the French left flank, coming down the sides of the mountain in very fine stile (open column of companies when the ground permitted).

The Artillery advanced in the center on the great Vittoria road, the enemy's right flank was also attacked. The musketry became very lively, the artillery open'd. Genl. Bradford led on the 24 Port. Infantry on the Pampeluno road, the enemy began to retire, everything advanced. The 24th could not force the gate on the bridge which shew' d marks of hatchets. The French fir'd on their left flank about 40 yards' distance from a colonnade prepar'd for musketry; some troops in the meantime getting in the French rear sent them off and we entered the town. The Brigade has suffer'd in men and officers.

29 June, in the evening we gave over the outposts to the Spaniards and return'd to Ocarzun, the soldiers were employ'd in making lots of fires to make the enemy believe the main body was up, while we look'd at the French filing through Yrun.

July 1st. The enemy left this part of the world and retir'd into France. St. Sebastian is garrison'd by 1600 French, the Spaniards have invested it, we must get heavy guns and mortars to fire them out.

If my map is correct from the bearings of Fontarabia, Yran and Andaye, the hill on which the French form'd their rear guard of about 2,000 as a signpost to the skirmishers of the rear guard placed along a causeway leading to it, was the isle of Pheasants celebrated for the interview of Charles the 5 and Francis the 1st to form some treaties, the Spaniards turned them out of it.[69] The Pyranees excited curiosity, we found very good roads and the elevation was by no means so great in this part, as many other ridges. I am sitting by a very good fire and enjoy its comforts. The enemy return'd the fire of a Spanish gun which they must have receiv'd from Bayonne.

---

69 The Isle of Pheasants (*Île des Faisans*) is on the Bidassoa river. In 1659 the Treaty of the Pyrenees, ending the 30 Years' War between France and Spain was signed there. The treaty was however between Louis XIV of France and Phillip IV of Spain.

King Jo sav'd a Gun and Howitzer at Vittoria but subsequently lost the Gun and entered France with the latter. Longa has taken Passages and sent near 200 prisoners to the rear. Everything Spanish is going to the front. 30,000 were at Burgos the other day. One would pause before letting loose such a set on France. Cruelty would sully success. The French would be forced to turn out the whole population to repel them. The Guns hid in the mountains, the biscuits conceal'd in caves, all is turning out. Longa has 4 months provisions for his people. Pampeluno is calculated to resist 6 weeks, all this depends on the quantity of artillery brought against it. We have a few 18-pounders with us many 16 taken among the 156 at Vittoria.

The money taken will never be known. Some soldiers divided it by each receiving a cap full. I have got nothing except a dog and ½ a piece of linen to cover the loss of the shirts you sent me. I will send you home some more money as soon as I can get another 100 out of the 400 they owe me.

I hear nothing of rank they have [3 or 4 words struck out].[70] We have French papers to the 21 June. They were bragging of their success over Minas near Roncesvalles. King Joe must sing "sad and mournful is the story of thy Roncesvalles fight"[71] or any other parody Lewis may write. Remember me to all our friends. I know nothing of the center and right columns. This Lord will play them more tricks yet. I have not received letters this last 50 days.

J. HILL

We are now in quarters round St. Sebastian. The Spaniards have the siege and outpost duty.

As Graham's weary men handed over their immediate duties, like Jack many reflected on their achievements in recent months. Wellington's army of 1813 had done remarkable things. Dejected, disorganised and ill-disciplined after the retreat from Burgos, they had recovered to march fully across northern Spain. They had outmarched, outmanoeuvred and outfought Joseph's army and ousted it from Spain.

---

70 This may relate to Jack's wait for confirmation of his Brevet rank of Lieutenant-Colonel in the Portuguese army, to which he was now entitled as a major in British service. He did not have to wait much longer.

71 The second epic poetry reference in this letter, this time to *La Chanson de Roland*, a French poem with the battle of Roncesvalles in 778 as its subject. The pass at Roncesvalles was one of those Wellington's main army was at that point defending.

Napier summarised: 'In this campaign of six weeks, Wellington with one hundred thousand men, marched six hundred miles, passed six great rivers, gained one decisive battle, invested two fortresses, and drove a hundred and twenty thousand veteran troops from Spain'.[72] The six-year long French occupation of the Iberian Peninsula, with the exception of Suchet's army in Catalonia and a few isolated outposts like San Sebastián, had been ended by a lightning campaign surmounted by a crushing triumph at Vitoria. Wellington shared his men's pride at what had been achieved. On 8 July he wrote 'There is not a Frenchman in Spain on this side [of the border], excepting within garrison...I have blockaded all the fortresses, and am about to attack San Sebastian, and am giving some rest to the troops, who have been a good deal fagged by their late exertions'.[73] A few days later he reported to London that preparations 'are already in great forwardness to attack the fort of San Sebastián, of which I am in hopes that we shall obtain possession in a short time after we have broken ground.[74] His optimism was, unfortunately for his army, to prove misplaced.

72 Napier, History
73 *Wellington Despatches*. Wellington to Bentinck 8 July 1813
74 *Wellington Despatches*. Wellington to Bathurst 19 July 1813

CHAPTER 13

INTO FRANCE

'I commanded the 5th Caçadores at the storm and capture of
St. Sebastián...was removed to the command of the 4th Portuguese
Regt. which was engaged in the passage of the Nivelle...
and also in the crossing of the Nive...I commanded the
4th Portuguese Regt. in the Battle of Orthes.

Statement of Service, 1816

The town of San Sebastián sits on a promontory on the Biscay
coast of Spain, just over ten miles from the border with France. A
soldier recorded how it appeared in 1813:

The town occupies the centre portion of a peninsula, formed by the
inlet of the sea on its western, and by the river Urumea on its
eastern side. At the extremity of the peninsula, immediately behind
the town, rises a high hill, of an oval shape, with rocky precipitous
sides towards the sea, and projecting so far beyond the isthmus on
its western side, as to form, with the aid of moles, a good harbour
for vessels of small burthen. On this hill is situated the Castle. The
town is fortified on the land side by a regular line of works
extending across the isthmus, having a large horn-work in front.
The water faces consist of only a single high wall, with no flank
defences but a few small towers, and quite exposed. Near the neck
of the isthmus, about 900 yards from the body of the place, is a
range of heights, level with the inland country, but overlooking the
isthmus. On this is situated the convent of St. Bartolomeo, and
immediately under it is the suburb of St. Martin; the former the
enemy had put into a state of defence, and occupied, and the latter
they had destroyed.
     On the land side, notwithstanding the proximity of the heights
of St. Bartolomeo, the place is unquestionably strong; but the face
next to the Urumea must be considered weak, because it can be

345

breached from the opposite side of the river, and approached at any time within half tide.[1]

This description was written fifteen years after the siege, so unsurprisingly outlines not just the features of the fortified town but also how Graham and his engineers, largely given free reign by Wellington at the start of the operation, chose to attack it.

Wellington could have blockaded San Sebastián, as he did Pamplona, the only other major Spanish town in north-west Spain still in French hands. After Vitoria, he could have invaded France; that was what many Frenchmen, and his own army, expected. But Wellington faced practical and political problems. As he admitted in his dispatches, his army needed time to recover and regroup after their remarkable recent exertions. His success had opened harbours along the north Spanish coast for allied use, enabling him radically to shorten his communications and supply routes to Britain: Bilbao, Santander and Passajes. 'Passages' as it was inevitably known to the British, was captured by Spanish troops on 30 June. On a small inlet surrounded by high cliffs a couple of miles east of San Sebastián, Passajes would become a main supply port for Wellington for the rest of the war, even though its narrow entrance meant it could not handle large vessels. Leaving a French garrison that close to this major node of activity would be almost inviting the French Governor of San Sebastián, the capable Brigadier-General Emmanuel Rey, to try to disrupt allied logistics. Another factor was that after Joseph's humiliation at Vitoria, Napoleon had transferred command of French forces in the western Pyrenees to Marshal Soult. Soult, like all his contemporaries who had tried, had not defeated a British-led force, but his aggressiveness had disrupted previous allied operations, including capturing and then relieving the first siege of Badajoz. Wellington knew Soult would try to relieve Pamplona and San Sebastián; indeed, Napoleon had ordered him to do this. Wellington therefore had to keep a strong military presence in the Pyrenean passes at places like Roncesvalles and Maya; he did not have the manpower to do that and blockade both San Sebastián and Pamplona.

Political questions also needed resolution before invading France could be contemplated. The Russian campaign of 1812 was disastrous for Napoleon, but his resilience was never better demonstrated than in early 1813, when he raised an almost wholly new army of over 200,000 men and aggressively deployed it. The Emperor's first campaign of that

---

1 *Twelve Years' Military Adventures in Three Quarters of the Globe* John Blakiston. Vol II 1829

year in northern Europe pushed the Russians and Prussians beyond the Elbe and led to the Armistice of Plässwitz and peace negotiations. As Wellington considered his next move, he knew a permanent peace might be agreed covering the northern, but not southern, European theatre. Such a peace might even exclude Britain entirely; if Wellington invaded France he might have to face the full weight of Napoleon's army and personal attention alone. Thus, the politico-military situation in northern Europe directly influenced that in the south, but the opposite was also true; when news of Vitoria reached the Russians, Prussians and Austrians it encouraged them to renew hostilities against France. While these matters were being resolved, Wellington concluded that there were tactical benefits in capturing San Sebastián. The possession of a larger port near the French border would be useful and would remove a potential thorn in his side. As well as the potential threat to Passajes, the continued presence of a French garrison in San Sebastián constrained Royal Navy presence on the north Spanish coast, while French, and US, naval activity nearby had already caused some losses of supplies and stopped the Royal Navy completely blockading the town from the sea. San Sebastián could also provide a potential port of embarkation for the army should that prove necessary despite the successes so far. With the momentum of his rapid advance across Spain stopped at the Pyrenees, San Sebastián in effect 'was the only forward option available to Wellington'.[2]

Wellington's first instinct was to deploy Spanish troops to capture the town. Graham's men had seen hard fighting even after Vitoria and San Sebastián was, after all, a Spanish town. He asked Graham 'whether the Spanish troops could carry on this concern, with a few English to assist occasionally to lead and assault, &c. It will be very desirable if this should be practicable, as it will save our English and Portuguese troops, of whom we have lost more since the 21st'.[3] Graham demurred, however, and a few days later, Wellington told him 'Upon consideration, I think you had better give Gen. Oswald charge of the siege of San Sebastián, with the 5th division and either Pack's or Bradford's Brigades...I do not think the Spaniards are yet to be trusted alone'.[4] So it was that Jack and his Caçadores were earmarked for another siege and the unpopular task of digging out batteries and trenches. 'There is no species of duty in which a soldier is liable to be employed, so galling or so disagreeable as a siege...I found much of that tone of mind among the various brigades which lay before San

---

2 *Wellington and the Seige of San Sebastián 1813* Bruce Collins 2017
3 *Wellington Despatches.* Wellington to Graham 4 July 1813
4 *Wellington Despatches.* Wellington to Graham 8 July 1813

Sebastian' said a contemporary.[5] The 5th Caçadores were positioned on some sand hills, known as Chofres, across the Urumea from the town. This would become the site of the main British battery, once they had dug it out. The peninsular on which San Sebastián sat had three main elements: the town itself in the middle, protected by its walls and a hornwork to its south, was overlooked on its sea side by a high, castle-crowned conical hill, Monte Urgull, and on its land side by the heights of Ayete, on which sat the convent of San Bartelomeo. Graham first sought to reduce and capture the convent, to provide additional, closer firing positions for the main bombardment and open the land approach to the town. After three days of bombardment, on the morning of 17 July, the convent was assaulted by two columns, Bradford leading the left one, comprising men from his own units, including '200 men of the 13th Portuguese regt., under the command of Major Snodgrass, of that regiment; an equal number under Lieut. Col. Macneagh [sic], of the 5th Caçadores, and supported by the 9th regt...Both attacks were made with such vigour and determination, that all obstacles were overcome, without the loss that might have been expected'.[6] Bradford's report of the action noted 'It affords me infinite satisfaction...that every individual of the brigade under my command performed well their duty', adding 'The convent was immediately carried by Major Snodgrass in the most gallant and spirited manner at the point of the bayonet, and that column forced its way with great difficulty thro' the ruins and adjacent gardens to attack the redoubt by the breach in the convent garden wall...The most determined attack was then made upon the redoubt...and the work was soon carried by the gallantry of the troops.'[7] The 5th Caçadores' losses were six men killed; two officers, two sergeants and seventeen men wounded.

The bombardment now began. Digging and hauling stores from Pasajes was exhausting work, overseen by Wellington's chief engineer, Jack's friend Richard Fletcher, now formally Lieutenant-Colonel Sir Richard Fletcher. Wellington, however, thought Fletcher's demands for troops for this purpose verged on the excessive: 'The officers of engineers and artillery don't appear to be very *light* in their demands of working parties' and two days later 'Sir R. Fletcher and Col. Dickson appear to be worse than usual in their demands for working parties; and unless they are forced to use the animals and carts at their disposal, whenever they can be used, they will work your men to death. I have known Col. Fletcher demand hundreds of men he could not use; and

5 Gleig, *The Subaltern* 1872
6 *Wellington Despatches*. Graham to Wellington 18 July 1813. 'Mcneagh' is a misspelling of 'McCreagh'.
7 Gaudêncio and Burnham *Fighting Cocks*

I am quite certain that much of the carriage of ordnance stores from Passages might be done by mules or carts.'[8] By 25 July, the walls were thought sufficiently breached to be assaulted. At low tide, to allow the troops room to advance along the river edge, 2,000 men from the 5th Division attacked. The assault failed, incurring over 400 casualties. San Sebastián was proving a tougher prospect than expected.

There was bad news from further east too, as Soult chose the same day to launch an assault through the Pyrenean passes. Wellington ordered Graham to suspend the siege of San Sebastián to enable the allies to concentrate on Soult's attack; the French advance was not stopped until three days later at Sorauren, just a few miles short of relieving Pamplona. After Sorauren, Soult retreated into France and the siege of San Sebastián resumed. Wellington took a closer personal interest, assigning additional heavy artillery and more men; after Burgos and the assault of 25 July, Wellington was keen not to have another failure on his hands. Yet more hard labour was the order of the day for the men. Preparing new and expanded batteries, digging trenches to bring the next assault force closer to the breaches with some protection and stockpiling ammunition all took time. It was a month after the first assault that the bombardment resumed, on 26 August. Jack's men had spent this time working hard; when a new assault was being planned, Bradford 'from the beginning, urged most anxiously the employment of [his brigade] in the attack, as they had had so large a share in the labor and fatigues'.[9] The French defenders had similarly not been idle; they rendered much of the damage done in the first bombardment nugatory with new defensive barriers and mines. French morale was also demonstrated on 15 August when they 'treated the blockading army to an illumination: this being Napoleon's birthday, an immense inscription with letters of fire six feet long, VIVE L'EMPEREUR, was visible on the high slope of Monte Urgull for miles around'.[10] Some 41,000 shot were fired during the second bombardment, the largest the allies undertook on the Peninsula: half as much again as at Badajoz, and more than four times as much as at Ciudad Rodrigo.[11] The date selected for a second assault was 31 August. The first attempt was felt to have used insufficient troops and

---

8 *Wellington Despatches*. Wellington to Graham 20 and 22 July 1813. Dickson was Wellington's chief of artillery.

9 *Wellington Despatches*. Graham to Wellington 1 September 1813

10 Oman, *History Vol. VII*

11 Collins, *San Sebastián* gives the figures based on contemporary records. 18,000 shot were fired in the first bombardment at San Sebastián, the bombardment of Badajoz used 26,500.

been uncoordinated; now a larger force assembled. This included the 5th Division again, keen to remove the stain of previous failure, Bradford's Brigade and a further 750 volunteers from other Divisions. Despite the danger, volunteering was 'a point of honour...Sergeants and men argued about their right to go'.[12] Novel tactics were also adopted: the line regiments of Bradford's Brigade would attack across the Urumea, wading through the shallows in broad daylight. It was low tide, but still the water was waist-deep: 'the Portuguese, who had advanced under intense fire, were assaulting both breaches'.[13]

Jack and his Caçadores were spared that ordeal, being detached to support the 5th Division. They were to position themselves in the trenches close to the walls, providing covering fire for the assault columns; their rifles were well suited for sharpshooting against the defenders. Jack was now formally in command of the battalion; on 10 July McCreagh was promoted to command the 3rd Portuguese Infantry, in the 5th Division. On Divisional duty in his new role, McCreagh would lead the covering parties into action; he may have specifically requested his former battalion for this force. The assault was scheduled for an hour before low tide, at around 11am:

> The morning of the 31st rose darkly and gloomily, as if the elements had been aware of the approaching conflict, and were determined to add to its awfulness by their disorder. A close and oppressive heat pervaded the atmosphere, while lowering and sulphureous clouds covered the face of the sky, and hindered the sun from darting upon us one enlivening ray, from morning till night. A sort of preternatural stillness, too, was in the air; the birds were silent in the groves; the very dogs and horses in the camp, and cattle on the hill side, gazed in apparent alarm about them. Moreover, as the day passed on, and the hour of attack drew near, the clouds gradually collected into one black mass directly over the devoted city; and almost at the instant when out troops began to march into the trenches, the storm burst forth.[14]

Under the Caçadores covering fire the assault columns made their way to the foot of the breach; as they struggled to climb it, British artillery fired over their heads to suppress Rey's defenders. One of these shots or, more likely, the fire that had begun to rage in the town reached a French magazine and blew it up. The disruption and damage from the explosion

---

12 Collins, *San Sebastián*
13 *An Ensign in the Peninsular War: The Letters of John Aitchison* W.F.K. Thompson (Ed.) 1981
14 Gleig, *Subaltern*

gave the allies their opportunity; British and Portuguese troops crossed the breach and entered the town. In the street fighting that followed, both sides were hampered by fire raging in the wind of the summer storm. At around 2pm Rey pulled his remaining troops back to the castle on Monte Urgull; the town of San Sebastián, or rather what was left of it after the fire had done its damage, had been captured. Many of those involved thought San Sebastián the toughest of all the sieges they had undertaken:

> in no instance since the commencement of the Peninsular War has it [the army] had more obstacles to encounter and in no instance - not even the capture of Badajoz - have they been more gloriously overcome. The conduct of every man engaged was so truly admirable, that no words in our language can do them justice - it required to be seen to be conceived; and when history should give to future ages the simple narrative of this day's deeds - they will excite admiration rather than belief. Portuguese troops acted their part excellently, and they are well entitled to participate in all the praises that can be bestowed.[15]

Another agreed about the prominence of the Portuguese units: 'It is impossible for troops to have behaved better than the Portuguese did in advancing to the breach of San Sebastián'.[16]

In his report to Bradford (who was ill and missed the assault himself) McCreagh was unshy of singling out his old battalion: 'It having been my good fortune yesterday as Colonel of the day in the trenches to conduct the covering parties to the assault and to lead them in over the Breach I think is but justice to report the excellent conduct and gallantry of two hundred men of the 5th Battalion of Caçadores who belonged to the covering party. They formed the head of my Column and their exemplary behaviour was remarked throughout'.[17] Colonel MacBean, who led the 24th Portuguese across the river, also singled out Jack's men:

> I have the honour to state to you that I advanced yesterday with a Battalion of the 24th Regiment across the Sands, fording the River and established myself on the Main Breach with some of the troops of the 5th Division. After waiting there for some time in expectation of a general advance, I ordered my Battalion with some of the 5th Caçadores to pass [climb] the Breach which they performed in a style the most gallant and praiseworthy, drove the Enemy from the

---

15 Aitchison, *Ensign*
16 Glover, *Hennell*
17 Gaudêncio and Burnham *Fighting Cocks*

ruins where they were strongly posted, and which were most difficult to pass, and succeeded in getting into the Town. I formed my Battalion near the church now the English Hospital, where I reported to Major-General Spry. I can say with satisfaction that my Battalion with some Caçadores were the first who passed the Breach, their noble example induced numbers to follow, nothing could surpass their steadiness and determined bravery.[18]

Graham's report of the action, sent to Wellington on the same day that McCreagh and MacBean wrote theirs, unfortunately omitted the detail their reports contained, but did at least acknowledge Jack's leading role:

The column of attack was formed of the second brigade of the fifth division, commanded by Major Gen. Robinson...and having in reserve the remainder of the 5th division, consisting of Major Gen. Spry's Portuguese brigade, and the 1st brigade under Major Gen. Hay, as also the 5th battalion of Caçadores of Gen. Bradford's Brigade, under Major Hill; the whole under the direction of Lieut. Gen. Sir James Leith, commanding the 5th division.[19]

Victory came at a high cost. Of perhaps 9,000 men committed to the assault, the allies lost over 2,300 killed, wounded or missing. The 5th Caçadores recorded twenty-one men killed and three officers and forty-eight men wounded of the 200 or so engaged. One casualty not officially recorded was Jack, who when writing his 1816 *Statement of Services* noted:

I commanded the 5th Cacadores at the storm and capture of St. Sebastián, and received a graze of a grape shot between my left arm and side.

His use of the word 'graze' implies this was not too serious a wound; possibly why he chose not to record it in his battalion casualty returns. He also knew that any wounded officer's name would appear in the list of casualties: Jack like many at the time would not want his family alarmed by seeing his name in casualty lists before a letter confirming his wellbeing reached home. Nevertheless, he had a lucky escape - a little either side and the shot may have removed an arm or been fatal.

---

18 Gaudêncio and Burnham *Fighting Cocks*
19 *Wellington Despatches*. Graham to Wellington 1 September 1813. The report was published in the *London Gazette* of September 14, 1813 (Issue No. 16778), the only time Jack's name appeared in a despatch published in the Gazette.

In 17 years of soldiering, it was the first wound caused by the enemy Jack had suffered. He had been badly knocked about in surviving the *Valk* in 1799 and had been bayonetted outside Copenhagen in 1807, but the former was the work of nature and the latter of one of his own men. From his first day of service, it seems Jack had one of the most important characteristics of a soldier, good luck. His friend Richard Fletcher did not. Standing on the beach near San Sebastián's sea wall watching the main assault go in, he was shot through the neck and died immediately. Jack does not mention either his wound or Fletcher's death in his next surviving letter, which implies he wrote at least one that is now lost. From where the 5th Caçadores were positioned, Jack was within yards of Fletcher when he was killed; another of his longstanding acquaintances gone. Fletcher would eventually be commemorated on the monument to his towering achievement, the Lines of Torres Vedras.

The capture of the town of San Sebastián remarkably did not mean the surrender of its French garrison. The French lost some 500 men during the second assault, but with the remaining 1,200 or so troops now in the castle, the allies settled in for further work. Cannon were moved closer, new batteries were dug and on 8 September a third bombardment began. But the defenders were too short of undamaged artillery to reply; to all intents and purposes the castle could not be defended any further. Rey sought terms and at midday on 9 September formally surrendered, his men marching with military honours into captivity, past British and Portuguese troops who lined the castle ramparts and the streets of the town respectively. San Sebastián was in a pitiful state: 'it is all destroyed except 4 or 5 houses...It *was* a beautiful town' said one who saw it.[20] A few days later Wellington received the news he wanted from northern Europe - the armistice was over; Austria had joined the Russians and Prussians in a renewed offensive. Having beaten off an attempt by Soult to relieve San Sebastián on the day of the second allied assault, Wellington was free to cross the Pyrenees and take his army into France.[21] Meanwhile, his army recovered. The 5th Caçadores received a draft of new officers; Jack made a memorable impression upon one of them, Captain Thomas Bunbury:

---

20 Glover, *Hennell*
21 If the second assault had been a day later, Jack would not have participated. Soult chose 31 August to attack across the Bidassoa near the villages of St. Marcial and Vera. Wellington asked Graham to release Bradford's Brigade to help repulse the French attack, but by the time his message arrived, the 5th Caçadores were already engaged at the breaches and Bradford's other battalions were wading the Urumea.

I joined the 5th Caçadores in the Basque Pyrennees. They were on bivouac in the heights of Lasacca, and commanded by Major Hill, commonly called Jack Hill, to distinguish him from two others of the same name in the Portuguese service. There was one other English officer in the battalion besides myself, viz.: Captain Dobbs, from the 52nd regiment...Hill was a most extraordinary character, from the 23rd or Welch Fusileers. He was accustomed to take wine very freely after dinner, and would then amuse us with the never-failing theme of the comparative merits, as leaders of armies, of Moses, Alexander, Bonaparte, and Wellington, but he always gave the palm to the Jewish leader, with whose camp regulations he seemed greatly enamoured. Hill was wont to attribute a great deal of the sickness in modern armies to epidemics, occasioned by the effluvia arising from reservoirs for filth, ordered to be constructed in our camps, and cited the 23rd chapter of Deuteronomy, 13th verse, as a far preferable sanatory regulation.[22] Thinking he was not serious, but only trying to pass off a joke on a newcomer, I told him I did not conceive Moses deserved the credit of the discovery, since it had been the practice of the whole family of cats from the creation. "Ah !" he replied, "Puss does it from instinct, but our leaders ought to be governed by more rational motives. You see that abattis," he said; "I have this day had it constructed to keep off our Brigadier, who is always finding fault with our bivouac, he will be here soon, and today I will have him on the hip." In fact it was not long ere General T. Bradford, with his aide-de-camp, made his appearance. Finding he could not penetrate the Major's sanctum, he began to call for him most lustily; while the Major, pretending not to hear, continued rubbing his hands together in great glee, until an orderly arrived, requiring his immediate attendance. The poor Major was obliged to remove his abattis the next morning.[23]

This is a fascinating glimpse into Jack's character and the type of man he was around camp. Bunbury wrote his memoires nearly 50 years later, but there is no reason to disbelieve him. Jack was, after all, a clergyman's son; the use of classical references echoes his letter of 24 March (see above), when he compared Napoleon to Alexander; his case against open latrines was arguably ahead of its time. His disdainful treatment of Bradford may indicate tension between the two men; that

---

22 'And thou shalt have a paddle upon thy weapon; and it shall be, when thou wilt ease thyself abroad, thou shalt dig therewith, and shalt turn back and cover that which cometh from thee'

23 *Reminiscences of a Veteran* Vol. 1 Thomas Bunbury 1861

Jack reported Bradford as 'always finding fault with our bivouac' is perhaps telling. That said, Bunbury's memoires are full of blunt and often mocking assessments of his fellow officers, most of whom were dead by the time he published. There *is* reason to question his assertion that Major John Hill was 'commonly called Jack Hill, to distinguish him from two others of the same name in the Portuguese service'. There were certainly other men called John Hill in the British army, but the only officers with that surname in Portuguese service were forenamed Dudley, Thomas and William; it is more likely that he was called Jack because he wanted to be.[24] Bunbury would later take over Jack's position; elsewhere in his book he complains of what he perceived as the soft treatment of the men of the 5th Caçadores by their previous senior officers. This may have some bearing on his painting Jack as an eccentric - though such a characterisation fits with Browne's pen-picture from Halifax. There was also good reason that Jack wanted to avoid Bradford. McCreagh's departure on promotion left Jack in command of the battalion, but his hopes of having this position confirmed were quickly dashed when a new Lieutenant-Colonel arrived, leaving him very unhappy.

25 Sep[r]. 1813
Frontiers of Spain

My dear Father,

I answer yours of the 5 Sep[r]. I do not recollect if I did not say to you in the beginning of the last winter, that the French were impudent dogs in dispersing themselves all over Spain immediately as we entered Portugal, considering we offered them battle a second time near Salamanca. You allude to some mistakes that have been made about the wounded; that gentleman has been three times dangerously wounded this campaign, but not confin'd a day - so the world gets on. Our near neighbours the French in this part of the world have not fir'd a salute for victories in the North, on the contrary, they say they have lost 70,000 and must retire across the Rhine.

I am glad William gets on well. I have written to Mr. Patterson the M.P. for Norwich, they say they are under obligations to me for civility shewn the son. I have begged that our fathers may correspond on the subject. I will get Mr. Julian to take home Col. Ellis' letter to Sir J. Warren.

---

24 *British Officers Serving in the Portuguese Army, 1809-1814* Lionel Challis
Journal of the Society for Army Historical Research 1949

As for myself, I am in a row with them as I consider myself ill used in their not giving me the Caçadores and MacCreagh forwarding the recommendations for the 5 Caçadores as he was then actually commanding the 3rd heavy regt. I suspect I shall only come off with the letter of thanks from the 5 Division. I am leaving the 5 Caçadores as I am superseded in them and lost a British Lt. Colcy. by being ordered to remain with them, the thing is in Genl. Packenham's hands. I am too sulky to enter long into this, but I will soon let you know the results. I have not seen Sutton. Ld. Berghussh is going abroad.[25]

Why did not my Mother add a postscript? I am glad she is to hear Catalani.[26] I think, with you, one is forc'd to look again and again to see whether it is a human frame that produces such tones. Your talking of both going to Exeter informed me my Mother was well.

We are working up to the knees in mud at entrenchments, our left wing is secure, supported by S. Sebastian. I hear firing in the direction of Pampeluno. We calculate it may fall by the 8th of October, then we may bring up our right flank through Catalonia. The breaches repair'd, the entrenched camp formed, we can detach to our right and finish the expulsion.

I have not heard before from you for 2 months, your last was directed well, if you mention Lisbon the letters go there and return by land.

The day after the surrender we came to the heights above Lessaca and the Biddisoa River. I was with Ellis yesterday; the 4th Dn. is part one side the river the other on this. It is constantly raining here, our men without camp equipage, they cannot keep themselves dry.

I will write again next week, there has been an affair in Catalonia, I know not the results. Remember me to all our Relatives.

Believe me ever your most affectionly [sic],
J. HILL.

---

25 John Fane, Baron Burghersh, son of the Earl of Westmorland, joined the 23rd as a captain in May 1805 and served on the staff of Sir Arthur Wellesley in the Peninsula, eventually being promoted lieutenant-colonel in December 1811. In September 1813 he was appointed Military Commissioner to the Headquarters of the allied armies in Germany.

26 Angelica Catalani, Italian soprano, renowned for the power and range of her voice (nearly three octaves). She dominated the London operatic stage for seven years, but Margaret Hill was lucky to see her as she gave her last performance at the end of the 1813 season and moved to France.

My Martinique prize money £25 has been paid into Chelsea hospital. I ask'd the Regt. on your information if they had heard anything of its being paid. I am writing to Cox and Greenwood to get it for me, it will pay my fees of Comm. as Major.

The 'affair in Catalonia' was Suchet's defeat outside Tarragona of a British force, in what turned out to be one of the last setbacks the allies would receive in Spain. The civility Jack showed to the son of 'Mr. Patterson the M.P. for Norwich' refers to Robert Dossie Patteson, formerly of the 23rd Foot, who Jack referred to as 'a very fine young recruit' in his letter from the Isle of Wight on 18 March 1804 (Chapter 5). By September 1813 Patteson was a captain in the 6th Foot, who were in the 7th Division at Vitoria. Perhaps Jack bumped into Patteson after that battle, the only time during the period when the two of them were in proximity to each other. It is also possible that Jack had written to Patteson's father in the wake of the battle at Etxelar on 2 August, when the 6th charged the French with what Wellington called 'a regularity and gallantry which I have seldom seen equalled'. Things in the 23rd Foot had obviously calmed down enough to allow Henry Ellis to write his letter to Admiral Sir John Borlaise Warren on behalf of Fred Hill, but Jack's description of his own circumstances shows how 'interest' could work against an individual. McCreagh's proposals for his succession in command of the 5th Caçadores presumably did not recommend Jack for the position; he was superseded in command of the 5th Caçadores by Lieutenant-Colonel Thomas St. Clair on 27 August 1813. St. Clair probably arrived at the battalion's cantonment around the end of September, approximately when Jack wrote his letter. The less than respectful behaviour towards Bradford recorded by Bunbury could have been because Jack suspected Bradford had denied him promotion and the command. As a substantive British major, Jack would have expected a Portuguese Lieutenant-Colonelcy. If Jack complained to his friend Ellis in the manner of this letter, Ellis may have spoken to General Edward Packenham who was no doubt as concerned as ever to further the careers of his beloved Fusiliers, especially someone he had commanded in the original Fusilier Brigade in Martinique. Whether any of this speculation is true, by the time Jack wrote his 'sulky' comments to his father, his promotion to brevet Lieutenant-Colonel in the British Army had been gazetted, on 21 September.[27]

What is not clear is which British lieutenant-colonelcy Jack believed he 'lost' by remaining with the 5th Caçadores, nor who 'ordered' him to

---

27 *London Gazette* Issue no. 16779, Tuesday September 21st 1813. 'To be Lieutenant-Colonels in the Army. Major J. H. E. Hill, of the 23rd Foot. Dated September 21, 1813'

do so. There was no such vacancy in 1/23rd; Ellis remained at their head at that rank. It is unlikely to have been in a different British regiment, not least as Jack would not have wanted (or perhaps been able to afford) to purchase it. At around this time, however, Lieutenant-Colonel William Wyatt, commander of 2/23rd since February 1808, was appointed 'an Inspecting Field Officer of a Recruiting District'.[28] Wyatt commanded 2/23rd during the retreat to Coruña and the Walcharen expedition, where his health suffered; his new appointment may imply he was no longer fit enough to lead them. There was a hiccup over Wyatt's succession when Charles Sutton, who was gazetted to the role, declined it.[29] Perhaps Ellis told Jack of this and asked if he was interested. It would have been a plumb post, not least as in 1813 2/23rd were based in Devon. But Wyatt's successor was to be Thomas Dalmer, who had seniority and first refusal. How this squares with Jack's claim he missed out by being 'ordered' to stay with the 5th Caçadores is unclear. Wellington's unwillingness to see experienced officers leave for appointments at home did not stop Dalmer going. But speculatively, if Jack had told McCreagh and/or Bradford of the possible opportunity and was told he would not be allowed to take it, that would have been more than enough further to sour his relationship with both.

Though missing out both on a senior British position and command of the 5th Caçadores, Jack was instead now appointed as Lieutenant-Colonel of the Portuguese 4th Infantry. Bunbury added a coda to his tale: 'Shortly after my arrival Hill was promoted, but as Marshal Beresford did not choose to give him a command, he was appointed Lieut.-Colonel to an infantry corps, where there was a Colonel; and Lieut.-Colonel St. Clair, on joining, succeeded to the command of the

---

28 William Wyatt had assumed command of 2/23rd in February 1808.

29 Sutton had seniority over both Jack and Thomas Dalmer; Jack's comment 'I have not seen Sutton' suggests he was aware Sutton was involved; he would certainly have known that the post was Sutton's to decline. The *London Gazette* announced Sutton as Wyatt's successor on 17 June 1813, but on 10 July 1813 Sutton was promoted Colonel in the Portuguese army, commanding 9th Infantry regiment; he must therefore have declined command of 2/23rd to stay in Spain (confirmed by his later receiving clasps for his Army Gold Cross for the battles of the Nive and Toulouse, and Portuguese medals for this period). Sutton's *Statement of Services* in the *Gentleman's Magazine* makes no mention of his commanding 2/23rd. Conversely, Thomas Dalmer's handwritten *Statement of Services* (RWF Museum Acc. No 0727) states that in 1813 he 'proceeded with the Army as far as the Pyrenees; from thence ordered to England to take the Command of the 2d. Battalion'. Presumably Sutton preferred higher rank in Portuguese service and Dalmer was rapidly called back to lead 2/23rd instead.

Caçadore battalion.'[30] This comment, however, underlines the unreliability of gossipy memoires written forty years after the event. The 4th Infantry in fact had no colonel (the position was vacant) and Beresford, as commander of the Portuguese army, approved Jack's appointment to command them. That said, his new appointment was formally listed as *agregado*, which means he was appointed as a supplementary officer. The reasons for this are complex. Lieutenant-Colonel Allan William Campbell, commander of the 4th Infantry since March 1811, was severely wounded at Sorauren on 30 July 1813. Command was assumed by the regimental major, António Eliseu de Almeida. With active operations underway, Beresford possibly felt the regiment needed a more senior officer; on 18 September 1813 Lieutenant-Colonel Richard Armstrong transferred from the 10th Caçadores to command them. Campbell was not expected to survive but while he lived it would be inappropriate for him to be superseded, so he was put on *agregado* status, leaving him formally still with the regiment. But curiously, Armstrong had also been severely wounded at Sorauren. When Campbell died from his wounds on 9 October 1813, Armstrong was still too ill to take up his new command, so the 4th Infantry continued to have no Lieutenant-Colonel present. Jack, newly promoted to the right rank and available due to the shenanigans in the 5th Caçadores, was therefore brought in to replace Campbell as the 4th Infantry's Lieutenant-Colonel *agregado*; he would command the regiment pending Armstrong's recovery.

Jack was thus able to adopt his new rank quickly and to obtain regimental command, though his position was somewhat tenuous: his command of the 4th Infantry depended on how long it took for Armstrong to recover, if he did. It is easy to see in these circumstances why Jack felt 'ill-used' in the Portuguese army. From his perspective, moving to the 5th Caçadores caused him to miss a majority in the 23rd Foot in 1811; then, despite leading the Caçadores through most of the last two years, and being entitled to a Portuguese lieutenant-colonelcy, he did not succeed to command when McCreagh left. Now, he had to stay in Portuguese service rather than take command of 2/23rd, even if Dalmer's accession there meant that opportunity never really existed. His letter from the 'Frontiers of Spain' is Jack's last surviving letter from the Peninsula; ironically, he was fulfilling the schoolboy prediction from his first surviving letter of 1796: 'once entered into a Regiment necessity forces the officers to go where...ordered'. Jack wanted to return to British service, Britain and Devon; but as a soldier he had no choice but to stay in Spain, in Portuguese uniform.

---

30 Bunbury, Reminiscences

One piece of news to improve his mood was that on the same day he was gazetted Lieutenant-Colonel, he was also awarded a medal. The Army Gold Medal was established in 1810 for officers who had commanded under fire in specified actions. One of those actions was the battle of Salamanca; Jack was duly sent his award by the Duke of York:

Major John Hill
5th Caçadores

Horse Guards
21st September 1813

Sir
The Prince Regent having been generously pleased, in the Name and on Behalf of His Majesty, to command that you should be permitted to bear a Medal, Commemorative of the Battle of Salamanca; I have the satisfaction to transmit to you the Medal, which with the approbation of His Royal Highness, has been struck upon the occasion; and to desire that you will acknowledge receipt of it.

I am, Sir, Yours
Frederick
Commander in Chief

A small indicator of Jack's pride in receiving this, and perhaps of his bureaucratic efficiency, is that he kept the original of this letter and noted on the back:

Salamanca Medal. Answered but it [is] possible the letter was lost in the Pacquet

Early in October, Wellington ordered his army across the Bidassoa and into France, outfoxing Soult by fording the river estuary near the sea, rather than upriver, where Soult had concentrated his army. The 5th Caçadores did not participate in the crossing but supported the movement from the Spanish bank. Captain John Dobbs, who had joined the battalion from the 52nd Regiment shortly before, later recalled: 'Lord Wellington got up his pontoons, and in the night of the 6th of October, in the midst of a violent thunderstorm, collected his troops close to the fords at the mouth of the river... I was engaged at the mouth of the river with Bradford's Brigade'.[31] Having secured the

31 Dobbs, *Recollections*

border, however, Wellington went no further immediately. Even Soult was surprised, believing Wellington could have pushed further into France had he so wished. The Allied commander was waiting both for Pamplona to surrender, to remove any incentive for Soult to make another attempt to relieve it, and for news of operations in northern Europe. At the end of October, the French governor of Pamplona finally sought terms; just over a week later came the news of Napoleon's defeat at Leipzig. Wellington's two conditions for further advances were met; he began to concentrate his army.

Jack's formal appointment as Lieutenant-Colonel of the 4th Infantry was dated from 15 November:

Head Quarters at Ustaritz, 12 December 1813
Order of the Day

By a decree of 15 November 1813, in consequence of a proposal made by His Excellency Marshal Beresford, Marquis of Campo Maior:…Lieutenant Colonel agregado of the 4th Infantry Regiment, the Major of the 5th Caçadores battalion, João Hill.[32]

Portuguese archives show, however, that Jack in fact left the 5th Caçadores on 29th October, arriving with his new regiment the next day.[33] Operations were expected soon and Beresford no doubt wanted the 4th Infantry's new commander in place without waiting for the formalities to be completed: even the Portuguese Commander-in-Chief needed formal approval for every appointment, and getting paperwork to Lisbon and back took time. Jack would anyway have wanted to get to know his new command as soon as possible; after his dispute with Bradford and McCreagh, he probably couldn't get away from them fast enough.

While many of its senior officers were British, the formation Jack was joining was uniformly Portuguese. His new regiment was part of the Portuguese 4th Brigade (commanded when he joined by Brigadier-General Archibald Campbell and from 23 November by Brigadier-General John Buchan), which was in turn part of the Portuguese Division (commanded by Major-General Sir John Hamilton). The 4th Brigade had until recently been detached from the Portuguese Division and temporarily assigned to Lowry Cole's 4th Division, which of course

---

32 *Beresford, Collecção das Ordens do Dia* 1813.
33 Gaudêncio and Burnham *Fighting Cocks*. Jack's appointment was not actually published until mid-December. The formal records are in the *Arquivo Histórico Militar* (the Portuguese military archive). The 4th Infantry Regiment's *Livro Mestre* (regimental book record) is PT/AHM/G/LM/B-04/10.

included the 23rd Foot. The brigade fought under Cole's command at Sorauren, so Jack may have obtained some insight into their abilities from his Fusilier friends - another reason for spending time with Henry Ellis recently. Portuguese line regiments contained two battalions; unlike British regiments, both usually deployed together in the field. Their authorised strength was 1,550; 760 in each battalion, plus thirty regimental staff. Below Jack the senior officers of the 4th Infantry were majors Henry Grove (late 80th Foot) and António Eliseu Almeida. Two other majors, Maj José Máximo Pinto and Brevet Major Caetano de Melo Sarria were detached from the regiment, the latter acting as Brigade Major. Jack's eight captains were Luís José Maldonado de Eça, Luís de Lemos Melo, Angus MacDonald (late 57th Foot), Pedro José Frederico, Ralph Dudgeon (late 71st Foot), Domingos Correia de Mesquita, Archibald Campbell (late 5th Foot), and Bernardino Mascarenhas da Rosa. A ninth captain, Dom Jerónimo Pereira Coutinho (Marquis de Soidos), was detached from the regiment. There were also ten lieutenants, nineteen ensigns or *alferes*, an Adjutant and Quartermaster for each battalion, plus a regimental Paymaster, Chaplain, Surgeon and Assistant Surgeon. Aside from Grove, McDonald, Campbell and Dudgeon, all Jack's subordinate officers were therefore Portuguese. One of his lieutenants, Luís de Moura Furtado would ultimately reach lieutenant-general, while Captain Luís José Maldonado de Eça would become a brigadier. One nuance that would have made Jack feel at home was that, except for the Grenadiers, the component parts of Portuguese Line Regiments were known as 'fusilier' companies. The soldiers were mainly conscripts, raised in the case of the 4th Infantry from Estremadura. Though present at Albuera, Arroyo de Molinos and Vitoria, the 4th had not been seriously involved, suffering few casualties. Jack was, however, taking over a regiment that was significantly understrength, both because the slow pace of recruitment rarely enabled Portuguese regiments to achieve their full establishment and because the 4th Infantry had suffered severe casualties in their most recent battle, Sorauren. As well as Allan Campbell, their Lieutenant-Colonel, they had lost nearly 250 men killed, wounded or missing. Indeed, so many of their officers had become casualties that by the end of the battle sergeants had been in command of most companies.[34] Jack probably still had around 1,000 men in his new command, but he also had a rebuilding job to do. He would not get much time to do it.

Joining his new regiment at Ariscum, south of Maya near the Spanish-French border, Jack learned another reason the 4th was

---

34 Gaudêncio and Burnham *Fighting Cocks*

understrength: the Portuguese government had stopped sending drafts to their front line regiments.[35] Yet the Portuguese Division remained an important component of the right wing of the army, together with the allied 2nd and 6th Divisions and a Spanish Division under General Pablo Morillo. Not least because of communications difficulties in this mountainous region, Wellington had placed all these formations under the direct command of General Sir Rowland Hill. Communications were hampered by the weather too; this late in the year there was snow, rain, mud and freezing temperatures. The Portuguese mostly had no tents to protect them from these conditions. 'The rain will destroy us if it lasts much longer; on the right it is snow' said Wellington on 31 October, adding the next day that Hill was 'up to his knees in snow'.[36] The Hill he meant, of course, was General Sir Rowland, but Wellington's comment could equally have applied to the newly appointed Lieutenant-Colonel Jack. Within a week of Jack's arrival, on 4 November, Hill's wing was ordered westwards into the Baztan valley near Urdax. They would be on the right of the sixteen-mile front of Wellington's army: around 82,000 allies facing some 62,000 French troops dug in along the hills beyond the Nivelle river. The move towards Urdax was delayed by the weather destroying the few roads that were available; Hill's wing did not reach their positions until the 8th.

The bad weather continued to add delay until the 10th, when attack orders arrived. The right wing would advance against French positions around Ainhoa, overlooking the bridge at Amotz. Their task was to capture both points while ensuring French troops from there could not redeploy to the centre, where the main attack would be. After a difficult night march, at around 6.30am Hamilton's Portuguese Division moved forward; the distance they had to go, and rugged terrain, slowed their advance relative to the divisions to their left. A French outpost near the foundry of Urdax retired after firing only a few shots. Continuing uphill, they reached the Nivelle river at around 11am and were exposed to artillery and skirmisher fire; ahead was the main line of French redoubts lining the summit of a high ridge thickly covered with bushes across a deep ravine. Each redoubt contained about five hundred men but, as Hill's divisions prepared to assault the redoubts 'to

---

35 *Arquivo Histórico Militar* PT/AHM/1/14/239/02 ms 5. Oman, *History Vol. VII*. Oman suggests this was due to the distance to the French border from Portugal, the impact on the Portuguese economy of Wellington's transfer of his supply ports from Lisbon to northern Spain and, possibly, Portuguese concern that now largely free from French occupation, Spain represented a renewed threat to them. There was also a belief that Portuguese units had been insufficiently recognised in Wellington's despatches compared to Spanish troops.

36 *Wellington Despatches*. Wellington to Hope, 31 October and 1 November 1813

their amazement, the French then flinched and retired, abandoning all the works'.[37] The attack in the centre had been so successful that the redoubts were being flanked, forcing the occupants to retreat or risk being cut off. At the top of the hill was a French camp with wooden huts, surrounded by minor earthworks. In his 1816 *Statement of Services*, Jack recalled that he led his men in 'the storm of the French entrenched camp on the 10th of November'. The French had set fire to the huts; the flames and smoke added danger, as an officer of another regiment recalled:

> The enemy's bivouack was the most complete we had ever seen, the huts were so admirably constructed, and the streets and squares so uniform. It had been well supplied with shops and canteens, but every thing useful had been destroyed; we found nothing but empty casks and bottles. Many of the huts had been set on fire, in which were a number of musquets, probably belonging to wounded men, who had been carried to the rear: many of them being loaded, went off occasionally, to the danger of the captors, long after the enemy were out of sight.[38]

While as another remembered:

> We passed on through their lines of defence, where they had been so long domiciled; their huts were extremely neat and comfortable, many had their green blinds over their little lattice windows; their neat little fireplaces, bedsteads of green boughs, shelves for their prog, and arm-racks, so like the natty Frenchman in camp. We found their rations uncooked, and plenty of onions and other vegetables, which were transferred *tout de suite* into our haversacks *en passant*. We pressed on with a running fire after them until sundown; then gave up the chase, stretched our weary limbs on the November sod, turned out the contents of our larder - a Dutch cheese, onions, biscuit, cold ration beef, and a little rum - and finished off the breakfast, dinner, and supper all at a go.[39]

Pushing past the fires, the allies came to another redoubt; when they attacked they 'saw the garrison leap down over the parapets and follow the other fugitives. Six guns, unspiked, were found in it, so hasty had the evacuation been'.[40] Campbell's Brigade, with the 4th Infantry, had

---

37 Oman, *History Vol. VII*
38 Cadell, *Narrative*
39 Bell, *Rough Notes*
40 Oman, *History Vol. VII*

formed the second line of Hamilton's advance. This and the lack of serious French resistance, meant they suffered few casualties (and probably gathered less loot). Jack's new regiment lost only four men killed and thirteen wounded, despite much of their attack being made across open terrain in sight of French artillery as they climbed towards the enemy redoubts. Not included in the returns is that during the attack Jack himself was injured 'in consequence of my horse falling with me'.[41]

Exactly when this happened is unknown; the only reference to it is in his 1816 *Statement of Services*. As this is the same note where he mentions leading his men in storming the camp, the accident probably took place after that (although he may have been able to remount or proceed on foot). He was in some discomfort in either case; it was later assessed that he needed hospital treatment, though he would be unable to undergo this for four months.

Wellington was triumphant about the victory on the Nivelle: 'we completely succeeded in carrying all the positions on the enemy's left and centre, in separating the former from the latter, and by these means turning the enemy's strong positions occupied by their right on the lower Nivelle, which they were obliged to evacuate during the night; having taken 51 pieces of cannon, and 1400 prisoners...In the course of the operations...we have driven the enemy from positions which they had been fortifying with great labour and care for 3 months'.[42] His subordinates were similarly pleased. Major-General Charles Colville, commanding the 3rd Division to the left of Hamilton's, wrote to his family:

> The day was one of the luckiest that ever came out of the heaven. The whole army moved forward from their respective points almost at the same moment at daybreak, and from the mountains behind, where many must have been beholders of the whole line of operations in one coup d'oeil, it must have been the grandest sight possible. Success was so general and everything went on so swimmingly, that I think it was altogether the most animating and...agreeable day of the kind I was ever engaged in.'[43]

Hamilton reported to General Hill:

---

41 Hill 1816 *Statement of Services*
42 *Wellington Supplementary Despatches*. Wellington to Bathurst, 13 November 1813
43 Colville, *Portrait*

I feel in every respect perfectly satisfied with the conduct of the division, and have received from Brigadier Campbell and Brigadier Buchan, commanding brigades, and Lieutenant-Colonel Tulloh, commanding the artillery, the most flattering reports of the good conduct of the officers, &c., under their command, who respectively have recommended the undermentioned officers: Lieutenant-Colonel Gomersal, commanding 2nd regiment; Major Jacintha, 14th regiment; Lieutenant-Colonel Hill, 4th regiment; Lieutenant-Colonel Jose Maria, 10th regiment; and Major Pampeluna, 10th Caçadores.[44]

In two years with the 5th Caçadores, Jack had never been mentioned in Bradford's despatches, despite his de facto command in McCreagh's absence; in less than two weeks with the 4th Infantry, he had been named by Hamilton, his divisional commander. Army officers always want recognition by their superiors; Jack would have been gratified finally to have received some.

A mention in despatches was not the only recognition Jack received at around this time. From home came news that, along with other local officers, on 2 November he had been awarded the freedom of the city of Exeter. He received a fine scroll recording:

City of Exeter

At a Chamber holden
By the Mayor Bailiffs and
Commonality at the Guildhall
Of the said City on Tuesday the
2nd Day of November 1813.

Resolved unanimously –
    That the Freedom of this City be presented to Lieutenant Colonel John Hill of the 23rd Regiment of Foot, Son of the Reverend John Hill Vicar of Hennock...in testimony of the high respect of this Body for the Bravery and Talents they have exhibited in several Engagements with the Enemy in the late Campaigns in Spain and Portugal under the Command of Field Marshall the Marquis of Wellington and the eminent services they have thereby contributed to render to their King and Country; and that the Town Clerk be requested to transmit to...them and Copy of this Resolution.

By Order of the Chamber

---

44 *Wellington Supplementary Despatches.* Sir J. Hamilton to Sir R. Hill, 11 November 1813

After the Nivelle, Soult moved most of his army towards Bayonne, which Wellington knew would be difficult to capture without significant loss. Moreover, the allied commander had self-imposed a reduction in his force, feeling obliged to return almost all his 20,000 Spanish troops to their own country. Only Morillo's Division, in Hill's right wing, stayed in France. The Spanish government had failed to provide either rations or pay; coupled with resentment following years of French depredation in Spain, hungry Spanish soldiers began to plunder local villages. This was firmly against orders; all provisions obtained locally by the allies had to be paid for. Wellington was desperate not to provoke French civilians to fight his army as the Spanish had against the French. As he put it himself:

> The conduct of the Portuguese and British troops has been exactly what I wished...But I despair of the Spaniards. They are in so miserable a state, that it is really hardly fair to expect that they will refrain from plundering so beautiful a country, into which they enter as conquerors; particularly, adverting to the miseries which their own country has suffered from its invaders...without pay or food, they must plunder; and if they plunder, they will ruin us all'...If I could now bring forward 20,000 good Spaniards, paid and fed, I should have Bayonne. If I could bring forward 40,000, I don't know where I should stop. Now I have both the 20,000 and the 40,000 at my command, upon this frontier, but I cannot venture to bring forward any for want of means of paying and supporting them.'[45]

Jack had told his mother in July (Chapter 12) 'One would pause before letting loose such a set on France. Cruelty would sully success. The French would be forced to turn out the whole population to repel them.' Wellington agreed: his troops were finding that disenchantment with life under the Emperor and the locals' ability to make money from selling goods to the allies made them not just accepted but welcomed by the French population. Jack and his colleagues were being treated more as saviours than conquerors; that attitude must not be risked.

With the loss of the Spanish, continuing bad weather, and lingering doubts about whether the victors of Leipzig would invade France from the north or offer Napoleon another truce, Wellington paused his advance again. On the 11th his remaining troops were ordered into camps slightly forward of the positions they had reached during the battle of the Nivelle. Hill positioned his men in the area around

---

45 *Wellington Despatches*. Wellington to Bathurst, 21 November 1813.

Espelette and Suraïde and probed towards the bridge on the river Nive at Cambo-les-Bains. The French destroyed the bridge and moved back towards Bayonne. This effectively abandoned the area between the eastern bank of the Nive and the Adour, leaving Wellington free to advance his right wing to the latter, a major supply route into the interior of France. Dominating the Adour might force Soult to abandon Bayonne for fear of being surrounded and trapped in the city, but the move was risky. The river Nive flows northwards, joining the Adour at Bayonne; crossing it would divide Wellington's army and leave an obstacle to reinforcement between the two halves. Soult could then concentrate his force against one part of the allied army, but Wellington believed the relative capabilities of the two armies mitigated the risk.

The Portuguese Division now received a new Portuguese commander, Major-General Carlos Lecor and Jack's Brigade a new British one, Brigadier-General John Buchan.[46] In the rain at daybreak on 9 December, the Division forded the Nive, the order to advance being transmitted simultaneously across Hill's command by the lighting of a signal beacon on a hill near Cambo-les-Bains. Lecor's division waded across in the wake of the 2nd Division, an officer in which recalled 'we waited some time for…the passage of General Buchan's brigade of Portuguese, who were not so fortunate as we were, they having had several men drowned in crossing'.[47] Once everyone was on the far bank, the bridge at Cambo was repaired and a pontoon bridge was also thrown over the river to ensure Hill's men could retreat or be reinforced as needed. French troops opposing the allied advance again retreated after minor resistance. The allies pushed forward to Villefranque, Lecor's men following the line of the main road, or *chaussée*, from St. Jean-Pied-du-Port to Bayonne. After a brief tussle, Villefranque was captured and the day's manoeuvres ended as the weather worsened: 'The afternoon and night of the 9th was extremely wet; the rain fell in torrents; and we had no covering whatever but our cloaks: we crouched around our fires, with our feet as close to them as possible.'[48] Overnight, Soult withdrew most of his troops to the western side of the river; dawn showed nothing in front of the allies. Hill pushed exploring parties over the hills past Horlopo and Mougerre and close to the south-eastern corner of the fortress of Bayonne itself. Finding the area between the Nive and the Adour unoccupied, Hill deployed his units in a three-mile arc along three hills between the two rivers, with

---

46 Wellington's despatches and other British sources spell the name 'Le Cor', but contemporary Portuguese military records have 'Lecor'. I use the latter, except when quoting from other sources.
47 Cadell, *Narrative*
48 Cadell, *Narrative*

the Bayonne suburb of Saint-Pierre-d'Irube ahead them. Jack, with the 4th Infantry in Lecor's Division, was positioned at the rear of the middle hill, quartered in hamlets and cottages along the *chaussée* or the sideroads which joined it there. On the 10th, Soult launched an attack on the other part of the allied line, west of the Nive. After two days of fighting with little progress he switched two divisions to the eastern bank and prepared to attack Hill. To avoid the two parts of his army being disconnected, Wellington had ordered a new temporary bridge, made from boats lashed together across the Nive near Villefranque and warned Hill to expect an attack. There was no movement on the 12th, but that evening flood water in the river washed away the boat bridge. Hill's wing could still be reinforced via bridges further upstream, but until the temporary one was repaired it would take hours longer to reach them. If attacked, Hill's 5,700 British and 7,500 Portuguese troops would need to be able to hold their ground for at least four hours until they could be supported. Hill's units would have difficulty supporting each other, as streams running between each hill were dammed; the marshy ground around the resulting ponds made the gaps between the hills largely impassable. Country roads crossed the hills on the left and right and joined the *chaussée*, which ran over the middle hill, about a mile back from the centre of the allied line, near the Horlopo knoll. This was where Lecor's Division, including the 4th Infantry and Jack, were positioned in reserve.

The morning of 13 December dawned clear and sunny but with the valleys shrouded in mist. Sounds of movement had been heard all night from the French lines and many enemy campfires were visible. 'The fog continued heavy, covering the vast masses of the French dimly seen; now and then, they appeared in solid columns like black thunder-clouds, as the mist rose spreading over a mile of ground'.[49] At around 7am the fog had lifted sufficiently for three enemy columns, some 23,000 men supported by artillery, to become visible advancing towards the allies. At around 8am the first shots were fired; 'for the next five hours the din was incessant'.[50] The main attack appeared to be against the allied left, where French success might cut off the prospect of reinforcement, even if the broken bridge were repaired. Buchan's Brigade were sent to support the line there, but the fighting quickly stalemated. Meanwhile, French attacks on the central and right hills were becoming far more challenging. In the centre repeated attacks and counterattacks by both sides had begun to wear down the Portuguese and British troops. The right-hand hill, where the village of Vieux Mouguerre stood, was being held by Major-General Byng's Brigade.

---

49 Bell, *Rough Notes*
50 Oman, *History Vol. VII*

One of his regiments was the 3rd Foot, the Buffs, who suffered so severely at Albuera. The Buffs were fighting hard, but they and the rest of Byng's brigade were being pushed back by overwhelming French numbers. By noon, allied troops on both the right and centre hills were in difficulty, the latter being at risk of being outflanked by French success on the former. Hill decided to counterattack, turning to the only troops he had available, Lecor's Division. Calling Buchan's brigade back from the left, Hill sent Lecor and Brigadier-General Hipólito da Costa's Brigade to reinforce the centre hill, while Buchan was ordered to climb the hill of Mouguerre and reinforce the right. Jack was marching to rescue the Buffs, who were in trouble on a hill to his right-front against the army of Marshal Soult, just like at Albuera.

Buchan's brigade 'crossed the valley, and ascending under a heavy flank fire from Soult's guns rallied the third regiment...it was now twelve o'clock'.[51] As Buchan's men neared the top of the hill, they deployed into line and, with the rallied remnants of the Buffs alongside, attacked. They were attacking an entire French division, under General Maximillian Foy, supported by horse artillery. But as at Albuera, the allied advance was unstoppable. 'On General Buchan reaching the ground, the enemy had got possession of part of the hill, viz. as far as the head of the mill-pond; but on being attacked, he gave way'.[52] According to Oman, the battle now became 'a running fight, in which the French were driven along the heights and ultimately down to the Adour. Buchan's Portuguese finished the game very successfully - losing 14 officers and 180 men before it was over, and capturing a gun'.[53] The term 'running fight' gives the impression that the French fell back almost immediately as Buchan's attack went in and did not return. But Jack's recollection, written just two years later, was that the hill was retaken and maintained, night putting a stop to the contest.[54]

Maintaining the hill implies there must have been at least one counterattack by the French. This is supported by the official history of the Buffs, which says 'this height was successfully maintained against all the efforts of the enemy to retake it' and by Wellington's dispatch after the battle (see below).[55] Buchan's success on the right also helped

---

51 Napier, *History Volume VI*
52 '*Details of the Action of the 13th December 1813, in Front of Bayonne*'. *The United Services Journal* 1834 Part III
53 Oman, *History Vol. VII*
54 Hill 1816 *Statement of Services*
55 *Historical Record of the Third Regiment or The Buffs*, Richard Cannon 1839. I have found no evidence that a gun was captured by Buchan's brigade, which is not mentioned in any after-action report. The official history of the Buffs claims they 'together with the other regiments of the brigade, carried, in superior style,

secure allied success in the centre: already under pressure from da Costa's counter-attack, 'at this moment Buchan's Portuguese and the Buffs were retaking the hill beyond the mill-pond, and rapidly driving back the enemy along its face'.[56] It was now the turn of French troops on the centre hill to fear being outflanked; they too fell back. Wellington now appeared on the field, having crossed the repaired bridge with reinforcements, but they were not needed; Hill's hard-fighting men had won the day alone. Wellington himself told Hill 'The battle is all yours'. By 3pm the French were back where they started. 'Our men threw up their caps in the air, and gave one long, loud, thrilling cheer, that echoed down the valleys amongst the retiring foe'.[57] Hill's losses totalled some 1,775; Soult's perhaps 3,300. 'At the close of the action, the dead and wounded along the high road and on the ground adjoining it were lying thicker than perhaps, in an equal extent, on any field of battle which took place during the war, not excepting Waterloo, although the latter continued eight hours, whilst this was over in three. Lord Wellington, in riding over the ground, remarked that he had never observed so large a number of killed on so small a compass' said one soldier later.[58] As night fell the troops bivouacked where they were: 'The days were short, and night closed upon the saturated field of blood, before we had time to light our fires and cook the wretched ration dinner; but still, with our half-gill of rum, after so long a fast, exercise, and excitement, it was an acceptable banquet. It came on now to pour rain like fury, and the bivouac was anything but agreeable, particularly to the wounded, among whom there was a multitude of hurts'.[59] The next day the clear-up began:

> We sent in a flag of truce to the French general to say they might carry away all their own wounded men from off our ground, and we would bury their dead; we had no hospitals nor medicos to care for them, and as prisoners of war they were not worth their

---

a hill on the French left which covered their manœuvres, and captured two guns; and this height was successfully maintained against all the efforts of the enemy to retake it.' Ignoring the point that Buchan's units were not of the same brigade, this claims two guns were captured and implies it was by the Buffs. It is not unusual for chauvinistic British historians to ignore the decisive Portuguese intervention; British regimental and other histories routinely fail to credit Portuguese units.

56 *Details, USJ*
57 Bell, *Rough Notes*
58 *Details, USJ*. The author of the article is anonymous but presumably was at Waterloo. He seems not to have witnessed Albuera, another field densely packed with casualties that Wellington also missed.
59 Bell, *Rough Notes*

rations. All was friendship and politeness now; our offer was accepted, and a line drawn out between us. Some trees were cut down and laid across the high road into Bayonne; our men collected all the wounded of the French, carried them down in blankets to this point, and handed them over. The sentries of both armies were planted along the line, not over six or seven yards from each other, as quiet and gentle as lambs! The hill-sides were perforated with cannon-shot, some places like a rabbit-warren, and dyed with blood...This "labour of love," in presenting so many disabled and useless soldiers to their country, lasted some days, and no end to groaning and moaning until we had them all removed. Two or three nights exposed to the rains left many of the unfortunates in a pitiable condition, for they had fallen in sand-pits, amongst brushwood, and in nooks and corners out of sight. The rains continued to over-shadow the scene of desolation all about us, and not a blink of the sun to cheer or warm the bivouac for many days.[60]

Like Waterloo eighteen months later, Saint-Pierre was a close-run thing but ended in decisive allied victory; it would prove to be Soult's last major offensive. Late on the day of the battle Wellington wrote excitedly 'I have the pleasure to inform you that Hill has beat them completely'.[61] His official report was more sober, but just as full of praise: 'I had the great satisfaction...in observing the conduct of Major Gen. Byng's brigade of British infantry, supported by the Portuguese brigade under the command of Major [sic] Gen. Buchan, in carrying an important height from the enemy on the right of our position, and maintaining it against all their efforts to regain it'.[62] Hill was similarly praiseworthy of Buchan's men: 'Brig. Gen. Buchan, with his brigade, gave very effective support in the early part of the day to the left; and subsequently was moved to the support of Major Gen. Byng's brigade, and contributed much to the success on that side.[63] Lecor, who had accompanied da Costa's brigade up the centre hill and did not see Buchan's attack in detail, reported 'the conduct of my troops was very gallant...I must also mention the gallant conduct of the corps commanders, Colonel Jorge de Avilez, 2nd Regiment, Colonel Luis Maria, 10th Regiment, Major Rodrigo Vito Pereira, the 14th Regiment's acting commander, Lieutenant-Colonel Hill, 4th Regiment, Brevet Major Pamplona, 10th Caçadores, and Lieutenant-Colonel Tulloh,

---

60 Bell, *Rough Notes*
61 *Wellington Despatches*. Wellington to Hope, 13 December 1813
62 *Wellington Despatches*. Wellington to Bathurst, 14 December 1813
63 *Wellington Despatches*. Hill to Wellington, 16 December 1813

the artillery commander.'[64] There was also independent testimony from another officer who recalled 'It is but justice to say that the Portuguese brigade, under General Buchan...behaved admirably'.[65] Jack had three of his officers and eighty men wounded in the attack. His letters from after the battle do not survive, he wrote with pride in his 1816 Statement of Services:

> I was engaged...in the crossing of the Nive, and in the battle which took place in consequence of the French attack on Lord Hill's Corps on the 13th Decr., when the two Battalions of the 4th Portuguese Regt. were ordered to secure a hill on the extreme right over the Adour, which the enemy had taken; this post was retaken and maintained, night putting a stop to the contest.

Today, atop the Croix de Mouguerre, the hill over which Jack led his regiment's charge, stands an impressive obelisk surrounded by weathered cannon. The monument commemorates Soult's defence of France. In French the inscription reads: 'From this height, which was taken and taken back at the battle of Saint Pierre D'Irube, views extend over the mountains and valleys of the Basque country. With inferior forces, foot by foot, Marshal Soult, Duke of Dalmatia, Lieutenant of the Emperor, defended this country for seven months against Wellington's army 1813 - 1814'. It is an appropriate place for a monument. The ground on which it stands saw perhaps the most intense fighting that took place during Wellington's invasion of France, and commands impressive views of much of the area that the armies disputed in late 1813. The monument stands on French soil; it is perhaps forgivable that the inscription fudges the point that the height was 'taken' by Soult's troops, but 'taken back' by Jack Hill and his colleagues from Wellington's army, in their memorable victory at the battle of Saint Pierre.

After the battles of the Nive, as the three days fighting on 10-13 December became collectively known, Soult expected Wellington to cross the Adour and besiege Bayonne; he positioned his army along the northern bank of the river to resist. Instead, according to Oman, the allies 'remained practically quiescent for the best part of a month'.[66] There were many reasons that Wellington did not immediately make further movements. First, after a long winter campaign his troops needed to be resupplied. Thomas Browne recorded:

---

64 Gaudêncio and Burnham *Fighting Cocks*
65 Cadell, *Narrative*
66 Oman, *History Vol. VII*

The Troops were in houses, & the great work of Shoemaking & mending, & repairing Clothes began. The Army was in a terrible plight for want of Clothing, & the Men had every Color on their backs, that would have done Harlequin credit. A considerable quantity of clothing, had arrived however at Passages from England, & small vessels were despatched from St. Jean de Luz to bring it to the latter place. As it arrived the different Corps or Regiments were allowed to come down from the lines into St . Jean de Luz, where they arrived successively. The day they marched into St. Jean de Luz, they halted, the day after they clothed from head to foot, & the day after that, they began their march [back] to the Army...Caps, Jackets, Trowsers, everything old, was thrown away.[67] Even then the Portuguese soldiers remained without much protection against the winter. It was not until 10 January 1814 that Wellington wrote to Beresford 'I...have given directions that the great coats for the Portuguese army may be brought round from Santander'.[68] Jack's troops must have been suffering without their coats, as the weather remained atrocious. One officer recalled: 'Every-body, who is old enough, recollects, I dare say, the severity of the winter of 1813-14. Even in the south of France, the frost was at times so intense, as to cast a complete coat of ice over ponds and lakes of very considerable depth; whilst storms of cold wind and rain occurred at every interval, when the frost departed'.[69]

As the end of 1813 approached Wellington wrote to London to explain why he was not pushing into France as quickly as armchair generals at home wished:

In military operations there are some things which cannot be done; one of these is to move troops in this country during or immediately after a violent fall of rain. I believe I shall lose many more men than I shall ever replace, by putting any troops in camp in this bad weather; but I should be guilty of an useless waste of men, if I were to attempt an operation during the violent falls of rain which we have here. Our operations, then, must necessarily be slow, but they shall not be discontinued.'[70]

Browne confirmed 'The weather had become so severe, as to prevent all idea of operations for the present. The roads, except the main road to

67 Buckley, *Browne*
68 *Wellington Despatches*. Wellington to Beresford, 10 January 1814
69 Gleig, *Subaltern*
70 *Wellington Despatches*. Wellington to Bathurst, 21 December 1813

Bayonne, became almost impassable, & in the transport of provisions, on Mules...from St. Jean de Luz to the several divisions on the right of the Army, a great number of these animals perished, from the depths of the roads, the scarcity of forage, & the extreme severity of the weather'.[71] One of those divisions on the right of the army was the Portuguese Division, suffering shortage of supplies as well as of coats.

Another reason Wellington largely stayed put was continued uncertainty about the situation in northern France. It was mid-January before he learned the Russians, Austrians and Prussians had crossed the Rhine. Even then he was dubious about their prospects: 'In regard to the operations on the Rhine, I confess that I feel no confidence in any thing that is doing. The Allies are not strong enough, nor sufficiently prepared, to invade France at all, or to do more than cross the Rhine in one great corps, and there blockade some one, two or three fortresses.'[72] But contrary to Oman's assertion of 'quiescence', things were far from quiet on the Adour. Wellington did plan to cross the river but first wanted to do three things: drag the main part of Soult's army eastwards, so it could not interfere either with either the crossing or the siege of Bayonne; weaken Bayonne's defences by forcing Soult to withdraw some of the troops inside it; and impede French use of the river to resupply the town. To achieve the last of these, the Portuguese Division spread eastwards along the river's edge. The possession of three islands upstream from Bayonne was disputed between the two armies; French fire from them could annoy the allies, but capturing the islands would help the allies control river traffic. The first and largest island, Île La Honce, was separated from the southern bank only by a narrow channel; on 20 December the allies brought up cannon that dominated the island, which the French then abandoned. Portuguese records show that two days later, one battalion of the 4th Infantry personally led by Jack attacked one of the other islands, probably the next along, Île de Broc. The island was being fortified by French civilian workers and defended by a company of Voltiguers from the 69eme line regiment, led by Captain Nicolas Marcel, whose memoires recalled his own heroic actions in the face of enemy assaults:

On December 22, my company was designated to go with two companies of the 76e to Île de Broc, in the middle of the Adour, we had to relieve the troops who guarded this island and had begun to build entrenchments there, because its possession was important for the movement of our boats. This island is only three feet above

71 Buckley, *Browne*
72 *Wellington Despatches*. Wellington to Beresford, 10 January 1814

the water level...On December 24, around midnight, a boat which had come loose, I don't know where from, was carried by the current up to an English sentry. This man, believing that we were landing, gave the alarm and the shooting began; as all the shots were arriving at our post, we also realized that we were being attacked and we began to defend ourselves. It was pouring with rain, the night was dark and the wind was blowing so hard that, out of ten guns, four did not fire, the spark being immediately blown away. If ever I found myself embarrassed, it was on this occasion: I did not have the order to withdraw and, had I wanted to, I could not have done so, because some soldiers of the 76e had seized the boat...I sent my lieutenant, M. Frédure, with twenty men to the end of the line where there was an easy place to disembark and I myself went to the other end to post a similar number...The rising tide was so strong that the island was completely submerged; the dyke on which I walked with my men was so narrow that I slipped and fell into the water; fortunately I knew how to swim. At that moment I saw what my old Voltigeurs were doing: several were on guard with water over their knees and they said to me: 'Captain, be calm, by the light of the water we will see if he arrives by boat and, if we are not killed, everything that disembarks will be bayoneted and thrown into the river'...I left my second lieutenant with the twenty men and returned to the centre: the enemy's fire still continued, but I saw that it was a false attack and I forbade that we respond to his shooting, the light of our shots was capable of indicating our locations and causing injury to many people... Around 2 a.m. after midnight, everything returned to calm.

On January 1, 1814, around 7 a.m., Captain Adjutant-Major Gugliéry came to wish me a happy new year and told me that the English had just asked the commander of Île de Broc to parley, but that, having been told to contact Bayonne, they had just aimed two pieces of artillery at the island, threatening to fire if the garrison did not leave immediately. As Gugliéry was leaving, the cannon was heard: I went to the water's edge and a corporal, who was on the island, told me that the companies were going to run out of cartridges. I immediately informed Captain Fournier who temporarily commanded the 3rd battalion: he quickly had a good number of them assembled, but there was no one to carry them in boats, the boatmen having fled at the first cannon shot: I then offered to go to the island with two peasants of good will who were willing to take charge of steering the boat. We had barely left the shore when the enemy directed their fire at our boat: despite everything, we continued, but, as soon as we landed, the 150 unarmed workers came and threw themselves onto the boat in crowds wanting to be brought back to the other side. Unfortunately, a cannonball hit the crowd, broke one man's thigh, injured five others and damaged the boat. I managed to bring order to this disorderly crowd...then I went to hand over the cartridges and transmit the orders to the commander of the island: in the short journey that I had to make to arrive with the soldiers who were fighting, I received three platoon fires and never had the bullets fallen around me in such abundance; when I returned I had the same honour which, I would have done without.

When I returned to our shore, all my Voltigeurs ran to congratulate me and presented me with brandy from their rations. Shortly after, the English were taken in flank by boats armed with cannons manned by French sailors and their fire slowed considerably. At this moment, Commander Guingret and my comrade Gugliéry came to ask me for details about my little trip to the island. I had not opened my mouth to explain when I received a bullet which passed through my shoulder and lodged under the armpit, where it found itself so well that it is still there.[73]

The dates in Marcel's account do not align precisely with those in the Portuguese archives, and there are unfortunately no further details of this attack from the allied side, though the battalion of the 4th Infantry lost one man in the action. The Portuguese Division were the only troops in the area, however, with Buchan's brigade at Briscous, alongside Île de Broc and da Costa's Brigade near Île La Honce. It seems highly likely therefore that it was the latter which captured La Honce and Buchan's which took Broc. No British troops were involved; presumably why Oman omits mention of these actions. The Portuguese Division thus had anything but a 'quiescent' Christmas and New Year, but Jack found time to organise an important ceremony:

It was in the church of the town of Honce that the 4th Regiment of Infantry received its new Colours, which were sent by the |Lisbon| Arsenal to replace the old ones which were in rags. The church's priest blessed the Colours at mass, after which they were attached to their respective poles from which the remains of the old ones were removed. These had left Lisbon on 5 May 1809 and had been carried in all campaigns of the war until only small pieces remained. At this point, Lt. Col. João Hill, who commanded the regiment at the time, gathered the Portuguese officers, and in the presence of

---

73 *Campagnes du Capitaine Marcel du 69e de Ligne en Espagne et en Portugal (1808-1814)* Le Commandant Var 1913

the priest and the French people, solemnly split the old rags and handed out a small piece of those glorious pennons to each officer who since 1809 had marched and fought in numerous combats and battles with those flags in their front.

This holy and solemn ceremony marked the end for these symbols of honour and love for the country, virtues which were constantly showed by those brave officers during the last five years.[74]

The islands now secured, Buchan's brigade moved further eastwards along the southern bank of the Adour, to the Joyeuse river, one of numerous tributaries that join from the south. Jack and his more than 1,000 4th Infantrymen moved to Bastide-Clairence, with the rest of the brigade at La Côte and the 3rd Division to their south at Bonloc.[75] In this advanced position, Jack's men were holding the extreme right of the allied line. On 3 January Soult determined to probe the strength of this part of the allied army; two French divisions, supported by cavalry, crossed the Joyeuse between Bastide-Clairence and Bonloc. The move outflanked the 4th Infantry's position, forcing them and the rest of Buchan's brigade to fall back about 5 miles towards Briscous. The 4th was the only unit to engage the French, in what Fortescue called 'a brisk fusillade' but managed their retreat without incurring a single casualty.[76] The rest of Lecor's division plus the 3rd and 4th Divisions moved up to support Buchan. The next day Wellington himself came to reconnoitre, but the weather was so bad that the allies could not regain the ground they had lost until the 6th. Wellington reported:

> The enemy collected a considerable force on the Gave d'Oléron in the beginning of the week; and on the 3d inst. drove in the cavalry piquets between the Joyeuse and Bidouze rivers, and attacked the post of Major Gen. Buchan's Portuguese brigade on the Joyeuse near La Bastide, and those of the 3d division in Bonloc. They turned the right of Major Gen. Buchan's brigade on the height of La Coste, and obliged him to retire towards Briscous; and they

74 *Historia Da Guerra Civil E Do Estabelecimento Do Governo Parlamentar Em Portugal*; *Vol. 4, part 2* Simão da Luz Soriano 1866. Translation by Moises Gaudêncio

75 A return in *Wellington Supplementary Despatches* entitled 'Brigading of the Army in the Peninsular' from the Adjutant-General's Office dated 16 January 1814 shows the 4th Infantry as having 888 'Effective rank and file'. Adding officers, NCOs and a share of 851 men from Buchan's brigade listed as sick brings the total under Jack's command to over 1,000.

76 Fortescue, *History* Vol. IX

established two divisions of infantry on the height and in La Bastide, with the remainder of the army on the Bidouze and the Gave.

Our centre and right were immediately concentrated and prepared to move; and, having reconnoitred the enemy on the 4th, I intended to have attacked them on the 5th, but was obliged to defer the attack till the 6th, owing to the badness of the weather and the swelling of the rivulets. The attack was made on that day by the 3d and 4th divisions, under the command of Lieut. Gen. Sir T. Picton and Lieut. Gen. Sir G. L. Cole, supported by Major Gen. Buchan's Portuguese brigade of Gen. Le Cor's division, and the cavalry, under the command of Major Gen. Fane; and the enemy were forthwith dislodged without loss on our side, and our posts replaced where they had been. I then ordered the troops to return to their cantonments, as the weather has again rendered all operations impossible for the moment; and the roads are in such a state, that it has become scarcely practicable to support the troops at the distance they now are from the sea-coast.[77]

Even for Jack and the 4th Infantry the whole affair had proved little more than a minor inconvenience, though it provided a rare occasion to fight briefly alongside his parent battalion. The Welch Fusiliers had only recently moved into their winter cantonments when the 4th Division were moved up. Lieutenant John MacDonald of the 23rd wrote home 'we had hardly got settled when we were ordered to support our right where Soult had moved 35,000 men, & after a disagreeable bitter campaign of a week, in very bad weather, we returned.'[78]

It was another month and a half before the weather was fine long enough for the roads to dry somewhat. The delay had one benefit: Soult's army had been weakened as Napoleon demanded he send troops back to Paris to hold off the central European allies. By the end of January, Soult had lost 14,000 experienced troops to that cause. Wellington was ready to begin his next manoeuvre, but did not plan to cross the Adour immediately. Rather he planned another outflanking movement, sending Hill's corps across the Joyeuse beyond the French left. He hoped this would force Soult eastwards, weakening his connection to Bayonne. Oman summed up the plan as 'turning Soult's left wing by the persistent advance of a large flanking column under

---

77 *Wellington Despatches*. Wellington to Bathurst, 9 January 1814
78 RWF Museum Object No. 5935. MacDonald letter of 23 January 1814

Hill...and by dislodging it in succession from the lines of the Joyeuse, the Bidouze, and the Saison...[force Soult to]...abandon those river-lines under pain of being taken in flank and rear by the turning column'.[79] Wellington would leave enough of his own troops outside Bayonne to watch the city, but Hill's right wing would be followed by most of his other divisions, under Beresford, to force Soult to redeploy or be heavily outnumbered. One unit left near Bayonne was Bradford's Brigade, so Jack's move to the 4th Infantry meant he escaped participation in yet another siege. On 12 February, General Hill was ordered to gather the 2nd, 3rd and Portuguese Divisions, a Spanish division under Morillo, plus a brigade of cavalry and a troop of horse artillery and 'be so good as put the above force in motion on the 14th inst., and move forward'.[80] Hill was aiming for the area between Bonloc and Hélette where he would both outnumber and outflank the French troops holding the extreme left of Soult's line, under General Jean Harispe.

As Wellington hoped, the French fell back as Hill advanced, but the next day, on hills near the Bidouze river around Garris, Harispe made a stand. It was a good position, but Harispe had only 7,000 men facing the 2nd and Portuguese Divisions with 12,000, while Morillo's Spanish Division was further south pushing around his flank. As Hill's advanced units, which included Jack and his 4th Infantry, approached the French position 'the day was far spent, and the 2nd Division and Le Cor's Portuguese were slowly forming in front of the French, vexing them with long-range artillery-fire and rather expecting them to retire.'[81] One soldier who was present later waxed poetically about the scene:

The evening of the 15th February, 1814, amidst the beautifully varied scenery of the Lower Pyrenees, was one of extreme loveliness; for though the early spring had not entirely obliterated all traces of winter, and the tops of some mountains were still clad in snow, yet the glowing sunset, with its ever-changing gold and purple, imparted to the magnificent display of mountain and forest, interspersed with fertile valleys, a richness and a colouring not to be described...from the earliest dawn of the day mentioned, the troops had been moving by a mountain-road, the light infantry clearing the way. In their course, they had successively dislodged their active enemy from the numerous abattis he had thrown across the road, and from the strong ground which he everywhere found, and of which he knew so well how to take advantage.[82]

79 Oman, *History Vol. VII*
80 *Wellington Despatches*. QMG to Hill 12 February 1814
81 Oman, *History Vol. VII*
82 Maxwell, *Sketches*

The leisurely allied deployment in front of the enemy was disturbed, however, when Wellington appeared and promptly ordered 'you must take the hill before dark'. The poetic soldier felt this would be a challenge:

> Immediately in their front was a deep precipitous ravine, which divided the height from a lofty hill close to the small town of Garris, on which a column of the enemy, 6000 strong, was in position. Both positions, together with the ravine between them, were rough forest ground; with portions, and particularly in the ravine, very thickly timbered...The streaks of evening had for some time, one by one, been disappearing, the more distant mountains were no longer distinguishable, and the shades of night were now settling darkly upon the height; but the order was literally and fully executed. Brief space had been given; time pressed; there had not been a moment to lose, and not a moment was lost. [83]

The allied troops moved forward. Pringle's brigade from the 2nd Division 'crossed the ravine and stormed the northern crest of the Motte de Garris, while Le Cor's Portuguese attacked along the high road and south of the hill...it turned out a very stiff affair...The attacking force had to cross the ravine, and then mount a steep slope under heavy musketry-fire'.[84] The allied pressure told, but not before both sides had charged with bayonets. Outnumbered, the French retreated towards St. Palais but their officers, unable to rally them immediately beyond the Bidouze river, only managed to stop them halfway to the next river, the Saison. The victorious and grateful allied troops found bounty on the hilltop:

> The enemy, not having anticipated so uncourteous an intrusion at so late an hour, had made extensive preparations for the comfort of his bivouack, in collecting large quantities of wood for his fires. Of this the regiment gladly availed itself, and that night its bivouack was far more brilliantly lighted than it usually was. Seated around the cheerful blaze, and while, with keen appetite, partaking of the simple supper which the havre-sack happened to supply, many a congratulation was exchanged between friends, and many an incident of the evening recounted. And there were few who did not, with grateful hearts, silently look up to Him who had given them the victory, and who had

---

83 Maxwell, *Sketches*
84 Oman, *History Vol. VII*

protected them in the execution of their duty. But, overcome with fatigue, it was not long before conversation began to flag; the various sounds of the bivouack gradually died away...Such was the action of Garris.[85]

Next morning, Hill's columns crossed the Bidouze at Saint-Palais; Harispe fell back again, beyond the Saison to Rivareyte. As during the advance to Vitoria, where Jack had been part of the outflanking column under Graham, Hill's outflanking of successive potential defensive positions forced Soult to retreat. Now, he had to abandon the line of the Bidouze and try to establish a new one behind the Saison. But that river was too long to be credibly defended by the four French divisions available. Just as Wellington wanted, Soult took units from around Bayonne to fill the gaps, leaving only a single division of regular troops, plus an inexperienced garrison, in Bayonne. Hill's men marched eastwards again on the morning of the 17th. Lecor's Division passed through Domezain heading for the bridge at Rivareyte. The 2nd Division got there first and plunged straight across the cold, deep fords. The bridge was captured with minimal resistance and Harispe withdrew yet again, to the Gave d'Oloron, around Sauveterre. Wellington's objective of pushing Soult and the bulk of his army well away from Bayonne now achieved, the allies stopped and consolidated. This puzzled Soult, who did not know that Wellington was planning another masterstroke. Riding back to Bayonne, the allied commander finally gave orders for the allies to cross the Adour. A line of small boats was strung across the river west of the city, where the French did not expect it; the move was almost unopposed. By the 27th, having stormed the suburb of St. Étienne, Wellington's army surrounded Bayonne; 15,000 allies were north of the Adour, 16,000 south. Wellington returned his attention to Soult.

The French line stretched north-westwards along the Gave d'Oloron from Sauveterre to Peyrehorade. At about 15 miles long, troops from one end could not easily reinforce the other. Wellington also had the attacker's advantage of determining where and when he would strike. He opted to reinforce his previous tactics, temporarily adding the 6th and Light Divisions to Hill's command, whose task would again be to turn the French left flank, still held by Harispe, by fording the Gave to his south. Beresford, now with just the 4th and 7th Divisions, would meanwhile demonstrate against the French line further downstream, holding them in place. On 24 February Hill's columns

---

85 Maxwell, *Sketches*

crossed the Gave at numerous points; some five divisions of infantry were opposed by a brigade of French light cavalry and two infantry battalions; they 'walked across the Gave with practically no loss'.[86] Jack and his regiment crossed via a pontoon bridge at Viellenave.

Soult ordered his entire army to retreat towards Orthez, concentrating his army west of the town, with his left anchored on it. Wellington reversed his tactics; he reinforced Beresford, on the allied left, ready to attack Soult's right. On the 26th, Hill took the 2nd and Portuguese Divisions with some cavalry forward from their camps around the village of Loubieng to occupy high ground on the south bank of the Gave de Pau overlooking the village of Départ and Orthez itself across the river. He was ordered the next day to throw his men across fords east of the town and get behind the French army. Early on 27 February Beresford's divisions attacked Soult's army on the hills northwest of Orthez. Hill ordered Buchan meanwhile to move his brigade against the 14th Century towered bridge across the Gave de Pau which enters Orthez from the south. Buchan's orders were 'to attempt to penetrate into the town of Orthez by the bridge, which the enemy had but imperfectly destroyed.'[87] But it was impossible to comply; the river there was unfordable; the barricades and fortifications were strong; and the whole area was strongly defended. Harispe's entire division was stationed in and immediately behind the town; even if Buchan had found a way through the defences on the bridge, his brigade would have had a tough street-by-street fight on its hands. As one officer who was there put it: 'There was a very handsome old bridge across the river at the town, fortified and mined. Above and below the bridge it was deep, and full of jagged rocks, and altogether a very formidable and dangerous place to run one's nose into without leave'.[88] It seems likely that Buchan concluded that pressing an attack on the bridge would pointlessly waste his men's lives, not least as his real job was to distract Harispe's defenders while the rest of Hill's column moved east to cross the river at fords upstream. Buchan's men therefore 'bickered across the river with Harispe's detachment in Orthez all the morning'.[89]

---

86 Oman, *History Vol. VII*
87 *Wellington Supplementary Despatches*. Wellington's *Memorandum of the Movement of the Troops in the Attack of the Enemy at Orthez on the 27th Feb., 1814*. Fortescue says 'The ancient bridge had been mined by Soult, but the masonry was so strong that only an insignificant breach had been made in it'. Fortescue, *History* Vol. IX
88 Bell, *Rough Notes*
89 Oman, *History Vol. VII*

The main fight, by Beresford's wing, was hard going. Soult's position was strong and he had broadly similar numbers at hand to Wellington. The sounds of battle carried to Hill's column: 'The cannonade and flashing of small-arms had now begun in earnest to echo down the river, through the town, and over the hills - all was in full play about nine o'clock, and continued all the day'.[90] But Buchan's diversion at the Orthez bridge meant Hill crossed the fords upriver almost without opposition: by early afternoon the 2nd Division, the rest of the Portuguese Division and the cavalry appeared behind the French lines. Soult again had no choice but to retreat, to avoid being surrounded. As Harispe abandoned Orthez, 'Buchan's brigade, finding the enemy gone, pulled down the obstructions on Orthez bridge, crossed the Gave, and marched up the Sault road, joining in the pursuit of Harispe'.[91] According to Wellington's report, Buchan's men got as far as the village of Sallespisse, about 4 miles from the bridge, before stopping. The main casualty of Buchan's engagement at the bridge may have been the mediaeval structure, itself where the fighting destroyed the parapets, though whether this was by allied artillery fire or French attempts to destroy it is unclear. Jack's 4th Infantry reported no casualties for the entire day, suggesting that taking the bridge was indeed deemed secondary to pinning down Harispe's troops while Hill circumvented them. Wellington told his brother 'we beat Marshal Soult, near Orthez, on the 27th. The action was for some time very warm, but I never saw troops get such a beating as they did; and they were saved at all only by the night'.[92] Officially, he reported 'I cannot estimate the extent of the enemy's loss: we have taken 6 pieces of cannon and a great many prisoners; the numbers I cannot at present report. The whole country is covered with their dead. The [French] army was in the utmost confusion when I last saw it passing the heights near the Sault de Navailles, and many soldiers had thrown away their arms'.[93]

In less than two weeks the allies, usually led by the 2nd and Portuguese Divisions of Hill's right wing, had marched some fifty miles, crossed five rivers, fought two battles and manoeuvred Soult's army away from both Bayonne and Bordeaux. After Orthez 'the infantry was tired out - the men...built large fires on which they frizzled their ration beef, and sank into heavy sleep early. The night was frosty, and the next morning it was a very stiff and rheumatic army which fell slowly into its

90 Bell, *Rough Notes*
91 Oman, *History Vol. VII*
92 *Wellington Supplementary Despatches*. Wellington to Wellesley 1 March 1814
93 *Wellington Despatches*. Wellington to Bathurst 1 March 1814

ranks, after the uncovenanted mercy of a small tot of rum, served out by a thoughtful head-quarters.'[94]

In the cold Jack must have been feeling the injuries he sustained at the Nivelle, but no time was allowed to recover. On 28 February General Hill was ordered to have his column in motion at daybreak, searching for Soult's army, which had reportedly retreated in the direction of Saint-Sever. By the end of that day the 4th Infantry had travelled about ten miles and was at Hagetmau. As they approached the French position on 1 March, their opponents again withdrew. Hill pursued along the southern bank of the Adour as far as Larrivière-Saint-Savin. The next day they continued to follow the river eastwards, the 2nd Division near the bank and the Portuguese Division about a mile further south. At around 2pm they found the French rearguard, under General Clausel, with two divisions drawn up on a wooded ridge behind the river Grave near Aire. Believing the French would again retreat when pressed, Hill did not wait until his full force arrived, sending the lead brigades of both divisions straight in. Barnes' of the 2nd attacked the French right and da Costa's of the Portuguese their centre. Barnes pushed the French back into Aire, but da Costa was repulsed. The day was saved by Barnes turning right and attacking along the ridge while Buchan's brigade arrived and advanced against the centre. When Barnes was reinforced by Byng's brigade, the French centre retreated. Hill was damning about the lack of leadership exhibited by da Costa during the fight and had him removed from command, describing him as 'unfit to command a brigade in combat... The conduct of the Portuguese troops since I had the honor to command some of them, had been so admirably good in all occasions, that you may easily imagine my surprise and distress with what happened on the 2^d, which I expect will not happen again'.[95]

After the combat at Aire, Wellington again halted. Most of his army rested for twelve days, while an expedition of some 12,000 men under Beresford went north to capture Bordeaux. Those left behind could recover from their recent exertions: 'In sixteen days we had marched nearly one hundred miles, passed over five large rivers, forced the enemy before us, captured over a thousand prisoners, six or seven guns, and magazines, and been everywhere victorious; let us now have a little rest to patch up our duds'.[96] But while the allies recovered, so did the French; on 13 March Soult marched his army back towards Hill's two divisions, positioned in the area between Aire and Garlin, ten miles to the south. Soult did no more than push Hill's cavalry pickets back from the river Leéz before Wellington reinforced Hill's line and offered

94 Oman, *History Vol. VII*
95 Gaudêncio and Burnham *Fighting Cocks*
96 Bell, *Rough Notes*

battle on the 15th. But Soult declined and the following day withdrew again. On the 18th the allied advance renewed. Hill, with the 2nd, Portuguese and Morillo's (Spanish) Divisions advanced towards Tarbes, fifty miles away. He was to pursue Soult directly, while the left of the army under Beresford, returned from Bordeaux, tried to cut the French off from Toulouse. Soult left three divisions on the hills beyond Tarbes to try to delay the allies, who reached the outskirts of the town on 20 March. The Light Division of Beresford's wing saw some sharp fighting to the north of the town, but the only delay Hill encountered was moving through the tortuous streets of Tarbes itself to cross the only nearby bridge over the Adour, which was so narrow that only four men could march abreast. Getting ten brigades across one after the other took a long time but by 4pm, Hill's units were across the bridge and in line. The allied army expected to be ordered to attack, but Wellington demurred. It was late in the day; his troops had been marching for hours and the French position looked strong. Instead, the army bivouacked for the night where they were. Overnight the French slipped away, following the rest of Soult's army.

Soult's delaying tactics worked; the allies could not stop his army reaching Toulouse. Wellington therefore followed him, with Hill's column following the river Garonne via Lannemezan, Monrejeau, Saint-Gaudens, Saint-Martory and Cazéres to Muret, on the outskirts of Toulouse, a total of 90 miles. Hill was cautious, however, as at around 13,000 men his wing was barely half the size of the army he was pursuing. The going was tough; the weather was poor and the roads worse. Hill took his time: almost a week to reach Muret from Tarbes; Soult, hurrying, got his army all the way to Toulouse in four days. Wellington knew taking Toulouse would be difficult; the town was surrounded by rivers and the allies would need to cross at least the broad and fast-flowing Garonne to be able to attack it. The first attempt was on 30 March, via a pontoon laid upriver at Pinsaguel, where the Garonne was narrower. Hill got his wing across, but was then unable also to cross the Arriege, which flowed into the Adour before Toulouse. The next day Hill withdrew his troops back to Muret. It would take Wellington over a week before he was finally able to get into position and attack Toulouse, but Jack had no part in that action. At around the time that he led the 4th Infantry across the Garonne and back, Lieutenant-Colonel Richard Armstrong finally arrived to take command of the regiment, sufficiently recovered from the wounds he received at Sorauren to assume the role Beresford had given him six months before. Jack's *agregado* status gave him no choice but to hand over command to Armstong. He could have stayed on with the 4th Infantry in a supporting role, but aside from the sense of demotion that implied, the injury he had received at the Nivelle was now so troublesome that, as he later wrote:

I took the opportunity of getting medical assistance, in consequence of my horse falling with me in the battle of the 10th Nov. (Nivelle), and was forced to undergo two surgical operations.[97]

According to Portuguese archival documents Jack officially started leave from the 4th Infantry on 29 April 1814, but he is not listed as being with them at the battle of Toulouse on 10 April. Nor did he list that action in his 1816 *Statement of Services*, which says he was superseded 'on the army arriving near Toulouse'. It seems likely therefore that soon after Armstrong appeared Jack went to the rear to have his injury assessed. The 29th was probably the date he was authorised to take leave of absence for the recommended surgery. The fighting was, in any case, finished by then. Wellington received news that the allies had entered Paris, and that Napoleon had abdicated on 11th April. The battle of Toulouse had been fought unnecessarily, though neither commander knew it. When Soult confirmed the news from Paris, the two sides signed a convention to suspend hostilities on the 19th.

There is unfortunately no record of what the two surgical operations Jack underwent were, nor where they happened. It is possible that he returned to Britain for the treatment; the facilities there were better, and he could recuperate more readily. Voluntary surgery at a time without anaesthetics or antibiotics was a painful and risky endeavour, so Jack must have been clear that he could not continue to bear whatever problems his injuries were causing. Assuming he returned to Britain, Jack would certainly have recuperated in Hennock alongside his family; he had been away from home for six years, since the 23rd embarked for Nova Scotia in January 1808. It was a significant day when the Hills were reunited with their firstborn son, though William and Fred were both still away at sea. A few months later there was more good news; Fred Hill passed his Royal Navy lieutenant's exam. Perhaps Ellis' letter on his behalf to Admiral Warren helped. By the time Jack left France, the rumours must have been strong that the rest of the British army would soon follow. Within a couple of months British, Portuguese, Spanish and German soldiers said their farewells to each other and to the Peninsular War. The comradeship between the British and Portuguese, who had fought alongside each other for so long, was

---

97 Hill 1816 *Statement of Services*

particularly strong. The Portuguese army had earned a well-deserved reputation with the British, though both were less enamoured with their Spanish allies: 'The Portuguese army was always well and gallantly led, fought well, and ranked next to the English troops in all ways…with an esprit de corps not so well understood amongst the Españoles. There was more genuine heroic pride amongst the ladies of Spain than in the ranks of the[ir] army.'[98] Jack would have agreed with this sentiment: immense pride in the men of the 5th Caçadores and 4th Infantry he had led, but as he had put it himself 'a little tinctured' by 'the antipathy the Portuguese have for the Spaniards'. Many of those Jack commanded would continue to serve their country, but political events in Portugal after 1820 tore the army apart; some who were brothers in arms in 1814 sadly became enemies in the civil wars that ravaged their country in the following years and that only ended in 1850.

Most battalions now travelled back to their home countries, but some of the British were shipped across the Atlantic, where war with America continued. They included fellow Fusiliers the 7th Foot, and General Edward Packenham. Packenham was killed at the battle of New Orleans, which like Toulouse took place after peace was agreed, but before those at the front knew. The Royal Welch Fusiliers were lucky not to be earmarked for this duty or a different overseas tour; they marched to Pauillac and on 14 June embarked for Plymouth, where they arrived on the 25th. They marched to Ivybridge on 5 July and then on to Dorchester, eventually arriving in Gosport, their base for the next nine months.   Their route of march took them close to Hennock; assuming he was not completely immobilised from his operations, it is impossible to imagine that Jack and others of the Hill family did not ride down to greet them as large numbers turned out to welcome the victorious army home. 'Every Regiment that landed was cheered, fed and regaled as though each man of it were some illustrious hero, until it seemed like dreamland to the poor fellows after having had years of fighting and starving and marching in inhospitable climes… in almost every town they passed through they were treated to as much meat and drink as they could use by their fellow countrymen.'[99]

Jack sensibly spent the rest of 1814 formally still in Portuguese Service, not resigning from the 4th Infantry until 13 December. He was far from the only British officer to do so, despite the end of the war. There was good reason for lingering: peace would inevitably bring reductions to the British army and half pay for

98 Bell, *Rough Notes*
99 Crook, *Bentinck*

officers who did not have a post in a British regiment to revert to. Those lucky enough to rejoin their British regiments would mostly resume lower rank than they enjoyed in Portuguese service, while keeping higher rank for as long as possible meant higher (and double) pay. While waiting for his immediate future to be determined, Jack probably looked back on his time in the Portuguese army with mixed feelings. He had transferred from the 23rd in mid-1811 because that was a route to promotion; the prospects of a majority within the regiment for its third most senior captain were slim - there was little likelihood of Ellis or enough majors departing to open positions for him. Purchasing a majority in another regiment was not an option he could afford himself and he would not have wanted his father to bear the cost. While he obtained the majority he sought, and later a brevet lieutenant-colonelcy, ironically if he had stayed in the 23rd a little longer, events conspired to completely change the situation, following the unforeseeable deaths and departures of so many above him. Yet if he had stayed, he may have been seriously wounded or lost his life, as many colleagues who remained with the Old Welch did. Ellis, his guiding star, soon ensured he gained a formal appointment as major in 2/23rd, even though Wellington's rules on experienced officers staying with the army meant he never physically filled the role. Whether or not he felt he had jumped to Portuguese service prematurely, he certainly found the camaraderie in his new role less attractive: 'Our society in this brigade is imperfect indeed' as he wrote in February 1813. Meanwhile, relations with McCreagh and Bradford deteriorated to the point that he left the 5th Caçadores in bad humour. It is not clear what caused this, though like many officers of the Fusilier Brigade, Jack believed Beresford had not properly recognised the Fusiliers' efforts at Albuera; it would not be surprising if he shared these views and caused friction. Maybe it was simply a personality clash. That said, he was proud to have led his two Portuguese units through difficult campaigns and numerous fights. While not getting the recognition he felt he deserved with the 5th Caçadores, he made up for that in command of the 4th Infantry. But even then, the good relationships he had built there, including with Buchan and Lecor, counted for nothing when Armstrong took command. By the end of 1814 though the future must have looked brighter. He was back in Britain, reunited with his family, recovering from his operations and about to rejoin the 23rd as the junior of Ellis' two majors. Thomas Dalmer, who had overtaken Jack by purchasing his majority in 1807, was the senior major. The long wars with France were over, Napoleon was exiled to the Mediterranean island of Elba and Europe was at peace.

'the 4th Portuguese Regt. were ordered to secure a hill on the extreme right over the Adour, which the enemy had taken; this post was retaken and maintained'. The memorial on the Croix de Mouguerre, the hill that Jack and the 4th Portuguese Infantry helped recapture during the battle of St. Pierre. The monument commemorates Marshal Soult's defence of France in 1813-14, not the allied victory in the battle

'Thank God the point is a little better' The prayer book which Jack carried at Waterloo. (Phillip Hill)

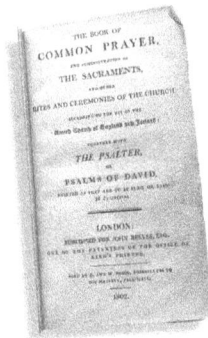

'The four and three quarter ball (iron grape) entered under the collar bone and came out through the blade bone behind.' The piece of heavy case shot which passed through Jack's shoulder at Waterloo, mounted on a base of metal taken from HMS Victory. The shot is approximately 42mm in diameter (Phillip Hill)

'This Gallant Officer': The memorial to Jack Hill in St. Mary's, Hennock

'Remember me to all, and believe me ever yours':
The Hill family vault, St. Mary's church. Hennock

'one of the finest young men in the Army': Henry Ellis, who at various times was Jack's room-mate, colleague and commanding officer (RWF Museum)

'Col. Pearson of the 23rd is extremely anxious to secure to that Regt. the Services of Capt. England as Major vice Hill'. Thomas Pearson, whose manoeuvres with Horse Guards heralded the end of Jack's army career (RWF Museum)

'present in every Field (except Minden) borne on the colours of the 23rd Regt': Jack's medals in the Royal Welch Fusiliers Museum, Caernarfon. From left to right, the Order of the Bath, Peninsular Gold Medal, Peninsular Gold Cross, Waterloo Medal, Order of the Grand Seignior of Turkey (RWF Museum)

'*once entered into a Regiment necessity forces the officers to go where it is ordered*': Another portrait of Jack Hill, possibly painted in Paris in 1816 or 1817 *(Phillip Hill)*

CHAPTER 14

THE LAST BATTLE

'horse killed and was hit in four places...an half-pound shot
struck on the left breast immediately below the collar bone and
pass'd out behind through the shoulder blade.'

Memorandum to the Duke of York, 1823

The army settled back into barracks in Britain. Those who had
commanded regiments 'under musketry' in the most recent battles
received medals; on 20 August 1814 Jack was sent awards for
St. Sebastián and the Nivelle. As he already held the Army Gold Medal
for Salamanca, these took the form of two bars, one battle named on
each, to be worn on the ribbon of that medal. There was no such
recognition for more junior officers, NCOs or rankers who had fought in
the war. Henry Ellis therefore arranged, and presumably paid for, silver
regimental medals to be issued to each man of the 23rd who had served
and survived. The medal listed each battle the recipient fought in, not just
on the Peninsula, but all Napoleonic battles the regiment had been in,
including Egypt, Copenhagen and Martinique. There were also new
honours to be added to the Regimental Colours: 'Peninsula', 'Albuhera',
'Badajoz', 'Salamanca', 'Vittoria', 'Pyrenees', 'Nivelle', 'Orthes', and
'Toulouse'. Jack was one of the few who had been at all the individually
named battles, albeit with the Portuguese army in most cases.

Medals and honours were welcome, but peace meant uncertainty
for soldiers. The British army was as large as it had ever been; even with
needing to protect colonies around the world it was unsustainably
sized. The government announced the abolition of 2nd Battalions;
2/23rd formally disbanded on 24 October. A few men deemed 'unfit'
were discharged and the most junior officers at each rank above
complemented numbers placed on half-pay; the rest joined the
remaining battalion, raising its strength to 1,197 NCOs and men. The
now single-battalion 23rd Foot was commanded by Henry Ellis,
promoted brevet colonel in June 1814 and knighted in January 1815.
Ellis was highly respected and, having been wounded in action no less
than eight times, lucky to be alive. The majors were Thomas Dalmer

and Jack Hill. Dalmer had sometimes been with 2/23rd, including as its last commander; he had seen marginally less action than Jack, but both were highly experienced and were brevet Lieutenant-Colonels in the army. As the autumn of 1814 came around, Ellis granted leave to every soldier that had been with the 1st Battalion when it sailed to Nova Scotia in 1808. Dalmer was not one of those, so assumed acting command while Ellis himself was away.

As the veterans enjoyed their leave and their less fortunate colleagues whiled away the days in barracks at Gosport, the leaders of Europe, the now Duke of Wellington amongst them, argued out the political settlement of the war at the Congress of Vienna. After many disagreements, offers and counteroffers, not to mention numerous balls and other entertainments, the outline of a deal was close when, on 26 February 1815, Napoleon escaped from Elba. Opportunistically capitalising on discontent and unrest in France, especially among his former soldiers, he generated such momentum on his march to Paris that he was restored to power on 20 March. The Emperor proclaimed his desire for peace, but Austria, Russia, Prussia and Britain declared him an outlaw and gathered their armies. While hoping to avoid war, Wellington, who considered 'Bony's conduct...very extraordinary' forecast that if fighting resumed 'the affair will be a serious one, and a great and immediate effort must be made.'[1] The four major allies had previously agreed to retain some 75,000 men each in central Europe until the Congress of Vienna concluded, though the need to send troops to North America meant Britain did not achieve this. Wellington was sent to command a 36,000 strong British, German and Dutch-Belgian army that had been based in the newly independent Netherlands since the end of the war. They were mostly not his Peninsular veterans, many of whom were in America. Wellington called it 'an infamous army, very weak and ill equipped'. He told the British government to 'reinforce the army in the Netherlands as much as you can' with more and better quality troops.[2]

Those reinforcements included the 23rd Foot. Leaving a detachment at Gosport, on 23 March with 'bands playing, colours waving and people cheering' forty-two officers, thirty-one sergeants, twenty-four drummers, thirty-six corporals and 611 privates embarked on the transports *Ariel, Percival and Poniana*, and on the 25th sailed for the Downs.[3] They took with them the Colours of the former 2nd Battalion, as Ellis decided those the 1st Battalion had carried through the

1 *Wellington Dispatches.* Wellington to Bughersh 13 March 1815, Wellington to Castlereagh 12 March 1815
2 *Wellington Dispatches.* Wellington to Castlereagh 18 March 1815
3 Crook, *Bentinck*

Peninsular war were in unfit state. Inevitably, they found bad weather; Lieutenant John Macdonald recalled: 'it came on to blow a tremendous gale of wind which lasted for two days, several ships parted their anchors thus were obliged to cut their masts to prevent running on the Goodwin sands, our ship drifted a considerable distance but a third anchor brought her up again, and we rode it pretty well, but you may easily conceive our happy situation for we had twenty officers packed together in one little cabin, the greatest part of course quite sick, and not able to go on deck, much less ashore, from the violence of the wind and rain, on the 29th we were put on board small sloops that carried about 50 or 60 men each and had a beautiful passage to Ostend'.[4] They arrived the next day. Jack, however, had gone ahead with a detachment to identify suitable quarters and supplies for the battalion; he had also endured another of his traditional bad sea crossings.

29 March [1815]
[Ostend]

My Dear Father,
    We arriv'd here two days since & were march'd near Nieuport, & are returning here on our way to Bruges - how much farther I cannot say. The rest of the Rgt. is not arriv'd nor my horses - I will go & see where I was put in march as a prisoner 17 years since. A variety of reports afloat - the King of France here & all the John Bulls running away as fast as possible, France is certainly divided in which case we shall get on finely - Bonaparte & his fiends must be swept from the face of the earth before the will [evaporates?].
    Excuse this short epistle but I want to relieve you of any anxiety in consequence of the very bad weather - some boats are missing but I think they are blown more on the Holland coast - remember me to Mr. Ley & Caroline, Mr W. and all our family unit. I am up to my ears in business to equip the people for a campaign.
    You will have heard of me from Wm. I hope he & the dog got home safe - my servant with all my keys on is with the Rgt.

Your most affectionate
J Hill

---

4 RWF Museum Object No. 5935. MacDonald letter of 3rd April 1815

Jack's military career had come full circle. Ostend was where he first saw action in 1798. Back after 17 years, he did not know that he would soon face his last battle.

Flanders was full of rumour. John MacDonald also noted opinion on Napoleon's return: 'We found every body at Ostend in great consternation, rumour said that a French army were on their march to attack it and the authorities feared Bonaparte had an organised corps in every town in Flanders. They were to assist his designs in making the Rhine the boundary of his Empire. There was a diligent search for spies at Ostend the night we landed but though every body knew they were numerous still they could not be made out, the public opinion here now appears to me much against him, (though still in favour of the French nation) as the spirited conduct of the Allies, and the fear of such immense forces as are collecting with the assistance of the mass of the French people who are decidedly against him, leaves but a sparse chance of his remaining long on the throne'.[5] On the 31st the regiment moved to Bruges, no doubt pleased that rather than marching they travelled via water, even if Macdonald called their transports 'large clumsy boats on a beautiful canal'. From Bruges they marched to Ecklo then Ghent, arriving on the afternoon of 2 April. In Ghent they found not everyone submitting to chaos; the dethroned King of France sought to uphold social standards: 'I saw Louis the Eighteenth yesterday and was even at his dinner table! What would Ann give to have been with me to see the Duke de Berrie, Conde d'Artois, but for fear they should doubt my veracity I must inform them that the King and Royal Family always dine in Public at last allowing all Ladies to enter, and yesterday he included all British officers in uniform, Victor, Augeriau, Marmont, Clarke, and a number of other French officers of the first distinction were at the table'.[6] Assuming MacDonald was correct that all British officers were included, we can assume Jack also dined at the King's table. After a few days around Ghent, on the 7th the regiment marched south to Oudenaarde. There, where the regiment had fought under Marlborough over a hundred years earlier, it remained for over a fortnight. When reviewed by Wellington himself on the 20th, the Duke was impressed, writing a few weeks later 'I saw the 23d the other day, and I never saw any regiment in such order. They were not strong, but it was the most complete and handsome military body I ever looked at.'[7]

The 23rd were assigned with 3/14th and the 51st Foot to the 4th Brigade under the command of Colonel Hugh Mitchell. Mitchell's

---

5 RWF Museum Object No. 5935. MacDonald letter of 3rd April 1815
6 RWF Museum Object No. 5935. MacDonald letter of 3rd April 1815
7 *Wellington Dispatches*. Wellington to Cole 2 June 1815

brigade was in turn part of the 4th Division, under Lieutenant-General Sir Charles Colville. The 4th Division was assigned to the right wing of the army, II Corps, commanded by (the now) General Lord Rowland Hill, under whom Jack served in 1814. On 24 April, the regiment moved into cantonments at Grammont (Geraardsbegen). After a week it temporarily moved back west to Renaix, as Hill suggested Colville should consolidate his division in case of a possible French attack in that direction. Colville was pleased to have the 23rd in his division, and called it 'good and strong'; he was less impressed by the climate, reporting to his brother on 5 May 'we had very raw, disagreeable weather for the first week, and to which succeeded very close and warm with thunder and lightning and heavy rain, and it is by no means settled or pleasant'.[8] On 9 May the 23rd returned to Grammont, which Wellington thought a better position either to resist any French attempt to cut off the British from the sea and their route home, or to join the rest of the army in protecting the main roads to Brussels. 'Col. Mitchell's brigade, which I understand is still at Grammont, had better, if the enemy move forward, join the rest of the army at Enghien, or rather Hal, unless it should be found that a serious attack is made upon the country between the Scheldt and the Lys', he told Hill.[9]

The 4th Division remained around Grammont for over a month. Meanwhile in London special recognition was awarded to senior officers who had served in the recent wars:

Whitehall, June 4, 1815

His Royal Highness the Prince Regent, acting in the name and on the behalf of His Majesty, has been graciously pleased to nominate and appoint the undermentioned Officers, belonging to His Majesty's Naval and Military Forces, to be Companions of the Most Honourable Military Order of the Bath.[10]

When eventually published in the *London Gazette*, the list of names ran to four pages. At the bottom of the third page was:

Lieutenant-Colonel J. Humphrey Edward Hill, 23d Foot

That publication did not appear until over three months later, however, and the letters formally informing the recipients individually were not sent

---

8 Colville, *General*
9 *Wellington Dispatches*. Wellington to Hill 9 May 1815
10 *The London Gazette* Saturday, September 16 1815

until a few days after that. While there may have been gossip around the camps at Grammont, Jack may not have known of his membership of the Order until well after the dramatic events the army would soon experience.

Life at Grammont meanwhile was pleasant and complacent, as MacDonald told his sister:

> We are in a delightful, plentiful country here covered with towns and villages & appearing much more like a garden or Gentleman's pleasure grounds in England, than the whole face of a country, we have been some time in Grammond, we have Generals Hill & Vivian, with all their staff, and the 51st and our regiment cantoned in it...we rise every morning at five to exercise the men for the campaign, at eight come home and breakfast, after breakfast take a book from a very good little library in the house and stroll into the garden, here we romp among the groves & banks till you choose to sit and eat fruit, of which there is the greatest abundance, the same as in England, about two, lounge out pay your visits & return at four to dress for dinner at the mess, at seven we generally ride out in the country for an hour or two...thus I have described our every days work, don't you sympathise with what we unfortunate soldiers have to suffer for our country, but then again we have grand races every Tuesday, and seldom a day without some review of eight or ten thousand men, which varies the scene...We speak nothing but French here, we have reports every day about the commencement of the campaign, but nothing certain, today they talk of a skirmish about thirty miles from here, but we are all quiet, and are all going to the races immediately. Deserters come in every day, about thirty have passed this morning, who all say that the French army will not fight against Louis the XVIIIth.[11]

An officer from another of Mitchell's battalions, a young Ensign called George Keppel of 3/14th, recalled 'time hung somewhat heavily on the hands of us officers...a swim across the Dender, or a stroll into Grammont, where we made acquaintances with the 23rd, 51st and 52nd regiments, formed our principal recreations...Races in a grand scale came off at Grammont on the 13th June. There was a strong muster of men of all ranks and of all arms. On that day I completed my sixteenth year, and passed my birthday very pleasantly'.[12] If Keppel made the acquaintance of the junior major of the 23rd Foot, the two might have found they had something in common. Keppel, later the 6th

---

11 RWF Museum Object No. 5935. MacDonald letter of 13th June 1815
12 *Fifty Years of My Life* George Thomas, Earl of Albemarle 1876

Earl of Albemarle, was the great-nephew of Frederick Keppel, the Bishop of Exeter who had ordained Jack's father in September 1773, and two years later appointed him rector of Hennock.

The allies intended to march on Paris, but the Austrian and Russian contingents were not yet close enough for offensive operations to commence. Each would provide significantly bigger armies than the 112,000 mixed-nationality troops under Wellington and the 130,000 Prussians under Field Marshal Gebhard von Blücher. Wellington saw no need to hurry, though: on 13 June he wrote to Jack's former commander in the Peninsula, Thomas Graham, now ennobled as Lord Lynedoch 'There is nothing new here. We have reports of Buonaparte's joining the army and attacking us; but I have accounts from Paris of the 10th, on which day he was still there; and I judge from his speech to the Legislature that his departure was not likely to be immediate. I think we are now too strong for him here.'[13] The intelligence was wrong; across the border, Napoleon knew that if he waited to fight defensively, he would be heavily outnumbered and could not possibly win. Always aggressive, he saw instead an opportunity to drive between Wellington and Blücher and defeat each in detail. If he could do that, he would capture Brussels, the audacity of which might be enough to force the allies to agree a peace deal. In the early morning of 15 June, having collected a mobile force of some 123,000 men, Napoleon took the initiative, crossed the border near Charleroi and split his army, sending separate columns to attack Blücher's Prussians and Wellington's multinational force, hoping to push them away from each other. That day, Wellington was apparently more concerned about the numbering of his divisions than about the risk of attack. Another of Jack's former commanders, Lowry Cole, was on his way to join the army; he and General Thomas Picton pressed Wellington that their divisions should be renumbered to the 4th and the 3rd respectively, the same designation as those they had led on the Peninsula. That Wellington was able to spend time on such trivia as Napoleon crossed the border indicates how unexpected a French advance was.[14]

Wellington responded as soon as he learned the truth. At 5pm on the 15th he sent urgent instructions for his army to consolidate: the 4th division would march immediately towards Enghien. Arriving on the 16th, it soon received orders to continue towards Braine le Comte. It was 'a trying march',[15] around twenty miles since leaving Grammont, much of it through searing heat followed by torrential rain, listening to the sound of artillery fire in the distance as part of Wellington's army met one

13 *Wellington Dispatches*. Wellington to Lynedoch 13 June 1815
14 *Wellington Dispatches*. Wellington to Clinton 15 June 1815
15 Cary and McCance, *Regimental Records*

French column, under Marshal Ney, at Quatre Bras while Napoleon found and defeated the Prussians at Ligny. On arriving at Braine the 4th Division camped for a few hours in a wheatfield before being ordered on again, another ten miles towards Nivelles. Mitchell's Brigade was first to leave. Up to this point, the 23rd had been marching in their lighter, and cooler, white linen forage jackets. Ellis, sensing that there was trouble in store, now ordered them into their red coats. Mitchell's Brigade arrived at Nivelles around the middle of the day on the 17th. As the 23rd's Regimental Records put it this was 'good luck'. As they approached Nivelles they saw wagons carrying wounded from Quatre Bras passing to the rear, but avoiding that fight was not the luck the Fusiliers' historians meant. Because Mitchell's marching had outstripped the rest of the 4th Division, his brigade alone joined the main part of the army. The disappointment of at least some of those in the rest of the division who were further back and did not participate in what followed was summed up by Sir Charles Colville himself, who later wrote 'I was not in the battle. I am not such a fire eater as to think it necessary to say that I have fretted myself at having been unavoidably absent from it, but at the same time am aware that I should have felt a proud satisfaction in being able to inform you of my having shared in the efforts of a day which must be recorded as perhaps the most important in modern history'.[16] History has indeed so labelled what was to happen on 18 June 1815, for the British and Prussian commanders had agreed that their bloodied armies should not move apart but should instead fall back in parallel towards Brussels; crucially, and despite his reverse, Blücher agreed to support Wellington if the latter chose to make a stand. With this commitment, Wellington ordered his army to concentrate on a ridgeline crowned by the farm and hamlet of Mont St. Jean, just south of a small town called Waterloo.

At Nivelles, Mitchell's brigade, now detached from the rest of their own division, caught up with the 2nd Division under Lieutenant-General Sir Henry Clinton and fell in with them, leaving at around 3pm. As they closed on the village of Merbe Braine, about halfway between Braine-l'Alleud and Mont St. Jean, the skies opened again. 'The rain came down in torrents, and in a few moments wetted us to the skin...For about an hour before sunset, the rain that had so persecuted us on our march, relieved us for a time from its unwelcome presence, but as night closed in, it came down again with increased violence, and accompanied by thunder and lightning...I threw myself on the slope of the hill on which I had been standing. It was like lying in a mountain torrent.'[17] The 23rd bivouacked for the night in a field outside Merbe in

---

16 Colville, *General*
17 Albemarle, *Fifty Years*

'torrents of rain, which drenched the unfortunate soldiers, who were lying out in the open, to the skin'.[18] Richard Bentick recalled however that not all were completely exposed: 'We had orders...not to put out our blankets but one or two or three others pulled them out against orders and put them over to keep the rain off. In the morning when the rain gave over we rung them out as well as we could. We put them in our Knapsacks again before any of the Officers saw us.'[19] The weather was not their only discomfort. Bentinck noted 'there was no food to be issued to the men so they were issued with a half liquor ration. It was a very dismal night', adding that as dawn broke:

> Then we began to look out for something to eat as we were all very hungry. We had not had anything for two days. Some of our men chewed the green ears of the young corn. There was a potato field close by and some of the men dug into the field with their fingers and their bayonets. I went to some house close by that the inhabitants had left but I could only find one barrel of thick beer. I drank about a quart of that and it filled my belly for a while for it was both a meal and a drink. As I was coming back to the regiment I happened to look behind me and I saw old Wellington coming behind me with two of his staff. They were coming to the Regiment but I got in as soon as I could and he said nothing to me nor I to him. I had not been back long when we had to fall in and form our lines. The Colonel was to make a speech and encourage the men. He said, "Now the 23rd we are going to have a hot day of it and mind you don't lose your character that you have gained before".[20]

It was going to be a hot day in more ways than Ellis meant. The weather on the morning of 18 June 1815 could not have been more different than that of the night preceding it. 'The day ...seemed to have been chosen by some providential accident for which human wisdom is unable to account. On the morning of the 18th the sun shone most gloriously, and so clear was the atmosphere that we could see the long, imposing lines of the enemy most distinctly'.[21]

Wellington's chosen position was a strong one, about three miles long along the ridge and covering two 'high roads' leading to Brussels. His line was centered on the road that ran directly from Charleroi through Quatre Bras to Brussels. The allied left extended eastwards to a

---

18 Cary and McCance, *Regimental Records*
19 Crook, *Bentinck*
20 Crook, *Bentinck*
21 *Recollections and Anecdotes of the Camp, the Court, and the Clubs* Captain [Rees Howell] Gronow 1877

set of buildings around Papelotte, while the right covered the Nivelles-Brussels road. Wellington thought Napoleon might outflank his right, which is why he had left some 18,000 men including most of Colville's division at Hal (Halle). The Nivelles road also potentially offered a route into his rear. He therefore placed some of his best troops across it. Detachments of Guards and Nassau units occupied a forward outpost, the outbuildings and château of Hougoumont, near the road, with the rest of the 1st (Guards) Division on the ridge behind. The 23rd moved in a column a short distance south from their overnight bivouac and were placed on the same ridge, behind the Guards and with their right touching the Nivelles road. The regiment's light company moved down the hill to help defend Hougoumont but, following his practice during the Peninsular War and with the bulk of Wellington's troops, the 23rd were positioned slightly below the crest of the ridge, where they could not be seen from across the valley to their front. Some officers would certainly have ridden to the crest from time to time to try to see what was going on, or to use the road that ran along it for communications. But for the first part of the day most Royal Welch Fusiliers would be in the disorientating position of hearing the battle but unable to see anything of it. Their vision was hampered initially not only by the hill but also by the tall, thick and wet crops that grew in many of the surrounding fields and in some cases reached as high as their headgear.

Napoleon had drawn up his army along a broadly parallel ridge some 1,000 -1,500 yards to the south. A major objective for him was to avoid the Prussians coming to the relief of the army across the valley. The Emperor had detached a significant force, some 33,000 men, to prevent that happening. As events turned out this was a mistake; the detachment neither impeded Blücher nor was available to Napoleon. As the sun rose on that Sunday morning, though, Napoleon faced his first problem. His army had been filing into position overnight but in the bad weather many had stopped short and were still marching in. The Emperor therefore waited until he had more of his units at hand. The rain of the previous days had also softened the ground so manoeuvering, especially moving cannon into position, was difficult. The delay surprised some of those watching from the allied line: 'There was, I should suppose, hardly any British soldier in the field that morning, who did not understand that we were there, not to give but to receive battle, and who was not surprised that hour after hour should pass away without any indication from the enemy that he intended to pay us a visit' recalled George Keppel.[22] Time was on Wellington's side, but at that point neither commander could be

---

22 Albemarle, *Fifty Years*

sure that the impending battle would not be over well before Blücher arrived. The French deployment was deliberately impressive; Napoleon placed his army in full view; martial music and cheering echoed to the allies on the opposite ridge. Many allied officers stood on their ridge trying to glimpse the man who had dominated Europe for much of their lives; some claimed to have done so, on his white horse across the valley. Cavalry was at both ends of the French line; on their left, directly down the Nivelles road from the 23rd, were the 2nd Cavalry Division under General Hippolyte Piré. In the centre of Piré's Division were the 2nd Company of the 4th Horse Artillery regiment, with four 6-pdr cannon and two 5.5-inch howitzers, commanded by Capitaine Gronier. When Gronier's gunners looked to their front their line of sight followed the Nivelles road, partially sunken as it passed Hougoumont; they were looking directly at where the 23rd Foot stood, just over half a mile away - within effective range of either a round shot from a cannon or an exploding shell from a howitzer.

Few battles of this era have a start time known with certainty; Waterloo is no exception. Some who were there claimed it started as early as 9am, others not until noon or after. Today, most historians accept that the first attacking shots, fired by French artillery, came in late morning, perhaps at around 11.30am. Before then, there had been plenty of gunfire to be heard across the soon-to-be battlefield as soldiers cleaned and tested their muskets, firing them without loading a ball to clear the barrel. The true opening of battle, however, was a French attack on Hougoumont, where the fight would ultimately go on all day, absorbing an ever-increasing part of Napoleon's infantry. Yet it was initially intended only as a diversion, to try to tempt Wellington to send more troops there and weaken the centre of his line at which, some two hours later, the Emperor aimed his entire 1 Corps, some 17,000 infantry. When the huge French force reached the top of the allied ridge, however, they were swept away by a massed advance of the British Union and Household cavalry brigades. None of these major features of the battle involved Jack and the 23rd, and yet the regiment was steadily accumulating casualties. Being on the reverse slope offered some protection, but balls that overshot the top of the ridge, either deliberately or accidentally, remained a threat. A man of the 51st, positioned to the right of the 23rd, recalled 'On the hill behind us was posted some 20 or 30 guns blazing away over our heads at the enemy. The enemy on their side with a battery of much the same force were returning the compliment, grape and shells were dupping about us like hail, this was devilish annoying.'[23] There was also the matter of

---

23 Wheeler, *Letters*

Gronier's gunners who had been targeting them and the rest of Mitchell's brigade along the Nivelles road. Keppel recalled: 'Fifteen years after the battle I was present at Paris…A French officer on duty entered upon a subject of his own choosing, but one generally avoided by his countrymen - "Waterloo." He told me that he was an artillery officer posted on the extreme left of the French line, and that his orders were to fire upon three British regiments the colours of which were respectively blue [23rd], buff [14th], and green [51st], thus proving, beyond all doubt, that it was against our brigade that his practice had been directed.'[24] To reduce the impact of the artillery, Lieutenant Robert Holmes of the 23rd's No. 8 Company recalled 'the Regiment deployed in line and lay on the ground, in consequence of the French having placed some Guns on the Nivelles road which killed one of our Captains and wounded some men.'[25] The captain may have been Holmes' own, as Captain Charles Jolliffe was killed while commanding No. 8 Company during the battle; his memorial notes that he was killed after being 'stuck by a shell'.[26]

By early afternoon more of the Guards had moved down the ridge to reinforce Hougoumont. At probably between 2 and 3pm Ellis 'perceiving an opening where his regiment might be employed with advantage'[27] ordered his men forward to help fill the gap in the allied front line the Guards had left, alongside several battalions of Brunswick infantry.[28] In the Brunswicker's ranks was Friedrich von Wacholtz, who had been in the light company square Jack led at Albuera, but this was no time to exchange greetings between former comrades. It may have been at around this time that Jack carried a message from the battalion. We do not know what the message was or who it was for; perhaps Ellis sent him to inform Clinton, under whose command the 4th Brigade were operating in the absence of Colville, of the regiment's movement. Jack later recorded that his horse, Honesty, 'carried me beautifully when [I was] sent on a message through a rye field seven feet high'.[29] Ellis' move of his regiment into the gap left by the Guards was the typically bold initiative of a man who had demonstrated his personal

---

24 Albemarle, *Fifty Years*
25 *Waterloo Letters* Major-General H. T. Siborne, 1891. Holmes joined 2/23rd as a 2nd Lieutenant in 1811, joining 1/23rd later that year in the Peninsula.
26 Jollife joined the 23rd in September 1805.
27 Cannon, *History of the Twenty-Third*
28 Fortescue says 'the Twenty-third from Mitchell's brigade was posted in the middle of the Brunswickers to give them the countenance of a veteran regiment', though gives no source for this precise positioning, which would place the 23rd towards the centre of Wellington's right. *History* Volume X
29 The horse's name no doubt had the obvious meaning, but may also have been named after the flowers of the mustard family that grow around Hennock in springtime.

courage repeatedly, but it was would have significant consequences: in solidifying the line Ellis moved his Fusiliers into danger.

As the 23rd adopted their new position, the fight around Hougoumont continued but there was something of a lull on their part of the field. Across the valley, however, French cavalry was seen to be forming; on the order 'prepare to receive cavalry' the allied battalions formed into squares. With bayonets fixed and front ranks kneeling, a static infantry square presented an unbroken hedge of spikes that no horse would willingly go near, coupled with a mass of firepower that could be lethal to anything within range. It also reinforced the men's confidence; touching shoulders with each other instilled reassurance in the face of what was coming. The company NCOs and officers stood immediately behind their men, while the field officers - for the 23rd Ellis, Dalmer and Jack - were on horseback in the centre of the square, near the colours and easily able to command and encourage their troops. At around 4pm a first wave of more than 4,000 French horsemen launched themselves at the allied lines between the two high roads. The magnificent scene burned into the memory of those who witnessed it: 'not a man present who survived could have forgotten in after life the awful grandeur of that charge. You perceived at a distance what appeared to be an overwhelming, long moving line, which, ever advancing, glittered like a stormy wave of the sea when it catches the sunlight. On came the mounted host until they got near enough, whilst the very earth seemed to vibrate beneath their thundering tramp. One might suppose that nothing could have resisted the shock of this terrible moving mass'.[30] But the squares did resist, they almost always did when the men kept their discipline. In the gaps between the squares was allied artillery, under orders to wait until the last moment before the gunners sought refuge in the squares or under their guns. One battery near the 23rd was Captain Cavalié Mercer's troop of the Royal Horse Artillery. Mercer later recalled:

I saw through the smoke the leading squadrons of the advancing column coming on at a brisk trot, and already not more than one hundred yards distant, if so much, for I don't think we could have seen so far. I immediately ordered the line to be formed for action - case-shot...The very first round, I saw, brought down several men and horses. They continued, however, to advance...the remaining guns as they rapidly succeeded in coming to action, making terrible slaughter, and in an instant covering the ground with men and horses. Still they persevered in approaching us (the first round had

---

30 Gronow, *Recollections*

brought them to a walk), though slowly, and it did seem they would ride over us...At last the rear of the column, wheeling about, opened a passage, and the whole swept away at a much more rapid pace than they had advanced, nor stopped until the swell of the ground covered them from our fire.[31]

The left of the first wave of French cavalry passed Mercer's guns and to the left of the 23rd's square. Mercer described them as 'very fine troops, clothed in blue uniforms without facings, cuffs, or collars. Broad, very broad buff belts, and huge muff caps, made them appear gigantic fellows.' They were the Chasseurs à Cheval of the Imperial Guard. Failing to have any impact on the squares they turned about and made their way back down the slope to regroup, having taken musket and cannon fire in both directions. There was a brief lull before another cavalry wave appeared, with different horsemen, but the same result. The cavalry attacks continued for some two hours; there is no consensus on how many waves there were over this period, though there were certainly at least two large and numerous smaller ones. One French source claims 'more than ten times they launched themselves on the English, and despite the fire, they reached their bayonets'.[32] A more recent history of the battle goes as high as sixteen.[33] The attacks involved every type of mounted soldier of the age - Curassiers, Lancers, Hussars, Dragoons, Chasseurs, Carabineers, Grenadiers à Cheval and even the Gendarmes d'Elite, the military police of the Imperial Guard. One of the 23rd's soldiers, Private Thomas Jeremiah, later recalled: 'The trembling of the Earth announced the Coming Charge...the flanks of the Columns of attack reached our own Regt. Whose iron ranks stood so firm as although they might kill us they could never Daunt us, at this trying moment our brave Colonel told us to be steady and wait well for his word of command which was strictly obeyed until they were within 30 or 40 paces of us then we opened a most Destructive fire which staggered their advancing Columns'.[34] Another recalled 'As they came thundering up, apparently determined to sweep the squares from before them, their defeat, as they recoiled from the deadly volleys, resembled a heavy sea pouring itself upon a chain of immovable rocks and then driven back. And amid all the tumult of this desperate action

---

31 *Journal of the Waterloo Campaign* Cavalié Mercer 1985
32 *Carnet de Campagne (1793-1815)* Colonel Tefcon 2003, quoted in *Waterloo: The Decisive Victory* Nick Lipscombe [ed.] 2014
33 *A Desperate Business: Wellington, the British Army and the Waterloo Campaign* Ian Fletcher 2001
34 The National Library of Wales MS 22102A; Autobiography of Private Thomas Jeremiah of the 23rd Regiment of Royal Welch Fusiliers (c.1837)

- the discharge of the artillery - the clash of arms - the shouts of the infuriated combatants - the groans and the shrieks of the wounded and the dying - the men behaved as on parade. In vain did desperate heroes among the French cavalry discharge their carbines and pistols at the squares to induce them to break the ranks.'[35] The successive French cavalry attacks surrounding the allied squares on the ridge at Waterloo has become an enduring image of the battle, and to an extent of the entire Napoleonic war. On the day itself, the courage and determination shown on both sides was recognised by those who were there:

> I am at a loss which to admire most, the cool intrepid courage of our squares, exposed as they often were to a most destructive fire from the French Artillery and at the same time or in less than a minute surrounded on all sides by the enemy's Heavey [sic] Cavalry, who would ride up to the very muzzles of our men's firelocks and cut at them in the squares. But this was of no use, not a single square could they break, but was always put to rout, by the steady fire of our troopes [sic]. In one of those made by the enemy a great many over charged themselves and could not get back without exposing themselves to the deadly fire of the infantry. Not choosing to return by the way they came they took a circuitous route and came down the road on our left [i.e between the 51st and the 23rd]. There were nearly one hundred of them, all Cuirassieurs [sic]. Down they rode full gallop, the trees thrown across the bridge on our left stopped them. We saw them coming and was prepared, we opened our fire, the work was done in an instant. By the time we had loaded and the smoke had cleared away, one and only one, solitary individual was seen running over the brow in our front…I went to see what effect our fire had, and never before beheld such a sight in as short a space, as about an hundred men and horses could be huddled together, there they lay.[36]

The initial cavalry attacks were imposing, but with each successive effort the horses and riders tired and the ground became more churned up, covered in dead and wounded men and horses and discarded equipment from previous attempts. The last few 'waves' were more bedraggled smaller groups of riders trotting or even walking to the attack. Wellington himself recalled: 'I had the infantry for some time in squares, and we had the French cavalry walking about us as if they were our own. I never saw the British infantry behave so well.'[37] If the

---

35 Crook, *Bentinck*
36 Wheeler, *Letters*
37 *Wellington Dispatches*. Wellington to Beresford 2 July 1815

cavalry was ineffective, however, the horse artillery that accompanied them was not. Infantry in squares was an attractive target for artillery who, as the cavalrymen withdrew to regroup, were now close enough to be able to fire case shot, cannisters filled with projectiles that ranged in size from musket balls to iron shot as big as a golf ball.[38] These spread from the muzzle on firing like projectiles from a shotgun, potentially killing or wounding across a wide area. As the 23rd suffered, Ellis called out to encourage his men: 'while our brave and beloved Colonel was reminding us of our former Exploits on the peninsula he received his Mortal wound just as he saw his commands obeyed'.[39] Ellis, mounted on his horse on the centre of the 23rd's square, had been 'struck with a musket ball in the right breast. Feeling himself faint from loss of blood, he calmly desired an opening might be made in the square, and rode to the rear. At a short distance from the field he was thrown from his horse while in the act of leaping a ditch; here he was found soon afterwards, much exhausted'.[40] Thomas Dalmer assumed acting command of the battalion with Jack, who had probably by now already had a near miss when a bullet grazed his left jaw, as his second in command. Their first job was to steady the regiment, who had seen Ellis fall: 'it required all of the attention of our own officers to restrain our Men for they were Burning with revenge for the loss of their Most

---

38 Soldiers of the day, from Napoleon downwards, universally called this 'grape shot', a name derived from early versions whose loose balls contained in cloth resembled a bunch of grapes. By the time of Waterloo, while a form of grape shot was still in naval use, land artillery rounds comprising shot in a container was properly called case or cannister, which came in 'light' (filled with musket balls) and 'heavy' (larger, golf ball-sized) variants.

39 Jeremiah *Autobiography*

40 Cannon, *History of the Twenty-Third*. The official records of the 23rd say Ellis was struck by a musket ball, as does the inscription on his memorial in Worcester Cathedral. It is possible this was a stray shot from near Hougoumont, though the range would be extreme. It could have been a ball from a pistol or carbine fired by a French cavalryman, for whom a mounted senior officer would be an attractive target. Fortescue claims (*History* Volume X) that French cavalrymen engaged squares with their pistols, though he calls this 'fruitless'. John McDonald wrote to his family 'We lost our gallant Colonel in the action of the 18th...we had repulsed two charges from the French cavalry and regiment being in square, when we observed a regiment of the Chasseurs of the Imperial Guard and making direct for us, our men remained steady as rocks and drove them back again with immense loss, but the poor colonel received a ball which finished his mortal career two days afterwards, he is universally regretted in the army'. The *Waterloo Roll Call* also says Ellis was hit 'in the breast, by a shot from a carbine'. Bentinck's recollection on the other hand was that 'a grape shot [sic] had stuck him in the breast', though it is not impossible that he was mixing up Ellis' wounding with Jack's.

Beloved Commander who had in so Many actions led the Regt. to Victory' said Jeremiah.[41]

As the cavalry attacks ended, at perhaps around 6pm, the artillery resumed. Jack dismounted and walked around the inside of the square, encouraging the men. After a while, he returned to his horse, in the middle of the square, to collect something from his saddle bags. As he was doing so, he had another near miss as a ball hit a cloak strapped across the front of Honesty's saddle. This may have been a piece of case shot from a French cannon, or a lucky musket shot by one of the French skirmishers who had managed to get as far as the eastern hedge of Hougoumont and were targeting the squares. Jack stepped back to see if Honesty had been hit, but both man and beast were unharmed. After muttering a few words to comfort the horse, Jack walked to the front face of the square. Despite the smoke that covered the field, he had identified a potential target and wanted to direct the men's fire on it. What Jack may have seen was the next French infantry advance, by two columns led by Lieutenant-General Bachelu and General Maximilien Foy, which advanced from their position near Hougoumont directly towards where the 23rd waited, still in square. This attack was quickly repulsed and, squeezed as it was between the dramas of the massed cavalry attacks and the later advance by the Imperial Guard, is sometimes unmentioned in summaries of Waterloo. But that the French infantry came to within musket range of the allied line is confirmed by Foy himself, who was wounded in the attack:

> I kept my left flank at the hedge [of the Hougoumont orchard]. In front of me I had a battalion deployed as skirmishers. When we were about to meet the English, we received a very lively fire of canister and musketry. It was a hail of death. The enemy squares had the front rank kneeling and presenting a hedge of bayonets. The columns of Bachelu's division fled first and their flight precipitated the flight of my columns. At this moment I was wounded.[42]

At about the same time as Foy was hit, Jack pushed through the closely formed front ranks of the square. As he did, an incoming round struck the head of a soldier next to him, showering Jack with part of the man's skull; a splinter hit near his eye. The posthumous Statement of Services later written by his son states that the unfortunate man was a 'Covering Sergeant'; if this is correct it may have been Sergeant-Major David

---

41 Jeremiah *Autobiography*
42 *Vie Militaire du General Foy* Maurice Girod de l'Ain 1900

Morrissey who was seriously wounded in the battle, dying the next day.[43] Jack was also struck in the face by stone fragments, possibly thrown up by a shell exploding nearby. The 23rd were receiving a serious bombardment: Holmes recalled that the battalion 'were suffering both from the French Guns and the fire from the garden of Hougoumont'.[44] The incoming rounds were taking their toll; there was no choice but to absorb it. 'Standing to be cannonaded, and having nothing else to do, is about the most unpleasant thing that can happen to soldiers in an engagement' said one who was himself standing a little further down the line from the 23rd.[45] Then, while in front of his battalion square with his face bloodied from his various wounds, Jack received another, far more serious one:

> an half-pound iron grape shot entered my left breast and materially injured the shoulder joint and passed out through the centre of the shoulder blade and lodged in my clothes.[46]

---

43 Hill, *Colonel Hill (CB) Services*. The 23rd had three sergeants killed at Waterloo, John Hudson, James Lefever and Joseph Shelly, but all three were company sergeants and would be unlikely to be acting as Covering Sergeant for a field officer.

44 Holmes in *Waterloo Letters*

45 *The History of Lord Seaton's Regiment (The 52nd Light Infantry) at the Battle of Waterloo* William Leeke 1866

46 Hill 1816 *Statement of Services*. It is impossible to pin down the precise timing of Jack's wounding. Clues are:
  – it was after Ellis left the field, as Dalmer was in command;
  – Jack said it happened when 'I went to the front face of the square and wanted to go out to the front in order to try to bring some musket fire to bear on the enemy'
  – That Honesty was killed 'A very short time after I was wounded'
  – In his 1816 Statement of Services he says that 'near the conclusion of [the battle] my horse was killed soon after the repulse of the French Cavalry'.
  – The medical report on his wound says he received it 'just as the action was decided'.
The French cavalry attacks ended at around 6pm; the height of the final French attack, by the Imperial Guard, probably occurred at around 7.30pm; Wellington ordered the allied general advance, effectively the final act of the battle, sometime after 8pm. The 23rd were apparently in square throughout this time. If the medical report and the *Statement of Services* are literal, then Jack's wounding may have happened as late as 7.30, in which case it is possible that he was trying to bring fire onto was the left-most column of the Imperial Guard, though the range would be extreme. Jack does not say this and Clinton's after-action report says the 23rd were in a supporting role at that point. It seems more likely it was after the French cavalry attacks ended, but when there was still French artillery in the area (which could have been

The shot caused massive damage and spun Jack round as he collapsed to the ground. Carried into the middle of the square, those who gathered around him included his soldier servant who described the bleeding as 'enormous beyond example'.[47] Jack's face was covered in blood from his eye wound, but remarkably he was still sufficiently conscious to clarify that this was not his main problem:

> they came round me and [said] he has got a ball in through his right eye, I then said the shoulder was the place. Col. Dalmer [asked] me some questions. I said, I had got just as much as I could carry off, & that I thought pretty nearly enough to finish me.

At the start of the battle, Ellis had called the regiment's officers to him and ordered that men must not leave the ranks to assist the wounded; every fit man who helped colleagues reduced the battalion's strength. Those wounded unable to make their own way to the rear were placed in the middle of the square. That day the 23rd suffered 101 killed and wounded; as they were not seriously engaged later, most of their casualties had been incurred by the time Jack was struck.[48] By then the inside of the 23rd's square looked like a charnel house. A good impression of the scene comes from an officer of another battalion: 'During the battle our squares presented a shocking sight. Inside we were nearly suffocated by the smoke and smell from burnt cartridges. It was impossible to move a yard without treading upon a wounded comrade, or upon the bodies of the dead; and the loud groans of the wounded and dying were most appalling. At four o'clock our square was a perfect hospital, being full of dead, dying, and mutilated soldiers.'[49] Another later recalled 'How cruelly the long strain told on the British squares is shown by one incident. Wellington had ridden up to the 23rd, and, peering through the smoke, saw what seemed to be a body of men a few score yards in advance. 'What square is that?' He asked. It was a square of the dead. The 23rd had held that position until the ranks of the living were congested and embarrassed by the

---

what he was looking to bring fire upon) at between 6 - 6.30pm, about the time of the Foy/Bachelu advance.

47 *Principles of Military Surgery* John Hennen 1830. Hennen's full report of Jack's wound and its treatment is at Appendix 2.

48 Clinton's report to Hill after the battle says 'the 23rd regiment, under the command of Major Dalmer, in consequence of Lt.Col. Sir B.W. Ellis [sic] being wounded, advanced as supports to the right of the attack' – i.e. the final advance of the allied army following the defeat of the Imperial Guard; there is no record of their engaging with the Imperial Guard. *Wellington Dispatches* Clinton to Hill 19 June 1815.

49 Gronow, *Recollections*

numbers of the slain. The colonel had drawn the survivors a little distance back to get clear standing-room, but the outline of a square, made up of the slain, still marked the original position of the regiment'.[50] This tale may be apocryphal, but it illustrates what the seriously overworked regimental medical staff faced. John Dunn, the regimental surgeon, was probably in one of the villages to the rear, perhaps at the First Corps Field Hospital in Mont St. Jean, where many of the regimental medical teams had been established to receive casualties. John Munro, one of the two Assistant Surgeons, had gone to minister to Ellis' wound. As the second most senior officer with the battalion, Jack therefore probably received priority attention from Assistant Surgeon Thomas Smith. Smith assessed the injuries as unsurvivable; Jack probably agreed. He was placed alongside the battalion's other wounded in the expectation that he would die, but he was carrying a prayer book and must have had an angel on his shoulder. By a remarkable stroke of the same luck that had helped him survive the *Valk* and numerous actions since then, the shot passed under his collarbone and through his shoulder blade but missed the principal arteries, veins and nerves passing down his arm. Still, he was in extreme danger and facing a serious challenge to survive.

By the time Jack was hit, Blücher had kept his promise to Wellington; the Prussians swept into the French flank. After a final attack by the French Imperial Guard was repulsed, Wellington's victorious army advanced across the valley toward the ridge the French had occupied throughout the day. Napoleon was finally defeated and fled for Paris. The recovery of the dead and wounded now began: the field was covered with up to 17,000 allied, 31,000 French and 7,000 Prussian casualties. Jack, now unconscious from loss of blood, was carried off the ridge, probably by his soldier servant or the regimental musicians, whose job included getting those unable to walk to the rear medical areas. They took him to a village adjacent to the field, possibly Merbe Braine where the battalion had bivouacked the night before; the medical field hospital for Rowland Hill's II Corps was also in this area. Jack's facial injuries were covered with lint and bandaged, his shoulder wound packed with lint and the joint and upper chest firmly covered using linen roller bandages. The dressings would absorb the blood and with the bandages would control the bleeding. Aside from the fortunate path of the shot, Jack was also lucky that it passed entirely through his body. A 'through and through' missile injury means pieces of clothing or other foreign material carried into the wound probably exited his

---

50 Courtesy of Colonel Nick Lock, RWF Museum

body with the shot, otherwise such inevitably filthy material would readily cause fatal infections. When he eventually came round, Jack found himself 'in the hands of a foreign surgeon', possibly one of the Dutch-Belgian medical staff, many of whom recently served in the French *Service de Santé*. His condition was described as 'faint, but collected; his arm numbed and immoveable, but very sensible to pain when touched'.[51]

Ellis, who received a nominally less significant wound, was far unluckier. Eventually found after falling from his horse, he was carried to a small building described as an 'out-house' or 'hovel'. There he finally received medical attention and his wound was dressed. Considered too poorly to move again he lay there all night and all the following day. As Surgeon Dunn's most important patient he received the best care possible, but during the night of the 19th the building he was in caught fire. Ellis was in danger of being burned to death, but Assistant Surgeon Munro rescued him 'with some difficulty'. The trauma of having to be moved under such circumstances on top of the damage from his wound was too much. Ellis, who had joined the 23rd just six months before Jack; who had shared quarters with him at Freshwater on the Isle of Wight; who had led the battalion since Nova Scotia in 1808; and who had survived wounds from the Helder campaign, Aboukir Bay, Albuera, Badajoz, Salamanca, and Pampluna, told the medical officer who was with him, probably Munro, 'I am happy, I am content, I have done my duty' and died. He was 32 years old. He was buried on the mound of a windmill at Braine-l'Alleud.[52] Wellington and the 23rd deeply lamented his passing; Jack called Ellis 'one of the finest young men in the Army'.[53]

As soon as he was deemed well enough to travel and transport was available (wagons were in short supply), Jack was taken to Brussels where hospitals had been established to care for some 50,000 wounded from Waterloo and the other battles of the campaign His danger was not over; hospitals were usually crowded and unsanitary. But those in Brussels at least did not suffer significantly from the fevers that often spread through such places. This was put down to the fighting having fortunately taken place before the 'sickly season'; the hottest days of summer when dysentery, malaria and various febrile illnesses became rife. The hospitals used for allied casualties were also in what was considered a healthier part of Brussels, which may have helped. Jack's serious wound needed continual supervision, and he was placed in the

---

51 Hennen, *Principles*
52 Cary and McCance, *Regimental Records*
53 Letter to J Ley 7 July,1815

care of John Hennen, an Irish surgeon who oversaw British casualties at the Jesuits Hospital, the largest in the city, where the Palais de Justice now stands. Figures from the time suggest the overall mortality rate of patients was about 10%. If surgery was necessary, however, the mortality rate could quadruple, with most fatalities by far among those who suffered amputation (not an option given the position of Jack's wound). Hennen was a highly experienced surgeon who served with the 40th Foot in Egypt and as a Staff Surgeon throughout the Peninsular War, being himself wounded during the crossing of the Bidassoa. He later wrote a standard reference book on military surgery, promoting approaches that were ahead of their time, such as the need for medical staff to be caring and to try to reassure their patients.[54] On the other hand he apparently 'always operated with a cigar in his mouth, a habit which even the Duke of Wellington condoned, for he had a high opinion of him'.[55]

Hennen recorded that Jack was placed under his care nine days after the battle, suggesting he arrived at the Jesuits hospital on 27 June. He was one of over 330 patients there and one of 13 who had suffered gunshot wounds to the shoulder.[56] Hennen had the bandages removed and studied the damage. In the shoulder he noted an artery 'awfully pulsating in situ' (Jack's less medical description was 'One great fellow showed his sides working in the wound'). Hennen reported the left 'arm was stiff, and all voluntary influence over it gone; and the slightest motion in dressing the parts was attended with exquisite torture'.[57] After removing a triangular piece of shoulder blade from the exit wound with his fingers, the wound was redressed, and the slow path to recovery went well until after five days Jack began to suffer acute kidney pain, so great he thought he would be better off dead: 'at one time I gave it up, during the paroxisms [sic] of suppression of urine, from inflammation of the left kidney.'[58] But after treatment with warm poultices and diet of thick drinks like bread soup, the pain from that source eased. Over the next few days the wounds were redressed twice daily. He may have been given laudanum, and almost certainly would have been placed on a contemporary anti-inflammatory regimen: venesection (bleeding), catharsis (purging of bowels) and/or emesis (induced vomiting). Hennen was a strong supporter of such measures, believing that the vigorous life of a soldier

54 *Wellington's Doctors* Dr Martin Howard 2002
55 *The Egyptian Campaign of 1801* Lt. Col. G A Kempthorne RAMC in *Journal of the Royal Army Medical Corps Vol. LIV* January – June 1930
56 *Waterloo After the Glory* Michael Crumplin & Gareth Gates 2019
57 Hennen, *Principles*
58 Letter to J Ley 31 July,1815

rendered their constitution better able to tolerate the treatment than civilians.[59] In addition, Jack would initially have been placed on a 'low diet', consisting perhaps of rice water, gruel and bread. Only as he slowly healed would his diet have been allowed to include wine, red meat and vegetables.

Around a week after the painful kidney infection eased, Jack felt well enough to write home. Proximity to Britain meant Wellington's report of the battle on the 18th reached London on the evening of 21 June. When news of major victories arrived, the *London Gazette* did not wait for its next edition but immediately published an 'Extraordinary' edition dedicated to the official report of the battle. It did so again on 22 June 1815, printing Wellington's dispatch in full, which is how the British public learned the name Waterloo, the town where Wellington had written his record. Wellington said 'It gives me the greatest satisfaction to assure your Lordship, that the army never, upon any occasion, conducted itself better', but noted that 'such a desperate action could not be fought, and such great advantages could not be gained, without great loss; and I am sorry to add, that ours has been immense'.[60]

Like every family waiting for news of loved ones, the Hill family probably did not immediately read the account of the battle, but first turned to the listed officer casualties. There, among the wounded they saw the entry 'Lieutenant-Colonel Hill, severely'. This scant note must have caused great distress for the Hills, not least because they could not have been wholly sure it meant Jack. Hill was a common enough name that there may have been others of the same rank and surname.[61] No first name was given and unlike almost every other entry, nor was a regiment stated. Moreover, while Jack held the army rank of lieutenant-colonel, his rank in the 23rd was major, adding to the confusion. But what if it was him? What did 'severely' mean? Had it already proved fatal? Ellis was listed as dead; clearly the 23rd were again in the thick of the fight. Family members wrote urgent letters to try to discover Jack's fate, but in the post-battle chaos as his regiment advanced with the rest of the army, Jack probably did not receive them. Given many in the 23rd thought he would not survive, any letters arriving there would have been

---

59 Howard, *Doctors*
60 *Wellington Dispatches*. Wellington to Bathurst 19 June 1815
61 The *Waterloo Roll Call* (Charles Dalton, 2nd Editon 1904) lists thirteen officers called Hill at Waterloo; three of them, all brothers of General Lord Rowland Hill, were Lieutenant-Colonels: Clement Hill of the Royal Horse Guards, Sir Thomas Hill of the 1st Guards, and Sir Robert Hill of the Royal Horseguards (Blue), who was also severely wounded in the battle, but whose full name and regiment was given.

handed to Thomas Dalmer, who may have been tempted to respond with very bad news. Finally, weeks after the battle, a letter from Jack's brother-in-law, Jacob Ley, found its way to the Jesuit's hospital. Ley had told Jack that on 1st July he had been awarded another medal for his Peninsular service, this one for the Nive. This was his fourth medal for that war, meaning he was now entitled to wear the Army Gold Cross instead of the gold medal: one of only 163 Gold Crosses ever awarded. In reply, and some two weeks after they read the report in the *Gazette*, came the letter the entire Hill family was desperate for:

Bruxelles
7th July,1815

My dear Ley,

I have written two letters home and one to town. In those home, I mentioned in consequence of my being wounded I could not go on in the pursuit, so that when I may join a party to go to Paris it must be at some distant period even now. Thank God the point is a little better, as to arteries bursting from the sluffing of the wound. One great fellow showed his sides working in the wound, now it begins to fill in.

The 4¾ ounce ball (iron grape) entered under the collar bone and came out through the blade bone behind. The wound behind is beginning to heal and the discharge is trifling. The front wound still continues to discharge very much, he is a most confounded ugly fellow, with a nasty red and bazoned face as big as a tea-cup. I have had a great deal to do to keep body and soul together, and have never yet been out of bed except when assisted by these people for the Doctors, to dress me twice a day. It was generally thought in the Army it was impossible for me to survive, but I hope the people not wounded were so much employed in the pursuit that none of them wrote home. In fact, I am put down as dead in one list. Some people coming over from Grammont to see us after the battle were told so, and when they walked into the room, said they were glad to find me in the land of the living.

The rest of our brigade got off very cheap; in fact, they were not with us when we followed up the French Cavalry in squares. You will see by the Gazette what a milling the poor old Welsh got. Excuse me for saying it, we have lost most of the oldest officers. Poor Ellis in a month or two would have been a General Officer, and we should have had the promotion without losing one of the finest young men in the Army.

In case I get over this, I think I shall make a campaign at the Horse Guards and try what they will do for me. I think it most probable I shall get 300 a year for this wound, as I do not conceive it possible that the arm can be re-established. I understand I may get 600 as my share of the Peninsular prize money. As for the Portuguese [service], I will, when in London, get some answer or other, tho' I may apply to the British Ambassador to that effect.

As for the medals, I get none for the last fight; the man who was commissioned by the British Government to pay the British off[ice]r[s] their British pay while serving with the Portuguese, he also is very much talked of. I stand with him in this point of view, he never would answer my letters. I desired Greenwood and Cox to write to him and say that in case he did not forthwith send me a copy of the balance due, I should report the whole proceeding in a memorial to the Secretary at War. He has not even answered this, so that I know now what to do, to bring everything into the highest department possible.

It was impossible for Bonaparte and Honesty to agree, his name was enough to get him sacrificed. I mentioned before to my Mother my servant seeing him buried. A very short time after I was wounded, Honesty got three shot, two cannon, one round carried off a fore leg, a shell destroyed the saddle but did not kill; he got also a musket shot in the chest, and poor fellow, he bled to death; he carried me beautifully when sent on a message through a rye field seven feet high; he was in the most beautiful condition you can imagine. We never had exactly a squabble. I was one day forced to tell him I was master and he always believed it after.

You cannot imagine how much I regret Honesty. When I was wounded, I was not on him but had gone up to him in the middle of the square, and took something I wanted from out of the holsters; while I was doing this a musket ball struck into the boat cloak strapped in front; I know not exactly if this ball went into him, I almost think not. However, I stept a few paces aside and said, if you are hit, old fellow, do not think I did it; from thence I went to the front face of the square and wanted to go out to the front in order to try to bring some musket fire to bear on the enemy. In endeavouring to get through the close ranks, I got the shot in my shoulder and five other wounds in my face. I knew when I got the [wounds] in my face, but do not [know] when the grape hit me. When I fell and they came round me and said he has got a ball in through his right eye, I then said the shoulder was the place. Col. Dalmer [asked] me some questions. I said, I had got just as much as I could carry off, and that I thought pretty nearly enough to finish me. Thank God, several days are now gone by, perhaps we may say of the most dangerous time, the other part of the time will be spent in seeing how far the shoulder joint will bring itself about again. A young Devonshire lad by the name of Clyde died here a day or two since, belonging to our Regt., shot in the lungs.[62]

Remember me to all our friends in Totnes and its neighbourhood, Miss Caroline and the little ones for me.

Yours most sincerely,
J. HILL

Throughout his treatment Jack's left arm was kept in a sling, but a few days later 'in an unguarded moment, he was induced to allow of the removal of the supporting bandage.'[63] Removing the sling caused intense pain to shoot through his shoulder and arm. Jack found the pain 'almost insupportable', his arm began to swell and went numb as the swelling compressed the nerve bundles in it, while his shoulder began bleeding heavily again and he became feverish. His arm was restored to its sling and after further treatment 'he was allowed a more nutritive diet, with some English porter'. Slowly, supported by adhesive strapping, the wounds finally closed with new or 'proud' flesh, a nickname for the newly formed granulations that fill in wound cavities. Jack even began to regain some limited use of his arm, though the medical staff told him his shoulder was unlikely ever to recover fully. As his fever diminished, he began to receive visitors and wrote home again:

July 31st 1815

My dear Ley,

As our last letters crossed each other on the road, I will venture this, tho' it may share the same fate, to tell you that I think you a strange fellow. Somehow or other you do things in your own way, and the strangest of all is that seven-eighths of the times you are right. Your designation of me as an unfortunate miserable wounded wretch, brought down compassion, and I had your letter after a very short passage. From Hennock it was as usual directed R.W.F. no comment, of course off went the letter to the Van of the Army that then happened to be at Paris, back it came with the letters from the army a month after the time.

Continue now to add Via Ostende, as I want nothing with Calais till I am fitted for the gaieties of Paris, if one can call the state they now are in enviable, having been the forces of recission

---

62 John Clyde was from Bideford, Devon. He joined the 23rd as a 2nd lieutenant in June 1811 and had previously been wounded at Salamanca.
63 Hennen, *Principles*

they have not spared then, particularly the Prussians. Imagine their turning one of the most beautiful apartments of one of the Palaces into the taylors shop where any Prussian soldier with a hole in his breeches might go and get it mended.

Blucher claims the column, but I believe there are difficulties put in by the other powers. The old chap says he wants the Prussian cannon out of it. I understand they none have been by any means nice, and the poor Parisians are praying for the British to occupy the town. I heard Gen[l]. Hill's corps was to go into q[uarte]rs. in Normandy - see how I have retailed you all the stale news which you will get so very much improved by the English daily newspapers in a second edition.

You must excuse my mode of writing, as every word nearly is shot flying, and the right arm forced to support the fingers of the left. I have written you first as I know you will communicate to Hennock before they will to you. I wrote W[ilia]m. I know not if I detail'd all my little sufferings, but at one time I gave it up, during the paroxisms of suppression of urine, from inflammation of the left kidney. As usual - "stocks vary", a day or two ago my left arm began again to swell very bad and brought with it fever. I was sent to [the doctors?] in lint and after 3 clearings and five washing-outs with a bucketful of whey and 30 hours' abstinence, I have got rid of all but the swollen arm, that of course will fluctuate perhaps for years, provided I live.

The Doctors sagaciously told me to-day they had little hopes of the shoulder being re-established. I always said, and did so at the moment they insisted I was killed by a ball through the eye, that the shoulder was completely smashed, some of them said the Humerus (ask Jacob if amidst my tower of Babel I have spelt this right) is not injured. I always insisted the upper part of the cup on the top of the shoulder was injured, and that they could feel the piece of bone broken off; now they find out I was right. The ball in passing through, struck with the greatest violence, it is true, the <u>lower</u> part of the joint which lifted the upper part and broke off part above. This is by far the most serious part of the job. Ask Dr. Cornish how he would pass an iron ball one & five-eighths of an inch, in close under the center of the collar and to pass out below the center of the shoulder blade and not kill the animal! In fact, it is one of the most astonishing wounds that has taken place, they asked me if I would give them leave to publish the case. I said the world was informed I was wounded and I should be very happy to hear them tell the world they had cured me.

I have two letters unanswered from Hennock, I will write them again in five or six days if I am in the land of the living. I have been making every enquiry from whom I got a present of fruit and flowers this morning. The servants hesitated about allowing the man to enter as I was suffering severely at the time in consequence of the arm being forced to be changed from one part of the bed to another. He said, Head of the Department of Police, I wish some of your flower fanciers had them. I am going to send them to Mrs. and Miss Julian who arrived here [to]day on their way to Paris, where they stay while the Regt. is in that part of the world.

Tell Caroline I hope I may next winter see her. The front wound wants about an inch to be filled up from the bottom, the back wound has never given so much trouble as the front, but I hoped it would have carried more of the discharge away, from its being lower. I forget if I was so much of a surgeon in my last. I believe I was more of a butcher, I told you of poor Honesty, we must have him in remembrance.

Kiss all the little girls for me, remember me to the boys when you write them. Say all the pretty things to the ladies in Totnes.

Tuesday! I wrote home Friday last - I know not but I have so many people calling on me that they will kill me with kindness. Many, many thanks to you for your very satisfactory [letter], my dear Caroline, you are always in my recollection.

J. HILL.

My Father tells me all the trouble he has taken to get the letters sent, his last was only mis-sent to Dock, but fortunately escaped Paris.[64] I am glad Salter gets on. Men and Money, - a son and a £1,000. It will be a month before I expect to go out of the house with impunity. The Doctors say, no man will be more laughed at than myself when I show the ball, the entry and exit to any medical people who have not seen it in this country progressing. Again adieu, the most affectionate friends of both of you.

And well, little lady, had the letter terminated on the other side, I tell you what time would have been, I would have taken you in my arms and kissed you all round the room for allowing your kind long letter of 8th July to go to Paris and not permitting me to get it till the 31st last night. Write to Hennock. Say I, this moment, just got their letter of 21st July jointly written by my Father and Mother. Remember me to Mrs. W. and children, never by any accident leave out <u>wounded</u>. Tell them their account of Fred is so very confused that much as I want to write to him, I know not if he

---

64 Dock was the original name of Devonport.

be in the Amphion or Albion, or on half pay. The Amphion report is very good, but will people in power let your men exchange when so many want employ of the most commanding interest.

This is the last surviving letter that Jack wrote home, and it is with some irony that almost his last words include an admonishment to his parents about both the contents and direction of their mail to him, just as some of his first from the army did. Many things had changed over his nearly 20 years of his service, but not his complaints about mail.

By 26 September Jack was strong enough to leave hospital. He was granted 'Commander-in-Chief's' leave to return to England for 'recovery of wounds.[65] The 23rd, meanwhile, had served under Thomas Dalmer through the follow up to Waterloo, including in the capture of Cambrai. Reaching Paris on 4 July, they camped in the Bois de Boulogne. Now they reflected on the losses they had suffered. Brevet Major Joseph Hawtyn (commander of the Grenadier company), Captains Charles Jolliffe (No. 8 company) and Thomas Farmer (No. 7 Company), Lieutenant George Fensham (Light company), two sergeants and nine rank and file were killed outright on 18 June. Henry Ellis, Jack Hill, Captain Henry Johnson (No. 6 company), and Lieutenants George Fielding (No. 5 company), William Griffiths (Grenadier company), John Clyde (No. 3 company), Anthony Sedley (No. 6 company), seven sergeants and seventy-one men were wounded. Some of those, including Ellis and Clyde, subsequently died. 2nd Lieutenant William Leebody and one private were killed in the assault on Cambrai, with another two men wounded: the last Royal Welch Fusilier casualties of the Napoleonic wars. While Jack and the others were still recovering, Wellington wrote:

Being aware of the anxiety existing in England to receive the returns of killed and wounded in the late actions, I now send lists of the officers, and expect to be able to send this evening returns of the non-commissioned officers and soldiers. The amount of non-commissioned officers and soldiers, British and Hanoverian, killed, wounded, and missing, on the 16th, 17th, and 18th, is between 12,000 and 13,000. Your Lordship will see in the enclosed lists the names of some most valuable officers lost to His Majesty's service. Among these, I cannot avoid to mention Col. Cameron, of the 92[d], and Col. Sir H. W. Ellis, of the 23[d] regiments, to whose conduct I have frequently drawn your Lordship's attention, and who, at last,

---

65 TNA WO 17/291 *Office of the Commander in Chief: 23rd Foot Monthly Returns to the Adjutant General 1815*

fell distinguishing themselves at the head of the brave troops which they commanded. Notwithstanding the glory of the occasion, it is impossible not to lament such men, both on account of the public and as friends.[66]

The 'glory of the occasion' was, of course, celebrated throughout the army and Britain, but the price was high. Colville wrote congratulating his men on 'the share they so fortunately had of the glorious and ever memorable battle', but ended his message with the sombre addition: 'An acquaintance of many years with Colonel Sir H. W. Ellis has fully impressed the Lieutenant-General with the loss to His Majesty's service as he cannot pass over, without offering his condolence to the 23rd Regiment on their loss the sense of the occasion alone can reconcile'.[67] The officers and men of the 23rd each gave a day's pay towards the erection of a monument to Ellis in Worcester cathedral. It cost in total £1,200. The inscription they chose called the marble sculpture 'a tribute to their respect and affection to the memory of a leader, not more distinguished for valour and conduct in the field, than beloved for every generous and social virtue'. Every mention of Ellis in Jack's letters underlines the respect and admiration he had for his friend.

Like many veterans of the Revolutionary and Napoleonic Wars, Jack was keen to see Paris, but he could not rejoin his regiment immediately. Instead, he went home to Hennock to complete his recovery. Many soldiers had recovered souvenirs of the battle; Jack took with him a unique one - the 'grape shot' that had passed through his shoulder, recovered from the folds of his waistcoat. It seems unlikely that when he showed this around in England he was 'laughed at' as the doctors in Brussels had predicted; more probably everyone was astonished and grateful to see him, as he put it, 'in the land of the living'.

---

66 *Wellington Dispatches*. Wellington to Bathurst 29 June 1815
67 Cary and McCance, *Regimental Records*

CHAPTER 15

THE MOST DISTRESSING
EMBARRASSMENTS

'Your memorialist at the period of leaving the Royal Welch Fusiliers
was the individual of the longest standing of either Officer or Private,
and had been present in every Field (except Minden) borne
on the colours of the 23rd Regt.'

Memorandum to the Duke of York, 1823

Jack was not the only man who found himself heading towards Devon
after Waterloo. The battle was not quite the end of the Napoleonic
Wars; pockets of Bonapartist resistance held out for some weeks
afterwards. Nor, contrary to Abba's assertion, did Napoleon surrender
there. But Waterloo certainly began a rapid demise for the man himself
and his eponymous era. Abandoning his army, much as he had in Egypt
and Russia, Napoleon could not cling to power, abdicating on 22 June
in favour of his four-year-old son, Napoleon II. On the 29th he headed
for the western coast of France, hoping to sail to America. On 8 July
Napoleon was rowed to a frigate off the Isle d'Aix, outside Rochefort,
the last French soil he would stand on. There it became clear that he
would neither be given a passport to the United States nor be able to
avoid Royal Navy patrols. Perhaps he finally empathized with
Villeneuve and the other Admirals he berated 10 years before for being
unable to get an entire fleet past the ever-watchful British sailors. On
the morning of 15 July, almost one month after Waterloo, Napoleon
boarded HMS *Bellerophon*, a Trafalgar veteran, and surrendered to her
captain, Frederick Maitland. He asked Maitland to transport him and
his small party of loyalists and servants to Britain, where he hoped the
Prince Regent, who he called his most powerful, constant and generous
of enemies, would grant him asylum.

On 24 July, *Bellerophon* arrived off Berry Head. Maitland had
been directed not to allow his passenger to disembark and anchored in
Tor Bay to await further instructions. Viewing the shore, Bonaparte
allegedly described Devon as 'a beautiful country' and told Maitland

the anchorage reminded him of a bay in Elba.[1] Great efforts were made to keep *Bellerophon's* secret, but the news soon leaked. Sightseers chartered boats to glimpse 'the ogre', who played to the crowd, walking the decks in uniform and lifting his hat to the throng. Maitland wrote 'you cannot imagine what a crowd we have here. The inns are full and the sea covered with swarms of small boats'. The bay was an easy hour or so's carriage ride from Hennock; it is tempting to speculate whether any of the Hills travelled to see the man their eldest sons had been fighting for twenty years. The French party pressed to be landed, but on the 26th *Bellerophon* moved to the more secure harbour of Plymouth to reduce any risk of escape. There she attracted even more attention, with reports of up to 10,000 people, some apparently from as far as Scotland, attending the Bonaparte show. Napoleon's hopes of comfortable retirement as an English squire were, however, dashed; on the 31st he was informed that he was to be exiled on St. Helena, in the southern Atlantic. *Bellerophon* returned to Tor Bay, where there was less risk of contrary winds. On 7 August Bonaparte and an entourage of twenty-six supporters transferred to HMS *Northumberland* and sailed south. The Devon coastline was Napoleon's last view of the country he had fought against for so long but never conquered. Disembarking on St. Helena on 17 October, he would spend much of the next six years recording his memoires. Like many retrospective memorialists the veracity of his account is not unquestionable.

For the victors of Waterloo came rewards. The *London Gazette* of 16 September 1815 formally announced the decision taken on 4 June to reward naval and army officers for the recent wars, including Jack's appointment as a Companion of the Most Honorable Military Order of the Bath.[2] The delayed publication implied the awards were for Waterloo, but there was another list for that with some names, including Thomas Dalmer but not Jack, appearing on both. The original nominations for both men were no doubt by Ellis. The letters enclosing the 'badge', or medal, and its ribbon were sent shortly after the *Gazette* appeared:

---

1 Presciently close to calling Torbay 'the English Riviera' as the local tourist authorities do today!
2 *The London Gazette* September 16, 1815

Horseguards

19th September 1815

Lieut. Col. J. Humphrey Edwd Hill
23^d Foot

Sir

I have the Prince Regent's Command to transmit to you herewith, the Ribbon and Badge of a Companion of the Most Honourable Military Order of the Bath, with his Royal Highness' gracious permission, in the name and on behalf of His Majesty, that you shall wear the same.

I am, Sir Yours,
Frederick
Acting Grand Marshal

Membership of one of the nation's senior orders of chivalry was a significant achievement for the son of the lowly Rector of Hennock. Jack also received an official-looking, largely pre-printed letter:

HIS ROYAL HIGHNESS THE PRINCE REGENT having been pleased in the Name and on Behalf of HIS MAJESTY, to nominate you a COMPANION of the Most Honorable Military Order of the Bath, it becomes my Duty to transmit the enclosed Paper, which I have to request that you fill up with a Statement of your Military Services, agreeably to the Regulations announced in the Gazette of the 4th of January last, and that you will address the same to me, under Cover, to the Secretary at War, London.

I beg leave to annex for your Information, a Statement of the Fees to be paid to me, as Officer of Arms attendant upon the Order, agreeably to the Rules and Ordinances appertaining to the Companions.

I have the Honour to be,

Your most obedient humble Servant,

GEORGE NAYLER,
Genealogist of the Bath and Officer of Arms attendant upon the Knights-Commanders and Companions.

£. s. d.

For the Escutcheon or Plate of your Name and Style to be affixed in Westminster Abbey	3	0	0
For recording the Statement of your Military Services in the Books appropriated to the Companions	2	16	8
For a Copy of the Rules and Ordinances	1	1	0
	6	17	8

One can imagine the ever-frugal Jack being less than impressed that the honour of a Companionship of the Order of the Bath implied an immediate cost of over six guineas, but he nevertheless wrote his summary *Statement of Services*, the first time he had recorded his long career in detail.[3] Jack's pride in his record is evident in his final entry:

> Brevet Lieut. Colonel J. H. E. Hill has been present in every field whose inscriptions decorate the Colours of the Welch Fusiliers, except Minden.[4]

When he wrote this, it was a true statement: the battle honour for the participation of 2/23rd in the battle of Coruña, fought while Jack and 1/23rd were in Nova Scotia, was not awarded until 1823. He could have made an even grander boast; not only was he at all 12 battles of the Revolutionary and Napoleonic Wars then named on the Colours of the Royal Welch Fusiliers, but he was also present at two granted as battle honours to other regiments, but not the 23rd.[5]

There was another medal that many more could take pride in. Ten days after Waterloo, Wellington wrote to the Duke of York to suggest 'the expediency of giving to the non-commissioned officers and soldiers engaged in the battle of Waterloo, a medal. I am convinced it would have the best effect in the army; and, if that battle should settle our concerns, they will well deserve it'.[6] Wellington's proposal was accepted; on 10 March 1816 Horse Guards issued a memorandum: 'The Prince Regent has been graciously pleased, in the name of and behalf of His Majesty, to command, that in commemoration of the brilliant and decisive victory of Waterloo, a Medal shall be conferred on every officer, non-commissioned officer, and soldier of the British Army,

---

3 Appendix 3
4 Hill 1816 *Statement of Services*
5 Jack was present for Egypt, Martinique 1809, Albuhera, Badajos, Salamanca, Vittoria, Pyrenees, Nivelle, Orthes, Toulouse, Peninsula, and Waterloo, all named on the RWF Colours. He was also at Ciudad Rodrigo and the Nive, not granted to the RWF. Engagements such as Burgos or Tolosa were deemed of insufficient significance to be distinguished from the all-encompassing 'Peninsula'.
6 *Wellington Dispatches*. Wellington to HRH the Duke of York 28 June 1815

present on that memorable occasion'.[7] It was the first such general award in the British army, with the name of the recipient stamped around its rim and able to be claimed by next of kin of those killed. All who received the medal were entitled to have the words 'Waterloo Man' assigned to their name in regimental records. There was also a financial reward: prize money for the Peninsula had been paid in stages throughout the war and was again after Waterloo. The amounts were scaled for rank; as a field officer Jack received £433 2s 4d.[8]

Jack's recovery continued, but his left arm remained unusable, and the extent of his incapacity needed to be assessed. He travelled to London for an examination by doctors at the Royal College of Surgeons. In consequence he was awarded an annual pension of £200, starting from 19 June 1816. The award was temporary, suggesting the examiners felt he might eventually regain at least partial use of the limb as the complete loss of an arm attracted a sum of £300, permanently.[9] By autumn 1816 Jack was sufficiently recovered to be ready to rejoin his regiment. Napoleon's defeat did not mean a return home for the whole army. An allied Army of Occupation was established, under Wellington's command, to try to underpin stability in France. Initially comprising some 150,000 men, of which the British contributed 30,000, its entire cost was to be paid by France. Wellington insisted that some of his best regiments were in the British contingent, so the 23rd Foot stayed and were reunited with their fellow Fusiliers, the 7th, and the 1/43rd in the 7th Brigade under the command of Major-General Sir James Kempt. The brigade was in turn part of the 1st Division, led by the Fusiliers' commander at Albuera, Sir Lowry Cole. As the wounded recovered and recruits from home arrived, the 23rd recovered their strength until by November 1815 they were 671 strong, with another twenty-nine about to arrive from Britain. Initially quartered in Montmartre, in February 1816 they moved to Hamelincourt, not far from Lille, where Jack was imprisoned in 1798. There they remained for some months, cantoned in villages around the town. As the first anniversary of Waterloo approached, a regimental dinner was planned, but abandoned 'as it might appear as if we meant to crow over and insult the feelings of the French. It was consequently resolved to spend the day in a jovial,

---

7 *Glory is Priceless!: Awards to the British Army During the French Revolutionary and Napoleonic Wars*, Lesley Smurthwaite in *The Road to Waterloo* Alan J Guy (ed.) 1990

8 Cary and McCance, *Regimental Records*

9 *Return of the Names of the Officers in the Army.* War Office 30 April 1818. Jack is one of eleven officers of the 23rd Foot recorded as in receipt of a pension for wounds.

but not in a tumultuous manner. We had horse-racing, gambols, and a dinner upon the ground. The *tout ensemble* of this *fête-champêtre* was delightful. Every thing went off in excellent style. About 60 persons sat down to dinner, when many appropriate toasts, and songs to correspond, were given'.[10] The regimental band was present and after the dinner dancing commenced, which 'was kept up with great spirit'. A toast was drunk to Ellis' memory, and a song specially composed for the occasion sung, including the lines:

> To Ellis, our Colonel, our friend and our pride
> Still, still on this day shall thy worth be remembered
> And still the full cup to thy memory shall flow
> Still, still in our hearts shall thy virtues be numbered
> Still loved, still respected, the tribute we owe.

At the end of September, the regiment moved to Cambrai, then in October moved temporarily to Denain for a review of the Army of Occupation by the Dukes of Kent and Cambridge, followed by a 'sham fight' directed by the Duke of Wellington. At the end of the month, they returned to Hamelincourt. Meanwhile, on 25 September Private Elias Williams travelled to England to help Jack with his packing and other preparations.[11] Jack and Williams travelled to France together and Jack formally rejoined the 23rd after almost a year and a half's absence, on 11 November 1816. Thomas Dalmer was confirmed as Ellis' successor in command; despite losses in the last campaign there were still some old faces to welcome Jack back to the fold. Jack found Dalmer suffering in contrast with the ghost of Ellis, with less than enthusiastic support from some officers. Lieutenant John McDonald wrote home from Montmartre in early 1816 'Now we have got a man at our head, with whom I have always been very good friends; but who has risen higher than he had any business to expect, and does not know how to behave himself towards his officers, & besides coming after a man who's memory even, is adored, you may easily conceive we see him as little as possible, in fact he is a little ugly, proud, passionate bachelor of fifty, who to give him his due does not trouble us very much but with whom it is impossible to be on any very friendly terms.'[12] If this attitude was typical among his officers, the battalion probably looked forward to the

---

10 Cary and McCance, *Regimental Records*
11 TNA WO 12/3975 *Regimental General Muster books and Pay Lists, 23rd Foot,* 1815 & 1816
12 RWF Museum Object No. 5935. MacDonald letter of 16th January 1816. Dalmer was in fact only around 35, not 50, years old at the time McDonald (who was 22) wrote.

return of the popular Major Hill; Dalmer almost immediately took leave, leaving Jack in command and not returning until March 1817. The regiment remained near Hamelincourt until April 1817 when they were ordered to garrison duty at Valenciennes.

On 7 July Thomas Dalmer asked permission to transfer onto half-pay; the men of the 23rd gossiped that Dalmer was ashamed when two of his men were hung for stealing from the locals.[13] This seems insufficient cause to resign command; Dalmer himself left no explanation, but the regiment was suffering disciplinary problems, for which Dalmer was accountable.[14] As senior major and Lieutenant-Colonel in the army, Jack may have hoped for promotion. He took acting command after Dalmer departed on 23 August, leading the 23rd at a review by the King of Prussia near Prouvy on 6 September, followed by a march back to Cambrai on the 10th for an assembly of the entire 1st Division. But on 28 September a familiar face returned as the regiment's new lieutenant-colonel: Thomas Pearson, whose departure in 1811 had cleared the way for Jack's majority. Posted to Canada, Pearson had reunited with his wife and subsequently fought in the War of 1812. In September 1814 he suffered a dangerous head wound but recovered and returned to Britain to command 2/43rd in 1815. They became a casualty of postwar army reductions; Pearson went on half pay, having extracted a promise from the Duke of York to 'give the utmost attention to your claim for Employment, whenever opportunities can be procured'; he exchanged with Dalmer a month later. Some officers may have been unimpressed by Dalmer, but Pearson's return was considered 'an evil day for the Regiment' by Richard Bentinck, who recalled his propensity for harsh discipline when a major. Bentinck soon found Pearson unchanged: 'When he came...to inspect them, for the first time as Colonel, two men came running in from five to ten minutes after he had ridden up. He at once called them out and ordered them 200 lashes each. When the flogging was over, he addressed his new Regiment, 'Now then', said he, 'I have only opened one eye yet; I'll warm your jackets if I have to open the other. If you behave yourselves I'll be as good as Colonel Ellis, if you

---

13 Crook, *Bentinck*

14 In *The Duke of Wellington and the British Army of Occupation in France, 1815-1818* (1992) Thomas D Veve records 'In the 23rd Regiment, General James Kempt remarked that he was thankful that the unit commander, Colonel Dalmer, went on half pay which allowed Colonel Pearson to take command and attempt to solve the unit's discipline problems. The next year Kempt reported the regiment much improved under Pearson's leadership'.

don't, I will be the Devil himself'.[15] Bentinck concluded Pearson had already delivered on his diabolic promise.

In October the 23rd returned to Valenciennes, remaining there until mid-1818. Pearson's enthusiasm for discipline was noticed: a report following an inspection by Kempt on 29 April 1818 noted 'It is impossible for any officer to evince more ability, zeal, and attention than Lieut.-Colonel Pearson has employed in his command of the 23rd'.[16] For all the drilling and inspecting, however, life in the Army of Occupation passed slowly, and while the 23rd established a Regimental School to improve the literacy of their men, and especially NCOs, aside from the occasional formal occasion and the inevitable paperwork its officers had plenty of time on their hands: perhaps too much. Those for whom hunting was a favoured pastime, like Jack, noted a General Order issued in November 1817 that warned hunting and shooting would be banned if more care was not taken to avoid damaging crops. Similarly, the use of fishing nets was banned to avoid destruction of fish stocks in the rivers, on which the locals depended.

While the political situation in France was far from stable, in 1818 the allies decided to withdraw the Army of Occupation. On 17 August 1818 the 23rd left Valenciennes for the last time and returned to Cambrai. Two months later, on 26 October, it marched for Calais, passing through Cantin, Lens, Lilliers, and Racquinhem. Calais was reached on the 31st. Jack may have taken a different route, as one of two surviving portraits of him, painted by Édouard Pingret is dated 1818. Pingret was a French artist who at the time was also producing portraits of other British officers. Jack may have sat for Pingret at Valenciennes or Cambrai, but family memory has it that Jack visited Paris, enjoying a romantic encounter (of which more later) and sitting for his portrait there. The Pingret portrait is a higher quality work and correctly depicts Jack wearing his CB, Army Gold Cross, Sultan's Medal, and Waterloo Medal (the other portrait, which is in a more naïve hand is unsigned and shows Jack incorrectly also wearing his Army Gold Medal.[17] Like many who had spent their lives fighting French armies, Jack would certainly have sought an opportunity to see the French capital if he could. Another possibility is that he made a (long) diversion to Paris while in Cambrai sitting on a General Court Martial in February 1817, but that would not fit with the date of the Pingret portrait. Whatever the truth, there is no record of Jack taking leave at any point while he was in France.

---

15 Crook, *Bentinck*
16 Cary and McCance, *Regimental Records*
17 As the Gold Cross replaced the Gold Medal, the two should not have been worn together, but it seems many soldiers chose to ignore the instruction.

Embarking on 1 November and landing at Dover next morning, the regiment was quartered in Dover Heights Barracks. They had little time to get comfortable. On 19 November the 23rd marched to Deal and embarked on two transports. Jack was aboard HMS *Defence* which left the Downs on 25 November and moored in the Cove of Cork on the 27th. Once disembarked the regiment was marched in separate 'divisions' towards Limerick. Jack led the first division, leaving Cork on 28 November and arriving in Buttevant on the 30th. There the battalion reunited before Jack and his division left on 9 December, arriving in Limerick the following day. Fully reunited in the New Barracks at Limerick, the 23rd was at full strength: 107 officers and NCOs; 800 rank and file and would spend almost the next four years in Ireland. For eighteen months they remained headquartered in Limerick, with detachments in villages in the surrounding area. It may have been while he was there, or perhaps more likely during almost two months' leave he took in May and June 1819, that Jack spent his idle time submitting his service record (and subscribing) to the grandly titled 'The Royal Military Calendar, or Army Service and Commission Book'. The five volumes of this piece, a military *Who's Who* claimed it listed 'The Services and Progress of Promotion of the Generals, Lieutenant-Generals, Major-Generals, Colonels, Lieutenant-Colonels, and Majors of the Army, According to Seniority. Jack's entry appeared at no. 1314 in Volume IV of the 3rd Edition of the work. It read:

1314. LIEUT.-COL.J.HUMPHREY EDWARD HILL,C.B.

Second Lieut. 23d foot, 29th July,1796; First Lieut. 6th April,1797; Capt. 3d Sept. 1803; Maj. 12th March,1812; and brevet L.-Col. 21st Sept. 1813. Served in Spain and Portugal, and was attached to the Portuguese army; he has received a cross for the battles of Salamanca, Nivelle, and Nive, and siege of St. Sebastian, at which he commanded Portuguese regs. He also served in Flanders, and was present at the battle of Waterloo. L.Col. H. is a Companion of the Bath.[18]

In June 1820 the regiment moved to Ennis and a few months later to Dublin. There Jack learned of his entitlement to further awards. In March 1820 King John VI of Portugal issued a decree establishing medals to be awarded in 'consideration of the remarkable service that the Generals, Commanders of Regiments and other officers have rendered me in the

---

18 *The Royal Military Calendar, or Army Service and Commission Book*. Volume IV, 3rd Edition 1820

chief battles which were fought, and the sieges which were carried on in the kingdom of Portugal, Spain, and France by the Portuguese troops and those of the Allies against the French'. After a lengthy and complicated process, a list was published of Portuguese and British officers entitled to these awards. *Tenente Coronel agregado* João Hill was named in the Portuguese equivalent of the *London Gazette*, the *Diário do Governo*, as being awarded the Silver Cross for two campaigns (1813 and 1814) and the Command Medal, with two 'leaves' for commanding the 5th Caçadores at San Sebastián and the 4th Infantry at the Nive.[19] But although the King decreed the right to wear the medals, designs for which were officially published, no actual medals were produced by the Portuguese authorities; anyone who wanted them had to have them made at their own expense. Portuguese officers were required to buy theirs from a specified manufacturer in Lisbon; entitled British officers could order the medals from different manufacturers (there is some diversity in the design of those that survive). Many simply did not bother, and it seems that Jack was one of these as there are no Portuguese medals in his collection.[20]

The regiment stayed in Dublin until September 1821 when it moved to Londonderry. Jack again took command of a division:

> The Division consisting of 2, 4, 5, and 6 Companies under the command of Lieutenant-Colonel Hill will march tomorrow morning at 6 o'clock agreeable to their respective routes, and will be quartered as directed in conformity to the scale laid down by Colonel Pearson. All baggage to be loaded this evening: a proportion of non-commissioned officers and officers' servants will form the baggage guard, and to be dressed in the most uniform manner. The men to march in their white trousers, and the cloth trousers to be most carefully preserved. All young soldiers to be under the command and superintendence of commanding officers

---

19 *Diário do Governo*, number 21 dated 24 January 1821. Jack was not awarded the Command Medal for the Nivelle. Moisés Gaudêncio suggests this is because, despite his commanding the 4th Infantry at the battle, the only part of his regiment engaged were its two grenadiers companies, who formed part of a composite advance guard under the command of Lt Colonel Donald McNeill of the 10th Regiment. Even they were only slightly engaged before the French pulled out; McNeill did not receive the medal either. Jack also missed out on an award for Orthez, which can only be because a of a harsh assessment that the diversion the 4th provided at the bridge was deemed insufficiently significant.

20 *The Gold Collars, Medals and Crosses Granted to British Officers by the Crown of Portugal in The Peninsular War* Charles Winter 1916 and private correspondence with Moises Gaudêncio.

of companies. All parades to be the same as at headquarters. The 1st Division of the Corps under the command of Lieutenant-Colonel Hill will commence its march for Londonderry at 6 o'clock tomorrow morning, and the 2nd Division under the command of Lieutenant-Colonel Keightley on the following day.[21]

On 14 November the regiment was ordered to Strabane, Jack's division again marching first. After a fourteen-mile march along the banks of the River Foyle, just as they arrived the orders were countermanded; they marched back to Londonderry. There they stayed until April 1822 when they moved to Boyle, 100 miles south. An inspection the next month concluded 'This corps is in a high state of discipline, perfectly equipped, and in every respect fit for any service.' Pearson's methods may have been unpopular with the men, but the results impressed. It was at Boyle a year later that news arrived that General Sir Richard Grenville, Colonel of the Regiment for Jack's entire career, had died. His successor was Major-General Sir Willoughby Gordon. Gordon wrote to Pearson expressing his 'pride in the national distinction of the corps, and in being associated with its long and hardly-earned [sic, i.e. hard-earned!] honours and reknown'.[22] For Jack, Grenville's passing perhaps indicated the changing times, as certainly did a significant change in his personal circumstances. On 19 April 1823 the *Morning Herald* contained the announcement:

MARRIED:

On Tuesday, the 15th instant, at Welsh Pool, Montgomeryshire, by the Rev. Wm. Clives, Lieut. Col. J. H. E. Hill, C.B. of the 23d Royal Welsh Fusileers, to Jane, the second daughter of the late James Turner, Esq. of that town. - At the same time, by the Rev. William Clive, the Rev. Richard John Davies, of Guilsfield, Montgomeryshire, to Eliza Elenora, the youngest daughter of the late James Turner, Esq., of Welshpool.[23]

Jane Turner was born on 20 January 1795; she married Jack at 28, almost 16 years younger than her groom. There is no documentary evidence of the circumstances in which Jack met Jane; perhaps her coming from Welshpool meant a Royal Welch Fusilier introduced them.

---

21 Cary and McCance, *Regimental Records*. John Keightley was a major with the 14th Foot at Waterloo and made brevet lieutenant-colonel after the battle. He transferred as a major to the 23rd in July 1816.
22 Cary and McCance, *Regimental Records*
23 *Morning Herald*, 19 April 1823

Letters from a Vicarage relates a family story from after they had met, as recalled by Enid Case, Jack's Great-Granddaughter:

> In Paris, in early 1815, on a summer evening, he was walking by the river with a lady on each arm; they were the Miss Turners, daughters of a Welshpool banker. One was the fiancée of Hill's Ensign Smith; the other, her elder, in nine years became his wife. He had seen a beautiful lady, with auburn hair, descending from a carriage, and (this really impressed him after so many years of heavy boots) with an elegant foot and ankle, and he fell in love. They met a soldier carrying a mattress; he asked what this was for. The soldier said it was for Ensign Smith who was on guard duty. Hill said 'Carry on. But dip it in the river first'! Peninsula men found newcomers very soft. Smith's fiancée must have thought him heartless: her sister began to fall in love.[24]

This is a charming story; it is true that two members of the 23rd, Jack and 2nd Lieutenant (not Ensign) Ralph Smith went on to marry the Turner sisters, Jane and Mary. There are, however, some problems with the tale. First, the 23rd was not in Paris in either late 1814 or early 1815; it sailed from Pauillac in southern France to Plymouth in June 1814 while Jack was undergoing his elective surgery and certainly was not in the French capital. When the regiment returned to the continent the next year it was based in Flanders, eventually marching to Waterloo. Jack could not have travelled to Paris during that time; no British officer would have been strolling the banks of the Seine after Napoleon restored himself to power. If Jack met Jane in Paris he must have done so during a visit to the French capital after he had rejoined his regiment in November 1816. The second problem with the tale is that Smith was hardly a 'newcomer'; he was with the 23rd at Vitoria, the Pyrenees, Nivelle, Nive, Orthes and Toulouse. This does not mean Jack did not play the trick of sending Smith a soaked mattress, but it was no prank on a new boy. If Jack and Jane met around this time, there is also no record of how they sustained their relationship over the (five or six, not nine) years between then and their marriage.

In May 1823 the regiment returned to Richmond Barracks in Dublin. The next month it was inspected by Major-General Sir Colquhoun Grant who commented: 'I have seen no corps surpass and scarcely any equal the Fusiliers, in appearance, movement, and discipline', high praise from a Peninsular and Waterloo veteran who was the former head of Wellington's intelligence service. Jack was only

---

24 Case, *Letters*

in his mid-40s, but he continued to suffer from his disabled arm; there is a suggestion that he was unable to use it to control his horse which must have frustrated him and apparently frustrated Pearson too. Perhaps also the tedium of garrison duty away from home in a peacetime army made him less enamoured with army life. Like many of his contemporaries, Jack seems previously to have considered active soldiering no profession for a married man, especially for those without independent means. As one rather poetically put it:

> The hazard of losing life, which a soldier is often called on to encounter, gives to his existence, as often as it is preserved, a value, it would, otherwise, soon cease to possess ... if it is painful at a certain age, to think, that, when you fall, no widow, no child, will drop a tear over your grave - it is, on the other hand, a comfort to know, that none are dependent upon your existence; that none will be left unprotected and in misery at your death.[25]

But now Jack did have someone dependent upon him; presumably the newlyweds also had ambitions to start a family. Moreover, rumours had the 23rd earmarked for overseas service; in November the regiment would be posted back to Gibraltar, not Jack's favourite place even as a younger man in 1802. As many had before him, he could avoid an undesirable posting by leaving the regiment, either by retiring and selling out, or transferring, possibly also going on half-pay. The former meant quitting the army but gaining the financial value of his majority (brevet promotions could not be sold); the latter meant a continued income, but one much reduced, at the nominal risk of recall to the Colours at some future point.[26] Jack was uncertain of the best course. Far from home, there were few he could turn to for advice; it seems likely that he discussed his position with his commanding officer and old comrade, Thomas Pearson, asking for three months leave to decide what to do. That was a mistake; Pearson's devotion to the efficiency of his regiment took primacy over any obligation he felt for Jack, his most senior subordinate and longest standing colleague. With an overseas posting imminent, Pearson declined to grant leave to a senior officer; instead, he proposed Jack follow Thomas Dalmer's example - exchange to half pay in another regiment. This was pure self-interest by Pearson; if the exchange was managed well, he could replace Jack

---

25 Sherer, *Recollections*

26 'Half pay' was a misnomer; pay was on a scale largely unchanged for 100 years; the actual amount was closer to quarter-pay. The service obligation was similarly dubious; few were recalled after the Napoleonic Wars ended. See Muir, *Tactics*

with someone he knew would fit the regiment. Apparently without Jack's knowledge, Pearson approached Horse Guards, noting that he deemed Jack unfit for service because of his injury. In the UK National Archives is preserved an undated but intriguing note that set off the chain of events which brought Jack's long army career to an unexpectedly sudden end:

> Submitted to HRH that Col. Pearson of the 23rd is extremely anxious to secure to that Reg$^{t.}$ the Services of Capt. England as Major vice Hill who retires on half pay & the Two Captains transferring to him already agreed.
> Captain England is a Capt. of 1811 & has been selected by HRH for the purchase of the Majority in the 92nd But if HRH should approve he might purchase that of the 49th, be removed to 23rd & the Majority from half pay go to the 49th leaving the Majority in the 92nd for any cause which HRH may fix upon, as the date matters not there, provided the Officer selected will join... Capt England's money having been lodged the Succession to a Majority could be completed at once if Capt. E. should succeed.[27]

England had served in five different regiments before joining the 23rd in August 1819. Like Pearson, he missed Waterloo; perhaps there was a commonality of envy between the two men against people like Jack - resentment against 'Waterloo Men' was far from uncommon in the army. England served with the 23rd for four years, during which time he clearly impressed Pearson, but in September 1823 began moves to purchase a majority elsewhere. When he heard of Jack's desire to avoid Gibraltar, Pearson saw the chance to declare him unfit, remove him and keep England in the regiment by taking Jack's position. The problem was that Jack had not yet decided his immediate future, despite Pearson telling Horse Guards he had. Horse Guards may have had some inkling that this was the case, not least because there was no application from Jack for permission to leave the 23rd. On 9 September the Military Secretary, Major-General Sir Herbert Taylor, wrote to the Commander-in-Chief in Ireland, Lieutenant-General Lord Combermere, asking him to speak to Jack personally and establish his intentions. Taylor must have specifically mentioned the problems Pearson perceived from Jack's disability, with the implication that he was not 'efficient'.[28] Combermere had his Military Secretary send Jack a copy of Taylor's

---

27 TNA WO 31/530 *Transfers 1823*. The content of this note suggests it was written before other loose letters in the same folder.
28 Jack's 1823 *Memorandum* to the Duke of York quotes from Taylor's letter 'His Royal Highness will readily give his utmost support to any application Lieut.

letter. Unfortunately, the text of this does not apparently survive, but Combermere's reply, enclosing a letter to his secretary from Jack, does.

Major General
Sir Herbert Taylor
&c &c &c

Royal Hospital
Dublin 22nd September 1823

Sir

In reply to your letter of the 9th Instant, desiring that I would call upon Major and Lieutenant Colonel Hill, of the Royal Welch Fusiliers, for his determination, whether he would resign his Commission in that Corps by the Sale thereof, or by retiring upon the half pay, I have now the honor to transmit, a letter from that Officer, requesting permission to exchange with Major England of the 49th Regiment, with a view to his obtaining three months leave of absence, for the purpose of consulting his Friends on the subject, before the expiration of which period, he will communicate to you his decision: which I request you will lay before His Royal Highness The Commander in Chief.

I Have the honor to be
Sir
Your most obedient humble Servant
Combermere LG[29]

Jack's letter makes it clear that Pearson's manoeuvres were previously unknown to him. Perhaps persuaded by Combermere, he seems to have accepted however that exchanging with English would buy time to decide what to do next:

Colonel Hill may address the Secretary at War for a pension in consideration of a wound which entailed such disability'.

29 TNA WO 31/530

Dublin 22 Sep$^{t.}$ 1823

Hon$^{ble.}$ Major Finch
Military Secretary
&c &c

Sir
 With reference to the letter of Major General Sir H. Taylor addressed to Lieu$^{t.}$ General Lord Combermere under date of the 9th ins$^{t.}$ and which you did me the honor to send me a copy of.
 I beg to state that the sudden and unexpected intimation therein contained, has given rise to the most distressing embarrassments. I however bend with humble submission to the wishes of H.R.H. the Commander in Chief, but beg for a short respite of three months in order to afford time to consult with my friends as to what will be the mode of quitting the service most advantageous to my interest.
 Perceiving by the concluding paragraph of Sir. H. Taylor's letter the desire of H.R.H. The Commander in Chief to have the R.W. Fusiliers efficient in Field Officers before embarking for Gibraltar, and my remaining in this Corps, for the period for which I solicit His Royal Highness' indulgence being inadmissible, and understanding that Major England of the 49 Reg$^{t.}$ is anxious to return to the Reg$^{t.}$, I beg to solicit leave to exchange with that officer, with the prospect of being granted the leave which I am so much in need of, at the end of which period, or perhaps sooner, my determination shall be notified to Sir H. Taylor either to sell or go on half pay.
 I have the honor to be Sir your obedient Humble Serv$^{t.}$

J Hill Major & L$^{t.}$ Co$^{l.}$
R.W.F. [30]

Another surviving memorandum records the outcome of Jack's appeal:

<u>23rd and 49th Foot</u>
Exchange between Major England & Brevet Lt. Col. Hill

<u>Sir H</u>

Under the circumstances of Lt.Col Hill's loss & the incapability of satisfying him in the 23rd Reg before the Embarkation, HRH will agree to his Exchange with Major England & shall dispose with his

---

30 TNA WO 31/530

signing the Certificate proscribed..., it being hereby understood that his object is not to join the 49th Reg^t but that he will either sell out of the Service or retire upon half pay within three months of the date of Exchange.[31]

[Different hand] Agreed 26 Sept.

The die was now cast: Jack would exchange with England and then decide his future. The *London Gazette* for Saturday 18 October 1823 duly announced:

23d Regiment of Foot Major Richard England, from 49th foot, to be Major, vice Hill, who exchanges

and below, the mirroring entry

49th Ditto Brevet Lieutenant-Colonel J. Humphrey Edward Hill, from the 23rd Foot, to be Major, vice England, who exchanges.[32]

Both appointments were dated 2 October 1823. Jack formally ceased to be a Royal Welch Fusilier on 30 September 1823.

The formalities were in place, but while Jack told Combermere he wanted time to consult his friends, it is not clear who these were. None of the close friends he had in his early days were still around; Ellis, James Mackenzie, Offley, Van Courtlandt and Keith had died in service; George Bradford had died in March 1818. George Mackenzie was still alive but was living in Australia. The only one of Jack's contemporaries available was Thomas Pearson, who had shown himself untrustworthy having, in Jack's perception, forced him out of the regiment he joined as a boy. Indeed, nobody else then serving in the unit, officer or ranker, had been there longer, or seen more action, than Jack. Even Pearson had joined later: in October 1796, after Jack was commissioned that July. With a little time to think, Jack now saw that exchanging to the 49th, the Hertfordshires, was a mistake; he did not need three month's leave to realise that. He may also have realised the potential financial disadvantage he had just incurred. The 49th was at Copenhagen, but was sent to Canada in 1802, where it remained until 1815. It had seen action in the War of 1812 and was a good corps; but it had nothing like the illustrious record of the Royal Welch Fusiliers. A commission in the 23rd might be more lucrative than one in the 49th; Jack had erred by

31 TNA WO 31/530
32 *London Gazette* Issue no. 17967 dated 18 October 1823

exchanging, rather than selling out as a Fusilier. On the day after he left the 23rd, even before he embarked for the mainland, Jack picked up his pen again and wrote directly to Horse Guards:

M General
Sir Herbert Taylor
&c &c &c
Horse Guards
London

Dublin 1 Octr. 1823

Sir

Having at last obtained leave of absence I have the honor to acquaint you that I have no wish to exchange into the 49th Reg^{t.} but prefer selling my commissions in the 23 Reg^{t.} if H.R.H. The Commander in Chief has no objection.

I was induced to consent to the exchange with Major England as the only alternative of obtaining leave of absence as will appear from the correspondence I have the honor to enclose.

As H.R.H. has been graciously pleased to consider my feelings on the subject, I cannot but think that after 28 years service in the Welch Fusiliers an exchange on full pay into another Reg^{t.} followed by a sale or half pay wants make my retirement most painfully unmarkable in the eyes of the army.

My resolution to sell will appear from the papers to that effect, which were returned and are herewith enclosed.

I have the Honor to be
Sir
Your most ob^{t.} Ser^{t.}
J Hill Major & Lt Col^{l.} R.W.F

It is not clear who Jack believed 'induced' him to agree to exchange with English, but it seems highly likely it was Thomas Pearson, not least because of the undated note describing Pearson as being 'extremely anxious' for an exchange to be arranged, and incorrectly asserting that Jack was planning to retire on half pay. There is some support for this speculative conclusion from two family notes: the posthumous record of his service written by his son James records that Jack 'Had to leave the Army…in consequence of being unable to manage his horse with his left hand', exactly what Pearson apparently told Horse Guards; a further note on Jack's career written in 1883 by his son-in-law records 'He through the jealousy of a Colonel newly appointed to the XXIIIrd & a friend of the Prince Regent, was reported as unfit any longer to manage his horse with his left arm (on account of the wound a most dangerous one received at Waterloo) and Col. Hill retired in disgust.'[33] Perhaps there is also a further hint in Pearson's own farewell letter to the officers of the 23rd when he left the regiment in 1830, which concludes with the oddly confessional lines: 'Human interest is ever liable to err and in no situation more so than in the exercise of command; be assured that in those instances when in the execution of public duty I may unintentionally have given pain, the fault has proceeded from the head, and not the heart and it is now only permitted me to hope...that when remembered it will not be with feelings other than those which I now in full sincerity of an overflowing heart subscribe myself your ever attached and truly affectionate friend.'[34]

He may have felt 'disgust' at his treatment but however aggrieved Jack was, to renegue on an exchange he requested was not a move likely to be well received at Horse Guards. It was not; Taylor scribbled a long and tetchy note across the back of Jack's letter:

HRH

His letters and the enclosures have been submitted to the Commander in Chief who orders me to acquaint him that in the arrangements connected with the Communications made to him it has been HRH's object that Major England should obtain the Majority of the 23rd Regt. and HRH has less hesitation in stating this & in adhering to that purpose as He had understood that Bt. Lt Col Dalmer had upon a former occasion consented to Major England's obtaining such appointment by purchase or by Exchange.[35] His R.H. therefore having agreed to his Exchange to the 49th Regt. with the clear view of the sale of his Majority in that Corps as stated in my letter to Lord Combermere of 26th Sept, does not wish now to admit of this Regiment that such Exchange should not take place previously to his retiring from the Service which he will be unlikely to do within 3 months from the date of

---

33 Hill, *Colonel Hill (CB) Services* and *Services of your Grandfather the late Lieut.t Colonel John Humphrey Edward Hill, C.B. XXIIIrd Royal Welsh Fusiliers*: Note by J.R. Race Godfrey to his son, Lieutenant S. H. Godfrey, 2nd Batt. The Lancers dated 21 March 1883

34 Cary and McCance, *Regimental Records*

35 This is Francis Dalmer, Thomas Dalmer's brother, promoted Brevet Lieutenant-Colonel for his 'conduct in the Battle of Waterloo', where he commanded No. 1 Company. Dalmer was serving with the 23rd in his regimental rank of Captain, having joined them in Ireland in May 1823. He was promoted to Major in the regiment after Jack left.

his Exchange. As this Exchange with Major England in the 49th takes place by His RH's desire he will just be required to pay the courtesy on the 49th & allow him to assess now that it he is very sensible of the manner in which he has read the Communications made to him throu' Lord Combermere.

Enclosures

Send copy to Lord Combermere suggesting it may be communicated to the officers of the 23rd Reg.

Does the last sentence suggest that the 23rd's officers had expressed disquiet at Jack's treatment? Whether or not this is the case, Jack did not want to be an officer in the 49th, nor go on half pay. He had only one choice and wrote again to Taylor.

> M General
> Sir Herbert Taylor KCH
> &c &c
> Horse Guards
> London

London Jany 24th 1824

Sir

 I have the Honor of requesting you to submit my application to the Commander in Chief, praying His Royal Highness to obtain His Majesty's permission to retire from the Service by the Sale of my Commissions in the 49th Reg^{t.}

> I have the Honor to be
> Sir
> Your most obedient
> Humble Servant
> J Hill

> Major 49th Reg^{t.} & B^t Lt Col^{l.36}

On 9 March the Regimental agents confirmed to Taylor 'that satisfactory security is lodged in our hands for the regulated difference

---

36 TNA WO 31/535 *Resignations 1824*

for the purchase of a majority for Captain Bartley of the 49th Regiment'
and Jack duly sold out. A week later the London Gazette announced:

> 49th [Regiment of Foot], Captain Robert Bartley to be Major, by
> purchase, vice Hill, who retires. Dated 5th February 1824.[37]

Jack's 28 years of military life had come to a messy end. Now financial
matters became important. He was relatively comfortable, having
received prize money from various campaigns, including the Peninsula
and Waterloo. Selling his majority in the 49th would have raised over
£3,000 (almost £300,000 today), even if he might have got more for
one in the 23rd. If he ever received the back pay he was due from the
Portuguese army, that would have provided a useful addition too.
Having lived in the army, or with his parents in Hennock, for his entire
adult life however, Jack needed money to establish his own household.
In civilian life he would have no regular income, other than his
temporary pension of £200, but his left arm was useless and he believed
he should be entitled permanently to the full £300 pension for the loss
of a limb. On 17 December 1823 Jack once again put pen to paper to
petition the Duke of York, as Commander in Chief, seeking a higher
pension. Jack knew the way the army did business well enough, and he
carefully referenced an implied promise of this in Taylor's letter to
Combermere of the previous September, coupled with a slightly more
expansive memorial of his career. The full text is at Appendix 4. The
memorial ended with the summary:

> Your memorialist at the period of leaving the Royal Welch Fusiliers
> was the individual of the longest standing of either Officer or
> Private, and had been present in every Field (except Minden) borne
> on the colours of the 23rd Regt. Your memorialist most humbly
> prays His Royal Highness that after being engaged in twenty affairs
> of importance, and seven sieges, once wrecked, once on fire at sea,
> after so many years of service and suffering, after twenty-eight,
> being obliged to return to Civil life, your memorialist adverts to Sir
> Herbert Taylor's letter to Lord Combermere dated 9th Sept. 1823
> in the paragraphs: 'His Royal Highness will readily give his utmost
> support to any application Lieut. Colonel Hill may address the
> Secretary at War for a pension in consideration of a wound which
> entailed such disability.[38]

---

37 *London Gazette* Issue No. 18009 March 13 1824
38 Hill 1823 *Memorandum*

But despite this previous promise of Royal support, no increase in his pension was granted; upsetting the Duke of York and his Military Secretary over the exchange with English cannot have helped his cause. The decision added to Jack's sense that he had been pushed out of the 23rd by Pearson and had left the army on poor terms. He considered an appeal to Viscount Palmerston, the Secretary at War. It is not clear whether he sent the letter, which survives only as a draft:

> My lord, the nature of the wound which I have received in H.M.S[ervice] having at length incapacitated me for active Duty, I am reluctantly compelled to give up the Military Profession, and as my income will consequently be much diminished, I request the favour of your Lordship's to direct that I may be re-examined by the medical board with a view to some addition being made to my present pension and flatter myself that the rank I held previous to being wounded at Waterloo with my previous services and subsequent sufferings give me some pretensions to your Lordship's Indulgent consideration.

Whether he sent it or not, the outcome did not change. His son's posthumous statement of service noted sarcastically that Jack 'Was refused the Pension…The Grateful County saved by this - One hundred pounds Sterling every year until his death'.[39]

Jack and Jane now focused on their life together, renting a house on the banks of the River Dart at Dartington, some five miles from Caroline and Jacob Ley at Ashprington. According to a contemporary advertisement Higher Hood House was owned by one John Wills Mapowder who continued to live next door. It was 'large, handsome, and commodious' with '3 sitting-rooms, hall, &c. on the first floor; large drawing-room, and 6 bedrooms on the second, with attics'. The gardens had 'a lawn in the front; Shrubbery and Gardens behind. The beautiful River Dart at an easy distance; and the new Road from Totnes to Ashburton conveniently near.'[40] The rent was £50 per year. Higher Hood House was a home in which to raise a family; Jack would live out the final years of his life there.

Marriage and departure from the army were only part of the most turbulent period in Jack's personal life. On 18 July 1824 Jack's mother, Margaret, died. She had been the recipient of most of Jack's letters; over fifty open with the words 'Dear Mother'. Four days after her death

---

39 Hill, *Colonel Hill (CB) Services*
40 *Exeter Flying Post* 21 Nov 1822

Margaret was laid to rest outside her husband's church, St. Mary's in Hennock. She did not live to see the birth of Jack and Jane's first child, John Edward, who arrived on 25 April 1825. A daughter, Jane Mary was born the following year. Jack's father John continued as Rector of St. Mary's, surviving his wife by nearly four years until on 2 April 1828 he died 'very suddenly, of apoplexy, aged 77.'[41] John's body was placed alongside his wife on 10 April. At a time when rectors routinely served their parishes for life, John's longevity in post was still notable: over 100 years later the entry for Hennock in a guide to Devon recorded (with significant inaccuracy about his elder sons): 'Among the vicars of Hennock was John Hill, whose 53 years of labour here ended in 1828. He had two warrior sons who fought all over the world, including Waterloo and Trafalgar. They both lived over 100 years, the father preaching peace here half the time, the sons going out to the wars.'[42] On 16 May, Jack, William and Fred attested to their father's will, which left significant sums of money to each of them and to Caroline. A week later, on the 22nd, Jack and Jane's second son, James Turner, was born, followed in 1829 by William Price and Charles in 1832. As the next generation increased, the last link to the previous one was severed when on 8 December 1833 Aunt Peggy, the Rev. John's sister, died. On 13 December that year she too was interred in the family vault.

There was further sadness to come. Jack's youngest brother Fred had followed William and Charles into the Royal Navy in around 1809, probably again as a gentleman volunteer, gaining his Lieutenancy in 1814 (when he first appears in naval records). Little is known of his career, other than Henry Ellis' introduction of him to the Admiral of the North American station. He may have served on William's ships, as it was normal practice for a Post Captain to take relatives aboard. Fred spent some of his career on the far side of the Atlantic, because he died at Arachat in Nova Scotia on 14 May 1834. Fred's passing meant that Jack, Caroline and William lost their father, mother, aunt, and only other surviving brother in less than ten years. After Fred's death, the surviving children of John and Margaret Hill placed a marble commemorative plaque to their parents, their three lost siblings and Aunt Peggy on the wall of St. Mary's. It reads:

---

41 *The Gentleman's Magazine and Historical Chronicle*, Volume 98, Part 11828
42 '*The King's England: Devon, Cradle of Our Seamen* Arthur Mee (ed) 1938. The claimed lifespan of Jack and William Hill is odd: the actual lifespan of both is clearly commemorated on the church walls.

IN MEMORY OF
MARGARET, WIFE OF THE REV^D. JOHN HILL, VICAR OF
HENNOCK, WHO DIED ON THE 18th OF JULY, 1824, AGED 67
AND OF THE REV. JOHN HILL, A.M. 53 YEARS VICAR OF THIS
PARISH, WHO DIED ON THE 2nd OF APRIL 1828, AGED 77.
ALSO OF THEIR CHILDREN, CAROLINE MARGARET, WHO
DIED 25th FEBRUARY, 1780,
CHARLES ABRAHAM, MIDSHIPMAN R.N.
SUPPOSED LOST IN A TENDER BELONGING TO H.M.S.
MINOTAUR, IN THE YEAR 1801 AGED 19.
ALSO OF MARGARET HILL, SISTER OF THE REV. JOHN HILL,
WHO DIED 8th DEC 1833, AGED 79.
ALSO OF LIEUT. FREDERICK C. HILL, R.N. SON OF THE REV^D.
JOHN AND MARGARET HILL, WHO DIED AT ARACHAT,
NOVA SCOTIA, MAY 14th 1834.

There is little trace of the life Jack and Jane lived thereafter with their children in the rolling hills of Dartington, near Totnes on the southern edge of Dartmoor. So far as his useless arm allowed, Jack no doubt continued his pursuit of field sports and like many old soldiers probably followed with interest the debates raging in the newspapers as contemporaries published their recollections, with greater or lesser detail and accuracy. Perhaps he occasionally attended Blundell's Old Boys days, held annually in the last week of August. Lieutenant-Colonel and Mrs. Hill's last child, Eliza Caroline, was born on 8 July 1836. But when Eliza was less than two years old, on 21 January 1838, Jack suddenly died. A few days later his body was carried back to Hennock; it was placed in the family vault on the 26th. In May the Gentleman's Magazine published his obituary:

Jan. 21. At Hood house, near Totnes, Lieut.-Col. John Humphrey Edward Hill, C.B. He was made Second Lieut. 23rd foot 1796, First Lieut.1797, Captain 1803, Major 1812, and brevet Lieut. Colonel 1813. He served in Spain and Portugal, and was attached to the Portuguese army; he received a cross for the battles of Salamanca, Nivelle, and Nive, and the siege of St. Sebastian, at which he commanded Portuguese regiments; he also served in Flanders, and was present at Waterloo.

Jane did not stay at Hood House and sold most of their household effects. The local newspapers carried the advertisements:

HOOD HOUSE, DARTINGTON, DEVON.

An excellent Horse, double and single London made Carriage Harness, Gig, Cart, nine Pipes of first rate Cider, 150 nitches of Reed, lot of good Hay, and Potatoes, Furniture, Carpets, Sofas, Wardrobes, Beds, and other Effects.

Mr. ROBERT TIPPETT, respectfully announces that he has been honoured with instructions to Sell by Auction on THURSDAY and FRIDAY, 5th and 6th days of April, punctually at Twelve o'Clock, the undermentioned

Furniture and Effects

Of the late Lieut. Col. HILL

Consisting of a large carpet 24 feet long, sofa, mahogany Pembroke table, what-not, bookstand, three deal wardrobes, several cupboards, three large desks, satin wood medicine chest, replete with every requisite for a family, two servants beds, bureau bed, bidet, mahogany crib, oak crib, dressing tables, and wash-stands, dresser with drawers and cupboards, large kitchen table, meat safe, meal hutch, salting tunnels, and salting pans, four washing trays, ten milk pans, butter bucket and scales, excellent large beam, scales, scales and weights, stone butter jars, coffee and pepper mills, two very handsome drawing-room and parlour stoves, two good modern kitchen ranges, smoke jack, three good guns, and appendages, kitchen and parlour fenders, blanc-mange shapes, forty dozen patent wine and porter bottles, and bottle racks, iron, furnace, and steamer, and a QUANTITY of BOOKS.[43]

This list of mundane household items includes a few that recall aspects of Jack's life: 'three good guns', reflecting his love of shooting; 'forty dozen patent wine and porter bottles', recalling reports of his pleasure at drinking at the mess table; and 'a quantity of books', which perhaps included those he asked his mother to obtain from Nova Scotia. At the same time the house was advertised for re-letting, Mapowder coincidentally having also died a couple of months after his tenant:

---

43 *Western Times*, 17 March 1838

DARTINGTON AND RATTERY, DEVON.

TO be LET for a term of seven years, from the twenty fifth day of MARCH inst..

subject to such conditions as will be produced at the time of letting, all those capital MESSUAGES, BARTONS, and FARMS, called Higher Hood, Lower Hood, North Hood, and a part of Putt's Tenement,

All situate lying and being in the parishes of Dartington and Rattery, in the County of Devon, lately occupied by Lieut. Col. Hill, and John Wills Mapowder, Esq.; in the following lots.

Lot 1. – All that capital MESSUAGE or DWELLING HOUSE, with a Shrubbery, the great Orchard, Gardens, and Green, called HIGHER HOOD HOUSE, containing together by estimation 4A, 3R, 37P, as lately occupied by Lt. Col. Hill, as tenant thereof, situate, lying and being in the Parish of Dartington, in the County of Devon.

...For Letting this desirable Property a PUBLIC AUCTION will be held at the house of William Leach, the King's Arms Inn, in Totnes, on TUESDAY the 3rd day of APRIL next, by 4 o'Clock in the afternoon.

For viewing the Premises, application may be made to the Hind at Lower Hood; and further particulars known of Mr. JAMES ELLIOT, Land Surveyor, Little Hempston, of Mr. JOHN BIDLAKE, Yarner, in Dartington, or at the Office of Mr. Farwell, Solicitor, Totnes.

Dated 17th March 1838.[44]

But although she left Dartington, Jane apparently stayed in Devon. The 1851 Census has her living in a cottage in Cheriton Bishop with her daughters Jane Mary and Eliza, together with two servants. By then John Edward had followed in the footsteps of his paternal grandfather, obtaining his M.A. at Christ Church, Oxford and holding a series of posts in the church including becoming curate of Welshpool in 1850. He became vicar there from 1865 and Proctor for the Diocese of St. Asaph

---

44 *Western Times*, 17 March 1838

in 1886. On 25 April 1850 he married Maria, daughter of Lieutenant-Colonel John Race Godfrey, a soldier in the Honourable East India Company's army. Like his parents, John Edward went on to have seven children: six daughters and one son, the latter also called John. Jack and Jane's first daughter, Jane Mary, cemented the Hill family's connection to the Race Godfreys when in November 1852 she married Lieutenant-Colonel Godfrey's eldest son; they went on to have six children, also making their home in Welshpool. Jane also later moved back there to live near, or probably with one of, her two eldest children.[45]

Jack and Jane's second son, James Turner, followed his father's footsteps, rising ultimately to the rank of Major-General in the Honourable East India Company army. In August 1857 James married Agnes Pennell; they would go on to have no less than eleven children, but apparently their honeymoon was interrupted by James' urgent recall to India after the outbreak of the Mutiny. Jack and Jane's 4th son, Charles Frederick, followed his three uncles' path into the Royal Navy. Eventually retiring as a Commander, he saw action in the Baltic during the Crimean War, being present at the capture of Bomarsund and the bombardment of Sveaborgh; he was gazetted on seven separate occasions for services against the enemy. Little is known about Jack and Jane's three other children. William Price also followed his father's footsteps, was commissioned in the 16th Foot, and rose to the rank of captain. In January 1860, however, newspapers reported the deaths the previous month 'at Funchal, Madeira, [of] Capt. William Price Hill, and Eliza Caroline Hill, son and daughter of the late Lieut. Col. J. H. E. Hill, C.B., of Hood House, Dartington, Devon.'[46] The circumstances of their deaths are unknown, but Eliza died on 22 December 1859 and William on the 24th; with deaths so close together, the cause may have been disease. William was 30 years old; Eliza just 23. Richard Hill, Jack and Jane's fifth and youngest son also died relatively young, at 35 years old in April 1870; like his brother William and his sister Eliza, he never married. The series of tragedies meant Jane outlived not only her husband but also three of her children; she survived Jack by fifty-two years. Towards the end of her life, she moved again to live with her son John in Montford, Shropshire, probably when he left Welshpool in 1886; Jane died in Montford on 8 December 1890, aged 96, leaving a personal estate of just over £1,400. She was not buried alongside Jack, but having never lived in Hennock that is unsurprising. Jack and Jane had only fifteen years together as husband and wife; they would spend eternity apart.

---

45 Jane's probate record lists her as having been 'formerly of the Vicarage, Welshpool in the County of Montgomery.

46 *The Bridgewater Mercury* 19 January 1860

CHAPTER 16

EPILOGUE

'His discharge of all the relations of his life was as exemplary, as his conduct in the field had been glorious'

Memorial plaque, St. Mary's, Hennock

A single tomb in a Devon village contains the remains of two brothers, one who survived Trafalgar and one who survived Waterloo. Perhaps other brothers participated in the two greatest battles of the Napoleonic Wars; few, if any, lie in the same tomb.[1] Jack's affection for William is clear from the many times he mentions him in his letters. Though the two served throughout the late Revolutionary and Napoleonic wars, they were rarely in the same theatre and never saw duty in the same place at the same time. Other than Christmas and New Year 1808/9, when they were both in Hennock for a month before Jack was recalled for embarkation to Nova Scotia, they barely saw each other in almost 30 years. William and Rose were living at Woodhouse Farm, just down the hill from Hennock, when William died in 1840. He too was placed alongside his family in the vault outside St. Mary's. William's wife Rose and their daughter, yet another Margaret, were later placed in the same vault. A commemorative plaque was also raised to William's memory in St. Mary's, which reads:

IN A VAULT WITHOUT THE CHURCH, ARE DEPOSITED THE REMAINS OF Wm. HILL, Esq R.N. POST CAPTAIN OF THE ROYAL NAVY, AND SON OF THE REV. JOHN HILL, MANY YEARS VICAR OF THIS PARISH, WHO HAVING SERVED HIS COUNTRY WITH DISTINCTION IN ALL PARTS OF THE GLOBE, AT THE GLORIOUS VICTORY OF TRAFALGAR, AND OTHER

---

1 One man is known to have been present at both battles: Lieutenant-General Miguel de Alava, an ADC to Wellington through the Peninsular War, was a Foreign Military Representative at Waterloo. He had been aboard the *Principe de Asturias* in the Spanish fleet at Trafalgar. In fiction, Richard Sharpe fought at both battles (on the British side).

MEMORABLE ACTIONS OF THE LAST WAR, DIED AFTER A
FEW HOURS ILLNESS THE 4th OF JAN 1840, AGED 56.
BELOVED RESPECTED AND LAMENTED.
ALSO OF ROSE PITT HILL, WIDOW OF THE ABOVE
BORN 23rd MARCH 1784, DIED 26th FEB 1868.
AND OF MARGARET THEIR SECOND DAUGHTER,
BORN 14th MARCH 1815, DIED 7th DEC 1867.

The third plaque on the same church wall offers an understated,
incomplete (and inaccurate) summary of Jack's service career:

TO THE MEMORY
OF
LIEUT. COL. JOHN HUMPHREY EDWARD HILL, C.B.
LATE OF THE 23rd REGT, ROYAL WELSH FUSILEERS,
ELDEST SON OF THE REVd. JOHN HILL,
FORMERLY VICAR OF THIS PARISH.

THIS GALLANT OFFICER COMMENCED HIS PROFESSIONAL
CAREER IN 1796, IN H.M. 23rd REGT OF FOOT, AND SHARED
IN THE RENOWN, THAT DISTINGUISHED CORPS ACQUIRED
IN EGYPT, THE PENINSULA, AMERICA, AND LASTLY AT
WATERLOO, ON WHICH MEMORABLE DAY HE WAS
DANGEROUSLY WOUNDED BY A GRAPE SHOT IN
THE SHOULDER, WHILST LEADING
THE BRAVE FUSILEERS TO VICTORY.

THE 4 PORTUGUESE REGT OF CACADORES, WHICH HE
FORMED, WAS COMMANDED BY HIM IN SEVERAL OF THE
PENINSULAR CAMPAIGNS, IN WHICH HIS ZEAL AND ABILITY
WERE SO EMINENTLY CONSPICUOUS AS TO OBTAIN FOR HIM
MANY HONORABLE MARKS OF DISTINCTION FROM HIS
OWN AND FOREIGN SOVEREIGNS.

HAVING FOR SOME YEARS RETIRED FROM THE ARMY, HE
WAS IN THE ENJOYMENT OF THE SOCIETY OF AN
AFFECTIONATE FAMILY, AND AN EXTENSIVE
CIRCLE OF FRIENDS: AND HIS DISCHARGE OF ALL THE
RELATIONS OF LIFE WAS AS EXEMPLARY, AS HIS CONDUCT
IN THE FIELD HAD BEEN GLORIOUS.

HE DIED SUDDENLY, ON THE 21st OF JANUARY, 1838,
AGED 59 YEARS.

The plaque's author was apparently confused by Jack's Portuguese army career as the tribute conflates the 5th Caçadores and the 4th Infantry, and he did not 'form' either unit. Jack and Jane's eldest son was only thirteen when his father died, so perhaps the text was written by William, who as a sailor was forgivably unfamiliar with his brother's foreign service.

Jack Hill literally grew from boy to man in the army. As a man, he undoubtedly had his eccentricities: Browne's description of his peculiar wardrobe and accounting habits (Chapter 8) are one indicator as, more debatably, are Bunbury's recollections from outside San Sebastián (Chapter 13). The family tale of his ordering the soaking of a junior officer's mattress in Paris fits the pattern too. Browne attributed such behaviour to Jack's being 'violently struck on the head' during the sinking of De Valk, but notably acknowledges that in 'his military duties...he was as correct as any Officer of the corps' and 'exceedingly beloved by the soldiers of his company'. Other evidence suggests a well-regarded colleague who cared for his men: in 1811 John Harrison called him 'the same sterling fellow as ever' (Chapter 9); Robert Patteson's father wrote in appreciation of the care Jack had taken with his son; Jack himself told of his checking on his company, then leaving them alone to enjoy Christmas in 1801; and there is the poignant story of his distributing the old battle-worn Colours of the Portuguese 4th Infantry among its officers at Christmas 1813. His empathy no doubt took its lead from his friend Henry Ellis; as a light company officer, he seems to have instinctively adopted the philosophy underpinning Sir John Moore's system of encouragement and emulation as the best way to deliver an effective and efficient force, as his men demonstrated in the hills of Martinique in 1809.[2] Despite being the son of a clergyman, there is little overt evidence of the strength of his religious beliefs, though like all officers of the time, he no doubt attended Divine Service every Sunday. That he was asked to perform the burial service for James Mackenzie in Egypt in 1801 and that he carried a copy of the Book of Common Prayer at Waterloo may suggest that, as was said of Nelson, he was 'a thorough clergyman's son [who] never went to bed or got up without kneeling down to say his prayers'.[3] Jack told his parents he 'prayed the Almighty out of his infinite goodness to return me safe to you and my Hennock friends once more' in his letter of Christmas Day 1801, and the opening of his first letter home after Albuera remembered to 'Thank the Almighty that He has again saved your son unhurt'. That

2 See The British Army's Legacy from the Revolutionary and Napoleonic Wars: Hew Strachan in The Road to Waterloo Alan J Guy (ed.) 1990
3 Nelson's Fleet at Trafalgar Brian Lavery 2004

said, his contemporary Walter Bromley, former Paymaster of the 23rd, later recalled 'it is a melancholy fact, that, among 1000 men of the 23d regiment, it would be difficult at times to procure even one Bible'.[4] What is evident, however, is that Jack was one of the earliest group of soldiers in an army that had increasingly professionalised; his career coincided with, and was part of, a transformation in effectiveness by both the British army and the 23rd Foot; he left the latter professionally acknowledged as one of the finest regiments of a fine army.[5]

Jack participated in six major overseas campaigns, travelling to four continents and fighting on three; he was at sea for over a year in total, sailing some 21,000 miles in the process. He was involved in nearly forty combat actions, three of them - Albuera, St. Pierre and Waterloo - seeing the most intense casualties by area of any battle of the period in which British soldiers fought. He was the only member of the Royal Welch Fusiliers, and possibly the only Englishman, to participate in all three. He was wounded 6 times, though only four times by the enemy, and three of these were during his last battle. He spent six months as a Prisoner of War after his first action and nearly drowned returning from his first campaign. By an odd coincidence, that first action, the Ostend raid, took place just 80 miles from his last, at Waterloo. Jack was undoubtedly lucky to be alive after both that first campaign, in Holland, and his last, in Belgium. Yet through all the fighting it is conceivable that he never killed anyone himself. Officers might carry pistols, but the chances of their hitting anyone with one was remote. They would draw their swords to direct and encourage their men, but most officers would consider it a failure if they had to use the weapon: their job was to control their company or battalion, not to engage enemy soldiers themselves. Jack never recovered the full use of his left arm after Waterloo and he may have been mentally scarred too, by the sinking of *De Valk* but also from the many close friends he lost, from James Mackenzie in Egypt to Henry Ellis at Waterloo. It would be surprising if his experiences had no psychological effect; despite the studied insouciance of most officers of the time, soldiers of the Revolutionary and Napoleonic wars were as subject to trauma from the experience of combat as the survivors of more recent wars. His incarceration in Lille apparently also affected him; one

---

4 *A Few Plain Questions and Observations on the Catholic Emancipation* Walter Bromley 1812
5 See Strachan, *Legacy*

reference claims that he later provided a weekly donation of fuel and writing materials to prisoners.[6]

Jack' own summary of his career was:

> after being engaged in twenty affairs of importance, and seven sieges, once wrecked, once on fire at sea, after so many years of service and suffering, after twenty-eight being obliged to return to Civil life.[7]

Such a long and distinguished career, especially through the Peninsular War and Waterloo, has inevitably brought comparisons with a certain fictional hero: Jack Hill has been called 'a real-life Richard Sharpe'. The author of that comment claimed Jack's story 'is every bit as worthy of a series of novels to rival Bernard Cornwell's *Richard Sharpe* character'.[8] That may be so, though his true story is remarkable enough. Hill and Sharpe marched many of the same roads and both ended their careers as Lieutenant-Colonels, so there are some parallels. That said Jack had a far better foundation in life than Cornwell's fictional hero, joined the army as an officer rather than being promoted from the ranks and (to the best of our knowledge) did not enjoy as many romantic entanglements, though it would have been surprising if he had mentioned such things in letters to his parents. With imagination, it is possible that the two met: in *Sharpe's Prey*, set during the Copenhagen campaign, Richard Sharpe, at that point a lieutenant, has an encounter with a captain and some men from the Royal Welch Fusiliers. The officer is not named, but it is nice to think that it may have been Captain Jack Hill.[9]

The award of the Waterloo medal pleased those who received it but disappointed many who missed that battle despite fighting throughout 'the Great War' as it was known for the 100 years after it ended. After many years of opposition, not least from the Duke of Wellington who considered Waterloo 'extraordinary', a Military General Service Medal (MGSM) was finally authorised on 1 June 1847. The medal formally commemorated service on land or at sea during the whole of the Revolutionary and Napoleonic Wars between 1793 and 1814, with

---

6 *Of What Value are the Letters of Lt. Col. J.H.E. Hill in Describing the Conditions of Service of an Infantry Officer, 1796-1815?* Undated typescript M R L D Lee, Blundell's School. I have been unable to verify this claim; if true, it may have been those incarcerated in Dartmoor Prison.

7 Hill 1823 *Memorandum*

8 Lock, *Sharpe*

9 *Sharpe's Prey* Bernard Cornwell, 2001

clasps awarded for each battle the recipient participated in. In fact, the earliest campaign for which a clasp was authorised was Egypt in 1801. Over 25,000 MGSMs were awarded to soldiers and some 21,000 to sailors, but many who qualified, including Jack, died before it appeared; next of kin were not allowed to claim the medal on behalf of deceased relatives. Had Jack lived, he would have been entitled to twelve clasps: Egypt (1801), Martinique (1809), Albuhera (1811), Ciudad Rodrigo (1812), Badajoz (1812), Salamanca (1812), Vittoria (1813), San Sebastian (1813), Nivelle (1813), Nive (1813), Orthes (1814) and Toulouse (1814), which would have been amongst the most awarded to any soldier.[10] William also missed his entitlement to the Naval version with one clasp, for Trafalgar.

The Reverend John and Margaret Hill founded a military dynasty that has continued almost to the present day. Not only did all four of their own sons join the military, but so did many of their grandchildren and great-grandchildren. The most recent member of the family to serve in the British army, Edward Hill, joined the Royal Welch Fusiliers in August 1996, almost exactly 200 years after his ancestor, that young man from Blundell's, did the same. A few family treasures survive as memorials of Jack, carefully preserved and handed down through the generations. They include maps of Spain and Portugal from the Peninsular War, the prayer book he carried at Waterloo and, most treasured of all, the shot that passed through his shoulder in that battle. The shot is now mounted on a brass stand, ironically shaped to resemble a rope-bound cannon, which bears the inscription 'This French Grape Shot at the Battle of Waterloo entered under the left collar bone & passed through the shoulder blade of the late Lieu^t. Col. J.H.E. Hill, C.B. 23rd R.W. Fusiliers'.[11] Jack's medals are held by the Royal Welch Fusiliers Museum in Caernarfon; at the time of writing they are displayed in a case alongside memorabilia of Henry Walton Ellis, which seems appropriate given how long the two men spent together in the regiment.

But the most significant relics of all are Jack's letters. When he was writing them, he of course had no idea they would be preserved, nor

---

10 The most clasps awarded was fifteen, to two recipients. Smurthwaite, *Glory*. Twelve-clasp medals were received by two Welch Fusiliers, Privates Hogg and McDonagh; had he lived, Henry Ellis would also have had 12. *Medal Rolls 23rd Foot – Royal Welch Fusiliers Napoleonic Period* Norman Holme & Major E.L. Kirby 1978

11 The brass is reputedly from HMS *Victory*, providing also a tenuous link to William, though he never served on her. It was probably commissioned by Jack's son Charles Frederick Hill, who was in possession of the shot while a captain in the Royal Navy in 1883.

read beyond the members of his immediate family. Fortunately, his family's pride in Jack's achievements ensured his words survived. In 1928 the letters were transcribed, by Reginald Montgomery Hill, Jack's grandson who sent a set addressed to his brother, Lt. Col. H. C. Hill DSO covered by a note inscribed 'Copy of Grandfather's (Lt. Col. J.H.E. Hill) letters during the Peninsular Campaign'. The copies included several interpretive notes written by Reginald. Decades later Reginald's daughter, Edith Case (née Hill), produced a typed version of these transcripts and in 1988 published a selection of extracts from them in her book, *Letters to a Vicarage*, edited by Jenny Currie. In 1999 Edith presented a copy of the typed transcripts to Major Robert Lake, Regimental Secretary of the Royal Welch Fusiliers. The copy she gave the RWF, now in the regimental archive, has pencil markings indicating the passages Edith selected in compiling her book; she also donated a folder containing photos of some of the original manuscript letters in Jack's handwriting. Edith also presented a copy of the typed transcripts to Blundell's. These were subsequently formally 'Bound and Presented to the History Department' of the school by Michael Casey, in gratitude for the support the school's head of history had given his two sons, both then pupils at the school. The red leather cover of this bound collection bears the words 'Letters 1793 - 1815 Lieut. Col. J. H. E. Hill O.B.', 'Old Blundellian' being Jack's first post-nominal and in this context arguably his most significant; he would not necessarily have disagreed. Jack's service with the British and Portuguese armies inspired many of his descendants to follow in his footsteps; his letters have inspired and been the subject of study by many pupils at his old school over the years and are still today – in 2025 Blundell's renamed one of the school's Houses 'Hill House' in honour of their distinguished former pupil. Almost 200 years after he died, Jack Hill's letters still provide a glimpse of the thoughts, experiences and life of an astonishing infantryman.

Appendix 1

The Loss of the *De Valk*:
Jack Hill's formal report*

To Lt. Col. Robert Brownrigg,
Secretary to H.R.H The Commander in Chief,
Horse Guards

In compliance with the orders of His Royal Highness the Commander in Chief, I have transmitted an account of the loss of the Valk Dutch Frigate; the principal part was written during my stay in the island of Ameland.

On the 27th October, 1799, the 23rd or Royal Welch Fusilier Regiment received orders to march from Colhorn to the Helder - on the 28th the Regt. arrived; and then embarked the following morning on board some Dutch fishing Schucts and stood out to sea, endeavouring to get on board some line of Battleships that were about 15 miles from the Mars Deep. The wind dying away, we were forced to put about, the tide making against us, on our return passing the Helder point, we were hailed from the shore and ordered to go on board some Dutch Frigate up the Harbour when it fell to my lot with Lieuts. Hanson, Vischer, Maclean, and Hoggard to go on board the Valk Dutch Frigate with the Grenadiers and two Battalion companies.

On the 30th Oct. we got under-weigh with the morning tide, when shortly an officer came on board and informed the Captain that he was to wait and receive some more of the regiment that were on the "Venus" Dutch Frigate which was found unfit for sea. The Valk let go her anchor. This was in all human probability an unfortunate delay, had we immediately put to sea, we had perhaps avoided our misfortunes, as all the ships that sailed that tide reached England the following evening.

We got out the following tide and all the next day had very fine weather; about 7 o'clock in the evening we were by our reckoning within 30 miles of Yarmouth, and the fire of one of the lighthouses was observed from the ship. The Captain did not like to stand in for the Harbour at night as he had no English Pilot or seamen on board nor had any of the Dutch seamen been in the Port.

At 5 o'clock the next morning the 1st of November the wind came round to the S. West and blew us off shore beyond the Dogger Bank. On the 3rd and

---

* The footnotes in this Appendix are Jack Hill's original comments in amplification of his own official report.

5th we had very severe weather indeed (and were at one time near the west of Norway).[1] On the 6th the wind was fair, so that we could lay our course; on the 7th it was against our going to England, but some of the Northern ports were open to us, the navigation of which was well-known to Captain Darcie, a naval captain in the Orange Service, who commanded in the Texel Island and who, with his wife, an Irish lady of Cork, were passengers.[2] As our allowance of water was reduced to a pint per diem, we entertained serous thoughts of running into one of them.

On the 7th the winds were light, yet still favourable tho' accompanied with a heavy swell. On the 8th, 9th, we had observations, on the 9th in the middle of the day it was imagined we were about 70 miles from Yarmouth. About 3 o'clock in the morning of the 10th of November, the ship first struck, 6 miles, we afterwards found, from shore.

I was wrapped up in my greatcoat asleep on the floor of the cabin and awoke with the shock. The Officer on watch immediately came down and said: "The ship is aground". We were on deck scarce a moment when she struck a second time, twice breaking her stern against the sands. I went immediately up to the Captain and asked him if he had any orders to give, that I would endeavour to get them carried into execution; he made me no answer whatever; I then asked him if he knew where we were; he said on the Lemon and Oar [Ower], a sand about 30 miles from Yarmouth. I pointed at this time to a long dark line in the horizon and inquired of him if it was not land. He answered, we were far enough away from any.

A knowledge of our situation was now spread thro' the ship, and a dreadful confusion prevailed thro' the whole, and to heighten the distress we had a number of women and children on board. A Serjeant's wife was in labour at the time the ship struck. It is impossible for any language to describe the scene. The Dutch sailors gave themselves entirely up, and trusted more to their prayers than their exertions; indeed, some of the British entertained the strange idea that Captain Martinius had betrayed them, and was running them on shore merely to destroy them, and in the paroxysm of their despair were going to throw him overboard to have the satisfaction, as they said to see him die before them.[3]

---

1 Part of the Mizzen Rigging gave way - this and the want of spare sails made it nearly impossible to endeavour to hove to windward in blowing weather. There was only one suite of sails on board the Frigate and that not a very good one, so that they were very cautious of using them in blowing weather. A part of the rigging belonging to the spinnaker gave way, and the Captain was very anxious in consequence.

2 Captain Darcie had the command of the Overgessel, a Dutch 64 and cruised with the British Fleet before Holland was over-run by the French. During this service he was at Cork, and married there. His command in the Texel Island was during the time the British were in N. Holland and was the depot for the natives to join the Orange party in arms.

3 Of the Dutch, scarcely 20, not including the officers, had been at sea before, and it was necessary for an officer to point out every rope they were to man, with his own hands.

After the Cap^n. did not exert his command, Lieut. Hoggard, who had some knowledge of sea affairs, was particularly active in attempting to get the sails thrust aback, and when we had beaten over our bank, he was the first person who observed it, saying, "Be steady, boys, and obey orders; she's afloat again."

There was at this time something said about letting go our anchor. I was at the time looking over the side of the ship, and observed a line of breakers into which the ship was drifting with her broadside; I pointed it out to the Captain, he said: "It is all over". The vessel was very soon in among them. The main-mast went overboard, breaking off about its middle and in its fall dividing the long boat. Lieut. Hoggard had got the pumps at work and continued them till the seas began to break over the ship. The guns were all drawn [unloaded] the evening before and were not reloaded. The gunner had been repeatedly called for, but no one could give any account of him so that we could not fire any signals of distress. I went down with the first Lieut. Dicharis and one of our Grenadiers who perished afterwards on the shore (nearly in the same manner as Lieut. Hoggard did) to break open the powder room.[4] The sea had been breaking over the ship some time tho' I obtained some canon cartridges and distributed them among the people around me; but in loading the sea washed me from my hold and spoiled the powder.

We had no guns on the quarter deck and all this was done in the waist of the ship which is the part nearest the water and where the waves came over with the greatest violence. I went again below and found a musket and pouch (which were hung up between decks and fortunately succeeded tho' the ship was fast filling from above). I went and placed myself on the wreck of the long boat and fired from 20 to 30 rounds. I afterwards found on inquiry that it was observed by some of the inhabitants of the island. While I was sitting here, Lieut. Hanson and Vischer came up and talked of cutting away the boat; I informed them it was of no avail as it was already destroyed by the falling of the mainmast: the small boat was stoved and upset full of people close along-side; two men continued to her till she drifted on shore, they were the first who were saved.

The mizenmast broke away near the top, some little while after the foremast went close to the board and destroyed a great number of people who were crowded upon its shrouds. On my hearing the vessel beginning to break up, I went to the forecastle where there were very few people, this part was kept stationary by the anchors at the catheads: (and perhaps from its form, got

---

4 There were a few exceptions - men who did not lose their presence of mind in the awful situation they were in. When Captain Darcie brought his wife on board I said to him: "This is no place for women, let us try to save the ship," to which he replied: "There is no chance, all is over." In going down to the Magazine, I was in a hurry, everyone was calling for the Constable to give the keys or show the way. A Private Grenadier here came to me and put his hand on my shoulder, saying: "Mr. Hill, 1f you do not keep cool, we shall be able to do nothing." The poor fellow got on shore and died on the beach his advice in all human probability saved my life.

embedded in the sands; it remained up to the moment we quitted the island and [was] driven within 300 yards of the beach).

On getting to the forecastle I laid myself down flat, to shelter myself from the seas, and was here spectator of the fate of my companions. The masts were laying to leeward entangled by the rigging and many persons on them. With a dreadful crash, I saw the quarter deck divide into 3 pieces.[5] The larboard piece first gave way covered with people, and floated gradually away, when it received a sudden check from the shrouds and other cordage and shook off the greater number, as it was brought back to the ship the waves breaking over her fell perpendicularly on it and beat off the remaining few. Captain Ludovic Martinius and Lieut. Hanson were standing on the deck when it divided and the next sea washed them away.[Ψ]

The after-part of the starboard next went and ten people, who perhaps had better secured their holds, only saved themselves. What became of the other (part) I know not. I remained with a few others on the forecastle, but the greater part thinking themselves safer on the bowsprit got out on it, when shortly the bows (forward, and now the only remaining part of the ship) falling on its broadside destroyed them all.

I was now with only 4 or 5 others adhering to the last portion of the vessel which remained. At this moment there was nothing to be seen but a great number of fragments and people floating to the leeward. As the forecastle had turned over, I found it impracticable to stay any longer in my then situation. I took, therefore, advantage of a large piece of the wreck that had given way near me, to get up on it, but this to my great disappointment was entangled in the cordage. I had just made up my mind to quit it, when a sea carried me from it.

I swam now for a piece which I found occupied by 2 Dutch sailors; in the act of swimming I was seized by the leg by a drowning man. I fortunately reached the piece of wreck and held on, the more I endeavoured to disengage myself the faster he held on. I therefore remained quiet till life was exhausted and felt no more of him, but in this encounter I received some very severe bruises. On this piece was a ringbolt. I requested them to let me pass my handkerchief through it (there was not room for all our hands) and by this means obtained a convenient holdfast. No sooner was this arrangement made, than all three of us were threatened with immediate destruction - the foremast was floating beside us. We expected every sea wd. bring it on us, and receiving a blow from it I determined to get out of its way, and swam to another piece, but it was a fragment very inconveniently shaped, it frequently turned round and got me under, here I was nearly lost having taken in a great quantity of water.

I quitted this fragment and in swimming hit on one I did not see that was large and convenient. I got up on it, but a difficulty arose, how to keep myself on. My left hand I now found was disabled, and it is among breakers [hard] to conceive the difficulty of keeping a station.

---

5 On this part the greater number of persons had collected. (Larboard piece of quarter deck.)

The sea had not subsided after the last gales. I fortunately recollected my braces and pocket handkerchief; with them, I lashed myself on, fastening them through the seams or cracks in the wreck, and getting them round my wrists (shortly after this it passed all the breakers, and came into smooth water then). I floated some hours in the dark, till the fragment grounded, after some hesitation I quitted it, finding I c'd touch the bottom and got upon the sand, and resting myself.[6]

The first thought that occurred was my being on a sand bank only left dry by the tide. The last conversation I had with Capt[n]. Martinius strengthened this idea - no one was in sight; all, I conceived, had perished buried in the waves, and my imagination suggested that in another tide I should partake of the fate of my companions. My limbs were benumbed, to recover the circulation I ran on the sands, when feeling something under my feet, I thought it seaweed but the daylight increasing I found it to be rushes. I now flattered myself I was in England, and as I advanced on the beach, I perceived the tracks of a wagon. Following its direction, I fell in with my two Dutch companions (with whom I had shared the advantage of the ring-bolt) supported by 3 of the inhabitants. I accosted them in English, and was surprised at being answered in Dutch from which I learnt I was in Ameland, not England. My helmet was washed from me, and one of the peasants good-naturedly took his hat from his head and put it on mine. They conducted us about 2 miles to an Inn where we found a good fire and two of the soldiers already, one of whom was my servant.[7]

Lieut. Hoggard with about 8 others was on the mainmast. When it first struck ground he perceived it and shook hands with his companions and said: "Thank God, my lads, you are once more in safety." They waited about 5

---

6 Up to this the original sent to Mathewson for the history of the regiment - Gibraltar.

7 On getting to the Inn and entering the room, I went to the window seat as the first resting-place. Here I remained absorbed in a variety of ideas and recollections, when my attention was called by the conversation of the soldiers recognising each other, and enquiring who else were saved; when hearing of so few, one said: "All our poor officers are gone". "And my poor master, too," said my servant, when I rose up with a Dutch hat, and greatcoat on, and made myself known and shook hands with them. I told them I would stay with them and do everything to get them sent to England.

On the mast on which Lieut. Hoggard floated to the beach, a dog also got on shore with the men on it; the dog formerly belonged to Major James Mackenzie, but latterly always lived with a private of the name of Wingfield, the animal never would leave the beach up and down which it used to walk howling, but when disturbed, or attempted to be caught, used always to run in among the sandhills. Every exertion that was made by the survivors to make him follow them or to catch him were ineffectual and the dog remained there when we left the Island. The first thing the inhabitants gave us was warm beer.

The bodies of the people washed on shore were buried the first day among the sandhills, but the inhabitants insisted on their being buried in consecrated ground and this brought about the arrangement carried into execution.

minutes when all except Lieut. Hoggard quitted the wreck, and some of the Regt. waded back and laid hold of him, but all their strength and persuasion could not force him away from the mast, he was perfectly delirious and talked in a very incoherent manner - asking down what street they wanted to take him - the poor fellows who had befriended him began now to be exhausted, and were obliged to take care of themselves, indeed, one of them the moment he reached the shore was seized in the same manner, and remained either insensible or delirious all that day and part of the next.

It is impossible to say with what attention and humanity the inhabitants of Ameland received us. The inhabitants had hoisted the Orange flag [Declared in favour of the Staadtholder] and all communication between the island and the continent was cut off. They treated us as friends and furnished us with clothes (as many had stripped themselves). The inhabitants would not allow us to pay for our provisions or any other necessaries.

The President of the Island came to us about 10 o'clock on Sunday Morning as he was going to Church and assured us that we should be taken every care of and sent back to Helder. I had the bodies of Maclean and Hoggard, which were the only officers washed up, brought to the Inn and coffins prepared for them and the President ordered them to be interred in his own burying-ground in the village of Holm [Hollum], my own disabled state deprived me of the satisfaction of following them to the grave. The body of Mrs. Darcie was also buried in the same place, about 150 others were buried in one large grave in a corner of the churchyard, with as much decency as circumstances would admit.

With respect to the cause of our misfortunes, I am incapable of forming an opinion; one day I remarked to the Captain that they had no log line on board, he said they sometimes carried one, and sometimes did not, and that the Dutch sailor could determine pretty exactly without. A copy of the log book with the Chart, etc., etc., were always on a table in the cabin. Captain Darcie assisted in revising the day's work. Mr. Vogel, the 2nd Lieut. appeared a very experienced seaman and with Capt. Darcie had been upwards of 20 years at sea.

The Valk, tho' a ship 30 years old, they informed me, in the severe weather of the 3rd and 5th, made not much water. In the night of the 3rd a heavy sea struck her and part went as high as the cross jack yard. Capt. Darcie and Martinius were on deck, and the next morning informed us of the great danger we should have been in, had it been more between ships. Whenever the weather was bad, Capt. Darcie used to keep watch as well as Capt. Martinius, we had ourselves great confidence in both. The behaviour of Capt. Martinius was polite and attentive during the voyage, and never did he make an improper use of liquor. My brother officers and myself had agreed to present him with a naval sword and epaulettes, as a token of his liberal and gentlemanly conduct; as we all lived together, we came to this resolution when we were anticipating the pleasure of being in England the next day.

We were obliged to remain a week in the island to recover ourselves, some of the men had fevers. I hired a fishing boat to take us to the Helder and agreed with a Dutch surgeon to accompany us, as so many stood in need of medical assistance. The inhabitants conveyed us in waggons to the shore and supplied us with 120-lbs. of beef for our use on the passage, copies of the agreements drawn up by the President of the Island I delivered to Lieut. General Sir James Pulteney at the Helder on our return. The Islanders were well affected to the House of Orange and there were not 100 Patriots (French party) in the Island. There was only one gun mounted as I was informed in the Island and that was on the part opposite Schelling near the spot where we were wrecked.

When I took leave of the President, I thanked him for his humanity to myself and my men. He then requested me to represent to our Government how thankful the inhabitants would be to have their fishing boats protected (which the British Admiral did). I feel myself infinitely obliged to His Royal Highness for the indulgence he has been pleased to grant me by a leave of absence, and if upon a perusal of the above narrative any questions may arise, I will obey his command as far as my recollection will serve.

I have the honour to be,

J. H. E. HILL,
Lieut. R.W.F.

[13 January 1800]

Lost in the Dutch Frigate

23rd Regt. Men	-	265
Women and Children	-	25
Dutch Seamen	-	115
Women and Children	-	12
Capt[n]. Darcie and Wife	-	2
		416[†]

Saved

23rd Regt	-	20
(Lieut. Hill and 19 Men)		
Dutch Officers and Men	-	5
Total		446

The crew was reported to me at 120, but I know not whether exclusion or inclusion of officers. This may make 5 or 6 difference.

The hire of the fishing boat was 130 Guilders ∟ £210. 16. 8. The surgeon for his attendance on the men while on the Island, 80 Guilders - English money = £26. 13. 4.[θ]

467

The following month Jack received a formal acknowledgement of receipt of his report:

Lieut. Hill
23rd Regt.
Hennock
Chudleigh

Horse Guards
Feb. 5th 1800

Sir
     I have been hitherto prevented by press of business [from] acknowledging the receipt of your letter of the 13th instant, which however, I lost no time in communicating to H.R.H the Commander in Chief who directed me to convey to you many thanks for the very interesting narrative which your letter contains of the melancholy loss of the Valk Dutch Frigate, & of the officers & men of the 23rd Reg^t. who were on board that ship.

I have the honor to be
Robert Brownrigg

Ψ The correct name of the captain of *De Valk* was *Lieutenant ter Zee* Dithmar Martinius (not Ludovic)

† The correct total of the figures is 419, and the total including survivors 444.

θ Jack's conversion rates are off. If 130 Guilders equated to nearly £211, then 80 Guilders cannot have equated to nearly £27. Moreover, according to the website historicalstatistics.org, in 1800 130 Guilders could buy around 76g of gold, which would cost £10 at the time, suggesting a conversion rate significantly different than Jack claimed. By the same gold conversion rate 80 Guilders would have been equivalent to about £6. Either Jack's maths was seriously faulty (and there is evidence for this immediately above in his inability to correctly total the figures for the lost and saved of the Valk); or he was ripped off by someone doing a local conversion. The third possibility, that he told the Duke of York inflated amounts to seek to obtain better compensation for his personal losses, can be surely ruled unthinkable for the loyal son of a clergyman!

Appendix 2

Medical report by John Hennen, extracted from *Principles of Military Surgery* 1830

The following appears to me an instructive and interesting case:-

CASE LXII.

Lieutenant-colonel H[ill] received a grape-shot of eight ounces' weight on the day of Waterloo, just as the action was decided. The ball entered precisely under the centre of the clavicle of the left side; raised the periosteum into a few small flocculi, and passed through the spine of the scapula close to its neck, lodging between the skin and his flannel waistcoat. Profuse hemorrhage, incalculable as to quantity, but designated by his servant and the surrounding soldiers, who had seen many hard fought days, as "enormous beyond example," instantly took place. He lay for dead for some time. On his recovery he found himself in the hands of a foreign surgeon at a village adjacent to the field, faint, but collected; his arm numbed and immoveable, but very sensible to pain when touched. I need scarcely say that he had been in extreme danger, when the assistant-surgeon of his regiment joined him, shortly after his wound. When he was placed under my superintendence, on the ninth day, suppuration was fully established, and on removing the dressings, some few splinters appeared around both the sternal and dorsal aspects of the wound. I was very curious to see the state of the artery; it lay awfully pulsating in situ, (which uncovered arteries are not always observed to do,) bare for about two inches in length, or I should rather say unconnected, for its surface was studded with healthy granulations of unequal size, from a pin's head to that of a pea; the plexus of nerves was bedded in granulations; the arm was stiff, and all voluntary influence over it gone; and the slightest motion in dressing the parts was attended with exquisite torture. The posterior wound was somewhat puffy, and a triangular piece of the scapula, easily removeable by the fingers, lay in it. No accident or interruption to the cure occurred till the 14th day, when a most

---

* This affection of the kidney, which the older surgeons imagined was a process of nature, to carry off peccant matters, and for which they, therefore, prescribed diuretic vulnerary decoctions, was here, I believe, entirely accidental; they supposed there was a direct passage from the vena azygos to the kidney.

acute pain in the region of the kidneys, and frequent ineffectual calls to make water, attacked him during the night.* By warm fomentations, and the use of mucilaginous drinks, this accidental symptom was removed. His cure then went on uninterrupted for some days; granulations of a healthy appearance spouted rapidly up in all directions; and the discharge, though copious, was of a very bland nature, and inoffensive in smell, until, in an unguarded moment, he was induced to allow of the removal of the supporting bandage in which his arm had hung since the receipt of the wound. Immediately after this the pain in the joint and all around became almost insupportable; the whole upper extremity, and particularly the fingers, became oedematous, numb, and tormented with an occasional prickly sensation; and the discharge was very profuse and gleeting, with large drops of an oily nature floating on it, which, both from appearance and from the spot whence they flowed, there was every reason to suppose were synovial. By restoring the arm to its former situation, and applying emollient cataplasms, these symptoms were relieved; and in a few days, as this increased discharge had very much debilitated him, he was allowed a more nutritive diet, with some English porter. The healing process was soon re-established; and, by the use of adhesive straps, the edges of this great wound were brought together, and a partial use of the arm was admitted of, with every hope of its regaining its full powers. His general health was completely restored; and he returned to England in the third month from the accident.

In another case, which occurred in the same action, a nine-ounce grape-shot passed nearly in the same direction, and was cut out beneath the clavicle; the patient recovered. How the arteries and nerves escaped in these cases, I cannot pretend to explain.

Appendix 3

Statement of the Services of Brevet Lieut. Col. J.H.E. Hill of the 23rd or Royal Welch Fusilier Regiment

1796   I had the honour of being appointed to a 2nd Lieutenancy in the 23rd or R.W.F. Regt. on the 29th July, and join'd in the October following.

1797   Promoted to a First Lieutenancy on the 3rd of April, and appointed by the Late Major-General J. J. Ellis to the command of his (the Lieut. Colonel's) Company, and continued at its head till promoted six years after.

1798   Was employ'd in the expedition to Ostend under General Sir E. Coote and was embark'd in H. M. S. "Harpy", Capn. Basely with a detachment of the 23rd Regt. on board which there was a party of Artillery with a 6-pounder. As this ship led in, the troops on board her were the first landed - Lieut. Coles of the Navy having charge of the sailors, but in getting on shore the boats were swamp'd on the beach and the ammunition spoiled. I advanc'd and surprised a signal station suppos'd to have been a battery, and remain'd in front of it till daylight when other troops disembark'd. On the succeeding day (20th Mar.) after some resistance, the whole were taken prisoners, conducted to Lille and confined in the Citadelles.

1799   Serv'd in the expedition to North Holland: on the 27th August, engag'd in the affair of the landing with the reserve under Colonel Macdonald, and in the repulse of the attack on the British position on the 10th Sept., and march'd with Sir R. Abercrombie's Column to Hoorn on the 19th Sept. Also engaged in our offensive operations on the 2nd October to the right of Bergen, and on the 6th Oct. in front of Egmont Op Zee.

1800   I was employ'd in the demonstration before Belle Isle Ferrol and Cadiz under Sir James Pultney and Sir Ralph Abercrombie.

1801   Under Sir Ralph Abercrombie, and landed in Abukir Bay on the 8th March with the Reserve commanded by Sir John Moore, having charge of the Lieut. Colonel's Company. I was also in the advance of the 13th March. And also in the battle of the 21st of March: on which day the 23rd Regt. moved up to the support of the 58th Regt. and halted about sixty paces from the front face of the ruined Roman buildings, the Light Company being in front, the Lieut. Colonel's company was on the left flank. The head of a French Column was observed entering through the broken wall on the left face; the dawn of day shew'd their hats, on which I wheeled the Company up in silence and gave orders to fire at about thirty-five yards' distance. During the 2nd discharge, Capn. Bradford brought up his Company on the right, and the late Col. Sir Henry Ellis his on the left; when the word "charge" was given, the openings gained and about three hundred and fifty prisoners made.

1802   At Gibraltar and returned to England in the month of September on leave of absence.

1803   Had the honour of being promoted to the rank of Capn. and got the Lieut. Colonel's Company.

1804   In England.

1805

1806   In Hanover during part of these years

1807   At the siege and capture of Copenhagen, and confined to my bed for three weeks in consequence of a soldier mistaking me in the dark during an alarm, and wounding me in the right side with his bayonet.

1808   Sail'd for North America under Sir George Prevost and proceeded to Barbadoes in the autumn.

1809   In the West Indies and commanded the Light (Rifle) Company in the advance guard at the taking of the Heights of Serrurier, and subsequent siege and final capture of Martinique, and returned to North America the same year.

1810   Sail'd from North America and arrived in Portugal in the autumn.

1811   Commanded the three Fusilier Light and Brunswick Rifle Company by order of Sir William Myers at the first siege of Badajoz and during the latter part of the Battle of Albuera. Lieut. Colonel Pearson, who led them into action, succeeded to the command of the brigade.

In the autumn appointed Major in the 5th Portuguese Cacadores.

1812   Promoted to the rank of Major in the 23rd or Royal Welch Fusilier Regt. I was with the covering part of the army at the sieges of Ciudad Rodrigo and Badajoz - and commanded the 5th Cacadores at the commencement of this campaign, at the Battle of Salamanca and Madrid: and superseded in the command after the capture of Valladolid. I was present at the siege of Burgos.

1813   I was engaged in the Battle of Vittoria, and in the affair of Segura and storm and capture of Tolosa by the left Column of the army.

I commanded the 5th Cacadores at the storm and Capture of St. Sebastian, and received a graze of a grape shot between my left arm and side: and had the honour of being appointed Brevet Lieut. Colonel, and was removed to the command of the 4th Portuguese Regt. which was engaged in the passage of the Nivelle and storm of the French entrenched camp on the 10th of November; and also in the crossing of the Nive, and in the battle which took place in consequence of the French attack on Lord Hill's Corps on the 13th Dec^r., when the two Battalions of the 4th Portuguese Regt. were ordered to secure a hill on the extreme right over the Adour, which the enemy had taken; this post was retaken and maintained, night putting a stop to the contest.

1814   I commanded the 4th Portuguese Regt. in the Battle of Orthes. On the army arriving near Toulouse, the Lieut. Colonel belonging to the 4th Regt. having recovered from his wounds, I took the opportunity of getting medical assistance, in consequence of my horse falling with me in the battle of the 10th Nov. (Nivelle), and was forced to undergo two surgical operations.

1815   In March I embarked with the Royal Welch Fusiliers for the continent, and was present at the Battle of Waterloo, near the conclusion of which my horse was killed soon after the repulse of the French Cavalry. A splinter of bone from some other body driven in the orbit of the right eye, two splinters of stone in my cheeks, a graze of a bullet on the left lower jaw, and an half-pound iron grape shot entered my left breast and materially injured the shoulder joint and passed out through the centre of the shoulder blade and lodged in my clothes.

Whenever the cure may take place, it is extremely doubtful whether the left arm will be of the slightest use.

Brevet Lieut. Colonel J. H. E. Hill has been present in every field whose inscriptions decorate the Colours of the Welch Fusiliers, except Minden

Hennock, Chudleigh, Devon. January, 1816

Appendix 4

Service Memorandum
to the Duke of York

His Royal Highness the Duke of York
Commander in Chief, etc.

The Memorial of Bt. Lieut. Colonel J.H.E. Hill
Humbly Sheweth
That your Memorialist Joined in:

1796	The 23rd or Royal Welch Fusilier Regt.
1797	Obtained a Lieutenancy, and appointed.by Colonel Ellis to command the Lieut. Colonel's Company.
1798	Ostend, having charge of a detachment to cover the Artillery, he was taken prisoner and confined in Lille.
1799	Holland, had the command of the above Company in every action, except on the landing; on returning embark'd on board the "Valk" Dutch Frigate, which being wrecked your memorialist reported to your Royal Highness his escape with twenty-four others, out of four hundred and forty-six persons.
1800	Employed on the coasts of France, Ferrol and Cadiz.
1801	Commanded a Company in the Egyptian Campaign
1802	At Gibraltar
1803}	England, promoted and obtained the late Lt. Col's Company
1804}	
1805}	Hanover, during the winter
1806}	
1807	Copenhagen, wounded in mistake by our own men.
1808	North America, appointed to the Light (Rifle) Company.

1809	West Indies, with the Advanced guard on the heights of Serrurier and at the final capture of Martinique.
1810	Portugal, joined the army in the lines of Torres Vedras.
1811	Spain, at the first siege of Badajoz, Battle [of] Albuera, appointed to do duty with Portuguese troops.
1812	Major 2nd Batt^n [RWF]. With 5th Cassadores before Ciudad Rodrigo, Badajoz, Salamanca, Madrid and Burgos.
1813	Vittoria, Sigura, Tolosa, St. Sebastian (there obtained the rank of Lieut. Colonel), Nive and Nivelle.
1814	Orthes and Toulouse.
1815	Waterloo, horse killed and was hit in four places - "an half-pound shot struck on the left breast immediately below the collar bone and pass'd out behind through the shoulder blade."

Your memorialist at the period of leaving the Royal Welch Fusiliers was the individual of the longest standing of either Officer or Private, and had been present in every Field (except Minden) borne on the colours of the 23rd Regt.

Your memorialist most humbly prays His Royal Highness that after being engaged in twenty affairs of importance, and seven sieges, once wrecked, once on fire at sea, after so many years of service and suffering, after twenty-eight being obliged to return to Civil life, your memorialist adverts to Sir Herbert Taylor's letter to Lord Combermere dated 9th Sept. 1823 in the paragraphs: "His Royal Highness will readily give his utmost support to any application Lieut. Colonel Hill may address the Secretary at War for a pension in consideration of a wound which entailed such disability"

It is most earnestly intreated that His Royal Highness may graciously be pleased to lend his assistance in placing your memorialist on the pension list as a Lieut. Colonel on three hundred a year, that rank having been obtained two years before the infliction of the wound.

And your memorialist shall as in duty bound ever pray.
J.H.E. HILL, Lieut. Colonel
late 23rd Regt., now 49th
London, 17th Dec. 1823

Appendix 5

Jack Hill's Contemporaries

These summaries of the careers of those of Jack's colleagues from the 23rd Foot mentioned in this book are based on material kindly provided from the records of the Royal Welch Fusiliers Museum, supplemented in a number of cases by additional research by the Author.

ABERCROMBY,
Hon. Alexander

Born 1784, fourth son of General Sir Ralph Abercrombie. Volunteer with 92nd Foot in the Helder Expedition of 1799; joined 2nd Dragoons as Cornet in August 1799. Promoted lieutenant 52nd Foot March 1800; transferred as captain to RWF on 21 May 1801; transferred as major to 81st Foot July 1806; lieutenant-colonel 28th Foot January 1808. Commanded the 28th at Buçaco and in the lines of Torres Vedras; commanded a brigade at Albuera. Also at the battles of Arroyo dos Molinos, Almarez, Vitoria, the Pyrenees, Orthes, Quatre-Bras, Waterloo, the storming of Peronne and the capture of Paris. Elected MP for the county of Clackmannan April 1817; retired from parliament 1818. Died unmarried at his country seat in Clackmannanshire, Scotland 1853.

BLANCKLEY,
Henry Stanyford

Born c.1787, possibly in Halifax, Nova Scotia; son of Henry Stanyford Blanckley. Commissioned 2nd lieutenant RWF on 16 October 1805; promoted lieutenant 31 July 1806; captain 21 May 1812. Carried the Regimental Colour at Copenhagen 1807 and possibly at the capture of Martinique 1809. Sailed to Lisbon with the battalion October 1810, shortly after marrying Elizabeth Forman (who remained in Nova Scotia). Served in the Peninsula from 1811 to 1813, including first Badajoz and Albuera. Selected for 'confidential service' (spying) by the Duke of Wellington. Listed for reduction in 1814, but appointed to the staff and was at Waterloo. Received the brevet rank of major on 21 June 1817; transferred to 13th Light Dragoons December 1818. Posted to India in February 1819, he subsequently died of liver disease, aged about 32.

BOOKER,
Gordon William
Francis

Born 20 October 1789. Commissioned ensign in 10th Foot May 1806; transferred as lieutenant to RWF on 14 May 1807. Wounded in the right hand at Albuera, on returning home became secretly betrothed to Loveday Sarah Glanville. Rejoined RWF in Spain; promoted captain 17 June 1813. Wounded at Roncesvalles 25 July 1813. Married Miss Glanville in 1814. Placed on half pay 25 December 1814. Assumed the surname and arms of Gregor by letters patent in 1826 when his wife inherited the Gregor estate, Trewarthenick, in Cornwall. Died in 1865; buried in Cornelly churchyard, Cornwall.

BRADFORD,
John George

Son of Reverend John Bradford of Ideford, Devon. Commissioned ensign in 32nd Foot; transferred as 2nd lieutenant to RWF on 7 February 1787. Promoted lieutenant 26 February 1790, was distinguished in the defence of Fort Tiburon in St. Domingo in December 1794. Promoted captain 13 June 1794. On returning from the West Indies Bradford was instrumental, with James MacKenzie (see below) in Jack Hill joining the RWF; they remained close friends through Bradford's service and beyond. Taken prisoner during the Ostend raid, served in the Helder and Egypt. Transferred as major to 58th Foot July 1803, creating the vacancy for Jack Hill to obtain a captaincy. Retired 1810 to Bishopsteignton, Devon. Died aged 50 1816; commemorated by a plaque in St. Mary the Virgin church in Ideford.

BROMLEY,
Walter

Baptised 27 February 1775 at Keelby, Lincolnshire; eldest son of Robert Bromley. Enlisted in RWF as a boy; served in the West Indies, Helder, Copenhagen, Egypt, Nova Scotia and the Peninsula. Having become a Sergeant, was appointed Quartermaster RWF on 12 June 1800; Paymaster to 2/23rd on 14 February 1805; returned to 1/23rd as Paymaster on 14 May 1807. Retired 1812, Drawing half pay until the 1830s. Bromley returned to Nova Scotia in 1813 as a social reformer, demonstrating enlightened attitudes towards Native Americans. He also worked with indigenous Australians between 1836 and his accidental death in May 1838.

BROWNE,
George Baxter

Born Liverpool 19 December 1788; second son of George Browne, a Liverpool merchant, and his wife Felicity Dorothea. Younger brother of Thomas Browne (see below), older brother of the poet Felicia Dorothea Hemans. Commissioned 2nd lieutenant RWF on 10 July 1806; promoted lieutenant 17 June 1807. Served with 2/23rd in 1808–9 including the retreat to Coruña and the Walcheren expedition. Joined 1/23rd in Spain in the spring 1811; present at the siege of Olivenza, first Badajoz, Aldea de Ponte, Ciudad Rodrigo, Badajoz (severely wounded), Salamanca (slightly wounded), Madrid, Vitoria and Roncesvalles (very severely wounded). Promoted captain 26 August 1813; listed for reduction and placed on half pay 1814. Never returned to full pay, possibly due to his wounds, but was promoted major unattached in August 1826; lieutenant-colonel November 1841. After retiring, appointed Joint Commissioner Dublin Metropolitan Police, holding the post until 1858. Died, aged 91, on 12 July 1879 at Clifton Gardens, Folkestone, Kent.

BROWNE,
Thomas Henry

Born Liverpool on 8 September 1787, eldest of seven children of George Browne, a Liverpool merchant and his wife Felicity Dorothea. Older brother of George Browne (see above) and the poet Mrs Felicia Dorothea Hemans. Commissioned 2nd lieutenant RWF on 28 October 1805; promoted lieutenant 18 September 1806. Carried the King's Colour at Copenhagen; served in Nova Scotia and Martinique (wounded). Sailed to Lisbon with the battalion October 1810 but remained with the RWF details at Belem, Lisbon. Appointed to the staff of the Adjutant-General in 1812, he was present at Salamanca, Madrid, Burgos and Vitoria (wounded in the head). Promoted captain 15 April 1813, he was present at the Pyrenees, Nivelle, Bayonne, Nive, Tarbes, Orthes and Toulouse. Placed on half pay in 1814, was subsequently appointed ADC to Lord Stewart (later Marquess of Londonderry) and served with him at the Headquarters of the Austrian and Russian Armies in 1815. Promoted major June 1817; lieutenant-colonel January 1819; colonel January 1837; major-general November 1846; lieutenant-general 1854. After retiring, he lived at Bronwylfa near St. Asaph, Flintshire. Lieutenant-General Sir Thomas Henry Browne KCH died, aged 67, on 11 March 1855 in Camden, London. In 1987 the Army Records Society published his journal, which includes invaluable commentary on events during his service and on some of his colleagues, including Jack Hill.

BUCHANAN, Peter	Son of Thomas Buchanan of Spittal, Stirling. Commissioned ensign 9th Foot in November 1790; transferred to RWF as lieutenant on 25 March 1794; promoted captain 20 January 1796. Died 6 April 1797, sparking a chain of regimental promotions, including Jack Hill's to 1st Lieutenant.
BURGESS, Samuel	A Sergeant, he was appointed Quartermaster 2/23rd 14 March 1805; held the post until succeeded by QM George Sedley (see below) on 14 April 1808.
BURGHERSH, Lord John	(John Fane, Baron Burghersh) Born 3 February 1784, son of the 10th Earl of Westmorland. Commissioned 2nd lieutenant 7th Foot in December 1803; promoted lieutenant January 1804; transferred as captain to RWF on 3 May 1805. Served on the expedition to Hanover and in Portugal on the staff of Sir Arthur Wellesley. Present at Obidos, Rolica, Vimiero, Talavera, Buçaco , Torres Vedras and Santarem. In June 1811 he married Priscilla Anne, daughter of Wellington's brother William Wellesley-Pole. Promoted lieutenant-colonel December 1811. Appointed Military Commissioner to the Headquarters of the allied armies in Germany, September 1813. Present at the siege of Huninguen and the campaign of 1814 in France, including the capture of Paris. Promoted colonel June 1814; placed on half pay in 1815. As his Majesty's Envoy Extraordinary and Minister Plenipotentiary at the Court of Tuscany, served with the Austrian Army in the campaign against Naples in 1815. In 1841 he was Envoy Extraordinary and Minister Plenipotentiary at the Court of Prussia. Succeeded his father as 11th Earl of Westmorland and Baron Burghersh in December that year. Promoted major-general 1825; lieutenant-general 1838. In 1851 he was at the Court of Vienna and was a special plenipotentiary at the Viennese Conferences in 1855. Appointed Colonel 56th Foot November 1842. Died in October 1859 at Apethorpe House, Northamptonshire and was buried there.
BURY, Thomas	Commissioned ensign 41st Foot in March 1790; transferred as lieutenant RWF on 28 February 1793; promoted captain on 22 April 1794. Taken prisoner when commanding the Grenadier Company during the Ostend raid in May 1798; served in the Helder (wounded) and Egypt. Promoted major 5 April 1801. Retired 10 December 1807.
CANE, James Frederick	Commissioned ensign 67th Foot July 1803; exchanged as lieutenant RWF 24 April 1804; promoted captain 16 June 1811. Served in Nova Scotia, Martinique and the Peninsula. Wounded at Aldea da Ponte. Placed on half pay in November 1814. Held the honorary rank of major.
CASTLE, Robert	Commissioned 2nd lieutenant RWF 19 January 1809. Died of wounds received at Albuera May 1811.

CLYDE, John

Christened 25 February 1795 in Bideford, Devon; son of John and Sarah Clyde. Commissioned 2nd lieutenant RWF 20 June 1811; promoted lieutenant 12 April 1812. Wounded at Salamanca, he rejoined 1/23rd from 2/23rd in March 1814. Served in No. 3 Company at Waterloo where he was seriously wounded. Died 3 July 1815. Jack Hill describes him as a 'young Devonshire lad', who was shot in the lungs and died in the Jesuits' Hospital in Brussels where Hill was also a patient. In 1889 the bodies of several officers, including Clyde, were removed to Evère cemetery and placed in a vault under the Waterloo Monument there. Clyde is the only soldier of the 23rd killed or died of wounds soon after Waterloo with a known grave.

COLLINS, George

Commissioned 2nd lieutenant RWF 27 May 1806; promoted lieutenant 14 June 1807. Served under Jack Hill in the Light Company in Nova Scotia and Martinique. Killed during the second siege of Badajoz.

COOKE, Samuel

Commissioned 2nd lieutenant RWF 1 March 1800. In a letter from Malta in December 1800 Jack Hill wrote of him 'Cooke is quite as ridiculous as ever, he has left our ship'. After the landing in Egypt, Cooke was seriously wounded at Alexandria in March 1801. In a letter of 27 March 1801, George Mackenzie (see below) wrote 'Poor Sam Cooke received a wound from a splinter of a shell which broke his right leg below the knee, & shattered it in so bad a manner as to render an amputation immediately necessary; which was done by Mr. Humphries [see below], who tells me that Cooke will do very well. He is in very good spirits, & will I conclude be sent home, with other officers who have lost their limbs, by the first opportunity. The Surgeon tells me that he never in his life saw any one bear an operation with such fortitude: he did not speak a word or utter a groan during the whole time. He is on board ship, & I have not seen him these few days. I have desired him to acquaint you with his arrival in England before he writes to his father & friends; and I have supplied him with what money I could spare, & I thought sufficient to carry him home.' Despite Mackenzie's optimism, Cooke died on 2 August 1801.

CORFIELD, Samuel

Born 12 March 1783, fourth son of Richard Corfield of Chatwall Hall, Shropshire, Surveyor General of Excise at Plymouth and Penryn and his wife Susannah. Commissioned 2nd lieutenant RWF 1 December 1804 he joined Jack Hill's company. Promoted lieutenant 31 October 1805. Served at Copenhagen and Nova Scotia. Died 20 March 1809, on the expedition to Martinique. Thomas Browne (see above) recorded 'one morning we heard that an Officer of the Light Company, Lieut. Corfield, a fine, healthy, active young man, had been taken ill a few hours before. At noon he was worse, and his head was shaved. Before Sun-set he had died'. Corfield was married twice, on 22 September 1797 to Ann Badman, then on 2 September 1808, to Mary Jordan.

COTTON, Stapleton (Lord Combermere)

Born 14 November 1773 at Llewenny Hall, Denbighshire; second son of Sir Robert Salisbury and Frances Cotton. Commissioned 2nd lieutenant RWF on 26 February 1790; transferred as lieutenant to 77th Foot March 1791; returned to RWF on 13 April 1791; purchased a captaincy in 6th Dragoon Guards February 1793. After action in India was eventually promoted major-general October 1805. Commanded a cavalry brigade in the Peninsula in 1808, distinguishing himself at Oporto and Talavera. Succeeded to a baronetcy on the death of his father in August 1809. Appointed to command Wellington's cavalry as brevet lieutenant-general in 1810. Present at Busaco, Fuentes d'Onoro, Salamanca (accidentally wounded the following day), Pyrenees, Orthes and Toulouse. Elevated to the peerage May 1814 as Baron Combermere of Combermere in the County of Chester, he took command of the allied cavalry after Lord Uxbridge was wounded at Waterloo and remained in France until the reduction of the army of occupation. Governor of Barbados and Commander, West Indies 1817 to 1820; Commander-in-Chief, Ireland from 1822 to 1825 (during which time he interviewed Jack Hill about his reported desire to retire). Promoted General in May 1825; appointed Commander-in-Chief, India. Made Viscount Combermere of Bhurtpore in the East Indies and of Combermere in the County Palatine of Chester; Privy Councillor 1834; succeeded the Duke of Wellington as Constable of the Tower and Lord Lieutenant of the Tower Hamlets in 1852. Made Field Marshal October 1855. He married three times, his first two wives both dying. Died, aged 92, at Clifton in February 1865; buried in St. Margaret's Church, Wrenbury near Nantwich, Cheshire. An equestrian statue in bronze was raised in his honour by the inhabitants of Cheshire.

DALMER, **Francis**	Younger brother of Thomas Dalmer (see below). Commissioned 2nd lieutenant RWF 10 March 1804; promoted lieutenant 18 April 1805; captain 10 December 1807. Served with the 2/23rd in the Coruña and Walchern campaigns. Joined 1/23rd in Spain December 1812. Present at Vitoria, the Pyrenees, Nivelle, Nive, Orthes and Toulouse. Promoted brevet major 26 August 1813; brevet lieutenant-colonel 18 June 1815 for his conduct at Waterloo, where he commanded No. 1 Company, he was thereafter listed with the unusual rank of 'Captain and Lieutenant-Colonel'. Promoted major RWF 16 October 1823. Went on half pay 10 July 1826. Died at the home of his sister, in London 2 October 1855.
DALMER, **Thomas**	Born c.1780 in Great Marlow, Buckinghamshire. Brother of Francis Dalmer (see above). Ensign March 1797; commissioned 2nd lieutenant RWF 22 May 1797. On the Ostend raid of 1798 but did not go ashore. Promoted lieutenant 12 June 1799, served on the Helder, Ferrol, Cadiz and Egyptian expeditions. Promoted captain 23 October 1804, served in Hanover and at Copenhagen. Promoted major 2/23rd 10 December 1807; served in Ireland and in the retreat to Coruña. Rejoined 1/23rd in Spain in 1811; present at Aldea De Ponte. Rejoined 2/23rd then again rejoined 1/23rd in 1812. Severely wounded at Salamanca; received the brevet rank of lieutenant-colonel. On recovery from wounds rejoined at Escurial near Madrid. In 1813 commanded the Light Companies of the Left Brigade of the 4th Division; present at Vitoria and the advance to the Pyrenees. Commanded 2/23rd until its disestablishment in 1814. Reverted to major in the now single-battalion regiment. Appointed a Companion of the Military Order of the Bath (CB) on 4 June 1815. Present at Waterloo, succeeding to command when Colonel Sir Henry Walton Ellis (see below) was fatally wounded. Commanded the regiment at Cambrai on 26 July 1815. Promoted substantive lieutenant-colonel and formally to command of the 23rd, he continued to serve with the Army of Occupation in France until exchanging with Thomas Pearson (see below) onto half pay 43rd Foot on 24 July 1817. Appointed Colonel 47th Foot April 1847; promoted major-general June 1838; lieutenant-general November 1851. Died 26 August 1854 at Hawkhurst, Kent.
DUNN, John	Appointed Assistant Surgeon 7th Dragoons July 1803; transferred as Surgeon 1/23rd on 10 September 1803. Served with the battalion, including at Waterloo until placed on half pay on 10 December 1823. Died at Plymouth on 5 December 1827.

ELLIS, Henry Walton

Born 29 November 1782, son of Lieutenant-Colonel John Joyner Ellis (see below) and his wife Sarah (née Walton). His father purchased a commission for him as ensign in 89th Foot when he was only a few weeks old. When the 89th disbanded later the same year the baby was placed on half pay. September 1789 brought onto full pay, aged 5, as ensign in 41st Foot; promoted lieutenant March 1792; captain-lieutenant December 1794; transferred to RWF 3 September 1795; promoted captain 20 January 1796; major 23 October 1804; lieutenant-colonel in command 23 April 1807; colonel 14 June 1814. Appointed KCB on 2 January 1815. Wounded at least eight times, including during the Helder expedition, at Alexandria, Albuera, Badajoz, Salamanca and the Pyrenees. Wounded by a ball in the chest while commanding at Waterloo, he rode to the rear but fell from his horse. When found he was taken to a shelter where his wound was dressed, but on the night of 19 June the house caught fire. Rescued by Assistant Surgeon Monroe (see below), Ellis died on 20 June, aged 32. Buried on the battlefield, the monument over his grave was later moved to the Wellington Museum; the location of his grave was thereby lost. The officers, NCOs and men of the RWF subscribed to a memorial in Worcester Cathedral which depicts the mortally wounded Ellis falling from his horse, supported by an angel holding a laurel wreath above his head, and with a soldier kneeling alongside. In 1839 the officers of the regiment paid for another marble slab to be placed in the church at Waterloo. Henry Ellis never married, but had two sons, Francis Joyner and Henry, both of whom were given commissions by the Duke of Wellington.

ELLIS, John Joyner

Born about 1750, the adopted, and probably natural, son of Henry Ellis. Commissioned in 1761 as a child; promoted lieutenant 18th Foot January 1773; captain-lieutenant March 1779; major February 1780; transferred to 89th Foot. On 27 August 1781 he married Sarah Walton at Hanley Castle church, Worcestershire. Transferred to 41st Foot in December 1787; promoted brevet lieutenant-colonel November 1790. Appointed to command the RWF 6 December 1793; promoted colonel 21 August 1795; major-general 18 June 1798. Having announced his intention to retire, he died in Bath on 30 October 1803 before he could sell his commission. His son, Henry Walton Ellis (see above) was refused permission to sell the commission on behalf of the family. John Joyner Ellis was buried on 2 November 1803 in St James's Church, Bath.

**ENGLAND,
Richard**

Born 1793, son of Lieutenant-general Richard England of Lifford, Co. Clare, and his wife Anne. Commissioned ensign February 1808 in 5th Foot; transferred as lieutenant to 14th Foot June 1809; transferred as captain to 60th Foot in July 1811; transferred to 65th Foot in November 1811; to 12th Foot in January 1812 and to RWF on 26 August 1819. Remained with the RWF until 4 September 1823 when he purchased a majority in 49th Foot. Returned to the RWF on 2 October that year, exchanging with Jack Hill. England was promoted lieutenant-colonel unattached on 29 October 1825; appointed to command 75th Foot from in July 1826 until July 1837 when he transferred to 4th Foot. Transferring again three days to 41st Foot, where he remained until July 1845 when he returned to the unattached list. Received the brevet rank of colonel in June 1838; major-general November 1851; lieutenant-general June 1856; general July 1863. He served in the attack on Flushing in 1809 and in Sicily in 1810-1811, before joining the army of occupation in Paris in 1815. While commanding 75th Foot he was appointed Commandant of Kaffraria and employed in the Xhosa war 1836-1837. Appointed Knight of the Hanoverian Guelphic Order (KH) in 1836. Commanded the Bombay Division in the Afghan war of 1842. Created KCB 29 September 1843, commanded the Third Division in the Crimean War as brevet lieutenant-general, including at the battles of Alma and Inkerman and the siege of Sebastopol. Elevated to GCB on 5 July 1855, and given 1st Class of Medjidie, a Grand Officer of the Legion of Honour and the Sardinian medal. Major-general of Division at the Curragh from August 1856 to March 1859. Became Colonel 50th Foot in September 1854, then Colonel 41st Foot in April 1861. He married twice: first in 1814 Anne Maria and second in 1844 Theodoria. General Sir Richard England GCB, KH died on 20 January 1883

ENOCH, John

Born at Carmarthen on 1 March 1785, son of Captain John Enoch of the Cardiganshire Militia. Commissioned 2nd lieutenant RWF on 30 March 1809. Served with 2/23rd in the Walcheren expedition before joining 1/23rd in the Peninsula in March 1811. Promoted lieutenant 15 August 1811. Severely wounded at Salamanca. Appointed lieutenant and Adjutant 1/23rd from 16 September 1813 to 1 January 1823; promoted captain on 22 July 1830; major 14 April 1846. Placed on half pay in May 1846. Became lieutenant-colonel, unattached, February 1851; colonel, unattached, November 1854. Died, aged 72, on 13 July 1855, while serving as Assistant Quartermaster-General.

FARMER, Thomas

Commissioned 2nd lieutenant RWF 14 November 1804; promoted lieutenant 29 October 1805. With 1/23rd in Nova Scotia and Martinique, sailing to Lisbon with them in December 1810. Severely wounded at Badajoz. Promoted captain 16 April 1812; served with 2/23rd until March 1814 when he rejoined 1/23rd. Killed while commanding No. 7 Company at Waterloo.

FIELDING, George

Born at Startforth, Yorkshire 14 January 1792. Commissioned 2nd lieutenant RWF on 24 May 1810; promoted lieutenant 7 November 1811. Joined 1/23rd at Pedrogao August 1811. Severely wounded 'in the breast and shoulder' at Badajoz; slightly wounded at Waterloo while serving in No. 5 Company. Promoted captain 6 June 1822; major 22 July 1830, commanding the Depot companies in Brecon. Died, whilst still serving, at Bath on 29 November 1830.

FENSHAM, George

Commissioned 2nd lieutenant RWF 20 April 1808; promoted lieutenant 4 January 1810. Served in the Peninsula. Killed at Waterloo serving in the Light Company.

FLETCHER, Thomas Lloyd

Commissioned 2nd lieutenant RWF 12 August 1803; appointed to Jack Hill's company. Promoted lieutenant 24 May 1804; captain in 2/23rd 19 June 1806. Commanded the rearguard during the evacuation of Coruña; locked the city gates on 18 January 1809 and brought away the keys (now in the regimental museum). Transferred as captain to 4th Ceylon Rifles March 1810; promoted major December 1827; lieutenant-colonel February 1835. Retired in 1846. Died 20 March 1850.

GRENVILLE, Richard

Son of the Rt. Hon. James Grenville and his wife Mary (née Smyth). Commissioned ensign 1st Guards in 1759; obtained the rank of captain in 1760 by raising an independent company; transferred to 24th Foot in May 1761. In 1761-2 he served in Germany as ADC to the Marques of Granby. Purchased captaincy in the Coldstream Guards 1772, accompanying them to America in 1776. Promoted colonel February 1779; major-general November 1782. Appointed Colonel, RWF April 1786, it was Grenville who recommended Jack Hill to the Duke of York for a commission in the regiment and who formally recommended all his subsequent promotions. Promoted lieutenant-general May 1796; general January 1801. Died in London on 22 April 1823.

GRIFFITH, John Scott

Born 7 August 1785. Hospital Mate from April 1806; became Assistant Surgeon RWF 7 May 1807. Served at Copenhagen, Nova Scotia and Martinique. In August 1809 became a staff surgeon in Portugal. Promoted Surgeon 15th Dragoons September 1812; returned to staff surgeon September 1813. Retired on half-pay in September 1814. Died on 31 May 1873.

GRIFFITH,
Thomas Edward
Allett

Commissioned ensign 81st Regiment October 1803; transferred as lieutenant RWF 16 May 1805. Promoted captain 7 November 1811. In 1807 he was employed in the Copenhagen naval arsenal in equipping captured Danish men-of-war. Retired on full pay to 2nd Royal Veteran Battalion June 1813; transferred to 1st Royal Veteran Battalion November 1819. Veteran battalions were later renamed invalid battalions; he was still receiving full pay in 10th Invalid Battalion in 1830.

GRIFFITHS,
William Atford

Born 14 February 1792, in Wrexham, Denbighshire. Commissioned 2nd lieutenant RWF on 14 March 1811 from the Denbigh Militia. Promoted lieutenant 13 May 1812. Served in the Peninsula in 1812 and 1813, including at Badajoz, Salamanca and St. Sebastian where he was wounded. He served in the Grenadier Company at Waterloo (wounded in the right thigh). With the RWF in Gibraltar 1823 to 1825; retired on half-pay March 1831. Died 10 March 1832.

HALKETT,
Alexander

Fifth son of Sir John Wedderburn Halkett 4th Bt. of Pitfirrane, Dunfermline and his second wife Mary. Commissioned 2nd lieutenant on RWF 31 March 1790. Promoted lieutenant 31 March 1793; captain on 25 March 1794. In the West Indies in 1795 he was wrongly reported dead; when the error was discovered he was reinstated. Taken prisoner during the 1798 Ostend raid and interned in Lille. He did not go on parole but remained behind with the men until all were exchanged. Major-General Sir Eyre Coote's despatch states that during the raid Halkett and an officer of the 11th Foot, 'eminently distinguished themselves by their cool intrepid Conduct during the whole Time'. Served as ADC to Sir Ralph Abercrombie in the Helder expedition and had his horse shot from under him. Jack Hill noted 'Halkett of ours, who is [Abercrombie's] Aide-de-Camp, had his horse also shot in the head, but it is yet alive'. Transferred as major to 15th Foot November 1799; as Lieutenant-Colonel to 93rd Foot August 1800; transferred to 104th Foot May 1810; appointed their colonel July 1810. Promoted major-general June 1813; lieutenant-general May 1825; general November 1841. Created a Knight of the Hanoverian Guelphic Order (KCH) 1837. General Sir Alexander Halkett KCH died in Edinburgh, aged 75, on 24 August 1851.

HALL, John	Born 10 April 1769 at Park Hall, Mansfield Woodhouse, Nottinghamshire, son of Urban Hall, Sheriff of Nottinghamshire, and his wife Mary. Commissioned ensign in 46th Foot August 1786. Promoted lieutenant 54th Foot September 1781; captain 46th Foot December 1794. Transferred as major to RWF on 18 January 1797. Promoted Lieutenant-Colonel on 12 June 1800 and commanded the regiment until placed on half pay 20th Foot on 14 November 1804. Promoted colonel in the army July 1810; major-general June 1813. Remained on half-pay until 1814, when pay was allowed to General Officers in lieu of regimental half-pay. Died, aged 53, on 26 July 1823 at Park Hall, and is buried in the family vault in the south chapel of Mansfield Woodhouse church. His obituary in The Gentleman's Magazine reads 'This gallant veteran commanded the Welch Fusileers in Egypt, served in the West Indies, and was present at the taking of most of the French West India Islands, by the expedition under the command of the late Earl St. Vincent and the late Earl Grey. Gen. Hall finished his military career in Holland and Flanders.'
HALL, Revis	One of six sons of Colonel Robert Hall, late 72nd and 39th Foot, of Topsham, Devon. Commissioned 2nd lieutenant RWF on 25 November 1808. Reported to 1/23rd at Valverde in Spain in April 1811. Killed at Albuera on 18 May 1811. A note by his brother William, published in United Service Journal reads: 'This young officer had not yet completed his seventeenth year, when he was thus prematurely cut off from his country and connexions. He had borne the King's colour of his regiment throughout the engagement, and it was not until its termination - even when the roar of battle had given place to the shouts of victory - that a stray shot struck him on the forehead, the effects of which proved mortal. This slight tribute will, it is hoped, be excused to a brother's memory'. In his letter of 18 May 1811, Jack Hill noted 'Hall the son of the Col. at Topsham...[is]...among our killed'.
HALL, Robert West	Commissioned 2nd lieutenant RWF on 15 January 1806. Promoted lieutenant on 8 January 1807. Served in Nova Scotia but fell ill on the expedition to Martinique. Thomas Browne (see above) said he was sent from Barbados in December 1808 to Nevis 'where he had some relations', to recover. Rejoined the battalion on 25 September 1809, travelling via New York to Halifax on the Packet ship. His health probably never fully recovered as he retired in April 1811.

HANSON, Henry Baggott   Commissioned 2nd lieutenant RWF on 20 July 1794. Promoted lieutenant on 12 October 1794. Taken prisoner during the 1798 Ostend raid and interned in Lille. He did not go on parole but remained behind with the men until all were exchanged. Participated in the Helder expedition; lost in the sinking of the Valk on 10 November 1799.

HARDING, Henry   Born c.1776. As sergeant-major he signed the regiment's loyal address in reply to the Nore mutineer's seditious handbill of 1797. In 1797–8 he organised a scheme for all ranks to subscribe one day's pay towards the cost of the war. Commissioned adjutant RWF on 14 April 1798; 2nd lieutenant and adjutant on 25 October 1799; lieutenant and adjutant on 1 March 1800. Resigned as adjutant November 1803 and retired by sale of his commission March 1804. Served in Haiti (1794–6), the Ostend raid, the Helder expedition and Egypt. In 1823 he married Anne, the widow of John Philipps MP, of Cwmgwili, Carmarthenshire. This was not his first marriage, as in 1808 Jack recorded in a letter from Nova Scotia: 'I saw Harding the other day. He is again married, I believe'. He died at Carmarthen on 14 September 1830 and has a memorial in St Peter's Church, Carmarthen.

HARRISON, John Christopher   Born 5 April 1788, seventh of thirteen children of Robert Harrison and his wife Elizabeth. Commission as a teenager in the Worcestershire Militia. Commissioned ensign 20th Foot in February 1805, transferred as 2nd lieutenant RWF on 7 March 1805; lieutenant 27 May 1806; captain 20 May 1812; major 29 October 1825; lieutenant-colonel 22 July 1830. Served at Copenhagen, Nova Scotia, Martinique, the Peninsula, France, Ireland and Gibraltar. Wounded at Albuera and Badajoz, the latter causing him to carry his right arm in a sling for the rest of his life (for which he was awarded an annual pension of £100). He missed Waterloo, reporting to the battalion in France on 24 November 1815. Commanded the Depot Companies from 24 July 1828 until taking command of the Service Battalion at Gibraltar on 22 July 1830. During his term of command the wearing of the Flash was disputed; Harrison established the regiment's right to the five black ribbons 'as a peculiarity to mark the dress of that distinguished Regiment'. Relinquished command 24 March 1837. Appointed a Knight of the Royal Hanoverian Guelphic Order (KH) on 25 January 1836. Died aged 83 on 31 March 1871 at his home, Mount Radford, in St Leonard's parish, Exeter.

HAWTYN,
Joseph

Commissioned cornet 17th Dragoons in October 1899. Promoted lieutenant August 1801; exchanged to 55th Foot December 1803; transferred as captain to RWF on 11 September 1806. Served with the regiment in the Peninsula, wounded at Badajoz. On 17 August 1812 he received the brevet rank of major in the army. Killed at Waterloo while commanding the Grenadier Company. Following his death his widow, Winifred, received an annual allowance of £80, commencing on 19 June 1815.

HOGGARD,
John

Believed to have been commissioned from the ranks as 2nd lieutenant RWF on 27 January 1797. Promoted lieutenant on 3 May 1799. Participated in the Helder expedition; lost in the sinking of the Valk on 10 November 1799. Jack Hill recorded that Hoggard had worked to help save the ship when she foundered and came ashore of Ameland island alive: 'Lieut. Hoggard with about 8 others was on the mainmast. When it first struck ground he perceived it and shook hands with his companions and said: 'Thank God, my lads, you are once more in safety'. They waited about 5 minutes when all except Lieut. Hoggard quitted the wreck, and some of the Regt. waded back and laid hold of him, but all their strength and persuasion could not force him away from the mast, he was perfectly delirious and talked in a very incoherent manner - asking down what street they wanted to take him - the poor fellows who had befriended him began now to be exhausted, and were obliged to take care of themselves'. Jack recorded that he arranged for Hoggard's body to be placed in a coffin, and that the mayor of the island had him interred in a burial ground the village of Hollum. His obituary in The Gentleman's Magazine for November 1799 recorded his last words as 'Thank God, my lads, we are again safe on-shore!'. This version also appears in the Naval Chronicle (though spelling his surname incorrectly).

HOLMES,
Robert Pattison

Born at Alconbury, Huntingdonshire 3 October 1790. Commissioned 2nd lieutenant RWF on 14 February 1811. Present at the siege of Ciudad Rodrigo; wounded at Badajoz by a musket ball in his right hand. Promoted lieutenant 12 December 1812, he was at the Nivelle, Nive, Orthes and Toulouse. Served in No. 8 Company at Waterloo where he was again wounded ('contused in the head by a musket ball'). Participated in the storming of Cambrai and the capture of Paris in 1815. Promoted captain 4 September 1823; major 17 December 1830; lieutenant-colonel 14 April 1846. He died of cholera at Montreal on 23 July 1849.

HUMFREY, Richard

Born 29 December 1772. Commissioned Surgeon RWF 18 November 1795 in succession to Surgeon John Warren (see below). Transferred as Surgeon to 1st Dragoons September 1803. Subsequently transferred to the 56th Foot in India, as in June 1808 Jack Hill wrote to him via his brother William. Humphrey went on half-pay 25 September 1814. Died, aged 69, at Bristol on 22 June 1843.

JAMES, John

Commissioned 2nd lieutenant RWF 24 May 1804; replaced Thomas Fletcher as 2nd Lieutenant in Jack Hill's company. Promoted lieutenant 30 May 1805; captain 21 January 1808; transferred to 89th Foot October 1808. Retired May 1811.

JENNINGS, George

Commissioned ensign 34th Foot in April 1805; transferred as lieutenant RWF on 19 December 1805. Killed on 4 September 1807 outside Copenhagen 'by a six pounder through the heart, died instantly', according to a letter from John Harrison (see above). Thomas Browne (see above) gives an account of his state of mind and says his death was from 'a single round shot . . . [which] carried off his head'.

JOHNSON, Henry Cavendish

Commissioned 2nd lieutenant RWF on 6 February 1805. Promoted lieutenant 26 May 1806; captain 14 May 1812. Served at Copenhagen, Nova Scotia, Martinique and on the Peninsula. Wounded at Badajoz and Waterloo where he commanded No.6 Company. Placed on half pay in 7th Light Dragoons May 1820. Died in Ireland 19 February 1853 aged 78.

JOLLIFFE, Charles

Youngest son of Thomas Samuel Jolliffe of Ammerdown, Somerset, former M.P. for Petersfield, and his wife Mary-Anne. Commissioned 2nd lieutenant RWF on 11 September 1805. Promoted lieutenant 5 June 1806; captain 14 May 1812. Served at Copenhagen, Nova Scotia, Martinique and on the Peninsula. Wounded at Orthes. Killed at Waterloo while commanding No. 8 Company. A memorial to him is in St. Peter's and St Paul's Church, Kilmersdon, Somerset.

JONES, Evan Born June 1771. Commissioned 2nd lieutenant RWF on 11 May 1791. Promoted lieutenant 15 May 1793. Deployed with the regiment to the West Indies. Soon after landing in Santo Domingo he developed yellow fever but, as described in his obituaries, was saved by 'a negro woman, his nurse, who wrapped him in a sheet or blanket strongly impregnated with vinegar, which arrested the rage of that dreadful malady'. Promoted captain-lieutenant 14 June 1794; captain 11 November 1794. On the Ostend expedition in 1798 but did not go ashore. Participated in the Helder expedition in 1799. Promoted major 24 July 1800; became senior major on 25 March 1801 after the death of James Mackenzie (see below) in Egypt. Promoted lieutenant-colonel to command 2/23rd on 23 November 1804; succeeded James Losack (see below) in command of 1/23rd in February 1807. Commanded in Copenhagen and retired after the regiment returned to England in November 1807. In 1808 married Anna Maria Kenyon, daughter of Robert Kenyon of Wrexham; lived at Gelliwig, Caernarvonshire. Died at Rose Hill, Wrexham on 25 March 1821.

JULIAN, Richard Became Paymaster RWF on 8 October 1812. Served on the Peninsula from December 1812 to October 1813. According to Jack Hill, after arriving at Lisbon Julian marched for over 3 weeks to join the battalion, who were stationed near Villa Real. Placed on half pay 23 October 1817. Died at Devonport 12 August 1836.

KEIGHTLEY, John Commissioned lieutenant 57th Foot July 1795. Promoted captain June 1803; transferred to 2nd Garrison Battalion June 1805. Served on the staff until becoming major 14th Foot January 1814. Present with them at Waterloo, he received the brevet rank of lieutenant-colonel on 18 June 1815. Transferred as major to RWF on 25 July 1816. Promoted lieutenant-colonel commanding the 11ᵗʰ Foot June 1825; exchanged to command 35th Foot in May 1835. Retired on 17 June 1836.

KEITH, William Sergeant-major in 27th Foot, appointed Quartermaster RWF on 31 December 1790 and Adjutant on 30 November 1791. Commissioned 2nd lieutenant 31 January 1794; promoted lieutenant 21 July 1794 (while still holding the appointment of Adjutant). In March 1798 relinquished the adjutancy on being made paymaster; promoted captain 18 February 1802; resigned the appointment of paymaster 14 May 1807. Wounded during the Helder expedition, he also served in Egypt, Nova Scotia, Martinique and the Peninsula. After Albuera was gazetted Major in the army but died September 1811 while still senior captain in the RWF.

LEAHY, John Thomas	Born September 1783 in Cork, Ireland. Commissioned 2nd lieutenant RWF on 6 April 1797; transferred to 69th Foot in October 1799; promoted lieutenant January 1802. Returned to RWF as captain 12 January 1805; received the brevet rank of major 27 February 1812. Commanded 1/23rd at Badajoz where he was severely wounded. Made substantive major on 17 June 1813. Placed on half pay of 7th Foot in 1815; returned to the active list as major 21st Foot April 1819; promoted lieutenant-colonel August 1821. In 1832–3 he led the 21st Foot to New South Wales, where it remained until 1839. He retired there in December 1835 and became a notable figure in Sydney and a JP. The Sydney Gazette and New South Wales Advertiser, Saturday 29 June 1839 records the death 'yesterday at the Club House, suddenly, John Thomas Leahy, Esq., late Lieutenant-Colonel 21st Royal Scottish Fusileers'
LECKY, Holland	Commissioned 2nd lieutenant RWF on 30 November 1793. Promoted lieutenant 19 July 1794; captain-lieutenant 4 April 1797. On the expedition to Ostend 1798, but did not go ashore. Transferred as captain to 60th Foot 20 June 1799.
LEDWITH, Henry	Commissioned 2nd lieutenant RWF on 23 February 1809 from the Longford Militia. Promoted lieutenant 11 July 1811. Served in the Peninsula. Slightly wounded at Albuera, again near Zubiri, north-east of Pamplona, in late July 1813, and again after the fall of San Sebastián . Died of wounds on 3 September 1813.
LEEBODY, William	A Volunteer with the 61st Foot, commissioned 2nd lieutenant RWF on 9 September 1813. Served in the Peninsula and at Waterloo. Killed during the capture of Cambrai on 24 June 1815.
LLOYD, Charles	Commissioned 2nd lieutenant RWF on 13 March 1796. Promoted lieutenant 30 November 1796; transferred to 25th Dragoons March 1797. Subsequently returned to the RWF and participated in the Ostend raid 1798 with the grenadier company; made a prisoner of war until released on parole. Transferred as captain-lieutenant 60th Foot in January 1799; returned again to RWF in that rank 20 June 1799; promoted captain RWF 11 January 1800. Wounded during the landing at Aboukir Bay. Transferred as major to 66th Foot In May 1804. Died in March 1809.

LOSACK, James Henry William	Born 4 March 1755 at Basseterre, St. Kitts, West Indies, son of Richard Hawkshaw Losack, Lieutenant-Governor of the Leeward Islands, and his wife Christina. Commissioned 2nd lieutenant 43rd Foot. Promoted lieutenant August 1773; captain October 1781; major March 1794; transferred to 82nd Foot May 1796; promoted lieutenant-colonel January 1798. Took command of 1/23rd on 14 November 1804, handing over to Evan Jones in February 1807. He retired 23 April 1807. Died 21 January 1810 at John Street, Fitzroy Square, London.
MacDONALD, Colin	Commissioned ensign 76th Foot in September 1779; transferred to 6th Foot in July 1794. Moved to RWF as lieutenant 10 July 1794. Promoted captain 5 January 1805. Served in Nova Scotia. At Martinique commanded the Grenadier company alongside Jack Hill's Light (Rifle) company in the assault on the heights of Surey. Awarded a grant of land in Nova Scotia by the Commander of the Martinique expedition and Governor General of British North America, Sir George Prevost. Jack notes in his letter from Halifax, N.S. of 15th June 1809 'Macdonald and myself between us lost 50 flankers killed and wounded, you may easily guess we must have been in the thick of it. Sir G. in consequence has given Macdonald a grant of land near Picton, his clan have emigrated in great numbers from the Highlands and have settled there, they wish him to come among [them]'. MacDonald did not join his family in a farming life, however, travelling with the battalion to the Peninsula. He died of wounds received at Albuera.
MacDONALD, Hon. Godfrey	Born 14 October 1775, second son of Sir Alexander Macdonald, 1st Baron Macdonald of Slake, Co. Antrim, and his wife Elizabeth. Commissioned lieutenant 70th Foot March 1796; exchanged with Captain James Richardson (see below) to be captain RWF on 25 April 1797. Wounded during the Helder expedition. In May 1803 he married Louisa Maria La Coast, daughter of the Duke of Gloucester and Lady Almeria Carpenter. Jack Hill's letter of 12 June 1808 notes 'Godfrey Macdonald, you know I suppose, married the woman he had at Battle, Keith saw them the other day surrounded with children of four sorts and with as great a variety of violincellos'. Promoted major 55th Foot February 1802; lieutenant-colonel and captain 1st Guards in February 1808; colonel June 1811. In April 1814 he assumed the name of Bosville by Royal Licence. Promoted major-general June 1814, he succeeded his elder brother as 3rd Baron Macdonald in June 1824 and in July 1824 resumed the name of Macdonald. Promoted lieutenant-general in July 1830. Died on 13 October 1832.

MacDONALD, **John**	Born c.1793. Commissioned 2nd lieutenant RWF on 26 October 1809. Promoted lieutenant 10 October 1811; captain 28 August 1827; appointed paymaster 16 October 1828. Served at Albuera and Salamanca, where he was slightly wounded, and at Waterloo. His final posting was in Gibraltar, joining the regiment from the Depot on 19 January 1829. Died, aged 37, at Gibraltar 9 January 1830.
MACKENZIE, **Frederick**	Born 1731, only son of William Mackenzie of Dublin and his wife Mary Ann. Commissioned 2nd lieutenant RWF on 31 August 1756. Promoted lieutenant 3 October 1757; lieutenant and Adjutant 11 May 1763; captain-lieutenant and Adjutant 22 November 1775; captain (resigned as Adjutant) 6 November 1776. Served throughout the American War of Independence, for which his diaries are an important record. Promoted Major 9 August 1780; appointed lieutenant-colonel 37th Foot October 1787. Placed on half pay March 1791, he raised and commanded the 1st Exeter Volunteers in 1794. Returning to full pay, he was appointed Assistant Barrack Master General in August 1799. Appointed Secretary to the Royal Military College in 1804; retired in 1814 to live at Teignmouth, Devon, where he died in 1824 aged 93. He was the father of James and George MacKenzie (see below).
MACKENZIE, **George**	Born Boston on 15 June 1775, the son of Frederick Mackenzie (see above). Commissioned ensign 37th Foot in January 1792. His entry in the Army Lists records the seniority of his rank in the army as 4 March 1782, which suggests his father bought him a commission when he was seven years old. Promoted captain November 1795; transferred to RWF on 8 June 1796. Promoted major 24 October 1804. Retired 15 May 1806. Moved to Australia where he acquired land on the Murray River near Freemantle, WA. Killed by a spear to the chest when attacked by indigenous Australians while thatching his house on 17 July 1830.
MACKENZIE, **James**	Eldest son of Frederick Mackenzie (see above). Commissioned 2nd lieutenant RWF on 11 August 1780. Promoted lieutenant 5 June 1783; captain-lieutenant 31 January 1794; captain 14 June 1794; major 11 December 1799. Mackenzie was instrumental in Jack Hill joining the regiment. Served on the Helder Expedition and in Egypt. Died on board HMS *Heroine*, lying off Alexandria on 24 March 1801. His body was brought ashore and buried the next day. His brother George Mackenzie (see above) wrote 'Bradford, Hill and myself saw it decently interred under a Palm tree'. Unable to find a Chaplain to perform the service, Jack was asked to perform the burial service.

MACLEAN,
Alexander

Commissioned 2nd lieutenant RWF on 12 October 1794. Promoted lieutenant 10 February 1796. Served on the Helder expedition, wounded at the battle of Alkmaar. Lost in the sinking of the Valk on 10 November 1799.

MACLELLAN,
Robert

Commissioned 2nd lieutenant RWF on 4 December 1806. Promoted lieutenant 22 October 1807; appointed Adjutant 1/23rd 17 March 1808. Wounded at Albuera and in the Pyrenees. Retired by the sale of his commission August 1814.

MEADE, Hon.
Edward

Commissioned ensign 40th Foot September 1799. Promoted lieutenant RWF on 6 February 1801. Killed during the landing at Aboukir Bay, at the time of his death he was still serving with the 40th Foot and was probably unaware of his promotion and transfer.

MERCER, James
Bradshaw

Commissioned 2nd lieutenant RWF on 12 September 1805. Promoted lieutenant 30 July 1806. Served in Nova Scotia and Martinique, sailing with 1/23rd to Portugal. He is listed in some records as having died in late 1811. Bentinck claims he was killed in a French raid on Rio Maior on 19 January 1811, but regimental records show him sick at Belem, Lisbon on 24 March 1811. He was presumably therefore wounded at Rio Maior and later died of his wounds.

MONROE, John

Commissioned Assistant Surgeon RWF on 26 May 1814, he was responsible for the rescue of the mortally wounded Henry Ellis (see above) from a fire after Waterloo. Placed on half pay 25 December 1818. In 1822 returned to full pay in the Medical Department and served in York Hospital. In 1823 he was stationed on the Isle of Wight and in 1824 in Canada. Appointed Surgeon to 58th Foot February 1839. Died while serving at Glasgow 10 April 1841.

MONTAGU,
Frederick
Augustus
Courtenay

Born c.1785, third son of George Montagu of Lackham, Wiltshire and his wife Ann. Commissioned ensign 4th Foot August 1799. Promoted lieutenant December 1800; exchanged to 81st Foot July 1803; transferred to be captain RWF on 21 March 1805. Killed, aged 26, at Albuera while serving as Brigade Major to Marshal Beresford.

MOORE, Charles

Appointed Adjutant 113th Foot May 1794. Commissioned lieutenant June 1794. When the 113th disbanded in 1795 he was placed on half pay until exchanging into the RWF on 4 March 1800. Initially posted as junior lieutenant under Jack Hill in the Lieutenant-Colonel's Company. Transferred to 2nd Royal Veteran Battalion in October 1803. Died in 1809.

MORRISSEY,
David

Born Templemoor, Tipperary, he was an optician before joining. Attested July 1804, aged 21 years. Promoted corporal January 1805; sergeant 25th January 1806; sergeant-major December 1813. Severely wounded at Waterloo; died of wounds on 19 June 1815.

MORSE, George Commissioned ensign 60th Foot 4 November 1795; transferred to be 2nd lieutenant RWF on 19 March 1796. Apparently committed suicide while on recruiting duty. He is listed as 'Dead' on 1 June 1796. When Richard Grenville (see above) asked the Duke of York to grant Jack Hill a 2nd lieutenancy, he noted 'I have just rec'd a letter from Lt. Col. Ellis to acquaint me that 2nd Lieut. Morse of the 23rd Regt. who was upon the recruiting service, has shot himself.' Morse's death opened a vacancy for Jack to be commissioned.

OFFLEY, Francis Needham Born c.1780, his probate document describes him as 'bastard'. His probable father was General Francis Needham, later 1st Earl of Kilmorey; the surname Offley was that of Needham's grandmother. Lieutenant 87th Foot in August 1795; transferred to RWF on 10 February 1796; promoted captain-lieutenant 5 April 1801; captain 26 May 1803; major 15 May 1806. Served on the Ostend expedition of 1798, but did not go ashore, on the Helder expedition and in Egypt. In 1804 he held a staff appointment in North America - Jack Hill says of him 'his uncle Gen¹. Needham has ordered him home from Newfoundland where he is employed as B[rigade] Major in consequence of there being nothing to do there'. Offley rejoined the regiment in time to serve in Nova Scotia where Jack said of him in 1808 'Offley is not quite so violent as formerly, he has turn'd a great farmer here for the mess, we have 40 sheep, Bullocks, etc' and in Martinique. Sailed with the regiment to Lisbon but then transferred to the Portuguese Army with the brevet rank of Lieutenant-Colonel. Appointed to command 1st Battalion Loyal Lusitanian Legion in December 1810; transferred 2nd Battalion LLL, later renamed 8th Caçadores, January 1811. Present with them at Fuentes de Oñoro. On departing 2/LLL he was described as 'indefatigable in his exertions to bring it to perfection, and who left it as fine a battalion as any in the service'. In August 1811 Wellington described him as 'a very good Officer'. Rejoined RWF after Albuera, but was court martialed on 15 October 1811 following an incident the previous month when he was alleged to have used 'violent, intemperate, and threatening' language with some Portuguese officers in a dispute'. Offley allegedly drew his sword and appeared to be trying to provoke a dual when one of the Portuguese officers struck him; found guilty of behaviour 'unbecoming an officer and a gentleman', he was suspended for 6 months from 1 January 1812. Returned to duty but was killed while commanding 1/23rd at Salamanca. Alleged to have ignored a plea for assistance by a fellow British officer during the battle, and to have himself been killed by camp followers while lying wounded on the field after the battle. He has a monument in St James's Church, Waresley, Huntingdon.

**PATTESON,
Robert Dossie**

Third son of John Patteson, Mayor of Norwich, MP for Minehead, Somerset and later MP for Norwich. Commissioned 2nd lieutenant RWF 31 December 1803, Patteson shared a house with Jack Hill at Freshwater, Isle of Wight and was subsequently appointed to his company, remaining with them on promotion to lieutenant 22 November 1804. Transferred to the 6th Foot November 1806. Killed at Fort Erie 17 September 1814.

**PEARSON,
Thomas**

Born 1781 at Podimore Milton, Somerset, son of the Reverend Thomas Horner Pearson. Commissioned 2nd lieutenant RWF 2 October 1796. Promoted lieutenant 25 April 1799; captain 7 August 1800. Served on the Ostend expedition of 1798 but did not go ashore, on the Helder and Ferrol expeditions. Wounded in the thigh during the storming of the Heights of Aboukir in Egypt. Promoted major 8 December 1804. Present at Copenhagen, served in Nova Scotia and in Martinique led the 'Light Battalion' composite unit, wounded in the leg during the capture of Fort Desaix. On 28 June 1810, at Alwington Manor, Westfield, New Brunswick he married Ann Eliza (Anna), daughter of Lieutenant-General John Coffin. Travelled with the battalion to Lisbon. Served at first Badajoz. At Albuera commanded a larger composite battalion of light companies, handing over command to Jack Hill when called to the command the Fusilier Brigade after the death or wounding of all its senior officers including Henry Ellis (see above). Wounded at Aldea de Ponte while again in command of the composite light companies. Promoted brevet lieutenant-colonel 30 May 1811; appointed to the staff in Canada. Second in command at Chryslers Farm on 11 November 1813, while on passage to Niagara he volunteered to join 2nd Battalion, Royal Marines at the storming of Port Oswego and was mentioned in despatches. Arriving at Niagara, he was 2nd in command to General Riall and commanded the Light Brigade. After the fall of Fort Erie, served in the withdrawal from Chippawa. Fought at Lundy's Lane, Niagara and at Fort Erie where he was dangerously wounded in the head. Returned to Britain in 1815, appointed to command 43rd Foot but went on half-pay when the regiment was reduced. Exchanged with Thomas Dalmer (see above) to command RWF on 24 July 1817. Promoted colonel 19 July 1821; remained in command of the RWF until promoted major-general on 22 July 1830. Dubbed a knight bachelor on 18 March 1835; promoted lieutenant-general on 23 November 1841. Retired 1843; appointed colonel 85th Foot that year. Lieutenant-General Sir Thomas Pearson, Kt CB KCH died at Bath on 21 May 1847; buried in the mausoleum of St. Swithin's Church. He and his wife, who died in 1859, have a memorial tablet in the church.

POTTER, William	Lieutenant in the 2nd West India Regiment in July 1795; promoted captain in October 1800; transferred to the RWF on 18 June 1807. Severely wounded at Badajoz and died shortly after.
POWER, George	From hospital mate, commissioned Assistant Surgeon RWF on 27 December 1801; promoted Surgeon 13 November 1806. Served at Copenhagen, Nova Scotia, Martinique, where he was wounded on the Heights of Surey, and in the Peninsular. Placed on half pay of the Medical Department July 1811. Published several works including: 'An Attempt to investigate the Causes of Egyptian Ophthalmia; with Observations on its Nature and different Modes of Cure' (London 1803) and 'Military Therapeutics' in The Edinburgh Medical and Surgical Journal (1823), which includes an account of the effects of corporal punishment in the 23rd Foot. Died on Bere Island, Co. Cork, Ireland on 18 April 1824.
ROSKELLY, Thomas	Commissioned 2nd lieutenant RWF on 8 July 1807. Promoted lieutenant 21 September 1808. Wounded on the Heights of Surey, Martinique. The London Gazette listed him as 'superseded, being absent without leave' in September 1812, but states he was reinstated in December.
SEDLEY, Anthony Gardiner	Born at Scart, near Ballyclough, Co. Cork, 10 July 1794, eldest son of George Sedley (see below). Commissioned 2nd lieutenant RWF on 1 August 1811. Joined 1/23rd in March 1812, Promoted lieutenant 16 July 1812. Served at Salamanca, Osma, Sabuganna de Morrilla (severely wounded, shot through the lungs), the Pyrenees, Vitoria, St. Sebastian and Waterloo (again wounded). Exchanged to half pay 8th Foot December 1818. Returned to active list as lieutenant 45th Foot March 1825. Promoted captain May 1835; transferred to 63rd Foot July 1836; promoted major September 1844; lieutenant-colonel September 1845; placed on half pay 1848; retired by sale of commission 1851. Appointed a Military Knight of Windsor; became Governor of the Military Knights 1875. Died 22 March 1876, possibly the last surviving recipient of the Waterloo medal.
SEDLEY, George	After serving in the Cork Militia, commissioned Quartermaster RWF on 14 April 1808. Served throughout the Peninsular War and at Waterloo. Retired on full pay 1827. Father of Anthony Sedley (see above). Died 19 October 1837, aged 71
SHAW, Richard	Commissioned ensign 81st Foot in September 1795. Promoted lieutenant August 1798; transferred as captain RWF on 24 April 1804; transferred to 6th Garrison Battalion April 1810. Died 1813.

SHAW, Thomas	Commissioned lieutenant 30th Foot July 1799. Exchanged to RWF on 19 December 1799; promoted captain 24 October 1804; transferred to 6th Garrison Battalion July 1807; promoted major June 1814; placed on half pay 1815; retired January 1826.
SKINNER, Philip Kearney	Born North America 1774, son of Brigadier General Cortlandt Skinner, a New York loyalist, and his wife Elizabeth, who fled to England in 1783. Commissioned 2nd lieutenant RWF on 16 November 1782. Promoted lieutenant 23 November 1785; captain-lieutenant 22 October 1793; captain 31 January 1794; major 1 September 1795. Became senior major 18 January 1797. Commanded the combined grenadier companies of 11th and 23rd Foot during the 1798 Ostend expedition. Taken prisoner and interned in Lille. He did not go on parole but remained behind with the men until all were exchanged. Transferred to 56th Foot as lieutenant-colonel December 1799; promoted colonel October 1809; major-general January 1812; lieutenant-general May 1825. Died Regent Street, London 7 April 1826.
SMITH, John Selby	A Volunteer with 18th Foot, commissioned 2nd lieutenant RWF on 5 April 1801. Promoted lieutenant 10 September 1803 and appointed to Jack Hill's company. Appointed Adjutant 24 November 1803; promoted captain 31 July 1806; relinquish the Adjutancy 30 October 1806; exchanged to 1st Foot December 1806. Retired by the sale of commission February 1818.
SMITH, Ralph	Commissioned 2nd lieutenant RWF in 1808. Promoted lieutenant 22 March 1810. Joined 1/23rd in the Peninsula, present at Vitoria, Pyrenees, Nivelle, Nive, Orthes, Toulouse and Waterloo. Placed on the half pay list of 53rd Foot in May 1823. He married Mary, daughter of James and Mary Turner of Welshpool, Montgomeryshire. Mary was the sister of Jane Turner, making him Jack Hill's brother-in-law. They had two sons and two daughters. He died at Ballymona, Co. Tipperary 31 March 1866.
SMITH, Thomas	Born at Rathin, Aberdeenshire 26 May 1789. Became a hospital assistant in March 1812; commissioned Assistant Surgeon, RWF, on 2 July 1812. Joined 1/23rd in the Peninsula in December 1812, present at Vitoria, Pyrenees, Nivelle, Orthes, Toulouse and Waterloo. It may have been Smith who first attended to Jack Hill after he was seriously wounded at Waterloo. Qualified as M.D. (Edinburgh) in 1825; promoted to be Surgeon RWF 13 July 1826. Served with them in Portugal and Gibraltar from 1823. Appointed Surgeon-Major to the Forces in Canada 1839. Placed on half-pay December 1846. Died on 29 April 1875 at Aberdeen.

STAINFORTH,
William George

Commissioned 2nd lieutenant RWF on 22 April 1802. Promoted lieutenant 29 December 1803; appointed Adjutant of 2/23rd 22 December 1804; captain 1/23rd 15 May 1806. Wounded at Albuera and Badajoz. Killed in the Pyrenees.

SUTTON,
Charles

Born 1775, eldest son of Admiral Evelyn Sutton of Screveton, near Bingham, Nottinghamshire. Commissioned ensign in 3rd Guards July 1800. Promoted lieutenant and captain December 1802, but soon afterwards placed on half pay. Transferred as captain to RWF on 26 May 1803; promoted major 23 April 1807; appointed Lieutenant-Colonel of Portuguese 9th Infantry August 1809. Appointed brevet rank lieutenant-colonel in the British army 30 May 1811. In June 1813 The London Gazette announced Sutton's appointment as lieutenant-colonel 2/23rd, but he declined the appointment and stayed in Spain to be Colonel commanding the Portuguese 9th Infantry. Served at Buçaco, Fuentes d'Onoro, Badajoz, Salamanca, Vitoria, Nivelle, the Nive and Toulouse. Receiving the Army Gold Cross with clasps for the Nive and Toulouse, and Portuguese medals for this period. Placed on half pay in the British army October 1814. Created KCB on 2 January 1815. Served as a brigadier-general in the Portuguese army from 12 October 1815, leaving Portuguese service in 1820 when all remaining British officers from the Peninsular War were expelled. Promoted colonel in the British army July 1821; appointed inspecting field officer of militia in the Ionian Islands January 1824. Died of an apoplectic stroke on 26 March 1828, aged 53, at his uncle's house in Bottesford, Leicestershire while on leave.

TALBOT,
Richard William

Ensign 66th Foot; lieutenant 105th Foot; captain 105th Foot; half-pay 85th Foot; exchanged to 5th Foot; exchanged to half-pay 33rd Foot in 1790; lieutenant-colonel commanding 118th Foot July 1794. Went on half-pay when 118th Foot disbanded. Exchanged to be lieutenant-colonel RWF on 15 March 1798. Commanded the regiment during the 1798 Ostend raid when he was captured and imprisoned in Lille. Promoted to be colonel in the army 1 January 1800. Retired by the sale of his commission to John Hall (see above) June 1800.

THORNHILL,
Edward

Commissioned 2nd lieutenant RWF on 17 April 1806. Promoted lieutenant 30 April 1807. Served under Jack Hill in the Light Company in Nova Scotia and Martinique. Transferred as captain to 45th Foot February 1810. Believed to have resigned December 1811.

THORNHILL, William

Commissioned 2nd lieutenant RWF on 16 August 1799. Promoted lieutenant 28 February 1800; captain 5 May 1804. While in Nova Scotia with the regiment in 1808, Jack Hill recorded that: 'Offley, Ellis, and Thornhill amongst them have purchased a small farm of about 16 acres for £110. There is now [sown] hay and a nursery [worth?] about £35 on it. The manure from the Fort and labour from the soldiers who are employ'd now in making proper fences will make it a valuable tract'. Exchanged to 7th Light Dragoons June 1806; promoted major April 1813. Served as ADC to Lord Uxbridge at Waterloo; severely wounded and made brevet lieutenant-colonel. Promoted substantive lieutenant-colonel August 1819; relinquished command of 7th Light Dragoons June 1825; listed as holding local rank employed in Europe until he died after 1850.

THORPE, Samuel

Born 28 July 1792, third son of Jonathan Thorpe and his wife Mary. Educated at Westminster School and Marlow Military College. Commissioned 2nd lieutenant in April 1807. Promoted lieutenant January 1808; joined 2/23rd on 14 January 1808. Served in the action at Lugo, at Coruña and on the Walcheren expedition. Reported to 1/23rd in Spain in March 1811. Present at the siege of Olivenca, first Badajoz and Albuera (wounded twice). Transferred as captain to 39th Foot April 1812. Severely wounded at Toulouse. Served at Plattsburg (War of 1812); returned to Europe for the capture of Paris. Placed on half pay September 1820; returned to full pay as brevet major July 1830; transferred to 27th Foot December 1831; placed on half pay February 1835. Died 19 December 1852 at Goff's Oak, Cheshunt, Hertfordshire.

TREEVE, Richard

Commissioned 2nd lieutenant RWF on 18 July 1805. Promoted lieutenant 29 May 1806; captain 1 October 1812. Served in Nova Scotia, but did not go on the Martinique expedition. Travelled with the battalion to Lisbon. Wounded at Albuera. Placed on half pay 2 May 1814. Appointed Barrack Master in Jersey in 1825, remaining in the appointment until he died 19 December 1852. Buried at Cheshunt, Hertfordshire.

VAN COURTLANDT, Jacob Ogden	Born in about 1777, second son of Colonel Philip Van Cortlandt of Croton-on-Hudson, New York State, USA, and his wife Catharine. His father fought for the King in the American War of Independence and thereby lost the family's property and possessions. Jacob was commissioned 2nd lieutenant RWF on 28 October 1795 having been on the half pay of the Provincials. Promoted lieutenant 1 June 1796. Taken prisoner during the 1798 Ostend raid and interned in Lille. He did not go on parole but remained behind with the men until all were exchanged. Promoted captain 25 June 1803. Accompanied the regiment to Nova Scotia in 1808 but, having been recently married, did not go on the expedition to Martinique, instead staying behind to command the detachment of 100 or so 'weaker' men left in Halifax. Travelled with the regiment to Lisbon. Served as Brigade Major of the Fusilier Brigade at Albuera. Killed at Aldea da Ponte on 27 September 1811. His widow received an annual allowance of £50, starting on 25 December 1815.
VISCHER, Harman	Ensign 9th Foot; transferred to be lieutenant RWF on 11 November 1794. Participated in the 1798 Ostend raid, was captured and imprisoned in Lille. Served in the Helder expedition but was lost in the sinking of the Valk on 10 November 1799.
WALLEY, William	Born c.1783. Commissioned 2nd lieutenant RWF on 13 May 1807. Promoted lieutenant 10 December 1807. Served at Copenhagen, transferred to 2/23rd. Served with them in the Coruña and Walcheren campaigns. Rejoined 1/23rd in Spain in April 1811. Present at first Badajoz, Albuera, Ciudad Rodrigo, second Badajoz (severely wounded), Vitoria, the Pyrenees, Nive, Orthez, Toulouse and Waterloo. Promoted captain 19 July 1815; placed on half pay 14th Foot April 1820. Died, aged 44, on 28 July 1827 at Birkenhead, Cheshire. He has a monument in Chester Cathedral.

WEST, James Dawsonne

Born c.1779. Commissioned ensign 86th Foot May 1796. Exchanged as 2nd lieutenant RWF on 1 June 1796 after General Grenville (see above) recommended him to the Duke of York. The recommendation almost prevented Jack Hill being granted a commission, as having already recommended one officer Grenville felt he could not suggest another. The Duke of York, however, consented to Jack Hill's appointment. Transferred to 60th Foot in August 1799; became lieutenant and captain 1st Guards December 1799; promoted captain and lieutenant-colonel August 1812; major and colonel 1st Grenadier Guards in July 1821. Retired 1827. Died, aged 52, 3 August 1831 at Great Malvern, Worcestershire 'after a severe illness'. His obituary in The Gentleman's Magazine records 'He served during almost the whole of the war, in Holland, the Peninsula, and France'. He has a memorial in St John the Baptist's Church, Mathon, Herefordshire.

WEST, Thomas

Commissioned 2nd lieutenant RWF on 6 April 1796. Promoted lieutenant 26 January 1797. On the 1798 expedition to Ostend, but did not go ashore. Sent on detachment to Horsham March 1800 when all regiments were required to provide men to participate in the Rifle Corps 'experiment'. Exchanged to 91st Foot in April 1800; promoted captain December 1800; exchanged to 2nd Foot in May 1803. Retired in 1805.

WYNN, Henry

Born c.1788, son of William Wynn of Rhagatt, Corwen, Merioneth. Possibly served as a volunteer in Egypt. Commissioned 2nd lieutenant RWF on 21 April 1803. Promoted lieutenant 10 March 1804; captain 29 September 1808; Adjutant 2/23rd from 22 May 1806 until 29 September 1808, but he was with 1/23rd in Nova Scotia and accompanied them to Martinique. Jack said of him in a letter of 1808 'Ellis, Offley, Power and Wynne are with us here... Wynne is the A^d., of as much use as nobody'. May have accompanied 1/23rd to Lisbon, but returned to 2/23rd to serve in the Walcheren campaign before rejoining 1/23rd in Spain. Severely wounded at Orthes. Commanded the Light Company at Waterloo. Died, aged 44, 18 June 1832. His obituary in The Cambrian Quarterly Magazine states: 'On the 18th of June, of spasmodic cholera, Captain Henry Wynn, of the Royal Welsh Fusileers. This distinguished officer joined the above regiment in Egypt, was present at the capture of Martinique, at Walcheren, throughout the Peninsular war up to the surrender of Paris, and at the battle of Waterloo. At Paris, his lady, after giving birth to a daughter, now 16 years of age, died, and lies interred adjoining the tomb of Abelard and Heloise in Pere la Chaise. He had been four times severely wounded, and had been complimented on several occasions for his conduct.' He has a memorial in St Mary's Church, Flint.

WYATT, William Edgell

Youngest son of Richard Wyatt of Egham, Surrey and his wife Priscilla. Commissioned ensign 29th Foot February 1793. Promoted lieutenant February 1794; captain-lieutenant April 1795; captain November 1796; major May 1803. Served with 29th Foot in the West Indies, Ireland, the Helder expedition (shot through the thigh during the landing) and Canada. Transferred to be lieutenant-colonel in command 2/23rd on 18 February 1808, assuming command at Loughera, Ireland. Commanded 2/23rd in the retreat to Coruña and on the Walcheren expedition, where he developed a fever which permanently affected his health. On 15 March 1811, in Guernsey, he appeared before a General Court Martial charged with (1) Scandalous and infamous conduct; (2) Absence without leave; and (3) 'improper language towards Paymaster Perkins on the 27th of May 1810, with a view to provoke the said Paymaster Perkins to a breach of his duty towards him as commanding officer.' Wyatt was honourably acquitted; Perkins was dismissed. Appointed Inspecting Field Officer of a Recruiting District 17 June 1813, handing over command of 2/23rd to Thomas Dalmer (see above). Appointed brevet colonel June 1814; nominated CB 4 June 1815. He married Harriet Fesey, daughter of Rev Thomas Smith of Bideford, Devon. Died on 17 May 1820; buried in Egham churchyard.

Bibliography

Primary Sources: Archives, Official Publications and Journals

The National Archives UK (TNA)

- WO1/179
- WO1/180
- WO 12 Series
- WO 17 Series
- WO 25/750
- WO 28/11
- WO 31 Series
- WO 76/218

Portuguese Archives

- Arquivo Nacional
- Arquivo Histórico Militar
- Collecção das Ordens do Dia

Royal Welch Fusiliers Archives

- Object 379. Letters of George Mackenzie
- Object 2682. Letters of Capt Gordon Booker
- Object 3777 Letters of Lt Col JHE Hill
- Object 5257b. Letters of Captain Thomas Farmer
- Object 5935. Letters of Lieutenant John MacDonald
- Object 7198. Letters of Col J C Harrison
- Officer Biographies of the Royal Welch Fusiliers, May 2011

The National Library of Wales

- MS 22102A; Autobiography of Private Thomas Jeremiah of the 23rd Regiment of Royal Welch Fusiliers (c.1837)

Blundell's School Archives

The Despatches of Field Marshal the Duke of Wellington During His Various Campaigns from 1799 to 1818, 1838

General Orders, Spain and Portugal

Return of the Names of the Officers in the Army. War Office, 30th April 1818

The Gentleman's Magazine

The London Gazette

The Royal Military Calendar, or Army Service and Commission Book

The Times

Y Ddraig Goch, The Journal of the Royal Welch Fusiliers, March 2000

Primary Sources: Memoires and Letters

'A Field Officer'	Four Years of A Soldier's Life United Services Magazine, 1844
'A Subaltern'	The Campaign in Holland 1799, 1861
Aitchison, John	An Ensign in the Peninsular War: The Letters of John Aitchison W.F.K. Thompson (Ed.). 1981
Albemarle, George Thomas	Fifty Years of My Life, 1876
Bell, George	Rough Notes by an Old Soldier, During Fifty Years of Service, 1867
Bunbury, Henry	Narrative of Some Passages in the Great War With France, 1854
"	Reminiscences of a Veteran: Being Personal and Military Adventures in Portugal, Spain, France, Malta New South Wales, Norfolk Island, New Zealand, Andaman Islands, and India. Vol. 1., 1861
Carr-Gomm, William Maynard	Letters and Journals of Field Marshal Sir William Maynard Gomm, G.C.B. Francis Culling Carr-Gomm [ed.], 1881
Cole, Sir Lowry	Memoirs of Sir Lowry Cole 1934 Maud Lowry Cole and Stephen Gwynn [ed.], 1934
Colville, John	The Portrait of a General, 1980
Cooper, John Spencer	Rough Notes of Seven Campaigns in Portugal, Spain, France and America During the Years 1809-10-11-12-13-14-15, 1869
Bentinck, Richard	The Very Thing: The Memoirs of Drummer Richard Bentinck, Royal Welch Fusiliers 1807 – 1823. Crook, Jonathan [ed.], 2011

Blakiston, John	Twelve Years' Military Adventures in Three Quarters of the Globe Vol II, 1829
Bromley, Walter	A Few Plain Questions and Observations on the Catholic Emancipation, 1812
Browne, Thomas Henry	The Napoleonic War Journal of Captain Thomas Henry Browne 1807-1816 Roger N. Buckley [ed.],1987
Cadell, Charles	Narrative of the Campaigns of the Twenty-Eights Regiment, 1835
Dobbs, John	Recollections of an Old 52nd Man, 1859.
Emerson, J	Recollections of the Late War in Spain and Portugal in Peninsular Sketches by the Actors on the Scene Vol. II W H Maxwell [ed.], 1845
Gleig, G R	The Subaltern, 1872
Green, John	The Vicissitudes of a Soldier's Life, 1827
Gronow, [Rees Howell] Captain	Recollections and Anecdotes of the Camp, the Court, and the Clubs, 1877
Hennell, George	A Gentleman Volunteer: The Letters of George Hennell from the Peninsular War, 1812-13 Michael Glover [ed.],1979
Hennen, John	Principles of Military Surgery, 1830
Hering, John Frederick	Journal of an Officer in the King's German Legion, 1827
Hill, John Humphrey Edward	Letters 1796-1815
	Statement of the Services of Brevet Lieut. Col. J.H.E. Hill of the 23rd or Royal Welch Fusilier Regiment 1816
	Memorial to His Royal Highness the Duke of York 1823
	Manuscript document Colonel Hill (CB) Services, written by Charles Frederick Hill, in the possession of the Hill family. Access granted by kind permission of Mr. Phillip Hill
	Services of your Grandfather the late L^t. Col.^{l} J.H.E. Hill. C.B. XXIIIrd Royal Welsh Fusiliers. Note by J.R. Race Godfrey to his son, Lieutenant S. H. Godfrey, 2nd Batt. The Lancers 21 March 1883.
	Letters to a Vicarage 1796 – 1815 Enid Case and Jenny Currie [ed.], 1988

Inceldon, Benjamin	Register of The Scholars Educated in Blundell's School 1770 – 1809.
Leeke, William	The History of Lord Seaton's Regiment (The 52nd Light Infantry) at the Battle of Waterloo, 1866
Marcel, Nicolas	Campagnes du Capitaine Marcel du 69e de Ligne en Espagne et en Portugal (1808-1814) Le Commandant Var [ed.], 1913
Moore, Sir John	The Diary of Sir John Moore Vol. I J F Maurice [ed.], 1904
Mercer, Cavalié	Journal of the Waterloo Campaign, 1985
Pringle, William	The Correspondence of Major General William Henry Pringle The Waterloo Association, 2021
Ross-Lewin, Harry	With the 'Thirty-Second' in the Peninsular and Other Campaigns, 1904
Sherer, Moyle	Recollections of the Peninsula, 1824
Siborne H. T.	Waterloo Letters, 1891
Thorpe, Samuel	Narrative of Incidents in the Early Military Life of Major Samuel Thorpe, KH, 1854
Tomkinson, William	The Diary of a Cavalry Officer in the Peninsular War and Waterloo Campaign 1809-1815, 1895
von Wachholtz, Friedrich Ludwig	Auf der Peninsula 1810 bis 1813: Kriegstagebuch des Generals Friedrich Ludwig v.Wachholtz (On the Peninsula 1810 to 1813: The War diary of General Friedrich Ludwig von Wachholtz) in Supplements to the military weekly by Major General v.Frobel, [Ed.], 1906
Walsh, E	A Narrative of the Expedition to Holland, in the autumn of the year 1799, 1800
Wheeler, William	The Letters of Private Wheeler 1809-1828 B H Liddell Hart [Ed.], 1951
Wyvill, Richard Augustus	Sketch of the Military Life, 1820

Secondary sources

Abell, Francis	Prisoners of War in Britain 1756 to 1815, 1914
Atkinson, C.T.	Gleanings From the Cathcart MSS Part V – The Younger Pitt's Last Venture: The Expedition to Hanover, 1805-1806. Journal of the Society for Army Historical Research Vol. 30 No. 121., 1952

Black, Jeremy	How the Army Made Britain a Global Power 1688 – 1815, 2021
Broughton-Mainwaring, Rowland	Historical Record of the Royal Welch Fusiliers, 1889
Buttery, David	Wellington Against Massena: The Third Invasion of Portugal 1810 – 1811, 2007
Cannon, Richard	Historical Record of the Twenty-Third Regiment or Royal Welsh Fusiliers, 1850
Cary, A D L and McCance, Stouppe	Regimental Records of the Royal Welch Fusiliers (Formerly 23rd Foot) Vol. 1 1689-1815 1921, Reprinted 1995
Chandler, David	The Campaigns of Napoleon David Chandler, 1966
Coelho, Sérgio Veludo	The Portuguese Caçadores, 1808 – 1814, 1995
Challis, Lionel S.	British Officers Serving in the Portuguese Army, 1809-1814 Journal of the Society for Army Historical Research, 1949
Collins, Bruce	Wellington and the Seige of San Sebastian 1813, 2017
Crumplin, Michael and Glover, Gareth	Waterloo After the Glory, 2019
Dalton, Charles	The Waterloo Roll Call (2nd Editon), 1904
Divall, Carole	Wellington's Worst Scrape: The Burgos Campaign 1812, 2012
de Chair, Somerset (ed.)	Napoleon on Napoleon, 1992
Edwards, Peter	Albuera: Wellington's Fourth Peninsular Campaign, 1811, 2008
Esposito, Vincent J. and Elting, John R.	A Military History and Atlas of the Napoleonic Wars Revised Edition, 1999
Fletcher, Ian	Wellington's Regiments, 1994
"	Galloping At Everything: The British Cavalry in the Peninsular War and at Waterloo 1808-15, 1999
"	A Desperate Business: Wellington, the British Army and the Waterloo Campaign, 2001
Fortescue, J W	A History of the British Army Volumes IV Part II (1906), Vol V (1910), Vol VIII (1917) & Vol IX (1920)
Fraser, Ian	Hennock: A Village, 2004

Gaudêncio, Moisés and Burnham, Robert	In the Words of Wellington's Fighting Cocks: The After-action Reports of the Portuguese Army during the Peninsular War 1812-1814, 2021
Gates, David	The Spanish Ulcer: A History of the Peninsular War, 1986
Girod de L'Ain, Maurice	Vie Militaire Du Général Foy, 1900
Glover, Michael	Wellington as Military Commander, 2001
"	The Purchase of Commissions: A Reappraisal Journal of the Society for Army Historical Research, 1980
Glover, Michael and Riley, Jonathon	'That Astonishing Infantry'; The History of The Royal Welch Fusiliers 1689 –2006, 2008
Graves, Donald E.	Fix Bayonets! A Royal Welch Fusilier At War 1796 – 1815, 2006
"	Dragon Rampant: The Royal Welch Fusiliers at War, 1793 – 1815, 2010.
Grehan, John	The Lines of Torres Vedras: The Cornerstone of Wellington's Strategy in the Peninsular War 1809-1812, 2000
Guy Alan J (ed.)	The Road to Waterloo, 1990
Haythornthwaite, Philip J	Wellington's Military Machine, 1989
"	The Armies of Wellington, 1996
Holmes, Richard	Soldiers, 2011
"	Redcoat: The British Soldier in the Age of Horse and Musket, 2001
Holme, Norman & Kirby, E L	Medal Rolls 23rd Foot – Royal Welch Fusiliers Napoleonic Period,1978
Howard, Martin R.	Wellington's Doctors, 2002
Keegan, John	The Face of Battle, 1976.
Kempthorne Lt. Col. G A	The Egyptian Campaign of 1801 in the Journal of the Royal Army Medical Corps Vol. LIV January – June 1930
Lavery, Brian	Nelson's Fleet at Trafalgar, 2004
Limm, Andrew Robert	'Fairly Out-Generalled and Disgracefully Beaten': The British Army in the Low Countries 1793-1814, 2014

Lipscombe, Nick	Napoleon's Obsession – The Invasion of England British Journal for Military History, Volume 1, Issue 3, June 2015
" (ed.)	Waterloo: The Decisive Victory, 2014
Lloyd, Peter A	The French Are Coming: The Invasion Scare of 1803-5, 1991
Lock, Nick	A Real Life Richard Sharpe: Lieutenant Colonel John Hill of the 23rd Foot, 2000
MacArthur, Roderick	British Army Establishments During the Napoleonic War Journal of the Society for Army Historical Research, 2009
Mackesy, Piers	Britain's Victory in Egypt: The End of Napoleon's Conquest, 1995
Mallinson, Allan	The Making of the British Army, 2011
McCarthy, Steve	The Loss of The Valk, 10 November 1799, 2024
McGuffle, T H	Recruiting the Ranks of the Regular British Army During the French Wars Journal for the Society of Army Historical Research, 1956
Mee, Arthur (Ed.)	The King's England: Devon, Cradle of our Seamen, 1938.
Muir, Rory	Britain and the Defeat of Napoleon 1807-1815, 1996
"	Salamanca 1812, 2001
"	Tactics and the Experience of Battle in the Age of Napoleon, 1998
"	Wellington: The Path To Victory, 1769-1814, 2015, plus additional commentary at https://lifeofwellington.co.uk/explore-the commentary
Napier, W F P	History of the War in the Peninsular and in the South of France, from the Year 1807 to the Year 1814 2nd Edition, 1833
Oman, Charles	A History of the Peninsular War Volumes IV (1911), VI (1914) & VIII (1922)
Parkinson, Roger	Moore of Corunna, 1976
Phillipson, Andy	The Raid on Ostend 1798: Combined Operations Against Revolutionary France, 2003
Polwhele, Rev. Richard	The History of Devonshire, 1793
Rathbone Low, Charles	Battles of the British Army, 1890
Riley, Jonathon	Officers and NCOs in the late 18th Century Army, 2013

"   A Matter of Honour: The Life, Campaigns and
                             Generalship of Isaac Brock, 2011

"   1813 Empire at Bay - The Sixth Coalition & the
                             Downfall of Napoleon, 2013

Sampson. M.   A History of Blundell's School, 2001.

Schama, Simon   Citizens, 1989.

"   A History of Britain, Vol. 3., 2002

Soriano, Simão da Luz   Historia Da Guerra Civil E Do Estabelecimento
                             Do Governo Parlamentar Em Portugal, 1866

Thomas, J E   Britain's Last Invasion: Fishguard 1797, 2007

Thoumine, R. H.   Scientific Soldier: A life of General Le Marchant,
                             1968.

Uglow, Jenny   In These Times: Living In Britain Through
                             Napoleon's Wars 1793 – 1815, 2014

Van Uythoven, Geert   The Secret Expedition: The Anglo-Russian
                             Invasion of Holland, 1799 2018

Veve, Thomas D   The Duke of Wellington and the British Army of
                             Occupation in France, 1815-1818, 1992

Ward, S G P   Portuguese Infantry Brigades, 1809-1814 Journal
                             of the Society for Army Historical Research, Vol
                             53, No. 214, 1975

Websites

www.blundells.org

www.britannica.com

www.devonheritage.org

www. FODA.org.uk

www.genuki.org.uk

www.nam.ac.uk

www.napoleon-series.org

www.rwfmuseum.org.uk

www.teignheritage.org.uk

www.ingramcontent.com/pod-product-compliance
Lightning Source LLC
Chambersburg PA
CBHW020341100426
42812CB00029B/3210/J